Visions of Reform

Visions of Reform

CONGREGATION EMANU-EL
and the JEWS of SAN FRANCISCO, 1849–1999

Fred Rosenbaum

JUDAH L. MAGNES MUSEUM
BERKELEY, CALIFORNIA
2000

Published by the Judah L. Magnes Museum
2911 Russell Street
Berkeley, California 94705

Cover and book design: Sara Glaser
Cover art: Detail, color etching by Max Pollak, 1940

ISBN: 0-943376-69-6 (paperback)
ISBN: 0-943376-68-8 (hardcover)
Library of Congress Catalog Card Number: 99-069417

Printed in the United States of America

FOR SEYMOUR FROMER

Table of Contents

Foreword

CONGREGATION EMANU-EL OF SAN FRANCISCO is one of the illustrious success stories of the diaspora. Established during the California gold rush of the mid-nineteenth century, it rapidly became the leading synagogue on the west coast of the still young republic. Many of its congregants, meanwhile, exerted a major role in the mercantile, civic, and cultural life of what was destined to become one of the great cities of America.

The development of Emanu-El, now celebrating its sesquicentennial, is a complex and multifaceted story filled with dramatic events and powerful personalities, great architecture and sublime music. And the temple has also been a place where important ideas have been passionately debated. During its formative years Reform Judaism itself was emerging and evolving, and the congregation was frequently embroiled in the often divisive issues of philosophy and practice encountered by the movement as a whole.

The origins of the synagogue also closely track the unfolding of the American saga and its attendant values manifest in the westward movement: ambition, change, achievement, and fulfillment. To some degree isolated on the edge of the continent, Emanu-El charted its own course, incorporating the spirit of a western frontier for Reform Judaism.

Yet, as the author shows, in the case of this large urban congregation, the theme of West Coast exceptionalism has its limits as well. For Emanu-El has also looked to New York for its inspiration. In its early years, much of its ultra-liberal religious orientation seems to follow that of its famous Manhattan namesake. In the critical second and third decades of the twentieth century it appears that its leaders were strongly influenced by the creativity of the Free Synagogue's Rabbi Stephen S. Wise. Even in our own day, the impress of thinkers such as Rabbi Lawrence Hoffman of New York's Hebrew Union College is reflected in a number of the temple's most promising initiatives.

But most of all, the institution has been shaped by the vision of its own leaders, an extraordinary group by any measure. The rabbis, cantors, board presidents, and executive directors who have given character and greatness to Emanu-El have been strong-willed and enterprising. They have taken part nationally and even internationally in controversies concerning the classical Reform liturgy, the absorption of East European refugees, the nature of American Jewish music, the establishment of the State of Israel, and, most recently, congregational programming and management. They have truly left us with multiple visions of Reform.

Above all, the eleven men who have held the post of spiritual leader at Temple Emanu-El have left their imprint on the congregation and on the community, and it is fitting that the present volume is organized primarily around their rabbinates. Their tenure has ranged from the relatively brief stewardship of Julius Eckman and Irving Hausman to the long hegemonies of Elkan Cohn, Jacob Voorsanger, Martin Meyer, Irving Reichert, Alvin Fine, and Joseph Asher (six rabbis who led Emanu-El during 115 of its 150 years).

Emanu-El provided the pulpit from which these dynamic—and very different—men led the congregation through times both glorious and difficult. These have included the construction of the great Sutter Street temple and later the masterpiece at Lake and Arguello, the city's Phoenix-like recovery from the disaster of 1906, the sponsorship of composers who would add immeasurably to the Jewish musical tradition, and the creation of community service programs that would extend the congregation's reach to the less fortunate.

But there have also been moments of conflict, misjudgment, and even disgrace. These have included the initially callous treatment of Yiddish-speaking immigrants at the turn of the century, strident opposition to

Zionism even in the midst of the Holocaust, and, finally, tragic misconduct on the part of a brilliant young rabbi in our own time.

Visions of Reform richly details all of these engrossing chapters in the temple's history. The author, Fred Rosenbaum, founding director of Lehrhaus Judaica, the Bay Area's innovative center for adult Jewish learning, has distinguished himself as an educator, teacher, and historian. He was first selected in 1975 to write about Emanu-El for the congregation's approaching 130th birthday. In *Architects of Reform*, published in 1980, he connected the modern era to that of the learned Jacob Voorsanger (after whom the synagogue's library is aptly named), who first penned *The Chronicles of Emanu-El* on the occasion of the temple's fiftieth anniversary.

Rosenbaum now draws upon new scholarship on the years before 1980, then picks up where he left off almost twenty years ago. In so doing the historian spins out for us the provocative tale of these last two eventful decades, offering us the story of an institution which confidently enters a new century in a posture of both change and continuity.

Stephen Mark Dobbs

Preface and Acknowledgments

THIS WORK IS AN UPDATED, revised, and much expanded version of *Architects of Reform*, the history of Congregation Emanu-El which I published in 1980. In both cases I was commissioned by the temple to write its institutional biography. But now, as then, I asked for and received wide-ranging editorial freedom both in the research and writing phases. I am grateful to the congregation for again entrusting me in this way with so important a responsibility.

I am also thankful for the opportunity afforded few historians to return to a book two decades after its publication in order to make it more relevant and engaging. Overall, I was pleased with the reviews of *Architects of Reform* which appeared in the early '80s, and the warm response I received from readers locally and nationally. For a second edition, several of my friends and colleagues recommended that I simply reprint the text and add two new chapters dealing with the past twenty years. But in addition to covering the contemporary period, I chose to rework a good deal of the history of the temple I had already written, from the Gold Rush to 1980.

For I was aware of much important scholarship that had surfaced since my original study, material that shed new light on many of the leading figures in the temple's history. During the 1980s, a full-length biography of Emanu-El's first rabbi, Julius Eckman, appeared, as well as two informative essays on Edward Stark (cantor from 1893 to 1913) and the oral history of Ludwig Altman (organist from 1937 to 1986). I myself published an article in 1991 on Irving Reichert (rabbi from 1930 to 1948) and the anti-Zionist American Council for Judaism in which he was a key leader during and after World War II. In 1995, a two-part essay was issued on the pivotal career of Martin Meyer (rabbi from 1910 to 1923). New information also became available on the lives of Jacob Voorsanger (spiritual leader from 1889 to 1908), the legendary Reuben Rinder (cantor from 1913 to 1959), and Joseph Asher (rabbi from 1968 to 1985).

Even a number of primary sources on the pioneer period, unavailable to me in the late 1970s, became accessible in recent years. The minutes of Congregation Sherith Israel, obtained in the past decade by the Western Jewish History Center, opened an important window on synagogue life in San Francisco during the second half of the nineteenth century. This was especially needed because Emanu-El's minutes were destroyed in the earthquake and fire of 1906. But one revealing annual report, from 1867, was found several years ago in the temple archives. I used that document as well as a trove of letters of Rabbi Julius Eckman from the mid-1850s, another source recently opened to researchers by the WJHC.

Perhaps most important, though, were interpretive works that deepened my understanding of the temple in the context of the history of the city of San Francisco, the Reform movement, and American religious life as a whole. The penetrating insights of Roger Lotchin and Peter Decker on the Gold Rush years (whose books appeared in the late 1970s but which I had not adequately utilized in my first study) proved immensely helpful as I sought to gauge the role of the Jewish community in the chaotic boomtown that was the Bay City in its first decade. Leon Jick's *The Americanization of the Synagogue*, Jack Wertheimer's *A People Divided*, and above all Alan Silverstein's *Alternatives to Assimilation* (a recent case study of Emanu-El along with three comparable synagogues in other regions of the country), provided me with a nationally focused picture of the evolution of Reform Judaism as I struggled, now for a second time, to find meaning in the vicissitudes of a single congregation. Studies by scholars such as Robert Wuthnow and Michael Quinn broadened my view even further as I attempted to make connections between Emanu-El's history and that of the religious expression of the American West in general. In sum, these works and others led me to address issues in the realm of social history which seemed more important now than they had twenty years ago: questions of gender, multiculturalism, urban life, spirituality, and regional distinctiveness.

But while I wanted to enrich my earlier history of Emanu-El, my major reason for undertaking this task was to tell the compelling story of the turn in the temple's direction in the past decade and a half. As one steeped in the congregation's history, I appreciated more than others the many changes that had occurred since 1985, a transformation both of style and substance in the areas of liturgy, music, education, community service, and rabbinic leadership. The physical plant was thoroughly renovated in these years; a preschool was established; the finances were put on a new basis; the membership swelled; the size of the budget and management staff more than doubled. Not even a serious scandal in the early '90s, involving the senior rabbi, could fundamentally slow these major developments.

It is the emergence of a different kind of congregation—large and inviting, variegated and vigorous—which, more than anything else, rendered my 1980 book out of date. My hope for this project, then, is that I have, in the latter part of the volume, captured the essence of the new Emanu-El, the new wine that has been poured into an old wineskin.

Of course, today's energetic Temple Emanu-El has much in common with earlier periods of innovation and experimentation in its history, most notably the remarkable rabbinates of Martin Meyer and his protégé and successor Louis Newman during the 1910s and '20s. At that time, too, a flexible and broadly based response to the changing needs of San Francisco Jewry revitalized and reconstituted the synagogue.

But no less striking have been the sharp contrasts from one era to the next as the synagogue has sought to adapt to a free and open society itself in flux. Competing visions of Reform have vied with one another throughout Emanu-El's history. Different strategies for ensuring the viability of the institution have been adopted, discarded, and tried again.

Through it all, the shifting nature of one congregation's identity across a century and a half has been part of something much larger that held me in its grip as I wrote this narrative: the challenge facing all of us who seek to reshape Judaism in order to sustain it.

THERE ARE MANY INDIVIDUALS who have helped make this book a reality. First and foremost, my deepest thanks go to Rabbi Stephen Pearce and Executive Director Gary Cohn for initiating the project and aiding me in every possible way. Both of them read major portions of the manuscript and made many valuable suggestions, all in the interest of clarity, accuracy, felicitous prose, and, above all, intellectual honesty. The high priority they place on preserving the history of their temple—in the tradition of the late Rabbi Joseph Asher, who engaged me to write the first version—should stand as a model for other synagogues across the country.

I am also grateful to Stephen Dobbs, himself a noted historian of Bay Area Jewry, for the care and concern he took in editing the entire manuscript. I benefited enormously from the knowledge he has gained from his lifelong affiliation with the temple, from his expertise on the history of the city of San Francisco, and from his firsthand experience with the inner workings of the Jewish community. The book was further improved by Naomi Leite's thorough and precise copyediting and Sara Glaser's keen and creative eye for design.

I also appreciate the input and encouragement of four of my closest friends and my sister, all of whom read parts of the work in its early stages: David Biale, Ken Cohen, Seymour Fromer, Harold Lindenthal, and Bobbi Leigh Zito. My thanks also go to several others whom I asked for advice as much as for information: John Rothmann, Terri Forman, Cantor Joseph Portnoy, and Rabbis Mark Schiftan, Helen Cohn, and Peretz Wolf-Prusan. In this regard I owe a special debt of gratitude to the late Rabbi Alvin Fine, who assisted me in countless ways in the preparation of both versions of this book, and who always lifted my spirits in the process.

Among the many archives and libraries in which I worked, the Western Jewish History Center of the Judah L. Magnes Museum in Berkeley is by far the most important, with its rich holdings of periodicals, personal correspondence, and institutional records. Susan Morris, now executive director of the Magnes Museum, always went the extra mile in locating the documents I needed. I thank her not only for her efforts but also for her enthusiasm.

As for the temple archives, I am grateful to Norman and Rose Grabstein for the thorough orientation they gave me to the many documents, photographs, and artifacts that have been preserved over the years by devoted congregants like themselves. Four temple staff members who cheerfully met my endless requests for data are Kathleen Safer, Sandy Barth and her predecessor, the late Muriel Cohn, and Dana Zimmerman, who was also of great help in gathering the illustrations for this volume.

I would also like to take this opportunity to acknowledge my debt to Rabbi William M. Kramer, the late Norton B. Stern, and their thirty-year-old journal, *Western States Jewish History*. Those who work in this field will know that over the years I have had my differences with Stern and Kramer on matters of fact, interpretation, and even propriety. I still take issue with them on several key points (most notably the cultural identity of the immigrants from Posen, among the region's earliest Jewish settlers). But in conducting my research for this project, I was struck again and again by the invaluable contribution they and their periodical have made to our understanding of the pioneer period. It is something that, in the heat of the intellectual battles I had with them as a young man, I had not fully appreciated. The fact remains that in writing the first four chapters of this book, I made use of more than two dozen articles from their publication—many of them written by Stern and Kramer themselves.

I interviewed twenty people for my original study two decades ago, and more than forty for this one. Nearly all of the interviews of the late '90s were recorded on audiotapes which are in my possession. I am thankful to all of those who took the time (in some cases many hours) to discuss with me their impressions of the congregation. In addition, I utilized seven key interviews conducted by Anita Hecht of Life History Services for the Edith S. Green Oral History Project, another aspect of the temple's sesquicentennial commemoration. I thank her for sharing those with me.

I am especially grateful to Robert Kirschner for granting me a ten-hour interview—with no subject off-limits—which he allowed me to record on audiotape. He also made available a raft of news clippings, photographs, and other documents dealing with his eleven and a half momentous years at the temple. Delving into his past at Emanu-El resulted in both pain and pride for Bob, but I could not have told the full story, either of his accomplishments or of his failings, without his help. I deeply appreciate his cooperation.

My final word of thanks goes to my partner in life, Dorothy Shipps, for her loving support and wise counsel every step of the way.

F. R.
December 1999

Visions of Reform

chapter one

Instant Metropolis

A tidal wave of humanity engulfed Northern California following the discovery of gold in the foothills of the Sierras early in 1848. With a suddenness unmatched in American history before or since, a remote and largely uninhabited region was rudely transformed into a monstrous center of commercial activity. By the end of 1852, the promise of new wealth had lured nearly a quarter of a million people, and the initial destination for almost all of them was San Francisco, the gateway to the Mother Lode. What had been an inconsequential Mexican outpost of eight hundred on the eve of the Gold Rush had fifty-six thousand inhabitants a decade later; it ranked as the fifteenth-largest city in the United States and its sixth-busiest port.

An unprecedented confluence of peoples descended upon the makeshift town from all parts of the country and from all over the globe. Foreigners, only 10 percent of the American population in the early 1850s, outnumbered the native-born in San Francisco, making it the most ethnically diverse city on the continent. Alongside Southerners, New Englanders, and a large contingent from New York City, came Chinese and South Americans, Polynesians and Europeans, Australians and North Africans. And among this "medley of races and nationalities," described by Hubert Howe Bancroft, were "the ubiquitous Hebrews," most of them Europeans, who had lived on the east coast of the United States only a few short years before undertaking the perilous trip to

California. A handful had come overland, defying rugged terrain, an un-
forgiving climate, and dangerous Plains Indians. But most of the Jews,
already veterans of one ocean voyage and embarking from a coastal city,
chose the sea route: the no less harrowing, five- to eight-month-long,
sixteen-thousand-mile journey "around the Horn," or the preferable
shorter route which broke the trip at the Isthmus of Panama but required
a crossing of mountains by mule and malarial swampland by canoe. A few
even came directly from Europe, the transatlantic trip adding thousands
of more miles to their odyssey.

The accounts of those who went by sea—and they had a great deal of
time to set down their thoughts—reveal the wonder they felt in experiencing the tropics for the first time: birds and fish they had never seen
before, sunsets unlike any in the northern latitudes, exotic tastes and
aromas that were new to them. But this was small consolation for the
monotony, the disease and discomfort, and at times the terror to which
they were subjected aboard the hundreds of old vessels that hastily had to
be put into service. Noting the bad food, the dirty, congested quarters, and
the lack of privacy, the cultural historian Kevin Starr likens their ordeal to
"spending half a year in a floating tenement."

Jews, a mere two-tenths of one percent of the American population at
mid-century, had a far higher representation among those daring enough
to undertake this adventure. They "numbered in the thousands on ships'
passenger lists" and doubtless constituted several percent of this great internal migration, arguably the most significant event in the nation's history
since the Louisiana Purchase nearly half a century before.

A significant few were proud and reserved Sephardim whose ancestors
had for centuries advised the rulers of Iberia, and who had been established in America—usually in a Southern port city such as Savannah or
Charleston—since colonial times. Fully acculturated and well educated,
they would play a vital role in the city and its Jewish community, particularly in the 1850s. There was also a sprinkling of Jews from France
(especially the province of Alsace along the Rhine), England, and Russian
Poland. But the majority by far hailed from the German-speaking lands
of Central Europe.

A virtual reservoir of Jewish immigration was Posen, in the kingdom
of Prussia, a province seized from Poland in 1793, where Jewish life in the

first half of the nineteenth century still approximated that of an East European *shtetl*. Living among ethnic Poles, the Jews here were more segregated, more pious, and more impoverished than anywhere else in the German states.

But the winds of change were beginning to be felt even in this bastion of traditionalism. Beginning in 1833 (just a few years after the birth of most of those who would later immigrate to California), Jewish children were required to attend the Prussian elementary schools. And the very decision to emigrate—itself breaking the long-standing pattern of passivity among East European Jews—indicated that the young men and women who left Posen were more modern and Western-oriented in their thinking than those who remained behind. The immigrants were Prussian subjects, travelling under Prussian passports, and, most significantly, spoke and wrote German as well as Yiddish. Once in America, they preferred to emphasize that German element of their binational provenance for reasons of social status. Yet to their chagrin, they were widely known as "Polish Jews" in the United States and frequently chided as "Polacks" by the other major German-speaking Jewish group in America.

These were the Bavarians, among the first of the German Jews to immigrate, and destined to achieve the most, particularly in the business world. Like the Poseners, they came from deeply religious, rural villages, spoke a variant of Yiddish as well as German, and were held back economically because of civil disabilities.

But here hopes for emancipation had been awakened as early as the eighteenth century. In the kingdom of Bavaria (as in the other southwestern German states such as neighboring Baden and Württemburg) the French Revolution had raised expectations among Jews that the thousand-year-old chains of persecution would finally be broken. Instead, in the wake of Napoleon's defeat, reactionaries on the German thrones crushed all hopes of legal equality, restoring medieval restrictions on occupation and residence, and even placing a quota on the annual number of Jewish marriages. Immigration for Bavarian Jewry was in this sense "a substitute for emancipation." But the economic motivation may have been even greater; particularly in the 1830s and '40s, it was the poorer Jews in the southern German states who chose to emigrate, young people who "could neither work nor marry."

From 1835 to 1880 almost two hundred thousand Jews from the German lands arrived in the United States. While it is true that most of them remained peddlers or small shopkeepers their entire lives, many became leading businessmen in their communities and a surprising number reached the pinnacle of wealth and status in the new land. Among these merchant-princes, a good portion made their fortunes in San Francisco.

But this lay years in the future. When they sailed through the Golden Gate in 1849 or in the early 1850s, they were very young men, often short on education, experience, and capital. Some went directly to the diggings to "see the elephant," the phrase used then to describe the world of the "real argonauts" at work in the gold fields, a phenomenon at once strange, dangerous, and of huge proportions. But most Jews realized from the outset that the merchant rather than the miner stood the best chance of attaining financial security. Often relying on a relative in the East who could ship dry goods—for which there was a terrific demand—they carried packs on their backs or opened small stores in San Francisco as well as in the coarse Sierra mining towns.

This first generation of Jews in the Bay City was twice as likely as non-Jews to remain in the area permanently. In other respects too, as we shall see, these early Jewish businessmen—who rarely drank to excess and usually kept within the bounds of the law—were a stabilizing, civilizing influence on frontier society.

Stability and civilization were badly needed in the wake of the invasion of the gold-seekers. A sprawling jumble of canvas tents and flimsy shacks, San Francisco during the first two Gold Rush years was ravaged by no less than six citywide fires, most of them the work of arsonists. Frequent floods and sandstorms hit the city. Rats and other vermin infested the area, which suffered a serious outbreak of cholera in 1850. And litter was everywhere: not only was garbage regularly dumped in the streets and the bay, but large quantities of goods that hadn't found a buyer simply lay rotting on the ground or washed up on the beach.

While there were few streetlamps until the mid-1850s, the town was illuminated by the light of its many saloons—centers for prostitution, gambling, and brawling as well as drinking. "Sports" in this city of young men gone wild included not only horseracing and bullfighting, but also cockfighting and bearbaiting. The muddy streets were rife with crime, including gang warfare and murder, but despite the formation of vigilante committees, justice was rare. Of fifty-four cases of homicide in the year ending in June 1851, not one was punished.

Even aside from onerous living conditions and recurring physical disasters, even apart from rampant vice and crime, the new arrivals were struck by the astonishing ethos prevailing in the boom town—an unbridled frenzy for quick riches. The norms of behavior they had learned in their short lifetimes about the value of work, money, and investment were severely tested as they saw fortunes made and lost in a day and masters and servants literally change places overnight.

The pioneer women provided some grounding, of course, and writers on the Gold Rush, and the Jewish experience in particular, are struck by the duty to their husbands they showed. There are many accounts of their resourcefulness on the journey and their quiet strength in making a home and raising a family amidst such chaotic conditions. At times they could also be found running their own small businesses, or teaching school. On the western frontier, more than elsewhere in the country at mid-century, necessity demanded that women work outside the home, and the relatively fluid social structure permitted it.

But there were very few women; this was a society largely without females, not only in the mining camps but even in San Francisco. Among the adult population in the city, men outnumbered them 6.5 to 1 as late as 1852.* And that small female contingent included many prostitutes, another side of the complex women's story among the gold-seekers.

Another San Francisco was emerging even in 1849, however. "Through the mud and stink and immorality," as one scholar has put it, "the unmistakable scent of respectability was in the air." While most of the transient youths gave little thought to the welfare of their community, there were indeed pioneers who cared about the rule of law, and about education, parks, culture, and religion. Most of these were businessmen and professionals who could see, even in the very beginning, that San Francisco had the potential to be the leading commercial center in the vast area from the Rocky Mountains to the Pacific Coast. They linked their own future to that of the new city.

*The demographic imbalance would right itself only gradually; by 1860, the ratio of adult men to women was 2.5 to 1, and parity was reached only in 1880.

The Jewish merchants were very much a part of that earliest "establishment." They sought permanence and security in their uncertain surroundings. Many thousands of miles from their families, they were also clearly longing for the emotional support their faith could provide: fellowship with their own kind, a link to the past and a connection with home.

IT WAS THESE IMPULSES that led to the first Jewish services on the West Coast, on Rosh Hashanah, 1849, when a group of perhaps thirty Jews, responding to a local newspaper notice, met in a wood-framed tent on Jackson Street near Kearny.* By Yom Kippur their number grew to nearly fifty. As they had no *Sefer Torah*, a sacred scroll made of parchment, a printed copy of the Pentateuch was used instead.**

The first Jewish organization in the West came into existence soon after these services. At the end of 1849, the First Hebrew Benevolent Society, comprised largely of Poseners and East European Jews, was founded to care for the sick and needy. Soon thereafter one of its leaders, Henry Hart, raised the funds to acquire two lots at the intersection of Vallejo and Gough Streets for a Jewish cemetery. In the fall of 1850, the Eureka Benevolent Society was established, primarily by Bavarian Jews. Its founder, the twenty-six-year-old dry goods dealer August Helbing of Munich, later reflected on the mix of social needs and charitable obligations felt by "the Jewish young men":

> We had no suitable way of spending our evenings. Gambling resorts and theatres, the only refuge then existing in 'Frisco to spend an evening, had no attraction for us. We passed the time back of our stores and often times were disgusted and sick from the loneliness of our

* Another version of the first service places the site on Montgomery Street, and the City of San Francisco has actually put up a plaque at that spot, but contemporary research tends to authenticate the tent-room on Jackson.

** The partial list of those present reveals the diversity of the nascent town's Jewish population. At least two were American-born: the Sephardi Joseph Shannon, who would soon be elected treasurer of the County of San Francisco; and Albert Priest of New York, who had come in by wagon from Sacramento. The Englishmen included Benjamin Davidson, soon to become an agent of the Rothschilds; Barnett Keesing, accompanied by his wife, the only woman present; and Lewis Franklin, of Silesian descent, whose store housed the worship services. Abraham Watters was a young merchant from Prussia; Samuel Fleishhacker was likely a relative of Aaron Fleishhacker of Bavaria, patriarch of the respected family of bankers and industrialists. Joel Noah, a dealer in dry goods, was of Hungarian descent.

surroundings. Besides, our services were in active demand; every steamer brought a number of our coreligionists, and they did not always come provided with means. In fact, some came penniless, having invested their all in a passage to the Coast. Some came sick and sore, and it needed often times a respectable portion of our earnings to satisfy all the demands made upon us.

High Holiday services that fall, for a considerably larger group than the year before, were held in Masonic Hall on Kearny Street, with "much pleasure felt at the cheering presence of many dark-eyed daughters of Judah." The Yom Kippur sermon, which has come down to us in its entirety, was delivered by the twenty-nine-year-old Lewis Franklin. He hailed from Liverpool but his Orthodox family's roots were in Silesia, like Posen a part of Poland that had been incorporated into Prussia.

Like the many forceful Christian preachers in San Francisco during the Gold Rush, whose favorite topic was the folly of greed, Franklin delivered a fiery oration, imploring each person present to "pause in your mad career 'ere it be too late." Invoking Ecclesiastes, among many other classical Jewish texts, he held forth:

> "Vanity of vanity, verily all is vanity," saith the preacher. Ye say wealth is to the possessor rank and life, and flattery and praise and envy salute your ears and ye are content. Ambition goads ye on, and ye would feign know no superior in the social scale. Man thou art a very idiot! These shining baubles…will take unto themselves wings, and flee from thee, leaving thou as naked as when thou wert first created.

He noted the familiarity with Jewish teachings of most of his listeners, but railed at their lack of piety: "Your very knowledge makes you doubly culpable." In particular, he castigated them for violating the Sabbath: "Hark ye at the terrible consequences! The soul of the Sabbath-breaker shall be cut off from his people."

In his thunderous demand for strict religious observance in the midst of raucous San Francisco, Franklin showed little interest in adapting Judaism to its new environment; his faith had to be rigid, for it was a shield of protection—against immorality, natural disaster, and his own loneliness. The presence in the city of two kosher boardinghouses during the Gold Rush years is evidence that he was not alone in clinging to tradition.

Franklin left San Francisco the following year and sailed back to

Europe at the end of the decade. But on that September morning in 1850, he also left a legacy to the Jewish community in the form of a challenge to construct a synagogue: "And I ask you," he exclaimed near the end of his exhortation, "shall there be no temple built to Israel's God?"

Yet this group did not hold services beyond Simchat Torah on September 29. It was torn apart by a serious rift between the Eastern and Western Europeans on matters of liturgy. Indeed, one of the two factions (probably the Bavarians, objecting to *Minhag Polen*, the traditional Polish ritual which Franklin likely used) had actually walked out of the Yom Kippur services. Despite the fact that the German and Polish rites were virtually identical textually, the differences in pronunciation, melodies, and minor procedures during the services were evidently decisive for immigrants seeking to replicate the religious experience they had known since childhood.

There appears to have been a semblance of unity at a series of meetings held in March 1851 to arrange for the observance of Passover and even to begin raising funds for a synagogue. By March 16, $4,400 had been collected from 182 contributors—more than half the number of Jewish households in town.

A meeting was called for April 6, inviting "the Israelites of San Francisco" specifically for the purpose of forming a congregation and electing officers. But alas, the group proved deadlocked on the question of who was to be elected community *shochet*, or ritual butcher, with the German and Polish sides (comprised largely of Bavarians and Poseners, respectively) each supporting its own countrymen as candidates. At the "stormy" public meeting, in the words of an eyewitness, the internal dissension in the room was so great that there could be no other decision that evening but to establish two congregations in the new city, just as there were two benevolent societies.

Such disagreements between the Bavarians and Poseners were common across America, and split many of the dozens of new synagogues formed by German-Jewish immigrants in the 1840s and '50s. One might expect San Francisco to have been different, almost two thousand miles from the nearest synagogue (in St. Louis) and in so many respects a social and cultural anomaly. But here too, age-old customs—as well as prejudice and mistrust—prevailed.

The regional pride—one leading researcher uses the word "arrogance"—of the Bavarians was based on more than a geographical distinction or a liturgical preference. Even at this early moment in the experience of Bay Area Jewry, social and class gradations were also evident: the Bavarians as a rule had arrived in America about a decade earlier than most Poseners and, in part because of that head start, were usually more successful in business. They tended to have more of a mercantile background than the Poseners, who were more likely to have been trained as artisans. They could identify fully with German culture, in vogue in America at mid-century, whereas Posnanian Jewry, as we have seen, was not allowed by other Jews to shed its Polish stigma.

This fragmentation within a religious group was hardly unique in Gold Rush San Francisco. The French Catholics worshipped apart from their Irish coreligionists, who were far below them on the social scale. Even the American-born Presbyterians were divided along sectional more than doctrinal lines, with Southerners and New Englanders early establishing separate churches.

As for the two Jewish congregations born in the same room on April 6, 1851, they would be as rival siblings ever since.* One was Emanu-El, meaning "God is with us," perhaps an expression of gladness for having arrived safely on the West Coast, perhaps forging a link with New York's synagogue of the same name, formed six years earlier by Bavarians. It drafted a charter on April 8, and filed it with the county clerk three days later. The incorporating document was signed by sixteen men, mostly Bavarians, but it also counted at least three native-born Sephardim.**

A recent study of the founders (including not only the sixteen who

*The controversy and confusion over which is the oldest congregation has also continued until the present day. Writing in 1900, Emanu-El's spiritual leader, Jacob Voorsanger, adamantly claimed that distinction for his synagogue, "a subject that, historically, admits of no discussion whatever," and determined the founding year of his institution to have been 1850. But in 1974, two researchers convincingly demonstrated that his conclusion was based entirely on a single misdated document. As they persuasively point out, no reference to either congregation—in newspapers or municipal records—exists before April 1851.

**The signers of the charter were Philip Runkel, Abraham Watters, Abraham Labatt, Samuel Marx, Moritz Schwartz, Simon Heiter, L. A. Levy Jr., Joseph Shannon, Rudolph Wyman, I. E. Woolf, A. H. Harris, J. J. Joseph Jr., S[amuel] Fleishhacker, J. Honisberger, Louis Cohn, and William Seligman. The original "Articles of Incorporation" was inscribed by Abraham Labatt's son, Henry.

signed the charter, but several dozen more who soon joined) reveals that they were typically in their early twenties, significantly younger even than the youthful founders of comparable German synagogues in other parts of the country. Their wives—or future wives, because many were not yet married—were much younger still. Nearly all the founding members were in commerce.

The other congregation, taking the name Sherith Israel—interestingly enough that of another New York synagogue, the oldest in the nation— included Englishmen, Poseners, and Jews from Russian-occupied Poland who met on the evening of April 8 and prepared an advertisement for kosher meat which ran in the *Alta California* two days later. Its bylaws stressed unwavering adherence to *Minhag Polen*, the Polish rite. Emanu-El began with sixty members, Sherith Israel with forty-two.

Given its later orientation, it is perhaps surprising that Congregation Emanu-El, in its infancy, was Orthodox. But this was the form of Judaism with which most of its members had been familiar in the small towns of Central Europe. Moreover, despite the clear commitment to making a new life in the West, the desire for acculturation was not yet fully awakened, and certainly not clearly directed, in the tumultuous early 1850s. On the frontier, even more than in the cities on the East Coast, the pioneers felt forced by necessity to relinquish Jewish practices in their daily lives. But this did not preclude them from founding synagogues that would put them back in touch with the Old World piety they had not so long ago left behind.

In addition to the importance attached to the office of *shochet*, Emanu-El's "Constitution" of 1851 decreed that services would strictly follow the *Minhag Ashkenaz* (traditional German ritual) and that members would be required to attend a *minyan* (the ancient requirement of ten men to constitute a quorum for prayer services) when notified. It also provided that no one married to a non-Jew was to be allowed to join and that any congregant taking a gentile wife automatically forfeited his membership.

YET THERE WERE HINTS from the outset that the congregation would gravitate toward liberal Judaism, itself barely in embryo. Emanu-El's first president was the Sephardi clothier Abraham C. Labatt, born and raised in Charleston, South Carolina, where in 1824 he had been active in the founding of the nation's first Reform congregation. Along with forty-six others, he had left his traditional synagogue, Beth Elohim, and organized the Reformed Society of Israelites, which shortened the services and introduced English into the liturgy. This lay experiment suffered greatly from the lack of rabbinical guidance, and would go no further than Charleston. But Labatt's presidency portended religious change—even if, for the moment, the recently arrived German-speaking majority seemed wedded to the notion of an Orthodox synagogue.

But reform would have to wait for a more pressing reason: the city and the congregation were in turmoil in the early 1850s. During Labatt's half-year term and the year served by his successor, the American-born Sephardi Joseph Shannon (both of them municipal officeholders, as well), there was more concern with survival than engaging in theological combat.

Less than a month after the founding of the congregation came the "Great Fire" of May 1851, destroying eighteen city blocks, or one-fourth of the entire "cloth and board" city. Ten to twelve million dollars of property was reduced to ashes, much of it belonging to Jewish retailers. Without any insurance companies operating in San Francisco at the time, and with underwriters in the East covering but a portion of the losses, many merchants suffered complete financial ruin. As one resident wrote home describing the calamitous spring of 1851, "Thefts, robberies, murders and fires follow each other in such rapid succession that we hardly recover from the effects of one horrible tragedy before another piece of unmitigated villainy demands our attention."

In June, many of the leading citizens, frustrated by an undermanned and ineffective police force and a corrupt judiciary, formed the first Vigilance Committee and took control of the city. No fewer than seven hundred men—among them about thirty Jews, including one of Labatt's cousins and several charter members of Emanu-El—joined the extralegal committee. For a month the vigilantes fought violent crime by bringing accused lawbreakers to its secret tribunals, trying them quickly and then dispensing "justice." Their main target was the "Sydney Ducks," gang members often of Irish ancestry who had immigrated to San Francisco via Australia, where some had spent years in that country's penal colonies. About half of the ninety men tried were set free due to lack of evidence, but one was whipped publicly and four others hanged.

During the turbulence that marked the infancy of the congregation, still in rented quarters on Kearny Street, its entire income was barely $1,500. But some progress had been made. A *Sefer Torah* was donated to Emanu-El in 1851 by the British philanthropist and guardian of threatened Jewish communities Sir Moses Montefiore; he may have learned of the needs of the San Francisco Jewish community through Benjamin Davidson, the representative in California of Montefiore's brother-in-law, Nathan Mayer Rothschild. A Torah reader, Cantor Max Welhof, was appointed in 1851, but at a nominal salary. The roughly one dozen children of the members were taught informally by the congregant Louis Cohn without compensation.

It was not until the spring of 1853, a few months after economic conditions had improved, that serious consideration was given to the erection of a synagogue. Emanuel Berg, the third president in two years, appointed a committee to acquire a suitable lot.

In addition to the rapid growth of the town's population, which now began to include a considerable number of women and children, it is possible that the thirty-five-year-old native of Bamberg, Bavaria, was also reacting to an outside threat in advocating a synagogue. To be sure, anti-Semitism was rare in the pioneer West, but newspapers such as the *Alta California* did print letters demanding a strict Sunday closing law, missives which often alleged greed as the motivation of Jewish storeowners who conducted operations on the gentile Sabbath. A flurry of these letters—often refuted by Jew and gentile alike—appeared late in 1852, while a petition, full of anti-Semitic slurs, urged the state legislature to enact a Sunday closing law.

Yet many months went by before the committee appointed by Berg announced that a site had been bought for the construction of a synagogue atop today's Nob Hill on California Street between Mason and Powell. The purchase price was $3,000, most of which was paid in cash. At its annual meeting on October 23, 1853, the congregation formally approved the acquisition of the lot and also elected as president the Bavarian dry goods dealer Henry Seligman. He was barely twenty-five years old. Serving until mid-1855, and again from 1857 to 1862, this member of a famous family of financiers exerted more influence on the congregation during its formative years than did any other layman.

In the late 1840s, Henry Seligman had been the last of a family of eight brothers and three sisters to immigrate to America from the tiny village of Baiersdorf (literally, "Bavarian village"). The men worked slavishly as peddlers, first in Pennsylvania and later in the South and upstate New York. Henry was preceded on the West Coast by two of his brothers, Jesse and Leopold, who sailed to San Francisco in 1850 with $20,000 of merchandise. Leopold almost died from malaria contracted during the Panama crossing, and Jesse was nearly killed when a stray bullet from a gunfight went through his hat. But the Seligmans prospered. In order to protect their goods from fire, they rented one of the city's few brick buildings. The gold they earned from their efforts was sent to New York, where the oldest brother, Joseph, traded it on the world market, laying the foundation for the mighty Seligman financial empire.

Henry and his brother William soon arrived in California as well, partly because the artistic Leopold, more interested in sketchbooks than ledger books, provided little help to Jesse. As in the East, the brothers did not abide by the Sabbath and dietary laws of their childhood. But they did feel an obligation to establish a congregation, even as they amassed a fortune in a rootless city that seemed driven only by money. Jesse and William joined Emanu-El, the latter as a charter member. Yet another brother, Abraham, later came out West and served for many years on the board of trustees. Henry, as president, directed efforts to construct a synagogue and engage a rabbi.

Only three weeks after his election, the congregation—still composed primarily of very young men whose future was uncertain—unanimously committed itself to raise $20,000 to build a house of worship. But the group of thirty in attendance at the special meeting decided to sell the California Street parcel and look elsewhere for a suitable spot. The site, with its commanding view of the Golden Gate, would later soar in value as private mansions and fine hotels rose alongside it. In 1853, however, two decades before the introduction of the cable cars that would make Nob Hill accessible, its high elevation ruled it out as inconvenient.

The California Street property was auctioned off, actually at a loss, but President Seligman found another piece of land early in 1854, nine thousand square feet six blocks north of the California site on Broadway between Mason and Powell. Known as North Beach even then, this was

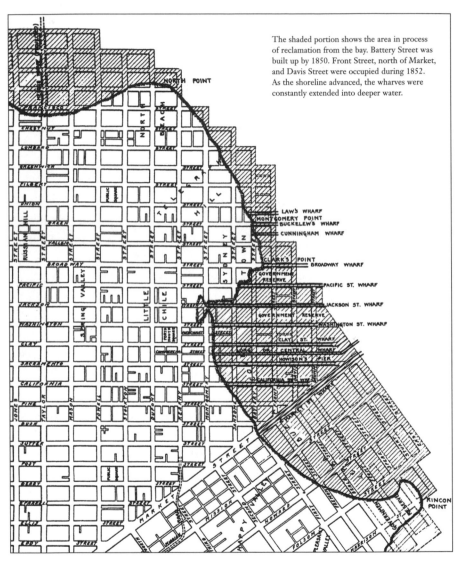

The shaded portion shows the area in process
of reclamation from the bay. Battery Street was
built up by 1850. Front Street, north of Market,
and Davis Street were occupied during 1852.
As the shoreline advanced, the wharves were
constantly extended into deeper water.

LAWS WHARF
MONTGOMERY POINT
BUCKELEW'S WHARF
CUNNINGHAM WHARF
CLARK'S POINT
BROADWAY WHARF
GOVERNMENT RESERVE
PACIFIC ST. WHARF
JACKSON ST. WHARF
GOVERNMENT RESERVE
WASHINGTON ST. WHARF
CLAY ST. WHARF
CENTRAL WHARF
HOWISON'S PIER
CALIFORNIA ST. LINE

NORTH POINT
RINCON POINT

MAP OF SAN FRANCISCO SHOWING BUSINESS SECTION
AND WATERFRONT, 1851–1852

a residential district in which many Jews made their homes. Stockton Street in particular, one block east of Powell, was considered a fashionable address for many Jewish merchants who enjoyed a short walk to their stores or warehouses in the city's business district.*

A design was accepted which had been estimated to cost $30,000, but when the contractors reported that there would be a 33 percent overrun, Seligman opted for the more modest plans which could be executed for the $20,000 voted upon six months earlier. In the spring of 1854, before the next deep downturn in the roller-coaster economy of the Bay City, ground was broken for the synagogue.

The young Henry Seligman (no doubt competing a bit with his brother James, who was one of the founders of New York's fast-growing Emanu-El) aimed high for his fledgling congregation in another respect as well: he convinced his fellow members, already hard-pressed by the building campaign, to pledge an additional $3,500 a year, the sum needed to retain a full-time rabbi.

Yet even at that lofty salary, three times the amount earned by an experienced physician or lawyer in those years, very few rabbis were available. Most of the nation's seventy-five congregations were led by cantors or laymen, for the yeshiva-trained rabbi was not a likely candidate for immigration to the "American Babylon." Only in the 1840s and '50s did a coterie of German-speaking rabbis come to the United States with the expectation that it would provide the proper atmosphere for their revolutionary interpretation of Judaism, strongly influenced by the Berlin Haskalah which Moses Mendelssohn had set in motion in the late eighteenth century. This movement, which crystallized in the German states during the liberal Napoleonic occupation, sought to end the ghettoized existence of Central European Jewry. It attempted to bring Jewish life more into line with that of the host country—economically, politically, socially, and even religiously. Thus, the Talmud was stressed less than the universal ethical message of the Bible, particularly the prophets. Many of the Hebrew prayers were removed from the service and often an organ

---

*The almost "instant spatial ordering" of the city in the early 1850s included a central business district between the bay and Montgomery Street, bounded by Market Street to the south and the Pacific Street wharf to the north. Most of the Jews lived in the nearby area to the west, beyond Dupont Street (renamed Grant Avenue early in the twentieth century).

was brought into the synagogue. Jews were urged to dress like their gentile neighbors, attend secular schools, and petition the German states for equal treatment under the law.

Few of the pioneer Jews in early San Francisco had been influenced by this movement in Europe; they came largely from rural hamlets which had remained traditional. But they would soon be profoundly affected by Reform Judaism, as it came to be known in America.

Its leader was the highly ambitious Isaac Mayer Wise of Bohemia, who had arrived in New York in 1846. After he had served for four years as the rabbi of Congregation Beth El in Albany, the board dismissed him because of his outspoken views. When Wise nonetheless continued to perform his duties, the president of the synagogue punched him in the face during Rosh Hashanah services, instigating a riot among the worshippers. Wise remained in Albany, forming a new congregation where he introduced the organ and, in 1851, mixed seating, the first time the family pew had ever been seen in a synagogue. But upstate New York proved too small a stage for him and by 1854 he was firmly ensconced at B'nai Jeshurun in Cincinnati, an expanding, young city which became the national headquarters of his new weekly, the *American Israelite*, and of the burgeoning Reform movement.

Wise was not the most radical of reformers; he forcefully advocated that his congregants close their businesses on the Sabbath, for example, and he believed that the divine revelation at Sinai was unique and "remains truth forever." But armed with philosophical principles such as "rational progress," which he had learned in Prague and Vienna, he sought to transform Judaism in America, a land he loved with a passion. He would steer a middle course when necessary, but his ultimate goal was to remake the Jewish liturgy, ritual, and credo to suit the values of the New World.

It was Wise's friend and like-minded colleague, Rabbi James Gutheim of Westphalia, whom Seligman invited to assume the Emanu-El pulpit. Gutheim had preceded Wise as the spiritual leader of B'nai Jeshurun, where he had brought in a choir and eliminated some of the prayers amidst a violent controversy not unlike the incident in Albany.

By the time of Seligman's invitation, however, Gutheim had been serving the Jewish community of New Orleans for several years, and he chose to remain at his post. For the Emanu-El pulpit he suggested Dr. David

Steinberg, his former classmate at the seminary of Münster, who also taught at that institution and stood in line to become its director. Seligman sent funds to Gutheim to book Steinberg's passage from Europe, but he too declined to come. Steinberg was aware that another Central European rabbi, already in America, was much interested in the Emanu-El position, and he felt it undignified to compete with him.

THAT WAS THE LEARNED JULIUS ECKMAN, who would become San Francisco's first congregational rabbi. He arrived in July 1854 and was soon asked to perform the ceremonies of laying the cornerstone both for Emanu-El and, two weeks later, for nearby Sherith Israel.

His credentials could not have been better: though born in Posen, he had earned a doctorate in classics at the University of Berlin. He had received his rabbinical ordination in the Prussian capital as well, from none other than Leopold Zunz, "the father of modern Jewish scholarship," who had been instrumental in laying the philosophical foundations for liberal Judaism in the German states. Because Eckman had also spent three years in London as a teenager, his English was flawless, and it was expected that his sermons would be as polished as those of any rabbi in America. Beyond all of that was his unquestionable dedication to the education of the young.

But he was far from ideally suited for the Emanu-El post, and it is clear that Seligman and the board of trustees had serious reservations about him from the beginning. Having come to San Francisco without a formal invitation, he was not engaged until late October 1854, after he had consecrated the handsome Broadway synagogue (on September 14) and led High Holiday services, all on a trial basis. Even then he was selected in large part because no one else was available; neither Gutheim nor the traditional Isaac Leeser, a highly respected cantor and journalist in Philadelphia with whom Seligman corresponded, could put forward any other name. Eckman was offered only a one-year contract and the salary was reduced to $2,000 from the $3,500 originally budgeted.

Perhaps the Emanu-El leadership was worried about the fact that he had lasted no more than a year at each of three different congregations in the South since immigrating to America in 1849. The Labatt family knew him—he had performed the wedding of Abraham's son Henry in New

Orleans—and although Henry would later become a close personal friend of the rabbi, the Labatts, among many others, harbored serious doubts about his ability to succeed in San Francisco.

But the substantial new house of worship seemed to demand a full-time rabbi. A solid, brick structure, with an attractive neo-Gothic facade, including buttresses and pointed windows and portals, it had a seating capacity of eight hundred. With a swelling list of members, many of them now joined in San Francisco by their wives and children, Seligman and his board felt that they could leave the pulpit vacant no longer.

Eckman lived on the West Coast until his death in 1874, but this first rabbi of Emanu-El had the shortest tenure of any in its history: only one year. Certainly a major reason for his failure was that he was not a member of Wise's camp and was at most a halfhearted reformer.

For reform was clearly Seligman's preference by the mid-1850s; he had to have been aware of the initiatives taken during this period not only by Rabbis Wise and Gutheim but also by New York's Emanu-El. Moreover, as the years passed, he and many of his fellow Bavarian businessmen

SAN FRANCISCO, SHOWING THE BROADWAY SYNAGOGUE, 1856

naturally began to feel more comfortable in their new home in San Francisco, and less in need of the precise religious experience they had known as children. If they had drawn strength and comfort from the Orthodox service during the traumatic and disorienting period of the Gold Rush, they saw themselves only a few years later as solid citizens of an emerging American metropolis. "The new focus of their lives was San Francisco," writes one historian of the change in sentiment among almost all ethnic groups in the city around the midpoint of this seminal decade, "and no hankering after the past could repel its demands. The narrow streets jumbled people up together; business, pleasure, educational, and ceremonial life multiplied their contacts; decentralization repeatedly uprooted them residentially; and the growing use of English gradually wiped out the main European criterion of nationality." In this dense environment of newcomers—in which people of different backgrounds mixed with one another even more than in other parts of urban America—religious insularity was beginning to erode as well.

By the mid-1850s there were no fewer than twenty-two Protestant churches in San Francisco, many of them with a high profile in the life of the compact city. It is unlikely that leading Jews did not have at least a passing acquaintance with the universal message of the Unitarians, the cultivated aestheticism of the Episcopalians, the tireless work on behalf of the poor carried out by the Methodists, and even the successful Sunday schools of the Baptists. They were annoyed at the Christian proselytizers in their midst (a problem throughout the country at this time), but also had to be aware of the dedicated, broad-minded preachers among the Protestants, some with advanced degrees from Harvard or Yale, who delivered their inspiring sermons in the streets and on the wharves as well as in the churches.

The Emanu-El membership—gradually and tentatively, to be sure—began to form a vision of an Americanized synagogue, shorn somewhat of its Jewish and German distinctiveness. They were groping toward a religious expression that, in their minds, was rational, dignified, and meaningful, and one that would not seem unduly strange to their non-Jewish neighbors, with whom they had such close contact. They hoped as well to resolve the growing contradiction between the lack of observance outside the synagogue, and the strictness of ritual practice within it.

Rabbi Julius Eckman

But Julius Eckman was not the man to lead Emanu-El in this new direction. While he saw the logic of some reforms, his pious childhood in a village in Posen evidently influenced him more than either his secular studies later in life or the open society of the West Coast. In general, he practiced and preached traditional Judaism during his year's tenure, despite the fact that most of the membership was leaning in the opposite direction. A choir of both men and women had been organized before Eckman's election, but in most other respects the services appear to have been Orthodox. "There are no innovations," a perceptive Alsatian observer wrote in 1855; "the synagogue services are more or less as still found in our humble villages," including a "gallery for the ladies."

Eckman did not insist on separate classrooms for boys and girls, and he also voiced his approval of the mixed choir. But his biographer tells us that even by mid-nineteenth-century standards, he was resistant to change when it came to the role of women. In contrast to Isaac Mayer Wise, for example, who favored not only family pews and universal suffrage but also the inclusion of women as synagogue board members, Eckman viewed their "so-called Emancipation" as "ridiculous foolery." He also felt strongly that the liturgy should remain almost completely in Hebrew, that the traditional two-day observance of most of the holidays be maintained, and that the worshippers walk and not ride to Sabbath services. Later he would object to the removal of skullcaps in the synagogue as well as changing the name of the Jewish house of worship to "temple."

But while Eckman resisted the radical reforms that appealed to Seligman, it is also true that he was willing to make some concessions to his times, and it is not inconceivable that he could have reached a compromise with Emanu-El's young lay leaders. Soon after his departure from the synagogue, he applauded the introduction of an organ in the sanctuary, writing that "the cultivated ear of our generation wants the aid of the refined arts in the service of religion as in…daily life." Asked by an Orthodox congregant if the organ may be played on the Sabbath, the rabbi curtly answered, "Fifty years hence our successors will wonder more at the question than the reply." While spiritual leader of Emanu-El, he agreed to suspend some of the stricter Talmudic injunctions pertaining to marriage and divorce, for which he was sharply criticized by the Orthodox Henry A. Henry, soon to become the rabbi of Sherith Israel. Indeed,

Eckman, who once told a friend that Judaism "is on the eve of great changes," might have fashioned a moderate version of Reform in San Francisco that could have had resonance even with the German-Jewish elite, despite its rapid Americanization.

Yet even if the theological differences he had with his flock somehow could have been resolved, Eckman's temperament was another matter. He seemed always at odds with his new surroundings. In a city of frenetic young men seeking quick profits, his manner was calm and ascetic. As one of his contemporaries wrote, "I do not think he ever felt at home amid the hurry and rush of San Francisco. He could not adjust himself to the people. He was devout, and they were intensely worldly." Eckman was appalled that his congregants would throw wedding receptions in downtown taverns, or that they would leave the synagogue (after services but before a public lecture) upon hearing that a steamer had arrived with mail and newspapers for the remote settlement. Most of all, he was distressed by the "madness in raving after riches" which he saw. A lifelong bachelor now past the age of fifty, the solitary rabbi lived in a garret on the most meager rations of food and water.

The only possession Eckman ever prized was his outstanding library, comprised of books in the many languages he read and studded with illuminated Hebrew manuscripts. He was a New Testament scholar as well as an expert on the Hebrew Bible, but his lonely life of austerity and introspection brings to mind the great religions of the Orient; perhaps it is not surprising that in the 1860s he seriously considered ministering to the Jews of Kai Fung Fu, China.*

The gentle rabbi, rarely without a black velvet cap on his head, related best to small children. He opened a Jewish school shortly after his arrival, the first on the Pacific Coast, which he headed while rabbi of Emanu-El and for many years after his ties to the congregation were severed. Known as Hefzibah (a term in Isaiah referring to the people of Israel), the popular school required its students to attend four class sessions during the week for instruction primarily in Jewish texts, as well as Sabbath services and a Sunday lecture. And Eckman wrote and published his own *Prayer-book for Children* and *Vocabulary of the Hebrew Tongue*.

*At least one historian states that Eckman spent several years in China, but in fact he never actually made the trip to Asia.

Certainly Hefzibah may be seen as a major step forward in the evolution of Jewish life in San Francisco. But Eckman's lack of administrative and business expertise, and his reluctance to charge reasonable fees, or any tuition at all for the children of the poor, ensured that the school, like its director, would always be in dire financial straits.

As for his congregational work, his utter lack of tact became painfully obvious within two months of his incumbency. When an official committee of Emanu-El congregants rescinded the license of a *shochet* whom he had earlier approved (the Orthodox Isaac Goldsmith, who also served Sherith Israel in this capacity), the "refined, peace-loving" rabbi surprised the entire city with the fury of his reaction: he published a haughty letter in the *Daily Herald*, denying the synagogue's right to oversee the ritual butchers, and singling out its proposed *shochet* for incompetence. Eckman claimed that he had personally seen the young man eat non-kosher meat, and that the "ignoramus" and "worthless character" lived in a non-kosher boarding house and worked in his butcher shop on the Sabbath.

Several days later a resolution demanding Eckman's resignation was introduced at a congregational meeting. It failed, but he was censured and President Seligman, embarrassed by the public airing of the issue, declared, "We are Reformers and do not take [such] matters so strictly."

The rabbi did not survive the annual assembly in the fall of the following year. Henry Labatt, the prominent attorney and son of Emanu-El's first president, exaggerated only slightly when he said that by then the only point of contention was whether Eckman should be asked to resign or just be summarily dismissed.

The issue that brought him down was more about rabbinical authority than kosher slaughtering, though the two were undoubtedly intertwined in Eckman's mind. His role model as a community rabbi was the devout Joshua Baer Herzfeld, the spiritual leader of Rawicz, Posen, when Eckman was raised there early in the century, and Herzfeld's frequent battles with the *shochtim* did not fail to impress the young Eckman with the need for tight rabbinical control of this key aspect of traditional Jewish life.

America was different, however, for the ultimate authority was lodged with the lay leadership, not only at Emanu-El, but at virtually all of the young German-Jewish congregations across the country. It is not that the pioneers were particularly knowledgeable, nor that they had in their minds an exact blueprint for the reform of the synagogue. What there was no confusion about, however, was the fact that they were in charge; in the last analysis, they were his employers. Eckman's attack on the board of trustees in the public press showed that he had no understanding of the role of the congregational rabbi in the New World.

But if Eckman was not suited for the pulpit, he had other skills that enabled him to make a deep and lasting impact on the pioneer Jewish community of the West Coast. After his dismissal, he turned with even greater vigor to his first love, education, co-directing a secular day school and a Jewish day-care center along with the Hefzibah venture. He retained most of the Emanu-El children in the supplementary school, but now, without congregational backing, he was forced to move Hefzibah out of the Broadway synagogue to shabby rented quarters a few blocks away. Yet the love the youngsters felt for their grandfatherly teacher evidently overcame the miserable physical surroundings. As a prominent San Francisco educator remembered her experience as his student in the late 1850s,

> It was a ramshackle, weird old building, falling into decay, full of strange noises and haunted corners; its halls and stairways unswept, and decorated with cobwebs and dust.…[H]ow slowly we ascended the rickety old stairs…how we held our breath and shivered with fear as we heard the rats…scurrying across the rafters; how we finally made a rush for the door of the room, to be welcomed by our dear old friend; to forget all our fears and troubles in the charm of his presence and the magic of his instruction.

At the same time, the irrepressible Eckman embarked on another consuming career—journalism. Beginning in January 1857, he published a newspaper, the *Weekly Gleaner*, which for the next six years was the most influential Jewish journal in the western states. Circulating along the entire Pacific slope, it offered long, scholarly essays on Judaica as well as news from Jewish communities throughout the world. Moreover, it followed developments in many of the remote settlements of Jews in the West—from the coast to the Great Salt Lake, from British Columbia to San Diego—reporting on their growing organizations and often mediating their religious disputes.

Although each issue of the *Gleaner* carried many advertisements, the failure of subscribers to pay their bills caused this enterprise, like the

Hefzibah school, to come close to bankruptcy on many occasions. In order to maintain them both, Eckman willingly worked long into the night, took his rest on a sagging couch in the newspaper office, and remained impoverished. Ultimately, he had to cease publication of his weekly, but continued as a journalist, serving in the late 1860s as the religion editor of another respected paper, the *Hebrew Observer*.

In 1863, he left San Francisco to accept a pulpit in Portland, Oregon. For a fifth time, he survived but one year as a congregational rabbi, typically resisting reforms and quarreling with the board. At another synagogue in Portland in the early '70s, from which he refused any salary, he seemed finally to have a measure of success. But by then his age and ill health mandated a return to San Francisco, where he had made so many friends. He continued to teach small children until his death in 1874.

For the most part, he gradually resigned himself to the fact that his religious pronouncements on matters of ritual such as *shechita*, or kosher slaughtering, often went unheeded. But, selfless though he was, he also sought pity from the public, complaining for example that he was dismissed from Emanu-El for being a "Polock." While there was only a grain of truth in that charge (because a doctorate from the University of Berlin was usually sufficient, in the minds of the Bavarians, to turn a Posener from a Pole into a German), he was on the mark with the following passage from an early issue of the *Gleaner*, an accurate self-assessment:

> All these [synagogues on the West Coast] do not maintain the one ordained teacher who [was] "found wanting" not in honesty, integrity or energy, nor in zeal and knowledge—not in self-denial and self-sacrifice. No, he was found wanting in PLIANCY, WORLDLY POLICY, and HYPOCRISY—hence in POPULARITY.

ON THE DAY OF THE DEDICATION of the Broadway synagogue, in the late summer of 1854, Emanu-El numbered 147 families, nearly twice the membership reported two years earlier. The colorful ceremony itself seemed to exude confidence in the future. Sixteen young girls in white dresses held blue ribbons attached to Torah scrolls as they accompanied the scroll-bearers seven times around the sanctuary.

But the next thirteen months, culminating with Eckman's removal in September 1855, saw another period of hardship and decline for the young congregation. A number of resignations resulted from the rabbi's ill-considered outburst on the *shechita* question, while several members of the small pro-Eckman faction left the following year when he was not reelected.

In addition, a series of bank failures led to a financial panic in 1855, seriously affecting every institution in the state. The indebtedness of the synagogue mounted rapidly in the spring, reaching $6,000 by May, a sum which had to be liquidated with new funds borrowed at an annual interest rate of 24 percent. Although the dues were raised from two to four dollars a month, the sexton was ordered to "take four dollars when he can get it, and if not to be satisfied with two." Seligman, "discouraged" at the sour turn of events, resigned the presidency in favor of past-president Emanuel Berg (whose own service to the congregation was soon cut short by death), and returned to New York on a long business trip; he would not occupy the presidency again until October 1857.

During the entire second half of the 1850s Emanu-El was without a full-time rabbi. At first, only $600 a year could be set aside for the minister's salary, a figure far too low to attract an ordained man. Later, when

HENRY SELIGMAN   EMANUEL BERG

$3,000 could be budgeted annually, the congregation was forced to wait three more years until one of the handful of rabbis fit for the post became available.

In the meantime, Emanu-El engaged a young man as "lecturer and teacher." Herman Bien, a charismatic, beguiling twenty-five-year-old, could not have been more different from Rabbi Eckman. A poet, playwright, and musician, Bien now led services, delivered sermons, and taught the young.

But in his quest to be appointed the permanent spiritual leader of the congregation, he feigned both a rabbinical ordination and a doctorate. It is true that in the German states his teaching had been supervised by the eminent reformer Rabbi David Einhorn, and that before coming to San Francisco in 1854 he had taught in a Hebrew school in New Haven, Connecticut. Yet Bien had only a passing acquaintance with classical Jewish texts. He bestrode the *bimah*, the platform between the ark and the congregation, with a distinguished white neck-cloth and a black cap embroidered with the words *Kadosh L'Adonai*, Hebrew for "Sacred to the Lord." But his sermons, though long on histrionics, were woefully short of substance.

Eckman was beside himself with anger at this turn of events, not least of all because Bien, half his age, had also decided to compete with him in the realm of journalism, publishing his own *Voice of Israel* at the same time the rabbi launched the *Gleaner*. The feud further divided the congregation because each editor carried letters from Emanu-El members fiercely critical of his rival's publication. Finally, Isaac Mayer Wise called a halt to the fray, scolding them both from Cincinnati:

> For God's sake do not, any of you, disturb the growth of the synagogue on the shores of the Pacific! It is a young and feeble institution, and craves your care and fostering. Retire both of you, and disturb not the peace.

Bien's theatrical sermons—delivered alternately in German and English, as were Eckman's—often carried a radically reformist message, but his lack of learning left the congregation highly skeptical. His initial ninety-day contract was renewed twice in 1856, first for four months and then, only by a slim majority, for another six.

Like Eckman the scholar, Bien the showman remained in San Francisco after his year in the Emanu-El pulpit. His newspaper was short-lived, but like many young men in the unformed early West, Bien tried his hand at many things, each time reinventing himself in the process. He ran a jewelry store for a while, staged two lavish productions of a play he had written, and then founded a second Jewish newspaper, the *Pacific Messenger*. When that went bankrupt in 1860, he simply started a successor called the *True Pacific Messenger*. And before he left the Bay City in 1864, he had opened—and closed—four different Jewish schools. One can imagine what Eckman must have thought of him as an educator.*

For its leading professional, the congregation next turned to a thirty-year-old Frenchman, Daniel Levy, whose life was almost as varied and colorful as Bien's, but without the affectation and fakery. Born in Lorraine, he had served under the direction of the French government as a Jewish-school principal in Algeria for several years. After arriving in San Francisco in 1855, he worked briefly as a businessman before returning to the field of education as a teacher at Emanu-El alongside Bien. Levy reorganized the religious school, beginning in the spring of 1856, in the newly remodeled basement of the Broadway synagogue. The following year he was given the additional appointment of "reader" (in effect, cantor) at the same time that the choir was organized on a permanent basis.** An organ, too, was introduced, by a slim majority, and although it produced some resignations it did not prove a serious threat to the unity of the congregation.

As early as October 1855, only weeks after Eckman's departure,

*Bien moved to Nevada where, in his maiden voyage as a politician, he was elected to that state's first legislature. But he soon left for New York where he married, had three children, and again worked both as a storekeeper and, for a short time, as a Jewish journalist. Later in life he did achieve his goal as a congregational rabbi, holding pulpits in Dallas, Chicago, and Vicksburg, Miss. But his bleak prospects in 1895 led to his death, most likely by suicide, at age sixty-four.

**With refreshing modesty, Levy made it clear that he had never held a cantorial position before, but his efforts were deeply appreciated by the congregation and he remained at both of his posts until 1864, when he returned to France, settling in Paris and making a distinguished career as a political journalist. He returned to San Francisco in 1871, however, and for the next four decades did more to further the cause of French culture than any other individual in the city. A teacher of the language at Boys' High School, he was also instrumental in such institutions as the French Library, Hospital Society, and National League, and was president of the local Alliance Française.

Emanu-El endorsed the resolutions of the Cleveland Conference—a path-breaking rabbinical conclave organized by Isaac Mayer Wise*—and resolved to study the heated question of religious rites. A year later a lay committee was actually charged with the task of "recommending a new mode of worship." But in this theologically muddled period, the service remained the Orthodox *Minhag Ashkenaz,* and Levy wrote home that the "ritual still teems" with prayers for the return to Jerusalem and the restoration of the Davidic dynasty, as well as references to the messiah and the sacrificial cult.

Like Wise he observed the Sabbath laws, but in other respects, particularly in the area of liturgy, Levy favored sweeping reforms for the Jews of the West. This could easily be brought about, he noted, because America lacked the centralization so prevalent in his native France, where "all the synagogues accept a single superior authority." Reveling in the freedom of his adopted land, he pointed out that

> a certain number of Jews find that they have the same principles and views on religion and worship, and behold, they promptly hold a meeting, adopt resolutions, form a congregation, assess themselves to build a new temple, name a committee qualified to revise the ritual and remodel the religious ceremonies, another committee to hire the salaried officials such as the teacher, officiating clergymen, and others. All this is done without the government having anything to do with it, with complete independence of action and spirit and without any concern for murmurs, the disapproval of the ignorant masses, or for the bitter criticism and the cries of anathema of the Orthodox fanatics.

Levy concluded early that "the future belongs to Reform." But he also knew that systematic and lasting changes awaited the arrival of a respected rabbi, preferably a nationally known man in Wise's circle who "could find here a fertile field for the seeds he would sow."

The lay leadership of the congregation was in clear agreement. Three prominent members wrote Wise in April 1857 that "Orthodoxy seems to

---

*To be sure, Wise's posture in Cleveland was one of compromise; he accepted a resolution declaring the "divine origin" of the Bible and the primacy of the Talmud in the interpretation of biblical laws. Still, the conference is usually seen as a victory for the moderate reformers because a committee, including Wise, was entrusted with the task of compiling a new prayerbook, *Minhag America.*

have but little sway among us, and, consequently, we have no hesitation in saying that a man to lead our flock should be of the New School." Wise himself considered the Emanu-El pulpit, but the congregation sought a well-known reformer still on the other side of the Atlantic, Dr. Elias Greenebaum, the astute district rabbi of Landau, in Bavaria. He had participated in the German rabbinical conferences of the mid-1840s that had laid the foundations for much of Reform religious practice; he had also fought, often successfully, for the easing of anti-Jewish legal restrictions.

In the summer of 1857, Greenebaum was unanimously elected rabbi and offered a six-year contract at $3,000 per annum plus traveling expenses. But like Gutheim and Steinberg before him, he disappointed the congregation by refusing its invitation.

YET JEWISH ORGANIZATIONAL LIFE TOOK HOLD in San Francisco during the 1850s, despite its remote location, its rootless, materialistic environment, its recurring economic crises, and its lack of strong rabbinical leadership.

By 1860 there were roughly ten thousand Jews in the western states, half of them in the Bay City, where they comprised about 9 percent of all the inhabitants—no small figure given the fact that the entire country counted only 150,000 Jews, even after it had absorbed the bulk of the German-Jewish migration in the 1850s. New York had about forty thousand Jews on the eve of the Civil War, but San Francisco was not far behind the other "larger" communities such as Baltimore and Philadelphia, which each numbered around eight thousand.

The city supported four permanent synagogues: in addition to Emanu-El and Sherith Israel, there was Shomrai Shabbes, a small group of Orthodox Polish Jews; and Congregation Beth Israel, founded in 1861 and also organized along traditional lines. For a while in the early 1850s there had even been a Sephardi congregation as well.

There were also the two benevolent societies founded at the very beginning of Jewish settlement. By the end of the 1850s the Eureka, with three hundred members, was the largest Jewish organization in the West. Like the First Hebrew Benevolent Society and the Chevrah Bikkur Cholim Ukedusha (established in 1857), it aided the needy, cared for the ill and indigent, and buried the dead. Women established mutual aid organizations of their own: the Israelite Ladies Society and the United Benevolent Society of Jewish Women.

In 1860, Emanu-El joined with the Eureka Benevolent Society to purchase a burial place on Eighteenth and Dolores in the Mission District, then an undeveloped part of the city. Known as the Home of Peace Cemetery, it adjoined a block bought at the same time by Sherith Israel and served the community for almost thirty years. President of the Cemetery Association was David Stern, another Bavarian who with his brother-in-law, Levi Strauss, created the company which in the twentieth century would become one of the world's great apparel firms.

The first lodge of B'nai B'rith in San Francisco, Ophir, was founded in 1855 by William Steinhart, a young native of Baden who also headed a thriving textile enterprise. Later in the decade a second was formed, Modin.

In the comparatively open atmosphere of the pioneer West, Jews also gained an early foothold in secular life. They belonged to the Odd Fellows as well as to lesser-known fraternal groups such as the Red Men, the United Workman, and the Foresters.

It was to the largest of these fraternities, the Masons, that Jews were especially attracted, and it is quite likely that Abraham Labatt was the Master of California's first lodge, which also included many other leading members of the Jewish community. Known in those days for their dislike of Catholics, the Masons reacted warmly to Jews, who comprised 12 percent of the San Francisco membership. This was a particularly high degree of integration, especially considering that any lodge member present on balloting night could block a candidate from joining by secretly casting the legendary blackball.

Emanu-El congregants in particular flocked to the Masons, about half of the men of the synagogue joining one of the city's sixteen lodges.* In part, business connections with non-Jewish Masons explain this high level of affiliation, but one scholar has emphasized instead the theological congruence between Reform Judaism and the liberal Protestantism which characterized Freemasonry. Committed to rationalism and universalism,

---

*For many other Jews in late-nineteenth-century San Francisco, Masonry appears to have been an alternative to synagogue affiliation; only about a third of all Jewish Masons also belonged to a congregation. But among those, the majority chose one synagogue, Emanu-El.

the Masons adamantly opposed what they termed the "ignorant superstition" of the Catholic Church as well as the "emotional fanaticism" of evangelical Protestantism. Moreover, they stressed the Hebrew Bible and monotheism in their elaborate rituals. But perhaps most impressive to Jews was the extensive work done by the Masons to aid the needy, their moralism being "exemplary" rather than "crusading."

Jews were also well represented in German cultural organizations such as the prestigious San Francisco Society, whose president at the end of the 1850s was the Emanu-El congregant and well-known physician Dr. Jacob Regensburger. Likewise, members of the synagogue were among the earliest pillars of the city's exclusive German social clubs. Joseph Brandenstein, the distinguished tobacconist who later led the German Benevolent Society, its hospital, and its old-age home, was devoted to the San Francisco Verein, founded in 1853, which became the Argonaut. Levi Strauss and Martin Heller were among the earliest leaders of the Alemanian Club, later known as the House of Concord and eventually the Concordia.* Central European Jews often spoke German at home in this first generation, and they basked in the respect most Americans then had for German culture.

Jews were active in civic affairs ranging from the volunteer fire department to the city's opera house and theaters. They played a prominent role in the press and helped found literary societies and the well-regarded Mercantile Library Association. As one visiting chronicler put it at the time, "Whenever an undertaking of public interest or benefit is to be carried out, the Jews are looked to first of all, because they are always ready to contribute."

But perhaps nothing is more indicative of their standing than their conspicuous presence among the vigilantes, the citizens' groups that seized control of the city in 1851 and again in 1856. The second episode, by far the larger of the two, enlisting eight thousand members and lasting for three months, has been termed a revolution by contemporary historians. Sparked by the assassination of a popular muckraking newspaperman,

*Within only a few years, however, these "German" clubs consisted almost exclusively of German Jews. In 1939, they merged as the Concordia-Argonaut.

the vigilantes came down heavily on alleged lawbreakers, hanging four (as in 1851), deporting twenty-five, and intimidating many hundreds more who left town on their own. Jews such as the well-known journalist Seixas Solomons, who was also very active in Emanu-El, served as officers in the five-thousand-man-strong military arm of the vigilantes.

They also formed a new political party which (along with its allies and successors) dominated San Francisco politics for the next two decades. In this "Revolution of 1856," Jesse Seligman played a major role as one of the powerful Committee of 21 which nominated the candidates of the vigilantes' highly successful People's Party.*

Moreover, the changing of the political guard in 1856—the defeat of Mayor Broderick's corrupt political machine, which he himself named Tammany—was clearly in the class interest of the Jewish merchants who in the main supported the vigilantes and then their candidates. The city would be run essentially by and for the businessmen until the mid-1870s.

Even at the beginning of the 1850s, however, Jews were highly active in politics. American-born Sephardim in particular led the way, providing a vital service for the Jewish community since the far more numerous Central Europeans were often not yet citizens, nor in full command of the English language. Not only were the first two presidents of Emanu-El, Labatt and Shannon, local officeholders, but, in 1852, two Jews were sent to the state assembly from San Francisco: Isaac Cardozo, uncle of the future U.S. Supreme Court justice Benjamin Cardozo; and Elkan Heydenfeldt (a Sephardic Jew on his mother's side), who later served as a judge.

The Jew perhaps most respected in non-Jewish circles was Heydenfeldt's older brother, Solomon. A native of the South, he left a thriving legal practice in Alabama, possibly because of his unpopular antislavery views. In 1851, soon after his arrival in San Francisco, he was nearly chosen by the legislature as a United States senator. The following year he became one of the three justices on the state supreme court, joining another Jew, Henry Lyons of Philadelphia. (Although born of Jewish immigrants from Frankfurt, Lyons does not appear to have practiced the

---

*Most of the nineteenth- and early-twentieth-century historians praised the vigilantes for restoring order, but contemporary commentators, focusing on the denial of rights to the accused and questioning whether crime was truly curtailed, have tended to be highly critical.

Jewish faith. Much the same may be said of Washington Bartlett, a distant relative of the Heydenfeldts, who was the first *alcalde*, or mayor, of the settlement by the bay, installed by the U.S. military in 1846.)* Heydenfeldt served for almost five years, rendering a number of important decisions for the fledgling state. Deeply committed to the rule of law, he was one of the few prominent citizens to speak out against the vigilantes. Regrettably, his outstanding judicial career is blemished by his ruling in 1854 disallowing the testimony of Chinese witnesses in any case involving a white person.

THIS JEWISH COMMUNITY, far from the Old World, faced relatively little anti-Semitism. True, Jews were numerous and easily identifiable, influential, and in some cases conspicuously well-off. In addition, the economy of the 1850s was one of boom and bust, and the latter naturally brought in its wake frustration and violence.

Yet the Jews were invariably spared their neighbors' wrath. Here, unlike other parts of the United States, much less Europe, they could not be viewed as "intruders." As one keen observer has put it,

> There was no aristocracy in California in 1849. There was only a ragtag gang of money-hungry pioneers of heterogeneous origins, welded together into a "frontier brotherhood community." As the "first families" became encrusted, they became encrusted necessarily in amalgam with the "first families" of the Jewish community.

At the same time, there were many other minority groups in California who, unlike the Jews, were racially excluded from entering that instant aristocracy, and who also bore the brunt of the masses' discontent. The American Indians were virtually exterminated; the Mexicans and Chileans often driven off their mining claims; the blacks segregated by law and prohibited from voting or testifying in court. But it was the Chinese who were the most common scapegoats in the pioneer period, and their plight in California recalls the ordeal of the Jews in Russia during the same years. Persecuted because they clung to a distinct ancient culture, they banded together for self-protection and were then accused of being "clannish."

---

*The following year, Bartlett officially renamed the town, known as Yerba Buena, as "San Francisco." He would be elected governor of California in 1886.

Jews were favored by the fact that California's historical experience differed fundamentally from that of Europe. The former, obviously, was not scarred by a thousand years of persecution emanating from the Catholic Church. There was, of course, a history of aggressive missionary activity on the Pacific Coast, first by Catholic orders and then by Protestant evangelists. But the remarkable diversity of the population precluded the dominance of any one religious group (with the later exception of the Mormons in Utah), and in this respect the West differed even from other regions within the United States. One historian puts forth the relatively benign image of the aquarium to capture the religious pluralism that took hold as early as the Gold Rush years:

> Throughout the wide spaces in God's western aquarium, there are schools of familiar (but easily startled) denominational species, there are slow-moving crustaceans, there are religious exotics from the depths and an occasional shark, there's the Mormon leviathan, and unchurched plankton are floating everywhere.

Whether it was the great distance from established religious centers, whether it was the emphasis on the individual and family as opposed to organizations of any kind, whether it was even the dramatic landscape that lent itself to a personal spirituality, somehow doctrinal and theological conflict lost its sharp edge west of the Rockies. Race was determinative as it was everywhere in America; religion was not.

Of course, antipathy to the Jews could extend beyond religious differences, and in Europe in particular it was often based on a deep-seated fear of Jewish "influence" and innovation—perceived as a threat to relatively static societies which still glorified the peasant and craftsman. Yet the entrepreneurial spirit that permeated the rapidly changing American West made this sort of modern anti-Semitism a rarity as well. Thus, in Germany and Austria—even in France—in the late nineteenth century, Jews came under heavy attack for their growing activity in such fields as industry, banking, transportation, retail trade, journalism, and politics. But their cousins, half a world away in California, were admired precisely because of their efforts at modernization; a new product such as Levi Strauss' copper-riveted jeans met usually with respect rather than resentment.

When anti-Semitic incidents did occur, they were met forthrightly, the young Jewish community intelligently using the resources at its command. Defamatory remarks in the Sacramento press in 1850 and the San Francisco papers the following year were strongly rebutted both by Jewish and gentile writers. We have seen that the anti-Jewish sentiments fanned by the agitation for a Sunday closing law in 1852 were also refuted in print, and may actually have contributed to the desire of Congregation Emanu-El to build a synagogue and strengthen itself in general.

The controversy over the Sunday closing law reached its most anti-Semitic stage in 1855, when the Speaker of the Assembly, William Stow of Santa Cruz, viciously slandered the Jews on the floor of the statehouse. He attributed Jewish opposition to the law to a desire to make a fast dollar and leave California. Stow, an adherent of the antiforeign, secretive Know-Nothing Party, important in the state in the mid-1850s, urged that a special tax be levied on Jews in order to drive them away.

His remarks were denounced by Isaac Mayer Wise and Isaac Leeser in the East and by Henry Labatt, who acted as the unofficial spokesman for the Jewish community of California. His incisive letter to the Speaker, printed in several western newspapers, skillfully exposed both Stow's ignorance and dishonesty. Without claiming any "superiority" for his people, Labatt enumerated the Jews' many contributions on the coast and then asked,

> How have they harmed you at all and in what respect? Have the Jews squatted upon your lands? If so, I have yet to learn who; the Jews are not squatters.
> Have they built grogshops to poison the people? Surely not; they are not rum-sellers. Have they filled your jails or taxed the state with criminal trials? Surely not; they are not robbers, murderers, or leading politicians [i.e. political bosses].

He concluded with the warning that "a numerous body of voters of this state will remember these facts, and I trust that every Jew will bear it in mind a long day." On another occasion, later in the 1850s, Jews used their political power, a bloc of 1,500 votes in San Francisco, to defeat a public school principal who had discriminated against a Jewish teacher.

The Sunday closing law passed the legislature, but it was declared unconstitutional in 1858 when Solomon Heydenfeldt, now in private practice, successfully defended a Sacramento Jew who had kept his store open on the Christian Sabbath. The court held that because he regularly shut his business on Saturday, he should be exempt from having to close on Sunday.

There was, however, a more subtle form of anti-Semitism beginning in the 1850s. As one scholar has revealed through his study of the San Francisco credit reports of R. G. Dun and Company (the forerunner of Dun and Bradstreet), Jewish merchants seeking commercial loans were held to a much higher standard than non-Jews:

> Jews were assumed not to possess character unless they proved otherwise. R. G. Dun almost always noted if a merchant was a "Jew" or "Israelite." If it was not accompanied with a positive qualifier such as "White Jew" or "an Israelite of the better classes," the religious affiliation more often than not carried with it an assumption of bad credit....A credit report on two German Jews who owned rather substantial assets warned: "They are Hebrews. May be good [for credit] *if well watched*; they are *tricky*."

But Jews prevailed in this regard as well, often borrowing funds from family members back East or even in Europe, or from other Jews in California. Like a number of Asian ethnic groups in late-twentieth-century America, their social cohesion and close family ties helped them overcome economic discrimination.

FROM THE OUTSET, San Francisco Jewry not only defended itself well, but it also felt a commitment to aid Jews in other parts of the world. In 1859, for example, Emanu-El congregants raised nearly $3,700 on behalf of their persecuted coreligionists in Morocco.

In January of that year, local Jews staged a mass meeting to protest an anti-Jewish outrage in Bologna, Italy, the kidnapping of a Jewish child from his house by papal police. Edgardo Mortara, aged six, had been secretly baptized by his nurse and was therefore considered a Catholic by the Pope, who placed him in a monastery rather than return him to his parents. The Vatican was flooded by a storm of criticism from America, and San Francisco's response was the largest of any city in the nation.*

---

*Unfortunately the Holy See never relented and Mortara, who identified completely with his captors, spent the rest of his long life as a devout Catholic. Ordained as a priest at the age of twenty-one, he served the Church as a popular preacher and, in his last decades, as a monk. He died in 1940, shortly before the Nazi occupation of his adopted land of Belgium.

More than three thousand people gathered in Musical Hall, called to order by Henry Seligman to hear a series of fiery speeches and resolutions.

The regional and class differences within the Jewish community were
bridged and the list of the conveners of the event reflects unity in the face
of crisis. They included the presidents of the two leading congregations,
the three benevolent societies, and the B'nai B'rith. Solomon Heydenfeldt, elected unanimously to chair the meeting, condemned the "act of
tyranny" and then reminded his audience of "the power of public opinion,
which, if excited properly in this instance, [will make] the Mortara case
the last of its kind the world will ever see."

A committee of ten was formed to draft resolutions expressive of the
sense of the meeting. Chaired by Henry A. Henry, rabbi of Sherith Israel
since 1857, who had also preached at Emanu-El during the High Holidays, it included influential journalists such as Manuel Noah and Seixas
Solomons, who acted as secretary. Perhaps most important of the committee's eight resolutions was that calling upon the United States
government to cooperate with the European countries in "their endeavors
to suppress religious intolerance and persecution, such as exhibits itself in
the Mortara case." The committee's declarations were speedily sent to
Moses Montefiore in London, coordinating a global effort to have the
Mortara boy released.

Rabbi Eckman, whose *Gleaner* had given extensive coverage to the
case, was rarely so impassioned. He delivered a speech identifying as the
villain "the superannuated Roman Canon Law…antagonistic to civilization, progress, and religious toleration all over the world." At the same
time, he sensed the danger of vehement anti-Catholicism overtaking the
huge crowd of Christians and Jews, a development which would also aid
the bigoted Know-Nothing Party. Bearing in mind the frequent outbreaks
of violence that had been directed against Irish immigrants in particular,
he urged that

> the deed of the Roman Executive [not be] instrumental in raising any
> ill feeling against Roman Catholics. We must not identify Catholics
> with Catholicism. For if the Mortara case has, as yet, not produced
> any other benefit, it has opened the eyes of the Christians of the
> world, and of Rome, and showed the great chasm which exists

between the living and the dead—between Catholics and Catholic Canon Law.*

Eckman's prudence was in sharp contrast to the inflammatory anti-Catholic remarks of Jewish leaders in other parts of the country, most notably Isaac Mayer Wise, who took the opportunity of the kidnapping in Bologna to castigate all priests as hypocrites. In the Far West, though, cooperation and mutual respect tended to characterize interfaith relations. The event in San Francisco's Musical Hall revealed not only proper restraint on the part of the Jews but also the good will of a number of prominent Christians, including several clergymen, who expressed their indignation at the Vatican and their sympathy for the Mortara family. The address of the civic-minded William Anderson Scott of Calvary Presbyterian—the leading minister in the city—was enthusiastically received; the Reverend Dr. R. P. Cutler of the Unitarian Church sent an open letter of support to the gathering and, the following day, chose the Mortara case as the subject of his Sunday morning sermon, "Religious Intolerance."

With the exception of the Catholic organs, the local press uniformly lauded the mass meeting. In the *San Francisco Times*, an editorial chastised Secretary of State Cass for his policy of abstaining "from all interference in the internal concerns of any other country." The paper pleaded that "it becomes *the sacred duty of our government* to protest against the Mortara *outrage*." That editorial and many others, as well as Cutler's sermon and the entire proceedings of the mass meeting, were all published in 1859 in a pamphlet on San Francisco's reaction to the Mortara case, and circulated throughout the city—an early document of highly effective Jewish community relations.

BY THE END OF THE HECTIC 1850s, enormous changes could be seen in San Francisco, and it was clear that the Jewish community had played a key role in transforming a crude frontier outpost into the undisputed

---

*The evening at Musical Hall was not without another indignity for Eckman, however, who had been asked to speak only to fill the time during which the resolutions committee worked on its draft. When the drafters returned to the stage to present their declarations, he was midway through his informative and eloquent speech—perhaps the most important of his career—but was not permitted to finish it.

center of commerce and culture in the American West. Of all the groups in the diverse metropolis, none could match the upward occupational mobility of the Jews who so often and so rapidly made the leap from peddler or small shopkeeper to solid merchant. "Almost all of them are doing well," claimed the Jewish world traveler I. J. Benjamin, who visited San Francisco in 1860, "a large part of the wealth of California is in their hands; they have acquired it by thrift and sobriety, by steadfast industry and toil."

To be sure, the Bay City also produced a great many spectacular failures in its first decade, "human wrecks" who were ruined by the vagaries of nature or the economy. The urban historian Peter Decker contends that, contrary to popular belief, economic opportunity was actually no greater in early San Francisco than in the East. But using quantitative analysis as well as contemporary accounts, he has shown that Jews were the exception. They "were more successful than others...for them, at least, the 'American Dream' was a reality." The self-discipline and mercantile skills which they brought with them and the social cohesion and community consciousness which they developed on the West Coast served them well in the almost Darwinian struggle that was nineteenth-century capitalism.

In 1858, Daniel Levy described the impact of this newly won prosperity on the daily life of the city and its Jews:

> Anyone leaving California in those days [the Gold Rush], not so long ago in time, but far removed by events, and returning today, would certainly not recognize it. Instead of the social chaos he had left, he would be pleased and delighted to find about a thousand Jewish families with pure morals and with homes that contained all the conditions necessary for comfort and even luxury. In place of the old and miserable hovels, ravaged by vermin and constantly exposed to total destruction by fire, he would see elegant brick homes or dainty and graceful cottages, hidden among trees and flowers; charming nests for people, where Americans have learned so well to shelter their domestic bliss.
>
> These families are linked by bonds of neighborliness and friendship. The ladies, almost all of them young, well brought up, more or less musical (there is a piano in every parlor), get together either for Saturday or Sunday visits, at the temple, at dances or at the theater, or for their charitable meetings. All this creates a charming and serene

social life. I do not think that many European communities can boast of as large a number of young and happy households living in affluence.

In only one decade a San Francisco Jewish identity had emerged. Much of it, as Levy indicates, was a bourgeois mentality, the result of recently gained wealth and respectability. Politically, it tended to be centrist or conservative; socially, it was tightly bound by convention; religiously, it was relatively unobservant. Money counted for a great deal in this Jewish community, and place of origin counted for even more. But from the very beginning Jews were also known for a generosity seemingly without limit—both in taking care of their own and in improving the city as a whole.

Perhaps most remarkable was the uncommon degree of acceptance, indeed respect, accorded San Francisco Jewry by the larger society. "Nowhere else," wrote the well-informed Benjamin, "are [the Jews] regarded with as much esteem by their non-Jewish brothers and nowhere else are they so highly valued in social or political circles."

All in all, it must have been exhilarating for the young immigrants who only a few years earlier had chafed under the repressive regimes of the German kings. Indeed, the Jews in the American West in the second half of the nineteenth century were the freest anywhere in the world.

But they did not take that freedom for granted, as shown by the wisdom and unity with which they faced their enemies both at home and overseas. They played an active role in the politics of a new country, not yet a century old, but also felt themselves tied to the fate of an ancient people, with a history three millennia in the making.

Those Jews who benefited most from the extraordinary opportunities that the open society offered them—successful businessmen and a sprinkling of professionals—usually were also members of Congregation Emanu-El, at the apex of the newly emerged Jewish community hierarchy. Through that institution, they were about to shape Jewish practice and thought to fit the unprecedented conditions of life on the Pacific Coast. It was the beginning of a never-ending process.

chapter two

ELKAN COHN
Temple on a Hill

Emanu-El became a Reform congregation, and one of the most important in the United States, under the guidance of Rabbi Elkan Cohn, who assumed his duties in the summer of 1860. He remained at his post until his death twenty-nine years later, enjoying the longest tenure of any rabbi in the history of the synagogue.

Unlike some of his successors, he was not cut out for the incessant political battles which inflamed the Jewish community. He took the unusual tack of refusing to polemicize his views in the bellicose Jewish press of his day; his sermons, half the time delivered in German, tended to be dry, convoluted, and even slurred. But if he lacked the instincts of the disputant, he more than made up for it in patience and persistence, qualities which, coupled with great learning, enabled him to be as effective a leader as any of the more outspoken rabbis who came after him.

His upbringing in the 1820s gave few hints that he would become the first liberal rabbi in the American West. Raised by devout grandparents in a hamlet in Posen, his childhood hours were filled with little else than the serious study of sacred texts. While still a boy, he was sent several hundred miles west to Braunschweig to be tutored by Rabbi Isaac Eger, son of the renowned Talmud scholar and standard-bearer of Orthodoxy in the German states, Akiba Eger the Younger.

But the premature death of Isaac Eger brought young Cohn under the wing of a Braunschweig luminary of a much different stripe, the historian Levi Herzfeld, one of the earliest Jewish practitioners of the critical method. Later a prime mover in the German Reform movement—an organizer of the Braunschweig Rabbinical Conference of 1844 and the author of a liberal prayerbook and treatise on matrimonial law—Rabbi Herzfeld was himself a young man during the period in which Cohn came under his influence. But the mentor was already preoccupied with the importance in Jewish history of social and economic factors, lessons which were not lost on the orphan from Posen.

At the age of twenty, Cohn left Braunschweig for the even more stimulating Berlin where, with Herzfeld's loving letter of recommendation, he both matriculated at the university and began his study for the rabbinate. He remained in the Prussian capital for a decade, the tumultuous 1840s, and followed a course of study similar to that of Julius Eckman, also a Posener educated in Berlin. Like his predecessor at Emanu-El, Cohn received a doctorate in classics and, having studied under the famed Zunz, among others, his rabbinical degree. The ardent student could also be found on the barricades in March 1848, fighting the repressive rule of the Hohenzollern king.

His first pulpit was in nearby Brandenburg, but in 1854 he received a call from America to succeed Isaac Mayer Wise at Congregation Beth El in Albany. He came with his wife and child. As vice-president of the Cleveland Rabbinical Conference the following year, he soon distinguished himself as one of the stalwarts of the newly born Reform movement.

Yet in 1860 he accepted the Emanu-El post only with the greatest reluctance. Forty years of age, and now the father of a second child, he felt settled in Albany and unprepared for the rigors of a frontier ministry. In this respect he had much in common with Thomas Starr King, the dynamic Unitarian minister who grudgingly gave up an established pulpit in Boston to come west at the same time the rabbi left New York. Like King, perhaps the most revered religious leader in the state's history, Cohn succeeded where others before him had not. Both men preached ethical universalism; both presided over the building of magnificent Gothic cathedrals by the same architect; and both were staunch abolitionists, helping to "save California for the Union." They were also warm friends. Cohn spoke at King's church, initiating permanent ties of friendship between the two groups. Each congregation aided the other in time of need, as we

RABBI ELKAN COHN

shall see, by making available its house of worship. And in the early 1920s the practice of holding joint Thanksgiving services was begun, a custom which remains in effect today.

King, exhausted by his labors, died early in 1864, less than four years after he had come to the coast. Cohn lived until 1889, but the terrific pressure of his position—very different from the life of scholarship he had pursued in Prussia—took its toll on him as well. Toward the end of his life, in his mid-sixties, he seemed like a man well past eighty.

AT THE BEGINNING OF HIS TENURE the new rabbi vigorously proceeded to reorganize the congregation. He concentrated first on the religious school, which had received an annual subsidy from the synagogue since 1858. Emphasizing ancient Jewish history as well as biblical Hebrew, Cohn made the institution a worthy competitor of the Hefzibah school, which still attracted the children of many members. In 1861, he inaugurated the confirmation program, the first class graduating on the festival of Shavuot in the following year. Later in the decade the school would be further developed with the aid of several of the congregation's lay leaders, such as the educator Lazard Cahn.

More controversial were the alterations Cohn made in the sphere of ritual. He removed many of the medieval hymns, or *piyyutim*; abridged the *musaf*, or "additional service" recited in traditional synagogues; and advocated a cycle of three years rather than one for the reading of the Torah. In 1861, he was able to abolish the lucrative but often "indecorous" practice of the *gaben*, contributions made by those called to the holy scroll. He also inaugurated Friday night services, probably the first rabbi in America to do so.

In addition, Cohn allowed men and women to sit together. He chose a Sabbath sermon to justify the change, invoking a well-known verse from Deuteronomy: "Assemble the people—men, women, children, and the strangers in your communities—that they may hear and so learn…" As one listener reported, the rabbi went on to complain that Judaism had far too long "excluded women from…many privileges to which they are justly entitled, but that the time had come when this evil ought to be remedied." There was no question now that Emanu-El was squarely in the camp of the reformers; among more than two hundred synagogues in the country at the beginning of the Civil War, I. J. Benjamin listed it as one of eight Reform congregations, the only one in the Far West.

The modifications provoked sharp criticism, but initially most of it emanated from outside the congregation. Though he received a stinging rebuke from the Orthodox Isaac Leeser in his influential Philadelphia journal, the *Occident*, Cohn was well received among his own flock, which extended his contract from three to five years after he had been in San Francisco only several months. In his annual report of October 1860, a joyful President Seligman said of the selection of his rabbi, "We could have made no better or wiser choice." He also declared that the synagogue was now too small for its 227 families—more than fifty of whom had joined in the past twelve months—and urged that a lot be acquired for the construction of a new house of worship. With great pride he predicted that Emanu-El, not quite a decade old, could soon become the largest Jewish congregation in America.

Only one year later, the board of trustees approved the purchase of a choice site in the center of the city, Sutter Street between Powell and Stockton (the location of today's well-known medical building at 450 Sutter). The price of the property, which belonged to Benjamin Davidson, was $15,000, more than half of which was raised within one month early in 1862 by the sale to the members of four-year, interest-bearing bonds.

By the end of that year the membership rolls had swelled to more than 260 households. Seligman, in his last annual report before moving permanently to Frankfurt am Main to handle his family's European interests, stressed the happy fact that California had suffered little from the Civil War "in the East": "I say we here on the Pacific Coast have been more fortunate; peace reigns in our midst, our homes and firesides are blessed with plenty, with all the comforts of life; commerce follows its usual channels, and is more prosperous than ever; [neither] discord nor strife exists among us."

Seligman was a staunch supporter of the Union, but there was a degree of pro-Southern sentiment in the state, some of which could be found in the Jewish community. Solomon Heydenfeldt, for example, urged the diplomatic recognition of the Confederacy and gave up the practice of law when the state legislature required of all attorneys a loyalty oath to the Union. And Rabbi Eckman, never averse to voicing unpopular views,

sympathized with the Confederacy as well, taking a stand against the war
and also advocating independence for the South.

But the overwhelming majority of Californians, and the Jews were no
exception, supported President Lincoln. The state meanwhile prospered—
and no one understood this better than the Seligman brothers—because
of the tremendous wartime demand in the East for wool, wheat, and, of
course, gold.

Yet Emanu-El endured its own version of a "civil war" in the first half
of the 1860s, including a "secession" which seriously sapped its strength.
Disunity was evident at the meeting at which Seligman bid the congregation farewell. No fewer than 179 members attended, presenting him with
a twenty-three-piece engraved silver serving set. But bitter strife erupted
at the gathering over the election of the sexton. By 1863, even as architects worked on blueprints for a new synagogue, two warring camps had
clearly emerged: those who supported the rabbi and those who felt that
his reforms had gone too far.

That year the anti-Cohn faction had much to complain about. During
the High Holidays, due to the sudden illness of Daniel Levy, the cantorial parts of the service were rendered by a celebrated Catholic concert
singer. Hoshanah Rabbah, considered a holy day by Orthodox Jews, was
not observed at Emanu-El; many of its more traditional members worshipped at Sherith Israel that day.

Cohn had tried to stem the tide of reaction against his reforms by
emphasizing "the need for a better and more proper observance of the
Sabbath." Nevertheless, he was ridiculed by the Jewish press as far away
as Mainz in the Rhineland. The *Occident* of Philadelphia deplored "the inroads and injuries which Reform has produced in San Francisco." Closer
to home, Eckman's *Gleaner* had criticized Cohn since mid-1861 for sermons such as the one in which he deprecated the wearing of *tefillin*, or
phylacteries, a practice he also described as "nonsense" to the shocked
father of a Bar Mitzvah boy.

The actual split, however, developed over the introduction of a new
prayerbook in 1864. In March, the board of trustees agreed to adopt the
moderate Reform version of the late Leo Merzbacher, a southern German
who in 1845 had become the first rabbi of New York's Temple Emanu-El.
His *Seder Tefilah* (Order of Prayer), compiled in 1855, was actually a

middle course for Cohn between David Einhorn's radical *Olat Tamid* and Isaac Mayer Wise's *Minhag America*, which hardly differed from the traditional *siddur*.

The Merzbacher prayerbook retained much Hebrew as the language of worship. But it also included a German prayer recited at the ark after the reading of the Torah, as well as hymns in that language sung before the sermon and at the end of the service. Moreover, it shifted the recital of prayers from the pews to the pulpit, causing an observer of the Merzbacher ritual in New York to term the worshippers "dummies" who merely sat back and listened to the service. Most important, though, adoption of the new form of worship meant abandonment of the time-honored *Minhag Ashkenaz*, which most of the members had known since childhood. Maintaining this Orthodox German rite was specifically required in Emanu-El's founding constitution, and had been the *raison d'etre* for the formation of two separate synagogues in 1851.

At the annual meeting in early November, Cohn's ally Louis Sachs, the Bavarian businessman who two years earlier had succeeded Seligman as president, won approval of the *Minhag Merzbacher* from the full congregation. But the opposition, feeling that he had violated parliamentary procedure, held its own meeting several days later, after publishing a notice in the local newspapers "to all members of the Congregation Emanu-El, who are in favor to organize a new Congregation."

In the meantime, it was decided to demand of Sachs a special meeting in order to reconsider the momentous vote. Such a meeting was held, on November 24, but, as Solomon Wangenheim, a young leader of the rebellious group, wrote, "no satisfactory settlement could be had, to remove all strife and discord, in fact no overtures for peace [were] mooted by our opponents."

Three days later, fifty-five members of Emanu-El signed a pledge to form a new congregation, Ohabai Shalome. Its minute book reveals that its members were not strictly Orthodox; they agreed that men and women would be allowed to sit together during services, for example. But they insisted that the Torah portion be read in its entirety each Sabbath (thus holding to the one-year cycle) and, above all, that the ritual remain the familiar *Minhag Ashkenaz*. Their deeply felt sentiments were perhaps best articulated by Joseph Mayer, elected the first president of Ohabai

Shalome on December 18. In his inaugural address (as paraphrased by
the secretary),

> he called God as his witness that he bore the old Congregation no mal-
> ice, had no unkind feeling towards them, but their principles and his
> own did not coincide. The memory of his deceased parents, his early
> education and childhood was still fresh in his mind. He honored and
> loved his parents and would do violence to his feelings if he did not fol-
> low their teachings and example.

Mayer died suddenly two weeks later, but the fledgling endeavor
had enlisted the support of many other prominent laymen such as Samuel Wand and Simon Koshland. While these men, along with Solomon
Wangenheim—Bavarians like most of the leadership of the new congregation—eventually rejoined Emanu-El, in its infancy Ohabai Shalome
took long strides. Within only one year it erected a substantial synagogue on Mason Street, engaged a rabbi, and increased its membership to
125 families.*

For Emanu-El the break could not have come at a worse time. In June
1864, the congregation had approved the expenditure of a huge sum—
$134,000—for the new synagogue, the cornerstone of which was laid
with a brief ceremony in October. Soon an additional amount needed to
be pledged, so that by the time of the defection the congregation owed
more than $150,000. It had counted 302 member-families in November
1864; the loss of almost sixty to Ohabai Shalome by the spring of the following year was a grave development. Despite the excitement generated
by the construction of the new house of worship, the rolls in October
1865 stood at only 267.

But Cohn and his lay leaders, strong individuals such as Sachs, Jacob
Greenebaum, and Martin Heller, were not ones to despair. They raised
the needed capital in a variety of ways: selling lifetime seats in the new

---

*One of the leading congregations of the city until its demise in 1940, Ohabai Shalome
constructed a larger house of worship in 1898, the Moorish-style Bush Street temple near
Laguna which still stands today, the oldest synagogue building in San Francisco. For many
years it served as a center for Zen Buddhism, but was nearly reclaimed by the Jewish community in the early 1990s as a home for the Western Jewish History Center of the
Berkeley-based Judah L. Magnes Museum. Those plans did not materialize, however, and the
distinctive wooden structure, situated in the neighborhood long known as Japantown, has
since reverted to the Asian community.

sanctuary; issuing bonds, now without interest; holding fundraising fairs; and putting on the market the Broadway synagogue, which was purchased for $19,000 by the San Francisco Board of Education. Nevertheless, $32,000, at an annual interest rate of 12 percent, was still owed a lending institution by late 1867. Nor could anyone predict that a strong earthquake in October of the following year would cause structural damage to the new building and require the expenditure of many more thousands of dollars.

Yet the loss of nearly sixty families, and the financial complications which necessarily followed, hardly slowed the timetable for the erection of the Sutter Street temple. In mid-1864, before the crisis, the date of completion had been set for Rosh Hashanah of the next year; in actuality the synagogue—approaching, with furnishings, $200,000 in cost—was dedicated on March 23, 1866, only six months past its scheduled completion date.

Louis Sachs

It was considered by many the most impressive building on the Pacific Coast. Its designer, the Englishman William Patton, had grown up among majestic Norman churches in Durham and York; for the Sutter Street site he planned nothing short of a medieval cathedral.

Active in the Gothic revival in his native land, Patton left a promising

The Sutter Street temple

career to sail around the Horn in 1849. He had tried his hand as a miner and a businessman before returning to his profession, but by 1863, with the creation of the Reverend Thomas Starr King's imposing Unitarian church, he had won recognition as one of the finest architects in California. He now turned his attention to Temple Emanu-El, which would become his magnum opus.

The big brick structure—80 feet by 120 feet—was not merely plastered with Gothic features, as had been the Broadway synagogue, but, as the architectural critic Allan Temko has written, "the arches, the pillars, the buttresses were built into the structure, as they would have been in a truly medieval church."

But Patton—whose address at the cornerstone-laying stressed the tolerated status of Jews in America—ingeniously wove many Jewish symbols into the Gothic plan. In this manner, he also intended to depart from the slavish adoption of various forms, such as Byzantine or Romanesque, which had characterized much of synagogue design in the past. His work, he felt, would mark a new era in Jewish architecture. Thus, the enormous, circular stained glass window above the portal sported not a rose motif under its rounded arch, but a Star of David. The six-pointed star was also inscribed on two other windows, as well as on the sides and bases of the two great towers. Between them, above the central gable and over a hundred feet high, were the stone Tablets of the Law.

Atop the graceful octagonal towers was the distinguishing mark of the Sutter Street temple, two bronze-plated domes which themselves tapered upward into smaller shining globes. One hundred sixty-five feet high, these gold-tipped spires were an integral part of the early San Francisco skyline: they were a prominent landmark for ships entering the Golden Gate; they could be seen by hikers across the bay in the Berkeley hills.

At first glance the domes appear to be a concession to the Moorish style of architecture which had characterized a number of major German synagogues built only a few years earlier. But, as Temko has pointed out, the domes, described by Patton as "pomegranate capitals which crown the towers," were probably meant to symbolize the headpieces of the Torah, known in Hebrew as *rimmonim*, the word for pomegranates. Nor is it difficult to imagine the broad central window, with its Star of David, as the breastplate of the Torah. In sum, Patton, a non-Jew, possibly in consultation with Elkan Cohn, may well have had his entire building depict the Scroll of the Law.

The interior of the synagogue also created a profound effect upon the worshipper. The sanctuary, with over five thousand square feet of floor space, and fifty feet high, was one of the largest vaulted chambers ever constructed in the state. In its pews of gleaming black walnut, twelve hundred people could be seated. Jewish symbols abounded here, too: high above the rosewood ark, itself carved and inlaid with Stars of David and Tablets of the Law, stood a dominating window containing a twelve-pointed star—one Star of David superimposed upon another.

The consecration of the temple that early spring day in 1866 began with a procession of children, followed by Cohn and Sachs, each carrying a Torah which was deposited in the ark. The rabbi delivered an hour-long address, but the most memorable performance of the evening was the chanting of the Sabbath prayers by Cantor Alexander Weisler, who had replaced Levy two years earlier. A pupil of the great Sulzer of Vienna, Weisler's "faultless" baritone voice, filling the glorious hall for the first

INTERIOR OF THE SUTTER STREET TEMPLE

time, made a deep impression on the reporter for the *Alta California* who wrote,

> The stranger became aware of how grand and beautiful—how harmonious and pleasant is the ancient tongue—the Hebrew—combining the euphony of the Spanish, with a comprehensiveness of expression unknown to other tongues, it embraces grace, melody and force; and as we gazed around the large gathering seated in an edifice combining all that modern art and taste can design, we were carried back mentally to the days of the ancient kingdom, when Israel was a power and a nation on the face of the earth, and yet, for all the years of adversity and trial which have beset them, they still realize to a great measure, by their indomitable perseverance, energy and talent, the same power which was wrested from them in the Holy Land.

THE ERECTION OF THE SUTTER STREET TEMPLE was part of the boom in synagogue construction throughout America in the 1860s, as German Jews everywhere seemed to reach a new level of wealth and acculturation and demanded elegant edifices to house their growing congregations. The United States census shows the value of synagogue property rising more than 450 percent in the decade to an aggregate of over five million dollars. Most impressive was New York's Emanu-El, which in 1868 spent an unthinkable $600,000 on a twin-towered sanctuary on Fifth Avenue and 43rd Street. Isaac Mayer Wise's famous Plum Street Temple in Cincinnati was also built at this time, in a style reminiscent of the Alhambra, and at a cost exceeding a quarter of a million dollars.

But the grand scale of the Sutter Street temple indicated that a Jewish commercial elite had crystallized in San Francisco as well—and within a shorter time than anywhere else. The house of worship opened its doors little more than a decade after the membership had struggled to build its first synagogue for one-tenth the cost, and only fifteen years after the birth of the congregation, when a few dozen men, almost all of them in their twenties, had agreed to dues of two dollars a month. They had come very far indeed.

Several dozen pioneer families in particular had been able to capitalize on the financial opportunities in a state virtually untouched by the Civil War. While trade had dominated the economy of the 1850s, the wartime

THE SUTTER STREET TEMPLE VIEWED FROM NOB HILL

demand for finished goods as well as raw materials contributed to the emergence of a diversified manufacturing sector in the following decade. Factories and foundries cropping up south of Market Street now supplemented the growing district of commerce and finance north of that broad thoroughfare.

Levi Strauss and his brother-in-law, David Stern, are examples of merchants who made the transition to manufacturing the goods that previously they had only sold. Rather than have the popular jeans produced by Strauss' brother in New York, they opened a factory in San Francisco and saved greatly on labor and transportation costs.

Businessmen also profited from the fabulously rich Comstock silver strike of 1859, on the eastern side of the Sierras, which produced hundreds of millions of dollars over the next two decades. Most of it found its way to San Francisco, now "rebuilt with Nevada silver." In 1864 alone, when the yield from the mines reached a new plateau, no fewer than a thousand new buildings were constructed in the downtown area. By the decade's end, banks, brokerage houses, and insurance companies crowded Montgomery and California Streets.

The completion of the transcontinental telegraph in 1861, and of course the railroad in 1869, further solidified San Francisco's claim as the unquestioned economic capital of the Far West. While the 1850s had been a decade of economic volatility, the '60s—during which the city's population nearly tripled—was one of almost uninterrupted growth. By the mid-1870s, when the business cycle suddenly turned downward, ten members of Emanu-El were reputed to have had an aggregate wealth of forty-five million dollars.

Most of the pioneer Jewish fortunes were made in the selling or manufacturing of clothing and other dry goods. As we have seen, Levi Strauss and David Stern were already established in this field during the Gold Rush years, as were August Helbing, William Steinhart, Louis Sachs, Lazarus Dinkelspiel, Samuel Wand, and many others. The 1860s saw the emergence of the Schwabacher brothers, the Hecht brothers, Abraham Gunst, and Raphael Peixotto, the latter one of the few Sephardim who were still leaders in an industry now dominated by Bavarians.

Later, Jews established most of the city's leading department stores, fine buildings, almost resembling museums in their elegance, in which could be found wares from all over the world. Raphael Weill of Alsace opened his White House in 1870; Adolph and Achille Roos, Isaac Magnin (aided immensely by his wife, Mary Ann), David Livingston, and Solomon Gump were among the Jewish pioneer retailers who built mighty enterprises that bore their names until late in the twentieth century.

Many others grew wealthy through the marketing of produce. William Haas and Frederick Castle, for example, accumulated great assets as wholesale grocers. Joseph Brandenstein together with the brothers Moses and A. S. Rosenbaum established a thriving tobacco dealership, as did Moses Gunst, Herman Heyneman, and the partners Mendel Esberg, Simon Bachman, and Julius Ehrman. Simon Koshland developed a tremendous business in wool and hides and for nearly two decades Isaac Friedlander dominated the state's trade in wheat.

Of course Jews were widely engaged in commerce in other American cities during the second half of the nineteenth century, particularly in retailing. In San Francisco, however, they were also to be found in activities where relatively few Jews in other regions of the country had made their mark. The brothers-in-law Louis Sloss and Lewis Gerstle, for instance, founded the giant Alaska Commercial Company soon after the territory was purchased from Russia, and enjoyed a virtual monopoly on the sale of its seals and salmon. In the 1870s, Aaron "Honest" Fleishhacker, who earlier had "grubstaked" the future "Silver Kings" James Fair and John Mackay, emerged as a leading manufacturer of cardboard boxes. Paper was also the business of Anthony Zellerbach, who opened a one-room basement store in San Francisco in 1870 and lived to see his concern become one of the largest of its kind in the world.

The brothers Daniel and Jonas Meyer broke new ground in the field of private banking as early as the 1850s. Later, Philip Lilienthal, who had worked closely with the Seligmans in New York and San Francisco (and married Henry's niece), established his successful firm, the Anglo California Bank of London. Perhaps most prominent in the realm of finance was Isaias W. Hellman, who in 1871 founded the Farmers and Merchants Bank in Los Angeles and much later moved to San Francisco to save the Nevada Bank, which he then merged with Wells Fargo. After the turn of the century his son, I. W. Hellman Jr., was counted among the city's outstanding bankers, as were the sons of Aaron Fleishhacker, Herbert and Mortimer, financial giants whose Anglo–London–Paris National Bank wielded enormous influence especially after World War I.

Jews were also conspicuous in the domains of insurance, stocks and bonds, and urban real estate. Michael Reese became one of the wealthiest men in the West through the buying and selling of real property, as did Adolph Sutro, whose profits from his tunnel through the Comstock Lode provided him with the capital to purchase one-twelfth of the acreage of the entire city of San Francisco.

DESPITE HIS WORLD-FAMOUS LIBRARY OF JUDAICA, Sutro, who became mayor in 1894, had little connection with Judaism save at the time of his marriage and at his burial. Michael de Young, one of the publishers and editors of the *San Francisco Chronicle*, was an American-born Jew of Dutch origin who forsook his faith, although Elkan Cohn did conduct the funeral of his brother Charles de Young, assassinated in 1880, and that of his mother. Yet these were the exceptions. Nearly all of the city's leading pioneer Jews publicly identified with some Jewish organization and the large majority joined Congregation Emanu-El, the Eureka Benevolent Society, the Concordia Club, and the B'nai B'rith.

On the High Holidays they filled the Sutter Street temple to capacity, alighting from great carriages driven by liveried coachmen. Here in formal attire, their women in luxurious furs, they listened to a sermon and exquisite liturgical music performed by a choir consisting mainly of non-Jews. "Many of our Christian friends were present" in the pews as well, beamed the temple vice-president in the annual report of 1867, proud that "they witnessed our impressive services."

This was the religious expression of the members of the San Francisco Jewish elite which coalesced during the Cohn era. For about a year, during the construction of the temple, they followed their rabbi's plea to shut their businesses on the Sabbath, but they soon departed from this practice and generally closed only on Rosh Hashanah and Yom Kippur. They also tended to observe Christmas, exchanging presents, decorating a tree, and sometimes feasting on roast pig.

Socially, they were a group unto themselves. At the temple not everyone was of their economic standing, of course, but with annual dues set at the considerable sum of $100 in the 1870s, hardly any member failed to belong at least to the upper-middle class.* Indeed, a recent study using census data has shown that by the century's end, all but one percent of the congregation were merchants or professionals; not one laborer or even "petty proprietor" could be found on its rolls. Moreover, the synagogue was segregated ethnically, with almost all of the members southern or western Germans, augmented by a few Sephardim and Alsatians.

For the Jewish aristocracy had little to do with East European Jews, whom they literally considered only one cut above the Chinese. Although the antipathy of the German Jews toward the *Ostjuden* would peak at the turn of the century, in reaction to the immigration of many Russian

*In 1877, the visiting Isaac Mayer Wise reported that *every* member of Emanu-El paid $100 a year, whereas an examination of the minute books of Sherith Israel in the mid-'70s discloses only about 15 percent of its congregants at that lofty level. About a third of Sherith Israel's membership paid three dollars a month or less.

refugees, it is clear that the aloofness of the Bavarians toward the Prussian "Polacks," which had polarized the Jewish community at its inception, continued unabated decades later. A notable exception was the B'nai B'rith, whose lodge lists after the Civil War reveal that young men from a wide variety of backgrounds belonged to the fraternal order. But for virtually every other Jewish organization on the Pacific Coast, membership seemed to be determined by an imaginary line of demarcation half a world away, somewhere to the east of Berlin.

Perhaps the keenest observer of this divide was Harriet Lane Levy, whose witty memoir of her childhood, *920 O'Farrell Street*, delineates the rigid social stratification of San Francisco Jewry during the last third of the nineteenth century. Her parents were pioneers who had arrived in the 1850s and had reached the upper-middle class by the following decade. They lived with their three daughters in a spacious, richly furnished home with a live-in Irish servant girl, were active in Sherith Israel, and were solid citizens in every way. They spoke German as well as English at home, but because Benish and Yetta Levy had been born in West Prussia (a province near Posen that had been Polish until 1772), all of the family members regarded themselves as inferior to the Bavarian Jews:

> That the Baiern [Bavarians] were superior to us, we knew. We took our position as the denominator takes its stand under the horizontal line. On the social counter the price tag "Polack" confessed second class. Why Poles lacked the virtue of Bavarians I did not understand, though I observed that to others the inferiority was as obvious as it was to us that our ashman and butcher were of poorer grade than we, because they were ashman and butcher....Upon this basis of discrimination everybody agreed and acted.

Harriet once participated in a debate at Emanu-El (which she won handily) and she and her sisters made friends with many Bavarian girls, but she felt "uncomfortable" in their midst: "Pleasure was rarely simple or unmixed with fear. I never completely belonged." And her mother put an end to any notion she or her sister Polly might have of ever marrying a Bavarian:

> "No Baier marries a Pole unless he is *krumm* or *lahm* or *stumm* [crooked or lame or dumb]."

"But if one fell in love with a girl?" Polly protested.

"If he fell in love, he'd fall out again," came the answer.*

The Jewish elite admired the Christian families of money and power, and to a large extent the feeling was mutual, but evidently both groups drew the line at intimate social contact. Jews "are welcome members of the best society," noted the prolific author Gertrude Atherton, herself a socialite, who wrote in the same sentence that "they are clannish and form an inner group of their own." And even from a vantage point a couple of rungs below the top of the ladder, Harriet Lane Levy could also sense this "pleasant disassociation which no one wished to change."

While "high society" was more accessible to the Jews in San Francisco than anywhere else in America, it is also true that exclusive haunts such as the Bohemian Club, the Pacific and Union Clubs (later to merge), and the Junior League admitted very few Jewish members. The Bay Area's first *Elite Directory*, published in 1879, included over two hundred Jewish households, 19 percent of the total list and more than twice the proportion of Jews in the general population. But nearly all of the Jewish names were printed on a separate list, with the notable exceptions of Levi Strauss and the dry goods importer Abraham Weil, who were on the Christian list only. Jews were interspersed among the general elite in the *Blue Book* of 1888, but accounts from the time reveal that relatively few of them were present at the lavish parties thrown by the Christian plutocracy. Not only were marriages to non-Jews unusual for the Emanu-El elite in the late nineteenth century, but so also were betrothals to anyone outside a circle of a few dozen German-Jewish clans. By World War I the city's Jewish aristocracy had become so inbred that it almost resembled the royalty of Europe.

If insular and sheltered, however, the lives of these privileged few

---

*Rebekah Kohut, who made a distinguished career as a social worker in New York and Europe, also spent her adolescent years in San Francisco in the late 1870s and early '80s and corroborates Levy's impressions in her autobiography, *My Portion*. The daughter of Rabbi Albert Bettelheim of Ohabai Shalome, Kohut writes of the "unhealthy rivalry among the congregations" and the tendency of the Jews to segregate themselves socially according to their European backgrounds—"to even a larger extent" than the community from which her family had come, staid Richmond, Va. As for Levy, the petty regional biases contributed to Kohut's ambivalent feelings toward Judaism during these years.

were also filled with culture and refinement. In the last three decades of
the century they built ornate Victorian residences on the beautiful
boulevard that was Van Ness Avenue before the earthquake; on sedate
Franklin Street one block west; and on the fashionable streets which
traversed them: Post, Sutter, Bush, Pine, California, Sacramento, Clay,
Washington, Jackson, and Pacific. In marbled drawing rooms and leather-
walled libraries, surrounded by precious works of art, they entertained
themselves lavishly. They were also frequently seen in public at the theater, the opera, and the temple.

Their children usually attended the city's better private schools and
were also tutored in French, music, and dance. Many of them entered
the University of California, in Berkeley, but some enrolled at Stanford
(where the Emanu-El congregant Louis Sloss was invited to join the board
of trustees) and a select few went east to Harvard. And a trip to Europe in
the tradition of the grand tour was de rigueur for the "finishing" of a young
person's education.

Most members of this American-born second generation assumed
positions in the family firm, but several went on to impressive accomplishments in the professions and the arts. Louis Sloss' son Marcus, for
example, became a justice of the state supreme court in 1906. Raphael
Peixotto, whose brother, Benjamin Franklin Peixotto, served as U.S. envoy
to Rumania in the 1870s, saw his son Ernest become one of the nation's
leading illustrators and his daughter Jessica become the first woman to
attain the rank of full professor at the University of California. Anne Bremer and Joseph Greenbaum, both related to leading pioneers, became
well-known painters, and Isaac Walter's son, Edgar, won fame as a sculptor.

The Jewish patriciate was not a closed caste, however. Those of
exceptional achievements, if modest means, were welcomed. Thus, the
acclaimed painter Toby Rosenthal, the son of a local tailor, was an honored guest in the houses of the rich, while Julius Kahn, a former actor
and son of a baker, was to represent San Francisco in the U.S. House of
Representatives for an unprecedented twelve terms. He was succeeded in
1924 by his wife, Florence Prag Kahn, who served an additional six terms,
the first Jewish woman in Congress. And the wealthiest Jews and non-
Jews fawned over the internationally known poet and Broadway actress
Ada Isaacs Menken, who came to town in the mid-1860s and created a

sensation with a role calling for her to ride horseback across the stage clad only in flesh-colored tights.

MENKEN, WHO WAS MARRIED AND DIVORCED FOUR TIMES in her short life (she died in Paris at the age of thirty-three), was obviously an anomaly in San Francisco, where most middle- and upper-class Jewish women kept well within the bounds of Victorian expectations. Yet it was not uncommon for the daughters of the pioneers to reject the traditional "woman's role" of self-sacrifice and duty to others, and strike out on their own into uncharted territory.

But often they had to contend with their parents' disdain. Jessica Peixotto, for example, a brilliant student both at Girls' High and at the Emanu-El Sabbath school, was forced to delay for a decade her studies at the university due to her father's objections. Harriet Lane Levy, meanwhile, had to struggle with the narrow-mindedness of her hard-bitten mother, who seemed to be obsessed with appearances. Yetta Levy lived in a seemingly constant state of disapproval, in

> a world where variation was perversity [and] nothing short of immolation could maintain reputation intact. A slight deviation from the norm, which was O'Farrell Street, a collar rolled back exposing a triangle of throat to the daylight, revealed its wearer to Mother as an eccentric; a broader step to the left and a girl's honor fell from her like a loosely buttoned petticoat.

Yet Harriet rose above the prim sensibility of her mother, and her adult life was one of art, adventure, and independence. She graduated from the University of California in Berkeley, never married, and along with Jack London and Frank Norris wrote for the *Wave*, an avant-garde journal.

As a free spirit, she was hardly alone among this first generation of San Francisco-born Jewish women. Her next-door neighbor at 922 O'Farrell Street was Alice Toklas, raised by her widowed grandfather, an Emanu-El congregant. With Alice, Harriet journeyed to Paris in 1907, where both women met Gertrude Stein, herself a Bavarian Jew who had grown up in Oakland in the 1880s. As is well known, Stein and Toklas fell in love and remained in France the rest of their lives, fully engaged in the world's most daring literary and artistic movements. Levy, too, was part of the circle that included Picasso, Braque, and Matisse, but eventually returned home to continue her life of letters in California. Years later, at a local monthly discussion group comprised of women writers, she discovered that a third Jewish girl on the same block had gone on to become an author with European connections, as well: Deborah Hirsh, "a nobody on O'Farrell Street," had married a wealthy Englishman and was "now Mrs. Orton of London, in the literary set."

While Harriet Lane Levy fulfilled her ambitions despite her mother's reproaches, another pattern has been described, that of "second-generation Jewish women in the West [receiving] from their pioneering mothers a legacy of self-confidence, self-reliance, independence and pride in achievement. Lacking trails to blaze or towns to build, some of these women became groundbreakers in new roles and occupations from which women had traditionally been barred." The Solomons women of San Francisco are a case in point. Hannah Marks Solomons was a bit of a rebel even during the Gold Rush years. An orphan, she was raised by an Orthodox uncle in Philadelphia and was brought out West in 1852 to marry a man she had never seen. After meeting him, she infuriated her family by breaking the engagement, a shocking act of defiance in mid-nineteenth-century America. Her brother, Bernhard Marks, himself a pioneer in Placerville, defended her, writing the relatives back East that "the cattle matching project" was "not...consistent with the spirit of an American education."

She took a job as a schoolteacher and in the early 1860s married the prominent Sephardi journalist Seixas Solomons, who had been an officer in the vigilantes and a community spokesman during the Mortara protest and who would later serve Emanu-El as secretary of the board of trustees. Sadly, though, Solomons became an alcoholic and the task of raising their five children fell entirely on Hannah. But her offspring went far with the values she imparted to them; not only did her three sons become noted professionals, but her two daughters broke new paths for women, one becoming a child psychiatrist, the other a forceful suffragette.

A female observer in the 1890s, worried that a stranger in town might get the wrong impression of the San Francisco Jewish woman, wrote,

> She appears always well-dressed, sometimes a little dashing in her apparel; with dusky, flashing eyes, brilliant cheeks, and a figure that

moves along with that swinging motion that indicates perfect health. With this hearty, well-groomed look, she seems a splendid creature physically, and one whose chief occupation does not extend beyond attention to her individual comforts or luxuries.

But stressing the accomplishments of Jewish women in the city in journalism, in the arts, in education, and even in medicine (a profession completely closed to American women a generation earlier), where they now accounted for six local physicians, the writer added that "the Jewess developed not alone physically but mentally and spiritually....She keeps pace with the world's advancement."

THE JEWISH COMMUNITY had its garish side of superficiality, snobbery, and scandal that made good copy for its scrappy journalists, who—next to feuding among themselves—loved nothing better than to expose the foibles of the Emanu-El elite in particular. Most aggressive of all was the multilingual bookseller Isidore Choynski, whose column in Isaac Mayer Wise's *American Israelite* showed all the restraint of a tornado. His "San Francisco Letter," featured in the nationally circulated Cincinnati paper, was invariably studded with incidents of humbug. His reporting ranged from the fact that the Concordia Club was filled with diners and poker players on Yom Kippur, to the item that upon the marriage of his daughter, the president of Emanu-El donated money to the "German" Eureka Benevolent Society but not to its "Polish" counterpart.

Many a spring Choynski ridiculed Cohn's ostentatious confirmation ceremony, "with its floral display that would do credit the Ninth Regiment on Decoration Day." He assailed the public oral examinations given the confirmands on Shavuot, in which "the handsomest and wealthiest misses...appear in silks and satins loaded down with borrowed jewelry for the occasion [and] shine for an hour as professors." Choynski also catalogued the vanity of the nouveau riche. A friend of Toby Rosenthal, he shared the artist's disappointment with the wealthy Jews who paid him well for their portraits, but who lacked the imagination to commission him for any other kind of painting. One well-to-do Jewish woman, referred to by Choynski as "Mrs. Shoddy," asked Rosenthal for a discount if he would paint not only her portrait but also the portraits of her two daughters.

The correspondent chronicled behavior which ranged from the bizarre to the depraved. Along with other Jewish journalists, for instance, he wrote of Joshua Norton, the rice speculator who had made and lost his fortune in the late 1850s only to reappear as "the Emperor of the United States and the Protector of Mexico." Until his death in 1880, he was a tolerated fixture in the city—and at Emanu-El, where he could be found most Saturday mornings—with his epauletted uniform, regal sword, and feisty dogs. Local restaurants indulged Norton I, honoring the scrip he issued for meals, but his coreligionists thought him enough of an embarrassment to deny him a Jewish burial.

Norton, whether a madman or simply a freeloader, was essentially a harmless, colorful addition to the city streets. But most of Choynski's other personal sketches were far less amusing. Often naming the principals involved—more than once an officer of the congregation—he told tales of blackmail, adultery, suicide, and even homicide. To be sure, the accuracy of Choynski's statements was at times open to question; his own editor often followed his pieces with a disclaimer and sometimes an outright refutation. Nor were the leading families of Emanu-El his only target. He also attacked women, the Orthodox, the poor, Chinese, American Indians, Christians, and all rabbis as a class.

Yet his dozens of columns in the 1870s and '80s can hardly be dismissed as merely the ranting of an irascible and inaccurate reporter. Taken as a whole, his impressions confirm an unmistakable thickening of social barriers within the Jewish community of the late nineteenth century. They also indicate that the Spartan virtues for which Jews were known in the 1850s were no longer intact one generation later.

CHOYNSKI RESERVED HIS MOST MORDANT CRITICISM for the Emanu-El congregant Michael Reese, a real estate baron, incessantly chiding "the prince of misers" for his habit of leaving restaurants without paying, haggling with local shopkeepers, and refusing to support his poor relations. But most damning in Choynski's view was the deaf ear Reese turned to philanthropic causes, for even in death the stingy bachelor provided only several hundred thousand dollars for charity out of an estate of many millions. Choynski even shared with his readers the cause—probably fanciful—of Reese's death. While visiting his father's grave in Bavaria, he vaulted over a cemetery gate rather than pay a toll and broke his neck. Martin Heller, the Hecht brothers, and even Levi Strauss were also labeled as tightfisted by the bookseller, who blamed the town's richest Jews for neglecting a raft of worthy projects. As he characteristically put it after failing to raise fifty dollars apiece from several millionaires, "These fellows...are more likely to plunk down twice as much on a pair of aces."

Yet in no other respect was Choynski more one-sided and unfair. For the fact is that during the Cohn period the Emanu-El elite firmly established itself as a philanthropic group; *noblesse oblige* became a paramount concern of the leading families, who would be known for their munificence ever since.

The Eureka Benevolent Society, founded in 1850, best exemplified that tradition. By 1889, the last year of Cohn's rabbinate, it counted no fewer than 831 members. Its assets, including a special fund for widows and orphans, amounted to nearly $150,000, the interest of which, along with additional donations, went to support the needy. That year seventy-five Jews received a small monthly stipend from the society and more than five hundred persons and families were given one-time cash grants.

In 1871, Cohn had chaired a meeting of prominent laymen which recommended the formation of a Jewish orphanage in San Francisco. With the aid of the B'nai B'rith's western region, District Four, funds were raised to open the Pacific Hebrew Orphan Asylum. The new building on Divisadero Street, an ample facility including playgrounds, was dedicated early in 1877, a year and a half before the B'nai B'rith completed its own substantial meeting hall. The most avid partisan of the orphan asylum was Samuel Wolf Levy, a member of Emanu-El's valued Alsatian contingent, who headed the institution for forty years and who also founded many kindergartens on the Pacific Coast.

The leadership of the orphanage was also concerned with sheltering the elderly, and already in the early 1870s land for this purpose was acquired on the outskirts of the city. The Hebrew Home for the Aged Disabled actually opened its doors in 1889 in rented quarters on Lyons Street, however, and a year later, when it merged with the orphan asylum, moved to larger surroundings on Lombard Street.

In the late 1880s leading Jews also founded Mount Zion Hospital. A meeting at the home of Frederick Castle resulted in the election of a board of directors; later a public gathering at the temple adopted bylaws and a constitution. The physical plant itself, the first Jewish hospital in the West, was dedicated in January 1897, a modest building of twelve beds along with surgical suites. Two years later a larger, fifty-bed unit was opened on Sutter Street between Scott and Divisadero. Even in its planning stages, the prime movers of the hospital faced the difficult philosophical question of whether or not it would serve only Jewish patients. Cohn spoke out in favor of a non-sectarian institution, a view shared by most of the Jewish community but opposed by a highly vocal minority.

In addition to local needs—and the hospital demonstrated that these included to an extent the well-being of non-Jews—the Emanu-El elite was also attentive to the plight of its coreligionists overseas. Indicative of this concern was the formation, in 1864, of a San Francisco chapter of the Alliance Israélite Universelle, an organization founded in Paris four years earlier with the goal of aiding persecuted Jews throughout the world. Daniel Levy, soon to resign from his position as cantor and return to his native land, was elected secretary. Cohn, who along with his wife spoke fluent French, served as president.

Particularly in the late 1870s and early 1880s, funds were raised in San Francisco, often through the Alliance, for the hard-pressed Jewries of Morocco, Turkey, Russia, Rumania, and even Palestine. Cohn received a personal letter of gratitude and encouragement from Adolphe Cremieux, president of the international organization for a decade and a half. Much like Moses Montefiore somewhat earlier, Cremieux, a member of the French parliament, epitomized the concern of emancipated Jews for their brethren still suffering under repressive regimes. And both figures were revered among the congregants of Emanu-El; Simon Koshland even named one of his sons Montefiore.

By the end of Cohn's rabbinate, then, the embryonic ganglia of Jewish organizational life in the 1850s had been manifestly strengthened and extended. It is true, as Choynski argued, that still more could have been done. At one point he even published a list of the donations to the orphan asylum in order to show that it was supported more by the masses of poor Jews, the fifty-cent-a-month givers, than by the opulent few. Another shortcoming—and one which Choynski was fond of pointing out—was the rivalry and duplication caused by the existence of many competing Jewish charitable institutions. Calls for the centralization of these agencies were voiced in the Jewish press as early as 1878, but the first step in this direction, the creation of the Hebrew Board of Relief, was not taken until the beginning of the new century.

But if Choynski was unsparing in his criticism, certainly non-Jews were in awe of the network of Jewish benevolence which they saw in the Bay Area. As Mary Watson wrote in her *San Francisco Society* in 1887, the Jews comprised the most charitable group in the city.

By VIRTUE OF BEING THE SPIRITUAL LEADER of the largest and wealthiest synagogue, the soft-spoken Cohn played the role of an unofficial "Grand Rabbi," in the words of Philo Jacoby, longtime editor of the local *Hebrew*. He was invited to the dedication of nearly every new synagogue in Northern California, even that of Ohabai Shalome; he spoke in Orthodox *shuls* as well as Reform temples. In 1883, he traveled to Los Angeles, a city of twenty thousand with perhaps six hundred Jews, where he addressed the small, struggling B'nai B'rith Congregation, decades later to be known as the Wilshire Boulevard Temple, then taking its first steps toward liberal Judaism.

Cohn was not quite the "ambassador to the gentiles" that many of his successors would be, but he did enjoy several deep friendships with non-Jewish clergymen. In addition to Thomas Starr King, who passed from the scene early, he was close to Horatio Stebbins, another important Unitarian minister; John Hemphill, the pastor of the Calvary Presbyterian Church; and Joseph Alemany, the Catholic archbishop of San Francisco. With Stebbins and Hemphill he fought for a cause which Eckman also furthered in the *Gleaner*, and which every future rabbi of Emanu-El would also embrace—that of the separation of church and state. It was the issue of public aid to parochial schools on which he chose to take a stand, firmly opposing that plan from the pulpit.

The rabbi represented the Jewish community at many municipal functions, and he was especially visible during the public outpouring of grief which followed the assassination of Abraham Lincoln. As part of a procession through town of twenty thousand mourners, he was among thirty-eight distinguished citizens of the West who served as pallbearers. He also officiated at memorial services for the fallen president held in the

Broadway synagogue. His most dramatic expression of sorrow, however, was rendered on the very day of Lincoln's death, when Cohn was informed of the shocking news just as he mounted the pulpit for Saturday morning services. He sank to the floor and burst into tears but then rose, quickly composed himself, and delivered a moving, impromptu eulogy which was printed in the *Alta California* as well as the Anglo-Jewish press. One of his few extant sermons, it reflects the synthesis of ancient Jewish values and modern American ideals which he sought so hard to create on the Pacific Coast:

> A great man has fallen. Arise, my brethren, and bow in humble devotion before God! Arise, and honor the memory of the blessed, whose life was a blessing to us, to our country, to the oppressed and afflicted, and to the human race at large....The great principles he so nobly and fully represented are the very nerve and essence of our people, and as long as there is upon our soil a mind to think and a heart to feel, these principles will be defended and upheld with the last drop of blood....Oh, he served God, in his love to man, the most glorious worship on earth!

WITHIN THE TEMPLE, Cohn found that he had an easier task of initiating reforms after the defection of the more religiously observant families to Ohabai Shalome. In 1869, for example, he broke the Sabbath laws by participating in a citywide celebration marking the completion of the Central Pacific Railroad. A move to censure him failed at a congregational meeting which also abolished the wearing of the *tallit*, or prayer shawl, by both rabbi and cantor. This time he was personally assailed by the traditionally-minded Rabbi Aaron Messing of Chicago, who had just decided to come out West, accepting the offer of Sherith Israel to become its next spiritual leader. In the pages of the *American Israelite*, Messing called Cohn a "false prophet" and "a 'messiah' who has converted the whole town into a Sodom. He rides around on the Sabbath with a cigar in his mouth and says that Moses and his generation invented the Torah and we have no part in it. He gets $6,000 a year and is a very rich man."*

---

*Messing came to the West Coast thinking that he could keep Sherith Israel in the Orthodox camp, but he had underestimated the reformist tendencies there and his tenure lasted only three years. He then took the pulpit of the more traditional Beth Israel, which he held until 1890. Fortunately, the ad hominem attack he leveled against Cohn was not characteristic of his long and productive rabbinate in San Francisco.

A few years later at Emanu-El, the ram's horn, or *shofar*, blown in almost every synagogue in the world on the High Holidays, was replaced by a cornet, a move greeted by Choynski, as we might expect, with leaden sarcasm:

> Perhaps you will consider me out of reason when I denominate the New Year's as the Day of the Cornet, but you know we are an enlightened, progressive people, and you know that our mode of worship has to conform to the appearance, the shadow, rather than to its efficacy, or substance....The plain, ungainly Shofar made way for the more modern cornet whose dulcet tones were [sounded] by a professional player, and all went merry, as though fasting belonged to bygone ages.*

The controversy over whether or not men should wear hats in the synagogue—a caustic and somewhat tedious debate since the completion of the Sutter Street temple—was finally resolved in 1881, when the board passed a resolution requiring the members to worship bareheaded. Soon thereafter, a visitor who insisted on wearing his hat had to be removed from the temple by the aged sexton, Maier Steppacher.

In 1886, Emanu-El introduced its most radical Reform measure of all: while retaining regular Saturday worship, it joined a handful of American and German congregations in moving Friday evening services to Sunday. But that proved abortive, lasting only about a year.

Cohn also departed from tradition at weddings and funerals. He willingly dispensed with the *huppah*, or bridal canopy, when asked; he often buried the dead in ornate caskets and without the customary shroud. While the rabbi did not perform intermarriage, it appears that a great deal of study was not always required for conversion.

THE NATIONAL REFORM MOVEMENT, which became a potent force in the 1870s, was of particular interest to Cohn, and he invited to Emanu-El one of its leading lights, Rabbi Max Lilienthal of Cincinnati, whose son, Philip, the dapper banker, was a prominent member of the temple. In July and August 1877, Isaac Mayer Wise himself visited San Francisco on behalf of the newly formed Union of American Hebrew Congregations and Hebrew Union College.

---

*Although the shofar did occasionally make an appearance during the High Holidays, it was not permanently brought back until the 1950s. During the turn of the century, the trombone was the instrument most often used in its place.

He arrived during an ugly summer, perhaps the most tumultuous months in the city's history during the long period between the Gold Rush and the Great Earthquake of 1906. A drought had led to rising food prices and severe unemployment; overspeculation in the Comstock Lode had resulted in tight money and falling real estate values. Many of the angry and frustrated jobless turned on the Chinese, now arriving in great numbers. Riots against them were incited by the demagogue Dennis Kearney, and order was restored only with the formation of a six-thousand-man Committee of Safety, armed with hickory pick handles, which subdued the mobs. Much like the vigilante days of the 1850s, leading Jews supported the extralegal measures; they feared for the safety of the Chinese, many of whom worked on the wharves as laborers for Jewish merchants or as servants in Jewish homes.

Violence occurred the very night of Wise's main address at the temple—he would speak at Emanu-El twice—and he wrote extensively of the social unrest in reports sent back to Cincinnati for publication in the *American Israelite.* Yet this hardly restrained his enthusiasm for San Francisco, "the city of miracles." He described its physical beauty and great wealth as vividly as its poverty and racism.

He was also impressed, on the whole, with Jewish life. A friend of Choynski, it is not surprising that he bewailed the fact that "two hundred dollars per annum pays a millionaire's bills to the congregation, charities, lodges, and orphan asylum all told." He lamented, too, the low level of religious observance, especially of the Sabbath. But he was deeply gratified by the proliferation of synagogues in the West, by effective leaders such as Cohn, and by the "gorgeous" temple which was packed for his lectures.

Emanu-El, on its part, was taken with Wise's eloquence and moved by his plea for unity "on this American soil...our Zion...our Mount Moriah." Only a few months after his departure the board opted to affiliate with the Union of American Hebrew Congregations, the first western synagogue to do so.

Important benefits were to be reaped by the synagogue through its membership in a national religious body under the direction of a forceful leader, interestingly enough another Protestant-style model which seemed appropriate for American Jewry in the late nineteenth century. The seminary, a combination of college and rabbinical school, would produce suitable clergymen to fill the great need for spiritual leaders that was felt especially on the Pacific Coast. Circuit preaching, another activity of the UAHC, would reach Jews in small, remote communities, again addressing a problem acutely felt in the Far West. The UAHC also offered inexpensive Bibles, a monthly newspaper, and other publications, and even functioned in part as a Jewish defense agency, monitoring anti-Semitism in America and also keeping a watchful eye on oppressed Jewish communities abroad.

Cohn and his lay leaders also hoped for aid from the UAHC in another vital area—Jewish education. The Sabbath school of Emanu-El was the largest in the city, with an enrollment of more than four hundred by the end of the 1870s, including many children of non-members who were warmly welcomed whether or not they could pay the tuition. But despite the focused efforts of many of the congregation's most capable laymen, its effectiveness was always in question. The prospect of improved textbooks and curricular materials, as well as access to nationally gathered data on religious schools, added much to the UAHC's attractiveness. With the founders of the congregation now in middle age, keeping their children and ultimately their grandchildren as members was seen as the key to viability in the future.

The Peixotto family understood this well. "Our children grow up in ignorance of the great truths of Judaism," wrote Benjamin Franklin Peixotto in 1867, shortly after he arrived in San Francisco for a three-year period, "[and] we are lacking in adequate teachers, preachers, and literature." He ardently supported Wise and the UAHC, and his brother Raphael later became president of Emanu-El's school board before assuming the presidency of the congregation itself.

Yet retaining the next generation was hardly a foregone conclusion. By the end of the 1870s, the number of Jews in the city had climbed to more than sixteen thousand, making it the second-largest Jewish community in the country, but only 16 percent of the Jewish families belonged to one of the seven synagogues in town. At the time of Wise's 1877 visit, the Emanu-El membership had dipped to 260 families, fewer than it had had a dozen years earlier, before it had opened the magnificent Sutter Street temple. Sherith Israel, which also built a large new house of worship after the Civil War, took major steps toward reform after the arrival of the dynamic

Rabbi Henry Vidaver in 1874 and now had close to the same number of congregants as Emanu-El. While there was as yet little direct competition for members with this "Polish" congregation, the Bavarian Ohabai Shalome, about half the size of the first two, was also ensconced in an ample synagogue and showed no signs of flagging.

Of more concern to the leaders of Emanu-El than rival congregations, though, was the mood of their own young people in the decades following the Civil War, a period in which mainstream religion in general was overshadowed by economic activity, scientific advances, and later political idealism. Jews reaching intellectual maturity in the last third of the nineteenth century "felt alienated," in the judgment of a leading historian of the Reform movement; they were often ambivalent about their German and Jewish roots and susceptible at times to the inducements of popular belief systems such as Christian Science, Ethical Culture, and even astrology and fortune-telling.

Others withheld spiritual belief of any kind. Toward the end of Elkan Cohn's rabbinate, the *San Francisco Examiner* described local Jewry as "a liberal-minded people [who read] the writings of the great Agnostics of the Age," and then went on to enumerate six contemporary philosophers—skeptics, freethinkers, and other radical critics of religion—which Jews "peruse at length."

Henry U. Brandenstein is an example of a self-proclaimed "agnostic" who refused to join the temple. His Bavarian-born father, the wealthy pioneer merchant Joseph Brandenstein, had been a pillar of Emanu-El since Rabbi Eckman had officiated at his wedding in 1855. But Henry, one of the first Jews to graduate from Harvard Law School, had other ideas. Returning to San Francisco in the early 1890s to set up his law practice, he became active in a myriad of Jewish organizations and later married Rabbi Cohn's granddaughter, May Colman. Yet he eschewed synagogue affiliation his entire life.

Brandenstein, who served on the city's board of supervisors and board of education, was a reform-minded Democrat. Other well-educated Jews of his generation were also drawn to the deep social problems of the Industrial Age, and favored strong remedies ranging from school reform and urban planning to anti-vice crusades. To be sure, his wife's grandfather, Elkan Cohn, was likewise committed to civic betterment and worked hard to build up a number of local institutions aimed at relieving every manner of human suffering. But in the temple Cohn's long, didactic sermons—delivered in German or heavily accented English—tended to focus more on the reform of Judaism than on the reform of society.

Women, meanwhile, could sit next to their husbands or fathers in the pews, but could not be members of the synagogue in their own right. With the exception of teaching in the Sabbath school, they were allowed but a small role in congregational activities. The younger women, far better educated than their mothers and much more inclined toward activities outside the home, often looked elsewhere to channel their energies.

Above all, however, it was the secular culture of San Francisco which lured the second generation, the sour events of the summer of 1877 notwithstanding. With its growing array of attractions, "The City"—the ninth-largest in the nation by 1880—had won the hearts and minds of the affluent American-born, sometimes at the expense of the synagogue. The many opera houses and theatres were a highlight originating in the Gold Rush years, but in the 1870s international recognition came for the variety and quality of the cuisine as well, the plethora of fine restaurants a consequence of the multicultural populace. Urban life had also become more amenable with the introduction of a good streetcar system and a network of cable cars. And San Francisco architecture was finally becoming more pleasing, too, with the construction of majestic downtown hotels, such as the world-class Palace in 1875, as well as rows and rows of charming Victorian homes with their ornamented facades and large bay windows. But perhaps most alluring was the opening of Golden Gate Park in this decade, a thousand-acre showplace of landscape architecture—even larger than its New York forerunner, Central Park—which stretched all the way to the ocean.

The founders of the congregation were also enamored of San Francisco, of course, but their European upbringing firmly linked them to the synagogue. It would be no small challenge for them to make Judaism relevant to their children born in this Eden on the Pacific.

THE LAST MAJOR PROJECT OF THE COHN YEARS was the establishment, in 1888, of a new cemetery of over seventy-three acres, on gently rolling hills in the farming town of Colma, in San Mateo County. The rapid population growth of the Mission District had compelled the city to demand the closing of the old burial grounds on Eighteenth Street which, in any case, were no longer adequate for the congregation of around three hundred families by the late 1880s.

Along with Sherith Israel, which was sold twenty acres of the San Mateo tract at cost—$350 per acre—the congregation built a mortuary chapel at the head of the avenue dividing the two cemeteries. Emanu-El, too, employed twenty acres, holding the remaining land for the distant future. This tranquil site, about ten miles from San Francisco, was the wise choice of Martin Heller, president of the congregation from 1880 until his death in 1894. The white-bearded Bavarian peddler-turned-dry goods dealer had made a fortune during the Civil War and invested it in urban real estate, constructing fourteen buildings in the late '60s and early '70s. In acquiring the cemetery, he not only ensured a serene resting spot for thousands of Jews, but also gained a tremendous financial asset for the temple for many generations to come.

Elkan Cohn, who consecrated the new Home of Peace Cemetery on Thanksgiving, 1888, was the following spring one of the first to be interred in its grounds. He had been in poor health since the death of his wife in 1879, and the loss of others near to him—his closest co-workers— exacted an additional toll. In 1884, the gifted cantor Max Wolff, who had succeeded Weisler a decade earlier, died at the age of forty-five after a long illness. A graduate of the Vienna Conservatory, and a man who could have spent his life on the operatic stage, Wolff had been chosen by the temple from a list of over two dozen candidates. His full baritone voice had thrilled worshippers on Sutter Street, and had made a deep impression on the visiting Isaac Mayer Wise.

But with Wolff's passing, the entire burden of the services fell upon the aging Cohn. An understanding temple board engaged a "junior rabbi" in 1885, Abraham Illch, an intense twenty-seven-year-old who was born in Albany, New York, while Cohn held a pulpit in that city. An outstanding student, Illch had been awarded a prize in mathematics as an undergraduate at Columbia and high honors for his doctoral dissertation in Semitics at the University of Leipzig. But he had been in frail physical condition since his childhood, and died only six months after his arrival at Emanu-El, his first rabbinical post.

His position was filled by Jacob Voorsanger of Holland, a minister of extraordinary ability and stamina, who soon succeeded Cohn as the spiritual leader of the temple—a position he would hold for almost two decades until his own death in 1908.

But for three years in the late 1880s the young Voorsanger, a lustrous career ahead of him, sat at the feet of the venerable "Dr. Cohn," as he called him. It was a time that he treasured. The elderly rabbi, now unable to perform many of his duties, often remained at home with his protégé, where he recapitulated his entire experience on the West Coast, recalling many friends and foes who had already passed away. Cohn thus provided a good deal of the material for *The Chronicles of Emanu-El*, the impressionistic history of the synagogue through 1886 which Voorsanger published at the turn of the century.

Cohn had reason to recount his three decades in San Francisco with much satisfaction, for he had won the major battles of his career. The long years he had devoted to scholarship as a youth later earned him the respect of congregants and colleagues alike, of vital importance in his struggle

CANTOR MAX WOLFF   RABBI ABRAHAM ILLCH

to reinterpret Judaism in a new land. His even-tempered manner and Job-like forbearance further ingratiated his followers and confounded his opponents.

He was, for more than half of his adult life, rabbi of "the Temple," the Sutter Street temple, whose massive brick walls and elegant, tapered towers spoke volumes of the strength, stability, and style he had brought to Reform Judaism in San Francisco.

chapter three

JACOB VOORSANGER
Axioms of Reform

Elkan Cohn instituted much of the ritual which would characterize the temple decades after his death. But it would be left to his successor, the Reverend Dr. Jacob Voorsanger, to articulate the philosophy of Reform Judaism in the face of a number of challenges at the turn of the century: a physical disaster, a political scandal, and, not least threatening in his mind, the arrival in San Francisco of thousands of Jewish refugees from Eastern Europe. As a scholar, a teacher, a preacher, and most of all as a publicist, this brilliant Dutchman became the most influential Jewish leader of his time in the American West.

Yet he was a self-taught man, a diamond cutter's son whose formal education ended with graduation from a Jewish high school in his native Amsterdam. He never received rabbinical ordination, and his doctorate, and even his bachelor's degree, both from the Hebrew Union College, were honorary rather than earned.*

Arriving in America in 1873 at the age of twenty, he worked initially

---

*A very different story of Voorsanger's early life is told in *Western Jewry*, written in 1916 by his successor at Emanu-El, Rabbi Martin Meyer. Here the Dutch immigrant is portrayed as the descendant of a long line of German rabbis and not only a graduate of the Jewish Theological Seminary of Amsterdam, but one of its finest students—biographical details repeated by more than one historian since. In 1983, however, after a close examination of archival material in Holland and America, the researchers Kenneth Zwerin and Norton Stern reached a startlingly different conclusion. Their persuasive account of Voorsanger's formative years must now be considered definitive.

as a cantor (coincidentally the meaning of the word *voorsanger* in Dutch) while he took elocution lessons from a private tutor. After holding three cantorial posts on the East Coast, his rabbinical career commenced with a call in 1878 from Congregation Beth Israel of Houston, Texas, where he would serve as the spiritual leader for eight years, spending virtually all of his free time in independent study.

When he came to San Francisco as the assistant rabbi of Emanu-El in 1886, it soon became obvious that intellectually he was more than the equal of his colleagues who had gone through a seminary or university.* Upon Cohn's death three years later, he was chosen as the senior rabbi.

Throughout his long tenure at the temple he distinguished himself as a man of letters. He edited San Francisco's *Jewish Progress* for a brief time, but far more influential would be the *Emanu-El*, which he founded in November 1895 and edited almost without interruption for thirteen years. A twenty-page weekly, it contained material on a high level: long, analytical articles on Jewish communities in Europe, Asia, and North Africa by its own foreign correspondents; fiction by authors such as Israel Zangwill and Sholom Aleichem; philosophical treatises by leading lights of American Jewry such as Solomon Schechter and David Philipson; biblical scholarship by Max Margolis and Moses Buttenwieser; and of course reports on local Jewish community life, filed by lay leaders. Voorsanger penned the incisive editorials and often an additional article of three or four thousand words. On the pages of the *Emanu-El* his thoughts were carried weekly to thousands of households up and down the coast and across America.

He was one of the luminaries of the Reform movement's radical second generation, along with men like Hirsch of Chicago, Krauskopf of Philadelphia, and Kohler of New York. Departing from Isaac Mayer Wise's goals of compromise with the Orthodox and uniformity in the ranks of American Jewry, these rabbis boldly declared their position in their Pittsburgh Platform of 1885:

> We accept as binding only the moral laws and maintain only such ceremonies as elevate and sanctify our lives, but reject all such as are not

*Usually referring to himself as "Reverend," Voorsanger never claimed rabbinical ordination, only that he had been "educated" at the seminary in Amsterdam, but Zwerin and Stern found no reference to him in the records of that institution.

The Reverend Jacob Voorsanger

adapted to the views and habits of modern civilization. We hold that all such Mosaic and rabbinical laws as regulate diet, priestly purity and dress originated in ages and under the influence of ideas foreign to our present mental and spiritual state.

Over principles such as these they waged war against the Orthodox and later the Conservatives (for whom opposition to the Pittsburgh Platform was probably the greatest stimulus for organization). And with only slightly less enthusiasm did the Reformers quarrel among themselves.

In accord with his colleagues, the foundation stone of Voorsanger's thought was an unshakable belief in human reason and human progress, concepts which pervaded much of Western philosophy at the end of the nineteenth century. His notion of "progressive, rational Judaism" replaced the traditional doctrine of supernatural revelation with Darwinian evolution, an idea of great currency at the time, not least of all for liberal theologians seeking to synthesize religion with the latest scientific advances. Voorsanger believed in a Supreme Being but held that evolution was God's plan for the world, and he deemed Judaism "divinely evolved" rather than divinely revealed. God grew in history only as the capacity of men's minds grew to accommodate Him.

His denial of the revelation at Sinai permitted him complete freedom as a biblical scholar, and his methods of textual criticism were radical; in this respect he parted company even with Elkan Cohn. Voorsanger's impact on the field of biblical scholarship—all the more impressive for his lack of formal training—can be judged by the invitation, near the end of his career, to translate the books of Jonah and Obadiah for the Jewish Publication Society's prestigious 1917 edition of the Holy Scriptures. He founded the Semitics department at the University of California in Berkeley, where he not only taught the theory of two Isaiahs but also the non-existence of Ezra, a Second Commonwealth date for Daniel, and the Gospels as *midrash*. In one of his well-publicized annual lectures at Stanford, he suggested a "power politics" interpretation of the canonization of the Hebrew Bible.

The notion of "the religion of reason" had implications far beyond the realm of biblical scholarship, of course. For Voorsanger it meant that everyday religious practice would have to be on the most dignified, intelligent, and comprehensible level possible. He despised nothing more than "external" ritual done out of habit or superstition. As he wrote on the fourth anniversary of the founding of the *Emanu-El*, "We find greater comfort in the struggle toward high ideals than in wrapping a carcass in a *tallith*." Attacking "legalism," also referred to as "rabbinism" or "oriental-ism," appeared to be one of the main tasks of the *Emanu-El*, especially in its early issues, as the following polemic reveals. Confronted with the prediction that the Reform movement would soon decline, Voorsanger agreed to ponder such an eventuality:

> The organ would soon disappear, so would the choir; the ladies would be relegated to the galleries, in charge of wardens who would ask them indecent questions. The *tallith* would make its reappearance and the national language would disappear from the prayer book. The second day of the holidays would be reinstated, and all the feast days would reappear. We would once more sit on the earth on the Ninth of Ab, and pray to return to a country which affords us neither home nor liv-ing; we would go unwashed to the synagogue that day. In our domestic rites we would have to alter much. We would sacrifice the barber; have our faces cleansed with lye, as green as grass. We would permit our beards to grow for thirty days in time of mourning and, surely, would wear the *pyes* which look so interesting. We would recite a hundred benedictions every day, turn our homes topsy turvy before the Passover, appoint *Shomerim*—stewards—who would superintend our meat shops, bakeries, butteries, dairies and vineyards, and level a tax on all victuallers or else pronounce their goods to be *Trefah*. We would reinstate our old prayers; thank God that we were not born women, read unctuously of the Talmudical chapter of the composition of in-cense, and on Sabbath pray for the continued prosperity of Babylonian universities which went out of existence eight hundred years ago...

But the question was how far and how fast to move away from "Ghetto Judaism." The moderate reformer Rabbi Spitz of St. Louis still subscribed to the ban on pork and the prohibition of smoking on the Sabbath, and dubbed Voorsanger a "radical" in his journal, the *Jewish Voice*. In his own paper, the Dutchman retorted with his usual acerbity: "Does a cigar stand between Reform and radicalism?"

For Voorsanger was a much more aggressive reformer than Spitz. He not only felt unbound by the dietary and Sabbath laws, but he also led services bareheaded, performed intermarriage, and introduced the revolutionary *Union Prayer Book*, which rendered most of the liturgy in English.

Yet there were important limits to his reformist tendencies as well. He argued that Rabbi Krauskopf had gone "too far," for instance, in advocating a rapprochement between Judaism and Christianity, and the reestablishment of a primitive religion embracing Jesus along with Moses and other prophets. Nor could he follow the lead of Rabbi Hirsch, who felt the Torah itself to be such an outdated relic that he actually removed the scrolls from his Chicago sanctuary.

Voorsanger also rejected extremism in the debate over the Sabbath question, which preoccupied the reformers around the turn of the century. Toward the end of Cohn's rabbinate, as we have seen, worship services at Emanu-El were actually held on Sundays. After a year they were moved back to Friday evening but, according to Voorsanger, only because people preferred a walk in Golden Gate Park to the synagogue on Sunday morning. "Our objections to Sunday services," he wrote in 1896, "are of no religious character."

A decade later, however, at the behest of the Central Conference of American Rabbis, he undertook a thorough study of the Sabbath question, which he now considered "the greatest issue of our modern religious life." In a seminal lecture delivered before the CCAR in Detroit, he conceded the economic and social obstacles standing in the way of Sabbath observance, but concluded that he was not yet prepared "to throw a three-thousand-year-old tradition overboard...not yet ready to confess that the future has nothing in store for our Sabbath but an assimilation with the national day of rest." Applying the brakes both to convenience and conformity, he declared that "Israel...must be a distinct spiritual entity."

As a final argument Voorsanger raised the specter of a schism. He wondered aloud whether recognition of the Sunday Sabbath might not lead to a sectarian movement threatening the very "solidarity and identity of the people whose teacher I am." In the same spirit as Erasmus, half a millennium before him, he called for reform but also for the preservation of harmony: "Members of the oldest spiritual confraternity, let us not hug the false ambition of becoming founders of the latest."

VOORSANGER'S CANTOR, EDWARD STARK, was also a man with a major national reputation. They both served at Emanu-El for roughly two decades, and during the fifteen years in which their tenure overlapped, 1893 to 1908, each was a perfect complement to the other, the cantor having no less of an impact on Reform sacred music than the rabbi had on liberal Jewish thought. At the peak of Stark's career, the early years of the new century before the earthquake, he was hailed in the local press as the leading cantor in America.

The son of a cantor and *shochet*, Stark was born in the small town of Hohenems on the western border of the Austrian Empire, very near Bavaria, where his family eventually moved. There he spent his adolescent years in the town of Ichenhausen, the ancestral village of the Koshlands, the Gerstles, the Levisons, and many other leading Emanu-El families, and emigrated to New York in 1871, at the age of fifteen. For the next two decades he worked in business with his older brothers, wrote and performed popular music, and served as a cantor in Brooklyn.

CANTOR EDWARD STARK

He would return to Europe for almost a year of formal cantorial train-ing, but Stark, like Voorsanger, was essentially an autodidact. He was influenced most by the renowned Salomon Sulzer (who himself had been born in Hohenems two generations earlier), a groundbreaker in blending traditional Jewish music with the great European compositions of his time.

Stark's father, Josef, was his bridge to Sulzer. The elder Stark had stud-ied in Vienna with Sulzer (who had become *Oberkantor* in the Hapsburg capital in 1826), and passed down to his son all that he had learned from the man often credited with creating the modern cantorate.

Edward Stark, though, may be said to have been instrumental in creating the modern *American* cantorate, for—as his job description at Emanu-El reveals—he was required not only to perform on the pulpit and direct the choir, but also to play a role in virtually all aspects of con-gregational life. He taught in the Sabbath school and even produced elaborate pageants for the holidays which the children performed at downtown theatres; he assisted at weddings, funerals, and unveilings, and not infrequently was the sole officiant; he shared the spoken parts of the services with Voorsanger, and in the Dutchman's absence led the services himself. It is not surprising that visitors to the temple sometimes mistook him for an assistant rabbi.

But of course the main task for which he was brought to San Fran-cisco—and later paid the high salary of $4,500 a year—was to provide the music for the worship service, and he more than met the temple's high expectations. For the choir of eight (augmented to twenty for the High Holidays), he hired only the best singers in the city. He paid them well but rehearsed them mercilessly—three full days a week during the three months leading up to Rosh Hashanah. A perfectionist known to be "quick in temper," he had the pulpit outfitted with an electric buzzer so that he could immediately signal any displeasure to the choir or organist, thirty feet above. His "angry rattlings" were frequent, but the critics were rarely displeased; Stark invariably received raves in the press, which in those days regularly reviewed High Holiday services.

Some saw a physical resemblance to Beethoven in the short and stocky cantor, but one contemporary—an admirer, no less—described him as "a squat, thickset dwarf." Not that it mattered, though, when people heard his magnificent baritone voice. He was inundated with requests for recitals of operatic, classical, popular, and sacred music throughout the Bay Area, and thrilled audiences with the "magnetic power" of a repertoire that ranged from Verdi to Victor Herbert.

Still, the consummate virtuoso seemed to hold something back for *Yizkor*, the memorial service on Yom Kippur afternoon, when he "sang as he sang but once in the whole year." Backed by a dozen outstanding players of string and brass instruments, as well as a harpist, Stark exhibited both perfect vocal control and an uncommon depth of feeling, "heavy with passionate sorrow."

He was also admired as a composer of Jewish sacred music, one of the most prolific of his day. He wrote for the organ, of course, which had been played with the utmost skill at Emanu-El from the 1870s until 1896 by Louis Schmidt, a church organist and also an accomplished violinist. In 1896 Schmidt was followed by the gifted Wallace Sabin, an English-born Episcopalian who became a Fellow of the prestigious Royal College of Organists and who would remain at the temple until his death in 1937, when he was succeeded by a young German-Jewish refugee, Ludwig Altman.

Writing at the end of Schmidt's career, it was almost as if Stark could look far into the twentieth century and foresee not only Sabin's four glorious decades but also Altman's extraordinary fifty-year tenure when he declared,

> An organ in the hands of a master, in one of his best moments of musical inspiration, is inferior to no source of the sublime in absorbing the imagination. The rush and concourse of sound has been not inaptly compared to the full and even volume of a mighty river; flowing onwards; wave after wave, occasionally dashing against some rock, till sweeping with momentary increasing vehemence, to the brow of a precipice, it rushes down, a wide-spreading and overwhelming flood.

Stark also wrote pieces for a musical ensemble containing instruments in addition to the organ, one including the harp and cello, another also adding the flute and violin. He was one of the first American synagogue composers to do so.

Much of the music heard at the temple at the turn of the century was similar in style to Protestant anthems and hymns, but Stark, like Voorsanger, set clear boundaries for his reforms. Indeed, as his biographer, Cantor Jeffrey Zucker, explains, his importance as a composer lies in the fact that, like Sulzer before him, he wove into the service traditional Jewish melodies set in a contemporary style; "he wanted to return the *nusach* to its rightful place in the synagogue." For the cantor, the *nusach*, or traditionally accepted way of chanting, was of course that of southern German Jewry, particularly fitting for a congregation comprised largely of Bavarians. But Stark's work was heard far beyond Emanu-El: in 1905, he set to music the "Shofar Service" of the *Union Prayer Book* and within a few years it was performed in Reform synagogues throughout America.*

Stark's compositions—usually short and simple—have not stood the proverbial test of time, however, and one authority on Jewish music attributes this to a "short-breathed sectionalism" in his technique. Another, complaining that Stark arbitrarily and abruptly changes keys, hears in the cantor's harmonic language the barbershop quartet so popular in those years.

Yet even for these critics, Stark's contribution was enormous; he was "head and shoulders above his contemporaries in the Reform temple, in overall skill and his determination to forge a musical service which had an emotional dimension." If his national popularity waned over time, his works continued to be performed at Emanu-El throughout the long career of his remarkable successor, Reuben Rinder, and can often be heard in the temple today.

As HE LOOKED DOWN FROM THE HEIGHTS of his elegant temple, filled with the ethereal music of Edward Stark, Voorsanger found much to criticize in the mass culture which had taken hold in American cities by the turn of the century. He deemed spectator sports "a public scandal of the most demoralizing character," condemning bicycle races along with prizefights. He lamented the growing popularity of the boardinghouse and hotel, which he felt exercised a negative influence on the young. In 1907, he prayed to be free "from the terror of the automobile." He was fearful of the women's suffrage movement as well as the great strides taken by labor unions.

---

*His hymns for schoolchildren were also circulated nationally and his award-winning setting of Psalm 27, "The Lord is My Light," was printed by the Bloch Company. The New York publisher also released the cantor's magnum opus—*Sefer Anim Zemiroth*, his musical setting of the entire *Union Prayer Book*, both for the Sabbath and the High Holidays—in four volumes beginning in 1909.

But for all of that, no native ever loved his country more than this immigrant. America's wealth and beauty, particularly in the West, never ceased to amaze him, but even more important was his feeling that in this country the Jews had the best opportunity to carry out their mission of moral righteousness and to spread their teaching of ethical monotheism. Here they were accepted, indeed respected, and he gloried in the fact that his sermons drew many gentiles and that non-Jewish children attended the temple's religious school. One of his congregants sat in the United States Congress; others had advanced to the highest positions in the fields of banking, insurance, commerce, and law. The occasional incidents of local anti-Semitism which came to his attention he considered minor aberrations.

While Voorsanger saw the Jews achieve so much in California, he did not believe that all other minority groups would have the same success. He had an affinity for the Irish and Germans, but was unable to transcend the intense anti-Chinese feeling of his times, writing in 1896, "The Chinese belongs to a non-assimilative race. He cannot mix with Caucasians. Like the ambassadors of foreign powers, wherever he goes he brings China with him. His food, his garments, his habits, his tastes and tendencies are all Chinese." Nor was he alone among his West Coast coreligionists in these sentiments. The Jewish press in California was uniformly opposed to the Chinese, despite rebukes for this stance from Jews throughout the rest of the country.

Precisely at the time when laws were passed to exclude the Chinese—1882—Russian Jews began immigrating to America in great numbers. Voorsanger doubted that they would adapt themselves to the New World as had their Western and Central European cousins. With trepidation he watched the Jewish population of New York City pass the one million mark after the turn of the century and stated quite bluntly, "We are confronted by an invasion from the East that threatens to undo the work of two generations of American Jews." In his view, "Russian Orthodoxy represents retrogressive forces that since the days of Mendelssohn refused every concession to the spirit of the times. That these same forces would upon American soil create an environment of Russian attitudes is only too patent."

The thousands of East European Jews who had immigrated to San

Francisco—comprising perhaps a fifth of the city's Jewish population by 1906—were an easy target for Voorsanger's powerful pen. He called their journalists "blackguards," their lay leaders "hypocrites," their itinerant rabbis "schnorrers." He feared that the area south of Market Street would become another Lower East Side, "another one of the reeking pestholes."

But his outright disdain was also mixed with genuine—if paternalistic—concern. With a number of his congregants he founded several institutions to alleviate the suffering of the unfortunate Yiddish speakers—and instruct them in American customs and values as well. As early as 1890, he formed the Russian-Jewish Alliance with the aid of Phil Lilienthal, director of the United Iron Works, where employment was found for hundreds of East European Jews.

Voorsanger was also instrumental in the creation in 1897 of the Jewish Educational Society, the forerunner of today's Bureau of Jewish Education. He was joined by two other esteemed local rabbis, Jacob Nieto of Sherith Israel and M. S. Levy of Beth Israel; Julius Kahn, then a state assemblyman; the president of Emanu-El, Raphael Peixotto; and the vice-president of the temple, Jacob Greenebaum. Angry that the B'nai B'rith closed the Free Religious School, which it had operated for five years, Voorsanger sought to provide Jewish education and training in civics to "the children of the proletariat." Servicing a variety of neighborhoods throughout the city—including the colorful colony of immigrant Jews "out the road" on San Bruno Avenue—the religious schools operated by the Jewish Educational Society counted almost three hundred pupils by 1904, earning Voorsanger's praise and encouragement.

Even more extensive was the spirited Emanu-El Sisterhood for Personal Service which he initiated in 1894, following the example set by New York's Temple Emanu-El half a decade earlier. Lilienthal's wife, Bella (daughter of New York's leading financier, Joseph Seligman), as well as prominent women such as Mathilda Esberg and Bertha Haas, served on the board of directors. The records for the year 1895 reveal that the Sisterhood's relief committee aided 1,350 applicants; its employment bureau found jobs for a third of the 234 seeking work. Several years later, emulating the ambitious settlement houses of New York, the Sisterhood opened a building on Folsom Street to provide classrooms for Russian immigrants, a kindergarten, and a gymnasium.

In 1905, Voorsanger's son, William, a German-trained physician specializing in tuberculosis, launched the Emanu-El Sisterhood Polyclinic on Seventh Street. Like the Folsom facility, it was located in the "South of Market" area heavily populated by East European Jews. Heading a staff of a dozen leading physicians, Voorsanger's busy clinic was soon absorbed by Mount Zion Hospital, which appointed the young doctor chief of medicine.

In the following decade the ambitious Sisterhood opened an attractive dormitory on Steiner Street for single, working Jewish women—a fast-growing group after the turn of the century—providing opportunities for vocational education as well as a warm, supportive atmosphere. This was the forerunner of the highly regarded Emanu-El Residence Club on Page Street, inaugurated in 1922, in a building designed by Julia Morgan, the West's foremost female architect. Many of the women housed in the Club through the 1920s were Yiddish-speaking immigrants; later it would welcome refugees from Nazi Germany.

The leading women of the temple founded the local chapter of the National Council of Jewish Women. At a meeting held at Emanu-El in the summer of 1900, called to order by Voorsanger, the dynamic general secretary of the NCJW, Sadie American, launched the organization with an inspirational address. Although he sometimes viewed the NCJW as a competitor of the Sisterhood, Voorsanger gradually came to appreciate the effective relief work done by the group, which would later open its own settlement house on San Bruno Avenue in the new immigrant quarter emerging on the outskirts of the city. He worked closely with the San Francisco section of the NCJW, providing not only advice but also courses for the women on both the Bible and current issues.

Organizations such as the Sisterhood and the NCJW not only eased the trauma of transition for thousands of immigrants, but often changed the lives of the native-born women who volunteered their services. These were high-powered "women's clubs" which took on much more responsibility than the "ladies' societies" that had come into existence in the 1850s, and they required considerably more in the way of organizational and leadership skills from their members.

As we have seen, a significant handful of Jewish women had achieved professional success in the last decades of the nineteenth century, but the overwhelming majority, particularly in the upper and middle classes, did not work outside the home. According to the census of 1900, nearly every Emanu-El household employed at least one live-in servant; it is not surprising that, in the words of Caroline Sahlein, president of the San Francisco section of the NCJW, many women sought "an outlet for the growing restlessness—the pent-up energies of those among us who for their leisure hours needed a new field of activity."

Through their voluntarism, they quietly began "a radical redefinition of behavioral norms," as one historian of American Jewish women has put it, their challenging activities taking them beyond the traditional role of the "enabler," or benevolent nurturer, to a new "sense of selfhood and gender consciousness." This transition is revealed in the records of Mount Zion Hospital, an institution whose lay leadership—both male and female— closely resembled that of Emanu-El.* Beginning in 1897, as the hospital's historians recount, "the auxiliary members...spent long hours...doing work in the kitchen and visiting patients in the wards. The hospital linens were their particular charge and, besides mending, the ladies would notify the directors whenever they saw the need to buy more."

But within a few years this limited role had become unacceptable to the women, and when their demands for increased responsibility were rejected by the all-male board, the Ladies' Auxiliary threatened to disband. The directors capitulated, however, asking for the women's help in fundraising in 1903 and appointing them to the committees of the board for the first time in 1909. Longtime board president J. B. Levison had to admit two years later that "the ladies have been of inestimable assistance in all committee work, and have absolutely silenced all apprehension as to the result of what was considered by some a hazardous experiment."

Although fairly conservative on women's issues, Jacob Voorsanger clearly foresaw the potential of female volunteers in the Jewish community and helped channel their efforts during this era of great human need. Seeing a myriad of Jewish relief organizations now operating in San Francisco, however, he felt that some sort of union was necessary. Even before the earthquake, which would force the city to address another huge

---

*At the turn of the century its sixteen-member Ladies' Auxiliary was headed by Frances Hellman, the wife of one of the city's leading bankers, I. W. Hellman Jr., and included Sophie Lilienthal and Bertha Haas, among several other prominent temple women.

dimension of human suffering, he argued for coordination and control of the many agencies, especially in the area of fundraising. One check covering all Jewish causes would "free every contributor from promiscuous begging, from unauthorized collections, from the constant annoyance of being interrupted by solicitors of the thousand and one charities which claim to have just title to support."

He did not live to see the Federation of Jewish Charities, which came into existence in 1910 and included such institutions as the Educational Society, the Sisterhood, and the hospital, but for over a decade his was the loudest voice urging its establishment.

ALL OF THIS BENEVOLENT WORK TO HIS CREDIT, it must also be noted that Voorsanger fought to restrict—and at times even to stop completely—the immigration of East European Jews to the United States. Alarmed that, due to the efforts of the Jewish philanthropic groups in London, steamship tickets were sold for less than ten dollars, he threw up his hands at this plot "to dump the riff-raff of Europe, the pauper element of the East End, upon the American communities."

As for those *Ostjuden* who had already arrived, he urged that they be removed from the great cities on the East Coast and "distributed over the full length and width of this country." In this regard he frequently encouraged such projects as Rabbi Krauskopf's National Farm School and carried reports in the *Emanu-El* on Jewish agricultural colonies. In particular, he favored the scheme of agriculturist David Lubin's well-capitalized International Society for the Colonization of Russian Jews, which put forward the desolate Mexican territory of Baja California for Jewish immigration.

But he rarely offered his own state for this purpose. In 1896, he praised Ephraim Deinard, the Haskalah scholar from Odessa who sought to establish a farming community in the West, but he warned, "Our people are in no humor just now for colonies. What with the unemployment, the hard times, and hot waves that kill the wheat, not to speak of the locusts and cankerworms....Our people have enough to do to take care of themselves."

When Deinard arrived anyway with thirty-seven Russian colonists from Philadelphia, Voorsanger became infuriated with "this madcap affair." Citing the failure of colonies in Sacramento and Tulare Counties, he

thundered, "The bringing of shiftless creatures from one place to another is but playing the ostrich." He felt compelled to raise the money to
send them back East, reporting several weeks later that twenty-three
"pseudo-farmers" had already departed and adding, "Those who remain
will have to shift for themselves—I told them not to come." Nor was the
Deinard affair an isolated case. The rabbi also discouraged Jewish colonization of the Salinas Valley and, in 1904, chastised some refugees of the
Kishinev pogrom, who settled in Colusa County, for not having notified
the local authorities in advance of their arrival. But the plan which en-
raged him most was the "foolish, senseless, suicidal business" of a Mr.
Cohn to establish Jewish farms east of the Sierras: "We must defeat this
nefarious scheme to colonize Nevada with Jewish *peons!*"

Months before his death in 1908, Voorsanger began to modify his
position on the East Europeans. A visit to New York in March of that
year showed him that "the processes of adaptation are already underway.
Anyone who compares the Jewish East End of New York of even a
decade ago with that of today will discern amazing changes and the unmistakable growth of tendencies in the direction of wholesome and loyal
Americanism."

At the same time, though, he was agitated by a new "grave danger to
the American-Jewish community"—the immigrant anarchist. Accusing
the political firebrand Emma Goldman of "moral insanity" and apostasy,
he concluded again that Jews should cooperate with the most rigid interpretation of the laws of immigration.

Nearly as serious a threat, in his opinion, was the Zionism expounded
by other Russian Jews. He believed the return to the ancient homeland to
be "one of the wildest of all wild dreams," writing in an open letter to
Simon Wolf, the influential Jewish lobbyist in Washington, D.C.,

> How would we compete? Look at the geographical location of Pales-
> tine. Is it not out of the way? What waterways does it possess, has it
> ever possessed to favor the development of commerce? What facilities
> has it for the founding of great industries? For competing with the
> great depots of the European and transatlantic countries?

His views on the "Turk-ridden land" were hardly altered by his own
trip to Palestine in 1907. Strong winds prevented his boat from landing at

Jaffa and, with much inconvenience and discomfort, he was forced to disembark at Beirut and journey south.

Aside from being impractical, the very idea of a Jewish state flew in the face of Voorsanger's notion of the Jewish mission: "We refuse to believe that the divine intention is the degradation of the Jew from his present lofty position as a world-teacher to again become the neighbor of mongrel tribes, on the very edge of civilization."

The Zionists, of course, were reacting to growing anti-Semitism in Europe at the turn of the century, and the *Emanu-El* carried detailed reports on the Dreyfus Affair, the Kishinev atrocities, and the election of the proto-fascist Karl Lueger as mayor of Vienna. But Voorsanger would not endorse "the degrading confession that the Jew is a beaten dog." Regarding even the blood-soaked Czarist regime, he believed that the "Jewish Question" would one day be solved by the Russian people themselves, who would overthrow authoritarian rule and put in its place a democratic government.

But underlying each of these objections to Zionism was simply the love of his adopted land. In the final analysis, California was his Zion and there could be no other, as the following paean testifies. Having chosen a vacation in Monterey over a rabbinical conference in Milwaukee, he wrote that his colleagues

> must resolve to meet with us next year if they wish to have foretaste of Eden. We will show them the country, rocks that await Alladin's magic key to unlock their treasures, all gold, platinum and quicksilver; plateaux on which the Almighty poured out all the blessings left over from the sixth day of creation. We will show them valleys now groaning with fruit and wheat and grain and valleys that know no barrenness in winter-time, the only fields in America in which the grass always remains green. We will show them our mountains, white-headed giants watching Hesperidean gardens, in which the golden apples are sweet and rich and luscious; mountains that are the store-houses of floods that rain down to bathe the valleys in their refreshing richness. And we will show them such flowers as they never saw before; our camelias and dandelions, our rich magnolias and jasmines, and our miles of wild flowers, carpeting the unploughed hillsides...
> We will remind them that this dear California is a gorgeous *edition de*

luxe of Palestine of old of which Midrash says with effusive tenderness that every spot in it has its hills and dales. Our holy land, our promised land is this golden spot, and we want the sages of Babylon to pay us a visit.

THE SEVEREST TEST OF VOORSANGER'S FAITH came in the early hours of April 18, 1906, "when suddenly the abyss yawned at our feet and it seemed that with the overturning of the world we would be lost forever." The massive earthquake, and the fires which raged for three days afterwards, destroyed more than half the city's buildings and claimed about three thousand lives.

One of the keenest observers of the catastrophe was J. B. Levison, an Emanu-El congregant who was second vice-president of the huge Fireman's Fund Insurance Company. He had attended the opening night of the San Francisco Opera on Monday, April 16.

> Wednesday morning I was awakened by something which is impossible to describe—a crunching of timbers—a roaring, apparently from above and below—and a jumping (the only word that seems to fit) of the house. It was most terrifying and frightful. I did not realize what the thing was, but had the feeling that it was a nightmare. Not until my wife screamed that it was a dreadful earthquake, and that I should try to get the children, did I awaken to full realization.
>
> I leaped out of bed but could not retain my footing because the house was still jumping. This can be better understood when I say that it took two or three attempts or lunges before I could get hold of the door leading to the room occupied by my sons John and Robert, nine and seven years of age, who were terrified beyond words.
>
> Trying to reach my brother I found that the telephone wires were broken. And there was neither light nor water. Here for the first time I appreciated the magnitude of the disaster.

Later, on the way to his office, Levison writes,

> I could obtain a view of the entire southern portion of the city....Half a dozen distinct conflagrations were raging and roaring in different sections, any one of which would have been a great fire. I realized then that the city was doomed.

Levison showed poise and presence of mind amidst the turmoil. He sent his family to the San Rafael summer house of his in-laws, the Gerstles, and turned his own home on Pacific Avenue into a refuge and temporary office for Fireman's Fund.* He saved nearly all the medical instruments of his brother Charles, one of the city's leading physicians.

Voorsanger accomplished even more. Working feverishly as the chairman of the mayor's food committee, he fought to spare the ruined city from famine, "the worst anarchist in existence." While monitoring isolated cases of price gouging and looting, he set up food stations throughout San Francisco. With a policeman's badge on his clerical coat, and the mayor's authorization in his pocket, he literally "commandeered store after store." As he wrote of his role in the critical days following the earthquake, "I was the biggest thief in the United States....I emptied grocery stores, drug stores, butcher shops, hardware establishments, [and] I was able to report to the mayor that the people were fed and that to the best of my knowledge there was not a hungry soul in San Francisco."

Still, terror reigned because of the aftershocks, the advancing fires, and not least of all the wild rumors that began circulating the morning of the disaster, when the city was cut off from outside communication for many crucial hours. The young journalist Paul Sinsheimer, nephew of the respected temple and community leader Henry Sinsheimer, wrote of the dread and delusion that gripped the populace:

> How widespread was the shock, we wondered. Had it reached Southern California? Had it gone east? How about Chicago, New York, Seattle, Portland? Then came answers to these questions, from whence no one knew. San Jose was destroyed, five thousand killed in Los Angeles, Portland overwhelmed by the river, Chicago wiped out by a tidal wave from the lake and New York swept into the Atlantic. Vesuvius had renewed its activity and eruptions were predicted in San Francisco. You can understand our state of mind with all those stories floating about and no evidence to contradict them.

*Several weeks after the fire Levison hit upon a scheme to salvage the Fireman's Fund Company itself, which owed roughly four million dollars in claims, much more than it had on hand. Rather than liquidate the firm and establish a new one, as his superiors Dutton and Faymonville suggested, Levison proposed to pay half of each claim in cash and the other half in company stock. The plan was eventually accepted by the board of directors and the policy-holders, and it not only rescued Fireman's Fund but became the standard form of insurance reorganization throughout the world.

The fire in San Francisco, though, was all too real; one could feel its heat throughout the city. As the flames spread westward it was thought that the width of Van Ness Avenue would finally contain the conflagration. But General Funston, commandant of the Presidio, felt that many of the mansions on the street would have to be dynamited or burned as well, among them the stately residences of Ernest Lilienthal, head of Crown Distilleries, and Marcus Sloss, who only months earlier had been named to the California Supreme Court.

But the bulk of the suffering fell upon the shoulders of the poor. Levison writes of "the grinding noise on the sidewalks of trunks and boxes dragged by the refugees on their way to the western hills." These were the newly homeless from Chinatown, North Beach, the Mission District, South of Market—indeed the entire eastern part of the city.

Among them were ten thousand Jews, according to Voorsanger's careful estimate, whose wooden shacks and cottages below Market had quickly become fuel for the flames. Many doubled up with friends or relatives in the unburned sections of town: the Richmond District, Hayes Valley, San Bruno Avenue, the Western Addition, and the area below Twentieth Street. Most camped out in Golden Gate Park or along the seashore as far south as the San Mateo county line. Of the quarter of a million people rendered homeless in April, forty thousand would still be living in tents as autumn approached. The Jews constituted about a tenth of the city's population in 1906, but their commercial and residential property accounted for a far greater proportion of the total fire loss, which approached a billion dollars.

Jewish institutions were ravaged. To be sure, newly built Sherith Israel, on California and Webster, suffered only minor damage and was soon used as a public building by the city. But the nearly completed Geary Street synagogue of Rabbi M. S. Levy (Congregation Beth Israel) was totally demolished by the earthquake. The Orthodox Russ Street *shul* was lost in the fire, as were the Emanu-El Sisterhood settlement house and clinic and the Jewish Educational Society. The Eureka Benevolent Society, B'nai B'rith Hall with its library of fifteen thousand volumes, and the Lombard Street Home for the Aged Disabled were all consumed. Destroyed too were the plants of each of the city's three Jewish newspapers. Even the Home of Peace Cemetery in San Mateo County was laid waste;

MOMENTS AFTER THE 1906 EARTHQUAKE, THE TWIN TOWERS OF
THE SUTTER STREET TEMPLE REMAIN INTACT, VISIBLE AGAINST
A CLOUD OF SMOKE FROM THE APPROACHING FIRE

eight hundred tombstones were overturned and the chapel was wrecked beyond repair.

The majestic Sutter Street temple was gutted, its proud domes down and only its stone walls standing; they alone survived the fire. Voorsanger wept openly as he realized the extent of the damage done to the synagogue where he had labored for twenty years and which had housed his congregants for forty. Many of his prized books were now ashes, as were the entire libraries of Elkan Cohn and Edward Stark. Burned beyond recognition was the Torah scroll which Moses Montefiore had sent the pioneers in 1851, as well as the minute books and most of the other records of the temple.

Even as he stood amidst the ruins of what had been the elegant interior of his synagogue, Voorsanger knew that the membership possessed the means to restore it. But what of the city's other Jewish institutions?

And what of the two thousand Jewish families now "houseless, helpless, totally ruined, destitute"?

He worked furiously on many levels. Reconstruction of the temple was left in the hands of President Henry Wangenheim and a powerful committee including Lippman Sachs, Julius Jacobs, I. W. Hellman, Simon Newman, and Marcus Koshland. Among six offers of temporary quarters, from three synagogues—including Sherith Israel—and three churches, they chose Reverend Hemphill's Calvary Presbyterian Church on Fillmore near Jackson.*

For other Jewish needs he sought outside aid. Beth Israel alone would require $75,000, he reasoned, to clear the debris and rebuild the Geary synagogue, an impossible sum for a congregation of 350 families, many of them recent East European immigrants. Adding the costs of the rehabilitation of the Russ Street *shul* and the Jewish Educational Society, as well as aid for the homeless, he arrived at a round figure of $100,000. But when the Jewish community of Portland sent an unsolicited donation of $5,000, Voorsanger returned the money; he wanted the rehabilitation of San Francisco's Jewish institutions to be a national priority, not a piecemeal process.

And he was disappointed. Although periodicals such as the *American Israelite* and *American Hebrew* were sympathetic, he had great difficulty persuading the newly formed American Jewish Committee—of which he was an executive board member—to commit itself to his cause. The funds were finally voted in November 1906, thanks to his personal appearance in New York, but by April 18, 1907, the first anniversary of the tragedy, no money had been received, and as a result Congregation Beth Israel was reconstructed with local funds, primarily from Emanu-El congregants.

The rabbi was even angrier with the National Conference of Jewish Charities, which a month after the earthquake had sent two observers to the Bay City on a fact-finding tour: San Francisco-born Judah Magnes, who had recently become associate rabbi of New York's Temple Emanu-El,

---

*Emanu-El remained at the Calvary Church lecture hall for four months until moving to larger quarters at the Reverend Bradford Leavitt's First Unitarian Church on September 8. Here, for one year, the congregation had the use of an office, classrooms, and a sanctuary. The Unitarians were returning a favor: in 1888 they had used the Sutter Street temple while their own house of worship was being constructed.

and Lee K. Frankel, superintendent of that city's United Hebrew Charities. The two eastern visitors held that the claim that ten thousand Jews were homeless was "exaggerated," concluded that two thousand seemed to them the correct figure, and recommended no aid at all.

Voorsanger was irate. He argued that Magnes, his former student, and Frankel had conducted merely a cursory investigation of three camps; they did not "take the time" to interview those refugees who had found temporary shelter but who were still in need of permanent housing. Similarly, he complained in August that millions of dollars in federal funds, intended to relieve the plight of the homeless, had been held up "in the high and mighty East."

But most of his wrath was reserved for his coreligionists across the bay. Oakland's First Hebrew Congregation (known today as Temple Sinai) housed and fed several hundred Jewish refugees during the week after the earthquake, but the San Francisco leader was offended that its rabbi, Marcus Friedlander, never came over on the ferry to confer with him. Worse was the telegram sent nationwide by the First Hebrew—without consulting San Francisco—asking aid for Oakland inasmuch as that community had to bear the costs of refugee resettlement. Voorsanger, in a

THE SUTTER STREET TEMPLE GUTTED BY FIRE AFTER THE 1906 EARTHQUAKE

wire of his own, deemed the appeal "indiscreet, injudicious, ill-advised." In the *Emanu-El* he dubbed the East Bay's leading city "a village" and ridiculed Friedlander, noting that he had once had the arrogance to refer to himself as "the only Jewish theologian on the West Coast."

VOORSANGER TOOK GREAT PRIDE in the rapid recovery of the city and its Jewish businesses and institutions. He saw many of his congregants reopen their firms on Fillmore Street or Van Ness Avenue, now San Francisco's busiest thoroughfares. Clothiers like the Livingstons, the Magnins, and the Roos brothers; the jeweler Joseph Dinkelspiel; and even the restaurateur Jesse Meyerfeld found business brisk at their new midtown locations. In the summer Voorsanger encouraged plans for improved lighting on Fillmore and an electric streetcar line across Van Ness. He pointed out in the *Emanu-El* that by August the city had already returned to 70 percent of its pre-earthquake population of almost half a million. Not surprisingly, then, he was outraged by press reports in the East which described San Francisco as "a total wreck" and its citizens as "a despairing mob."

A magnificent symbol of the city's revival was the restored Sutter Street temple, which opened its doors on September 1, 1907. Soon after the catastrophe the board of directors opted to shelve plans—discussed since 1900—for a new building on Van Ness. The design of architect Gustave Albert Lansburgh had already won the gold medal at the Paris Salon in 1906, but, as President Wangenheim explained, the congregation would restore the original structure and remain on Sutter Street "until the future looks brighter and more secure." Not only was the inflated cost of building materials a factor, but also weighing heavily against the option of moving was the fact that the temple's Van Ness lot was now in the heart of the city's business district—hardly an improvement over the location at Sutter and Powell.

Lansburgh, a thirty-year-old Jewish architect who would later have dozens of California buildings to his credit, was entrusted with the restoration.* He did not replace the bulbous twin domes which had been

---

*Born in Panama and raised in San Francisco, Lansburgh was an Emanu-El congregant during most of his adult life. He designed the B'nai B'rith building, the Concordia Club, and the Orpheum Theatre in San Francisco and Temple Sinai in Oakland. In 1924, he became a consultant on Emanu-El's Lake Street temple.

THE RESTORED SUTTER STREET TEMPLE

such a notable feature of the city's skyline since 1866, leading Voorsanger to remark, "Russian domes have no place on a synagogue." Squat towers were erected in their place and yet, because most of the surrounding buildings had been leveled, the restored Sutter Street temple seemed, for the time being at least, even taller and more imposing than the original.

Inside he converted the sanctuary's two small lateral galleries into lounges, thus improving the temple's acoustics. Specially selected Oregon pine was used for the ceiling, from which were suspended ornate chandeliers in the shape of six-pointed stars. An enormous new Kimball organ was installed as well as a pulpit, hand-carved in weathered oak, and an ark, the curtains of which could be drawn by the push of a button. Sunlight filtered into the august room of worship through opalescent glass windows.

The cost was almost $100,000; restoring the cemetery required another $60,000, and money from the temple's insurers was coming in at a trickle. Voorsanger took a voluntary cut in salary from $750 to $500 a month, and Cantor Stark—as well as the sexton, secretary, and custodian—followed suit, but their action, in effect for half a year, was more a gesture than anything else; the temple had no difficulty raising the needed funds even in such stressful times. Membership actually increased a bit during the year 1906, approaching four hundred families by the late fall.

Kevin Starr has written that the devastation wrought by the earthquake and fire was initially viewed as a welcome challenge in many quarters, "giving back to San Francisco the sense of mission and excitement known by pioneer forbears. [They] seized upon this notion of renewed frontier, this chance for quickening of purpose and regeneration of spirit."

These were also Voorsanger's sentiments. His address on the bright Sunday afternoon of the rededication was characteristically studded with many allusions to the Hebrew prophets that aptly portrayed the suffering and rebirth of San Francisco. To cap the occasion, Cantor Stark set the uplifting Thirtieth Psalm to music interwoven with strains of "America."

But it was the analogy to the early California pioneers and their struggle against adversity which was stressed most of all, for the recent crisis had linked Voorsanger's generation with theirs. He paid special tribute to "Father Jacob" Greenebaum, who had arrived in California in 1851 at age twenty and who had been treasurer of Emanu-El at the time of the original dedication of the Sutter Street temple a year after the end of the Civil War. Invoking the memory of Greenebaum's contemporaries, many to whom Voorsanger had paid final tribute in the past decade,* he exclaimed, "We inherited more than their names, their wealth or achievements; we inherited their faith, their courage, their unequaled patience, their inflexible piety, their high moral character—else how could we have withstood that awful time of trial?"

In sum, the calamity only reinforced his belief in his community's special role in the world. He concluded, "So shall this beautiful edifice, reconsecrated to its high mission, serve indeed as the sacred emblem of the redeemed city by the Gate, its beauty restored, its sins purged, its temples rebuilt, its children reunited in [their] mission."

---

*In 1907 alone the temple lost two of its pioneer patriarchs: Abram Anspacher, the former president known as "Old Man Benevolent," and Julius Jacobs, the insurance man who also served as assistant United States treasurer.

THE GREAT EARTHQUAKE AND FIRE was not the only calamity San Francisco's Jewish elite faced in the year 1906. For on November 15, the city's political boss Abe Ruef, the well-educated son of Alsatian-Jewish immigrants, was indicted by the grand jury for extortion. Named along with him was Mayor Eugene Schmitz, the man whose political career he had made.

In the months that followed, a federal prosecution team—headed by Francis Heney and the famous detective William Burns, and aided by the sugar magnate Rudolph Spreckels and the muckraking editor of the *Bulletin*, Fremont Older—built a massive case against the two, who had been in power for more than five years. By the spring of 1907, Ruef faced sixty-five counts of bribery in addition to the extortion charges. Heney sought to prove that he had bought the favor of the mayor and the board of supervisors with "legal fees" from such sources as the Parkside Development Company, Pacific States Telephone and Telegraph, Pacific Gas and Electric, and the United Railroads.

With a few exceptions, such as J. B. Levison, the city's Jewish leadership stood by Ruef, who was defended by the distinguished attorney Henry Ach, an Emanu-El congregant who had been active in local politics. Rabbi Nieto of Sherith Israel—ironically, the site of the first trial—served as the main courier between the accused and the prosecution; he was virtually a member of the defense team. On Nieto's advice, indeed assurance, Ruef agreed to "turn state's evidence" by pleading guilty to one count of extortion in exchange for immunity on all other charges.

But the deal fell through. The prosecution was not satisfied that Ruef had "told all he knew," despite the grueling interrogation by Detective Burns. Unable to convict corporate executives like Patrick Calhoun and Tirey Ford of the United Railroads, Prosecutor Heney cancelled the immunity contract and in January 1908 made it clear that Ruef would have to stand trial again—on every one of the charges.

Rabbi Nieto, "stunned" at this turn of events, took his story of the prosecutor's duplicity to the press. The *Emanu-El*, breaking its silence on the case, ran a rare banner headline: STARTLING REVELATIONS IN THE GRAFT PROSECUTIONS AS DISCLOSED BY RABBI NIETO. Its front-page editorial, apparently written by Voorsanger, was a fierce

polemic even by his standards. Referring to "a chapter of disgrace unequaled in the history of San Francisco," it went on to accuse the
prosecution of suborning perjury, claiming that the promise of immunity
was withdrawn because Ruef had not implicated innocent men.

There was more to this defense of Ruef by leading Jews than simply
the fact that he was one of their own, or that the rabbis felt that they had
been deceived. Politically the trials divided the city between the supporters of the prosecution, who included the leaders of organized labor, and
the backers of the defense, which generally consisted of the business community. Voorsanger, along with most of the Jewish establishment, joined
the latter. He lauded the contributions to San Francisco of Ford and Calhoun, both on trial for bribing Ruef, and demanded "a square deal for
the indicted." Pleasure at their acquittal—as well as the overturning of
Mayor Schmitz' conviction on a technicality—was expressed by Rabbi
Bernard Kaplan of Ohabai Shalome, who wrote the *Emanu-El* editorials
after Voorsanger's death.

Both men also delivered blistering attacks on the "perverse" press,
namely the *Call* and the *Bulletin*, which they felt had "poisoned the public mind against those charged with wrong-doing." Voorsanger reported
from Paris in January 1907 that due to the "exposure of all the political
filth," San Francisco was "considered one of the most infamous communities extant." He predicted that business would suffer as a result, a theme
which Kaplan reiterated in two dozen articles.

The leading rabbis were also dismayed at a number of strikes in 1907
and 1908 which retarded the city's recovery. Voorsanger was especially
angry with the carmen's union, which crippled the United Railroads for
many weeks; he urged his readers to ride the trains despite scab labor.
Kaplan attacked the powerful head of the Building Trades Council, P. H.
McCarthy, who had caused all work to stop on the new downtown Mills
Building. Eventually, labor and the prosecution split with one another;
when McCarthy ran for mayor in 1909 he was opposed by Heney himself.
The *Emanu-El*, wishing to have little to do with either, supported the
unsuccessful candidacy of a little-known Republican businessman.

In order to spare the Jewish community further embarrassment, Ruef's
conviction and sentence—fourteen years, of which he served four and a
half at San Quentin—were completely ignored by the *Emanu-El*. But the

journal carried letters of prominent Jews urging his parole, and in an editorial demanded his early release. The weekly even took exception to Stephen Wise's comment that "Israel is not responsible for Ruef's sins," and rebuked the New York rabbi for assuming the convicted man guilty: "Wise is a brilliant and eloquent young man but not of a well-balanced frame of mind."

While the defense's analogy between Ruef and Dreyfus (on trial in the previous decade) was ludicrous, there was indeed a bit of anti-Semitism injected into the trials of the political boss, the only one of the accused to go to prison. Heney was charged by the *Emanu-El* with excluding Jews from the grand jury, to which he replied that "some of the best men" on the panel were Jewish. A year later, at the defendant's second trial, Heney revealed the prison record of the potential juror Morris Haas, a fact which the obscure middle-aged family man had kept secret for twenty years. Pointing a finger at the humiliated Haas, he then shouted, "He is an ex-convict and he is a Jew, and this defendant Ruef is a Jew." The *Emanu-El* expressed deep sympathy for Haas even after he returned to the courtroom several months later and shot Heney in the head before taking his own life in his jail cell.* Other anti-Semites were put in their place by the sting of Voorsanger's pen. When a local pastor used the Ruef case as an occasion for venting anti-Jewish remarks that were published in the *Bulletin*, Voosanger's reproach elicited a letter of apology to the *Emanu-El* the following week.

More telling, though, is the relative lack of anti-Semitism considering that "a small, weak, nervous Jew," as Ruef was characterized by a Midwestern priest, had come to symbolize the city's corruption during more than two years of sensational trials. Coming on the heels of a horrendous physical disaster, and coinciding with a period of labor unrest and a sizeable immigration of poor East European Jews, the Ruef affair certainly had the potential for stirring a wave of anti-Jewish sentiment throughout the Bay Area.

But it did nothing of the kind. Not only were anti-Semitic utterances rare, but the public refrained even from retaliating against Jewish

---

*Heney's life was saved because he happened to be laughing; the bullet entered his mouth and lodged in the jaw muscles below his left ear. After Haas' suicide, suspicion fell on Police Chief Biggy, who himself suffered a mysterious death soon thereafter.

politicians. Congressman Julius Kahn, a Republican in a traditionally Democratic district, was reelected as usual. Edward Wolfe (a member of Congregation Beth Israel) was again sent to the state senate, and Lippman Sachs, vice-president of Emanu-El, received the second highest number of votes of the twelve members elected to the "Reform" board of supervisors in the fall of 1907.

Again it was the Asians who were abused during these years of turmoil; they and not the Jews became the scapegoats. Ruef himself, before his fall from power, contributed to the suffering of the Chinese. A member of the committee on their relocation, formed after the earthquake, his aim was to prevent their return to the desirable section of the city near Nob Hill, which they had long occupied. Hoping to create a new Chinatown in Hunter's Point, or even beyond city limits in Colma, he detained many Chinese both at the Presidio and in North Beach.

His plan ultimately failed, but an even greater controversy erupted later in 1906 regarding the more recently arrived Japanese. Resentful of the rapid success of these enterprising people—often stereotyped in the press as shrewd and conniving—San Francisco reacted by segregating Japanese children from whites. The Chinese School, rebuilt after the earthquake, was renamed the Oriental Public School and designated as the only one in the city that would admit Japanese. Mayor Schmitz and the San Francisco Board of Education, headed by Ruef's brother-in-law, Aaron Altman, eventually rescinded the order, but only after a promise was made to them by President Roosevelt that Japanese laborers would be excluded from California in the future.

Yet, had there been no Asians on the West Coast, it is still hard to imagine that Voorsanger's generation of Jews would have been singled out for persecution, even during the years of 1906, 1907, and 1908. For the leading Jewish families not only enjoyed wealth, political influence, and social standing, but were genuinely respected by the gentiles. Like their fellow San Franciscans, they took the Great Earthquake and Fire and the Ruef case in stride.

IN 1908, ON A TRIP DOWN THE CALIFORNIA COAST that he cherished, Voorsanger was stricken with a heart attack which proved fatal. He was fifty-six. He had had a cardiac condition, aggravated by his unrelenting efforts on behalf of the city during the earthquake. Exhausted, he had nevertheless left in November 1906 for a long-planned trip to Europe and the Middle East, accompanied by his devoted wife, Eva, and daughter, Rachel, the second youngest of seven children. Rachel's death, shortly after their return in the spring of the following year, drained him physically as well as emotionally.

As reserved as he may have seemed at times, he was a man for whom personal relations took precedence over everything else. If his friends included financier Jacob Schiff, railway magnate Leland Stanford, and university president Benjamin Ide Wheeler, he could also patiently prepare restless teenagers—such as Judah Magnes, Martin Meyer, and his own son Elkan—for the rabbinate. His smoke-filled study on California Street, lined with thousands of books, was open to all. Here this large, muscular man often held one of his children while he read long into the night.

Jacob Voorsanger, who counted among his accomplishments the mastery of thirteen languages, was one of the most learned men in the American West. But he remained unable to transcend the spirit of his age; he was rooted in the nineteenth century the way a "mighty oak"— words invoked to eulogize him—is rooted in the soil. He stereotyped the immigrant Jew and the Chinese in America; he was blind to the significance of anti-Semitism and Zionism in Europe. Of the twentieth century he anticipated little, save the Federation of Jewish Charities, and that California would one day be "the star of the American Empire."

While he was the catalyst for much of the good work done by his congregants in the immigrant quarter, his vision of the temple itself was that it ought to remain a rather exclusive domain. He seemed untroubled by the fact that the synagogue was comprised almost entirely of prosperous merchants, that Russian Jews numbered less than one percent of the membership, or that the congregation counted so few young people. Indeed, the average age had risen to fifty-three by 1900, and only one of every seven Emanu-El members was under forty. Voorsanger appeared content too with women playing a minor role in the synagogue, even as they began to have a major impact on the Jewish community through their own organizations.

Yet the threads of fairness and probity which run through his career are undeniable. He not only printed articles by those with whom he disagreed, but invited many of them to his temple as well. He loathed self-proclaimed mystics, "swindlers who trade on the credulity of society," but he brought the Galician kabbalist Naphtali Herz Imber to San Francisco, and listened attentively to his lecture. He deplored Zionism, but presented his congregants with the movement's two most attractive and convincing American advocates—Judah Magnes and Stephen Wise. For all the repugnance he had for the East European Jews, he nevertheless spoke annually to a packed house at Congregation Beth Israel on the second day of Rosh Hashanah and in 1904 he led a highly successful appeal on behalf of the victims of the Kishinev pogrom. In sum, it is true that he remained a product of his age to the end, but he was one of its finest.

Cantor Stark lived until 1918, but his health too was ruined by overwork in the period following the earthquake: he assumed most of the rabbinical duties when Voorsanger went abroad in late 1906, then took the helm again for a year and a half following his colleague's untimely death. He resigned in 1913 after suffering a stroke—while hurrying to a High Holiday rehearsal—that would leave him incapacitated for the remaining years of his life.

But his premature retirement, at age fifty-seven, might well have occurred anyway due to the new rabbi, Martin A. Meyer, for whom Stark's elaborate cantorial work seems to have been a low priority, a superfluous luxury for the enjoyment of the elite. Indeed, as early as 1910 his role in the service was cut down and his salary reduced.

In the second decade of the century, with a new, young rabbi and cantor in place, Emanu-El would take a different direction, one of expansion, innovation, and democratization that Voorsanger and Stark hardly could have imagined. But the two self-educated savants left an indelible mark on the temple, a permanent legacy of intellectual excellence and exquisite, original music. Voorsanger's radical Reform theology, which he articulated so aggressively, would soon be eclipsed; but it would return again and again in future generations.

chapter four

MARTIN MEYER

Temple and Community

A heady atmosphere of recovery permeated the entire decade following the earthquake. Forests of steel frames sprang up in downtown San Francisco as hundreds of thousands returned to their city and their jobs.

The dizzying heights reached by the resurgent spirit were best evidenced by the Panama-Pacific International Exposition of 1915, which celebrated the rebirth of the city as well as the opening of the Panama Canal. It drew the astounding total of nineteen million visitors in less than ten months. And members of the Emanu-El elite were well represented among the civic leaders responsible for this sparkling array of art, architecture, and technology on the newly built marina. Julius Kahn used his seniority in Washington to win the approval of Congress, which had seriously considered New Orleans for the site. He was aided in his appeal by Leon Sloss, one of the vice-presidents of the Exposition; the tobacconist Alfred Esberg, chairman of the project's budget committee; and Robert Roos, whose French mother gave a lavish reception in her home for President Taft when he broke ground for the World's Fair in 1911.

The prospect of planning a model city by the Golden Gate caught the imagination of some of the most prominent women affiliated with the temple. The witty Bostonian Hattie Sloss, wife of the former California Supreme Court justice Marcus Sloss, chaired the women's board of the Exposition. A vice-president of the board was the novelist Bettie

Lowenberg, founder of the Philomath Club (a cultural society for the city's leading Jewish women) and also originator of the Exposition's Congress of Authors and Journalists. Caroline Sahlein, active in the women's suffrage movement and president of the San Francisco Council of Jewish Women, also dedicated herself to the great pageant.

Music for the extravaganza was entirely the province of J. B. Levison, himself an accomplished flutist. Provided the staggering budget of $665,000, he was able to bring the Boston Symphony Orchestra by special train for a two-week engagement. From war-torn Europe came Camille Saint-Saens, at the pinnacle of his career, to conduct three concerts and compose a special work, "Hail California." The German conductor Karl Muck—whom the well-intentioned Levison tried to keep away from Saint-Saens—and the revered Polish pianist Paderewski bolstered the list of foreign figures at the fair. Levison also insisted on an Exposition orchestra, comprised of eighty musicians, which performed in Festival Hall, often accompanied by the Exposition choir. Beyond all of this he arranged for no fewer than ten bands, including the incomparable ensemble of John Philip Sousa.

Nor was the Exposition the only outlet for the public-spirited during this period. In 1910, after the death of his brother, Sigmund, the banker Ignatz Steinhart offered the city the marvelous aquarium which bears his family's name. Jews were also becoming conspicuous as patrons of the arts. Mrs. Sloss and Mrs. Koshland were already known for holding musicales in their homes, and the swarthy, stocky Albert Bender—son of an Irish rabbi—helped many an aspiring young artist as well.

America's entry into World War I provided the Jewish elite with further opportunities for service. Mortimer Fleishhacker, active in banking, utilities, and manufacturing, was California's federal mediator for industrial disputes during the war; he settled the prolonged strikes of the shipbuilders and ironworkers. His nephew Albert Schwabacher served as the state's federal fuel administrator. The prominent attorney Jesse Lilienthal headed the local United War Work Drive, which raised over a million dollars for seven citizens' groups. Sigmund Stern's cultured wife, Rosalie, turned an entire floor of her home into a workshop where Red Cross volunteers sewed hospital dressings.

Rabbi Martin A. Meyer

Others served the Red Cross in Europe, such as Alma Levison (whose brother Charles became a lieutenant colonel in the Hospital Corps overseas), and Emanu-El's rabbi, Martin Meyer. Voorsanger's youngest son, Elkan, who had been junior rabbi of a congregation in St. Louis, left for France in May 1917 and became the first Jewish chaplain of the American Expeditionary Force. Moving up in rank from private to captain, he remained in Europe well after the armistice as the head of the Jewish Welfare Board, the extensive organization which concerned itself with the well-being of Jews in uniform.

This sort of wartime public service was duly noted in the *Emanu-El*, where brief sketches of the most active were featured in a special box under the heading "Jews in War Work." But with the exception of Congressman Kahn, there was little of the flag-waving we might have expected of Jewish civic leaders at this time. Very few anglicized their names, for example. Despite the fact that they were almost all the children of German immigrants, few felt any great necessity to make speeches proclaiming their loyalty—for they knew no one could seriously doubt it.

Jewish institutions claimed the attention of the elite as well. Mount Zion Hospital, badly hurt financially during the uncertain months following the earthquake, opened the doors of a new, well-equipped facility in the summer of 1912. The $100,000 gift of I. W. Hellman in memory of his late wife, Esther, was augmented by bonds in order to raise over a quarter of a million dollars needed for construction.

By 1910 the leading families could no longer postpone a decision on the late Jacob Voorsanger's proposal for the consolidation of the Jewish community's charitable and educational institutions. With the disaster of 1906 a recent memory, and the number of needy East European Jews increasing steadily, it was clear that relief work would have to become more effective: volunteer agencies would have to be overseen by professionals; duplication of services and fundraising efforts could no longer be tolerated. Justice Sloss became the first president of the newly organized Federation of Jewish Charities, which raised $165,000 annually by 1913. Not surprisingly, over two-thirds of the forty-six-member board of governors came from Emanu-El's ranks, including the two vice-presidents, J. B. Levison and Henry Sinsheimer, a wool merchant who had been active in several of the Federation's constituent bodies such as the Eureka Benevolent Society.

THE TEMPLE ITSELF underwent a period of profound reorganization in the second and third decades of the century, largely due to the vision of Voorsanger's young successor and former pupil, Martin A. Meyer. Thirty-one years old when he assumed his duties early in 1910, the handsome San Francisco-born rabbi had not been the first choice of President Wangenheim. He had much preferred established scholars such as William Rosenau of Baltimore, who declined to come west.* But Meyer, who had first served in Albany and later at Temple Israel in Brooklyn, where he helped organize that borough's Federation of Jewish Charities, was distinguished in his own right. Valedictorian at Hebrew Union College, he continued his study of Semitics in Palestine and at Columbia University, where he earned a doctorate for his original research, later published under the title *History of the City of Gaza*.

During his thirteen years at Emanu-El he wrote an important pamphlet on the Jewish view of Jesus and compiled the useful (though hardly authoritative) *Western Jewry*, essentially a collection of short biographies of prominent California Jews. Yet neither serious scholarship nor highly developed "theories of Judaism" would characterize his rabbinate as they had that of his predecessor. For he was far more interested in practice than in theory. If Voorsanger had been the architect of Reform Judaism on the West Coast, it remained for Martin Meyer to build its edifices. But in major areas he would depart from his predecessor's blueprints, relying instead on his own instincts in planning for the storms which would batter Jewish life in the new century.

The tall, blond minister, son of an immigrant businessman from Hanover, Germany, was very conscious of his San Francisco birthplace. Along with Judah Magnes, his senior by two years, and Elkan Voorsanger and Edgar Magnin, both slightly more than ten years his junior, Meyer comprised the first generation of California-born Reform rabbis. They

---

*An embarrassing incident occurred when it appeared that Wangenheim, searching for Voorsanger's successor in the East, offered the job not only to Rosenau but also to Rabbi Abram Simon of Washington—without consulting his board of directors in either case.

venerated their European teachers, but they were also eager to assume the mantle of leadership themselves. Martin Meyer's return in 1910 to the city of his birth was yet another indication that the pioneer period of Western Jewish history had come to an end.

Like Voorsanger, the stern Meyer attacked the typical "evils" of his day such as apartment houses, "slumming" parties, and prizefights. But he prodded temple members in a way the Dutchman never had: he wanted them to question their all-too-comfortable accommodation with the larger gentile society.

For he was deeply concerned about the weakening ties to Judaism of his congregants, many of them now two full generations removed from their immigrant forebears. In an intimate memoir, Frances Bransten Roth-mann captures well the attenuated Jewish identity of the Emanu-El elite in those years, and the challenges faced by the new rabbi. Writing of the sheltered, privileged lives of her mother and aunt—Florine Haas Bransten and Alice Haas Lilienthal—Rothmann stresses their interest in Jewish philanthropy and volunteer work. But though the sisters attended High Holiday services (without their "recalcitrant" husbands, who refused to accompany them),

> they knew little about Jewish rites. The menorahs, the beautiful lights adorning their Franklin Street homes, were merely artifacts ornamenting their dining and living rooms. We might dine on gorgeously glazed hams, but only fish was served on Fridays. As bacon sizzled in the kitchen, Mother worried endlessly about our Catholic nurse's lenten diet. These were not intentional or prejudicial defiances; they were merely part of the world the sisters knew and lived in. Of course they had heard about old Jewish traditions, but they were felt to be part of a different world, a world of old *tantes* living in backwards Bavarian villages. Mother spoke to me about one of these old aunts who refused to light her fire against the bitter cold because of the Sabbath. Her account sounded foreign and fascinating, as though they were speaking of different beings on a faraway planet.
>
> As a child, I never heard my aunt or mother use words such as *yahrzeit, shiva, mikveh,* or *chuppah.*

Early on, Meyer expressed his dismay that many temple members (and the Haas sisters were good examples) celebrated Christmas and Easter and not Hanukah and Passover. He also voiced his alarm over the fact that some congregants, particularly women, were attracted to the popular Christian Science Church.

To fight these trends, Meyer, who had become a Bar Mitzvah at the traditional Congregation Beth Israel, sought to restore a number of Jewish ceremonies—such as baby naming and praying for the ill—which had fallen into disuse at Emanu-El decades earlier. He urged the temple choir to recruit a higher proportion of Jews. To be sure, he never attempted to bring more Hebrew into the service, nor did he wear a *kippah* (skullcap) or *tallit* (prayer shawl). But he refused to sanctify intermarriage under any circumstances.

Most important, though, was Meyer's grand new concept of the role of the temple, one far more broadly based than that of Voorsanger. Focusing on the future of American Jewry, the young man hoped above all to unify his badly fragmented people. He sought to bring the immigrant and the native-born Jew closer together; he tried to make peace between the Reform and the Orthodox; he advocated Zionism, women's rights, and community service. In sum, his mission as a pulpit rabbi was that of a builder and a healer of the entire Jewish community, and his vision was ultimately reflected in the Lake Street temple, completed shortly after his untimely death. While the elegance of its sanctuary would be unmatched by any house of worship in the American West, its adjoining "temple house" would distinguish it as an ambitious "synagogue-center," open to all forms of Jewish expression and accessible to people from every walk of life.

Meyer's inclusive approach bears a striking similarity to that of two other brilliant Reform rabbis of his generation, Judah Magnes and Stephen Wise, who both became internationally known for their foresight, idealism, and courage. No doubt he drew strength from their highly publicized crusades on behalf of East European Jews, their passionate advocacy of Zionism, and their uncompromising stand for social justice. Wise in particular, about half a decade older than Meyer, had an enormous influence on the San Franciscan. As a young rabbi in Brooklyn during the latter part of the century's first decade, Meyer witnessed at close range the huge success of Wise's Free Synagogue across the river in Manhattan. This was an experimental *shul* that ministered to the wealthy "uptown" German Jews as well as the downtrodden newcomers on the Lower East Side. In addition to an extensive cultural and educational program, and inspiring sermons delivered by its charismatic spiritual leader, it employed a dedicated social worker on its staff to direct its many community service initiatives.

Meyer left New York to take the Emanu-El post just as the Free Synagogue moved its worship services to Carnegie Hall, where Wise regularly drew a crowd of thousands. But the two corresponded frequently during the next thirteen years and Wise's biographer states that Meyer was "greatly liked and admired" by the country's most influential rabbi, who enlisted him as an ally for many worthy causes. Wise was also familiar with the specific challenges facing West Coast Jewry; he had earlier served for six years as the rabbi of Portland's growing congregation, Beth Israel, where he had been installed by Jacob Voorsanger.

But it must also be noted that in style, if not in substance, Meyer was far less of a maverick than Magnes or Wise, who deeply angered the Jewish establishment at times. As young rabbis, both had negative experiences at New York's Emanu-El, for example, just the sort of bruising, public conflicts with the board that Meyer managed to avoid in San Francisco. In an open letter in the national Jewish press, Wise refused the post of head rabbi on Fifth Avenue after learning that the pulpit was not "free" (in the sense that the rabbi could speak his mind on any subject he chose), but rather under the control of the leading laymen. He thus sardonically credited Emanu-El's powerful member Louis Marshall as the unwitting "author and founder" of his alternative Free Synagogue. Later Wise even founded his own rabbinical seminary, the Jewish Institute of Religion, which rivaled the Hebrew Union College until the two finally merged in 1948. And the perennial gadfly Judah Magnes, an associate rabbi at Emanu-El, resigned in 1910 amidst the board's dismay at his objections to the assimilationist practices of some of his most prominent congregants. Even earlier, following another unpleasant encounter, Magnes had given up his pulpit at Brooklyn's Temple Israel for the same reason—and was succeeded by Martin Meyer.

Such blunt confrontations were foreign to Meyer's nature, however. Innovative though he was, he could also work within the established framework of Jewish institutional life. He refused to play the role of *enfant terrible* which could have been his; he was nothing if not proper.

Still, he was capable on occasion of taking great risks in exposing the inadequacy—some might say hypocrisy—of his flock's religious expression, as the following broadside demonstrates. In 1915, objecting to Rabbi Emil Hirsch's glorification of the German Jews' achievements in America, he contended that it had been only

> the accident of history that brought the so-called German Jews to this land ahead of the Russian....They have been far more interested in their Americanism than in their Judaism. Like a certain popular actor they have always tried to get a wave of applause by frequent waving of the Stars and Stripes....For the most part, as we take it, the German Jew is a Jew because he can't help it; his neighbors insist that he remain a Jew even after he joins the Christian Science Church.

Standing Voorsanger's theories on their head, Meyer pinned his hopes on the East European Jew,

> who wants to remain a Jew because he feels the call of blood and the promise of the spirit. Frankly, the future of the Jew in America will be in the hands of the Russian-descended contingent, not only because of the preponderance of numbers but chiefly because he is conscious of his Jewish affiliations and anxious to perpetuate the traditions of his people.

Furthermore, in the spirit of Magnes and Wise, Meyer viewed internal dissension as American Jewry's "greatest folly and weakness," and refused to tolerate the attacks on Orthodoxy which had been characteristic of Voorsanger and which still flowed from the pens of many Reform rabbis. Soon after becoming editor of the *Emanu-El* (a post he would hold, however, for barely a year) he reminded his readers, "If we are not the children, we are certainly the grandchildren of that Orthodoxy."

He reached out to Yiddish-speaking Jews in a number of ways. He became the director of the Jewish Educational Society, begun by Voorsanger. With his encouragement, and I. W. Hellman's generosity, the Esther Hellman Settlement House was erected on San Bruno Avenue at the end of 1918. The Hebrew Immigrant Aid Society (HIAS) was also established in San Francisco with his help, and for many years he served as vice-president of the local chapter. Guardian angel of the Young Men's Hebrew Association, of which he was president from 1916 to 1918, he was instrumental in its move to an ample three-story structure on Haight Street where young immigrants had the use of club rooms, a social hall, and other facilities. During World War I, he also was active in the formation of the American Jewish Congress, an expression of the East Europeans' urge to create a democratically elected national Jewish assembly.

Unlike his predecessor, he actively encouraged the immigration of East European Jews to America and to the Bay Area in particular. While he saw the value of agricultural colonies for the new arrivals, he specifically recommended San Francisco to them, pointing out that a shortage of labor had long been one of the city's problems.

In 1916, he invited Mary Antin, author of the famed immigrant tribute to America, *The Promised Land*, to the temple. However, his concern for the *Ostjuden* did not begin with their arrival at Ellis Island, but extended directly to Eastern Europe. During World War I, Meyer worked tirelessly on behalf of tens of thousands of starving Jewish civilians literally trapped in the cross fire between the two warring sides on the eastern front. A rally for the war sufferers in 1915, at which Meyer introduced the philanthropist Nathan Straus, packed the Emanu-El sanctuary. By February of the following year a committee consisting of the rabbi and his wife, Jennie, as well as I. W. Hellman, Cora Koshland, Mortimer Fleishhacker, and others, had raised more than a quarter of a million dollars for the cause, surpassing every city in the country except New York. Just as dramatic were the protests led by Justice Sloss after the armistice, against the pogroms that erupted along the borders of the new Soviet Union.

The most important bridge to the immigrant Jews was undoubtedly Cantor Reuben Rinder, whom Meyer brought to the temple in 1913. He was born and raised in a small town in the province of Galicia, near Lvov (under Austro-Hungarian rule but populated by Poles, Ukranians, and Jews), where he learned to sing from his devout uncle. The youth journeyed to New York at the age of thirteen, shortly after the death of his parents, briefly attended the Hebrew Theological Seminary, and soon became the cantor of a small *shul* in Brooklyn. Four years later he moved to Manhattan's B'nai Jeshurun, the largest Conservative synagogue in the five boroughs.

REUBEN RINDER SHORTLY AFTER HIS
ARRIVAL IN SAN FRANCISCO IN 1913

Young Rinder also fell under the influence of Rabbi Stephen Wise and would occasionally sing at the Carnegie Hall services, which were held Sunday mornings. It was on Wise's recommendation that Meyer engaged the twenty-six-year-old, who readily negotiated what must have been a startling transition from a Galician *shtetl*, via New York, to San Francisco's Reform "cathedral."

Once on the West Coast Rinder and his wife, Rose—herself brought up in a Hasidic village—mixed easily with all segments of the Jewish community. They were to be frequent dinner guests in the opulent homes of the Koshlands, Slosses, Ehrmans, Hellers, and Sterns, families who would enable Rinder to make a stunning impact on the world of Jewish music for almost half a century. But the Rinders—whose social activities also included a Yiddish-speaking circle called the Sholom Aleichem Group—were an integral part of the immigrant community as well.

The cantor administered the Sabbath school and taught the confirmation class at the Esther Hellman Settlement House, known simply as "the Club" to the immigrants and their children. Here, on San Bruno

Avenue, young people were provided with the same Jewish education as their more well-to-do contemporaries on Sutter Street. They also learned American table manners, such as how to use a napkin. One alumna of the Club remembers of the well-dressed Emanu-El women who oversaw activities that "they certainly could not imagine us mixing with their children." But there was more here than simply a patronizing attitude, revealed by the great attention to detail paid by Rinder, Sidney Ehrman's wife, Florence, and above all the beloved teacher, Grace Wiener, whose father had been the Emanu-El sexton. At the annual confirmation ceremony, for example, the stage was exquisitely decorated and each girl was given a great bouquet of flowers. While a liberal approach to Judaism was taught, the laws of *kashrut* were strictly observed at the Club so as not to confuse these children from Orthodox homes, or offend their parents.

BOTH MEYER AND RINDER voiced strong Zionist convictions in and out of the temple; in this sense they were part of a tiny minority among the Reform clergy in America. For the rabbi, conversion to Jewish nationalism had been a gradual process. His year in Palestine shortly after the turn of the century made him doubt the Zionists' "rosy accounts" of the land, leading him to contend in 1911 that half a dozen other countries would be better suited for Jewish colonization.

By 1915, however, he had been won over to the cause. Much like Louis Brandeis, who epitomized American Zionism in these years, the terrible suffering of the Jews during World War I convinced Meyer of the need for a refuge in Palestine. But the contacts of both men with the rich cultural life of the East European immigrants provided them with a second argument in favor of Zionism: they viewed the Jews as a nation, not merely a religious group.* In November 1915, Meyer chaired a mass meeting at Dreamland Rink on behalf of the Jews of Palestine, who found themselves in dire straits due to the war. Early the following year he was named to the advisory council of the Federation of American Zionists, which included men like Felix Frankfurter, then professor of law

*Meyer had one final reservation, though. He had to be assured by Brandeis that non-Jews would also have the right to become citizens of the proposed Jewish state. Apparently he did not want his Zionist affiliation to appear inconsistent with the strong position he took at home on the separation of church and state.

at Harvard, whom he brought to the temple after the Balfour Declaration in November 1917.

On the local level he was joined by a handful of his congregants, such as the colorful Confederate veteran Leopold Michels; the wealthy cigar manufacturer Morgan Gunst; and the president of the San Francisco Bar, Jesse Lilienthal. But the city's Zionist chapter did not attract a sizeable portion of Emanu-El's members. Nahum Sokolow spoke at the temple in 1922 but, according to one local historian, Chaim Weizmann was spurned by the board of directors two years later.

The anti-Zionist position taken by most of the city's Jewish elite was articulated by Julius Kahn, who carried the fight to the Paris Peace Conference in 1919. There he presented President Wilson with a petition opposing the creation of a Jewish state, signed by almost three hundred prominent American Jews, including Emanu-El congregants such as I. W. Hellman and Justice Sloss. The Republican congressman—who two years earlier had been responsible for initiating the Selective Service System— stated, "For me the United States is my Zion and San Francisco is my Jerusalem. And if I have to make a choice between my country and my Judaism, that choice is not difficult. I shall stand firmly and forever for my country."

Meyer, who even during World War I rarely voiced patriotic feelings, was not one to be swayed by Kahn's "double loyalties" argument. Nor was he discouraged by the indifference to Zionism of most of his flock. With his characteristic foresight, he wrote in the *Emanu-El* (which remained anti-Zionist under the long editorship of Jacob Voorsanger's brother, A. W.) that "the twentieth century will be notable in Jewish history for the reintegration of the Jewish people among the peoples of the earth."

Rinder, meanwhile, lent his unusual talents to the movement. In 1918 he composed the stirring "Battle Song of Zion" for the Jewish Legion of Palestine. The first stanza, in a minor mood, typifies the diaspora. The second, employing the sound of the shofar, reflects hope for the end of the exile and for a new and virile life in Palestine.

Women too were drawn to the cause of Zion. "Rowie" Rinder, as she was dubbed by her husband, initiated San Francisco's first Hadassah chapter in 1916. In the East that year she had heard inspiring speeches by Wise, Brandeis, and Weizmann; soon thereafter, at a national Hadassah conference, she was encouraged by Mary Antin to organize a group in San Francisco. The turnout was unexpected: 250 women appeared at a small room in the St. Francis Hotel. Hattie Sloss became the president, Mrs. Moses Heller the treasurer.

But this early success was short-lived. Apparently few of the women, including Mrs. Sloss and Mrs. Heller, understood the nationalist aims of Hadassah; they believed it to be simply a charitable organization for the uplifting of Palestine. When, in 1918, the national office insisted that its members be Zionists, Mrs. Sloss resigned and the entire San Francisco chapter disbanded.

Mrs. Rinder was able to reorganize Hadassah several years later, along clear-cut Zionist lines. She was aided by a few temple members, in particular the wife of Dr. Henry Harris, who assumed the presidency of the group. But the battle at Emanu-El to win support for Jewish nationhood would remain an uphill struggle for decades to come.

MEYER'S ZIONISM and his links with the East European Jews constituted only one phase of his revolutionary rabbinate. He was just as intent on surmounting physical barriers as cultural ones. Keenly aware that those living in small rural communities, especially in the western states, were often completely cut off from Jewish life, he declared in 1910, "Had we the proper spirit we would not wait for them to come to us, we would be active in organizing our fellow Jews wherever they be found."

He hoped that the Jewish Chautauqua Society would provide an antidote. One of its founders and leading fundraisers, and ultimately its Pacific Coast director, Meyer never ceased to praise this organization which brought speakers on Jewish themes to small communities throughout the nation.

With the same goal in mind, in 1912 he established the Emanu-El Correspondence School, an attempt to educate young Jews in remote areas. A nominal fee for postage and handling entitled a child to weekly mailings of literature on Jewish history, ethics, and culture. Completed assignments would then be sent to San Francisco. School secretary Milton Sapiro, one of Meyer's young favorites who later became a local judge, reported an enrollment the first year of thirty-five, from spots as far away as Idaho and Utah.

Closer to home was his concern, expressed as early as 1910, about an imminent exodus to "the suburbs." The style excepted, his analysis in the *Emanu-El* could have been written in the final decade of the twentieth century as well as in the first:

> The rapacity of the landlords of San Francisco has made the rents so high that decent, modest living in the city has been made well-nigh impossible. The carnival which the forces of evil-import have enjoyed on this side of the Bay has suggested to fathers and mothers of growing children that it was better for them to rear their children under more favorable moral circumstances.

His efforts to help the struggling Jewish communities of the suburbs were legion. In 1913, he established monthly Friday evening services and a religious school across the bay in Alameda. Two years later he opened a branch of his own religious school down the peninsula in San Mateo; it continued to function well past mid-century. During the High Holidays he arranged for services to be held in the Richmond District and in Fresno, Chico, San Leandro, Vallejo, and other towns throughout Northern California. In particular, he kept a watchful eye on Berkeley. In 1914, he helped organize a small traditional congregation by providing not only financial assistance but, more importantly, the services of his protégé, Louis I. Newman, then a graduate student at the University of California.

Like Voorsanger, Meyer lectured for over a decade in the Semitics department at the university, but his role on the campus took him far beyond the classroom. In 1916 he was instrumental in forming the Menorah Club—forerunner of the Hillel Foundation of the following decade—which presented cultural programs aimed at the university's 150 Jewish students.

Meyer even felt an obligation to the Jewish inmates of the state's prisons and mental hospitals. During the first decade of his rabbinate he headed the State Board of Charities and Corrections and often visited the Alcatraz, San Quentin, and Folsom prisons. In 1920, as a result of talks with Federation director I. Irving Lipsitch, he was convinced of the need for an organization to put this work on a more regular basis. To do so, he created the Jewish Committee for Personal Service in State Institutions, encouraged by the local rabbis and funded by federations throughout the state. As his caseworker, Meyer engaged William

Blumenthal, who reported a total of 524 potential wards: 120 in prison or reform school, seventy-nine in homes for "the feeble-minded," and 325 in mental hospitals. Later the rabbi was able to involve a corps of volunteers from the newly formed Emanu-El Men's Club.

His vision stretched not only from the suburbs to the farms, and from the university to the jails, but also from Northern California to the nation as a whole—particularly in the field of Jewish learning. Appalled at the often low intellectual level of the rabbis of his day, "the ignorant men who occupy the pulpits," he urged that minimum standards of education be adopted nationally and constantly reiterated that the Union of American Hebrew Congregations, and its seminary in Cincinnati, would have to be strengthened.

As for the laity, Meyer hoped that the publication and dissemination of Jewish books would make an impact. As honorary vice-president of the struggling Jewish Publication Society, he often castigated American Jewry for its "indifference" to the support of scholarship: "We get as much from Europe in a six-month period as we get here in a dozen years." The Jewish Chautauqua Society published Meyer's two-volume teacher's manual, *Methods of Teaching Post-Biblical History*, but one of his most common complaints was the lack of proper textbooks for religious school students. Regarding primary and secondary education as well as high scholarship, he pointed to the need for "a Jewish public which will encourage it, appreciate it, support it."

IN HIS TEMPLE WORK he concentrated on two groups which had been neglected—women and youth. Although Voorsanger had founded the Emanu-El Sisterhood for Personal Service, to which Meyer also gave wholehearted support, this effective organization saw relief work in the community as its main task and played only a small role in the activities of the congregation. For the specific purpose of serving the temple, Meyer formed the Women's Guild in 1917. The first president was Sophie Gerstle Lilienthal, still in black mourning dress for her husband, Theodore (brother of Phil and Jesse Lilienthal), who had died more than twenty-five years earlier. This auxiliary of one hundred women worked to attract new temple members; in the '20s its frequent social gatherings brought dozens of families into the Emanu-El orbit.

In 1921, the year after women were finally allowed to vote, Meyer succeeded in winning for them privileges at the temple as well. They were now permitted to join in their own right and not only in their husband's name. At this time too, Sophie Lilienthal and Caroline Sahlein became the first female members of the board of directors.

With his sixth sense for fathoming social trends, the rabbi well understood the need to integrate women into American synagogue life. Predicting (along with Stephen Wise) that they would one day serve as rabbis, he wrote in the spring of 1922 that the emancipation of women in Judaism would necessarily follow their emancipation in the general society: "Woman the world over has come out of her classical and medieval seclusion to take her place at the side of her brothers. She will never go back, come what may, to the gallery or the harem."

No less urgent, however, were programs for young people. Shortly after his arrival he assumed complete responsibility for the religious school, which had been reorganized after the earthquake by the eminent William Popper, professor of Semitics at the University of California, but which had since slipped in enrollment to roughly two hundred.

The school met Sunday mornings in the basement of the Sutter Street temple, in rooms which Meyer found wholly inadequate. He was willing to postpone construction of a new temple for several years, but he insisted on a new schoolhouse, voted by the congregation in the summer of 1910 and occupied by the spring of the next year. Located at Sutter and Van Ness, eight blocks from the sanctuary—on land the temple had purchased before the earthquake—the three-story brick annex was highly functional. Costing a modest $30,000, it included ten classrooms, a lecture hall, and a chapel.

The new building was a resource which seemed tailored to Meyer's ministry. Beginning in 1911, it housed the "Free Synagogue," High Holiday services for people in the community who could not have been seated in the sanctuary, which was filled almost to capacity. Milton Sapiro and Philip Wascerwitz were responsible for the first year's services; others of Meyer's "boys" would later take charge of this unique program of "temple hospitality" which lasted through the 1920s.

Meyer especially relished the fact that non-temple groups made use of the school building. Federation gatherings and Chautauqua Society meetings were common; classes of the University of California Extension were welcomed with particular warmth.

But the Sunday school benefited most from the facility. Over a hundred new students were added to the rolls in 1911 alone and registration increased steadily over the years. By 1917 the annex itself had become overcrowded—with over five hundred pupils in seventeen classes—and rooms in a nearby office building had to be rented. Members of other congregations were not permitted to send their children to Emanu-El's popular school, but children of the unaffiliated were accepted without charge.

The academic year of 1918–19 witnessed a setback, though. While Meyer was in France with the Red Cross, John Altman, who administered the school in his absence, had to cope with a citywide epidemic of typhus during the late winter.

But rapid growth continued in the early '20s. In addition to the school in San Mateo, classes were held in Masonic Hall and at Mission near Eighth, for the convenience of those who lived some distance from the temple. Yet the Sutter and Van Ness building alone boasted 545 registrants in 1921, with an average attendance of 484, and a "normal class," taught by the rabbi, which trained future teachers. Meyer's success was not due to any drastic changes in the curriculum. More committed than Voorsanger to the teaching of Hebrew, he was as frustrated by the lack of student interest. No more than thirty a year ever registered for a course in the ancient language. But youngsters—especially teenagers—were drawn to the school because of a range of activities which gave them a sense of their own self-worth. Charity drives, for example, often netted over $1,000 from the school itself.

The pride of the school was its slick literary magazine, the *Scroll*, which appeared as many as six times a year. After one false start—a "Young People's Page" in the *Emanu-El* which fell flat—Meyer hit upon the correct formula in 1913. The journal sparkled with articles on current affairs, clever anecdotes, short stories, and items on local Jewish history. An enthralling fictional account of a jury trial was written in 1917, for example, by thirteen-year-old Assistant Literary Editor Matthew Tobriner, in the 1970s and '80s a California Supreme Court justice. The boys and girls who worked on the *Scroll* each year, after avidly reading the publications of other religious schools around the country, understandably concluded that theirs was one of the best of its kind anywhere.

Another source of excitement was the annual Hanukah play, and again it was one which bore little resemblance to the productions of other temples. In collaboration with the young Milton Marks (future state assemblyman and father of the well-known state senator) or another lad from the rabbi's circle, Meyer somehow found the time to write an original play for the occasion. His 1913 effort, *God Is One*, published by the Bloch Company, was distributed nationally.

The rabbi took the initiative in other areas as well. He encouraged the formation of an athletic league among the city's Jewish schools, and, in 1918, had the temple sponsor a Boy Scout troop, number 17, with consequences no one could have then foreseen. Under the leadership of a scouting fanatic, Arthur "Pie" Myer, Troop 17 became in the '20s one of the most active groups of its kind in the nation, a position it would hold for over four decades.

A similar success was the all-male Pathfinders, which Meyer founded in 1921. Composed at first of thirty post-confirmands who met every other week in the rabbi's home, this cultural and service organization grew in size and scope in the interwar period to involve not only high school but college students, as well.

As a result, he developed a personal bond with a cadre of young men who would provide the Jewish community with a reservoir of leadership for the next two generations. They marveled at his private library of Judaica, the most extensive on the West Coast, were awed by his sermons, and hung on his every word in his confirmation classes. On Saturday afternoons his home was open to them, but many arrived early on Sabbath mornings to watch him shave and then walk with him to the temple.

Leo Rabinowitz, for decades the Bay Area's leading Zionist organizer, was a member of Meyer's inner circle of young men and a teacher at Emanu-El's school despite the fact that his father, Joseph, was the cantor of Congregation Beth Israel. Lloyd Dinkelspiel and Richard Sloss, who would each serve as president of the temple in the late '30s and '40s, were also "Dr. Meyer's boys," as was John Altman, a future temple vice-president who had his own key to the rabbi's house. The philanthropist

Daniel Koshland, who would later become an Emanu-El vice-president as well as a central figure with the Federation, was yet another introduced to social responsibility at the feet of Martin Meyer.

Others entered the rabbinate. Benjamin Goldstein, whom Meyer nurtured as an adolescent, became the first director of the Berkeley Hillel Foundation in 1928. William Stern, the son of an Orthodox rabbi, was persuaded by Meyer to study at Hebrew Union College; in the '20s and early '30s he held pulpits in the Midwest and South before beginning a tenure of almost a third of a century at Oakland's Temple Sinai.

His best-known disciple, however, was Providence-born Louis I. Newman, who had come to Berkeley in 1913 as a nineteen-year-old graduate student in Semitics. An ambitious scholar, active in the Menorah Club, and through Meyer's efforts the spiritual leader of Berkeley's Congregation Beth Israel, Newman was closely shepherded by Meyer until he left in the fall of 1916 to work at Rabbi Stephen Wise's Free Synagogue and take his doctorate at Columbia.

Newman would remain in New York for eight years before succeeding his mentor at Emanu-El, and their correspondence during this period reveals much about both men. In letter after letter they discussed Professor Popper's *Studies in Biblical Parallelism*, on which the precocious Newman had collaborated, and the young man's own massive, unwieldy Ph.D. thesis concerning the Jewish influences on Christian movements through the ages. They also shared thoughts on current affairs, and Newman's white-hot Zionist rhetoric was curbed somewhat by his teacher, who detested "bickering" in all its forms. Headstrong though he was, Newman took the criticism well: "If you find me off the track, please set me right." The student always addressed his mentor as "Dr. Meyer," but shared with him his most personal concerns. He sought his counsel before accepting any new position, such as the offer, in 1917, to become traveling secretary of the Intercollegiate Menorah Association: "I would hesitate to enter the Menorah despite its many advantages unless, Dr. Meyer, you who have guided my life so generously feel convinced that the step is correct." He asked Meyer's advice on dealing with an anti-Zionist colleague at the Free Synagogue, on whether or not to deliver a sermon in Carnegie Hall before he had been ordained, and even on how to approach Rabbi Wise for a raise. When Newman broke off his marriage engagement, he assured Meyer, "I have done nothing faithless to my calling as a rabbi," and was gratified that his advisor had talked to the young woman's father.

Meyer, fifteen years older than Newman, assumed a fatherly role toward the man whom he—along with Stephen Wise and Sidney Goldstein of the Free Synagogue—ordained in 1918. He constantly warned Newman to look after his health and not take on too much: "A broken-down rabbi at twenty-seven is a particularly useless person," he jested. But he also lost his temper at times with those closest to him, and Newman was no exception. When Meyer found out, for example, that Newman had acquiesced in his exclusion from the Menorah Association's Tenth Convention, he wrote, "You acted like a cad....If your present attitude is to be typical of your future, I would advise you to sweep streets rather than enter the rabbinate." Months went by before the devastated Newman would be forgiven.

MEYER WAS THE STAUNCH ADVOCATE of a new temple even before World War I. He saw the schoolhouse quickly become inadequate, with over fifty children crowding into a single classroom at times. The walls of the sanctuary were slowly crumbling and the interior could not even be properly heated.

But more than merely a new house of worship, he envisaged a complex of buildings that would bring Jews together for social, athletic, charitable, and educational purposes as well—serving not only his own congregants, but the entire Jewish community. Calling his concept "the Temple of the Open Door," he boldly unveiled it in January 1920, at one of the most eventful annual meetings in the history of the institution:

> Community service is the word of the day, not only on the basis of economic waste of a plant which is idle the greater part of the week and the year; but because we feel that any church or synagogue deaf to the possibility of social and community service is doomed....One thing is certain, that just a house-of-prayer idea for weekly services and religious school instruction is apt to be barren.

Not the least important consequence of the new temple idea, Meyer realized, would be the lessening of class consciousness among the city's

Jews. His congregants, roughly 450 families in the early '20s, were segregated from the rest of the community by their ability to pay the dues—close to $100 a family as the absolute minimum. He would soon call for a $50 fee for two High Holiday tickets in the back rows of the sanctuary, to which, after a three-year fight, the board agreed. He was angered too that without exception non-members were required to pay the temple $200 for his services at a funeral. A new temple, he reasoned, might accommodate up to a thousand families, a much broader cross-section of the community. Arrangements would be made for those in modest circumstances to become members; in any case they would be permitted to enjoy the temple's facilities. This all-embracing vision of Emanu-El—of which the new structure would be the linchpin—could not have differed more from that of his predecessor.

Of course there was more to this momentous shift than the difference in outlook between Voorsanger and Meyer. The decade following World War I ushered in an unprecedented period of synagogue building across the country, the number of structures doubling during this era of prosperity and population growth.

Especially popular was the notion of the "synagogue-center"; almost every large American city saw the rise of at least one such grand, multipurpose edifice. In later years there would be a split, as the "center" came to denote a separate institution—the Jewish Community Center, or JCC—usually independent of any synagogue. But the 1920s saw a marked tendency to place Judaism and "Jewishness" under the same roof.

Certainly Rabbi Mordecai Kaplan's notion of "Judaism as a civilization" afforded an ideological justification for this trend; in 1917 the renowned theologian laid the cornerstone of a nine-story Jewish center on the Upper West Side which, he said, "will endeavor to have us work, play, love and worship as Jews." Stephen Wise, New York Jewry's other titanic figure, had no comparable building for his Free Synagogue, but his activism indicated as well how far the definition of a synagogue could reach.

But recent research has revealed that the idea of the "open temple" was first broached decades earlier by Reform rabbis—usually American-born pragmatists hoping to attract young people—who tried to recast their synagogues from a worship-centered shrine into a many-faceted home. The concept was advocated at the turn of the century perhaps most forcefully by Rabbi Moses Gries of Cleveland's influential Tifereth Israel, who declared that "a new spirit is widening the walls and purposes of narrow synagogues and temples [because] every effort and activity of life, all work and pleasure, are within the province of religion." This approach was opposed by many older, foreign-born Reform rabbis, who doubted the wisdom of providing the young with "amusement and spiritual entertainment which has no connection with religious life." But the idea of a "synagogue-center" rapidly gained ground and was heartily endorsed by the Central Conference of American Rabbis, which established its Committee on Social and Religious Union well before World War I.

The well-informed Meyer was undoubtedly mindful of all of these developments as he pondered the new synagogue and sought to overcome perhaps the most profound dichotomy in American Jewish life, that between the spiritual and the secular. He met with some resistance, but felt by the beginning of 1920 that his influence in the congregation had reached a symbolic peak and that he would get his way. He had just celebrated the tenth anniversary of his coming to Emanu-El; the previous spring he had been given a raise to $14,400 a year and had become the only rabbi in the West with a contract for life. In June he had delivered both the baccalaureate sermon at Hebrew Union College and the commencement address at the University of California.

His congregants followed his lead. After his dramatic presentation at the January 1920 annual meeting, the membership moved to create a committee for the purpose of securing a suitable site. President Wangenheim appointed a group of five, which included the department-store owner David Livingston, who soon became chairman.

By the end of August the committee had a list of many possible locations, most of them fairly close to the center of the city. One site that was nearly purchased was a lot in Lafayette Square only two blocks west of Van Ness, of which Marcus Koshland was one of several influential advocates. Another plot that was almost chosen was at Pierce and California, about half a mile to the west of the busy commercial avenue.

But the site committee had difficulty making a final decision. Not until the summer of 1922 did it purchase a property: a large, level tract (288 feet by 120 feet) more than a mile and a half west of Van Ness at Lake Street and First Avenue (later renamed Arguello Boulevard). Located in

Presidio Heights, and very close to Pacific Heights, this fashionable residential district had attracted many of the wealthier congregants in the past decade. The Sutter Street building was sold for $410,000, and the Lake Street site, in addition to three small buildings on property adjoining the lot, was purchased for $140,000.

The forty-three-year-old industrialist Louis Bloch, now chairman of the building committee and within three years to become temple president, was charged with outlining the basic requirements for the new structure. These would be guidelines for the eminent team of architects headed by Sylvain Schnaittacher, John Bakewell, and Arthur Brown Jr. The sanctuary, he wrote in March 1923, would have to seat at least 1,800, half again the capacity of the old synagogue. The religious school would need to include twenty-five classrooms, a library, and an assembly hall for seven hundred, equipped with a kitchen, stage, and projection booth. Finally, Bloch suggested a "community house," if possible, for athletic activities.

ON JUNE 27, while the board of directors and congregants were preoccupied with the plans for the new temple, a shocking event occurred: Rabbi Meyer was found dead in his home. His wife entered his study very early on Wednesday morning and discovered his lifeless body.

Although it would never be admitted publicly, all the evidence seemed to indicate that the leading rabbi in the West had taken his own life. Because he had spoken at the St. Francis Hotel only hours before his death, and played golf earlier that day, his family and friends first hypothesized a sudden stroke. But the coroner found potassium cyanide in his stomach, a chemical Meyer used to mount butterflies.

The *American Israelite* suggested that someone had poisoned the forty-four-year-old rabbi, and there also exists the possibility—accepted by the San Francisco Police Department after a brief investigation—that he drank the lethal substance by mistake. Much more likely, though, in the opinion of those who knew him, was that he was driven to suicide by some agonizing crisis in his personal life.

But what could it have been? It seemed to several of his colleagues that he was not the same after he returned from service with the Red Cross during World War I. In eulogizing his lifelong friend, San Francisco-born Rabbi Rudolph Coffee noted that "the harrowing labors with the wounded and dying burned their impress on his soul, and he returned a disillusioned man." Meyer's health had been poor for three years before his death: he was hospitalized for several months in 1920 due to "stress and exhaustion," and then needed a lengthy vacation outside the city. Not long afterward he had operations for gall stones and appendicitis.

He was also suffering from a serious hearing loss, which some said contributed greatly to his despondency. Other congregants believed that he had had an inoperable brain tumor as well, the diagnosis of which led to his suicide. There was also a more disturbing rumor that circulated at the time: that he was culpable of sexual misconduct and unable to face the prospect of being found out. Although each of these theories has been advanced over the years by highly regarded temple leaders, no further evidence has been found to support any of them. It appears that he died by his own hand, but the immediate cause of Martin Meyer's final act continues to elude us.

IT WAS PROBABLY NOT A COINCIDENCE that the last article he wrote for the *Emanu-El* was an obituary, for the aged Rabbi Joseph Krauskopf who had passed away in Philadelphia. Only one week before his own death, Meyer extolled Krauskopf with phrases that also applied to himself:

> Few, if any, equaled him in incessant, self-sacrificing devotion to the duties which he had assumed. The secret of his outstanding success lay in this as well as in his unusual powers as an organizer and an advocate. The congregations to which he ministered...knew him as an indefatigable worker and much of the spirit of these communities as well as their successful institutional life can be credited to his labors.
>
> Hundreds of young men came under his personal influence...they are living memorials of his great work.
>
> As a preacher and teacher [he] was easily one of the best—not the scholar that Hirsch was, not the passionate orator that Stephen Wise is, but possessed of an eloquence all his own.

To this, though, must be added Meyer's prodigious ability to grasp the forces that would shape American Jewry in the future. Within his temple he cultivated the women and the youth, but he rarely conceived of his flock apart from the entire Jewish community. He reached out to the

Zionists, the Orthodox, and immigrants; he ministered to the isolated, the impoverished, even the imprisoned. He generated support for national Jewish organizations and overseas giving, both budding endeavors in this pivotal period.

Taking a broad and encompassing view, Martin Meyer offered a fresh, new definition of both Judaism and the temple. His vision was fully formed as early as 1920, but it would be no less compelling at the century's end.

chapter five

LOUIS NEWMAN
The Renascent Twenties

The forceful Louis I. Newman was chosen in the spring of 1924 to succeed the late Martin Meyer. Thirty years old, he was the youngest man ever selected as the spiritual leader of Temple Emanu-El. But he possessed the ability and the will to bring his mentor's dreams to fruition.

Although he had been ordained without attending a seminary, his career held as much promise as that of any young rabbi in America. "Tall, erect, and spare," he spoke with a dramatic delivery that made some think of Moses exhorting the ancient Israelites. He had spent five years at the Free Synagogue under Stephen Wise before becoming associate rabbi of Manhattan's large and wealthy Temple Israel in 1921. Two years later, a collection of his sermons was published, "typical illustrations of what is preached from month to month in the liberal Jewish pulpits across the country." Entitled *Anglo-Saxon and Jew*, the slim volume was widely noted for its strident, positive expression of Jewish identity in the face of anti-Semitism and assimilation. In July 1924, he was asked to deliver the invocation at the Democratic National Convention, held in Madison Square Garden.

Newman's scholarly reputation was also established early. In 1922, he completed his doctoral dissertation in Semitics, which was soon published as a monumental seven-hundred-page volume dedicated to Martin Meyer. Actually four distinct books, *Jewish Influence on Christian Reform*

Movements caused a controversy in academic circles. To be sure, it was attacked by academic giants such as George Foote Moore and Paul Radin, both of whom faulted the young man for his loose terminology and weak conceptual framework. They argued that a sixteenth-century Christian humanist's knowledge of Hebrew, say, hardly constituted the Jewish "influence" on the Reformation which Newman claimed. But even these critics had to applaud him "for bringing together so many hitherto scattered facts." His "valuable mine of material" was praised in the *Saturday Review* as "compilation and research unusual in this day of outlines."

Beyond all of this he was a man with a passionate love for the arts. He was a poet and a playwright, a lyricist and a literary critic. And just as Newman himself was more than a pastor, so he conceived of Judaism as more than a faith. His formative years in New York toward the end of the immigrant era, precisely the period in which Mordecai Kaplan developed his philosophy of "Judaism as a civilization," had vividly shown him the ethnic, cultural, social, and nationalist dimensions of his people, as well as the religious. His apprenticeship under Stephen Wise further deepened his understanding of *klal Yisrael*, the overall unity of the Jewish people. It was with this all-embracing definition of Jewish identity—in some respects even more developed than that of Martin Meyer—that he pursued interests ranging from architecture to Zionism. As he wrote in 1923, in a short piece entitled "On Being a Jew," "Men move in groups; hence I will accept my own group and, through it, make my little contribution to life. My group is the peer of all other groups; and even if it were not, I would strive to make it so. As it happens my group is the aristocracy of history."

Louis Newman assumed his duties at Emanu-El in August 1924, the month ground was broken for the new temple. He remained for six years before returning to New York, a period that may be termed the congregation's halcyon days. It was a time of artistic creativity, limitless prosperity, and unbounded optimism. The harsh struggles of the pioneers and the trauma of the earthquake belonged to earlier generations; no one yet knew that the years ahead would be marked by the Depression, the Holocaust, and bitter strife over Zionism. The mid- and late '20s was an interlude of almost magical qualities and, especially for those who were young then, one which came to an end all too soon.

RABBI LOUIS I. NEWMAN

NEWMAN HAD PLAYED AN IMPORTANT ROLE in the building of Temple Israel's new synagogue on the Upper West Side, an elegant house of worship with an ample adjoining building that included a small theater. In San Francisco he applied himself to the same task with his characteristic blend of intensity and imagination.

First he fought for the "temple house," advocated by Meyer and Bloch but by the fall of 1924 still far from approval by the board of directors. Influenced by Mordecai Kaplan on this matter as well, Newman wrote, "The Temple House movement with its basketball games, dramatics, dancing classes and social interests is a complete refutation of the idea that the Reform Temple is purely a theological institution."

He joked about rabbis wanting "a *shul* with a pool," as the synagogue-center was dubbed by the mid-'20s, but he was serious about the benefits to be derived from secular activities at the temple. He even went so far as to compare the symbiotic relationship between worship in the sanctuary and group activities in the temple house with the relationship between Judaism and Zionism: "The Temple House is a 'piece of Palestine' in the community wherein, it is hoped, religious interest will, and often does, flower."

Newman had to fight hard for this vision. He was opposed by powerful men such as Harold Zellerbach, soon to become the head of the giant paper company founded by his pioneer grandfather. President of the YMHA, he argued instead that the erection of a well-equipped, citywide community center would fill the social, cultural, and athletic needs of the city's Jews. In 1923, a survey done in San Francisco by the New York Bureau of Jewish Social Research had recommended a JCC; approval by a local study committee and the Federation came in 1925. In the opinion of Zellerbach, who would later become temple president, and several other prominent congregants, the temple house constituted needless duplication.* The tenacious rabbi carried the day, however, and the board approved a five-story temple house, including not only classrooms, offices, and a library, but a gymnasium and theatre as well. Seating around nine

---

*Zellerbach headed the JCC building fund campaign which, beginning in 1930, raised over $600,000. Dedicated in November 1933, the JCC is located on Presidio and California Streets, only half a mile east of Temple Emanu-El.

hundred, the Martin A. Meyer Auditorium in particular bore Newman's stamp. The sloping floor was his contribution—a feature he demanded in the main sanctuary as well—and he also insisted on a stage equipped with headlights, footlights, backdrops, a curtain, and dressing rooms.

Including the temple house, the price tag for the entire complex came to over $1,300,000—more than fifteen times the average cost for an American synagogue constructed in this period. With the help of the able businessman Henry Mayer, president of the congregation from 1922 to 1927, Newman undertook the responsibility of raising the funds. Because they knew that future operating expenses would be high, they rejected the idea of a mortgage; the new buildings would be paid for in cash. Since $450,000 was on hand, mostly the proceeds from the sale of the Sutter Street temple, roughly $850,000 had to be solicited.

From the sale of seats in the new sanctuary, $250,000 was expected. In effect, members purchased the right to occupy the same seats each year

THE LAKE STREET TEMPLE UNDER CONSTRUCTION, 1923

(upon payment of annual dues, of course), just as their grandparents had in 1866. In the old synagogue, 543 seats were "owned" by congregants in 1924; Mayer proposed to buy them back for the amount at which they were originally sold, up to $225. This cost the temple almost $100,000, but it now offered for sale all 1,672 seats in the new house of worship at prices as high as $850. Two-thirds of the sanctuary was quickly subscribed, yielding nearly $350,000 or a net profit of approximately a quarter of a million dollars.

The status-conscious finance committee established sixteen different categories of seats in a chart which precisely reflected the socioeconomic stratification of the membership. Rows 2 to 11 were considered the most desirable, but even within this choice section, designated AA, a seat on the aisle cost $850 while one in the middle of the row could be had for $750. At Row 15, the beginning of Class B, the price fell sharply to $450 and declined every few rows thereafter. The last four rows on the main floor went for $75 a chair; the back rows in the balcony were only $50.

In this manner, less than a quarter of the membership accounted for more than half the revenue. But the temple would be required to lean even more heavily on the wealthier families, since $600,000 was needed even after the sale of seats.

A special meeting was held on December 9, 1924, to collect pledges toward this vast amount. After an impassioned address by Newman, Marcus Sloss, acting as chairman, asked to hear the donations of those present. A contagious feeling of pride swept through the packed gathering on Sutter Street and the response of the membership was tremendous. Over $320,000 was promised that evening alone, to which $45,000 was added within the next two weeks. The remaining quarter of a million dollars came in steadily over the following four years, so that the new temple was not only completed but also free of debt well before the onset of the Depression.*

A published list of the donors of December 9 reveals contributions from 260 families, of which forty-eight pledged $2,500 or more. These

---

*Other congregations were not so fortunate. In 1930, Temple Sholom of Chicago erected an imposing synagogue of about the same size—and cost—as Emanu-El, but took out a mortgage of $700,000. Within a few years it nearly went bankrupt because of the crushing debt.

leading families, nearly all of them with pioneer roots, accounted for $234,000, more than two-thirds of the money raised.*

Later that winter, on a rainy Washington's Birthday, the cornerstone was laid by President Mayer with the same trowel used for the Sutter Street cornerstone in 1864. Newman, who in half a year at Emanu-El had seen virtually all of his proposals for the new temple accepted, delivered an eloquent address in which he said, "Here shall stand one of the rarest buildings in all the land."

HIS PREDICTION CAME TRUE on the weekend of April 16, 1926, exactly twenty years after the earthquake, with the dedication of the new sanctuary. The elaborate exercises included speeches by Mayor James Rolph; the president of Stanford University, Ray Lyman Wilbur; local Christian clergymen; and a dozen rabbis from throughout the West. The dignitaries and the public were awed by the house of worship, designed primarily by Arthur Brown Jr. in the prime of a sterling career that included San Francisco's splendid, domed City Hall in 1915. At that time he had also served as associate architect of the Panama-Pacific Exposition. In the 1930s he would design the War Memorial Opera House and, with two others, the San Francisco–Oakland Bay Bridge.** The well-educated, well-traveled Brown was a non-Jew who nevertheless chose the medium of the synagogue to express many of his personal religious ideas.

After considering both cut granite and marble as possible materials, the building committee finally chose steel and concrete, for once bowing to economic considerations. The notion of an interior of great, grey walls soon led Brown to his main motif—an imposing dome set on four enormous arches. As he wrote several months after the dedication,

*The largest contributors—at $20,000—were E. S. Heller and Sidney Ehrman. Marcus Koshland gave $15,000; Jacob Stern and Frances Hellman, $10,000 each. Fannie Haas pledged $7,500 and sixteen families followed with gifts of $5,000.

**Brown, who died in 1957 at the age of eighty-three, also had to his credit the Hoover Library at Stanford; Cowell Hospital and the Library Annex on the campus of the University of California, Berkeley; Coit Tower and the Federal Building in San Francisco; and the mammoth Department of Labor Building in Washington, D.C. He also designed the Pasadena City Hall, the domed tower of which became a symbol of the Southland, popularized in the mass media.

THE LAKE STREET TEMPLE NEARING COMPLETION

Of all the architectural forms yet imagined by the mind of man, the dome is, I feel very strongly, the most superb, the most noble and most deeply inspiring. There are other forms of great and imposing beauty, Gothic spires, Roman basilicas, great temples, but the dome surpasses them all in impressive nobility and beauty. It is most appropriately used when men wish to give material form to most exalted sentiments.

He was influenced by St. Peter's Cathedral as well as the Dome Church which houses the tomb of Napoleon at the Invalides in Paris. But his clearest model was Hagia Sophia in Constantinople, the church built during Justinian's reign and considered the masterpiece of the Byzantine Age. Like the sixth-century shrine, Emanu-El's dome appears to float, "a great, golden bubble, lofty, soaring in the sky," as one observer wrote in 1926. This effect, realized for the first time in Hagia Sophia, is the result of spherical triangles, called pendentives, which connect the square formed by the arches to the circular rim of the dome. The appearance of buoyancy in both structures is further provided by closely spaced windows around the entire base.

The exterior of the dome—at 150 feet almost as high as Hagia Sophia—was surfaced in tile described by Rabbi Newman as "autumn red." Against the light blue California sky it appears at times earth-colored, at times a deep gold.

The symbol of the dome, conveying a sense of unity, also has its place in the variegated world of synagogue architecture. Undoubtedly Brown was aware of the outstanding domed temples built in the latter half of the nineteenth century in such cities as Florence, Berlin, and Nuremberg. In the early 1920s a number of archaeological discoveries pointed to its use in ancient Palestine, causing Lewis Mumford to advocate its "consistent" adoption in America in order to create a coherent architectural style which would give the stamp of Judaism to a synagogue, as plainly as the baroque gives the stamp of the Jesuit order to a church.

This was the intention of Alfred Alshuler, whose study of an excavation in Tiberias gave him the inspiration for the domed Isaiah Temple of Chicago, completed in 1924. That year also saw the erection of Cleveland's spectacular Tifereth Israel (soon thereafter to be known simply as "the Temple"), with a hemispheric dome of almost the same proportions as Emanu-El.

But these Midwestern synagogues, as well as their European precursors, were lavishly decorated in the Moorish style. Isaiah's dome, for

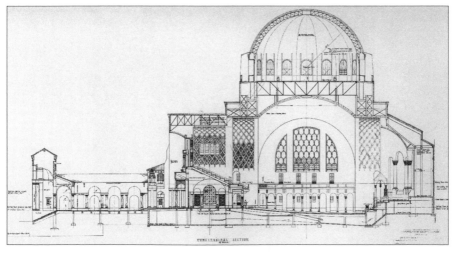

THE LAKE STREET TEMPLE

THE LAKE STREET TEMPLE, 1925

TEMPLE COURTYARD AND ENTRANCE TO THE
MAIN SANCTUARY VIEWED FROM LAKE STREET

example, rests on an octagonal enclosure and is topped by a Mohammedan minaret. Emanu-El, on the other hand, with its four arches and relative lack of adornment, effects a feeling of bold simplicity again reminiscent of Hagia Sophia.

Mumford was likewise impressed by the clean-cut, almost geometrical relationship of the dome to the subordinate cubical masses of the temple house and offices, the more utilitarian requirements of the complex. He singled out the "intelligent" design of the San Francisco structure and its Byzantine forerunner to prove the maxim that "everything in architecture is either a cube or an egg." The cloistered courtyard of the temple group, with its fountain and grandiose portal, was the ingenious idea not only of Brown but also his associates, John Bakewell and Sylvain Schnaittacher, an Emanu-El congregant. This atrium, which opens onto both the sanctuary and the temple house, was a feature not only of Byzantine architecture but of Solomon's temple as well. It has also proved to be highly practical. Worshippers gather in the courtyard before services, prepared for prayer by its mood of seclusion. In the patio one is struck by the intricate stone sculpture above the temple's entrance—a lion-headed theme. This was the work of Edgar Walter, the son of Jewish pioneers, and Robert Howard.

If the ancient world provided the main motifs, the new temple was also distinctly Californian. The open-air courtyard, with its low, cloistered, russet-roofed walls, brings to mind a Spanish mission. A consultant on the project was Brown's teacher, the eminent Bernard Maybeck, and his contribution may be felt in this seemingly effortless blending of indoor and outdoor spaces.

Brown and his associates anticipated the most common criticism of the complex: the cold, almost icy feeling engendered by the sparse interior of the immense sanctuary. Byzantine columns of antique marble were employed along the sides of the hall, supporting the balconies, but the soaring walls and ceiling—sweeping curves of colorless concrete—remained unbroken by any decoration. Even the six giant chandeliers appeared insignificant in so vast a chamber.

But this stark rendering—exaggerated further because of the contrast with the bright blue, gold, and red of the vestibule ceiling—was precisely Brown's intention. As Newman later explained,

There is a rugged and potent barbaric splendor in the edifice which is achieved with an almost too great simplicity of decoration. Whether fresco work or medallions on the mighty arches would improve the character of the auditorium is as yet an open question. The chief impression of the beholder is of vast and almost primitive power. Thus the heroic mood of the ancient Hebrew warrior is fused with the mysticism and rationalism of the modern Jewish worshipper.

Harris Allen, editor of the *Pacific Coast Architect*, concurred. He wrote of "a great quiet auditorium, which is so impressive as to be almost startling. The effect…is that of utmost dignity, power, peace. I cannot agree with any suggestions for the decoration of these walls. Where should it begin? Where end?"

The austere design of the interior serves to focus attention on the ark, for which Brown constructed a large, pyramid-topped stone canopy, or ciborium, held in place by four columns of the same dark marble used along the sides of the room. The ark itself, in the form of a nine-foot-high jewel box, was donated to the congregation in February 1927 by the three children of the late Marcus Koshland. Among the most noted Torah chests extant, this three-thousand-pound masterwork is not attached to a wall of the synagogue but stands freely, as did the ark which the ancient Israelites carried in the desert. The thick bronze doors and sides of the case wear the banners of the twelve tribes of Israel, along with dozens of

THE LAKE STREET TEMPLE. LEFT: INTERIOR OF THE MAIN
SANCTUARY. RIGHT: THE CIBORIUM AND ARK

enameled rubies and sapphires. Inside the ark are delicately executed biblical scenes in gesso plaster. The California artists George Dennison and Frank Ingerson studied biblical specifications for three months before beginning a year's work on the project in London, where a centuries-old foundry on the Thames was selected. Their finished product created a sensation in British art circles before it was shipped to San Francisco.

Behind the ciborium, with its resplendent ark, a curved stone grille conceals the entire console of the organ, a four-manual Skinner with more than five thousand pipes. Ernest Skinner himself spent several weeks in San Francisco to supervise, with Cantor Rinder, the nearly perfect placing of this extraordinary instrument which can even simulate the sound of the shofar.

The temple house, in large measure the work of Schnaittacher—who did not live to see its completion—was dedicated in January 1927. Later that year, the American Institute of Architects selected Temple Emanu-El as the finest piece of architecture in Northern California. The awards committee honored it as "a glorious building…beautifully planned and modeled…realizing to the highest degree the expression of its religious character."

THE NEW TEMPLE AND NEWMAN'S DYNAMISM resulted in a near doubling of the membership in the late 1920s. From 565 families at the beginning of 1924, the rolls jumped to 710 one year later, 890 at the end of 1926, and over a thousand by the last year of the decade. In accord with the plan put forth by Newman's predecessor, the temple also included roughly two hundred "associates" by 1929. These were less well-off families paying but forty dollars a year, for which they could enroll their children in the Sunday school, subscribe to the bulletin, use the temple house facilities, and receive two seats for the additional High Holiday services, now held in the Martin Meyer Auditorium. Newman remarked in 1930 that five thousand people were in some way affiliated with the congregation. In 1925, before the new temple was completed, a single Kol Nidre service was held at the Civic Auditorium. Drawing over eight thousand people, it was hailed as one of the largest worship experiences in American history. Like several other services in this period, it was broadcast throughout Northern California.

Great strides were being taken toward Newman's goal of a vibrant, multifaceted Jewish community revolving around the synagogue. Soon after his arrival he inaugurated the *Temple Chronicle*, an attractive weekly bulletin of activities which often included an excerpt from one of his sermons. Only four pages, it proved highly effective, particularly after April 1926, when the board of directors voted unanimously to cease all advertising in the *Emanu-El.**

The early volumes of the *Temple Chronicle* charted the progress of an exciting endeavor, the Temple Players, which involved many of the congregation's most energetic young people. This drama group was formed, at Newman's urging, by Paul Bissinger, a student of acting at Stanford, who served as director. Conrad Kahn (son of Julius and Florence Prag Kahn, both members of Congress), Charles Levison (later Lane), and Mortimer Fleishhacker Jr. were also active in the popular club; there the young Fleishhacker met his future wife, Janet Choynski (granddaughter of the pioneer journalist). In the late 1920s, the Players presented five full-length plays in the Meyer Auditorium.

Their most successful effort by far was the production of S. An-Ski's *The Dybbuk*, which attracted more than eight thousand people to a two-week run in the fall of 1928. For this unusual piece of theater—a story of exorcism drawn from medieval Jewish folklore—the lionized Nahum Zemach was engaged as the director. He had founded the celebrated Habima troupe in Moscow during the revolution but, with his troupe, left the Soviet Union in 1926 due to its repression of Jewish culture.

At Emanu-El, with Cantor Rinder as his interpreter, Zemach rehearsed with the fifty-five-member cast for two long months. Critics were unanimous in their praise of the detailed sets, the eerie lighting, and the inspired acting, particularly of Carolyn Anspacher in the role of Leah, the girl possessed by the soul of her dead lover.

But *The Dybbuk* meant much more than the artistic success reported in the press. With its lay participation, its thoroughly Jewish theme, and

---

*A feud had developed between the aging A. W. Voorsanger, still the journal's editor, and Newman. Evidently, the volatile rabbi was angered when the paper, on its own, solicited his congregants for an ad congratulating the temple on its new edifice. Newman, who had been a contributing editor of the *Emanu-El*, resigned his post and devoted all of his journalistic talents to the *Temple Chronicle*.

CAROLYN ANSPACHER TAKES CENTER STAGE IN THE
TEMPLE PLAYERS' PERFORMANCE OF *THE DYBBUK*, 1928

its full use of the new facility, it demonstrated more than any other event in the 1920s the enormous potential of the temple house concept.

The youth groups, too, benefited greatly from the increased membership and the move to Lake Street. Meeting on Sunday evenings, the Pathfinders often attracted college students from the University of California, who would spend the night at their parents' house and then take the ferry back to Berkeley for Monday morning classes. They enjoyed themselves over milkshakes at Simpson's, on Second and Clement, but their meetings—at which prominent community leaders often spoke—were serious affairs; procedure was governed by Robert's Rules of Order and no one could enter without a jacket and tie. These young men also served the temple as teachers in the religious school, High Holiday ushers, stagehands, and countless other roles. The Pathfinders had been a select society, choosing its members in the manner of a college fraternity, but Newman persuaded its leaders to open the club to any interested youth.

The rabbi's well-liked wife, Lucille, meanwhile formed the female counterpart of the Pathfinders—the Reviewers—which was highly successful during her husband's tenure in San Francisco.

The Boy Scout troop sponsored by the temple was headed by the legendary "Pie" Myer, who arrived in 1922 and remained for more than forty years. His Troop 17 was known as the "Eagle Machine" because of the high number of its scouts who reached that coveted level. The two-week camping trips this oil company executive ran were rigorous, but he was even more demanding as a swimming instructor; training his boys at the spacious Sutro Baths, he produced many of the city's outstanding aquatic athletes.

Myer, who was also the advisor of an East Bay Boy Scout troop, interviewed not only all potential members but their parents as well. When the father of one boy in Troop 17 mentioned half-jokingly that Myer himself was not wearing regulation socks, the scoutmaster was so deeply offended that he refused to speak to the man for the next ten years.

Meetings were held in the temple gymnasium on Friday evenings, when the pressures of school were farthest from the boys' minds. The rabbi naturally fought hard to move Troop 17 away from direct competition with services, but Newman had finally met his match. Neither he nor any of his successors could prevail over "Pie" Myer.

The religious school did not enjoy the numerical growth of the temple as a whole, but the new complex, which included thirty classrooms, added much to Sunday mornings. Drama was especially popular, and several plays a year were performed by students in the Meyer Auditorium and reviewed in the *Scroll*. Elaborate festival celebrations, such as a pageant for Sukkot, were held in the temple court.

Newman emphasized Hebrew more than any of his predecessors, raising its status from that of an elective to a major part of the curriculum in each of the school's twenty-four classes. By the end of the decade each student received at least one-half hour weekly of instruction in the language of the Bible—one-third of the total class time.

In the summer of 1929, the temple engaged Rabbi Melbourne Harris to supervise the school. With the title of Director of Religious Education and Activities, the freshly ordained Oaklander became the first assistant rabbi of Emanu-El since the late 1880s, when Jacob Voorsanger served under Elkan Cohn. Newman continued to teach the confirmation class, which now numbered over fifty high school sophomores annually.

But despite a professional director, a large, well-equipped physical plant, and an array of extracurricular activities, the school had difficulty competing with "the California out of doors," in Newman's words. The rate of absenteeism, about 25 percent, was more than twice that of the years immediately following World War I. Worse was the fact that roughly half the members' children were not even enrolled. As capable a woman as Hattie Sloss, head of the Sunday school committee in the late '20s, was frustrated in her attempts to motivate the parents to take a greater interest in Jewish education. "Nothing in this world is perfect," she wrote in one annual report, "and neither is our school."

While discipline in the temple's religious school has been a problem in every era, the children of the late 1920s may have been the rowdiest of all. Marshall Kuhn, later a distinguished Jewish educator both at Emanu-El and elsewhere, remembered his own Sunday school experience during the Newman years as "just horrible." He spoke of the time a model Passover seder held in the gymnasium suddenly erupted into a raucous food fight. A mortified Cantor Rinder summarily dismissed the hundreds of children who were in the room.

Louis Heilbron, who like Kuhn would also serve as principal of the religious school, began teaching at Emanu-El as a nineteen-year-old college sophomore in 1926. He recalls the great emphasis placed on "social life" in those days, noting that many of the older girls came to Sunday school wearing the orchids or gardenias their boyfriends had given them Saturday night: "I'm not sure it was religious fervor that brought them to religious school," he said. "It was rather to talk over what happened the night before."

UNLIKE VOORSANGER, who praised the hardy spirit of his flock at the rededication of the Sutter Street temple, Newman wondered aloud whether his generation was worthy of its pioneer forebears. For the 1920s had brought a revolution in manners and morals which troubled the somewhat straitlaced rabbi. He lashed out in his sermons at what he termed "the new paganism"—the obsession with jazz, sports, alcohol, and above all sexuality—which he perceived in those only a few years younger than himself.

Unparalleled prosperity and advances in technology powered this new way of life, but Newman preferred to attack its intellectual antecedents. His favorite foe was Freud, who had "unloosed a veritable Pandora's box of demons." By replacing "I ought" with "I wish," according to Newman, the author of *Beyond the Pleasure Principle* had sanctioned "moral laxity" and "fatalistic animalism." "Psychoanalysis has become God," he thundered from the pulpit, "and Freud its prophet." Newman—the father of three sons—was a staunch defender of the institutions of marriage and the nuclear family, both under heavy attack in this period. Like Stephen Wise, his talks before young people in particular stressed fidelity for husband and wife and chastity for the unmarried. In 1927 both rabbis entered into a series of debates against Judge Ben Lindsey of Denver, the nationally known proponent of birth control and divorce by mutual consent. "Judge Lindsey," stated Newman, "dismisses the need for continence too lightly."

In contrast to his predecessor, Newman could not tolerate the rapidly changing role of women in this turbulent decade. He blamed "the young girl for the troublesomeness of the new youth," objecting not only to her short skirts and smoking in public but also to "the new type of woman who believes that a career with complete financial independence is preferable to the life of the home and the family."

He felt that balmy California, with its fads and cults, was particularly vulnerable to the new social order and even voiced fears that "nature worship" might one day replace religion. In his fifth anniversary sermon at Emanu-El he concluded that "Jewry, like other religious groups...is being overborne by the threat of prosperous, ease-loving, pagan pleasure-seeking."

At the same time he fought against fundamentalism, which was also gaining ground in the 1920s. He led the opposition to the Miller Bill, which would have granted students release time from public schools for religious education. Likening it to Bible-reading in the classroom and to the attack on the teaching of evolution, he upheld the principle of separation of church and state in a widely circulated pamphlet, *The Sectarian Invasion of Our Public Schools*. Along with Rabbi Nieto and state assemblyman Edgar C. Levy (an Emanu-El congregant who later became Speaker of the lower chamber), Newman lobbied against the bill in Sacramento and was instrumental in its ultimate defeat.

Even something as seemingly harmless as release time meant that on some level children would be segregated in the public schools according to faith, a proposition Newman could not accept. As he testified before the California assembly, "This may be the age of hysteria, as the advocates of the Miller Bill argue, but we will add to it still another confusing and discordant element, if we pass [it]."

In July 1925, only three months after the defeat of the Miller Bill, the Scopes Monkey Trial opened in Tennessee. Newman, alarmed at the strength of the anti-evolutionist movement, publicly repudiated its leader, the three-time presidential candidate William Jennings Bryan. In an open letter to Middle America's folk hero, published in the local press, the rabbi turned Bryan's famous campaign slogan around, writing, "You shall not crucify mankind upon a cross of ignorance." Where Christian fundamentalism crossed the line into anti-Semitism, as it did on many occasions in the 1920s, Newman was quick to retaliate. In 1927, taking another cue from Rabbi Wise, he joined the nationwide protest against Cecil B. de Mille's inflammatory film, *King of Kings*. Two years later he condemned the American tour of the Freiburg Passion Play, which portrayed Jews as Christ-killers.

STRONG STANDS SUCH AS THESE were applauded by nearly every Emanu-El congregant, but on other issues—when he made the Jewish people as a whole his greatest priority—his was the minority opinion at the temple. He was rigid in his refusal to perform intermarriage, for example, leaving that pastoral duty to Cantor Rinder, who had married Jew to non-Jew during the rabbinate of Martin Meyer. But Newman went beyond his predecessor in assailing intermarriage both in print and from the pulpit. "True liberalism," he contended, "does not encourage the breakdown and deliberate disintegration of historic peoples." This principle, so often and loudly articulated, cost him the support and friendship of a number of his most prominent congregants, among them Louis Bloch, president of the temple in 1927, whose daughter married a non-Jew without the rabbi's blessing.

Others objected to his making Hebrew a requirement in the religious school and his plans for instruction three days a week rather than merely Sunday mornings. As Harold Zellerbach later remarked icily, "Newman would have been better off at a Conservative synagogue. Here we're Reform, you know."

But it was on the question of Zionism that he was most at odds with the membership. Again he embraced Meyer's position, but voiced it much

more stridently. His denunciation of the Reform movement's disapproval
of Jewish nationalism was merciless, as illustrated by the following sermon, delivered at the commencement of Stephen Wise's Jewish Institute
of Religion and printed in the *Temple Chronicle*:

> The most flagrant blunder of Reform Judaism is its opposition to
> Zionism. If it continues to be "dead against" Zionism it will soon be
> entirely dead. [Reform Judaism] lives off the profits of Zionism, but it
> refuses to acknowledge its indebtedness. It assumes to have a mission
> but excommunicates any dissenter who seeks to fulfill the mission by
> championing unpopular political or economic causes. Fifty years after
> these causes are vindicated, Reform Jews claim credit for the heroism of
> the iconoclasts they repudiated in the hour of danger. The only good
> radical in the eyes of a Reform Jew is a dead Jew.

Newman, who spoke throughout the West on behalf of the United
Palestine Appeal, was known as a fierce nationalist even in Zionist circles. He was the first Reform rabbi to endorse Vladimir Jabotinsky's
militant Revisionism which called for a Jewish state on both sides of the
Jordan River.

Like Jabotinsky, Newman was impatient with the sluggish pace of the
Zionist movement in the '20s, both in Palestine and America. Particularly after the Arab riots of 1929, he came into direct conflict with the
Jewish Agency; he blamed the bloody disorders on the "colossal blunders" of the Weizmann administration, by which he meant negligence,
corruption, and weakness toward Great Britain.

He soon became one of the most outspoken critics of Louis Lipsky,
Weizmann's lieutenant who had headed the Zionist Organization of
America since 1921. Joining forces with the Brandeis-Mack faction,
which had been on the sidelines through most of the decade, Newman
publicly called for Lipsky's resignation:

> The catch phrases of the last ten years have spelled tragedy and disas-
> ter. The hour calls for calm, self-sacrificing statesmanship. We must
> turn a new page in American Zionism. We must set our house in order.
> American Zionism must not destroy itself, for our failure will be
> Jewry's failure and we will rightly be accused of having deserted our
> world-enjoined duties to Palestine.

Along with Julian Mack, Stephen Wise, Jacob de Haas, and others, Newman succeeded in effecting a complete restructuring of the ZOA in June 1930. At the tumultuous conference held in Cleveland that month he was named to the eighteen-member national executive committee charged with running the organization.

Newman's loudly proclaimed ideology was not the only source of friction between the rabbi and congregation, however. It was felt that he was standoffish—that, preoccupied with the great issues of the day, he had little time for personal interaction. Often he was so deep in thought that he would pass acquaintances on the street without even acknowledging them.

Still, the persistent young man was deeply respected by the membership, his critics included. His exhilarating sermons—and he excelled at nothing more than at oratory—were well attended even in this "pagan" age. In a sense, most of the congregants were grateful for his critique of their assimilated, "pleasure-loving" lifestyle. He served as their conscience in the era of the bootleggers and flappers, a role which he relished as well.

But at the end of 1929, Newman handed in his resignation, effective the following summer, to accept the offer of Temple Rodeph Sholom, on New York's Upper West Side near Central Park. He chose to return to the lively neighborhood of apartment houses and brownstones—dense with Jewish intellectuals—in which he had thrived in his twenties as a graduate student at Columbia, a rabbinic intern at the Free Synagogue, and a pulpit rabbi at Temple Israel. At the large and active Rodeph Sholom, which opened a magnificent synagogue-center only months before his arrival, he would remain for forty-two years until his death in 1972. As had been true of Stephen Wise's tenure in Portland, Newman's half decade in the "Far West," as he put it, would turn out to be a relatively brief interlude in a long career centered in Manhattan.

To those who were closest to him, his decision hardly came as a surprise. They knew that he considered New York "the center of centers," and San Francisco a mere province. He had made the long cross-country train trip several times during his tenure at Emanu-El, always conveying a glowing description of "the amazing city." In California he missed the Broadway shows, a good newspaper, Stephen Wise, and a thousand other things. As Rose Rinder remembered with a smile, Newman never felt that he would remain permanently in the West. When, shortly after his arrival in San Francisco, he went with her husband to buy a piano for his growing family, he first asked the salesman the price of shipping it to New York.

The president of the congregation, Samuel Dinkelspiel, tried desperately to convince Newman to stay. He closeted himself with the rabbi for many hours, but to no avail. It was almost as if he knew that Newman's departure would signal the end of the temple's golden years.

c h a p t e r   s i x

REUBEN RINDER

Music and Humanity

T he 1920s was also the decade in which Cantor Rinder came into
his own as a force in the world of Jewish music. He was himself
a composer and a performer, but his greatness lay in his impact on others.
His penetrating mind discerned musical genius; his warm personality
nurtured it; his generous friends financed it. Until his death in 1966,
Rinder the catalyst matched prodigies with patrons. No individual in the
twentieth century did more to enrich the music of the synagogue.

Yet there are those who remember him primarily as a pastor. He served
as the congregation's spiritual leader while Meyer was in France at the
end of World War I. After the rabbi's death, in 1923, he undertook the
pastoral duties of the temple for more than a year until Newman's arrival.
But even when both the rabbi and assistant rabbi were in residence, it was
frequently the cantor upon whom the congregants called to perform marriages and funerals, to counsel the troubled and visit the housebound.

His exceptionally long tenure—more than half a century of service at
Emanu-El—accounted in large measure for his being asked to perform
rabbinical functions. He had known as small children many of those he
later married; he had been close for decades to many of those he buried.
The rabbis, towering figures though they were, came and went. Rinder
remained, seemingly forever, as the presence signifying continuity.

No one could have been better suited for this role. Dubbed "Mr. Chips"
in his later years, this gentle, silver-haired man—a bit absent-minded—

exerted a comforting, almost healing influence on those with whom he came in contact, from disruptive schoolchildren to the ailing elderly. Regarding Albert Schweitzer, whose life he had studied, Rinder once noted that "the peculiar sensitivity which marks the musician at the same time arouses within him the deepest sympathy with all human experience," a tribute which fits the kindly cantor himself. The rabbis of Emanu-El were respected; Rinder was beloved.

IN THE MINDS OF THE CONGREGANTS, the year's cycle of Jewish holidays was bound up inextricably with him. He not only appeared on the *bimah* for fifty-three years, but the receptions at his home—his wife Rowie's annual Passover seders and break-the-fast suppers following Yom Kippur—became a tradition as well.

From 1928 to 1940, he presented a concert of Jewish music each Hanukah at the Washington Street mansion of Marcus Koshland's widow, Cora. Hundreds of her friends, including many non-Jews, would gather around the fountain in the marble hall of their thirty-room residence, a replica of the Petit Trianon in Versailles. The afternoon of liturgical and folk music would end with the kindling of scores of menorahs, flooding the house with light. Then refreshments would be served, usually hot spiced wine.

Mrs. Koshland would sponsor similar events on Sukkot and at other times during the year as well. Often the Emanu-El choir, with soloists such as Dorothy Warenskold and Leona Gordon, would be present. The temple organist, Wallace Sabin, and later Ludwig Altman, who succeeded him in 1937, would play the ample organ which Mrs. Koshland had installed for these occasions, an instrument moved to the Meyer Auditorium following her death.

On an even grander scale were the annual musical events which Rinder held at the temple beginning in 1922. Open to the public, free of charge, were performances of Handel's *Judas Maccabaeus*, *Israel in Egypt*, and *Esther*; Mendelssohn's *Elijah*, *Athalie*, and *Hymn of Praise*; Gaul's *Ruth*; and many others. These oratorios and cantatas were often performed by an ensemble from the San Francisco Symphony and a chorus, directed by Rinder, of about a hundred voices, the Emanu-El choir joining that of

CANTOR REUBEN R. RINDER

Stanford, the University of California, or San Francisco State College. Soloists included such well-known personalities as Nelson Eddy. The temple itself sponsored these concerts. During the Depression they were no longer presented annually but every few years; yet even then the leading families, particularly the Koshlands, added their own gifts to the temple's funds, insuring the splendid quality of these affairs. Honegger's *King David*, which was performed at Emanu-El in 1949 and 1952, was originally presented twice in the 1930s at the War Memorial Opera House, where Alfred Hertz, director of the San Francisco Symphony Orchestra since 1915, featured violin solos by the orchestra's concertmaster and Rinder's friend, Naoum Blinder. But it was the cantor himself, as narrator, who provided "the most thrilling episode," in the opinion of one reviewer, "an extraordinary example of musical declamation that had both intonation and rhythm and tremendous dramatic power."

EARLY IN HIS CAREER Rinder was preoccupied with the fact that nearly all the great religious music of Europe and America had been written for the church and not the synagogue. Of course, he admired the work of his illustrious predecessor, Edward Stark. But he was also certain that the poetic grandeur of the Hebrew prayers, as well as the vast body of traditional Jewish folk music, could be even more effectively utilized in the modern synagogue service. A conscious effort would have to be made, however, in order to turn creative musical minds toward liturgy. "American Israel," he lamented, "contents itself with a meagre musical output." He would use all the resources at his command to produce "a Jewish Palestrina."

His own liturgical output includes a number of hymns (such as "Thou Ever Present Friend," "As Pants the Heart," and "Hymn to Peace") performed frequently in the temple. Also, he set to music the threefold benediction which often closes the Reform service as well as that of several Christian denominations. But his most widely heard work by far is his arrangement of Kol Nidre, eventually adopted by several hundred American congregations. This familiar prayer, ushering in the Eve of Yom Kippur, had been eliminated from the Reform liturgy in the late nineteenth century. After his arrival in 1913, Rinder reintroduced it at Emanu-El with Rabbi Meyer's full approval. The cantor's own 1925 arrangement speeded its acceptance throughout the country, and in 1937 it was broadcast nationally on NBC radio.

For the publication of his Kol Nidre he was willing to remove the words which the early Reformers had feared would offend gentile ears: "Forgive us for all the false vows we have vowed." For despite his *shtetl* upbringing and traditional training, he had little difficulty adjusting either to Reform liturgy or theology.

But he felt that the *music* of the Reform service—much of it having been written by those with weak ties to the Jewish past—would have to be enhanced. In 1927, he founded the Society for the Advancement of Synagogue Music with the idea of awarding a prize for the best interpretation of the rhymed hymn which concludes the Sabbath and festival services—the spirited "Adon Olam." Announcements of the contest were placed in journals throughout the world and although the cash award was only $500, no fewer than ninety entries were received.*

On the advisory board of the society sat America's foremost Jewish composer, Ernest Bloch, who lived in San Francisco from 1925 to 1930. Rinder had been instrumental in bringing the great man to the Bay Area, and he would play a central role in Bloch's career during its most fertile years.

It was on a train trip east that the cantor decided, "on the spur of the moment," according to his wife, to stop in Cleveland and meet Bloch, the Swiss immigrant who directed that city's Institute of Music. Bloch was already world famous, having composed in Europe such major works as his Symphony in C-sharp Minor, *Shelomo*, the *Israel Symphony*, and the opera *Macbeth*. But he admitted Rinder immediately, ahead of a long line of people waiting to see him, with the greeting, "Anyone coming from San Francisco has priority over anyone else."

Rinder informed Bloch that a director was being sought for the recently chartered San Francisco Conservatory of Music, supported in large part by the Emanu-El elite. Unhappy in Ohio, and longing to live in the city about which he had heard so much, the forty-four-year-old composer

---

*The panel of three judges, consisting of the musicologist Albert Elkus, the son of a pioneer Jewish family; Alexander Fried, a local music critic; and Cantor Joseph Rabinowitz, Rinder's counterpart at Congregation Beth Israel, conferred the first prize on the French composer E. Bonnal.

ERNEST BLOCH

responded enthusiastically. Rinder, upon his return, spoke to the school's co-founders, Ada Clement and Lilian Hodghead, who soon traveled to Cleveland themselves and convinced Bloch to teach at the conservatory in the summer of 1924. At the end of the following year, he became the school's director at an annual salary of $20,000.

Although Bloch was frustrated when plans to merge the conservatory with the University of California fell through, his five years in the West constituted a rare period of contentment in a life otherwise marked by deep ruts of hypochondria and depression. As he wrote to Albert Elkus in 1927, "I have felt around me, in Frisco, an atmosphere of kindness, friendship, good camaraderie which have gone to my heart. Like a desiccated plant—and this is what I was when I came—I feel life come back again to me, as if fresh, good, healthy water was uplifting me."

His professional life flowered as well. In addition to teaching a series of popular courses at the conservatory, which he would head for almost the entirety of his stay, he wrote some of the most important works of his career in the Bay Area. His *Four Episodes for Chamber Orchestra*, influenced by his frequent visits to San Francisco's Chinese Theatre, won the first prize of the 1927 New York Chamber Society competition.

The symphony *Helvetia*, an ode to his native land and its people, was completed in 1929 and named the co-winner of the Victor Company Symphonic Contest.

But the most enduring work of his San Francisco period was his *America: An Epic Rhapsody*. It had been germinating in his mind from the day in 1916 that he had landed in New York, but he needed a decade to "absorb America," which had seemed to him "like another planet." For the sweeping tribute he appropriated a wide range of folk music—Indian songs, spirituals, tunes of the Old South, sea chanteys, and jazz—which he unified organically with his own simple, powerful "Anthem." This composition was unanimously chosen by a five-judge panel (Leopold Stokowski, Serge Koussevitsky, Walter Damrosch, Alfred Hertz, and Frederick Stock) as the winner of yet another contest, that sponsored by the magazine *Musical America*. At the end of 1928 it was performed in seven cities and in San Francisco twelve thousand people packed Exposition Auditorium to hear it. Yet a number of critics ridiculed the piece, and there were even those who wondered if a foreign-born Jew ought to be writing American music. For Alexander Fried, however, Bloch had produced "the greatest symphonic work thus far written in this country."

Rinder, meanwhile, sought to interest him in composing a service for the synagogue. Yet Bloch was reluctant to do so. Several of his works had been on Jewish themes, and even a kind reviewer of *America* felt compelled to write that "the Indians in the symphony dance with Hasidic feet." But a religious service was another matter. He had had little in the way of Jewish education and his deepest convictions were universalist. Bloch's oft-quoted lines of 1916 reflect the Jewish component of his work:

> It is the Hebrew spirit that interests me—the complex, ardent, agitated soul that vibrates for me in the Bible; the vigor and ingenuousness of the Patriarchs, the violence that finds expression in the books of the Prophets, the burning love of justice, the desperation of the preachers of Jerusalem, the sorrow and grandeur of the book of Job, the sensuality of the Song of Songs. All this is in us, all this is in me, and is the better part of me. This is what I seek to feel within me and to translate in my music—the sacred race-emotion that lies dormant in our souls.

But, as Ruth Rafael has pointed out, the lesser-known first part of the statement is equally revealing:

It is not my purpose, not my desire to attempt a "reconstruction" of Jewish music, or to base my work on melodies more or less authentic. I am not an archaeologist. I hold it of first importance to write good, genuine music.

Still, he agreed to take home a copy of the *Union Prayer Book* and study it. When Rinder succeeded in soliciting a gift of $3,000 from Daniel Koshland and his friends, Bloch finally agreed to embark on what is often considered his most impressive work of all—*Avodath Hakodesh*, or *Sacred Service*.

Ten thousand dollars were soon added to the Koshland stipend by New York philanthropist Gerald Warburg, himself a cellist, who had been informed of the project by Rinder while in San Francisco for a performance. This enabled Bloch to leave the conservatory in February 1930—and San Francisco two months later—in order to work on the *Sacred Service* in a remote mountain village in the Swiss Alps. For more than two years he remained in seclusion, mastering the Hebrew language, analyzing Jewish liturgy, and ultimately writing the first Jewish service by a modern composer of stature.

It was a process full of pain. His health, never good, had broken down completely during the Atlantic crossing, and his letters to Rinder complained of liver trouble and neuralgia, muscle aches and insomnia. After bewailing the "commercialism" of America, he returned to his native land only to discover how hard it would be "to find a refuge against the tourism, the noise, the horrid hotels which have spoiled this country." Furthermore, his friends and relatives had vanished during the three decades he had spent in Western Europe and the United States; he had returned only to "cold, rain, and loneliness."

But he found relief in his work. As he wrote the cantor several weeks after his arrival,

> What has helped me the most and is slowly giving me my balance and may…bring me peace and restore my soul is the Jewish service. Slowly I have absorbed it.…It has impregnated me. It is becoming mine. I have *memorized* it slowly, and now I know it *all by heart*.…I declaim it, aloud, amidst the rocks and forests…and when I cannot sleep at night, I recite it!

In long letters to Rinder he described the emerging masterpiece. "I had, literally, to *fight* for each note," he confided, but his most excruciating task would be to weld each of the segments he had composed into a unified whole:

> The defect of all the services you showed me was that they were very small fragments, unrelated arias, recitations, choirs, with no nervous system, no circulatory system, no directing brains in them....I felt one could—one *had* to give *Unity* to all that, for Unity is the basis of our religion.

He shared with Rinder not only an outline of the entire five-part service but its underlying philosophical—indeed cosmological—premises as well. Bloch asked the cantor's opinion on the definition, pronunciation, and syllabification of key words in the Hebrew text, and asked him to suggest a Hebrew title for the work. A portion of the morning service which the cantor had set to music—"Tsur Yisrael," or "Rock of Israel"—appeared *in toto* in Bloch's final manuscript.

Avodath Hakodesh, unveiled in Turin, Italy, in 1934, would not be performed at Emanu-El until March 28, 1938, nearly a decade after its conception, by a proud Rinder who also took the role of recitant. Presented by the Federal Music Project of the WPA and sponsored by the temple and seven of its most prominent members, the evening was a stunning triumph. For Bloch had reached the lofty goal he had set for himself: through his music he succeeded in conveying the universal and ethical dimensions of the Sabbath service. As Alfred Frankenstein wrote in the *San Francisco Chronicle*,

> The service is built up from the vast, primordial roots of religious emotion. It speaks at times with an epic grandeur paralleled only in Handel and Bach, with an awful, subdued sense of mystery and wonder akin to the final meditations of Beethoven, with a soft lyric breath like that in the "German Requiem" of Brahms. All of which it resembles not the slightest for it is altogether Bloch, a Bloch who has put aside the rugged hammer-and-tongs dynamism of his abstract instrumental music to brood for a while over an age-old poem that has a thousand meanings or one meaning and is here revealed in a new and supremely beautiful context.

The composer, still in Europe, was thrilled with the news of his San Francisco success, and chose this moment to reveal his feelings to Rinder once again. Reflecting on the genesis of *Avodath Hakodesh*, in his typically agitated prose, he wrote,

> It seems *yesterday* to me that *you* approached me with the idea of the Service—you are in fact the *godfather* of this work—you felt instinctively that it would liberate in me, from me, a whole world which (wanted?) needed to take shape…and you know what happened then! And how, amidst terrific sufferings and pains of childbirth…this work…was born.

IN THE SPRING OF 1948 Rinder commissioned a second classic Sabbath service, that of the highly prolific and versatile French composer Darius Milhaud. Ten years had passed since the premiere of the Bloch service at the temple, and twenty years since it had been commissioned. The long interval was due to the fact that the few world-famous Jewish composers who would have agreed to undertake the task—Leonard Bernstein was one who refused—seemed inappropriately secular and avant-garde to the cantor. A service would have to be rooted, at least to some extent, in tradition.

Although not an observant Jew, Darius Milhaud, born in Aix-en-Provence, took great pride in his Jewish origins, which reached back to the Middle Ages on both sides of his family. His paternal great-grandfather had been a biblical scholar at the time of the French Revolution; his mother's ancestors had been established in Italy since the Spanish Expulsion, one of them having been a medical advisor to the Pope in the fifteenth century.

Milhaud, nearing the age of fifty, had composed more than two hundred musical works—from operas and symphonies to ballads and film scores—when the Nazi invasion of France forced him to flee with his family to the United States. Teaching musical composition at Mills College in Oakland, he quickly came to the attention of Rinder as well as the leading temple families, who often invited him and his wife, Madeleine, to musical events in the city. His countryman and coreligionist Pierre Monteux, conductor of the San Francisco Symphony Orchestra beginning in 1935, not only performed several of Milhaud's works but also arranged for the composer himself to lead the orchestra's rendition of his *First Symphony*.

The Milhauds attended the Rinder seder each year—where Darius would charm those present by singing "One Only Kid" in Provençal—and it was in the midst of the Passover meal of 1948 that he was commissioned to compose his *Sacred Service*. When the cantor mentioned at table that Milhaud would be an excellent choice to write a service for the temple, Mrs. E. S. Heller (daughter of the pioneer banking giant I. W. Hellman) hastily offered to fund the project. Without hesitation the Frenchman accepted. In stark contrast to Bloch, that summer he would compose the piece in Paris in a mere two months.

Gracious and even-tempered though he was, Milhaud would not let anyone forget for a moment that he was one of the world's outstanding living composers. In 1954, after returning from a trip to Israel where he had seen his opera *David* presented in Jerusalem, he shocked guests in the Rinder home with a rebuke of the conductor: "I want performers of my work, not interpreters." But the cantor, who had brought out the best in the troubled and excitable Ernest Bloch, was also equal to the delicate task of criticizing the prodigy of Provence. Well aware of Milhaud's facile, almost nonchalant style, he persuaded him to work out in depth at least

DARIUS MILHAUD

one segment of the service, insuring that one "big number," as temple organist Ludwig Altman remembered, would emerge from the Frenchman's efforts. This was "Hodo al Eretz," the prayer for returning the Torah scroll to the ark, which is highly developed counterpointally and written for a large number of voices.

Milhaud, who would live until 1974, fails even to mention the *Sacred Service* in his autobiography, but it must nevertheless be reckoned as one of the highlights of a spectacular career. Conducted by the composer himself, despite his painful arthritis, the premiere was held at the temple on May 18, 1949. A 150-member chorus from the University of California sang the work, accompanied by the San Francisco Symphony Orchestra. Rinder, as he had done in the Bloch service, recited the spoken prayers against a musical background.

The *Sacred Service* is remarkably restrained for a man who in his youth had been so deeply affected by Brazilian dance music and American jazz. The *Chronicle*'s Alfred Frankenstein actually found the work too evenly paced, but was overwhelmed by its "simplicity, dignity, magnificently fluent melody," and "classic clarity." Fried likewise granted that it might be found dull, but he too stressed the "subtle beauty" of the "deep-felt and original" composition.

Bloch's *Avodath Hakodesh*—among the world's most frequently performed modern Jewish services—is generally considered the more symphonic and dramatic of the two. Yet on some levels the Milhaud effort compares favorably even with its Swiss precursor. It is better suited for the organ, Altman explained, and actually superior liturgically, in that individual parts of it are more easily selected for use in the synagogue. In this respect he compared the Bloch service to "a never-ending carpet." At Temple Emanu-El, birthplace of both masterpieces, Milhaud's has been the one more often heard.

IN THE LAST DECADE OF HIS CAREER Rinder commissioned two more works, both of them by Israeli composers. Earlier than most, this dedicated Zionist understood the cultural consequences of Jewish statehood; through the medium of sacred music he sought to bring the raw pioneer spirit of the new country into liberal synagogues throughout the Western world.

During his first trip to Israel in 1953—the gift of a grateful congregation on the occasion of his fortieth year of service—Rinder met Marc Lavry. Born in Riga, he had come to Palestine in 1935 and soon established himself as one of the Yishuv's leading composers. With the founding of the state he had become musical director of the Israeli Broadcasting Station, a post which made him a celebrity in the fledgling land.

With fascination Rinder saw the members of a kibbutz declare a holiday during a visit from Lavry. All work ceased as the patient, unassuming master spent the day teaching people of all ages and conducting the kibbutz orchestra. Impressed as much with his manner as his music, and feeling that Lavry, who had written the first Israeli opera, epitomized the young nation itself, Rinder commissioned him to write a service. The cantor promised him but a thousand dollars, thinking that, if necessary, he could donate that sum himself. For the Israeli, however, this represented a considerable amount, and he quickly began work on the task which would preoccupy him for the next two years.

Due to the generosity of Mrs. Heller, Dan Koshland, and others, not only was the fee offered by Rinder raised, but funds also became available to bring Lavry and his wife to San Francisco for the premiere. The composer preferred the earliest possible date for the performance, writing Rinder in the fall of 1954, "I have indeed labored nights and days, I may actually say I lived with this composition. I am now looking forward to this premiere as for the birth of a daughter. I must give birth and desire to see the child." March 11, 1955, was chosen, marking the temple's 105th anniversary. Lavry himself conducted the eighty-member chorus composed of the choirs of Emanu-El and San Francisco State College.

To the throng which filled every available seat in the sanctuary, it soon became clear that this long service (which includes both the evening and the morning Sabbath prayers) was far different from its predecessors. The rhythm of the desert is heard here, in almost Arabic-sounding folk songs described by one critic as "angel-music of the soft, quiet, luminous and gently tuneful variety." But others were disappointed with the work, which they felt to be shallow and uneven. Several experts believed that Lavry, the author of many a film score, had fallen much below the rarefied heights of truly sacred music. Merely excerpts of the service were ever published, and these only in simplified versions.

Although he held it to be of "outstanding merit," Rinder admitted that Lavry's endeavor was not in the class of Bloch's or Milhaud's. But he understood that the significance of the Lavry service went beyond the quality of the music. In the words of Rabbi Wolli Kaelter, regional head of the Union of American Hebrew Congregations, who congratulated the cantor, "The work occupies a unique place in the history of Jewish Sacred Music because it marks the first major contribution of the land of Zion since ancient times to the Song of the Synagogue. At the same time, it forms the most direct link between Israel and Reform Judaism."

It was for these reasons that Rinder attempted to gain a wider hearing for the piece, succeeding, for example, in persuading Congregation Beth El of Detroit to present it in March 1958. The service, which Lavry dedicated to Rinder, also marked a turning point in the composer's career. He made invaluable American contacts through the cantor, such as Rabbi Louis Newman, with whom he would later collaborate on an opera, *Tamar*. Upon returning to his Jerusalem studio, he soon finished two compositions based on biblical themes. As he wrote to Rinder in 1957, "You really opened before me the field of oratorial and sacred music. You inspired me."

Rinder's second visit to the Holy Land, in 1962, resulted in the final commission of his career, that of Paul Ben Haim, the German-born dean of Israeli composers. Rather than an entire service, the cantor now felt the need for closing anthems. With the charming Ben Haim, in Tel Aviv and Jerusalem he selected three psalms—the Fourth, Twenty-third, and One Hundred Forty-seventh—to be set to music.

Ben Haim, sixty-five years old, had earlier written the first symphony composed in the Jewish state as well as a number of highly regarded choral works. His *Sweet Psalmist of Israel*, performed in 1959 by the New York Philharmonic, caused Leonard Bernstein to remark that despite the composer's Munich origins and training, his "themes and tunes are unmistakably Israeli....What he gives us is an inner image of what King David's music must have sounded like."

The *Three Psalms*, presented at the temple on May 17, 1963, is considered among his finest works. "A mood of fresh, melodious innocence, as if the poems came from a high-spirited adolescence of the human race," was Alfred Frankenstein's comment. Ludwig Altman, who felt that because it was published in Israel Ben Haim's work did not receive the attention it deserved, held that the superb composition may be ranked alongside Bernstein's famous *Chichester Psalms*.

The *Psalms* ("Supplication," "Consolation," and "Praise") had its premiere at a festival of sacred music honoring Rinder on his fiftieth anniversary with the temple. In addition to the *Psalms*, the evening included two movements of Bloch's *Avodath Hakodesh* as well as a recently written work of Darius Milhaud, *Cantate de l'Initiation*, which he conducted himself. Much like the concert marking his forty-fifth year with Emanu-El—at which excerpts of the Bloch, Milhaud, and Lavry services were performed—the jubilee was a living testimonial to Rinder's immense accomplishment. Five decades seemed almost a brief period for one individual to have brought so many of the world's leading composers into the synagogue.

BUT FOR ALL OF THAT Rinder cared more about the musicians themselves than about their music; and he was as interested in those with the potential for greatness as he was in those who had already become great.

The decade and a half following World War I was the period of child prodigies, when, as Rose Rinder recalls, "One child after another sprang up—from where? Out of the blue, with this talent....This hasn't happened since."

Yehudi Menuhin was less than two years old when he was discovered by Rinder. His Russian-Jewish father, the stubborn Moshe Menuhin, had lived for several years in Palestine before immigrating to New York. There he took as his bride a girl of Khazar and Tartar ancestry whom he had known in Tel Aviv. Their firstborn was to become one of the most sensational child prodigies of the century.

After a miserable stint as a Hebrew teacher in the drab industrial town of Elizabeth, New Jersey, in 1918 Menuhin moved his family to the Bay Area, where he would eventually administer the Jewish Educational Society and become a teacher of Hebrew at Emanu-El. At first they lived in Berkeley, in a two-room shack cluttered with piles of old newspapers and magazines. Arriving on Rabbi Meyer's request to interview Menuhin for a teaching position, Rinder heard the baby singing, on key, a Hebrew arpeggio. He declared the child a musical genius.

The parents, who soon moved to Hayes Street in San Francisco, would smuggle the two-year-old into the Curran Theatre, where he became enraptured by the solos of Louis Persinger, then concertmaster of the symphony orchestra. For his fourth birthday, Yehudi wanted a violin and Persinger to teach him how to play it.

Both wishes would be granted, but not without some initial frustration. His first instrument was a mere metal toy (the gift of one of his father's well-meaning colleagues) and, sobbing with disappointment, he threw it on the ground. But Rinder, after testing the child and determining that he had perfect pitch, arranged for the reluctant Persinger to take him on. With Moshe and Yehudi he drove to the concertmaster's home, but the cantor asked the often hotheaded father to wait downstairs while he led the boy, now five, up to the study. There Yehudi played the Lalo Concerto, and Persinger immediately agreed to be his teacher.

Persinger, "who [set] high my sights from the beginning," Menuhin later wrote, "took extraordinary pains with me." One lesson a week soon became five, and eventually they worked together every morning for three hours until the youngster went to Europe in 1926.

That trip, on which he would study with Georges Enesco and return an internationally known figure, was financed by Sidney Ehrman. For once no prodding from Rinder was necessary. The tall, urbane attorney (brother-in-law of Mrs. E. S. Heller) had heard the first full-length recital of the child, not yet nine, at the Scottish Rite Hall. But his offer of a year in Europe for Yehudi was initially refused by Mrs. Menuhin, who dreaded the breakup of her family and also felt ashamed of the need for outside donations. Ehrman overcame the first objection by offering to underwrite the expenses abroad of the entire family, which included Yehudi's two younger sisters, themselves budding pianists. The second doubt he erased with his noble, selfless manner. "He adopted us," writes Menuhin in his autobiography, "not simply for a subsidized year or so, but unto his heart for life, and we children promptly recognized the bonds of kinship by calling him Uncle Sidney. My own father apart, no man has had greater title to my filial affection, not even my revered masters Enesco and Persinger."

Isaac Stern was another musical genius unearthed by Rinder. Born in the Ukraine in 1920, he had been brought to San Francisco by his parents while still a baby. His father, an artist in Russia who had to settle for the occupation of house painter in California, suffered from chronic heart disease. His mother, noticing that her son seemed to have talent at the piano, brought him before the cantor.

Rinder observed that, like Menuhin, this child had perfect pitch. But his fingers seemed somehow unsuited for the keyboard, so Rinder suggested that the eight-year-old try the violin. Mrs. Stern bought the instrument; Rinder purchased the bow.

The boy, who attended Emanu-El's religious school, studied the violin with Robert Polak, Persinger's successor as concertmaster of the city's symphony orchestra. Rinder found him a patron in the form of Jennie Baruh Zellerbach, mother of J. D. and Harold. He also arranged for his friend, Dr. Henry Harris, to treat Isaac's ailing father.

The young violinist, diligent though he was, did not make the phenomenal progress of Menuhin, and Mrs. Zellerbach eventually gave up on him. But Rinder, never at a loss for backers, contacted the elderly Miss Lutie Goldstein, who resided at the Mark Hopkins Hotel, where she dispensed the fortune of her brother, an unmarried Southern California businessman. She heard Stern at the cantor's home and was more than a little doubtful that he would ever succeed. Only after Rinder "begged her," as Rose Rinder later remembered, did she agree to support him for a two-year trial period.

Goldstein's enthusiasm had to be periodically rekindled, but she lived to see her "investment" pay off handsomely. Stern, who left Polak to study with Naoum Blinder at the conservatory, played with the San Francisco Symphony Orchestra at the age of eleven. He gave his first concert in New York four years later, in 1935; his Carnegie Hall debut in 1943 enhanced his reputation even further.

Like Menuhin, Stern remained close to Rinder in later life. On the evening following the sacred music festival marking his forty-fifth anniversary with the temple, a testimonial dinner for the cantor was held in the Gold Room of the Fairmont Hotel. Menuhin sent a recording of good wishes as well as a composition for the occasion. Stern performed in person and also voiced deeply felt gratitude to his earliest champion.

In the late '20s and early '30s other exceptionally gifted children came before Rinder, a veritable parade of infant prodigies. There was the pianist Ruth Slenczynski—so tiny at age four that her exacting father had to devise an extension of the foot pedal for her—who stunned European audiences before she was seven; Miriam Solovieff, a violinist who studied both with Polak and Persinger, and, at age twelve, gave a recital in the Hollywood Bowl; and Leon Fleisher, who at fifteen became an internationally known concert pianist following his debut with the San Francisco Symphony Orchestra.

BY THE MID-1930S Rinder's attention had shifted from children to adults—German musicians whose careers appeared to have been ruined by Hitler's rise to power.

The renowned violinist Bronislaw Huberman, who would form the Palestine Philharmonic Orchestra from the ranks of refugees, got his first big push in America from the cantor and his friends. In town for a solo concert at the Opera House in early 1936, Huberman met Rinder for lunch at the St. Francis Hotel. The Polish-born master was already admired in the West for having refused to appear with the Berlin conductor Wilhelm Furtwaengler, citing the silent acquiescence of the German intellectuals to Nazism. He had subsequently toured Palestine and told Rinder of his dream: to organize there a symphony orchestra of refugee musicians. The cantor was so strongly moved that he could not finish his meal. When Huberman explained that the one obstacle to the plan was money, Rinder rushed to the phone and called several of his favorite contributors, all of whom promised to help.

A reception at the home of Hattie Sloss yielded $5,000 in one evening alone. Later, on the night of Huberman's performance, Rinder accompanied him to the home of a potential donor who in return for her gift wanted only to have the great virtuoso at her dinner table. He said that he never ate a full meal before a concert, so on his plate were put a hard-boiled egg and a check for $1,000.

Encouraged by the response of San Francisco—where the Jewish community became the first in the country to allocate him funds—Huberman canvassed the entire nation and soon collected a quarter of a million dollars. Albert Einstein became the honorary president of the orchestra;

Hattie Sloss and Cora Koshland were members of its first board of directors. At the end of the tumultuous year of 1936, only ten months after Huberman had voiced his idea to Rinder over lunch, the Palestine Philharmonic Orchestra (later to become the famed Israeli Philharmonic) opened its first season in Tel Aviv. Its conductor was Arturo Toscanini.

In the 1950s Rinder and his wife touched the lives and careers of a number of Israeli musicians studying in the United States. The young pianist Max Pressler, in town for a contest at the Legion of Honor, stayed with the Rinders and practiced on their piano. Hoping to calm him down before the event, Rose Rinder told him of a similar competition among violinists decades earlier, which Yehudi Menuhin had entered and in which he had finished only second. "So, you see," she said, "your whole future does not depend on this." Composed, Pressler went in and proceeded to win the $1,000 first prize.

The cantor raised funds for the penniless pianist Amiram Rigai to study for a year in this country. He also aided Itzhak Perlman—the youngster stricken with polio—now one of the world's foremost violinists.

OF MORE CONSEQUENCE TO EMANU-EL was Rinder's discovery of Ludwig Altman, a Jewish refugee from Germany who became the temple organist and choir director in 1937, a post he would hold for the next half century.

Born in Breslau in 1910, his talent was evident early. At the age of eighteen, a composition he had written—though one that he passed off as his father's—was performed by an orchestra in his hometown. He was soon accepted at the prestigious State Academy for Sacred Music in Berlin, one of thirty admitted among 160 applicants, and studied under the renowned Hans Joachim Moser. While at school in the capital, the young man played the organ for the famed Berlin Philharmonic Orchestra and also worked as a freelance music critic for the German-Jewish press.

But shortly after Hitler seized control of Germany in 1933, Altman was expelled from the State Academy on a pretext. He found work as an organist at synagogues in the Berlin area and during his last year under the shadow of Nazism, 1936, was engaged by the ornate Oranienburgerstrasse synagogue, the largest in the country. In his mid-twenties, he was offered life tenure at this fabled institution.

Heeding his mother's advice, though, he emigrated to America instead, and was later able to bring over his parents. After a brief period in the East, he arrived in San Francisco, where he had relatives, and took a number of part-time positions including that of piano teacher at the Esther Hellman Settlement House. This was a job he disliked but, due to financial pressures, held for many years. Fortunately, he was also hired as an organist by the Christian Science Church in Berkeley, as well as many other churches in the Bay Area. In 1940, he became the organist of the city's symphony orchestra, a position he would hold for four decades.

But from 1937 on, his "main job" was that of organist at Temple Emanu-El. He began as a substitute for the aged and infirm Wallace Sabin at Emanu-El, sitting next to the Englishman at the keyboard and playing the difficult pieces that the older man could no longer master. After Sabin's fatal heart attack several months later, Rinder chose young Altman to replace him.

While he inspired congregants with his extraordinary virtuosity at the Skinner organ, he and his well-educated wife, Emmy, a German-Jewish refugee whom he met in San Francisco, also delighted the temple family with their refinement, congeniality, and humor.

But unbeknownst to many temple members, Ludwig Altman also carved out an international reputation as a scholar and a composer as well as a performer. He unearthed first editions of organ works of Bach, Beethoven, Mendelssohn, Mozart, and Telemann. He wrote prizewinning pieces for cantor, choir, and organ. He was the organist at the Carmel Bach Festival for seventeen years and a fixture at the Legion of Honor, where he played Sunday afternoons for more than a generation; beyond all of that he concertized in Europe every summer in the 1960s, '70s, and early '80s.

In 1964, he returned in triumph to Berlin, giving a moving recital in the landmark Gedaechtniskirche. It was attended by Professor Moser as well as several others with whom he had studied at the State Academy in the early 1930s. Altman met Thomas Mann in San Francisco in 1943, and frequently corresponded with the Nobel laureate in the years that followed. He played in orchestras conducted by such luminaries as Leonard Bernstein, Sejii Ozawa, Arthur Fiedler, and Bruno Walter, the idol of his youth.

LUDWIG ALTMAN

Yet he was always self-effacing, uncomfortable with any praise save that he was "the best organist in the Richmond District." He was also a "team player" at the temple, where he worked about one-third-time—with health insurance, pension, and paid vacations, but without a contract for fifty years—enjoying an excellent relationship with Rinder, to whom he always remained grateful for giving him his start. Altman, not only the organist but also choir director at Emanu-El, "diplomatically" let the cantor, who was also music director, select the pieces for each service. This was a good division of labor for both individuals and for the temple. As Altman realized toward the end of his life, his success outside the synagogue may have actually dampened any potential rivalry between the two artistic giants:

> If the cantor [Rinder] had worried about my wanting to run the music at the temple, all my outside activities—church jobs, the orchestra, the Bach Festival, and the summer tours—would have shown the contrary. So while all this worked so well for me at Emanu-El, the combination of a cantor and a musically ambitious young Jewish organist could have produced problems particularly if the organist expected to be and became musical director.

This is the reason, Altman explained with regret, that so few gifted Jewish musicians of the younger generation choose to become synagogue organists; it would be difficult not to "outshine" the rabbi and particularly the cantor. Indeed, Altman himself was the only Jewish organist in the temple's history.

Still, it would be hard to imagine any real covetousness arising between him and Rinder. In a field known for its "prima donnas," neither of these men seemed to have a jealous or conceited bone in his body.

RINDER'S ONLY BOOK, *Music and Prayer for Home, School, and Synagogue*, appeared at the end of his career. A project on which he spent four years, the handbook is a compilation of dozens of hymns and chants as well as a complete Sabbath service. A unique feature of the nationally distributed work (published by Hebrew Union College with temple support) is the printing of the music on the same page as the words, rather than merely in the back of the book. In addition to age-old compositions, he included examples of his own arrangements, as well as those of Cantor Stark and Ludwig Altman, and works of the three composers he had commissioned to write services: Bloch, Milhaud, and Lavry.

In 1959, the year of the publication of *Music and Prayer*, Rinder retired, the board of directors naming him "Cantor for Life." It was largely Rose Rinder's doing. She hoped to relieve her seventy-two-year-old husband of the burdens of the job he had begun in 1913.

LEFT: CANTOR AND MRS. RINDER. RIGHT: CANTOR RINDER AND RABBI ALVIN FINE

Rinder had actually lost his fine baritone singing voice well before World War II. He continued to recite the spoken parts of the service, but the cantorial portion was chanted by Stanley Noonan, a Catholic with a magnificent delivery as well as a deep understanding of Judaism. Mrs. Rinder felt that the congregation, having become somewhat more traditional under Rabbi Fine in the 1950s, needed a performing cantor. The promising young Joseph Portnoy, an affable, sweet-voiced tenor, was brought out from the East as Rinder's successor.

But Rinder continued to sit on the *bimah* and remained active in the community. As in years past, he served as chaplain of the local American Guild of Organists; secretary-treasurer of the Northern California Board of Rabbis; and a member of the board of directors of the Bureau of Jewish Education.

In the fall of 1965, while reading the Torah, his speech suddenly became incoherent and he had to be helped to his seat. Soon afterward he suffered lapses of memory as well. The doctors found a brain tumor, and within a year he was dead.

A dozen Jewish organizations and more than a hundred individuals sponsored a memorial dinner for him at which the Reuben R. Rinder Forest in the Galilee was established. Louis Newman, who flew in from New York to honor his close friend of over half a century, concluded his speech with the words, "It is said in the Zohar that 'there are halls in heaven which open only to song.' Rob Rinder has unfolded to three generations these celestial heights because of his love of melody and his devotion to his fellow man."

Equally noteworthy was a fiery address which Newman had made almost forty years earlier, in May 1927, just prior to the beginning of Rinder's extraordinary period of accomplishment. Indicting Reform Judaism on many counts, as he was wont to do, the rabbi declared it "sterile of inspiration, poetry, and art."

Rinder's life work, as much as Newman's, stands as a refutation of that statement. For in the end, by bringing great music into the synagogue he did more than that. The cantor brought the dimension of beauty to modern religion.

c h a p t e r   s e v e n

IRVING REICHERT

Years of Rancor

The 1930s and '40s, the most momentous decades in the entire post-exilic Jewish experience, were also the most agonizing in the history of Temple Emanu-El. The Depression, the ascent of Hitler, American anti-Semitism, the Second World War, and above all the Holocaust created feelings of despair hitherto unknown to Bay Area Jewry; in addition, the viciously fought battle over the merits of Zionism produced the highest degree of internal dissension that the community had ever experienced.

Emanu-El's rabbi during the seventeen uneasy years from 1930 to 1947 was Irving F. Reichert, who assumed the pulpit at the age of thirty-six after serving at two New York congregations during the 1920s. Unlike his predecessors, Martin Meyer and Louis Newman, he was not a critic—but rather a fierce defender—of the ultra-liberal Judaism that had taken form in the late nineteenth century and that would later be known as Classical Reform. In this respect, as well as in his awesome skills as an orator (he had won several statewide debating championships as a college student), Reichert had much in common with Jacob Voorsanger, who had occupied the same post a generation earlier. Like the Dutchman, he was unable to adjust his thinking to the needs of a changing world—a serious flaw at the turn of the century, a fatal one in the 1940s.

Along with his brother, Victor, who also became a Reform rabbi, he grew up in pre-World War I New York and developed rock-solid faith in human reason and progress. His class at Hebrew Union College, that of 1921, was the last to be ordained under the presidency of Kaufmann Kohler, one of the early, radical leaders of the Reform movement; Reichert's philosophy hardly differed from that of the Pittsburgh Platform drafted by Kohler in 1885.

At the core of this system of beliefs, aimed at integrating the Jews into American society (or perhaps justifying what had already taken place), was the "fundamental fact that Judaism is a religion, *and a religion only.*" Despite the presence in this country of millions of East European-born Jews and their children, Reichert derided their culture as "either a phrase or a fetish, no more than that, dependent on kitchen recipes, musicians, painters and story-tellers, but not on God." And, even after the Holocaust, he chose as the highest priority of his career vehement opposition to Zionism, which was in his view "a retreat from the highway of Jewish destiny and achievement in America to the dead-end street of medieval ghettoism."

But if Reichert would define a Jew solely according to religion, he also made amply clear his displeasure with many traditional religious practices. When, in the years following World War II, many Reform congregations introduced the *kippah* and *tallit*, added more Hebrew to the service, or instituted rites such as the redemption of the firstborn, he lamented "the decline of an historical mission." With words which Voorsanger could have penned in the 1890s, he asked,

> Why this revival of archaic Orthodox ceremonies and customs which were eliminated only after a long and bitter struggle, discarded because they were superstitious survivals or irrelevant anachronisms? Do they really think that the religious anemia which afflicts American Jews can be healed by these medieval nostrums?

Rather than observance, his Judaism—which, he granted privately, came very close to the teachings of the Unitarian church—emphasized belief and conduct. His concept of God, "a quest, a vision, and a goal," was that of an eternal trend in history towards peace, justice, and freedom—not for the Jews alone, but for all the peoples of the world. In this struggle for redemption, "from Moses to Lincoln," Reichert viewed man as God's indispensable "co-worker."

Rabbi Irving F. Reichert

Thus, his sermons were normally filled with the searing ethical message of the Hebrew prophets, a fraternity in which he included Jesus. In "The Duty of Hating," for example, one of the many nationally broadcast talks which he delivered in the late '30s, he cited Amos' blistering indictment of ancient Israel, along with the prophet's conclusion that impending doom would be avoided only if "the masses could be aroused to such fierce hatred of the prevailing evils that they would rise up in their wrath and destroy them utterly." But the shepherd of Tekoa merely set the stage for Reichert's critique of his own inequitable society:

> How much liberty do we want? Do we want it only for white men and not for others? How much justice do we want? Do we want it only for people of wealth and power, or for the humble and friendless too? You may depend upon it that this is a situation in which only an angry social conscience will get results.

Few laymen, he felt, shared his understanding of the primary role of the rabbi: that of identifying society's ills and motivating his flock to cure them. He subordinated administrative, pedagogical, and even pastoral duties ("time- and energy-consuming activities…a digression") to "preaching," by which he meant something very specific. As he told his colleagues at a national convention of the Union of American Hebrew Congregations,

> Preaching that claims to be interested in the spiritual welfare of men but ignores the slums that degrade them, the politics that exploit them, the industrial conditions that enslave them, the international relations that slaughter them—well, to my mind that kind of preaching is the apotheosis of futility, the superlative illustration of sanctimonious ineffectiveness.

HIS PASSION FOR LIBERAL CAUSES seemed insatiable. He supported Harry Bridges, Tom Mooney, and the Scottsboro Boys; he was active in the ACLU, the California Conference of Social Workers, and the National Committee for the Defense of Political Prisoners. To the temple he invited speakers ranging from Eleanor Roosevelt to Howard Thurman, a local black minister.

Reichert's board of directors consisted primarily of Republican businessmen, but he made no secret of his admiration for the New Deal.

In 1933, he was appointed by General Hugh Johnson to the state advisory board of the National Recovery Administration as vice-president for Northern California, a post in which he arbitrated dozens of labor disputes.

Soon after taking office, however, he clashed openly with Governor "Sunny Jim" Rolph (who had been the popular mayor of San Francisco for almost two decades, and a speaker at the dedication of the Lake Street temple in 1926) regarding the rights of striking farmworkers in California's Central Valley. When vigilantes and local police terrorized twelve thousand of them—through arrests, brutal beatings, and even murder—Reichert and his friend Lincoln Steffens sent a telegram to Rolph, and the press, holding him "responsible for any further outrages."* The rabbi then publicly threatened the growers, including some of his own congregants, with a cutoff of federal farm relief if the laborers were treated unfairly.

The strike was settled in time for the harvest, but another bloody incident later that fall caused an indignant Reichert to denounce the governor once again. In San Jose, a mob of thousands lynched two confessed murderers and kidnappers hours after Rolph proclaimed that he would not call out the National Guard to protect them. Following the ghastly act, he actually commended the hangmen for "the best lesson California has ever given the country."

With the nation's attention transfixed on the Lindbergh kidnapping case—Bruno Hauptmann had been arrested only weeks before the San Jose atrocity—public opinion may well have been in Rolph's favor. For Reichert, however, the deed had brought only "humiliation and shame" to California, where more lynchings had occurred than anywhere else outside the South. Along with Marcus Sloss and twenty-three other prominent citizens, including former President Herbert Hoover, the rabbi issued a statement deploring the action and its "laudation" by the state's chief executive.**

Reichert had far fewer allies a few years later when he urged sanity in

---

*Rolph responded to the pressure not by calling out the National Guard, as Reichert had hoped, but merely by enforcing the ban on concealed weapons throughout Kern and Tulare Counties. He did act, however, to prevent the local sheriffs from "starving out" the strikers.

**The statement was also signed by two local Christian clergymen who were Reichert's allies on many occasions: Caleb S. S. Dutton, of the Unitarian Church, and Archbishop Edward Hanna. Stephen Wise, meanwhile, demanded in New York that Rolph be impeached.

the face of another avalanche of hatred—that which crushed Japanese Americans following Pearl Harbor. Less than one week after the United States' entry into the war, he delivered a sermon protesting the "unpardonable attacks and outrages upon American citizens of Japanese parentage whose loyalty to our country is as unyielding and assumed as that of President Roosevelt himself....We Jews ought to be among the very first to cry down the unjust persecution of the foreign-born in our midst whose patriotism is equal to ours."

He openly objected to the wartime confinement of Japanese in detention camps and, in early 1944, offered to help speed their reentry into society. To this end, "only decency," as he put it, he organized the American Committee on Fair Play. His courageous actions stemmed from the same sense of social justice which had impelled him to defend the fruit pickers a decade earlier. As he told his congregation at that time,

> Ask any Jew what he thinks of tyranny, of cruelty, or of oppression, and you are posing a rhetorical question. But are we who have such a passion for liberty, are we who are the historic crusaders for freedom, willing to defend these principles when they are challenged in our own backyard? This is the true test of liberalism.

YET FOR ALL OF HIS UNIVERSALIST LEANINGS, no one could fault him for minimizing the ordeal of his own people. His protest against the Nazi regime was the earliest and most forceful of any rabbi on the West Coast.

He went to Germany in the summer of 1933 as a special envoy of the American Joint Distribution Committee. Hitler had been in power less than five months, but Reichert already realized the "hopeless lot" of German Jewry. In a prophetic sermon delivered on Rosh Hashanah of that year, he painted a horrifying picture of a community "of 600,000 of our fellow Jews." Sixty-five years later, the attorney Louis Heilbron, who had been principal of the religious school in the early and mid-'30s, vividly recalled that moment as "the most moving and most impressive sermon I have ever heard in the temple." As Reichert reported,

> German Jewry, like Israel of old over whose mangled body Amos sang his plaintive lament, lies prostrate and fallen. Its once thriving industries are shattered, its brilliant professional life is extinguished, its wealth confiscated, its influence destroyed, its opportunity annihilated.

The illustrious contributions of its men of letters feed flames around which hooligans dance and caper....

As to how German Jewry will specifically solve its problem...this much seems certain: the more fortunate thousands will emigrate and the more miserable hundreds of thousands will be killed, or shunted off into social if not actual ghettos, condemned to degradation by a constant stigma of inferiority.

He continued by taking American Jewry to task for its "incomprehensible" complacency and "appalling niggardliness." The Jews of Britain, France, and Holland had given generously, he noted, but expressions of sympathy appeared to be the only contribution from the western side of the Atlantic.

As a first step, then, he urged a much higher level of giving to the Jewish National Welfare Fund, of which he soon became campaign chairman:

There is no longer any justification for delay or parsimony. The very least we can do is to protect this proud and heroic element in Jewry from the ravages of famine, disease, and destitution, and make it possible for some of them to escape from the living hell of Germany into the free atmosphere of other lands.

Secondly, he urged his listeners to join the national boycott of German-made goods. Siding with the American Jewish Congress and Stephen Wise (with whom he was at odds on many other issues), Reichert declared that for a Jew to do otherwise would be to "subsidize his own degradation." He addressed himself to the argument of those who opposed the boycott—groups such as B'nai B'rith—that Hitler would counter with even harsher measures against the Jews. Quite perceptively, he held that further persecution would result less from any actions world Jewry might undertake, than from domestic prosperity with which Hitler would be able to justify all of his policies, anti-Semitism included.

Late in 1933, Reichert formed and assumed leadership of the Campaign for Relief of the Victims of Nazi Oppression, an organization whose speakers' bureau included many eminent Christians. He lectured throughout Northern California, detailing the terror wrought by Hitler and also debunking the myths about Jews circulated by American anti-Semites. Often referring to himself as "ambassador to the gentiles," he scheduled more than fifty speaking engagements a year in the mid-'30s and was active in a dozen local civic associations.

Evidence of the high esteem in which he was held in the Christian community is the fact that he was able to prevail upon the San Francisco Board of Education—again in the crowded year of 1933—to remove all religious references from Christmas celebrations in the public schools.* Later in the decade, in order to check a rash of anti-Semitic incidents that had broken out in the Bay Area, he and six other leading Jews** formed the Survey Committee, forerunner of the Jewish Community Relations Council. Reichert was "invaluable whenever we needed anything from the Christian clergy," remembered Eugene Block, the lively newspaperman who became the committee's executive director. For example, the rabbi was instrumental in forcing the hateful Father Coughlin off the air locally by persuading the Protestant minister whose radio station carried the Sunday diatribe to cancel the program. Reichert approached him as "one man of the cloth to another," recalled Block, who felt that success probably would not have been achieved had the committee simply pressured the station's advertisers.

As German-Jewish refugees began to arrive in San Francisco in large numbers, the rabbi made their well-being one of his and the temple's highest priorities. He personally sponsored many immigrants, and one grateful German rabbi presented him with a Torah scroll, the only possession he had managed to salvage from his hometown. In 1937, Reichert again visited Nazi Germany to learn more about the refugee situation; his trip further confirmed the observations he had made four years earlier, and added a new urgency to his admonitions.

Weekly classes for immigrant women, meanwhile, were organized at the temple by Guild president Mrs. Joseph Ehrman Jr. (daughter of the governor of Oregon, and the socialite whom Reichert would later marry after the death of his first wife, Madeleine). There they would discuss mutual problems of adjustment and also learn about American institutions; at

---

*He was aided by the two Jews on the seven-member board of education—Philip Lee Bush, an engineer who was also on the temple board; and Mrs. Conrad Prag, mother-in-law of Julius Kahn. Another ally was a longtime member of the board of supervisors, Jesse Colman, who was active in Emanu-El and many other Jewish institutions.

**The seven were called together by the distinguished attorney Jesse Steinhart, one of the few members of the city's Jewish elite who did not appear on Emanu-El's membership rolls.

one point Hattie Sloss even arranged for voting machines to be brought over from City Hall. The Men's Club, despite the Depression, found employment—to be sure, usually manual labor—for dozens of German-Jewish breadwinners.

Attempts were also made to integrate the refugees into synagogue life. Special High Holiday services, largely in German, were held for them in the Meyer Auditorium without charge. By 1937, fourteen German-Jewish children were enrolled in the temple religious school, most of them with tuition waivers.

Emanu-El's programs for immigrants were replicated throughout the nation, but it is also true that few refugees joined the temple until well after World War II. Most could not afford the dues, which remained high throughout the '30s. Many were also uncomfortable with the ultra-Reform services at Emanu-El; for even if they had attended liberal synagogues in Europe, these were usually comparable to Conservative congregations in the United States. Perhaps most important was the fact that these people—driven from their homeland and still traumatized by the experience—wanted to be left to themselves for a while. The organization which aided them most was their own "Council of '33"; a few years after the war they founded their own synagogue, B'nai Emunah, in the city's Sunset District.

But obviously there was far less of the tension—stemming from cultural and class distinctions—which had characterized relations between the Emanu-El elite and the East European immigrants a generation earlier. Many of the '33ers, as this wave of newcomers was known, had been prominent in business, the professions, and the arts during the Weimar Republic. The leading members of the temple did not need to be told that they, too, might have been impoverished refugees had their grandparents not left Bavaria in the nineteenth century.

DESPITE HIS HATRED FOR HITLER, until the attack upon Pearl Harbor Reichert loudly opposed America's entry into the Second World War. No doubt he sought to refute the most frequently heard claim of anti-Semites such as Charles Lindbergh during those years: that American Jews were trying to "push" this country into the war. On this point he even clashed publicly with the man who had appointed him to the National

Recovery Administration board several years earlier, Hugh Johnson, who in 1940 appeared to echo Lindbergh's sentiments.

Beyond this was the rabbi's belief in the utter futility of armed conflict, a conviction bordering on pacifism which he held until December 7, 1941. As he declared on a national radio network soon after the war had broken out in Europe,

> You blind men, fumbling with your broom-straws in the Veteran's Hospital that overlooks the Golden Gate, whose shimmering glory you can never know—you won the last war! You share-croppers, scratching the dry crust of earth for crumbs to feed your wives and children—you won the last war! You bankers and brokers whose war profits built such costly tombs for your gassed and shattered sons—do you hear me? You won the last war! Thousands slain and hopelessly mangled; 200 billions of property destroyed; a national debt of 40 billions; ten millions of unemployed—and who can count the cost in human suffering and spiritual values! And we won the war.

But after Pearl Harbor there was no one more committed to victory then Reichert. He declared in *Newsweek* that American Jews were "prepared to give everything."

Beginning in 1942, servicemen were invited to High Holiday prayers at Emanu-El that began at six rather than eight in the evening, because of the danger of a night attack on the city. In 1944, five hundred men and women in uniform met for their own services in the Meyer Auditorium. The Women's Guild set up a canteen at the synagogue for those stationed at the nearby Presidio, who were also welcome to use the gymnasium. The temple house was made available at no cost to any group connected with the war effort, and a surgical dressings unit of the Red Cross was installed on the third floor.

The administration of the temple itself was also affected. Attendance at services dropped sharply due to gas rationing, for example. By the end of the war, the religious school was completely without male teachers, who in 1941 had comprised half the faculty. Reichert himself served as principal.

In his sermons, he spared his congregants none of the painful facts of the times; by May 1943, earlier than most, he had recognized the true nature of the catastrophe in Europe. As he accurately said of those who had already been slaughtered, including his own in-laws,

They were not killed on the battlefield, where they might bravely have met a patriot's death. They were not casualties of bombing raids, victims of the terror that knows no race or creed, but falls from the skies indiscriminately upon a whole community. They did not starve to death, sharing on terms of equality with their Greek and Polish fellow-countrymen the famine which the apostles of the New Order created.

No, these two million Jews were never even given a chance to share common suffering and common sacrifice....They actually boarded them into cattle-trains, or hermetically sealed freight cars without food or water—old men and little children, terror-stricken women, and men who had been leaders of culture and enlightenment in their communities—and they sent two millions of them off to be butchered in slaughter-houses, to face firing squads in lonely forests, to starve to death or die of disease in the pestilential ghetto of Warsaw.

Again he drew upon the words of the Hebrew prophets, now for their "compassion and courage in days of disaster and suffering." He invoked Isaiah, who had comforted a ravaged Jewish people in Babylonia with the promise of immortality: "Not the captives but the conquerors disappeared. The small voice of Jerusalem outlived the great clamor of Nineveh."

Also in the tradition of Isaiah, he inspired his people with a vision of the future. Less than two months after Pearl Harbor he declared that "the real problems will come after the last shot has been fired," and he filled his wartime sermons with allusions to world federations, an international police force, and Roosevelt's Four Freedoms. Just as Voorsanger's faith in human progress had been left intact by the earthquake and fire, so was Reichert's liberalism unaltered by the war and the Holocaust.

ALONG WITH EVERY OTHER RESPONSIBLE JEWISH LEADER in America, Reichert turned his thoughts towards the resettlement of refugees even while the war still raged. He felt that the remnant of European Jewry should be free to enter Palestine if it so desired, and he opposed Britain's perfidious White Paper of 1939, which had severely limited Jewish immigration to the Holy Land.

But he drew a vital distinction between rescue, relief, and rehabilitation on the one hand, and Jewish statehood on the other. Against the latter he struggled with every resource at his command. It would cost him his reputation and not that alone.

He had gone on record against Zionism as early as 1931 and delivered a speech to that effect before the local chapter of the Zionist Organization of America. But he did not publicly address the explosive issue again until January 1936, when—despite his oft-stated desire not to add to Jewry's burdens in a time of crisis—he felt compelled to rebut the American Zionist ideologue, Ludwig Lewisohn, who had recently aired his views in the *Atlantic Monthly*. In a widely reprinted sermon, Reichert articulated his main argument: the radical Reform belief that Judaism is a religion only, and that nationalism is "alien to the historic traditions of Israel." Repeating the formulation of his teachers at Hebrew Union College, he proclaimed, "Jewish states may rise and fall, as they have risen and fallen in the past, the people of Israel will continue to minister at the altar of the Most High God in all the lands in which they dwell." He even objected to the claim of centrality in Jewish history for the Holy Land: "Israel took upon itself the yoke of the Law, not in Palestine but in the wilderness at Mount Sinai, and by far the greater part of its deathless and distinguished contribution to world culture was produced not in Palestine but in Babylon and the lands of the Dispersion."

But this lengthy sermon, entitled "One Reform Rabbi Replies to Ludwig Lewisohn," was far more than a theological tract; it also contained the political premise which Reichert would put forth with increasing desperation over the next two decades: that the existence of a Jewish state would threaten the tolerated status of Jews in America and even play into the hands of the anti-Semites. Known as the "dual loyalties" argument, he phrased it as follows:

> One wonders what the Gentile world makes of all this [Zionism]. It is notorious that anti-Semites, when other arguments fail, sometimes succeed in prejudicing even friendly Christians against the Jew by quoting this type of nationalistic propaganda to convict us out of our own mouths for being a nationality imbedded within a nation. There is too dangerous a parallel between the insistence of Zionist spokesmen upon nationality and race and blood, and sinister pronouncements by Fascist leaders in European dictatorships....We may live to regret it.

Moreover, it was clear that the rabbi abhorred the combative style of the Zionists, to which he referred as "truculent." But he responded to their shrill rhetoric with a vicious attack of his own: "No swashbuckling, saber-rattling Nazi ever used more provocative language." Later he would castigate them for their tactics as well, accusing them of "extortion, character assassination, intimidation, and blackmail."

IMPRESSED BY THE LONG STRIDES taken toward the upbuilding of Palestine, the Reform movement in the interwar period retreated from the militantly anti-Zionist position of its founding fathers to one of neutrality. In 1935, the Central Conference of American Rabbis resolved to "take no official stand on the subject of Zionism."

Reichert, in the interest of harmony, voted for the proposal and, for more than six years after the Lewisohn sermon, held his anti-Zionist sentiments in check. But by 1942, a large number of his colleagues—particularly those younger than himself—had come to embrace political nationalism; for them the need for a safe refuge in Palestine now outweighed all other considerations. That year the CCAR passed a resolution supporting the creation of a Jewish army, making it clear to the minority—one of whose spokesmen was an irate Reichert—that the 1935 neutrality formula was no longer in effect. When the new, Zionist-minded president of the CCAR, Rabbi James G. Heller, refused to expunge the resolution from the record, ninety-two non-Zionist rabbis (labeled the "goy nineties" by their opponents) called their own conference in Atlantic City.

Only weeks before they assembled, in June 1942, the atmosphere was further charged by David Ben-Gurion's much-heralded speech at New York's Biltmore Hotel, demanding that the Jewish Agency replace the British Mandatory Administration in Palestine. The Biltmore Program, or statehood, had finally become the official policy of the Zionist movement, for which it hoped to receive the endorsement of American Jewry.

The rabbinical conclave in Atlantic City, in which Reichert played a leading role, countered with a manifesto of its own. Reprinted by the rabbi in the *Temple Chronicle*, it held that "the day has come when we must cry, 'Halt.' A dual citizenship in America is more than we can accept."

The gathering also led to the formation, several months later, of the American Council for Judaism. With the main purpose of combatting Jewish nationalism, this organization was born out of discussions held in the summer and fall of 1942 among a number of rabbis: Reichert; Morris

Lazaron of Baltimore; Edward Nathan Calisch of Richmond, Virginia;
Samuel Goldenson of New York; Louis Wolsey (dubbed "Cardinal"
Wolsey by the Zionists) and William Fineshriber, both of Philadelphia;
and Elmer Berger of Flint, Michigan. The philanthropist Lessing Rosenwald, who had been chairman of the board of Sears, Roebuck and
Company, received the rabbis in his mansion in Jenkintown, Pennsylvania, where he agreed to assume the presidency and underwrite the
expenses of the group. Berger, young and energetic, and obsessed with
the cause, became the ACJ's executive director, a post he would hold until
after the 1967 War.

Reichert assumed the office of national vice-president and official
spokesman for the ACJ in the West. By mid-1943 he had quietly organized the San Francisco section, soon to become the most successful ACJ
branch in the United States. According to Berger, only Houston—where
the leading Reform congregation actually barred Zionist congregants from
full voting membership—approached the Bay Area's level of ACJ activity.

Reichert drew his leadership almost exclusively from the board of
directors of the temple. Perhaps his most prominent co-worker was
Monroe E. Deutsch, who served as the first head of the local chapter.
Born in San Francisco of pioneer parents, this professor of classics was
not only provost and vice-president of the University of California,
Berkeley, but also president, in 1943 and 1944, of the city's prestigious
Commonwealth Club.

The two vice-presidents of the local ACJ were Reichert and Hattie
Sloss, who often hosted meetings in her home. The clothier Grover Magnin served as treasurer, and Daniel Hone, a well-known attorney, served
as secretary. Other executive committee members included Mrs. Joseph
Ehrman Jr. (Reichert's future wife); Dan Koshland; Mrs. Maurice Goldman, wife of a wealthy Houston realtor; and Harry Camp, a successful
hat manufacturer who was a close friend of the rabbi.*

More cohesive and better organized than their counterparts in other
cities, and facing weaker Zionist opposition than elsewhere, each member

*The board of directors was rounded out by J. D. and Harold Zellerbach, Sydney
Ehrman, Mrs. I. W. Hellman Jr., Newton Bissinger, and Robert Levison, whose brother
George would later head the ACJ. One influential temple board member was conspicu-
ously absent from the ACJ's ranks—Madeline Haas Russell.

of the board personally solicited a hundred people from a list of his or her friends and acquaintances; the local chapter sent out a packet of information on its aims along with a membership application to three thousand others.

Reichert chose the occasion of his Kol Nidre sermon of 1943 to make a plea for members. In this talk, the most important of his career, he told the hushed audience of two thousand the significance of the debate on Zionism: "No more serious issue will face us as Jews during our lifetime and the lives of our children." After reiterating the critique of Jewish nationalism contained in his reply to Lewisohn, he now emphasized a theme which would pervade his speeches for the next decade—the fundamental dishonesty of the Zionists.

He shocked the congregation by relating an incident which had occurred at the American Jewish Conference, a forum held several weeks earlier in New York on the subject of Zionism. Present were representatives of most of the nation's leading Jewish organizations, who voted their overwhelming support of the Biltmore Program—statehood. Reichert claimed, however, that the proceedings had been manipulated by the Zionists "at every point." He revealed that a delegate to the conference—past-president of the temple, Lloyd Dinkelspiel, a non-Zionist—was at the last moment unable to attend, but was registered as being present and voting in favor of Jewish statehood. "It is on the basis of such a vote," the rabbi lamented, "that we, and the entire...public are asked to believe that now all American Jews share the ideals and aspirations of the Zionist Organization of America."

With the Kol Nidre exhortation, entitled "Where Do You Stand?" Reichert had passed a critical juncture in another respect: he no longer felt obligated to urge restraint on the divisive question. On the contrary, he demanded of his congregants that they "make a decision...and take a place on one side or the other," that they join either the Zionist Organization of America or the American Council for Judaism.

NO ONE ACTUALLY WALKED OUT ON THE SERMON, but the partisan speech did result in several resignations, which the temple could ill afford. Also dismayed were most of the servicemen in the audience, many of them on their way to the Far East. Heated exchanges ensued, such as the

scene caused on the following Sabbath when the ardent Zionist Rose
Rinder, in a most uncharacteristic fit of anger, compared the rabbi to
Hitler within earshot of many worshippers.

But on the whole Reichert was sustained by his congregants, many of
whom joined the ACJ; by February 1944, the San Francisco section
boasted an enrollment of over a thousand. The chapter's correspondence
with the main office in Philadelphia reveals that by the time its membership
peaked the following year, at somewhere approaching 1,400, it constituted
almost one-third of the ACJ's national enrollment. The San Francisco
chapter also produced enough revenue to send the hard-pressed main
office about $20,000 annually in the mid-1940s. This comprised nearly
30 percent of the operating budget, and (leaving aside Lessing Rosenwald's large personal contribution) almost one-half the funds raised by all
of the chapters combined.

The local chapter drew large crowds to events such as Memorial Day
services at the temple and speeches by Rosenwald and Elmer Berger at
the Jewish Community Center. A program devoted to the contributions
of the Jews of California featured distinguished speakers in the areas of
agriculture, law, medicine, social welfare, and music, as well as young ushers dressed in cowboy costumes. In explaining the strength of California
Jewry from the Gold Rush to the present day, one of the lecturers quoted
Emanu-El's pioneer rabbi, Elkan Cohn, who had written that "while
Israelite, it had known no other nationality than that of American."

The leading families in particular rallied to the cause, and nearly every
one of them supported the ACJ—at least until late 1947, when statehood
appeared likely. For them Reichert's idea of Judaism as a religion and not
a nationality was hardly unfamiliar; it had been expounded in the temple
as a key precept of the Reform movement by Jacob Voorsanger early in
the century, coinciding with the youth of many of those who would join
the ACJ during World War II.

Far more important, though, was their limited understanding of the
inherent dangers of the diaspora, a naiveté shared virtually nowhere else
during this terrible time. Having lived in benevolent San Francisco for
generations, they enjoyed, as Kevin Starr has said, an almost unique
"sense of well-being." Even in the 1940s, when world Jewry could not have

been more vulnerable, San Francisco Jews were in the midst of a "golden age" in terms of their influence. Largely due to their philanthropy and political fundraising, as one historian has shown, the German-Jewish gentry received nearly a third of the mayor's appointments to municipal boards and commissions, a proportion that "could not be matched in any other American city."

Overgeneralizing from their own sheltered experience, it seemed to them that integration of the Jews into the host country was the natural order of things, and anything else merely an aberration. They were hardly ignorant of the Holocaust, or unmoved by it. But they failed to grasp its wider implications regarding Jewish powerlessness in the twentieth century. As Reichert said less than a year after the fall of Hitler, when the rest of world Jewry was still in trauma,

> Does anyone who has not completely surrendered to cynicism believe that the Germany of Kant and Goethe will not one day be resurrected, that the land which produced a Mendelssohn and a Lessing, a Luther and a Niemoeller is doomed forever to remain a graveyard of human liberty? I, for one, do not believe it. In 1290 the Jews were driven from England; in 1391 France turned them out; in 1492 Spain exiled them. Then as now, prophets of doom frenetically screamed that for all time to come no Jew would ever tread again those lands of bigotry. But you know how sadly lacking in perspective was that view.

But it was especially when they considered their own future in America that the Emanu-El elite feared Zionism more than anti-Semitism. The latter, they felt, could eventually be overcome with the help of gentile allies. A Jewish state, on the other hand, would be an ever-present wedge between the Jew and his friends. He would now be seen as more distinct, the member of a national minority group. And no guarantees existed that the state would not be communist, theocratic, or a dozen other things that could cause American Jewry embarrassment at the very least. There was no assurance either that the foreign policy pursued by a Jewish nation would not clash with that of the United States. In sum, the Jewish patriciate of San Francisco believed that a century of achievement could somehow be invalidated by the actions and statements of David Ben-Gurion, half a world away.

Of course, most other San Francisco Jews angrily dismissed this worry of being accused of "dual loyalties" and were infuriated by the ACJ in the mid-'40s. But there was almost no organized opposition to it until the end of the decade. The local ZOA, with its limited resources, felt that it had little to gain and much to lose from an all-out public feud with the city's most prestigious Jewish leaders. When, immediately after World War II, their great moment of opportunity finally arrived, the Zionists held rallies, disseminated literature, and took much pride in the fact that donations to the Jewish National Welfare Fund, much of which went to Palestine, doubled in 1946 alone to almost 1.5 million dollars. Young Saul White, rabbi of the fast-growing Congregation Beth Sholom, soon to join the Conservative movement, reprimanded the ACJ by name in March 1946 at a Zionist rally attended by five hundred people. But this was the exception, not the rule, until after statehood. More typical was the lack of response to Reichert on the part of Rabbi Morris Goldstein of Sherith Israel, whose brother, Israel, spiritual leader of New York's B'nai Jeshurun, was one of the leading Zionist spokespersons in the country.

Countless individuals, though, wrote the rabbi of their displeasure with his position. One affecting letter was sent by a German-Jewish refugee in June 1945:

> There are still a few thousands of European Jews on the march. Where are they going? How can our conscience permit us to let them shift for themselves? Should they get down on their hands and knees and beg to be admitted to any country in Europe?...You as a scholar and a rabbi should try to unite our people, not divide them, and should consent to let the majority rule....The majority here wants to work for a Palestine whose doors will be open for wandering and oppressed Jews....We need a Jewish homeland and we need it now.

He replied in a courteous but firm tone:

> I do not believe that a Jewish state in Palestine at the present time is either desirable or necessary, and that it will not only fail to solve the Jewish problem, but will complicate it enormously....I too believe in Jewish unity, but only on the basis of a common loyalty to our faith. I do not believe in Jewish unity for political purposes.

Reichert also fought against the rising tide of Zionism nationally, but on this front he had little to show for his efforts. He forcefully pleaded his case at the biennial assembly of the Union of American Hebrew Congregations early in 1946, only to see Zionists come to dominate that body as well as the Central Conference of American Rabbis. With George Levison, soon to become president of the local ACJ, he sought out Bartley Crum, the San Francisco attorney who was a member of the Anglo-American Committee of Inquiry, charged by London and Washington with devising a solution to the Mid-East crisis. But many hours of declamation failed to budge his pro-Zionist leanings in the slightest. Several months later, Hattie Sloss reported another attempt, again in vain, to change the opinion of Herbert Hoover. Even if the ACJ could point to some success in the Bay City, its hopes to prevent the creation of a Jewish state were beginning to dim.

IN 1946 THE RABBI ALSO HAD TO FACE the prospect that his ten-year contract, soon to expire, would not be renewed. Dissatisfaction with his avoidance of pastoral duties had been brewing for many years. He had conducted less than half the temple's funerals, for example, while his predecessors had officiated at more than two-thirds. Visiting the sick and bereaved was another job he did not relish. But he felt that his critics ("reluctant to face him frankly," as he wrote in an annual report) were unreasonable. He loved to tell the story of the woman who threatened to resign from the temple when he failed to pay her a condolence call on the death of her poodle.

There were also those who believed that Reichert—who had grown up in modest circumstances—had catered too much to a half dozen well-to-do families at the expense of the rest of the congregation. Despite the monthly tea parties for new members at his home, his bad memory for names and faces damaged him with scores of people whom he failed to recognize on the street or in the synagogue. Nor could it be said that he was popular with the children of the temple.

But most glaring was the deterioration of the institution itself. Membership had declined steadily from over a thousand families in 1929 to fewer than seven hundred by the end of the war. Enrollment in the religious school during these years had slumped from 536 to 202. Sabbath services were also poorly attended; Reichert attracted an average of only one hundred worshippers in 1946, less than a quarter of those who had regularly heard Newman, Meyer, and Voorsanger. The Pathfinders, Reviewers, and Temple Players had all disbanded.

Obviously, it was unfair to blame such a state of affairs on one man. Certainly the Depression—during which the operating budget was cut 4 percent annually for each of several years—and the war were not conducive to growth. Melbourne Harris, the temple's assistant rabbi, resigned in 1931, only one year after Reichert's arrival, and was not replaced until the young Morton Bauman was engaged to run the religious school in 1938. He remained only two years, leaving the synagogue with only one rabbi, and of course Cantor Rinder, throughout the 1940s.

Also, it could be argued that there were a number of tangible accomplishments during the Reichert period. Louis Haas, who served as temple president for seven years during the 1930s, spearheaded the construction of a new mausoleum, for example. At the end of the decade, Emanu-El was chosen by the national Reform movement as the site for its biennial.

Most important, though, was the addition of a new sacred space in the temple. In 1940, a large gift from the Guggenhime family resulted in the completion of the small, tranquil chapel later dedicated to the memory of Reuben Rinder. Using a minimum of ornamentation, a young local architect, Michael Goodman, was able to create a chamber well-suited to quiet contemplation. With its vaulted ceiling, hand-carved ark and pulpit, colorful stained-glass windows, and intricately designed chandeliers (which cast the shadow of a menorah on the carpet), the chapel provided congregants with a place of worship both intimate and elegant.

But this was small consolation to a number of board members who saw other Reform temples make tremendous strides while Emanu-El was in retreat. Sherith Israel, for example, under the leadership of Rabbi Morris Goldstein, tripled its membership from 1932 to 1946, surpassing its wealthier rival in numbers. And in Los Angeles, Edgar Magnin's Wilshire Boulevard Temple established itself in these years as one of the largest and most active synagogues in the country.

With an eye to improving the administration of Emanu-El, the full-time position of executive secretary, already a feature of many leading East Coast synagogues, was created by the board of directors. The amiable

Louis Freehof, a Denver attorney and brother of the prolific scholar Rabbi Solomon Freehof, was chosen for the post in the summer of 1946.

But Richard Sloss, president of the temple, felt that changes more far-reaching might be necessary. He asked Harold Zellerbach—a longtime friend of Reichert and the man who had actually engaged him in 1930—to join the board in order to evaluate the synagogue and its rabbi. He was to assume the seat of his brother J. D., who had recently been appointed United States ambassador to Italy.

The iron-willed corporate head, who in the past decade had played only a minor role in temple affairs, accepted Sloss' invitation but only on the condition that he have a free hand in restructuring the institution. Sloss and Dan Koshland, the influential vice-president, agreed.

Zellerbach's first task, as he put it, was one of "hearing complaints." He soon came to the conclusion that he needed the help of an outside consultant and, over the objection of several board members, selected a non-Jew for the task: Gene K. Walker, an advertising executive who, along with Zellerbach himself, had recently helped in the reorganization of a local black church.

HAROLD ZELLERBACH

The Walker Report, three months in the making and paid for by
Zellerbach personally, was released to the board of directors on May 15,
1947. It was a devastating description of the synagogue which, according
to the author, "in the minds of many non-members is a citadel of snobbishness, controlled by and operated for a few favored families."

While it stopped short of calling for the removal of the rabbi, it concluded that his "attitude" would have to be changed, and noted the need
for "warmth and friendliness" on the part of the entire professional staff.
Walker compared the administration of the temple to "a ship with many
propellers all working at cross-purposes rather than in synchronization."
The board, too, was rebuked, its members accused of absenteeism. Board
membership was perceived as merely an "honorary office," wrote Walker,
but it was, in fact, "a grave responsibility."

The twenty-page document included a series of recommendations
aimed primarily at attracting new members from among the city's many
unaffiliated Jews. Above all, it urged the adoption of a uniform dues system,
an end to the "scaling of the house," whereby the location of a family's
High Holiday seats was a function of how much it paid. "The publication
of a price list," Walker emphasized, "seems to suggest that those with the
largest pocketbooks are most entitled to religious satisfaction."

Just as the board began to deal with the disturbing conclusions of the
Walker Report, however, it appeared that the temple was experiencing
some sort of recovery, with a net gain of 104 members during the year
1947. This was the first indication of the postwar revival when throughout
the country Jewish war veterans, now married and thinking ahead to the
religious education of their children, were beginning to swell the ranks of
synagogues. Emanu-El, in particular, benefited from the activity generated
by Zellerbach, the new president, as well as the organizational abilities of
Lou Freehof.

But Zellerbach felt that Reichert had had no part in the temple's rally.
In November 1947, he held a day-long hearing on the subject of the
rabbi's contract, in which "witnesses" testified pro and con, and he reached
the decision that Reichert should not be retained. On November 29—
ironically the day on which the United Nations voted to partition
Palestine and create the first Jewish state in two thousand years—Zellerbach phoned the rabbi and advised him to resign.

With supporters such as Monroe Deutsch, Hattie Sloss, and Lloyd Dinkelspiel, he initially opted to fight for his job. Deutsch, desperately defending "one of the ablest pulpit orators of our time," came before the board and made an impassioned speech, touching on a variety of issues:

> A rabbi is not a janitor or a street-sweeper, to be hired and fired at pleasure. He should have [an initial] period of probation—a brief one, such as three or four years—and then have security; you cannot wipe out the seventeen and a half years which Irving Reichert has served this congregation and served it brilliantly.
>
> You cannot use a rabbi's services till he is on the threshold of age and then turn him adrift, at a time when he would be unable to continue in his profession, for which he has trained himself for so many years. Why?…In short, because of his age and his position on Zionism, his career as a rabbi would be permanently and completely ended, if his contract were not extended.…
>
> The whole matter is now public gossip. It cannot be concealed. The dismissal of the leading rabbi in San Francisco will be a stigma on Temple Emanu-El.…To thrust him out…could not be understood by our Christian friends, and naturally so. What explanation would you give? What could you give?…I feel that it would blacken the name of this congregation and the Jewish community as a whole.

But the board of directors—swayed by a second lengthy report, written by Zellerbach himself and highly critical of Reichert's entire career—voted not to rehire him. He was, however, granted a substantial pension and the title Rabbi Emeritus.*

To be sure, the leading families had admired Reichert for his anti-Zionist crusade, and one suspects that they might even have overlooked his shortcomings at the temple in order to retain so effective a spokesman for their views. But by the time his fate was decided, they no doubt had second thoughts on the matter. Since the end of the war they had heard the harrowing cry of the Jewish remnant in Europe for a refuge; by the fall of 1947, with the UN in the process of partitioning Palestine, they had to face the fact that, like it or not, Jewish statehood loomed as a distinct possibility. Were Reichert to be sustained, they felt, the temple

---

*Much to Zellerbach's displeasure, Reichert was represented in his negotiations with the board by the influential Lloyd Dinkelspiel. The rabbi received $10,500 a year, more than two-thirds of his 1947 salary, until April 1955.

would be frozen in a militantly anti-Zionist posture, whatever the years ahead might bring. It was a risk that most of them preferred not to take. This is not to say that unwavering opposition to Jewish nationalism cost him his pulpit, but clearly it weighed heavily against him once Independence came into view.

Very few of the other leading congregational rabbis associated with the American Council for Judaism were still at their posts by 1949. Morris Lazaron, the longtime spiritual leader of the Baltimore Hebrew Congregation, was forced to step down because of his anti-Zionist views. But most of the others were nearing seventy years of age by 1946—Calisch was over eighty—and retirement was a course they might well have taken in any case. Reichert, however, was in his early fifties and felt that he had many years of active service ahead of him.

A NUMBER OF EMANU-EL MEMBERS hoped to join a new congregation which he would form, but he chose instead to leave the rabbinate in order to work for the American Council for Judaism on a full-time basis as executive director of the western region. Within a few months he was provided by Berger and Rosenwald with an annual salary of $10,000 plus expenses, a secretary, and an office on Market Street.

But many of the ACJ's most respected backers dropped out in May 1948, after Independence and American recognition. As Lloyd Dinkelspiel put it, "If it's good enough for my country, it's good enough for me." Walter Haas, Dan Koshland, and even Hattie Sloss' son Frank also voiced doubts about the ACJ which letters from Berger could not allay, despite his prediction that Israel would soon "drift into the Russian orbit."

Haas' skepticism toward the ACJ may have resulted in part from the Zionist leanings of his daughter and son-in-law, Rhoda and Richard Goldman, who "used to argue" the point with him. Like many in the pioneer families' younger generation, they were inspired by the creation of a Jewish state in the wake of the Holocaust; indeed, the ACJ had virtually no members under thirty.

Moreover, the chapter's hopes of broadening its base beyond the temple now appeared more remote than ever. "Certainly all of our members belong to the Reform," wrote Hattie Sloss to Berger early in 1949. And she could point to no more than a single rabbi on its shrinking rolls.

Despite Reichert's long and strenuous trips throughout the West, he could report no real success anywhere. In Los Angeles, he was shunned by Rabbi Magnin and had to "reactivate" a dormant chapter where there was "difficulty in maintaining the interest of the members, especially [those] on the executive committee." Of Denver, he wrote Berger in August 1949, "the group needs constant attention and prodding," and Portland, he complained a month later, "appears to be coming apart at the seams."

Yet far more serious than these setbacks were the inherent contradictions—much more intractable after statehood—in the anti-Zionist position of the San Francisco chapter itself. One issue the local board could not resolve in the late 1940s was the question of whether members of the ACJ should also contribute to the United Jewish Appeal. Even before Independence, Sidney Ehrman discontinued his $100,000 annual gift. Reichert, who long admired the philanthropic work accomplished by American Jewry in Palestine, encouraged donations to the UJA, but Berger, the more dogmatic of the two, stubbornly opposed ACJ members aiding Israel in any way. He even voiced criticism of George Levison, who in 1949 headed a local fundraising campaign for the Hebrew University–Hadassah Medical School.

The personal style of both Reichert and Berger also posed a major problem for the ACJ locally. A lengthy letter written to Berger in 1949 by the gracious Hattie Sloss, who would remain a member until her death in 1963, was quite telling in this respect: "Let us be sure that we do not step over the lines of good taste....We can be much more effective [if we are] constantly amiable and retain our good manners, than...in excitement or anger."

Long known for its discretion, the Jewish gentry was simply not as eager for political combat as were Reichert and Berger or even some of their lay counterparts in other cities. They sought to lead the Jewish community, not hopelessly divide it—which they feared would result from the maximalist goals and belligerent tactics of the ACJ's professional leadership. This circumspect attitude was perhaps best expressed by Alice Haas Lilienthal in explaining the apparent contradiction in her long affiliation with both the ACJ and Hadassah: "First of all, they're both philanthropic. Second of all, I wouldn't want to offend anybody."

A wholehearted commitment to the ACJ was in any case problematic for people whose attachment to Jewish causes of any kind—if anti-Zionism may be called a Jewish cause—was a limited one. These grandchildren of pioneers, fully integrated in San Francisco's high society, had many other interests and concerns in life, from the opera and the symphony to the local museums and universities. Faced with the prospect of a malevolent, open fight over the merits of Jewish nationalism, they opted to turn their attention elsewhere. Thus their high degree of acculturation ironically served to brake their anti-Zionism.

In this sense, one can appreciate the failure of the ACJ even in San Francisco, its most promising terrain. Obviously its prospects were bleak after the spring of 1948. But even earlier, when membership rolls were over a thousand, one senses that support for the ACJ was "a mile wide and an inch deep." A large number of members were two-dollar-a-year subscribers who had simply responded to an appeal with a prestigious letterhead and who would drop out in a few years. Moreover, it seems the wealthy elite also held back from making a full commitment. Even in the middle and late '40s, Berger's desperate fundraising appeals always fell short of his needs; given the means of these old families, the relatively modest sum of $20,000 donated annually in this period by the Bay City members raises the question of whether they truly believed in the cause. There was no local equivalent of Lessing Rosenwald, a philanthropist willing to devote major resources to this fight.

The history of the ACJ in San Francisco does reveal the extent to which the Jewish elite of the city could turn its back on world Jewry as a whole; in essence, the pioneer families followed the lead of their rabbi in embracing anti-Zionism even in the midst of the Holocaust. Yet the story of the ACJ also demonstrates the limits of that position. The ever-cautious Jewish patriciate was unwilling to create a schism over the issue and uncomfortable with the abrasive approach of Reichert and even more so Elmer Berger. "Ashamed" of themselves, as Dan Koshland admitted, the great majority of the pioneer families would come to accept Zionism and regret their ACJ affiliation.

BUT REICHERT, aided by George Levison, Hattie Sloss, and above all the Ehrman family, continued the uphill struggle *after* Independence, now with more virulence than ever. His main concern at this time was that American Jewish youth, "indoctrinated" with Zionist ideology, was "developing a split-personality neurosis." He petitioned the Union of American Hebrew Congregations to keep nationalism out of religious school textbooks. The rabbi also fought the propagation of the Hebrew language and of course the encouragement of *aliyah*, or immigration of Jews to Israel. Preventing Ben-Gurion from "Zionizing" the American Jew was also the goal of Moses Lasky, a leading San Francisco attorney active both in the local and national ACJ. He glibly compared the influence of Israel in America with that of the Communist Chinese across its border in Korea: "Zionism uses the state [of Israel] as a sort of haven north of a Yalu River to subvert our American view of Judaism and to herd us into a new ghetto. We shall not bomb north of this Yalu, but we must keep watch along the river line."

Reichert, meanwhile, was distressed by the Brandeis Camp Institute in Southern California, the innovative programs of which often simulated Israeli kibbutzim. In a letter to its chief sponsor, Judge Louis Goodman, Reichert compared the camp to the German American Bundist Youth, since youngsters were conditioned to believe "that they were actually in Palestine"—and demanded that it be closed down. Berger, meanwhile, suggested that Reichert find out whether or not the camp's director, Shlomo Bardin, was an American citizen. If not, he wrote, Judge Goodman (who had ignored the ACJ's claim) "would probably be a little embarrassed." The rabbi also attacked the camp publicly on a speaking tour for the ACJ through the South late in 1949. At the Nashville synagogue of Rabbi Arthur Hertzberg, he stated that "it bears an ominous resemblance to similar enterprises which not long ago Americans found extremely repugnant."

With the help of Berger, to whom he wrote an average of twice a week in 1949, Reichert planned an advertising campaign for the ACJ in the local *Jewish Community Bulletin*, which in 1945 became the successor of the *Emanu-El*. He hired a public relations consultant to lay out a series of vivid ads which appeared in the paper throughout the fall. That of October 7, for instance, featured a Boy Scout playing a bugle in front of an American flag. Ben-Gurion's statement, "Our next task...consists of bringing all Jews to Israel...[and] we appeal chiefly to the youth," was run under the heading, "ZIONISM SAYS." Under "WE SAY" appeared the words, "This land is YOUR land—this flag is YOUR flag. Son, that thrill

ZIONISM SAYS ➤

WE SAY:

This land is YOUR land — this flag is YOUR flag

Son, that thrill you feel when you salute the Stars and Stripes, when you sing "The Star-Spangled Banner," is shared by all of your 149,000,000 fellow-Americans.

YOU have the grandest birthright on earth

Freedom of speech, freedom of worship, freedom of thought, the right to work at the job of your choice—to travel or live where you please in this miracle-land of 48 states of breathless beauty and boundless opportunity.

WAKE UP—Count Your Blessings

This is your country, your homeland, your land of promise. Sure, it's not perfect, but it's not finished yet. That's part of your job—our job—all together, Jews, Catholics, Protestants.

Honor your flag! Honor your Faith!

Build your life firmly on these two loyalties—God and Country. Keep them both strong!

THINK IT OVER!

The American Council for Judaism

AMERICAN COUNCIL FOR JUDAISM ADVERTISEMENT IN SAN FRANCISCO'S *JEWISH COMMUNITY BULLETIN*, OCTOBER 7, 1949

you feel when you salute the Stars and Stripes, when you sing the Star Spangled Banner, is shared by all of your 149,000,000 fellow Americans."

The *Bulletin* printed the ads only after a furious altercation involving the Zionist Organization of America and the Survey Committee. Reichert, angry about the delay, naturally felt that he was being denied his constitutional rights. Earlier in the year he had learned that Zionists in Seattle and Portland had tried to cancel a speaking tour in the Northwest which he had undertaken on behalf of the National Conference of Christians and Jews.

In the most scathing terms he knew, he denounced what he saw as an attempt to muzzle himself and others. Likening Zionism to McCarthyism (which he also publicly opposed in the early '50s), he declared before the national convention of the ACJ in Washington,

> The Jewish nationalists have a lot of money. They have slick advertising experts. They control the Jewish press. They know how to influence politicians. They are not too troubled by moral scruples. They are skilled in the techniques of smear. They have made people afraid to think, afraid to speak, afraid to disagree. They have turned rabbis into puppets and made moral cowards of community leaders. They justify any means that serves their ends, and smash all opposition with a club they call "unity."

But this speech, delivered early in 1952, was the last national ACJ event he would attend. For the next few years he drifted away from Berger, whom he gradually came to perceive as little more than a propagandist for the Arabs. With its attack on Israel and its people, Reichert felt that the ACJ was attempting to influence American foreign policy not unlike the Zionists themselves.

The official break came in July 1956, when, as the rabbi indicated in his letter of resignation, the ACJ adopted the "incredible and outrageous" proposal that the Department of Justice investigate the United Jewish Appeal. The ACJ's position was no doubt connected to Moses Lasky's seventy-two page exposé of Zionist fundraising in America in the same year, in which Lasky concluded, "The bulk of funds raised by the UJA... passes to Israel in a manner defeating final accountability....The ends to which the funds are put include governmental purposes in the U.S. and Israel, and indoctrination of American Jews in Zionist philosophy."

For Reichert, this attempt to sever the philanthropic bond with Israel had rendered the ACJ "a pariah among Jewish organizations." Only one month earlier, he had written a letter to the *Bulletin* urging San Francisco Jews to contribute to the Federation campaign. He noted, too, that he could not accept the Arab demand to "turn back the clock to November 1947," for "history has made its decision. It is just as silly to refuse to recognize that Israel is a sovereign nation, as it is to assert that all Jews everywhere should regard Israel as their homeland."

Yet these sentiments marked little change in his basic position; since Independence he had accepted the *fact* of Israel's existence and stressed that he wished its population no harm. But until his death, in 1968, he held Zionism to be the most pernicious force in the Jewish world; and he never ceased from pointing out its "dangerous" implications for the American Jew in particular.

Moses Lasky too resigned from the ACJ only a few years after Reichert, and for many of the same reasons. Although he still opposed Zionism, he felt that "the [ACJ]'s strident public affairs campaign, its carping at Israel, its concern for the Arabs, has gained us nothing but enmity."

A few other prominent temple members, though, remained on its rolls even after the Six Day War, most notably the late August Rothschild and Charles Tanenbaum, who even today heads the national philanthropic fund. But the San Francisco chapter of the ACJ ceased to exist in any formal sense by the 1970s.

IRVING REICHERT LIVED OUT HIS LAST YEARS in profound disagreement with virtually the entire Jewish community. For three years in the late 1950s he served as part-time rabbi at a new synagogue on the edge of the city, Temple Judea, and was instrumental in changing the name of its suburban street—on which several churches are also located—to Brotherhood Way. But few other congregations opened their doors to him; his many offers to conduct High Holiday services, free of charge, almost always went begging.

His personal life also caused him unbearable pain. Despite his remarriage, he never overcame the death of his first wife in 1960. Nor, despite his universalism, had he ever truly recovered from the marriage of a daughter, during World War II, to a non-Jew. But in the opinion of his embittered son, Irving Reichert Jr., a prominent local attorney, the rabbi was wounded most deeply by his career-long fight against Zionism—ending in defeat that could not have been more absolute. In 1968, at the age of seventy-four and in poor health, no longer able to endure the ostracism of the community, according to Reichert Jr., he took his own life.

Erudite and charming, articulate and courageous, he could have been one of the most influential rabbis in America. Even Reichert's critique of Zionism, had it been properly harnessed, could have been a positive contribution. Had he been willing at least to see the value of statehood, he could then have played the often effective role of the liberal gadfly. Like Judah Magnes, whom he admired, he could have authoritatively spoken out against sectarianism and militarism, and perhaps advocated the cause of the Palestinian refugees. But by opposing the very creation of the state, even after the Holocaust, he isolated himself from the rest of the Jewish people. He and the ACJ came to be regarded initially as the enemy and later simply as a nuisance.

Compromise on his conception of the role of the rabbi—which was something akin to an ancient prophet—also would have been to his advantage. Had Reichert developed closer ties with his congregants and their children as a pastor, he probably would have been better received as a preacher. But compromise was not his way.

chapter eight

ALVIN FINE

Postwar Revival and Neo-Reform

Harold Zellerbach pinned all of his hopes for a revitalized temple on a young native of Portland, Oregon, who was already considered by many to be the outstanding orator in the American rabbinate. He was only thirty-two, but his service as a U.S. Army chaplain during the war had matured him far beyond his years.

Alvin I. Fine assumed his duties at Emanu-El in the summer of 1948, and for the next sixteen years dominated Jewish life in the Bay Area as had no other person since Louis Newman in the 1920s. A Labor Zionist, a foe of McCarthyism, and a fighter against racial discrimination, Fine felt the heat of controversy every day of his tenure at Emanu-El. But, like Newman, he was admired for his integrity and intelligence even by those with whom he did battle. He provided the congregation, whose membership increased by more than half while he served as its rabbi, with the harmony and vitality that had been sorely lacking since the Depression.

Fine, not sure he wanted a pulpit, nearly turned the position down. Still shaken by the carnage he had witnessed as a freshly ordained rabbi in the Pacific theater and the many funerals of young men he had had to perform, he envisioned a career in the academic world. So after his return to the states, he accepted a post in Cincinnati as the assistant to the internationally known archaeologist Nelson Glueck, the new president of Hebrew Union College.

One of Fine's duties was rabbinic placement, and early in 1948,

Harold Zellerbach arrived at the college with another congregant, his attorney Philip Ehrlich, in order to fill the opening at Emanu-El. After lengthy discussions with the San Franciscans, Fine recommended several candidates. The next day, Dr. Glueck informed him that they had rejected all of his suggestions. But Fine's disappointment turned to astonishment when his boss continued, "They want you, Alvin."

Glueck, influenced by Zellerbach's promise of a big gift to HUC if he could persuade Fine to take the job, encouraged his assistant to go to California and meet with the search committee. After much deliberation, Fine agreed. At the interview he openly discussed his long-held Zionist inclinations, which "raised some eyebrows." But afterwards, Zellerbach, accompanied by Dan Koshland, co-chairman of the committee, took him aside and simply said, "We'd like you to become our rabbi."

Koshland's brother was well acquainted with the young rabbi's abilities. They had met during the war in China, where Robert Koshland had been an air force colonel. Chaplain Fine, upon Robert's request, had conducted the military funeral of the Koshlands' cousin, Lloyd S. Ackerman Jr. After coming to San Francisco, Fine courted and married Ackerman's beautiful young widow, Elizabeth, a romance that captured the imagination of the entire congregation as well as the watchful columnist Herb Caen.

The temple's second rabbi during this era, who served for thirteen years, was Meyer Heller. He was handpicked by Fine, who had known him well at HUC, where he had compiled an outstanding academic record. He came to Emanu-El in 1950, at the age of twenty-nine, and was given the task of directing the fast-growing religious school. With his warm, easygoing manner and his deep concern for those who sought his counsel, "Rabbi Mike" affected his congregants, and especially their children, in a different but no less important way than did the nationally known Fine. As he often put it, he played "Mr. Inside" to the senior rabbi's "Mr. Outside." Everyone remarked upon "the great team" they made, a staff rounded out by the revered Reuben Rinder, now in his last decade of active service, and Lou Freehof, who vastly increased the effectiveness of the temple with his administrative expertise and personal warmth. Aided by a group of influential, dedicated lay people and spurred by favorable demographic trends, Fine and his colleagues made the '50s at Emanu-El a decade of growth and excitement.

RABBI ALVIN I. FINE

GRADUALLY, BUT UNMISTAKABLY, there was a shift away from the Classical Reform of the Reichert years toward the more traditional approach which observers such as Marshall Sklare have labeled "Neo-Reform." The pioneer families were as influential as ever in setting the course of the temple, but the composition of the rank and file was now changed by the addition of hundreds of new members, largely German refugees and the children of East European immigrants, who often felt that Emanu-El had gone too far in severing its links with the Jewish past.

Most important in this regard was the attitude of the new rabbi. A child of Russian immigrants, he had been raised in the "transplanted *shtetl*" of South Portland, where his mother kept a kosher household and his father was a board member of the Orthodox First Street *shul*. Fine would later come under the influence of the distinguished Rabbi Henry Berkowitz of Portland's large Reform congregation, who "wouldn't let a day go by" without encouraging him to enter the rabbinate. But loving memories of the vibrant, Yiddish-speaking community of his childhood would remain with him the rest of his life.

At Emanu-El, Fine was the first rabbi in eighty years to wear the *tallit*, to be sure not the traditional prayer shawl but rather a narrow vestment known as a stole. He also reinstituted the actual blowing of the shofar during the High Holidays, instead of having its sound merely simulated on the organ or by a trumpet player from the city symphony, as had been the practice in the late 1930s.

Later he attempted to introduce at least a modicum of Hebrew into the school curriculum. With Heller, Rinder, and later Cantor Joseph Portnoy, who joined the staff in 1959, he expanded the Bar Mitzvah program—in which about a quarter of the thirteen-year-old boys enrolled in the school now participated—to two classes a week for two years. He introduced popular family services (on Friday evenings, beginning at 7:30) and, with articles in the *Temple Chronicle*, tried to increase the level of observance in the home. Unlike his predecessor, he did not sanctify intermarriage.*

But the most pronounced difference between Fine and Reichert was their position on Jewish nationalism. Fine attempted to lower the volume of the divisive debate, but he made it clear to everyone where he stood on

---

*Decades later, however, Fine altered his views on this question and officiated at several mixed marriages.

U.S. Army Chaplain Fine conducts a "worry clinic" for soldiers in the lounge of the American Red Cross Town Club in Kunming, China

the issue. A member of the Labor Zionist Organization of America while still in Cincinnati, he joined the local chapter immediately upon arriving in the Bay Area and quickly became one of its most active fundraisers. He also was one of the initiators of the sale of Israel Bonds in Northern California. In 1948, he participated in a march in San Francisco for the new nation sponsored by the American Jewish Congress, and later became a member of its militantly pro-Zionist national board.

He addressed the question of Zionism from the pulpit for the first time on a Friday evening in October 1949. (Earlier Fine had prepared an address on Jewish nationalism to be delivered before the Commonwealth Club, but the speech was cancelled after he refused the unusual request that he submit an advance text.) Carefully tracing the age-old yearning to return to the Holy Land "in the consciousness of thousands of Jews in every period," he spiritedly refuted the arguments of his predecessor:

> American democracy, in its best and highest definition, does not reduce American nationalism to a jingoism which requires me to wrap myself in the American flag as I walk down Market Street....Loyalty to America

does not require me to give up my Judaism in any part, or to renounce my feeling of kinship with my people all over the world. American democracy does not require this narrow, totalitarian conformity characteristic of fascist states....

If the slanderous label of "divided loyalty" will be applied to one group of Jews in America, it will be applied to all, even to those who wrongfully and falsely render the charge.

At the temple the major forum for the often heated discussion of these ideas became the religious school committee. Textbooks mildly favorable to the Jewish state, such as Roland Gittelsohn's *Modern Jewish Problems* and Mordecai Soloff's *How the Jewish People Lives Today*, were considered objectionable by several members. But Fine and Heller got their way on the issue of educational materials and therefore were outraged when, in 1951, Elmer Berger, executive director of the anti-Zionist American Council for Judaism, singled them out in a public address as examples of Zionist rabbis who had been forced by their congregation to drop pro-Israel texts. In a stinging letter sent to every one of his colleagues in the Central Conference of American Rabbis, Fine described the incident and denounced the statement by Berger as "a complete fabrication and utter falsehood." He held that "the only fragment of truth is that the rabbis referred to are Zionists." Berger had probably been guilty of wishful thinking more than anything else, but neither he nor any other Jewish leader in the country could now have any doubt about the impact of the new rabbi on the orientation of the temple.

The change in rabbinical leadership at Emanu-El was of special significance to Rabbi Maurice Eisendrath, president of the Union of American Hebrew Congregations since 1943. Fearing the marginalization of Reform Judaism, he was waging a struggle to lead the movement away from its dogmatic ideological position of the prewar years and into the mainstream of American Jewish life. Toward this end, he was instrumental in the late '40s in moving the UAHC headquarters from Cincinnati to New York, then the indisputable center of world Jewry. Encouraging social action, support of Israel, and a more normative religious expression, he invigorated the movement, which tripled its membership across the country to 150,000 by 1953.

Rabbi Eisendrath regarded Fine as one of his ablest and most trusted commanders in the field. He and Nelson Glueck prevailed upon him to line up contributors for the combined campaign of the UAHC and Hebrew Union College, and the *Temple Chronicle* was often filled with information on both institutions. In the late '50s Fine also had a role in the establishment of the Reform seminary's new West Coast campus in Los Angeles.

Not only did the amounts given to the UAHC and the college rise substantially, but three of Emanu-El's most prominent congregants now assumed leadership positions in the national Reform movement. Dan Koshland was chosen to serve on the UAHC executive board; Harold Zellerbach became a member of the HUC board of governors; and Ben Swig, the colorful hotel magnate who had arrived in San Francisco in 1946, served both as vice-chairman of the UAHC and head of the Combined Campaign.

Eisendrath called upon Fine for more than financial support. In 1957, he faced a rebellion in the ranks of the UAHC at its biennial convention in Toronto. In the wake of the Sinai War, a number of Reform leaders, influenced by the American Council for Judaism, questioned the UAHC's Zionist stance; others objected to the liberal views it voiced on social issues in America. Eisendrath implored the young rabbi to send as many Emanu-El congregants as possible to the convention, assuming that they would vote down any initiatives of the Classical Reform synagogues. As he wrote to Fine, "I know such delegates will reflect your inspiration and guidance and will, therefore, prevent any possible retreat from the positions which the Union has taken during the past decade."

But Eisendrath, although he survived Toronto, was a bit too sanguine. A number of Emanu-El congregants, particularly among the old families, never changed their views on Israel or their Classical Reform approach to Judaism. Mortimer Fleishhacker Jr., president of the synagogue in the early '50s; Hattie Sloss; August Rothschild; and George Levison, among others, remained leaders in the ACJ during the Fine era despite his outspoken opposition to that organization.

Still, they never interfered with their rabbi's freedom of the pulpit. When Hattie Sloss wanted the congregation to hear the views of Morris Lazaron, one of the ACJ stalwarts, Fine, with Fleishhacker's help, was able to withhold the invitation to the Baltimore rabbi.

But well into the 1960s, the temple office was still barraged with a spate of objections to the support of Israel voiced by its rabbis. Heller and Fine would mark each "Zionist crisis" by dropping a penny into a vase in the senior rabbi's office. "At the end of the year we would empty it," remembers Heller, "and usually find fifteen or sixteen cents." There was dismay too about the changes in the mode of worship, and some of those who phoned in complaints were so upset that they greatly exaggerated the extent to which Fine had altered the service. Several claimed he had worn a skullcap, or introduced more prayers in Hebrew, neither of which was true.

IN THE EXPANSIVE FINE PERIOD, a new level of lay involvement was reached in the temple, the Federation, and the community as a whole. Harold Zellerbach was at times resented at Emanu-El for his blunt manner, but no one could deny that his five-year presidency had profoundly recast the institution. More than any other individual, he had been responsible for replacing Reichert with Fine, but his sense of duty hardly ended with the arrival of the new rabbi. He worked closely with his "racehorse," as he dubbed the young man, advising and encouraging him with memos he would sign "Coach." The goal he set for the temple—where he had become a Bar Mitzvah by Jacob Voorsanger in 1907—was uncomplicated: increased membership and lay involvement. As he told Fine, "I want the lights on seven nights a week."

Two other descendants of pioneers upon whom the rabbi could always count were Dan Koshland and Walter Haas, brothers-in-law who had made their fortunes as the heads of Levi Strauss and Company, and who would die just a few days apart in 1979 at ages eighty-seven and ninety, respectively, rich in honors and community esteem. Although less active in the temple than Zellerbach, they played a greater role than did the paper manufacturer in the wider community, particularly in the Jewish Welfare Federation, of which Haas became president in the late '50s. In contrast to their attitude to Zionism before and during the war— indifferent at best—they now contributed vast sums to the United Jewish Appeal. Along with the proverbially magnanimous Madeleine Haas Russell, the extended "Levi Strauss family" invariably accounted for one-quarter of all the funds raised by the Federation.

Yet another member of the Jewish elite, Lloyd Dinkelspiel, was co-chairman of the study group which, in 1955, recommended the merger of the Jewish National Welfare Fund with the Federation of Jewish Charities. The new organization, known as the Jewish Welfare Federation of San Francisco, Marin County, and the Peninsula, brought in almost two million dollars annually in the late '50s. By emphasizing Israel, the beneficiary of most of its funds, the Federation became an increasingly attractive outlet for the energy, talent, and philanthropy of most of the city's leading Jews. As Rabbi Fine recalled, the early study missions to the Middle East were far more exciting than committee meetings held at the temple to set the requirements for confirmation students.

But for all of its dynamism, Fine was concerned about the secular orientation of the Federation and the fact that it rarely took the synagogues into account. With foresight, he wrote a long letter in 1962 to the Federation's top executive officer, Sanford Treguboff, declaring,

> The Federation...faces a choice: either it will confine itself to fund-raising and the rendering of "caretaker" services to a declining and dwindling Jewish community, or it will become actively and profoundly involved in the sacred work of preserving Judaism as a vital religious and cultural force in America. If the latter choice is made, as it must be made, then the Synagogue and Federation (including its local agencies) will have to establish exceedingly close relationships, in order to make a united effort toward the ultimate purposes and goals of Jewish life.

He concluded with the thought that the professional leadership of the Jewish community would have to take the initiative in this cooperative venture. "If we do not do this now," he wrote, "then I doubt that it will be done at all in our time."

The temple, the Federation, and its agencies, most notably Mount Zion Hospital, competed with one another for the attention of the Emanu-El elite, but it must also be noted that Jewish causes constituted but one area of interest for the heirs of the old families, who in the postwar decades added substantially to the outstanding contributions they had already made to the civic and cultural life of Northern California.

Among the leading beneficiaries of their largesse were the local institutions of higher learning. At the University of California, Berkeley, Zellerbach Hall was built in 1967 to house both a spacious auditorium and a playhouse. A decade earlier, Walter Haas, with the aid of the trust fund of his wife's aunt, Lucie Stern, had provided the university with the clubhouse and swimming pool of the sprawling Strawberry Canyon Recreation Center. And this merely foreshadowed philanthropy on a much grander scale toward the end of the century, when the Haas family would endow both the business school and a new sports arena for the university.

Similarly, Mills College received Lucie Stern Hall and the Walter A. Haas Pavilion. At Stanford University, the main theatre for the performing arts, Dinkelspiel Auditorium, was donated in 1957 by Lloyd Dinkelspiel, president of the board of trustees, in memory of his late wife.

The civic activities of these and other pioneer families have ranged from public health to public television. But some would argue that it is as patrons of the arts that they have been most deserving of credit. Their generous support of the opera, the symphony, the theater, the ballet, and the museums has helped make San Francisco one of the nation's outstanding cultural centers.

THE LAYMAN TO WHOM FINE WAS CLOSEST, Benjamin H. Swig, was not a member of one of the old families, but rather the first lay "outsider" to influence seriously the course of the Jewish community of the Bay Area. Like the grandchildren of the pioneers, he contributed freely to non-Jewish causes, such as the Jesuit-run University of Santa Clara, to which he gave many millions of dollars. But the road he traveled was a very different one from that of the city's native Jewish aristocracy.

Swig was past fifty when, after World War II, he settled in San Francisco and proceeded to develop a real estate empire which included the Fairmont, St. Francis, and Bellevue Hotels. Up to that point his life had been spent in the greater Boston area where his father, a Lithuanian immigrant, had been instrumental both in founding a Conservative synagogue and in battling the strident anti-Semitism of his neighbors from the seat he won in the Massachusetts state senate. In this respect Boston, among American cities, was at the opposite end of the scale from tolerant San Francisco. Ben Swig did not attend college, but earned his "master's degree" as a shoe salesman and was twice wiped out financially before becoming in the 1940s America's leading broker in the field of chain stores.

In Swig, who headed the Jewish National Welfare Fund drive soon after his arrival, the Bay Area gained a contributor whose yearly gift to the Fund and Federation was second only to that of the Haas-Koshland-Russell clan. Even more important was his style of conspicuous giving. His trademark was the grand gesture, like his gifts of new luxury automobiles to Israel's President Yitzhak Ben-Zvi and Prime Minister David Ben-Gurion. He was also an outstanding fundraiser; in this area his tactics were likened to a sledgehammer by his biographer.

Fine worked intimately with Swig, who was "practically a father" to the young man,* on an array of causes such as Israel Bonds, the United Jewish Appeal, Brandeis University, the Hebrew University of Jerusalem, and the national Reform movement. They were also allies in the temple, where Swig served for six years on the board of directors, three of them as secretary.

It was this persuasive partnership that created the Benjamin H. Swig Camp for Living Judaism. Early in his tenure at Emanu-El, Fine had participated in two Jewish youth conferences at Asilomar and had come away convinced of the need for a rural retreat at which teenagers in particular could experience Judaism free from the distractions and pressures of the city. Swig suggested a superb location, the two-hundred-acre Kathleen Norris estate in the Santa Cruz mountains, which he had nearly bought for the Columbia Park Boys Club. The regional office of the UAHC, as well as a number of local Reform rabbis, joined Swig and Fine in raising funds for the project.

But they were frustrated because their grand vision of Jewish life in the West was not shared by the board of Emanu-El, which opposed the plan. The restless real estate man therefore secured the property for the UAHC through his own gift and loan. Camp Swig, as it has been known since 1965, has been one of the key elements in the revival of Reform Judaism in Northern California. With its imaginative summer and weekend programs and its respect for tradition, it has brought hundreds of young people each year—among them many who had not responded well in the Sunday school setting—to an appreciation of their Jewish identity. It strongly influenced dozens who later entered the rabbinate, several of whom would make their mark at Emanu-El.

*Years later the Fine and Swig families actually did become linked when the rabbi's nephew married Ben's granddaughter.

THE PRESENCE OF BEN SWIG also enhanced the influence of San Francisco's Jews on politics—locally, statewide, and even nationally. The old families, of course, had been active in politics since the Gold Rush. In the 1920s, the Emanu-El elite helped two of its own, Jefferson Peyser and Jesse Colman, become influential members of the city's board of supervisors. Colman, a grandson of pioneer rabbi Elkan Cohn, served for a record twenty-six years.

With a number of exceptions, most notably Madeleine Haas Russell and Harold Zellerbach, the descendants of the pioneers tended to favor Republicans in this era. Ben Swig was a Democrat, however, who worked for Adlai Stevenson in 1952. In 1956, as Stevenson's national campaign treasurer, he rallied the California contingent at the Democratic National Convention (one of four at which he would be a delegate) to the side of the losing candidate for the vice-presidential nomination—John F. Kennedy. He was a devoted friend to Pat Brown, whose nomination for governor he seconded at the California Democratic Convention in 1958, and whose two successful campaigns for that office he co-chaired. In 1966, Swig was also the first to console Brown after his loss to Ronald Reagan as they watched the disappointing returns on television together. Pat Brown, together with his son, Jerry, himself a two-term governor, sat in the front row of the temple at Swig's funeral in 1980.

It was through Swig that Fine became close to the elder Brown as well as to former California governor Earl Warren. On one occasion, Swig chartered a yacht out of Vancouver for a cruise on which he invited the Warrens and the Fines. The rabbi made a deep impression on Chief Justice Warren, who later let it be known that he would want him to co-officiate at his funeral, a task which Fine was called upon to perform in the scandal-ridden Washington of mid-1974. Richard Nixon was present at Warren's funeral, and Fine's eulogy was criticized in some quarters because of a number of alleged indirect references to Watergate. The rabbi responded that the subject was the integrity of Earl Warren, but added the old maxim, "If the shoe fits, wear it."

In San Francisco, Swig played a major role in the mayoral elections, supporting John Shelley in 1963 and Joseph Alioto in 1967 and again in 1971 with sizeable contributions. Their opponent in each election happened to be an Emanu-El congregant, the Republican Harold Dobbs, a longtime supervisor who received the backing of Dan Koshland and Walter Haas. Until 1974, when individual campaign contributions were limited to $500, other San Francisco politicians, often Jewish, were also the beneficiaries of large donations from the Swig family. Milton Marks Jr., a liberal Republican state senator (who would later switch parties), and Robert Mendelsohn, a former supervisor who ran unsuccessfully for several other posts, were both supported by the owner of the Fairmont. But two other local Jewish officeholders, Dianne Feinstein, elected mayor in 1979, and the man who opposed her, Supervisor Quentin Kopp (later a powerful state senator), have not always been in the Swig camp.*

Obviously, the large contributions which Swig made over the years entitled him, at the very least, to "the ear of the mayor" as well as others at City Hall, no small matter to him in his thirty-year fight to develop downtown San Francisco. In this regard, another prominent Democratic donor and East Coast native who belongs to the temple, Walter Shorenstein, president of the enormous Milton Meyer real estate company, has wielded almost as much clout. It was Shorenstein's house at which Jimmy Carter stayed when he was in San Francisco for the second presidential debate of 1976.

LIKE SWIG, Rabbi Fine was often urged to run for office but always refused. Yet he too made a deep impact on San Francisco politics that continued long after his resignation from Emanu-El.

He placed no concern higher than that of social justice, in his view "as much of a *mitzvah* [commanded deed] in Judaism as penitence and prayer." Particularly in the field of civil liberties, his voice was one of the most eloquent and effective of any rabbi in the country. He revealed the religious roots of his social conscience perhaps most clearly in his address commemorating the American Jewish Tercentenary, delivered at the Washington Hebrew Congregation early in 1955:

It is for us to seek the *right* way—not merely the easy or the safe way.

We who have known slavery and segregation—poverty and persecution—humiliation and homelessness, but who have emerged triumphant

---

*Of these four public figures, only Kopp has no connection with the temple. Mendelsohn and Feinstein (who was confirmed at Emanu-El by Alvin Fine) have been congregants as was Marks who died in 1998.

must, forever, lead in the struggle against these iniquities whenever they are inflicted upon any man or any people, anywhere.

In Judaism we not only make a sanctuary of the synagogue. We also expect the synagogue to help transform the world into a sanctuary.

He was headed in this direction while still a child, affected profoundly by his older, Russian-born cousin, Rabbi Jacob Weinstein. An alumnus of Reed College (later to be Fine's alma mater) and a Labor Zionist, Weinstein was a radical critic of American capitalism even before the Depression. In 1930 he assumed the pulpit of San Francisco's Sherith Israel, where his engaging sermons were heard by the city's poor and unemployed, who, dressed in overalls, often crowded the synagogue to capacity. Yet he was forced to resign in 1932 because of his outspoken views. Weinstein left San Francisco and later went to Chicago, where he made an outstanding career as the rabbi of Kehillat Anshei Ma'Ariv Congregation (known as KAM), but after 1948, through his protégé, Fine, his influence was again felt in the Bay Area.

Like his mentor, Fine did not shrink from attacking American foreign policy, even in the midst of the Cold War. In 1949, at the Thanksgiving service held annually with the First Unitarian Church, he urged an immediate moratorium on arms production. His widely reprinted sermon, by his own admission "idealistic," also suggested amending the UN charter in the direction of world government. Two years later, with Rabbi Saul White of Congregation Beth Sholom and several other clergymen, he publicly voiced his doubts about the rearmament of Germany and Japan and the involvement of the United States in the Korean War.

But it was domestic issues that, from the beginning, were his main concern. Only a few months after arriving in San Francisco, Fine became embroiled in a free-speech controversy by joining a group of clergymen in sponsoring the public lecture of Dr. Hewlett Johnson, an avowed communist. Known throughout the world as "the Red Dean of Canterbury," this distinguished-looking head of one of Britain's oldest institutions was also an editor of London's *Daily Worker;* several years later he journeyed to Moscow to accept the Stalin Peace Prize and was subsequently barred permanently from this country by the State Department. But Fine believed that the reverend had a right to be heard during his visit to San Francisco. He accepted the invitation of the organizer of the event, Episcopal bishop

Edward Parsons, a longtime battler for human rights whom the rabbi deeply admired, to sit beside Johnson on the lecture platform.

The following spring, Fine attracted national attention for a speech delivered at the convention of the International Longshore and Warehouse Union. With Harry Bridges, the head of the ILWU, facing deportation charges because of alleged communist activities, the rabbi chose not to give a perfunctory address welcoming the delegates to San Francisco. Instead, he pointed to the darkening clouds of political repression on the horizon and urged the leaders of organized labor to remain strong whatever the future, "frightfully obscure and terribly uncertain," might bring. He spoke on May 4, 1949, before the emergence of Joseph McCarthy and the arrests of Julius and Ethel Rosenberg, but he well understood that a period of peril had already begun: "Spectacular excitement over spy-hunts and loyalty tests and treason trials and the curbing of intellectual freedom on the American campus has created an atmosphere of friction and fear and suspicion; and in the confusion many honest citizens are under attack. Freedom, always so fragile, always jeopardized by hysteria, is under attack too."

Early in the new decade he fought "political witch-hunting," as he put it, by lobbying against the state senate's "Tenney Bills" which, among other things, allowed any employer to summarily discharge a "subversive," who would then not be entitled to unemployment insurance. Similarly, in 1952 he was a sponsor of the statewide Federation for the Repeal of the Levering Act, the law which required a loyalty oath for all public workers. In a sermon given at the temple, Fine attacked the loyalty oath required by the University of California. When a number of congregants objected to his position, he responded by presenting a debate on the subject before the Men's Club, a very active auxiliary in those years. Because the speaker in favor of the loyalty oath, University of California regent John Francis Neylan, refused to participate in a face-to-face confrontation, a second evening was scheduled for his opponent, Professor Charles Muscatine. Most of those who packed the temple house for the two events, recalled Fine, were won over to Muscatine's side by his persuasive, low-keyed approach. Soon thereafter, probably as a result of Fine's outspoken opinions on the loyalty oath and other matters, an FBI agent came to the temple and questioned him at length about his political activities.

IN ADDITION TO BISHOP PARSONS, Fine had an important ally in another veteran civil libertarian, the educator Alexander Meiklejohn, who in 1920 had been a founder of the national American Civil Liberties Union. The rabbi, who had been a member in Cincinnati, was encouraged by Parsons and Meiklejohn to join the board of the Northern California chapter. He accepted in 1954 and, near the end of the decade, began a two-year term as board chairman. Through the ACLU, then at the height of its influence in San Francisco, Fine and his co-workers were able to counter many of those threats to personal liberties which had not faded from the scene with McCarthy.

To be sure, they did not embrace the cause of every victimized person who came to their attention. Fine refused, for example, to take an active role in defending Morton Sobell, serving a thirty-year sentence in Alcatraz for conspiracy to commit espionage. Tried along with the Rosenbergs, Sobell had been convicted on highly questionable evidence, but the rabbi followed the lead not only of the national ACLU but also the UAHC, neither of which could perceive in the case any abridgement of civil liberties.

Far more often, though, Fine did lead the Northern California chapter directly into the line of fire. He despised the work of the House Un-American Activities Committee (HUAC), for instance; during his chairmanship, the local ACLU held many hearings and seminars in order to educate the public about the damage being done by Inquisition-like investigations. After college students picketed a meeting of the HUAC held in City Hall, a clash ensued between Fine and San Francisco's conservative mayor, George Christopher. When Christopher subsequently appeared in a documentary film on the incident made by the FBI, he referred to the protesters as "dupes of known communists." With Ernest Besig, the indefatigable executive director of the ACLU, Fine went to the press with a statement branding the film "a fraud" and attacking Christopher for his bad judgment. The mayor's final comment on the subject seemed to prove them correct: "If the film is a fraud then I am in good company. J. Edgar Hoover and all the FBI supports my feelings in this matter." A year later, in 1962, Fine again assailed Christopher when the latter proclaimed "Anti-Communist Week" in San Francisco to coincide with the Christian Anti-Communist Crusade of Fred Schwarz. The rabbi also frequently spoke out against that fanatic as well as the dangerous John Birch Society, declaring from the pulpit,

> I believe that the extremist ideology of the reactionary right poses the same threat to the security of our nation and its democratic society as communism. Actually, the "far out" right may be even more of a threat because it is better able to wear certain masks of respectability. But, behind any mask, both extremes are tyrannical and totalitarian.

On the question of whether another band of bigots—George Lincoln Rockwell's American Nazi Party—had the right to distribute its hate literature, Fine answered in the affirmative. He generally agreed with the position of the national ACLU, which actually defended in court a Nazi who was assaulted while distributing anti-Semitic leaflets. According to the rabbi, "concern with the dangers and pitfalls of censorship and its threat to constitutional guarantees of freedom of speech" were at least equal to "concern with the question of obscene literature."

Like every rabbi in the temple's history, Fine was a staunch defender of the separation of church and state. As such, he was delighted with the U.S. Supreme Court decision of 1962 eliminating prayer in the public schools. In letters to elected officials, statements to the press, and talks given throughout the Bay Area, he tirelessly explained the logic of the Court's holding. Above all, he hoped to prevent the decision from being circumvented by an act of Congress or a constitutional amendment.

Unfortunately, he was at odds on this issue with another courageous San Francisco clergyman and close friend, James Pike, who referred to Fine as "my pastor." A successor of Edward Parsons, this famed bishop of the Episcopal Diocese of California eventually faced charges of heresy for his fearless investigation of the historical Jesus and for his progressive views on birth control and the ordination of women. He was also a philo-Semite who twice spoke at Emanu-El and who shared many of the ideals voiced by the rabbi. Fine consoled the bishop after the death of his son, and delivered the main address at the testimonial dinner following Pike's resignation in 1966. According to Pike's wishes, Fine also gave one of the eulogies at his memorial service after his life was mysteriously cut short on an expedition in the Judean desert.

Yet in the summer of 1962 they publicly disagreed on the Court's decision. Pike, in addition to everything else a legal scholar, testified before the Senate Judiciary Committee in favor of a constitutional amendment guaranteeing voluntary prayer in the public schools. To Fine, the churchman's views were "surprising" and "disquieting," terms he shared with local reporters. With his characteristic concern for the rights of the individual, he explained, "To say that a prayer in a public school is optional and not compulsory does not solve the problem. It merely places the nonparticipating child in the role of an involuntary nonconformist or even anti-religious in the eyes of his classmates."

But his strong opinions on this delicate issue did not weaken the rabbi's excellent relations with the local Christian clergy, a tradition at Emanu-El since the congregation's inception. Fine spoke several times at Grace Cathedral, for example, where his friend Julian Bartlett was the dean. He also appeared on a weekly television show, *Problems Please*, with Bartlett and a Catholic priest, Monsignor Mark Hurley, later to become the bishop of Santa Rosa. It was through a lengthy correspondence with Hurley, one of the participants in the Second Vatican Council, that Fine was able to convey his views in Rome at a time when the Church was finally reformulating its relationship to Judaism.

FROM LEFT: RABBI FINE, BENJAMIN H. SWIG, FATHER TOM BOWE OF THE SAN FRANCISCO ARCHDIOCESE, AND EPISCOPAL BISHOP JAMES PIKE

FINE, THE PERENNIAL LIBERAL, admitted that, like Jacob Weinstein, he was the champion of many lost causes. As one of the eleven members of the mayor's Fair Rent Committee, for example, he had to report in 1953 that only five of 693 landlord-tenant disputes could be mediated.

But he never lost his faith in the ability of government to ameliorate society's ills, as his long and laborious struggle against racial discrimination reveals. As early as 1949, he urged legislation governing fair employment practices and, along with others active in the Council for Civic Unity, lobbied for a decade and a half to bring it about, constantly bombarding every member of the board of supervisors with letters. He testified several times at City Hall, often citing the pragmatic reasons for fair employment, such as the availability to business and industry of a previously untapped labor market. In 1957, though, he took a different tack:

> Being a religious man, it is my conviction that justice, sooner or later, will prevail. Whether it comes about only after additional human frustration, suffering and degradation, or by the peaceful and orderly process of law, depends in large measure on what you, as guardians of the public trust and welfare of *all* citizens, decide concerning this proposed measure.

In 1964, the rabbi's goal was finally realized with the creation, by Mayor John Shelley, of an emergency committee on minority employment, the embryo of the Human Rights Commission. Fine was the only charter member of that body still at his post (having served as chairman of its two major committees, Youth and Education, and Employment) when at last he resigned in 1980.

He used the prestige of his pulpit to combat intolerance in other ways as well. For once subordinating his fears of censorship to other considerations, he attacked the degrading blackface minstrel shows still performed at San Francisco high schools in the 1950s. Later, with Bishop Pike, he publicly opposed the overly harsh sentence meted out to a black physician arrested at a civil rights demonstration. In September 1963, he was one of the leaders of a local rally protesting the church bombing in Alabama that left four little girls dead. He used the occasion to urge passage of the stalled Civil Rights Bill, a plea he would voice two months later to another grief-stricken audience, that mourning the death of President Kennedy.

Martin Luther King Jr., extolled by Fine as "a modern Moses," was honored with a reception in Emanu-El's Guild Hall. Afterwards, King asked the rabbi to show him the sanctuary. As Fine later recalled,

> I took him into the temple and we went up to the altar. I looked at his face as he was standing there, looking at the ark, and could see the meditation that was going on. When we walked out and got to the foyer, he stopped and looked at me and said, "I want to thank you...for bringing me into this sanctuary; it refreshes my spirit for the enormous job that lies ahead of us."

The rabbi reached out to many other African Americans during his career, seeking their friendship long before the celebrated civil rights struggle of the 1960s. He was very close to Dr. Howard Thurman, for example, the prolific writer and spiritual leader of the Fellowship Church of All Peoples, who lectured at the temple frequently. Maya Angelou, the celebrated poet and author of several memoirs on the African American experience, visited Fine and even discussed conversion to Judaism.

RABBI FINE WITH MARTIN LUTHER KING JR.,
RALPH ABERNATHY, AND AN AIDE

The most famous African American to adopt the Jewish faith had his interest in the religion first sparked at Emanu-El. Sammy Davis Jr. was performing at the Fairmont's Venetian Room when Fine had the idea of asking him to speak to the religious school on the theme of brotherhood. He accepted, and afterwards toured the temple, leaving with a list of books on Judaism. A few weeks later, he confided to the rabbi his desire to become a Jew. As Davis noted in his autobiography, *Yes I Can*, he felt that there was an affinity between the Jewish and black histories of suffering, and he was deeply affected by the concepts of justice which pervade the Mosaic teachings. Fine, though, did not immediately encourage the conversion. He was not concerned with the fact of race, nor did he doubt the entertainer's sincerity, but he did feel that the act might be interpreted by the news media as a publicity stunt. He suggested that Davis see Hollywood rabbi Max Nussbaum, who brought him into the Jewish fold.

IN 1964, FOR THE FIRST TIME, the congregation formed a committee on religion and race, the outgrowth of a citywide conference held the previous year. Chaired by John Gorfinkel, dean of Golden Gate Law School, the main work of the committee was a resolution opposing Proposition 14, an amendment to the state constitution which would have invalidated not only the recently passed Rumford Fair Housing Act, but any past or future legislation limiting discrimination in the sale of real property. Although this bid for segregated housing was eventually ruled unconstitutional by both the California and United States Supreme Courts, the initiative won a majority of the votes in San Francisco and two out of three statewide. The margin of victory would have been even greater had it not been for the opposition of most of the state's religious leaders. At Emanu-El, the "No on 14" resolution of the committee on religion and race was also approved by the board of directors and mailed to every congregant. It marked the first time in its history that the temple had ever formally taken a position on a ballot measure.

The Women's Guild (now known as the Sisterhood) and Men's Club, meanwhile, held a number of joint activities with the Reverend Hamilton Boswell's Jones Memorial Methodist Church, including a clothes drive for disadvantaged blacks. In the spring of 1965, Rabbi Joseph Weinberg, Heller's young successor, flew to Selma, Alabama, to participate in the historic civil rights march on the state capitol. There, along with some of the most respected rabbis in the country—men like Arthur Lelyveld and Abraham Joshua Heschel—he was arrested and jailed for peacefully protesting the denial of equal voting rights. Upon his return, the ninth-grade class at the temple presented the popular assistant rabbi with a plaque, part of which read, "You have walked the way of the prophets."*

The feeling of solidarity with the African Americans which swept through the congregation was well expressed by Reynold Colvin, active in the Men's Club and the committee on religion and race and later to become president of the temple. In a "meditation" (the term given to the frequent lay sermons at Emanu-El, which Fine encouraged), he declared, "Bigotry, however polite, arrogance, however polished, and injustice, however rationalized, are observed with resentment and felt with pain by the descendants of those who were slaves in Egypt."

Fifteen years later, in 1978, arguing before the United States Supreme Court, Colvin would represent Allan Bakke, a white student who claimed that, despite his qualifications, he had been denied admission to medical school because of his race. In taking on the case, Colvin represented a position that was antithetical to that of almost every major black organization. Although another Emanu-El congregant, Justice Matthew Tobriner, wrote the only opinion against Bakke when the case first came before the California Supreme Court, most temple members agreed with Colvin. Bakke seemed to them to be the victim of a rigid system of racial quotas that did not square with the earlier call for equality.

Long before the Bakke decision, the Jewish-black alliance had been seriously strained. The militant black nationalists of the late 1960s—and nowhere was their rhetoric more inflammatory than in the Bay Area—repudiated their former allies, who themselves were now turning inward in the wake of the Six Day War. San Francisco was spared the race riots and bitter confrontations over housing which undermined relations between the two groups in other cities, but a panel discussion on black anti-Semitism held at the temple at the end of 1966 was an early indication of a changing relationship in the Bay Area as well.

---

*Weinberg was later to serve for many decades as the senior rabbi of the Washington Hebrew Congregation, the largest Reform synagogue in the nation's capital.

If, in retrospect, the Jewish preoccupation with civil rights in the early
'60s may be labelled "naive," the charge of hypocrisy, later leveled by radicals of both groups, is blatantly unfair. Like Pope John XXIII and John F.
Kennedy, in this historic if brief era of good will, the magnificent African
American preachers of non-violence such as Martin Luther King stirred
age-old hopes for deliverance deep in the collective Jewish soul. Having
suffered the traumas of immigration, anti-Semitism, and the Holocaust
only decades earlier, many Jews felt a genuine kinship with another oppressed people. In a sermon in 1963, Alvin Fine articulated these feelings:

> Our fellow citizens—our brothers of the Negro community are the
> 20th Century Israelites. They march from oppression to freedom—
> from humiliation to human dignity. They march not only for their
> own sake, but also for the sake of all other human beings—and we
> march with them, for we have made the same march ourselves. We ask
> for nothing to be given as a patronizing grant. It is rather that we sim-
> ply insist on translating into civil, social and economic rights what
> every human being already possesses by *divine right*.

FOR TWO YEARS BEFORE FINE ARRIVED in San Francisco, membership
in the temple had been increasing rapidly. But during his tenure the rolls
swelled even further, growing from around a thousand families in 1948 to
a high of 1,540 households by 1964. As early as 1950, each High Holiday
service needed to be offered twice to accommodate the enlarged congregation. A proud Harold Zellerbach predicted that Emanu-El would soon
grow to two thousand families.

A number of factors accounted for this gain besides the magnetism of
the new rabbi. In California and elsewhere, the two postwar decades constituted not only a prosperous period, but also one in which "organized
religion" and the family played a relatively large role. The Jewish population of San Francisco grew by several thousand during this period, largely
due to the arrival of young families from the East and Midwest.* In these
years, too, Emanu-El regained the lead in the spirited competition for
members between the city's two great Reform synagogues. In the 1930s

*In his *Report on the Jewish Population of San Francisco, Marin County and the Peninsula*,
Fred Massarik estimates a total of 46,616 Jews in the city in 1959, an increase of nearly six
thousand from 1939.

and '40s, Rabbi Morris Goldstein had drawn part of Reichert's flock to Sherith Israel; now, in the latter half of his long rabbinate, he was losing families to his sister congregation.

This sustained growth was the main reason for the "democratization," to use Fine's term, which began at Emanu-El in the late 1950s and '60s. The addition of almost two thousand new people made it clearer than ever that the system linking the dues schedule with High Holiday seating, in use since the 1920s, was both impractical and inequitable. At the urging of G. Marvin Schoenberg, the businesslike social worker who succeeded Freehof as the temple's executive secretary in 1959, the board eventually abolished the thirty-seven membership categories and adopted the "Fair Share Plan." In use at a number of other large congregations, this arrangement geared each family's dues to its income rather than the placement of its seats in the sanctuary. In 1962, for example, a household earning $10,000 a year was asked for an annual contribution of about $150; those with incomes of $20,000 were obligated for $300; and "$500 or more" was requested of those earning over $30,000. (A couple under thirty or a single person would be asked to pay half the "fair share.") Several years later, Schoenberg, a former Federation worker, modified the plan, setting the annual dues of many a congregant by himself, a practice which occasionally produced an irate phone call.

The temple did not adopt Fine's recommendation of unassigned seating; families that had occupied the same pews for many years continued, in most cases, to do so. But now no new member could reserve a seat in the front rows simply by paying higher dues. Schoenberg also began to phase out the seat "ownership," which in 1924 had helped finance the construction of the temple, by discouraging their sale or transfer. By the mid-1970s, less than two hundred remained, a number that has declined to several dozen today.

The temple's annual operating budget rose rapidly, reaching almost a quarter of a million dollars by 1960, the fourth highest of any synagogue in the United States. Revenue from dues, however, was actually lower than that at comparable congregations, for under the Fair Share Plan, almost half the membership taxed itself at the lowest rate—$135 annually.

Fortunately, Emanu-El could draw on other sources of income. The Home of Peace Cemetery, for example, showed a surplus in almost every one of the Fine years, money which could be used for temple programs. In 1954, an extensive addition to the mausoleum was built and attractive garden vaults were constructed a decade later. Soon after he assumed his post as executive secretary, Schoenberg engaged Fred Platt, already on the staff, to manage the cemetery, and also went about building up the Perpetual Care Endowment Fund, which passed the one million dollar mark in the early '60s and doubled by the following decade.

Funds for capital improvements, meanwhile, were raised in special anniversary drives every five years. The dazzling, week-long centennial celebration of 1950, at which Isaac Stern and Yehudi Menuhin performed and Governor Earl Warren, Rabbi Maurice Eisendrath, and Pastor Howard Thurman spoke, brought in $127,000, primarily due to the efforts of Dan Koshland and Louis Heilbron. About half that sum went to retire the deficit which had accumulated since the war; the rest went into renovation of classrooms, the sanctuary, and the mausoleum. Later in the decade the gymnasium was converted into a reception area, Guild Hall. In 1960, anniversary funds became available to install the new Jacob Voorsanger Memorial Library and to make some cosmetic improvements

LEFT: RABBI FINE WITH ISAAC STERN AND HATTIE SLOSS
RIGHT: RABBI FINE WITH YEHUDI MENUHIN BEFORE HIS
PERFORMANCE AT THE CONGREGATION'S CENTENNIAL CONCERT

to the Meyer Auditorium and the temple house offices. Schoenberg, who would face a raft of fiscal problems in the post-Fine era, looked back on the late '50s and early '60s as the proverbial "good old days": "Membership was up and inflation was down."

ALSO TO EXPAND in the postwar years were the temple auxiliaries. The Men's Club and Sisterhood enjoyed a combined membership of over a thousand, even before Fine's arrival. The Emanuelites, a social group primarily for singles, founded in 1947, reached an enrollment of nearly two hundred within a few years.

In the late '50s, Rabbi Heller organized the spirited Emanu-El Temple Youth (known as ETY) by recruiting members from the religious school's alumni association; in the mid-'60s Rabbi Weinberg would develop ETY further, inspiring countless teenagers. Taking advantage of the baby boom, ETY had a membership of around 125 high school students under the supervision not only of Weinberg but also a dedicated youth worker, Bob Michels. Its newsletter reflects a wide range of social and community service activities which created strong, lasting friendships.

Like the Pathfinders during the days of Rabbis Meyer and Newman, ETY instilled a sense of social responsibility in many youngsters, a number of whom became influential leaders in the Jewish community in later decades. John Rothmann, for example, who as a youth was deeply affected both by Fine and Weinberg, later distinguished himself as an activist for a myriad of causes including Zionism, Soviet Jewry, and Holocaust remembrance. Douglas Kahn, president of ETY in 1968, became a Reform rabbi and has served for many years as the powerful executive director of San Francisco's Jewish Community Relations Council.

No part of the temple grew faster than the religious school, however. Enrollment, which had doubled in the last two years of Reichert's rabbinate to about four hundred students, stood at 1,151 by the peak year of 1960, with the confirmation class at well over a hundred. Even by the mid-'50s, when registration approached a thousand, the thirty classrooms could no longer comfortably hold the entire student body, and classes had to be split between Saturday and Sunday mornings.

In his thirteen years as school director, Heller could point to a number of positive developments besides the tripled enrollment. In addition

RABBI FINE INSPECTS A CHALLAH WITH RELIGIOUS SCHOOL
STUDENTS IN THE TEMPLE COURTYARD

to a faculty of about fifty, he utilized many of the post-confirmands as teaching assistants; they remained at the temple Sunday afternoons to attend the high school, which also tripled during the Fine era to sixty students. In this way almost half the students continued their Jewish education beyond the confirmation.

An excellent rapport existed between Heller and the youngsters. On the one hand "Rabbi Mike" was almost like a big kid himself, playing ball near his home with the children of the temple. On the other, he provided patient and understanding counsel to the school's troubled youth. One example among many was that of an insecure girl from a broken home, whom Heller helped by always taking her as his first partner at the youth group dances he chaperoned.

Yet the religious school had severe problems, not the least of all being discipline. Although the attendance figures were high—87 percent on an average weekend morning in 1960, for instance—a number of boys and girls ducked out of class and either hid inside the great dome or left the temple premises during most of the brief instructional session. Learning in the classroom itself was often disrupted by children who resented the

RABBI MEYER "MIKE" HELLER MEETS WITH
EMANU-EL TEENAGERS AT HIS HOME

fact that their parents had forced them to attend. Other students eagerly looked forward to Sunday school, but solely as a means of socializing with their friends.

Hebrew, or something like it, was learned from a textbook used throughout the Reform movement at the time, entitled *Rocket to Mars*. It taught students the letters and sounds of the alphabet, but strung the characters together to form English words, rather than Hebrew, and told a story of the exploration of outer space, devoid of Jewish content. One pupil wrote a letter to his relatives in Israel in this "language," and, believing that he had been learning modern Hebrew, was disappointed to find out later that not only the characters but also the words differed from English.

Heller, of course, understood the built-in limitations of any program which provided, for most of the students, only two hours of instruction a week for no more than half the weeks of the year. As he indicated to the congregation in his tenth annual report, "We know that the amount of information that we can impart to our children represents only a minute fraction of what Judaism and its tradition has to offer. The most that we can hope to do is to instill...a positive attitude to their faith, a

pleasant association with the temple and a sense of loyalty to Judaism."
But the biggest obstacle in the way of an effective religious school was
often the attitude of the parents. Without the adequate reinforcement of
Jewish practice at home, as Heller frequently noted, the school was fated
for futility.

Among the adults, however, a significant minority of congregants did
manifest a new interest in Jewish learning, and two structures were created
to meet that need. At Rabbi Fine's urging, a committee was formed in
1950 with the purpose of establishing a museum and archive at the temple. Founded seven years later with Bess Altman as its first chairwoman,
the museum's gallery (located in the main sanctuary, its vestibule, and
alongside the Rinder Chapel) has featured rare documents and ceremonial objects as well as several changing exhibits each year by well-known
Jewish artists such as Peter Krasnow, Max Pollak, Jacques Schnier, and
many others. A modern sculpture by Schnier, permanently exhibited in the
sanctuary's vestibule, was acquired by the museum through the Elizabeth S.
Fine Memorial Art Fund. This was established by the rabbi and his children
soon after his wife's death at age fifty-seven, in 1973, after a long illness;
the entire museum was renamed in the memory of Mrs. Fine in 1980.

An ambitious program of adult education, the Temple Emanu-El Institute of Jewish Studies, was inaugurated in 1962. Organized and headed
for years by laymen such as Reynold Colvin and Ludwig Rosenstein, the
Institute, meeting weekly, soon drew over two hundred people to half a
dozen courses. In addition to Fine and Heller, the permanent faculty
included Rabbi Joseph Gumbiner, director of the Berkeley Hillel Foundation, and Elliot Grafman, the affable retired rabbi from Long Beach
who would later serve for eight months as the congregation's interim
spiritual leader. Courses were also taught by local scholars such as Walter
Fischel, the eminent professor of Semitics at the University of California,
and Ephraim Margolin, a faculty member at Hastings College of the Law.

In the spring of 1964, the Institute was opened with a lecture by America's foremost Jewish philosopher, Abraham Joshua Heschel, who had
been one of Fine's teachers at Hebrew Union College. Words of wisdom
he had imparted to Fine more than twenty years earlier remained in the
rabbi's mind for the rest of his life. When Fine, in his senior year at
HUC, won the award for the best sermon preached by a student, Heschel,

like everyone else, was taken with the extraordinary depth and richness of
the young man's speaking voice. For the sage, though, this was a God-
given trait that placed a lifelong obligation on his student. He took Fine
for a walk and exhorted him to "make sure that everything you ever say is
worthy of that voice."

THE HESCHEL ADDRESS was to be one of the last programs of Fine's
rabbinate. He was still in his mid-forties, but in the spring of 1961 he had
suffered a heart attack and it had taken him almost a year to resume most
of his duties. In January 1963, he submitted his letter of resignation,
effective eighteen months later. President Samuel Jacobs implored him
to remain at the temple, offering to add another rabbi to the staff so that
he could cut down his merciless schedule, but Fine refused, not wanting,
as he put it, to "diminish" the role of the spiritual leader of Emanu-El.

In the summer of 1958 Fine had left for a year's sabbatical in Europe
and Israel with his family, but by the early '60s he was exhausted by the demands of a position which had contributed to the death, in office, of three
of his six predecessors. Because he was considered the unofficial spokesman for Northern California Jewry, he was normally the first called upon
to represent the Jewish community at public functions and to give statements on controversial issues to the press. The fact that his congregation
included some of the wealthiest and most influential people in the state
made many feel that his support was essential for the success of almost
any Jewish cultural or charitable endeavor. As he explained, "Anybody who
wanted anything came to the rabbi of Emanu-El." But the most crushing
burden that he carried was the pastoral work required by a congregation
of five thousand people.

He was also "discouraged," as he wrote Jacobs in October 1961, "with
the meager interest, response and participation that we are able to evoke
from so large a membership." The consummate orator was especially dis-
heartened by the attendance at Sabbath services. A total of sixteen
thousand would hear him on the High Holidays, but late Friday evening
prayers (discontinued a few years after he left) and Saturday mornings
each drew an average of about 225 worshippers.

Rabbi Heller, who was quickly given to understand that he was not
being seriously considered to succeed Fine, handed in his resignation just

weeks after the senior rabbi. The search committee was seeking a man with a national or at least statewide reputation. "Rabbi Mike," despite his many talents, had long been in the shadow of Alvin Fine, as well as Reuben Rinder and Lou Freehof. The adults of the temple often attended his masterfully constructed sermons for the High Holiday youth services, yet few could imagine him in the role of head rabbi. He moved to Los Angeles, where he worked for several years as the associate of Rabbi Max Nussbaum. At the end of the '60s, he became the rabbi of Temple Emanuel of Beverly Hills, where he has served with distinction ever since.

Freehof, another member of the postwar team, resigned in 1959 to become executive director of the Sinai Memorial Chapel, a position affording him a key role in many facets of the Jewish community until his death in 1980. By mid-1964, among the remarkable staff of the '50s Rinder alone remained at Emanu-El, and he had but two years to live.

Fine was offered many attractive posts, including one with Robert Hutchins' Center for the Study of Democratic Institutions at Santa Barbara. He chose, however, to remain in the Bay Area, where in addition to serving on the Human Rights Commission he became a professor of

RABBI FINE SHORTLY AFTER HIS RESIGNATION FROM THE TEMPLE

humanities at San Francisco State University. Here, during a sixteen-year career (the same length of time he had served at the temple) he developed and taught an immensely popular course on the history of his beloved city by the bay. Indeed, an entire cadre of teachers was needed for the heavily enrolled San Francisco course; its members called themselves the "Fine Fellows" and met regularly under his leadership. No less important was the active role he played in upholding academic freedom on the campus, particularly during the violence of the late '60s.

He came to the aid of the community during another harrowing time, the immediate aftermath of the assassinations of Mayor George Moscone and Supervisor Harvey Milk. Only hours after the shootings, on November 28, 1978, acting mayor Dianne Feinstein asked him to address a mass meeting the following day at the Civic Center, not far from where the killings had taken place. True to form, he comforted the huge crowd—both sorrowful and angry—with an eloquent, reassuring plea for unity in the memory of two compassionate leaders.

LARGELY DUE TO HIS FRAGILE HEALTH, Fine was not a frequent visitor to Emanu-El after his retirement, but the appearances he did make rank among the most moving events ever held at the temple. In 1990, marking the 140th anniversary of the congregation, he and Rabbi Heller once again shared the *bimah* and led Saturday morning services.

He also participated in the installation of all four of his successors. But perhaps most touching was the eightieth birthday celebration that the temple held for him in 1996. Fine had long before declined the title of Rabbi Emeritus—he thought it inappropriate for a man who had resigned in his forties—but now he accepted the rare honor of "Rabbi Laureate," bestowed by a congregation that continued to adore him a third of a century after he left the pulpit. Emotional tributes were delivered by Louis Heilbron, one of the members of the selection committee in 1948; Paul Matzger, immediate past president of the congregation, who had become a Bar Mitzvah under Fine's tutelage in 1952; and Rabbi Heller, who lauded his "mentor [and] older brother."

This was also the occasion for which the temple had commissioned a musical rendition of the rabbi's enduring poem, "Birth Is a Beginning." It was the fifth time this sublime verse had been set to music. Written in the mid-1950s as a prayer of consolation for the *Yizkor* service on Yom Kippur afternoon, the work has since become part of the Reform canon, published in the High Holiday prayerbook *Gates of Repentance*, as well as the *Rabbi's Manual*. It distinguished Fine as a modern psalmist.

Birth is a beginning
And death a destination
But life is a journey
    A going—a growing
    From stage to stage.

From childhood to maturity
And youth to age.
From innocence to awareness
And ignorance to knowing;
From foolishness to discretion
    And then perhaps to wisdom.

From weakness to strength
Or strength to weakness—
    And, often, back again.
From health to sickness
    And back we pray, to health again.

From offense to forgiveness,
From loneliness to love,
From joy to gratitude,
From pain to compassion,
And grief to understanding—
    From fear to faith.

From defeat to defeat to defeat—
Until, looking backward or ahead,
We see that victory lies
Not at some high place along the way,
But in having made the journey,
    stage by stage
A sacred pilgrimage

Birth is a beginning
And death a destination
But life is a journey,
A sacred pilgrimage
Made stage by stage—
From birth to death
To life everlasting.

"Birth Is a Beginning" comforted the temple family at a memorial service marking the death of Alvin Fine early in 1999.

LIKE HIS PREDECESSOR AT EMANU-EL, Fine spoke out vigorously on behalf of the oppressed, but unlike Reichert he never alienated himself from the Jewish people. On the contrary, he guided the temple back into the mainstream of the Reform movement—itself drawing closer to the rest of world Jewry—in terms of ritual, Zionist ideology, and cooperation with the Union of American Hebrew Congregations and Hebrew Union College. "I wanted to move...into the next century, not the last century," he recently recalled. "It was a new time, the postwar period, in our society and religious life." He struck the balance between the universal and the particular that was needed to reunite the synagogue. As he declared in 1949, invoking an ancient parable, "The universal principles are like windows that let in the light, but if the house is fallen, woe to the windows."

Similarly, in the manner of Meyer and Newman a generation before him, he was quick to act on the changes he perceived in American Jewish life. At the temple's 105th anniversary in 1955, he explained,

We learn from the past, but we do not live in it. We live in the present, but we are not bound to it. With hope and confidence we look to the future—but we shall not postpone or neglect all things waiting for it. The present moment, in which the past and the future mingle mysteriously, is our moment of opportunity and responsibility.

It is true that circumstances favored him at nearly every turn. He inherited a divided synagogue, but also a reservoir of good will from a congregation wishing to overcome the ordeal of the Reichert years. The issues with which he grappled were formidable, but he was not called upon to deal with the Vietnam War or black militancy during his tenure as rabbi of Emanu-El. Nor was the civil libertarian forced to address another raft of controversies which fully emerged only after he left the temple, such as drug use, gay rights, and the new feminism. He was also spared the flight to the suburbs, which later contributed heavily to the temple's loss of membership, and the spectacular growth of the Federation after the Six Day War, which challenged the influence of the synagogue in a variety of ways.

Still, given the force of his personality, it is hard to imagine this man not succeeding had he remained for a second decade and a half. Like most congregational rabbis, he published little, but, like very few, the spoken word never failed him. His rare ability to inspire an audience, first evident in the acting he did at college and in civic theater, may have been his main asset as the spiritual leader of Emanu-El, for he reached people not only from the pulpit but also through two popular weekly television programs. Yet, even though Fine enjoyed the status of a celebrity, he also maintained close relations with congregants and colleagues and so he was trusted as much as he was admired.

His resignation—an anticlimax to a stellar rabbinical career—forced the congregation once again into a period of redefinition, precisely at a time when American society itself was embarking on painful years of self-examination.

chapter nine

JOSEPH ASHER
Verities for a Volatile World

A s Fine's successor, the temple chose his close friend and former classmate at Hebrew Union College, Irving Hausman. He had been the spiritual leader of Temple B'nai Israel in Sacramento and the Jewish voice in the state capital during the entire period that Fine had served in San Francisco. For the eloquent Hausman, who had sought the Emanu-El pulpit in 1948, the invitation of the board of directors sixteen years later fulfilled his greatest ambition.

As a child, Hausman had immigrated to America from Eastern Europe, but he was completely at home in the sedate world of Classical Reform Judaism that had been spawned by German Jewry. Dignity, decorum, and the ethics of the Hebrew prophets were at the center of his religious vision.

The new rabbi was also interested in Jewish culture and, shortly after his arrival in August 1964, established a fund to acquire objects of art for the temple museum and to underwrite lectures and musical events. The following year, a concert of sacred music helped commemorate Emanu-El's 115th anniversary, with Robert Commanday conducting the Oakland Symphony Orchestra and Chorus in Mozart's *The Penitent David* as well as two psalms composed by Yehudi Wyner and Ludwig Altman.

But the tall, vigorous Hausman was at his post only a little more than a year when he was stricken with a rare virus which left him partially paralyzed and in great pain until his death in 1985. The mysterious disease hit him on the Sabbath of Repentance, between Rosh Hashanah and Yom

Kippur, and, although he later showed some improvement, he was never fully able to resume his duties.

He demonstrated much courage. Refusing to give up his large confirmation class, for example, he met with the one hundred students in two groups in his home. Before leading Sabbath services, he would rest on a cot in an anteroom off the sanctuary and then undertake a slow, tortuous walk to the pulpit. Finally, after more than two years of such physical punishment, the board felt that it would be impossible for him to continue as rabbi. At the end of 1967, he reluctantly agreed and sent a letter of resignation to the temple president, Dr. Ernest Rogers, effective almost immediately.

Fortunately, the elderly Elliot Grafman was available to serve as interim rabbi until Hausman's successor could begin his tenure in September 1968. Grafman, who had conducted High Holiday services in 1961, after Fine's heart attack, and who had also served as a popular teacher in the high school and the Institute of Jewish Studies, was counted as a warm friend by many congregants.

The assistant rabbi during the period of Hausman's illness was Richard Zionts, a native of Pittsburgh, Pennsylvania. Like the interim rabbi, he accomplished more than anyone could reasonably expect during the difficult transitional years of the mid-1960s, which also saw the death of Cantor Rinder. Zionts worked particularly well with teenagers and, under his supervision, ETY continued to thrive as one of the most active temple youth groups in the United States. He also showed himself equal to the task of substituting for the incapacitated senior rabbi. In the fall of 1965, for example, this young man, a mere seminary student the previous spring, was asked on short notice to deliver the Kol Nidre sermon to two combined audiences of nearly four thousand people. In his fourth and final year at Emanu-El, after working under Hausman and Grafman, Zionts helped introduce Joseph Asher, the new rabbi, to the congregation. Zionts was still in his twenties when, in 1968, a grateful board of directors raised his rank from assistant to associate.

RABBI JOSEPH ASHER was selected after the most exhaustive search in the temple's history. One fatigued member of the eighteen-person

Rabbi Joseph Asher

committee confided that never had he "been engaged in a more arduous, long-lasting, and difficult task."

Asher would remain for seventeen years, from the late '60s to the mid-'80s, one of the most turbulent periods in the history of the country and especially the San Francisco Bay Area. His deep learning, his continental manner, and above all his personal integrity afforded many congregants a sense of stability in a tumultuous world. Others, particularly young people, sometimes felt he was "out of touch" with the rapidly changing times. But all respected him immensely.

The rabbi, who was called to Emanu-El in June 1968, had had an unusual career and an unusual life. The scion of an unbroken line of Orthodox rabbis going back six generations,* he fled his native Germany for England in 1938 at age seventeen. He left just before Kristallnacht on the advice of his ophthalmologist, the half-brother of Hermann Goering, who told him that the inflammation of his tear ducts was a far less serious threat to his well-being than that posed by the Nazi regime. Completely opposed to the racist ideology propounded by the notorious field marshal of the German Reich, the eye specialist was actually a philo-Semite who treated many of his Jewish patients free of charge in the late 1930s. And he was in a position to know the horrors in store for the Jews—not only because he had gleaned information from his half-brother, but also because Hitler himself was in his care for an eye disease caused by a gas attack during World War I.

Dr. Goering referred Asher to an ophthalmologist in London, where the youth enrolled in the highly traditional Tree of Life Yeshiva. But it was also in England that he would gravitate toward Liberal Judaism, influenced by the famed social worker Sir Basil Henriques, as well as Lily Montagu, the fervent female preacher who had established the World Union for Progressive Judaism.

In the summer of 1940, the young rabbinical student, along with tens of thousands of other German-Jewish refugees, was interned by the British

---

*It was Asher's father, Jonah Ansbacher, who made a key break with his traditional forebears by embracing the neo-Orthodoxy of the nineteenth-century luminary Rabbi Samson Raphael Hirsch. Rabbi Ansbacher was as accomplished in the world of secular scholarship as he was in Judaica. Though tightly bound by Jewish law, he was an astronomer and a mathematician, an Arabist and a classicist.

FROM LEFT: JOSEPH ANSBACHER (LATER ASHER) AS A RABBINICAL
STUDENT IN LONDON; ASHER INTERNED BY THE BRITISH AS
A FRIENDLY ENEMY ALIEN; ASHER AS CHAPLAIN OF THE
EIGHTH AUSTRALIAN EMPLOYMENT COMPANY

as a "friendly" enemy alien. His confinement at a converted racetrack was not especially bad, but the two-month voyage to Australia which soon followed proved to be the most horrendous experience of his life. Aboard the HMT *Dunera*, Asher and his shipmates were stripped of all their valuables and locked in the hold without sanitary facilities, sleeping accommodations, or adequate food supplies. The sadistic captain and crew, later court-martialed by an apologetic British navy, devised daily tortures for their human cargo—aimed more at the two thousand Jews on board than at the four hundred German POWs. Miraculously, there were only three deaths before the ship reached Sydney.*

Conditions improved in Australia and the internees, many of them prominent professionals, organized an array of cultural activities in their camps, including religious services, a drama group, a symphony orchestra, and even college courses accredited by the University of Melbourne. But liberation did not come until February 1942, when the Australian government, now at war against Japan, realized the full extent of its labor shortage. Asher was first assigned onerous work as a fruit and vegetable picker but in the spring was permitted to join the army, where he served

---

*The pain and humiliation of the *Dunera* incident—resulting in fear of water and occasional sleep disorders for the rest of his life—was something Asher kept from all but his family until 1979, when a fellow internee related his experience in the local *Jewish Bulletin*. The rabbi called in a reporter the following week and unburdened himself of his story.

as the acting chaplain of a refugee unit. Later he became the assistant rabbi of Melbourne's large Liberal synagogue, where he was greatly influenced by the senior rabbi, Hermann Sanger, a German refugee who had succeeded in establishing Reform Judaism in Australia.

After the war, Leo Baeck and Lily Montagu called Asher back to Germany to be a liaison chaplain between the British occupational authorities and the Jews in the DP camps. His main office was in Bergen-Belsen. He had already been ordained by the Tree of Life Yeshiva—having finished the program by correspondence from Australia—when in the late 1940s he came to America and attended Hebrew Union College in Cincinnati in order to familiarize himself further with the teachings of the Reform movement. His first American pulpit was in Florida; his second, Alabama, where he also took a degree in law from the state university. In 1958, he became the spiritual leader of Temple Emanuel in Greensboro, North Carolina.

There he remained for a decade, the most crucial period in the struggle for civil rights in the South since the freeing of the slaves. Asher promptly identified with the cause of the blacks. He supported the nation's first sit-ins, held at Woolworth's lunch counter in Greensboro, and spoke at North Carolina A&T at the request of its student body president, Jesse Jackson. Within his congregation, Asher explained the need for equal rights to many who wished to maintain the racial status quo, including the influential owners of Cone Mills, a company that had been active in North Carolina since the nineteenth century and which was now one of the state's leading employers. One of the requirements to be met by the confirmation class, meanwhile, was to befriend the first three black teenagers admitted to Greensboro's high school.

Asher won many over to his side by drawing upon his own experiences as the victim of prejudice and discrimination. In response to the violent protests during the integration of Little Rock's schools and the controversy over the use of federal troops, he reminded his congregants that as a schoolboy in Germany he too had faced jeering crowds, the difference being that there the government did not protect him.

Despite his work on behalf of civil rights, the small-town rabbi would have been little known outside the South had it not been for a controversial article which was published in *Look* magazine in April 1965.

Enunciating the religious universalism which would also characterize his rabbinate in San Francisco, Asher wrote that "the time [had] come for those who hate Germany and the Germans to take a new look at their feelings."

The article had been prompted by a visit to his old school, the Staatliche Gymnasium in Wiesbaden, from which he had been the last of seven Jews to be expelled during the Third Reich. Addressing high school students, he felt that he had won a "spiritual victory in reducing bitterness and converting it into the stuff of which civilized human relations are made." He looked up a former classmate, only to learn when they met that thirty years earlier the boy had scribbled "*Judd*" (kike) next to Asher's name in the school yearbook. But the rabbi felt no "animosity" in his heart, "only compassion."

A storm of criticism greeted the *Look* article, not least because of the sensational title which the editors chose for the front cover of the issue's five million copies: "A Rabbi Asks: Isn't It Time We Forgave the Germans?" Thousands of letters poured into his Greensboro office, the overwhelming majority of them negative. *Look* printed replies from two former concentration camp inmates who took exception to the rabbi's position because, in their opinion, he hadn't suffered enough to be an authority on the subject. Nor could he leave the matter behind him when he went west; his advocacy of a rapprochement between Germans and Jews was protested by a number of refugees and others who picketed his first Kol Nidre service in San Francisco.

IT WAS CLEAR FROM THE BEGINNING that the demand for social justice would be a centerpiece of his rabbinate. Like many of his colleagues, at the end of the '60s he opposed the Vietnam War but, like very few of them, he tackled another heated issue, that of busing. "Since when is the neighborhood school so sacred?" he asked, concluding that busing, far from being a dirty word, might well be the lesser of two evils. In 1972, he actively campaigned for the election of George McGovern.

He fought for many progressive causes through the American Jewish Congress, serving as president of the local chapter for two years in the mid-1970s and later as national vice-president. He ardently supported AJC programs such as legal assistance for the elderly poor, an experience reserve bank to help new business ventures, and nursing home certification, both in print and from the pulpit. He was also a staunch advocate of Mount Zion Hospital, which was funded in part by the Jewish Welfare Federation but served primarily non-Jews.

In his sermons he frequently dealt with questions often ignored by the Jewish community, such as world hunger, arms control, and the murder of thousands of Jehovah's Witnesses in some of the new African republics. The Asher years, following the Six Day War, coincided with a period in which Jews increasingly worried about their own; they were preoccupied not only with Israel's security but also Soviet Jewry and black anti-Semitism. Yet his was a far wider perspective, seeking to transcend parochial Jewish concerns. In discussing any political development, he was annoyed by the question "Is it good for the Jews?"

Asher even deemed the Holocaust indicative of "a universal threat to humanity." Appointed to the U.S. Holocaust Memorial Council by President Carter in 1980, he broke publicly with those members who saw only the distinctively Jewish nature of the catastrophe:

> I would regret the Council to fall into the trap of single-issue orientation that so fragments our country. I support Jewish Particularism. But not as an end in itself. Only as it leads to a Universalism which our prophets envisioned for us to aspire.

During his five-year term he rarely missed a meeting of the council, an organization instrumental in creating the impressive U.S. Holocaust Museum on the Capitol Mall, which would open its doors in the following decade. And he established a close friendship with the council's chairman, Elie Wiesel, whom he brought to San Francisco to address the congregation. But he also incurred the wrath of several other council members, who chafed at his emphasis on the figure of eleven million, rather than six million, murdered by Hitler. For the rabbi wanted to ensure that the non-Jewish victims of Nazism not be given short shrift. His own ordeal during the war had shown him firsthand the basic human drive of survival and the commonality of all people.

But if Asher was an all-embracing humanitarian and a political liberal, he was decidedly conservative as a social and cultural critic. His sensibility was that of a man accustomed not only to the refinements of German

RABBI ASHER WITH ELIE WIESEL

culture, but also to the respect for convention one encounters in the British Empire as well as in small Southern cities such as Tuscaloosa and Greensboro. So he was offended by much of what he saw on the streets of San Francisco beginning in the late '60s, though his lively curiosity drew him again and again to ponder its meaning.

This urbane European intellectual found it worth his while to familiarize himself with the language, music, and attitudes of the counterculture. He reviewed Charles Reich's *Greening of America*, referred to Jimi Hendrix and Janis Joplin in the *Temple Chronicle*, and wrote at length on the subject of hallucinatory drugs. He praised the young for their interest in nature and ecology, but he also tore off the "veneer of flower petals" which covered the "love and peace generation," as evidenced by his cutting comments on the Rolling Stones' ill-fated rock concert at Altamont:

> Viewing the event, there came to mind the picture of the proverbial lemmings inexorably drawn to their own destruction. A peaceful pasture invaded by a quarter of a million youngsters writhing for a few hours in a kind of unreal ecstasy leaving behind them heaps of trash. Is this what man visits on nature?

Throughout the '70s and early '80s, the rabbi attacked other examples of mass culture "assaulting our senses and intellects." He mocked fads such as peace symbols worn as jewelry, or antiwar slogans made into bumper stickers. Graphic movies such as *The Godfather*, *A Clockwork Orange*, and *Straw Dogs*, he felt, contributed to the atmosphere which led to such terrorist acts as the Munich massacre, and popular television shows like *Let's Make a Deal* were part of the mediocrity which "penetrates, ... saturates, strangles our lives at every turn." Asher bewailed "the total lack of subtlety" which had come to characterize the mass media in those years. As he wrote in the *Temple Chronicle*,

> "Telling it like it is," leaves little to our imagination. The tendency to speak one's mind seems to be concerned more with the act of speaking than with the substance of what is said. To communicate violence, we project an imagery of gallons of blood and searing flesh. To communicate love, we need naked bodies engaged in fornication. To communicate perversions, we need to enact them in full view.

A man of impeccable manners, for whom language was all-important, he was alarmed by the foul words which had come into vogue in so many quarters: "All we shall have accomplished by our contemporary directness will be to destroy what few niceties there are left in human relations."

In this regard he was also uncomfortable with the rhetorical "excesses" of feminism. Nor did he feel an affinity with San Francisco's large and vocal homosexual community, whose leaders he viewed as contentious and provocative.

FOR ASHER, the Jewish community itself was threatened by the forces of vulgar sensationalism and crass parochialism at work in the society at large. In this sense he repeatedly criticized Rabbi Meir Kahane's Jewish Defense League for its blind extremism, but his most publicized conflict arose with another group on the periphery of the Jewish community, Berkeley's Chabad House. Established in 1972, this outpost of the Lubavitcher Hasidim attracted attention for its zealous attempts to increase the level of observance among Jews throughout Northern California. In 1975, one of the young Chabad rabbis, Chaim Drizin, arranged for a giant Hanukah menorah—donated by the rock impresario Bill Graham—to be erected on public land in San Francisco's Union Square. During a ceremony which drew much media coverage, Drizin himself was lifted in a crane to light the 3,500-pound, twenty-two-foot candelabra.

Asher protested vehemently, his remarks carried in the *San Francisco*

Examiner as well as the *Jewish Bulletin*. On one level he objected to what he viewed as a violation of the principle of separation of church and state, deeming the Chabad menorah "the newest challenge to the Bill of Rights." He reasoned that the Jewish community would now be on much weaker ground in objecting to similar behavior on the part of Christians, such as the display of the cross on public buildings. Beyond that, he felt that the whole spectacle, "an exercise in showmanship," was simply in bad taste. In the *Temple Chronicle*, he asked his readers "if a giant menorah really intensifies Jewish values," and if they "really [wanted] to secularize Hanukah as Christmas has become secularized."

Nearly all of the Bay Area's Reform rabbis agreed with Asher, but he was sharply criticized by several of his Conservative and Orthodox colleagues, not only for his views but also for having aired them in the press. The Jewish Community Relations Council formed a committee, including one of its own professionals and two laymen, to try to reach a compromise for the following year. Its work resulted in the menorah being moved to a privately owned site at the Stonestown shopping center, five miles away. Beginning in 1977, however, it was returned to Union Square; Chabad House has retained that location ever since, creating a San Francisco tradition which draws thousands of people each Hanukah.

Asher chose to remain silent after it was clear that he had lost the battle over the giant menorah. But throughout his long rabbinate he continued to take a dim view not only of Chabad, but of other alternative groups as well, from the "pied-pipering" of the local House of Love and Prayer founded by the singing *rebbe*, Shlomo Carlebach, to the Jewish Renewal Movement of New Age rabbi Zalman Schachter-Shalomi.* These charismatic spiritual leaders and their passionate followers sought to breathe new life into a postwar American Judaism which they felt had become divorced from the concerns of young people. But to Asher these grassroots movements, among others, were upstart organizations which not only offended his German-Jewish sense of decorum, but also challenged the centrality of the synagogue. Nor could he welcome the *havurah* movement, the new rituals and liturgies created for women by feminist Jews, or

---

*Despite Asher's antipathy, Carlebach—whose nearby center was supported by a number of Emanu-El congregants—performed in the temple courtyard in September 1969, on the anniversary of the Babi Yar massacre.

the emerging worship communities for gays—all of which seemed to thrive on the West Coast.

On Rosh Hashanah morning, 1972, he used the term "spiritual bankruptcy" in referring to this popular religion that had arisen outside the walls of the synagogue and that in his mind threatened institutional Judaism: "Jewish militants, Jewish radicals, Jewish communes, Jewish vegetarians, Jewish homosexuals, Jewish coalitions, Jewish mystics, even Jews for Jesus, every one of whom grinding their own axes without much regard for the Jewish community as a whole....There is more grandstanding than substance in all of this." With the sardonic humor that was his trademark, he then asked, "How about a minyan motorcycle gang? That could get a sixty-second spot on the evening news and a half column in *Time* magazine."

In the late '70s Asher was worried about the allure of cults for Jewish youth, but he cautioned against the rise of "Jewish cults" just as strongly. For him the blossoming of interest in Jewish mysticism and meditation in particular "represented a primitive sentimentality, a submission to our coarsest rather than our most exalted needs."

Joseph Portnoy, the temple's cantor and educator throughout the entire Asher era, fully agreed with this assessment. For him, too, the new "Jewish spirituality" provided little in the "search for answers to religious questions." He would later soften his position, but as late as 1986, when so many of the alternative Jewish cultural expressions had become commonplace, he seemed to echo the rabbi—in style as well as substance— lamenting the rise of

> an idealized shtetl culture incorporating [its] crassest elements...with the dissemination of Yiddishkeit as its major objective. Music groups such as Hot Borscht and Klezmerim are [now] the performers of "authentic" Jewish music. How long will it be before a bagel and lox amulet is produced to be worn along with the Chai and Mogen David as yet another symbol of Jewish identity? What has become of Jewish rectitude, dignity, self-respect?

Asher and Portnoy, then, were not about to borrow from the new impulses invigorating American Jewry in the '70s and early '80s. On the contrary, they sought to protect the temple from what they regarded as the contaminating influences of Jewish showmen and charlatans.

THERE WAS ALSO A DEGREE OF PRESSURE for religious change from within the temple itself, but the rabbi and cantor steadfastly maintained Emanu-El's basic mode of worship. Many of the younger members had been influenced by Shabbat retreats at Camp Swig, where they often sat in a circle and sang traditional Jewish songs to the accompaniment of a guitar. Some asked for a more intimate and participatory worship experience at the temple as well, if not in the main sanctuary, at least through alternative services in the Rinder Chapel or the Meyer Auditorium. Older members, including some of the synagogue's leaders, were often impressed with the more traditional services they attended at the biennial conferences of the Union of American Hebrew Congregations. Here they were exposed to a good deal of Hebrew in the liturgy, to skullcaps and prayer shawls, and to the sort of Jewish music one might hear in a Conservative or even Orthodox *shul*. Many congregants, especially if they had not been brought up with the Emanu-El brand of Judaism, wondered if the Classical Reform service could give way to a religious expression that would be a bit more in the mainstream.

Asher and Portnoy gradually introduced a few traditional practices such as the *hakafot*—festive, circular processions on Simchat Torah in which the children are showered with candy.* Moreover, the Bar Mitzvah boys and Bat Mitzvah girls began to chant rather than speak their Torah and Haftorah portions, and a few wore skullcaps and prayer shawls as well.

Of course, the most important liturgical innovation during the Asher years was the introduction in 1976 of the new Reform prayerbook for the Sabbath, *Gates of Prayer*, and, three years later, *Gates of Repentance* for the High Holidays. They added more Hebrew and a number of traditional prayers to the service, while rendering the English translation in language more contemporary and accessible. But these were all changes about which the rabbi was "very ambivalent."

A number of congregants from the old families were loath to replace the old *Union Prayer Book*, which despite its archaic expressions and outdated theology had served the temple since the turn of the century. Asher saw their point, arguing that "there is something to be said for the majesty

---

*This Central European custom was especially appreciated by the German refugees—then reaching their sixties and seventies—who comprised the majority of those in attendance not only on Simchat Torah but on every other holiday as well, save Yom Kippur and Rosh Hashanah.

of that old English style...reminiscent of the King James usage....To reduce it to the common vernacular might well make the prayers somewhat banal." Nor was he enamored of the inclusion in the weighty Sabbath tome of sixteen distinct Friday evening and Saturday morning services, many of them, such as the neo-Hasidic, reflecting just the sort of alternative approaches to liturgy that he rejected. Still, he allowed that "the [revised] text retains a poetic character," and in the end Emanu-El—with the aid of a gift from its Sisterhood—joined the overwhelming majority of Reform congregations in the country (though not its famous namesake in New York City) in adopting both new books. Asher himself refrained from making a recommendation on this matter; the decision was entirely that of the ritual committee and the temple board.

In other respects, he succeeded in retaining many Classical Reform features. The clergy at Emanu-El did not cover their heads when leading services, for example, and almost all of the congregation went bareheaded as well. The Sabbath and High Holiday liturgy continued to include a prayer for the welfare of the nation, spoken while "My Country 'Tis of Thee" was played on the organ;* and the *amidah*, usually a silent prayer performed while standing, was here read responsively by a seated congregation. Nor at that time were there *aliyot*—the practice, even in the large majority of Reform synagogues, of calling honored members and guests to the *bimah* to recite the blessings over the Torah portion.

Worshippers were also struck by the very formal, stylized quality of the services, frequently referred to as "cold." But Cantor Portnoy pointed out that this style was mandated by the architecture of the sanctuary, a vast, austere hall that hardly lends itself to hand-clapping and communal singing. At the end of the 1970s, he employed the term "high church" to describe the temple on Saturday mornings, adding, "We offer some of the world's greatest liturgical music but, like Grace Cathedral or St. Mary's, we have less room for experimentation and innovation than a smaller house of worship somewhere off in the suburbs."

---

*Portnoy saw no reason to jettison the American patriotic hymn, and recalled that the synagogue at which he had first served as cantor, in Richmond, Virginia, played the tune "Old Oak Tree" during *Yizkor* instead of the time-honored "El Molay Rachamim." "Even that is justifiable," he said, "because of the emotion it has elicited from the congregation for more than half a century."

Even aside from the regal setting of the main sanctuary, Portnoy allowed recently that he "wouldn't have *dared* to introduce" (his emphasis) a different style of music that was "less church-like or secularly classic [and] more folk-like, or 'Jewish.'" The cantor had sung in an Orthodox *shul* as a teenager and was capable of initiating a more eclectic repertoire, but he felt that Cantor Rinder (who sat on the *bimah* until the mid-'60s), organist Ludwig Altman, and Rabbi Asher would have objected to any new departure in this regard. There is no doubt, too, that many Classical Reform patterns of the past were retained in deference to the pioneer families.

In 1980, the temple reinstituted, on a once-a-month basis, the somewhat less formal Friday evening family service with a late starting time that had been offered in the Fine years. But the rabbi was annoyed by the persistent requests for more far-reaching religious changes, some of them even going beyond the mode of worship. In a pointed piece in the *Temple Chronicle* in 1982, he lambasted the inconsistent "pick and choose" mentality of those he derided as "mindless Traditionalists." Using as an example the recent directive of Camp Swig not to serve milk with meat—despite the fact that the meat was not kosher—he claimed that in the swing to more tradition, there is invariably "a darker side as well...a corruption of Jewish law and ritual posing as the real thing." A year later he seriously questioned the motives of those advocating "the restoration of customs and rituals which we had abandoned as archaic and irrelevant for the twentieth century." He accused some Reform Jews of trying to "placate Orthodoxy's attempt to delegitimize them" with nothing more than "a fad for nostalgia and contemporary Jewish chic," warning that in any case this was a debate that they could never win.

He, for one, was not about to compromise the essence of the Emanu-El tradition of dignity and prophetic ethics, elegance and refined spirituality. To make this clear, he even titled one of his last courses at the temple's Institute of Jewish Studies "Reform Judaism—With No Apologies."

"I know that there are only a few congregations like this left," he stated in 1979, "and I feel an obligation to preserve this one." With a resolve perhaps not unlike that of his Orthodox forebears, he insisted: "There is room for us in San Francisco. Not everyone's taste runs to the rock music at Winterland. There is also an opera house in this city."

IF, WITH THE BENEFIT OF HINDSIGHT, Asher's views on the alternative Jewish expressions which emerged during his rabbinate seem unduly rigid and behind the times, on another key issue events have borne him out as remarkably prescient. With his characteristic courage he became one of the first rabbis of a major congregation to criticize Israel publicly, plunging him into a serious controversy which cost him a number of congregants and close friends. It revolved around his election, in February 1977, to the national board of Breira (Hebrew for "alternative"), an organization of leading Jewish intellectuals openly critical of Israel's policies toward the Palestinians. Although Breira's rolls included such prominent rabbis as Eugene Borowitz and Wolfe Kelman, its position that Israel negotiate with the PLO was viewed as misguided by most major Jewish organizations, and outright disloyal by some.

Asher's Zionist "credentials" were such that it is surprising that his motivations were questioned. A lifelong supporter of Jewish statehood, he was honored for his work on behalf of Israel Bonds—sold at the temple for the first time after his arrival—with a special dinner in 1969. The following year, he and Brian Lurie, the youthful assistant rabbi, launched the first annual confirmation class trip to Israel, an ambitious six-and-a-half-week summer tour in which thirty-six students participated. Asher won the approval of the board of directors for the program—no easy task—and also secured funds for scholarships. Lurie, who was very popular with the temple's teenagers, led the trip; it has since become a community-wide venture. Moreover, Asher demanded of his congregants and his rabbinical colleagues "sacrificial giving" to the UJA campaign, and on this score not even his most caustic critic could accuse him of hypocrisy; he annually contributed about a tenth of his salary to that cause alone.

But in keeping with his disdain for triumphalist nationalism—emanating from any quarter—the rabbi did not view Israel as a sacred cow. Beginning in the early '70s, in sermons, writings, and even a course taught at the temple, he focused his congregation's attention on the internal problems of the Jewish state, topics often overshadowed by the looming drama of war and peace. Distressed in particular by the narrow-mindedness of Israel's religious establishment, "zealots…who impose their prejudices upon the people," Asher devoted one of his monthly messages in the *Temple Chronicle* to a wry report about Israel's chief rabbi's practice of rating the "kosher level" of the country's restaurants with asterisks a là the *Guide Michelin*. Following the Yom Kippur War, he also expressed his concern about the conflicts between young and old, Arab and Jew, Ashkenazi and Sephardi, soldier and civilian—contradictions only temporarily hidden by the external threat.

Breira addressed itself to these issues, as well as what it regarded as a "garrison state mentality" governing Israel's foreign policy. For Asher, any criticism of the state had for too long been considered "tantamount to treason." As early as 1973, he declared that "we have the right—nay, the duty—to insist that its uniquely Jewish character not be submerged in the aping of other nations."

Yet a number of Jewish leaders saw Breira as a threat to Israel's security. They alleged that several of its spokesmen, such as Arthur Waskow—a New Age rabbi with whom Asher found fault as well—had had ties to left-wing organizations opposed to the very existence of a Jewish state. A lengthy pamphlet circulated by the Zionist Organization of America drew parallels between Breira and the American Council for Judaism, and suggested that many of its rabbis (most of whom were Hillel directors) had been duped into becoming propagandists for the PLO.

Asher, who along with Leonard Beerman of Los Angeles was one of the few congregational rabbis to join Breira, saw his role as that of toning down radicals like Waskow and raising the level of responsibility and maturity of the nascent organization. This point was evidently lost on his detractors, however, a number of whom dubbed him "the new Irving Reichert." A conspicuous article in the *Jewish Bulletin* on Asher's Breira connection resulted in many complaints being phoned in to temple president Myer Kahn—and a few resignations as well. Feeling that he was no longer wanted at the local ZOA, the rabbi quietly resigned from its board of directors. Federation executives, meanwhile, were unhappy with what they felt to have been his bad judgment. And, as in the aftermath of the *Look* magazine article, he was the recipient of several death threats.

As in past crises Asher was greatly supported by his wife, the former Fae Snyder, daughter of the leading *shochet* of Sydney, Australia, and highly active in temple activities. She exerted a calming influence on her husband, who finally agreed not to discuss Breira in public in order to avoid the sort of dissension that had paralyzed the congregation in the

1940s. The issue was further defused with the fading of Breira from the national scene even before the Sadat peace initiative.

Moreover, Asher did not shrink from coming to Israel's defense when he felt the circumstances warranted it. Although he opposed the invasion of Lebanon in 1982, he also expressed his dismay with "the dramatic rise of resentment against Israel," including "odious and malicious" comparisons between Prime Minister Begin and Hitler—some of them even made by Jews. Fearing a "crumbling of our attachment" to the Jewish state, he firmly declared, "It is one thing to be sharply critical of the Government of Israel and some of its leaders.…It is another thing for some of us to use this episode [of the war in Lebanon] to take flight from our obligations to the State of Israel, and to sever ties with her."

Yet the notion that the Jews of the diaspora have an "obligation to speak out" on Israel remained axiomatic for him until the end. He did not live to see the 1992 election of the Labor government, which would openly negotiate with Yasir Arafat, but he felt much vindication in 1985 when Shimon Peres, as prime minister, ended the war in Lebanon and began to speak of a new relationship with the Palestinians. Writing that summer, shortly before his retirement from the temple, and proudly reflecting on more than a decade and a half of acting "as a goad" on the Israel issue, he could not resist noting that "only now [are] the very voices ignored for so long… appropriated for the conventional wisdom."

WHILE THE LEADERSHIP of the Jewish Welfare Federation was unhappy with the rabbi's outspoken criticism of Israel and his affiliation with Breira in particular, this was merely one aspect of the uneasy relationship between the temple and the JWF throughout the '70s and early '80s. For Asher had a major philosophical disagreement with the Federation: just as he felt the centrality of the synagogue was threatened by the proliferation of small, grassroots Jewish organizations, so he saw it endangered by what he termed "a secular, or civil religion replacing the sacerdotal." He believed that the "financial means test" applied by the Federation had jaded all of American Jewry and that "precisely because the synagogue applies a test beyond the financial one, it has become little more than a tiresome necessity."

Moreover, he argued, the Federation too closely resembled a giant corporation, with business ethics rather than Jewish values as its guiding principles. This posed a particular problem, the rabbi and some of his lay leaders felt, because the JWF was no longer solely in the business of raising and allocating funds, but had become an "activities" organization—entering the social, educational, and cultural fields in which the synagogue had once been predominant. And, according to Asher, the Federation lacked the spiritual underpinning of the synagogue needed for such tasks.

Whether or not this critique was justified, it was clear to everyone that during the Asher era the Federation had eclipsed the temple as the most powerful force in the Jewish community. According to Reynold Colvin, who served as president of Emanu-El as well as Jewish Community Relations Council chairman and JWF vice-president, federations across the country had "drained away substantial resources" from synagogues and other Jewish organizations. Although not necessarily critical of this development, which came about as a result of Israel's unprecedented needs, Colvin, Myer Kahn, and others felt that it constituted one of the major problems the temple faced in the decade and a half following the Six Day War.

By the late 1970s Emanu-El leaders were a little in awe of the local Federation's ability to raise over ten million dollars a year, a figure which had doubled since the beginning of that decade (and which would double again by the late 1990s). "With its high-powered organization, and the appeal of Israel," said one temple president from that time, "[the Federation has] ways that we don't have to make you feel guilty if you don't give."

Competition for lay leaders was also spirited, with the JWF drawing most of its top people from the temple. Since its inception in 1910, the overwhelming majority of the Federation's presidents have been Emanu-El congregants; in 1979, for example, the six highest elective offices were all held by temple members. Rabbi Asher, who well understood the lure of the Federation's exciting missions to Israel—which often included an audience with the country's political leaders—wrote ruefully that he could not organize missions to meet Talmudic sages such as Moses Maimonides or the Vilna Gaon.

The attractiveness of the JWF may have partially accounted for the fact that the descendants of the old families held far fewer positions of leadership in the temple during the Asher years than they did during the rabbinate of Alvin Fine. Less active than they had been formerly in Jewish affairs of all kinds, save the arts, the younger descendants of the pioneer families in particular tended to gravitate toward the Federation and some of its agencies—when they sought involvement at all.*

Ironically, the executive director of the San Francisco JWF in those years was not only a rabbi, but also Joseph Asher's former assistant at Emanu-El. After leaving the temple in 1971, Brian Lurie worked for the United Jewish Appeal of Greater New York for a year and a half before returning to San Francisco to become, in his early thirties, the youngest major federation director in the country. He succeeded brilliantly in the Bay Area, transforming the JWF into one of the leading federations in North America. In the early 1990s, he went back to New York, this time serving as the head of the UJA, arguably the top post in the field of Jewish communal service in the entire diaspora.

He did not have a warm relationship with Rabbi Asher, and gave little credence to the older man's critique of the Federation. In Lurie's view, the term "secularization" has no meaning in the Jewish tradition, and he rebutted his former colleague by asking the question of whether caring for the aged or finding someone a job is not a religious act. Rather than a debilitating competition for leaders and dollars, he felt that a harmonic, supportive relationship prevailed between synagogue and federation, the latter being the "instrumentality for creating community," the former concentrating on family. The attraction of Israel may draw people to the federation, Rabbi Lurie conceded in an interview at the end of the 1970s, but it is the congregational rabbi who is present at the most dramatic points of the life cycle—circumcision and baby naming, Bar and Bat Mitzvah, confirmation, marriage, and death. "We can't compete with that," he added.

Whether or not the rapid rise of the Federation bore part of the blame, there was no doubt that the temple played less of a role in the

*There were notable exceptions, though. Lloyd Dinkelspiel Jr. would most likely have been chosen president of Emanu-El, like his father and grandfather before him, had he not suffered a fatal stroke while still in his prime. In 1977, however, his sister, Frances Green, was the first woman to become president of the Federation.

Jewish community in the '70s and early '80s than it ever had before. True, visiting dignitaries such as Golda Meir and Abba Eban were introduced to the community in the sanctuary, which was also the site of a huge citywide rally during the Yom Kippur War. But it was the Jewish Community Relations Council of the Federation which became the closest thing to a policy-making body for the Jews in the Bay Area, not Temple Emanu-El, nor any other synagogue. And just as those in the Christian ministry no longer seemed to wield the influence of a Parsons, Pike, or McGucken, so the local rabbinate during this period came to lack the charismatic leaders who had guided the course of the Jewish community in years past.

Asher himself freely admitted that he was on the defensive. Contending with the Federation on the one hand and alternative religious expressions on the other, struggling against demographic and economic tides, and facing a flock ever more cynical and critical, during increasingly unstable times, he also felt very much alone.

DESPITE THESE PROFOUND CHALLENGES, Emanu-El in the Asher era maintained its high intellectual and aesthetic standards.

Among his many roles the rabbi believed preaching to be the most important; his sermons were as carefully constructed and polished as those of any clergyman in the Bay Area. Not only were they always written out in advance, but they even included diacritical marks in red ink indicating when he was to raise or lower his voice. Drawing upon his extensive knowledge of European civilization as well as Jewish tradition, his cultivated talks from the pulpit often resembled top-flight university lectures. As his admiring colleague Rabbi Robert Kirschner later put it, "Rabbi Asher was by aptitude and temperament a true intellectual.... [He] never stooped to conquer: he sought the heart by way of the mind. His sermons were more thoughtful than theatrical, more akin to discourse than homily."

He was sometimes criticized for being a highbrow, a sort of Adlai Stevenson of the rabbinate, but he felt that his audience, primarily college graduates, could follow him quite well. In any case, he preferred to talk over the heads of some than insult the intelligence of others.

It is this commitment to the life of the mind that also accounted for the appearance at Emanu-El of some of the most provocative thinkers of the day, such as Bruno Bettelheim, Richard Rubenstein, William Sloane Coffin, Irving Howe, Lucy Dawidowicz, Yehuda Bauer, and Martin E. Marty. The Institute of Jewish Studies, meanwhile, counted among its faculty virtually all the leading academicians of Judaica at the Bay Area's colleges and universities.

In the arts, too, the temple continued to be true to its illustrious past, with the descendants of the pioneer families playing a generous supportive role. In the area of fine arts, the most impressive project of the entire postwar period was the completion, in 1973, of two enormous stained-glass windows for the sanctuary, a gift of Walter and Elise Haas and Madeleine Haas Russell. These replaced the deteriorating amber glass that had been part of the original, unembellished design in the mid-1920s.

Originally Marc Chagall was asked to design the new windows. Although he was in his mid-eighties and living abroad, he showed much interest in the project; but his protective wife prevented him from undertaking the task. Elise Haas, a woman with a keen understanding of art, then recommended the versatile Californian Mark Adams. A student in the 1940s of the famous abstract painter Hans Hoffman and a master of the art of tapestry design as well as stained glass, he devoted two years to the windows. In the end, he created two radiant, nonrepresentational interpretations, "Water" and "Fire," for the east and west balconies, respectively.

The temple board accepted the expensive gift only by a very close vote. A number of prominent congregants strongly objected to any interference with the deliberate austerity of the domed chamber, intended to enhance the contemplative aspect of prayer. But once the great windows were installed (the single-handed accomplishment of fabricator George McKeever), virtually everyone was delighted by the vivid color "that dances across the sanctuary, adding…warmth and enchantment."

Each window, comprised of two thousand pieces of glass, includes over two hundred different hues. Adams "seems to say," his biographers write, that "only by entering the temple…you can look out the windows and see the true nature of the universe around you. It is perhaps his response to religious mysticism that makes it possible for him to create these awesome spaces so charged with meaning."

The temple was further adorned in 1976 with the presentation by Lucille Bush of an intricate mosaic for the south wall of the courtyard, in honor of her late husband, Philip, born in San Francisco more than a hundred years earlier. In 1979, replacing altar cloths that had been stolen from the sanctuary several years earlier, the congregation dedicated three new tapestries for the *bimah*: cloths for both the upper and lower altars, and coverings for the pulpit benches. Designed by the husband-and-wife team of Yael Lurie and Jean-Pierre Larochette, of the well-known Aubusson school of France, the fabrics were woven locally by Ruth Tannenbaum and the San Francisco Tapestry Workshop. The tapestries, financed by a number of leading families through special subscription, were a long-term project of the energetic museum committee.

Four years earlier, under the leadership of Nadine Rushakoff, a UC Berkeley graduate who would later become the first woman to serve as president of Emanu-El, the committee exhibited the works of five historic California Jewish painters—Toby Rosenthal, Joseph Greenbaum, Ernest Peixotto, Anne Bremer, and Joseph Raphael. Co-sponsored by Berkeley's Judah L. Magnes Museum in 1975 in honor of the congregation's 125th anniversary, *The Creative Frontier* included seventy-seven paintings that were placed on view at the temple and in the East Bay. In 1982, a twenty-fifth anniversary retrospective demonstrated that the Elizabeth S. Fine Memorial Museum possessed one of the leading collections of any synagogue museum in the country. A few years later, under the leadership of the dedicated congregant JoAnne Levy, the Fine Museum was accepted as a member of the Council of American Jewish Museums—a further indication of its high standards.

To commemorate the temple's 125th anniversary, the Sisterhood presented the city with an unusual gift: a biblical walk and garden including seventeen trees and plants for Golden Gate Park's Strybing Arboretum. This was the initiative of Marian Levy, one of many strong leaders of the women's auxiliary in this era.

Another active Sisterhood president was the community-minded Sylvia Stone, influenced by the shining example of Hattie Sloss a generation earlier. Stone also belonged to an intimate discussion group known as "Our Crowd West" that included devoted longtime Emanu-El members such as Lucille Bush, Rebecca Rosenstein, Reggie Goldstine, and Rowie Rinder—all of them avid supporters of the temple's cultural initiatives.*

In this period the performing arts flourished as well. The Temple Players, revived in 1973, presented *The World of Sholom Aleichem* in December of that year. The production was made possible by the Jennie Baruh Zellerbach Memorial Fund, which Harold Zellerbach had established in memory of his mother. Three years later *The Dybbuk* was performed in the Meyer Auditorium by the New Habima Production Company; among those present on opening night were members of the Temple Players who had staged the enthralling drama with so much fanfare in 1928.

The tradition of Reuben Rinder was also continued, with the temple making notable contributions in the field of music. Ludwig Altman's highly praised organ recitals, for example—in the '70s and early '80s an annual event at Emanu-El sponsored by the Goethe Institute—thoroughly enriched the musical life of the city. The temple was also the setting for the yearly performances of the San Francisco Civic Chorale, usually accompanied by members of the Symphony Orchestra.

Moreover, in addition to musical renditions of the *kedushot* (prayers inserted into the *amidah*, a core element of the service) by both Mark Lavry and Paul Ben Haim, Emanu-El commissioned two full-length works during the decade. In 1970, marking the temple's 120th anniversary, Cantor Portnoy engaged Seymour Shifrin to set the Book of Chronicles to music. The Brandeis University professor produced a highly modern, five-part work drawn from the texts of Isaiah and Job as well as Chronicles; the piece was so challenging to the chorus, soloists, and orchestra that initially Portnoy found it impossible to have it performed. A few years later the intricate avant-garde work, reminiscent of Arnold Schoenberg, was played in Boston by that city's symphony orchestra, accompanied by the New England Conservatory Chorus. It was declared "monumental" by a local reviewer.

---

*These older women—capable and confident, witty and worldly—were not only caring to one another (several of them lived in the same apartment building on Jackson Street) but also gracious and hospitable to everyone else at the temple. Among others in this coterie have been Golda Kaufman, Helen Gorfinkel, Sylvia Reback, Delphine Heilbron, Emmy Altman, and Florence Grafman. Fae Asher, of course, played a major role both in the Sisterhood and in Our Crowd West, which has seen a number of its key members pass away but continues to this day.

CANTOR JOSEPH PORTNOY AND ORGANIST LUDWIG ALTMAN (SEATED)

For the 125th anniversary of the congregation, and the fiftieth anniversary of the Lake Street temple, Portnoy, through the Zellerbach Fund, commissioned a sacred service based on the new Reform prayerbook. For the task he chose Sergiu Natra, professor of music at Tel Aviv University, who had immigrated to Israel from Rumania in 1961. The cantor worked closely with Natra, playing a role not unlike that of his predecessor in the Bloch service. On three occasions he journeyed to Israel to consult with the composer and aided him greatly in blending the highly original music with the Reform liturgy.

Dedicated to Portnoy and his wife, Ruth, the *Avodat Hakodesh* was first performed on May 15, 1976, with Joseph Asher and Arnold Magid (assistant rabbi from 1975 to 1979) participating along with the cantor, Ludwig Altman, and the Emanu-El choir. Later published by the prestigious Israel Music Institute, the work was hailed by Alexander Fried, who decades earlier had reviewed the services of Bloch and Milhaud. "It spreads warmth and lyric appeal," he wrote in the *Examiner*. "The music has heart and buoyancy."

YET NONE OF THESE ARTISTIC TRIUMPHS seemed to stem the loss of congregants; membership declined in each of the fifteen years after 1964.

Although in the late '70s and early '80s the official count seemed to have bottomed out at around 1,200, a significant number of those on the rolls were really inactive members who had neither paid dues nor attended temple events in years. It was later estimated that by 1985 the actual size of the congregation had dipped to around a thousand, a loss of a third since the days of Rabbi Fine.

Even more disheartening was the rapidly dwindling religious school, directed by Cantor Portnoy since 1965.* Enrollment had fallen well below 250 by the mid-'80s, barely a fifth of its size a generation earlier. It was difficult to attract qualified teachers, and Muriel Cohn, the beloved secretary of the school, freely admitted that many instructors wandered from the curriculum. No doubt, the two-hour-a-week Sunday session (supplemented by a two-year, twice-weekly Hebrew program for those wishing to become a Bar or Bat Mitzvah) provided a limited framework for serious Jewish learning. But if some parents were dissatisfied, clearly the main reason for the sharp drop was the declining number of congregants with school-age children.

For Emanu-El was not only shrinking; it was also aging. As the last president of the Asher era, Walter Newman, remembers, "When I first got on the *bimah* [in the capacity of president, early in 1985], I looked out at the audience and saw nothing but gray hair."

Searching for an explanation of this troubling loss of young families, temple leaders—both lay and professional alike—blamed the erosion on the flight to the suburbs. They often cited as evidence a demographic study published in 1972 which revealed that the city had lost 26.5 percent of its Jewish population, or 12,270 people, since 1959.** Nearly all of this "exodus" was comprised of families with school-age children—the backbone of most congregations—who had tended to move to Marin County

---

*Portnoy was given responsibility for the school both because he held a doctorate in education from New York University and because the temple board felt that he would provide the school with continuity, something that would have been lacking had it remained the province of the assistant rabbis, whose tenure was normally limited to two to four years.

**According to the nationally known demographer Fred Massarik, who conducted surveys on behalf of the Federation in both 1959 and 1972, the Jewish population of San Francisco had fallen during these thirteen years from 46,616 to only 34,246. By 1972, Jewish children under fifteen years of age numbered only about four thousand, down 55 percent from 1959. By contrast, those over sixty remained constant at roughly 10,500.

or the Peninsula, two areas where the Jewish population soared during this period.

Although San Francisco experienced an influx of Hispanics and Asians in these years, it saw relatively little of the racial friction, usually between blacks and Jews, which sometimes spurred the move to the suburbs in the East and Midwest. But skyrocketing housing prices, a deteriorating public school system, and an increase in violent crime all did their part to reshape the social contours of the Bay Area. No longer was the city seen by the white middle class as the ideal place to bring up children.

In the face of this powerful and seemingly inexorable trend, coupled with the congregation's sharply rising expenses in the inflationary 1970s, two temple presidents, Raymond Marks and Myer Kahn, even mentioned merger with Sherith Israel as a distinct possibility. The two large urban synagogues had existed since the Gold Rush, but now the ominous shift to the suburbs raised the prospect of radical remedies.

But what was the true demographic picture as the temple reached the critical juncture of the mid-'80s? Another Federation-sponsored demographic study, conducted in 1986 by Brandeis University professor Gary Tobin, offers a snapshot of the situation just as the Asher era came to an end. It reveals that the sociological profile of San Francisco Jewry had indeed been transformed since mid-century, but in complex ways that presented both problems and opportunities for the temple.

First, the sheer size of the Bay Area Jewish community was impressive: it had soared to almost a quarter of a million, and was now virtually tied with four other communities as the third largest in North America. To be sure, San Francisco had grown the least of the eight counties in the region. But while the city now comprised less than a quarter of Bay Area Jewry, even its Jewish population had increased 12 percent since 1959. Now numbering about fifty-two thousand, it had more than replaced the steep losses of the 1960s and early '70s.

Less encouraging, though, were the changes in the size and composition of Jewish households in the Bay Area; these were most pronounced within the city limits of San Francisco. Whereas 22 percent of the city's Jews lived alone in 1959, that number shot up to 32 percent by 1986. It was striking that only a little more than half of all Jewish adults were now married (by far the lowest level in the Bay Area) and those who were married reported fewer children than their coreligionists in the suburbs. The average household size of San Francisco Jewry was a scant 2.1, significantly smaller than that of the region as a whole and one of the lowest of any Jewish community in North America. While the city showed a disproportionately high number of Jewish senior citizens (19 percent, compared with a Bay Area average of 14 percent), it was the percentage of young adults that was most remarkable: more than a fifth of the city's entire Jewish population was aged twenty-five to thirty-four (the other Bay Area counties averaged only one in ten), and about half of that large cohort of more than ten thousand Jews had arrived since 1980.

For many of these young people, joining any synagogue, to say nothing of Temple Emanu-El, was the farthest thing from their minds. A good proportion of them were men who were drawn to San Francisco specifically because they wished to become part of the large and strident gay subculture that had emerged in several of the city's neighborhoods early in the 1970s. This seems to be borne out by the fact that within this key age group, Jewish men outnumbered Jewish women by a ratio of 3 to 2. While hundreds of Jewish gays attended the memorial service held at Emanu-El for slain gay activist and city supervisor Harvey Milk, himself a Jew, few of them ever returned to the temple. Those who opted to join a synagogue generally chose Sha'ar Zahav, formed in 1977 expressly for homosexuals.

Aside from the gays, there were many other people in the city—especially young singles and married couples without children—who chose not to join Emanu-El or any other synagogue because of a general aversion to "establishment" institutions. Those whose attitudes had been formed in the late '60s often regarded "organized religion" as irrelevant at best. And, Tobin's study showed, if they had arrived in recent years from the East or Midwest, free of the social pressure exerted by their parents or extended family, there was even less of a chance of affiliation. But this is not to say that they were therefore cut off from any Jewish experience. On the High Holidays, for example, many of them attended one of a dozen alternative services in the Bay Area that required neither membership nor even a financial contribution.

No doubt the demographic dominance of the young, unattached newcomers accounted in large measure for the city's appallingly low rate of synagogue affiliation—only 25 percent by the mid-'80s, far below the rest of the Bay Area and barely half the national average. But there were other factors as well that had given San Francisco Jewry the dubious distinction of having perhaps the lowest percentage of synagogue members in the country: the high rate of divorce and increasing number of single parents who felt uncomfortable in the synagogue; the lack of interest on the part of recently arrived, foreign-born Jews such as Israelis and émigrés from the Soviet Union; and, not least of all, the relatively high rate of mobility: half of the city's Jews expected to move to another neighborhood (though usually remaining in the Bay Area) within the next three years. And, as in communities throughout the country, the rising financial cost of joining a congregation was reported as a major obstacle for virtually all subgroups.

Yet this was not the entire story told by the 1986 study; other demographic and social trends in the '70s and '80s actually boded well for the temple. Despite the small size of the average household, there were more Jewish families with children than had been thought—a belated "baby boomlet" was in the making. Almost seven thousand Jewish children aged fourteen and younger lived in the city in the mid-'80s, many more than in the early '70s and nearly as many as the halcyon period of the late 1950s.

Most of these were the children of the baby boomers, whose attitudes about many things—including synagogue affiliation—were changing in the '80s. Many of course still clung to a '60s-style anti-institutionalist bias; but there were also those among them who thought that a synagogue might meet some of their social and cultural needs, as well as provide a Jewish education for their children and a meaningful spiritual experience for the entire family.

Among the new arrivals in the '80s were a significant number of high-earning young couples who had been transferred to the San Francisco branch of a major corporation.* Others, working in small business or the professions, also came to view synagogue membership in a different light, especially if they had children. Indeed, the 1986 study revealed that

---

*The city's economy had been transformed since the '60s, losing many of its manufacturing jobs but gaining white collar positions, especially in real estate, insurance, and finance. This was reflected in a boom in the construction of downtown office buildings in the first half of the '80s, in part a result of San Francisco's growing trade with the Pacific Rim.

almost half of the city's vast group of unaffiliated Jews were considering a synagogue in the future; this was a decidedly higher percentage of potential members compared to 1959, when the same question had been asked. Not surprisingly, those among the unaffiliated who were most likely to have plans to join were the newly arrived families with school-age children.

Although denominational distinctions seemed to matter less than ever before, the unaffiliated tended to identify themselves as Reform Jews, the category that far outnumbered any other designation, especially for young people. San Francisco did not see the resurgence of traditional Judaism witnessed in many other urban areas; whereas one in seven of the city's Jewish population had identified themselves as Orthodox a generation earlier, that number dropped to one in twenty in 1986, with a large fraction in this category over the age of seventy.

Few welcomed the soaring rate of intermarriage in the '70s and early '80s; Professor Tobin disclosed the startling fact that in almost half of the marriages involving Jews in the Bay Area between 1981 and 1986, the spouse was of another faith. In an additional 17 percent, the bride or groom had converted to Judaism, leaving only about a third that could be called "in-marriages" between two born Jews. This was an intermarriage rate almost five times as large as that of 1960, and one of the highest in the country.

But like the Jewish population as a whole, almost half of the intermarried families who were unaffiliated said they were considering synagogue membership in the future. This represented a group of thousands of young marrieds in the city and clearly a special opportunity for Emanu-El, whose rabbis and cantor performed intermarriage—in contrast to the clergy of most other Reform congregations. Of course interfaith couples were welcome at most other synagogues, too, but with its extensive "Introduction to Judaism" course, its universal ethical message, and its uplifting, Americanized worship service, Emanu-El seems to have had a particular allure for those of another faith.

So while there were those in the Asher era who saw the downward drift of Emanu-El as inevitable, there were others—even before Tobin's study made it into print in 1988—who sensed in the trends of the '80s an opening for the temple. A certain type, they felt, could revitalize the congregation if only they could be induced to join: baby-boomer couples in their thirties, perhaps with children, perhaps intermarried. At the same time, more could be done to attract singles, and among them single parents.

There were very few younger congregants at Emanu-El by the mid-'80s; this was the group, including the children of many older members, which the temple had largely lost to other synagogues—especially Sherith Israel—in the past decade and a half. There an amiable and effective young rabbi, the native San Franciscan Martin Weiner, had followed the veteran Morris Goldstein in 1970 and succeeded in attracting younger members in particular. But the large majority of young Jews in the city had joined no congregation, and many newcomers were arriving every year. Couldn't Emanu-El win hundreds of these households, adding not only new members but also a new vibrancy?

Even the most optimistic knew it would be difficult, though, for this was a cohort for whom personal choice meant everything. They would not join the temple—or any other organization—unless they were convinced it would meet their individual needs.

THE NEED TO ATTRACT NEW MEMBERS was made especially pressing in the mid-'70s by sharply rising costs. The physical plant had become increasingly expensive to maintain, requiring a custodial staff of five full-time employees, as well as vast outlays for heat, light, and power. By 1979, after more than fifty years of use, major repairs were needed—among them an upgrade of the heating and plumbing systems as well as weather-proofing, sandblasting, and cleaning the entire exterior, including the great dome.

Although this half-million-dollar capital project would be dwarfed in size by a mammoth renovation of the temple a decade later, it nevertheless proved a daunting task. While longtime member John Samter, an electrical engineer, oversaw the repairs, President Nadine Rushakoff, Richard Dinner (the son-in-law of Ben Swig), Dr. Ernest Rogers, and others went about raising the funds. But as one of the temple's professionals noted at the time, "it has become increasingly difficult to ask the wealthy families to bail us out of any financial crisis that arises." So for the first time in Emanu-El's history a special assessment was levied on the entire membership: for two years each family was required to add 20 percent beyond its dues to fund the maintenance costs.

There was also a concerted attempt to trim the temple's operating budget, which—including the cemetery—had passed the one million dollar mark in the 1970s. Annual deficits were not infrequent during the Asher era, and although the debt was retired through "anniversary drives" every five years, financial difficulties seemed chronic.

It was a fiscal dispute that led to a major conflict with the the Union of American Hebrew Congregations. The temple's request for a waiver of its payment for 1975 (about $38,000, half of which was to go to Hebrew Union College) was refused, and for a while it appeared that Emanu-El—after an affiliation of nearly a century—might actually be forced to leave the UAHC. But the negotiations remained cordial, if somewhat tedious, with an understanding Rabbi Alexander Schindler, president of the UAHC, taking an active role. Finally, a compromise was reached, termed by temple president Myer Kahn (himself a member of the UAHC board) the "most important accomplishment" of his three-year term.

The compensation of the clergy and other staff were kept relatively low, meanwhile, a fact which few people outside the temple leadership fully appreciated. Despite the public's image of Emanu-El as a bastion of wealth and privilege, the senior rabbi and cantor actually earned barely two-thirds of the average salary of their counterparts at other leading Reform congregations in the Bay Area. And it was next to impossible to find money for new initiatives and programs, recalls Cantor Portnoy: "We were constantly discusing funding,…how to economize.…It was very stultifying and limiting.…That was the stricture within which we all worked."

For their part, the lay leaders were worried about large financial obligations looming just over the horizon. As early as 1980, Nadine Rushakoff publicly stated something that many had left unspoken: the fact that virtually all the key staff would be of retirement age by the middle of the decade. In the early '80s, Asher and Portnoy were in their sixties; so were the two top administrators, Executive Director Marvin Schoenberg and Cemetery Administrator Fred Platt. The internationally renowned organist, Ludwig Altman, spry though he was, had passed seventy. Not only would they all need pensions, but their replacements would likely require larger salaries and the new rabbi possibly a house provided by the congregation, as well. Fortunately, in 1982 the Swig family took the lead in creating a fund that would generate retirement benefits for the senior staff in the amount of 60 percent of their salary. But it was still clear that the impending "changing of the guard" at Emanu-El would seriously affect the financial condition of the temple along with everything else.

NADINE RUSHAKOFF, an unusually active board president who served a four-year term beginning in 1978, struggled valiantly to shore up the temple during this difficult period. Unhappy with talk of Emanu-El "as an empty house" and irritated by constant criticism "that our congregation is of the senior-citizen variety," she was more than willing to institute some changes "to actively encourage the younger generation to affiliate" and "to provide activity for every age and interest group."

She and her husband, the respected physician Oscar Rushakoff (known simply as "Rush" to his friends), regularly opened their home to new members as part of a program called "Getting to Know You." She also played a role in the formation of a new auxiliary, the Emanu-El Temple Club (ETC), offering activities for both single and married members under forty-five. This was the forerunner of a similar group created a few years later, New Encounters Forum, which also held educational, religious, and social events for the congregation's younger adults. The temple conducted a family weekend at a resort in the Santa Cruz mountains in 1978 and, two years later, with the aid of a grant from the children of the late Daniel Koshland, a retreat for board and committee members at the Sonoma Mission Inn.

Rushakoff also responded to members' requests by encouraging Rabbi Asher to offer an additional Friday evening service at 7:30 on the first Sabbath of each month. For many congregants, especially working people with children, the long-standing 5:30 starting time was inconvenient. Moreover, the early service—still known in those days as "vespers"—was conducted in precisely thirty-three minutes each week, and some felt it to be too methodical.

To be sure, there were a handful of young people who did attend regularly. They enjoyed the communal singing (which was not a feature of the Saturday morning service), and found it "a wonderful way to wind down from the week." As Reynold Colvin's son Andrew recalls, "You always knew who you would see there....What I liked [about the service was that] I knew exactly when it was going to start and when it was going to end. One of the beauties of Judaism *is* the repetition." But many others preferred a livelier, more varied worship experience. The new family service was thus intended to be more informal and festive and was followed by a reception with light refreshments, an *Oneg Shabbat*. Although it only lasted for a few years in the early '80s—until an overworked clergy found it too burdensome—the family service reflected an awareness at Emanu-El that some alternative to the orderly vespers was needed.

Also in an attempt to accommodate members' needs, in the late '70s the temple opened a branch of its religious school in rented quarters in southern Marin County. Offering mid-week Hebrew instruction, this was a bid to retain the young families who had moved to the attractive suburbs across the Golden Gate Bridge.

Perhaps most important, though, Rushakoff worked with Asher to reconceptualize the position of the junior rabbi. In 1979, Asher had become one of the first senior rabbis of a large congregation to appoint a woman assistant, Rabbi Michal Bourne. This made an important statement to his critics, who had claimed that he was unwilling to change with the times. A Long Island native, the tall, slender young rabbi, whom many felt resembled a fashion model, was comfortable with the temple's Classical Reform orientation. Likeable and caring, she was much appreciated by a number of families who delighted in the way she related to their toddlers.

Unfortunately, as she recalls, her job description didn't "play to [her] strengths." Having entered Hebrew Union College without a strong background in Judaica, she had not fully made up deficiencies in Jewish studies and in the Hebrew language in particular. She fell short during her two years at Emanu-El, especially as a teacher of older children and adults.

Along with Asher, Rushakoff concluded from the experience that the second rabbi should no longer be a "trainee," as she told the congregation in an annual report, but rather someone experienced as both an educator and a pastor.

Bourne's successor was an individual of uncommon intellectual ability. Rabbi Robert Kirschner, appointed in 1981 at the age of thirty-one, had graduated Phi Beta Kappa from Stanford and had already taught on the college level as a lecturer. For the past two years, he had served as the assistant rabbi and educator at Congregation Beth Am, a fast-growing synagogue in the nearby suburb of Los Altos Hills.

He had also distinguished himself as one of the best students in his class at Hebrew Union College. His rabbinic thesis, a vast, ambitious treatise on rabbinic responsa during the Holocaust, had won the praise of Rabbi Alexander Schindler, who helped the young scholar obtain a grant to prepare the manuscript for publication.

Shortly before he was engaged at Emanu-El, Kirschner had been accepted into the rigorous doctoral program in UC Berkeley's Department of Near Eastern Studies. The temple allowed him to pursue his degree—as a full-time student—even while he shouldered his considerable rabbinical responsibilities. Early on, he won the prize awarded to the university's top student in Judaica.

It was clear from the beginning that Kirschner was more than just the next in a succession of assistants to the senior rabbi. He came to Emanu-El with the title of associate rabbi and, with the help of funds from the Sisterhood, a large new study was built for him on the second floor of the temple office suite. At the outset he developed an excellent working relationship with Asher, who shared the pulpit with him almost on an equal basis.

The personable, athletic father of three children (a fourth would be born to the Kirschners within a year and a half of his appointment), and a

LEFT: RABBI ASHER WITH ASSISTANT RABBI MICHAL BOURNE
RIGHT: ASSOCIATE RABBI ROBERT KIRSCHNER

talented guitar player, composer, and song leader, he quickly became popular among the younger families in particular. But congregants of all ages were impressed by the depth of the young man's learning.

THE ADDITION TO THE STAFF of a highly gifted associate rabbi and the programmatic changes fostered by Rushakoff made an impact which continued through the presidency of her successor, corporate lawyer Bruce Denebeim, originally from Kansas City. But it was Walter Newman, whose presidency began early in the pivotal year of 1985, who saw the need for far more sweeping changes; he felt it imperative for the temple virtually to reinvent itself to face the challenges of the rest of the century.

It is hard to imagine a man better suited to help bring this about. His grandfather, Simon Newman, one of the state's leading agriculturists (and the man for whom the town of Newman, near the family's huge farm in the Central Valley, is named), had been president of the temple early in the century. Walter, very proud of his forebear's contribution to Emanu-El, broke the pattern of the 1970s and early '80s, which had seen the old families play a reduced role in the leadership of the synagogue. And like Harold Zellerbach, president of the temple during such a critical moment a generation earlier, Newman's pedigree no doubt strengthened his hand as he presided over major changes.

But Newman, again like Zellerbach, whom he much admired, had a great deal more than a respected name. From the time that he led men into battle as a twenty-one-year-old infantry officer in the Normandy invasion, he had been a natural leader. A successful real estate developer and corporate executive, he also served his beloved city for many years as president of both the planning and redevelopment commissions.

As the powerful president of the Fine Arts Museums of San Francisco, he had presided over the complex and delicate merger of the De Young Museum and the Legion of Honor, reconfiguring the staff structure in the process and instituting the practice of advance tickets for specific time slots. He also arranged a series of traveling "blockbuster" shows, most notably the King Tut exhibit, which drew 1.3 million visitors— one of the greatest attractions in the history of San Francisco. Newman didn't want the museum to be a "deadly" place where "things weren't happening," he said recently of his work in the 1970s to revitalize the institution. "I love to see people come in....I'm a populist."

The man who influenced Newman most was his father-in-law, the legendary civic booster and bon vivant Cyril Magnin, San Francisco's first chief of protocol. Working for two decades as a top executive in Magnin's firm, the respected women's specialty store Joseph Magnin Company, Newman learned the importance of public service from a man whose devotion to his city knew no limits. He came away with another vital lesson, as well:

> Through Cyril Magnin I learned that youth was the driving force in our whole society....That's where the energy came from....Cyril used to say, "I want young people around me; young people know how to dare; they know how to take chances." I remember taking twenty-five-year-old girls, giving them a pen and saying go out and buy millions of dollars worth of merchandise.

These were also Newman's sentiments regarding Emanu-El. As an influential board member even before he assumed the presidency, he "felt strongly that youth had to be attracted to the temple, and youth attracts youth. What we needed was a new generation."

The respect and gratitude the key lay leaders felt for the five men reaching retirement age in the mid-1980s was profound. Joseph Asher in particular was revered, Newman calling him a "great, great rabbi." But as Newman also recalls, the hour had arrived for a new and younger team: "As happens in so many different organizations, there comes a time for renewal and reorganization....It was the turning of a big page and I had to be the one to turn it."

By early 1983, Rabbi Asher himself agreed with this assessment and began to make plans to step down. He had received a raft of honors in the prior few years: an honorary doctorate from Hebrew Union College; a special medal from West German president Richard Weizsaecker, who brought him to Bonn as a distinguished guest; and of course his appointment to the U.S. Holocaust Memorial Council, which led to his saying the *kaddish* in the White House as part of a Yom Hashoah commemoration.

But in San Francisco, he was tiring from his many battles—both within and without the congregation—to maintain Emanu-El's distinctive

RABBI AND MRS. ASHER TRAVELING IN PRAGUE

direction. Given too the financial problems facing the temple, and the impending retirement of almost all his closest colleagues, he faced a rough, uncertain road ahead.

Moreover, the health of this hard-driving man—a heavy smoker who got little physical exercise—was beginning to flag in the early 1980s. Although he stuck to a demanding schedule until his retirement and never missed a day due to illness, he was nevertheless in pain his last few years at the temple, suffering from serious back problems and from the disease that ultimately claimed his life—a yet-undiagnosed case of prostate cancer.

After a total of nearly four decades of bearing the burdens of a pulpit rabbi—responsibilities which Asher took more earnestly than most—he hoped finally to be free to pursue his many other interests, which included writing, teaching, and travel. Above all he craved the time needed for serious study.

In March 1983, he informed the personnel committee of his desire to retire at the end of January 1986, the month of his sixty-fifth birthday. But he also asked for a half-year sabbatical, which the board granted, so that he could actually leave his duties in mid-1985. He was given the title of

Rabbi Emeritus and an office in the temple, and, along with his much-admired wife, Fae, was honored at a special Sabbath celebrating seventeen years of devoted service. He seemed at peace with his decision when he formally announced it at the annual meeting in January 1984: "Not that I am obsessed with my age or that I subscribe to the notion that young is necessarily better, but I do believe there comes a time to let go."

Marvin Schoenberg, about half a decade older than Asher, had expressed a desire to step down as early as 1981, but the board had convinced the capable executive director to stay on for several more years. He resigned at the beginning of 1984 after more than a quarter of a century on Lake Street. Fred Platt, the cemetery administrator, had had an even longer tenure—thirty-five years; he left a short time after Schoenberg.

Cantor Portnoy too felt he "had had enough" after twenty-seven years. Frustrated with the declining membership in the synagogue and especially the dwindling enrollment in the religious school, he felt that he and Asher "had tried to make certain changes, but nothing affected the outcome." The cantor felt especially burdened by the responsibility of directing the religious school for more than two decades, and gave up his educational portfolio in 1985, a year before his retirement from the temple.

But among the retirees of the mid-'80s, the man who had served the longest—and would be one of the hardest to replace—was the organist and choir director, Ludwig Altman. At the age of seventy-six, after half a century at the temple, he had finally wearied of his duties and resigned his position. Not only a lavishly gifted musician, but also a gracious personality, he would be showered with honors both by Emanu-El and many other institutions until his death in 1990.

Within the space of eighteen months, five key posts had turned over. On the senior staff, only Kirschner remained, and he had come on board a mere four years earlier. And the sum of this unprecedented number of personnel changes was even greater than its parts. For collectively these long-serving, disciplined men had set not only the agenda but also the tone of the synagogue—refined, if a bit reserved; erudite, if at times elitist. Whatever the strengths and shortcomings of their style, however, it was obvious by the mid-'80s that something very different would necessarily arise in its place.

ON THE EVE OF ANNOUNCING HIS RETIREMENT, Rabbi Asher surprised many by launching a new and highly ambitious initiative that would
preoccupy him for the remainder of his rabbinate and for several years
beyond. He urged the temple to create a senior citizen life-care facility for
the local Jewish community, a fifty-million-dollar project which would
provide middle- and upper-income retirees not only with handsome
apartments, but also with recreational facilities, a health center, skilled
nursing if necessary, and many other services.

At the annual meeting early in 1983, he invoked both the Eureka
Benevolent Society, founded during the Gold Rush, and the Emanu-El
Residence Club, which aided immigrant women in the 1920s and refugees in the '30s. Placing the proposed retirement community in the same
context, he declared, "I can envisage our temple once again being in the
forefront...meeting a social need in the community. And more than a
social need. It is a religious imperative which we would affirm in this
way." His model was the Sequoias, well-appointed condominiums for
older adults in a high-rise atop Cathedral Hill, administered by the Presbyterian Church. Clearly this was not a project calculated to capture the
imagination of the young people the temple was trying to attract. But a
Jewish equivalent of the Sequoias, Asher believed, would bring high visibility to the temple and a crowning achievement to his rabbinate.

Initially he made a great deal of headway. With backing from the
temple board, and a substantial grant from Walter Haas Jr., extensive feasibility and marketing studies were conducted in 1984 by Crown
Research, a nationally known consulting firm. Hundreds of Bay Area
Jews expressed interest in moving into such an "assisted living" complex,
a fact Asher frequently cited when he advanced the proposal from the
pulpit and in print.

In 1986, an ideal facility in the center of the city became available, the
newly constructed Daniel Burnham Court on Van Ness Avenue. Catty-
corner from the Concordia Club, to which many Emanu-El congregants
in this age group belonged, the complex included almost two hundred
and fifty residential units (most of them one-bedroom apartments selling
for about $215,000) as well as roughly a hundred thousand square feet of
commercial space.

Although a powerful temple committee came "very, very close to culminating a deal," as one of its members recalls, Daniel Burnham Court was not acquired by the Jewish community, and the retirement center envisioned by Asher never materialized. Despite the fact that the rabbi had access to some of the leading philanthropists in the city, the complexity and scale of this project—which, among other things, required federal funding—simply proved too great for the synagogue to undertake.

Asher was also frustrated by his failure to obtain grants from foundations (which could not justify using their resources to subsidize luxury residences), but he was certainly gratified that he had sensitized the Jewish community to this vital issue. As had so often been the case in his long career, he proved more adept in articulating prophetic ideals than in actually effecting institutional change.

Aside from this disappointment, though, his few retirement years were remarkably productive, despite his worsening health. He accepted a part-time college teaching position at the Kirchliche Hochschule in West Berlin, where he thoroughly enjoyed sharing his vast store of Jewish knowledge with German students two generations his junior. They responded avidly, not only to his deep learning but also to his warmth and wit. "Everyone there loved him," recalls one young woman whom he mentored, Charlotte Fonrobert, who was nineteen and had never met a Jew before. With Asher's help she soon came to Berkeley's Graduate Theological Union to pursue Jewish studies, earned a doctorate, and went on to become an assistant professor of Talmud at the University of Judaism.

At the end of his life Asher was absorbed by the "incomprehensible puzzlement" of the land of his youth. He struggled to understand first how the Holocaust could have been authored by the nation of *Dichter und Denker*, of poets and thinkers, and second, how Central European Jews could have been caught unawares by the impending catastrophe.

But most of all, he focused on the glorious intellectual life of German Jewry, especially the synthesis between classical Jewish thought and Western Enlightenment principles—the product of a succession of philosophers beginning with Moses Mendelssohn in the eighteenth century and ending with Franz Rosenzweig in the twentieth. For Asher, this line of thought—which sought, albeit in vain, to integrate the Jews into a pluralistic society—had as much, if not more, relevance for American Jews than did the more insular Jewish civilization of the East European *shtetl*.

The contributions of German Jewry was the subject of the last course the rabbi emeritus offered at the temple, in the fall of 1988.

It was also the theme of the festschrift, a volume of essays celebrating his career, which his friends and colleagues began preparing in the late '80s for his seventieth birthday in 1991. *The Jewish Legacy and the German Conscience*, a handsome publication subsidized by the temple and published by the Judah L. Magnes Museum, included articles by internationally known authors ranging from Immanuel Jakobovits, the chief rabbi of the British Commonwealth, to Elie Wiesel.

Asher's own piece discussed the remarkable intellectual odyssey of his scholarly father, Rabbi Jonah Ansbacher, who successfully bridged the worlds of Jewish orthodoxy and secular learning; who, incarcerated in Buchenwald, saw his synthesis collapse during the Holocaust; and who recreated it in postwar London, where he lived for a quarter of a century as a loyal British subject. As he pondered the vicissitudes of his father's unlikely life, Asher no doubt included himself as well when he spoke of the German Jews' "fierce attachment to the world around them. Their commitment to Western civilization has been second only to their commitment to Jewish values."

But sadly, the publication of the festschrift was a posthumous honor. The rabbi, confined for many months to his San Francisco home, where many of his former students, colleagues, and congregants came to visit, passed away in late May 1990.

RABBI JONAH AND ROSA ANSBACHER

More than a thousand people came to mourn him in the temple, deeply moved by the eulogy delivered by his son, Raphael, himself a Reform rabbi who had built up a vibrant congregation in suburban Walnut Creek and a man with a strong physical resemblance to his father. As the lanky young man mounted the *bimah*, his long arms swinging out from his sides with the same body language as Joe Asher, many were struck once more by the length and strength of the "chain of rabbis" in the family, an unbroken line of seven generations. Those sitting in the sanctuary, most of them his former congregants, also knew how apt was the son's characterization of his father as

> a *Seelsorger* [a German term meaning "curator of souls"] who took special care with every bride and groom, every Bar Mitzvah family, every bris, every simcha and bereavement. That tightly wound energy, his consummate reliability, penetrating wisdom and generous smile were like that of an overseeing curator who takes particular pleasure and concern in every individual work of art.

A month before his death, the board had voted to name the cloistered temple courtyard—an inviting enclosure graced with a fountain, sculpture, and trees—in his honor, a fitting gesture, as Rabbi Raphael Asher explained on the occasion of its dedication in 1992: "My father considered this sanctuary to be holy ground. And there was much in the secular world he considered to be crass and profane. But imagine, if you will, the courtyard as a kind of holding zone between the two worlds, an anteroom....That is where Dad liked to be!"

JOSEPH ASHER'S RABBINATE may be viewed in the context of a group of German-born rabbis who made a deep impact on the American Reform movement in the postwar decades and who remained active into the 1980s and in some instances even the '90s, men like Alexander Schindler, president of the UAHC; Alfred Gottschalk, head of Hebrew Union College; scholars such as Jakob Petuchowski and Gunther Plaut; and leading congregational rabbis such as Max Nussbaum, Joachim Prinz, and Gunter Hirschberg. Even if they had left Germany while still children, they brought with them that disciplined attitude toward work and study so ingrained in Central Europe's prewar generations. As outsiders to an extent, they were often sensitive to aspects of American life, and of course American-Jewish life, which many native-born simply took for granted.

Asher was surely such a disciplined contrarian; always the gentleman, he nevertheless went against the grain of his times. In the period of Jewish particularism which followed the Six Day War, he was often critical of Israeli policies and preached universalism even in regard to the Holocaust. During the years in which American Jewry was refreshed by popular, alternative forms of Judaism, he viewed the temple almost as a fortress and too often kept out the creative and salutary along with the faddish and superficial. He found himself at odds with groups as disparate as the Lubavitcher Hasidim and the local Federation.

Yet the unwavering principles of this man, rooted in the Old World, provided most of his congregants with a sense of comfort and continuity during a period of social upheaval. In a time of increasing moral relativism and self-indulgence, he would not alter the ethical standards to which he held himself and others. He was thus a welcome constant for Emanu-El members, who often felt inundated outside the synagogue by a surfeit of change.

It is also true that the temple was not in a dynamic, expansive mode under the spiritual leadership of Joseph Asher; he was less of an innovator than some of the rabbis who preceded him or came after him. But he was as much a guardian of the Emanu-El ethos as any who ever occupied the pulpit; his rabbinate had something in common with that of Jacob Voorsanger and Irving Reichert, both of whom, like him, served just under two decades. Of course he had none of the political conservatism of Voorsanger, nor (despite the overheated accusations of some of his detractors) the anti-Zionism of Reichert. But like them his role was that of a resolute keeper of values and verities, a conservator who could sometimes be contentious. His goal, as theirs, was the preservation of a particular kind of Reform Judaism at the temple, not an unchecked expansion that might ultimately dilute its distinctive qualities.

For he felt there were some things even more important than attracting large numbers. He saw a great danger, as he wrote just before his retirement, "when the synagogue tailors its style merely to evince popularity." For him, the synagogue was "the spiritual and durable anchor of the Jewish people [and] an anchor's effectiveness is determined not by how many tie up to it, but by its intrinsic firmness."

As a rabbi, he was something of an anchor as well, not moving with the swift currents that swirled around him, but possessed of an inner stability and integrity that steadied his flock. As the temple entered the 1990s—without Joe Asher—no one knew how much these traits would be missed.

chapter ten

ROBERT KIRSCHNER
Fallen Star

Joseph Asher was succeeded in mid-1985 by his young associate, Robert Kirschner, whose six-and-a-half-year tenure as senior rabbi would resemble a Greek tragedy—a rabbinate of extremes unlike any in the history of the institution. Through the power of his charisma he brought the temple to unprecedented heights; through the weakness of his character he brought disgrace on himself and plunged the synagogue into one of the gravest crises it had ever faced.

When he resigned at the end of 1991, amid allegations of sexual misconduct, there were feelings of loss and anger as well as betrayal. But above all, the temple was engulfed in a sea of sadness: for a brilliant career cut short, a family torn apart, and a circle of women deeply hurt. Yet his contributions to Emanu-El rank among the greatest of its rabbis; his sudden fall could not erase the fact that, far more than any other individual, he was responsible for rejuvenating the temple in the late '80s and setting it on the upward course it would take for the rest of the century.

Kirschner, only thirty-four years of age, was chosen in the spring of 1985 by a slim majority over much older and more experienced candidates, some of them nationally known. He was the temple's only junior rabbi to be elevated to the top post since Jacob Voorsanger nearly a century earlier. Even the beloved Mike Heller, who was well over forty and who had served with great distinction for more than a dozen years, had not been selected in 1963 to succeed Alvin Fine. Moreover, in terms of

297

the guidelines of the Central Conference of American Rabbis, Kirschner was far from eligible to lead one of the largest Reform congregations in the country. He had been ordained only half a decade earlier and had served only two years as the assistant at Congregation Beth Am and less than four years as the associate at Emanu-El. He had never held a pulpit of his own.

But with Walter Newman as his champion, the search committee, chaired by Bruce Denebeim and Frances Green, was ultimately swayed by the young man's scholarship, sermons, and rapport with the congregation's young people. Initially Rabbi Asher (who had no formal role in the process) had preferred a man of national standing to succeed him, but he too was eventually persuaded that his junior colleague, who had served him so diligently and so loyally, was the appropriate choice to head the temple.

Kirschner's swift ascent was all the more remarkable because of his humble origins. He and his two sisters grew up in Los Angeles, in the diverse working-class area that would later be known as South Central. His father, who had never finished high school, was a short order cook and his mother a switchboard operator.

Tensions between blacks and Jews ran high in this part of the city, and contributed much to Kirschner's lifelong preoccupation with questions of race and ethnicity. In 1965, when Bob was fifteen, the family joined in the widespread "summer of white flight" that followed the Watts riots, moving a few miles away to the modest Westchester district near the L.A. airport.

Although all four of Kirschner's grandparents were born in Russia, there was little Jewish observance in his home in Los Angeles. While his father in particular had great respect for Judaism, the family never lit candles for the Sabbath nor had a proper Passover seder. But the boy became a Bar Mitzvah at a small, struggling Conservative *shul* and had many other positive Jewish experiences at Hess-Kramer, a progressive summer camp run under the auspices of the Wilshire Boulevard Temple. For many years there—first as a camper and later as a counselor and dining-room manager—he was also able to pursue his passion for basketball and guitar.

He eventually enrolled in the religious school of the wealthy Wilshire Boulevard Temple and was confirmed by its regal rabbi, Edgar Magnin. But the boy who had grown up near Watts never felt comfortable in this "bastion of privilege," as he remembers it, and was also put off by its

RABBI ROBERT KIRSCHNER

Classical Reform orientation, ironically the mode of worship he would inherit a decade and a half later at Temple Emanu-El:

> It seemed like a church. There were pews, the rabbis wore vestments that made them look like Presbyterian ministers rather than rabbis, everything was in English, there was a pipe organ, there was no cantor, [but rather] a choir—these heavenly voices that came from hidden precincts up there.…The whole experience was quite alien to me at first.

The youth excelled in school and "had the necessity of being elected president of everything"—his ninth-grade class in junior high school, his temple youth group, and his high school, where he somehow defeated the captain of the all-city football team. Although crushed by rejection letters from Harvard, Yale, and Princeton all on the same day, he won a full-tuition scholarship to Stanford, where he entered college in 1968.

Again, he felt somewhat uncomfortable with his classmates of "much more privileged backgrounds…who had gone to private schools, who on their term papers would put an initial instead of writing out their first name." Even by his senior year he didn't know better than to go to his interview for a Rhodes scholarship dressed in jeans and cowboy boots.

Kirschner worked as a hasher and dishwasher in his fraternity and played the guitar in local coffeehouses. He was caught up in the social activism of the late '60s which permeated the campus, but was drawn more to religion than to politics. The co-editor of the Stanford literary magazine, he was especially interested in modern novels with religious themes. He was inspired by the fiction of Elie Wiesel, who spoke at Stanford, and with whom he corresponded, but was drawn even more to Christian authors such as Kazantzakis, Dostoyevsky, and Unamuno, who deeply influenced him with their "spiritualized figures who somehow had an aura of goodness and serenity, who had an effortless way of accomplishing things and who were seemingly touched by God." In this respect he was even taken by the character of Jesus in the movie *Ben-Hur:* "You see him from the back, never from the front; you see the flying locks in his hair; you see these faces as he's speaking…and these faces are transfigured by hearing him."

Kirschner recalls that he was attracted to "these *figures* [his emphasis]…who became a magnet for other people…as much as to their ideas," and he developed a desire to lead in this way himself: "There was something narcissistic, I think....I seemed to need the validation; I wanted somehow to be recognized."

After a very brief stint at Berkeley's Pacific School of Religion, a nominally Protestant institution, he chose instead to enter the rabbinical program of Hebrew Union College in 1974. He had married a non-Jewish woman a year and a half earlier, a young bank secretary from a small town in the Central Valley whom he had met in Palo Alto. A Baptist, she agreed to convert to Judaism and the two soon went off to the HUC campus in Jerusalem.

While he was in rabbinical school, later in Los Angeles and then in Cincinnati, the couple had two children and Kirschner worked part-time to support his family even as he demonstrated to his professors an unusually high proficiency in classical Jewish texts. For his two-volume rabbinic thesis, he translated and annotated thirty-five rare responsa on the Holocaust, a work that was eventually published by Schocken Press.

His first position was assistant rabbi of Congregation Beth Am in the affluent suburb of Los Altos Hills, only a few miles from Stanford. He served under the avuncular Sidney Akselrad, a rabbi in the latter part of a long and productive career, who was deeply respected and beloved by his congregants, especially as a pastor. But Kirschner, whose main duty was the administration of the large religious school, had an unsatisfying experience at Beth Am. No longer in the rarefied world of citing rabbinic responsa and Talmudic passages, he was now "worried about religious school teachers...showing up on time, kids' soccer schedules and car pools and chaperones and youth groups and all things junior rabbis do— I wasn't crazy about it."

He sensed a lack of respect from some of the leading lay people and also felt stifled in not being given enough opportunities to deliver sermons or make hospital visits. "It wasn't a good fit and I wasn't happy," he recalls, and within a short time he planned on leaving the rabbinate for a career in academia. In the spring of 1981, his second year at Beth Am, he was accepted by UC Berkeley's doctoral program in Near Eastern studies.

But before he enrolled that fall, he heard of a junior rabbinical position at Emanu-El and "on a bit of a lark" drove up to San Francisco in his 1955 pickup truck for the interview. Later that day he learned from

Rabbi Asher that he had been hired. Initially, the Emanu-El appointment was in Kirschner's mind a station along the way toward his goal of becoming a professor. He and his wife, Reesa, "a full-time mom," now had three children, and the raise in salary which the temple offered was most welcome. But even more important was the fact that he would now be much closer to Berkeley than he had been on the Peninsula, and that the congregation would permit him to undertake the arduous course of study that he had mapped out for himself at the university.

But there was an unexpected benefit as well that came with the new post: a respect for the office of the rabbi which Kirschner had not enjoyed in the suburban congregation. Here the flock "still look[ed] to the rabbi as a kind of holy man," he later wrote; this was evident to him at the job interview itself:

> I was prepared for the grandeur of Emanu-El's majestic synagogue. But I was not prepared for what I encountered inside. I was escorted to the board room, where the search committee was waiting. There were some twenty people seated around a long table. All of them were watching the door. The moment I walked in, every one of them stood up.
>
> It may have simply been *derech eretz*, good manners. But at the time it seemed to me that their gesture meant more than that....In this congregation, as I have since learned, the office of the rabbi is invested with singular stature....With that spontaneous gesture, they honored what I represented. It was not unlike the ancient example of Rabbi Hanina, who equated the rabbi with the Torah. Respect for one, I would argue, is still an expression of respect for the other.

He joined the staff with the title of associate rabbi and thrived under the mentorship of Joe Asher, "everything a senior colleague could be." With his own retirement in view, Asher encouraged Kirschner's scholarly aspirations, generously shared the pulpit and hospital visits with him, and even sent invitations to major community events his way.

His working-class sensibility could still cause awkward moments for him, though. Soon after he joined the staff, a board member was "so distressed" upon seeing his old pickup truck, which didn't even have a lock on the driver's side door, that he solemnly told him, "This will not do for a rabbi of Emanu-El."

But to his own surprise, the young man who had originally seen his work at the temple as a transition into academe gradually grew to savor his rabbinical duties, especially at this high-profile urban synagogue with its long, storied past.

> I found that I liked...the opportunities I had and the way people responded, whether it was a sermon or a class, even visiting the hospital regularly. I felt this sense of privilege.
>
> The congregation won me over: the sanctuary, the people, its leaders and [the rank and file], too....My first experience [at Beth Am] had been quite stressful most of the time, [but] this was different.

So although he was fully immersed in his doctoral studies, working on his dissertation and beginning to publish scholarly papers in leading academic journals, he made a bid for the position of senior rabbi. And like so many other things he had wanted in his life, it came his way.

His wife was "thrilled" when he was chosen. To be sure, Reesa Kirschner "had a lot of trepidation about being the [senior] rabbi's wife," particularly as she followed Fae Asher, one of the women best suited for this role in the temple's history. Reesa had some self-consciousness about being a "Jew by choice" and had neither a deep knowledge of Judaism nor a college education. But the promotion meant a great deal for her family, which had grown by yet another child in 1982. They had rented a tiny two-bedroom house, and all four children—the oldest was nine—had to share one room, sleeping in two bunk beds. Now, for the first time, the Kirschners had a home of their own, a large, handsome house on Fifth Avenue which the temple helped them purchase through a liberal equity-sharing agreement. With his salary more than doubling to roughly $100,000 annually, "she knew and I knew," he recalls wistfully, "that this would mean security for the first time in our life together."

THE YEAR 1985 would prove to be as pivotal for the temple as any in this century. Like Alvin Fine in 1948 and Martin Meyer in 1910, a dynamic and very young rabbi, born on the West Coast, took over the reins of leadership from an erudite but much older man who had been highly respected but also somewhat resistant to change. The sense of anticipation was almost palpable, as Kirschner recollects: "I had the feeling that people were just waiting for something to ignite at Temple Emanu-El."

The installation itself was a grand event which reminded many of the heady days of a generation earlier. Thousands of people passed through the temple during an open house early in September, an entire weekend of events culminating in a Sunday evening ceremony which featured such notables as then-Mayor Dianne Feinstein, whose home is adjacent to the temple and who later joined the congregation. The many prominent Christian clergymen in attendance included Father John Lo Schiavo, president of the University of San Francisco; the Very Reverend Alan Jones, who had just become the dean of Grace Cathedral; John Quinn, the city's respected archbishop; and Cecil Williams, the buoyant pastor of Glide Memorial Church. The installation sermon was given by Uri Herscher, executive director of Hebrew Union College, who had been one of Kirschner's teachers in Cincinnati. Joseph Asher, speaking warmly of the close ties he and Kirschner had formed over the past four years, installed his colleague, and Alvin Fine delivered the benediction. The new senior rabbi, very moved by the presence of his mother and two sisters—his father had died many years earlier—spoke eloquently of the "profound honor to receive this sacred responsibility" from Rabbi Asher's hands, which he would "always measure by his exalted standard."

RABBI KIRSCHNER AT HIS INSTALLATION WITH
WALTER NEWMAN AND MAYOR DIANNE FEINSTEIN

Even congregants who failed to attend the proud and joyful occasion could not but notice that change that had come to Emanu-El. The monthly *Temple Chronicle* was transformed overnight from a staid bulletin, hardly modified since the 1920s, to a much bigger and more attractive two-color catalogue of events, with larger photos and a far greater array of stories. A smart new logo—of the domed sanctuary—now adorned all publications as well as the prominent display ads which the temple ran with increasing frequency both in the Jewish and the general press. In addition, synagogue operations were computerized in mid-1985, affecting everything from billing and membership records to payroll and budgets.

Much of the credit for the temple's fresh image was due to the flair for publicity of Irwin Wiener, the executive director who arrived late in 1984, about half a year before Kirschner took over the duties of senior rabbi. The middle-aged New Yorker had served for more than two decades as a Jewish communal worker and educator and had a national reputation for shepherding synagogues through times of transition. He accepted the Emanu-El post with a mandate from President Walter Newman both to oversee the many new staff appointments and to reinvigorate the congregation. He would serve for six years, his tenure coinciding almost exactly with that of Kirschner. Respected for his competence and creativity by the staff and lay leadership alike, he wielded much influence during these years of excitement and expansion.

But it was the handsome young senior rabbi whose star far outshone all others. With his first Kol Nidre sermon he propelled himself into the front ranks of the national Reform movement. He also galvanized the congregation as no one had in decades.

With surpassing courage, and poise to match, he addressed perhaps the most sensitive subject in America, the AIDS epidemic, a year before President Reagan would even utter the word—well before official declarations from the nation's religious movements or even compassionate statements from its leading clergymen. And he urged Emanu-El members not only to be sympathetic to the victims of the disease, but also to support a concrete project of comfort and healing.

It had taken Kirschner more than a year to reach this point. In the spring of 1984, he delivered a routine Sabbath sermon on homosexuality, which he *"thought* was quite enlightened at the time,"* arguing that while

Jews should not favor the abrogation of civil rights for gays, Judaism does not endorse homosexuality as the divinely intended form of sexual expression. He also took issue with Sha'ar Zahav, San Francisco's largely gay synagogue, decrying the title of its congregational bulletin—the *Jewish Gaily Forward*—as making a mockery of the great New York newspaper that had been revered since the turn of the century.

Attending services that morning was Sha'ar Zahav's president, Dr. Michael Rankin. The physician had been invited by a close friend—an Emanu-El congregant "very much in the closet"—who had known of the sermon in advance and who had dreaded the impending attack upon his sexual orientation by a rabbi he admired. In the temple to lend his friend emotional support, Rankin was so pained by Kirschner's remarks that he wrote him a lengthy letter revealing the injury his comments had caused not only to the gays in the synagogue that Sabbath but also to their families. He described as well his community's struggle with a fatal epidemic which had already claimed many hundreds of lives in San Francisco, including several members of Sha'ar Zahav.

The rabbi called Dr. Rankin immediately and then met with him. From their meeting he learned a great deal about the plague which at that time—before the isolation of the virus and the discovery of AZT—was reaching its peak. That Friday evening Kirschner attended services led by Rankin at Sha'ar Zahav and, after much study and reflection, in August 1984 gave another Sabbath sermon at Emanu-El in which he recanted his harsh judgment of several months earlier:

> The words of the Torah and the sages...have not changed since last April, but my own thinking has....A law that says the homosexual is an abomination and deserves to die does not reflect divinity. In fact, as far as I'm concerned, calling such a law the word of God is a kind of blasphemy—a smear on God's name.
>
> Our religion [is] not against homosexuality. Judaism stands for loving, respectful, and responsible human relationships—wherever and between whomever they occur.

Later, he told Rankin that he would visit AIDS patients in San Francisco, which had the highest mortality rate from the illness in the country; it was his first such encounter—on the day before Yom Kippur Eve of

1985—that resulted in the catalytic Kol Nidre sermon. He had been called to comfort a young Jew dying from AIDS and, despite his fear of accidentally contracting the disease, he felt determined to go.

Kirschner was appalled by the fact that the AIDS hospice, on Divisadero Street south of Geary, had to be so well hidden. Because of concern that the neighbors would try to have it evicted if they learned of its existence, the hospice had neither a sign nor even a house number; one reached it through back stairs behind an auto repair shop. In the rabbi's words, "It had to be ashamed to speak its name."

He was ushered into the room of a moribund, emaciated man eagerly awaiting his visit, whose first words were, "Where's your yarmulke?" When Kirschner responded that he didn't wear one, the dying man said, "Wear mine," and put his own skullcap on the rabbi's head.

He asked Kirschner to say the prayer for the dead for him. At first the rabbi refused to recite the *kaddish* for a living person, but after the man told him that he had no one to say it for him, Kirschner agreed. After he left the hospice, he "knew exactly what to talk about" on the following evening. He scrapped what he had earlier prepared for Kol Nidre; he now had another subject.

This is the background of the powerful sermon that began with Kirschner's reference to the cruel treatment of lepers described in the Bible and the Talmud: "not only to be afflicted with disease but to be despised for it...not only to suffer but to be forsaken...not only to die a terrible death, but to be accused of deserving it." Those with leprosy, today called Hansen's disease, are no longer stigmatized, he went on, "but now there is a new multitude of sufferers to fear and shun. Theirs is the new dread affliction, the new mark of doom: AIDS."

Although he stated that no caregiver accidentally exposed to AIDS had ever contracted it, he well understood that "we are still afraid" and that "the fear of contagion is itself contagious and likely to persist." But he went much further in focusing on why "we shrink from people with AIDS." It is "not only because they are sick but because we don't like how they got sick. Like the ancient leper, the AIDS patient suffers not only the torment of his illness but the stigma of it. He is shunned not just for what he has but for what he is. His life, and now his death are regarded as a kind of disgrace."

Kirschner declared his rejection of the injunction in Leviticus, which would be read in the sanctuary the following day, on Yom Kippur afternoon, making homosexuality punishable by death. "Reform Judaism departs from the Torah on occasion," he said, and "a belief in...God, to my way of thinking, cannot be reconciled with a judgment of anathema upon homosexuals, or lepers, or any other of His children....Each of us, in our unique being, is the work of His hands and the bearer of His image; each of us—even someone with AIDS."

Pointing out that the local Jewish press had not carried an article, an editorial, or even a letter of sympathy for AIDS victims, or a word of outrage at the ostracism they had suffered, he asked his listeners to "imagine what the gay community must feel at this moment, and imagine what they must think of our silence."

He related for his audience of almost four thousand not his own experience the previous day at the hospice, which he felt too private to reveal, but rather a visit made by his friend, a Catholic priest, to the AIDS ward at San Francisco General Hospital. Father Michael Lopes saw a patient whose body was riddled with the purple lesions of Kaposi's sarcoma, his face bloated and his mouth full of fungus. But, as Kirschner continued, "beneath the mass of lesions [Lopes saw] a person, a human being hurting so badly that the mere presence of a visitor was a benediction."

Then the rabbi made a rare plea from the *bimah* for funds, for special hospital beds on Ward 5B costing over $1,000 each:

> Let us, as a congregation...establish a temple fund for the care of people suffering from AIDS. Let us start out by donating a few hospital beds, and then let us see what else we can do. Let us together fulfill the exalted commandment to comfort the sick and the dying who need us and deserve our kindness, not our lectures.

The response to the sermon was extraordinary. When he returned to his office between the two Kol Nidre services he found many notes of encouragement and even a check that had been slid under the door. The next evening, at a break-the-fast gathering at their home, Richard and Cissy Swig made a substantial donation to the cause. Within a few weeks more than $20,000 had come into the temple for AIDS relief, and a committee, headed by Dr. Ernest Rogers and including Dr. David Goldberg,

DR. ERNEST ROGERS WITH RABBI KIRSCHNER

chief of medicine at Marshal Hale Memorial Hospital, was formed to allocate the funds.

The sermon, published in *Reform Judaism*, energized the entire movement on the issue. Only a month after Kirschner spoke, the UAHC passed a strongly worded resolution urging an extensive program of education, more government funds for research, and an end to discrimination against AIDS victims. It also called for the formation of a committee on AIDS; Kirschner, Dr. Rankin, and Sha'ar Zahav's activist rabbi, Yoel Kahn, were the three San Franciscans among the twenty-five delegates chosen as charter members. One of the early meetings of this nationally constituted group was held in the board room of Emanu-El.

The interdenominational Northern California Board of Rabbis endorsed the UAHC resolution early in 1986, and leading Christian clergymen followed suit as well. Episcopal bishop William Swing, the Reverend Cecil Williams, and Archbishop Quinn all spoke out in support of AIDS victims during the months following the rabbi's sermon.

The temple, meanwhile, used the contributions it continued to receive over the next few years to establish outpatient services for those with AIDS at San Francisco General and Mount Zion Hospitals and to assist several hospices, including the highly regarded Shanti Project. It also helped the families of AIDS patients with counseling, referrals, and hospitality, and addressed the crisis with a series of workshops and conferences. At the end of 1987, Emanu-El and Sha'ar Zahav won the UAHC's social action award for their AIDS relief work; the following year Kirschner was appointed to the special HIV Epidemic Task Force formed by the city's progressive mayor, Art Agnos. Perhaps most gratifying was the infusion of hope the "AIDS sermon," as it came to be known, gave the gay community. As Dr. Rankin recently said, "We felt for the first time that we weren't alone in this."

The sermon's influence on temple members was also profound. For some it was the most compelling sermon they had ever heard. More than a dozen years later, Andrew Colvin vividly remembered the "passion and compassion" of the rabbi's message: "I can still picture him and what he said; it had as distinct an impression on me religiously as my son's Bar Mitzvah and the day I got married. I can't tell you how shocked I was when I realized what he was talking about....It gave people a sense that there was something they could do."

On that Kol Nidre, Kirschner had made the connection between Judaism and community service that would be be the watchword of his rabbinate. For the first time the congregation heard the poetic declaration of social commitment that he would often repeat:

> God has no other hands than ours. If the sick are to be healed, it is our hands, not God's, that will heal them. If the lonely and frightened are to be comforted, it is our embrace, not God's, that will comfort them. The warmth of the sun travels on the air, but the warmth of God's love can travel only through each one of us.

WITHIN A YEAR AND A HALF of his famous AIDS sermon, he tackled an issue no less difficult, and requiring no less fortitude—that of black-Jewish relations. Here too an experience in Kirschner's life led him to motivate the congregation to take practical measures in grappling with a major social problem.

He had of course been engaged with racial issues since his boyhood near Watts, and his younger sister's marriage to a black psychiatrist had brought the problems faced by African Americans into his own family.

But it was a civil rights march in rural Georgia, early in 1987, that convinced him more than anything else that "there are still wounds that take generations to heal, wounds that prove fatal if ignored."

The rabbi had answered the call of the Reverend Cecil Williams to march in protest of an ugly incident a week earlier. "We need you, brother," said the ebullient black pastor, who explained that a racially mixed group of marchers celebrating Martin Luther King Day in the small town of Cumming, Georgia, had been physically attacked by the Ku Klux Klan.

One of three rabbis in the Bay Area contingent of about 125 who flew overnight to Atlanta, not far from where the episode had taken place, Kirschner was pleased to see that almost twenty thousand protesters from all over America had descended on all-white Forsyth County. But the civil rights marchers were met by more than a thousand sheet-clad white supremacists, who jeered them with the most obscene racist and anti-Semitic epithets imaginable. At one point, amidst great noise and confusion, KKK members lifted their Grand Dragon into the air and Kirschner thought he had seen an apparition: "[He was] suspended there, high above the others, white sheet flapping in the wind as he lifted his arm in a Nazi salute....As a Jew, it was like looking at the specter of evil. I knew then why it was important to be there."

During the march the rabbi met the pastor of San Francisco's Third Baptist Church for the first time. He walked arm in arm with the Reverend Amos Brown for a while and learned that the Third Baptist was one of the oldest black churches in the West, established, like Emanu-El, in Gold Rush times.

The two clergymen decided that they needed to work together after they returned home. Despite the fact that relations between the two groups had soured in the mid-'80s, due in part to disparaging remarks against Jews made by Louis Farrakhan and Jesse Jackson, the rabbi was sure that he had a reliable ally in Amos Brown. "It occurred to me," Kirschner told the *San Francisco Examiner*, "that if we could walk together in Georgia, we could walk together here." But both men were committed to more than a public gathering, to "something concrete and lasting."

The rabbi and minister arranged for a joint worship service to be held every year on Martin Luther King Day, a lively event which still continues today, more than a decade later. But they also announced, at the first joint service in 1988, a well-conceived program aimed at improving the lives of African American children in the inner city.

This was the initiative soon to be known as "Back on Track," an after-school tutorial program that began with a handful of youngsters and grew to about two dozen by the end of its first year. The tutors, who came largely from Emanu-El (though also from the church), worked with youngsters on weekday afternoons at the Third Baptist—only two miles from Emanu-El, but bridging, as Kirschner said, "the huge divide between the Western Addition and Presidio Heights."

With the support of the rabbi's friend Ramon Cortinez, superintendent of the city's school system, and under the direction of a professional educator, the tutors provided assistance with homework as well as general help in mathematics and English composition. Although focusing primarily on children in the third through sixth grades, the program soon grew to encompass those from kindergarten to high school, and by the early '90s counted close to a hundred students annually, each of them paired with a volunteer tutor.

For co-leader of this demanding project, Kirschner tapped a young woman who had recently returned to her native San Francisco after many years on the East Coast, Alison Geballe, granddaughter of the famed

JUDI NEWMAN MEETS WITH A YOUNG STUDENT
AS PART OF THE BACK ON TRACK PROGRAM

philanthropist Daniel Koshland. Feeling strongly that "every kid should have a mentor," she and her counterpart, Leon King of the Third Baptist, worked with devotion to develop the program, which eventually resulted in marked improvement among the younger children in particular. In the spring of 1994, a grateful congregation honored Geballe and Jeremy Paul, a member who had served many years as a tutor, with its first "Beacon of Light" community service award. Back on Track, which has also brought leading African American intellectuals to the temple for its fundraising events, "has been a wonderful way of cementing better race relations," said Walter Newman recently, who himself had taught in the program for four years. "People across generational boundaries were willing to participate," remembers Don Buder, a young attorney who had joined the temple in 1985, largely because of Kirschner, "and we were always warmly embraced by the Third Baptist."

Many other initiatives in the realm of community service took shape in the late '80s, all of them part of what Kirschner termed "the lighthouse effect," referring to Emanu-El as an institution "on the moral and spiritual horizon of our community" and leading the way for society as a whole.

Following only the AIDS relief effort and the Back on Track program in importance was the temple's major drive to help the city's homeless. Once again it originated with a sudden awareness in the rabbi's mind, this time triggered by his young son on a rare shopping trip the two of them made one evening to the department stores on Market Street. Jesse Kirschner expressed his amazement in seeing his father step right over a homeless man lying on the sidewalk. "I didn't even see him," remembers the rabbi, who was struck by the realization that "these guys are just becoming part of the curb; and we need to do something about it."

He chose the annual joint service with the Unitarian Church, on Thanksgiving of 1987, to deliver a major sermon on the issue of hunger and homelessness. He titled it "Cosmetic Compassion," to make the point that he was speaking not of a single, annual gesture but rather of "a continuing commitment to help the needy of our city not only today but tomorrow and the day after that."

For this venture he enlisted the well-known Adele Corvin, a respected leader in the Jewish community who had also been president of the United Way of the Bay Area. She headed a task force that spent several months visiting a great number of service providers; Central City Hospitality House, a homeless shelter in the Tenderloin district, was finally selected as the temple's partner.

Hospitality House, a twenty-year-old nonsectarian institution with a special program of outreach to homeless youth, would be the beneficiary of roughly $10,000 from the temple each year. But even more was done than providing needed financial assistance at a time of government cutbacks in aid to the poor. To raise the self-esteem of the homeless, the shelter conducted an extensive program in the creative arts, and Emanu-El opened its doors to provide space to display it. The temple also served as a place where congregants dropped off clothing and canned goods for the needy, a practice, to be sure, that was not unusual for a church or synagogue, but one not often seen at Lake and Arguello. Many of the younger congregants in particular volunteered for the homeless initiative, which like the AIDS relief project was singled out for praise by Mayor Agnos.

But there were also some who raised doubts. In an article in the *Temple Chronicle*, Lou Kamen stressed the complexity of social problems such as homelessness and recommended a limited role for the temple. Others worried that the emphasis on social action might diminish the synagogue's liturgical or educational mission. And there was also criticism from the Jewish Community Federation (as the Jewish Welfare Federation was now known), which felt that the temple was beginning to compete with its own extensive network of service agencies.

Kirschner, though, would not be moved from his position that the synagogue was a vital partner in the philanthropic process, "not only the conduit of money but the generator of concern." Very aware of prior chapters in the history of the congregation, such as Rabbi Martin Meyer's outreach to immigrants early in the century, he felt he was "restoring, not inventing" Emanu-El's role in trying to remedy society's ills. In the fall of 1988, he sent out a booklet, called the *Emanu-El Light*, to every temple household, outlining the impressive array of community service projects he had spawned and inviting donations and volunteer time. As he told a newspaper reporter at the time, "The synagogue should not be confined to where people are married and buried. The synagogue, because it is the preserver of the most exalted Jewish ideals, must also be

MURIEL COHN, LONGTIME EMANU-EL CONGREGANT AND STAFF
MEMBER, VOLUNTEERS AT A HOMELESS SHELTER AS PART OF A
TEMPLE-SPONSORED COMMUNITY SERVICE PROGRAM

the implementer of those ideals. Otherwise we become a museum of
Jewish relics."

His energy and creativity in this area seemed to have no end. "Con-
cerned about Jewish insularity," as he put it, he inaugurated the Asian-
Jewish Friendship Coalition, which through cultural and educational
events sought to link the temple with the Chinese, Japanese, Korean, and
Southeast Asian communities of the Bay Area. With the aid of congregants
Richard Hall and popular newscaster Wendy Tokuda, Hall's Japanese-
American wife, the initiative began with a highly successful screening at
Emanu-El of the documentary film *Unfinished Business.* Chronicling the
internment of American citizens of Japanese origin during World War II,
the film was followed by a panel discussion which included the director
as well as one of the men whose stories were featured.

Later Kirschner brought a renowned Japanese choir whose specialty
was Hebrew music to perform in the temple. But he was even more
active in the political realm, working with a consortium of activist organizations to better the lot of the state's fast-growing contingent of recently
arrived Asian immigrants, a group that was frequently exploited. He also
sought to reduce racial prejudice against the Chinese in the temple's
own environs through his leadership in the Richmond District Neighborhood Association.

By 1990, Asians comprised almost a third of the city's population, and intermarriage between Jews and Asians was occurring with increasing frequency. Still, some congregants and staff members felt that Kirschner had gone too far afield in his outreach to a people that historically had far fewer ties to Jews than did other minority groups such as African Americans. He readily admits that it was not his most successful endeavor and, unlike some of the other initiatives, had "little lasting effect." But he also felt the necessity of "holding out our hands to our neighbors in the community.... The issue is not only compassion for Jews but Jewish compassion for all."

Early in 1988, he and Irwin Wiener launched a program to serve the deaf. Under the leadership of Emanu-El member Debra Heaphy, who had lost her hearing as a teenager, a congregation-within-a-congregation was formed to remedy the lack of services for the Jewish deaf in the Bay Area. The first event of the Emanu-El Community of the Deaf was a signed reading of the Purim *megillah*; interpreters were soon provided for other holidays as well, in addition to classes, lectures, and many other temple programs. In the following year, Kirschner brought a deaf rabbinic intern to lead Sabbath services for an overflow crowd in the Rinder Chapel. But most moving was the Bar Mitzvah of a deaf boy in 1990, a child unable to hear since the age of eighteen months. Studying intensively with the Emanu-El clergy and a speech therapist knowledgeable in Hebrew, the Marin seventh-grader overcame his disability and chanted his portion of the Torah and *haftarah*.

Beyond all of this there was a program of providing Sabbath meals to the frail elderly and the creation of a communal chaplaincy to meet the needs of the transient and unaffiliated. The rabbi also took a strong stand in the local press on statewide political issues: he actively opposed the lottery; he called for a letter-writing campaign to protest cutbacks in public education; and he fought the "English Only" proposition which among other things would have ended bilingual ballots.

And there was a major effort to aid the victims—Jewish and non-Jewish—of the Loma Prieta earthquake in 1989. Kirschner's plea for contributions at the Friday evening services following the disaster netted around $40,000, which the temple allocated to seven relief organizations. For many months Emanu-El also housed the city's Korean Presbyterian

Church, whose own building was condemned after the earthquake and ultimately demolished. Once again, Mayor Agnos was grateful for the temple's efforts and spoke at Friday evening services to convey his thanks to the congregation.

Taken as a whole, the vast amount of community service beginning in the mid-1980s redefined the very purpose of the congregation. Of course, a strong commitment to social justice had been voiced by virtually every rabbi at Emanu-El since the turn of the century. And nationally, the Reform movement had distinguished itself in this area for decades. But Kirschner went far beyond statements of concern for the disadvantaged: he created opportunities for his congregants to become personally involved in alleviating their plight.

The synagogue formed a new community service committee, headed by Don Buder, to oversee the various initiatives. Buder and Kirschner also set up a charitable foundation (a separate non-profit corporation) to allocate funds to the various agencies with which the temple was paired, as well as other local groups seeking to relieve human suffering. The Emanu-El Community Service Fund, an unprecedented endeavor in synagogue-based philanthropy, has grown to around a million dollars today.

A part-time program coordinator, Judi Newman, joined the staff and worked on many of the social action efforts. In the last year of Kirschner's tenure, she reported that the list of volunteers for these activities had grown steadily to several hundred. It showed a remarkable level of participation from a congregation that had not been known for activism among the rank and file.

Many of those who rallied to Kirschner's causes were younger members who, like him, had been on the college campus in the idealistic '60s and early '70s. Buder, who had graduated from UC Berkeley's Boalt Hall, was but one of a cohort of idealistic young professionals who gravitated to Emanu-El in the mid-'80s. They were comfortable with the rabbi's language of social engagement and eager for the sort of involvement with the wider community which he urged.

Rhonda Abrams, for example, a student activist at UCLA from 1968 to 1972 who became the local executive director of the Anti-Defamation League only six years later, "joined the temple because of Bob" in 1986:

"He touched a chord integrating personal values and religious expression; you felt good about it; you felt you were making a difference....Here we could be doing the right thing and also be doing it as Jews."

As Andrew Colvin remembers, just as he voted with enthusiasm for Bill Clinton in 1992, so was he deeply impressed with Kirschner: "He was able to connect with me...because I felt him to be a person of my generation." Another young board member in the late '80s, Stephen Dobbs, also saw the temple's transformation into a "responsible social force" as a most welcome development, aptly terming the synagogue a "congregation of conscience."

Those in the older generation had their qualms at times. But they too were won over by Kirschner's highly principled and well-reasoned advocacy of his programs. Almost everyone felt pride in the greatly enhanced role their rabbi and their temple were now playing in the larger community. And with the synagogue's aggressive attempts to "repair a broken world"—fulfilling the age-old obligation known as *tikkun olam*—they also felt increased pride in their Jewish heritage.

IN LIGHT OF THE SWEEPING CHANGES he effected at Emanu-El, it is perhaps surprising that Kirschner altered the liturgy very little. The grandchild of East European immigrants, a boy who became a Bar Mitzvah in a Conservative *shul*, his initial experience with the Classical Reform service as a teenager in the Wilshire Boulevard Temple had been "very negative." Moreover, he had been trained as a rabbi in the 1970s, when both the students and the faculty of the seminary were turning toward Jewish traditionalism.

But he had come to appreciate the beauty of the Emanu-El service as the temple's associate rabbi, sharing the *bimah* in the early and mid-1980s with Asher, Portnoy, and Altman, men he deeply respected. It was also clear that the highest rung of lay leadership was very comfortable with the status quo in this regard. To introduce a more participatory, traditional service could cost him some of the good will that he had worked so hard to create. In any case, Kirschner didn't think the entire issue of worship services "mattered very much"; it was for him "neither as a child, a rabbinical student, or a rabbi...ever a significant expression of Jewish commitment."

This may also explain why he chose to revitalize the congregation with community service initiatives rather than embracing "alternatives" in the realm of prayer, such as Jewish spirituality. For Kirschner was always more comfortable in the arena of prophet than priest.

Similarly, when he first came to Emanu-El in 1981, out of deference to Joe Asher he readily agreed to follow the older rabbi's lead and perform intermarriage. While at Beth Am, however, he had steadfastly refused to marry Jew to non-Jew.

So while Kirschner adhered to Emanu-El's distinctive religious style— unique in Northern California—it was never out of the strong convictions his predecessor had held. This meant that in the larger Jewish community, the new senior rabbi would be anything but the staunch defender of Classical Reform principles that Asher had been. Indeed, Kirschner tried to break down the sectarian barriers separating Jew from Jew with the same zeal with which he sought to bring all Jews into greater involvement with the problems of society as a whole.

Within his own denomination, he established much closer links with the other Reform congregations in the city, co-sponsoring numerous holiday celebrations and public lectures with Sherith Israel and Sha'ar Zahav. He was esteemed at the latter synagogue, which honored him in 1990, not only for his undaunted efforts on the AIDS issue, of course, but also because of his leadership in the struggle to ordain openly gay men and lesbians. His incisive essay, "Halakhah and Homosexuality: A Reappraisal," published in *Judaism*, was widely circulated at the conventions of the Central Conference of American Rabbis in the late '80s and early '90s and gradually helped bring the Reform movement to a position of tolerance on the question of homosexual rabbis.

But he also reached out to the Conservative and even the Orthodox movements, precisely at the time of a dangerously widening rift between traditional and liberal Jews. Only a few months after his installation, he boldly announced an exchange of pulpits with a small Orthodox synagogue near the temple, Magain David Sephardim. Its twenty-eight-year-old rabbi, Hayyim Kassorla, recently ordained by Yeshiva University, had much impressed Kirschner with his willingness for dialogue, and the two decided to use the upcoming 850th birthday of Maimonides to bring their two congregations together.

RABBI KIRSCHNER ON THE *BIMAH* OF THE ORTHODOX
MAGAIN DAVID SEPHARDIM CONGREGATION

They each delivered a lecture on the twelfth-century philosopher in
the other's synagogue. Kassorla preferred not to speak in the Emanu-El
sanctuary, but his presentation in Guild Hall, and Kirschner's at Magain
David, were highly successful, drawing a combined attendance of more
than seven hundred people.

With 1986 producing a rash of violent attacks in Israel motivated by
religious zealotry, Kirschner chose to devote his Rosh Hashanah Eve sermon to "the disgraceful squabbling among the Jewish people." While he
catalogued the acts of vandalism perpetrated by the ultra-Orthodox, he
also took secular Jews to task for their incendiary retaliation. Above all, he
urged reconciliation, and toward that end offered to open the Emanu-El
pulpit to any other rabbi wishing to address the congregation on the
religious issues dividing world Jewry—questions such as conversion,
observance, revelation, and even patrilineal descent, the latter a controversial measure recently approved by the UAHC. Characteristically, he
put forth a plan of action accompanying his concern:

> For the sake of Torah, for the love of the Jewish people, sanctimony
> must be set aside. For all the rabbis in our community to exchange

pulpits for even one Sabbath would send a message of conciliation more powerful than a thousand speeches. It would remind the Jewish world that we are still one people, the House of Israel, tied in a single garment of destiny.

We are so busy fighting over the [Torah] scrolls that we have forgotten to open them. We are so adamant about what they say that we have forgotten what they mean.

Kirschner joined in a pulpit exchange later that year which received national attention. A young Orthodox rabbi, Michael Samuel of Congregation Chevra Thilim, participated, along with Professor Jacob Milgrom, Kirschner's dissertation director at UC Berkeley, who also served as the part-time rabbi of Ner Tamid, a Conservative synagogue. Each rabbi spoke during successive Sabbath services at the other two congregations, with Kirschner teaching the weekly Torah portion and urgently calling for mutual understanding. The San Francisco experiment was hailed as "unprecedented" by one of the most respected Jewish leaders in the country, Rabbi Irving Greenberg, who earlier had warned world Jewry of an impending civil war.

The "who is a Jew?" issue meanwhile escalated in Israel during the election year of 1988, with an attempt by the religious parties to amend the Law of Return and exclude non-Orthodox converts to Judaism from automatic citizenship. Kirschner found himself in the midst of the controversy. Representing Hebrew Union College (on whose board of governors he now served), he made an emergency trip to Israel as one of twenty-five prominent delegates of the Coalition for Jewish Unity. He met with Prime Minister Shamir, Foreign Minister Peres, President Herzog, the chief rabbis, and dozens of other Israeli leaders, including some of those campaigning for the amendment to the Law of Return. All the while he voiced his objection to "any effort to divide our people by the legislative action of the Knesset."

Upon his return he wrote a letter to every congregant assuring them of his "resolve to defend Jewish pluralism." And he held a community-wide forum at the temple to discuss the crisis, in which he was joined by three others who had just returned from their own lobbying efforts in Israel: the president of the Federation, Annette Dobbs; its executive director, Rabbi Brian Lurie; and Mayor Dianne Feinstein, born of a non-Jewish mother, who voiced "pain and outrage at the prospect of having her Jewish legitimacy challenged." Kirschner showed remarkable restraint, telling the anxious audience of eight hundred that "the ultra-religious are not villains....[They] are pious Jews who mean well but who see the world differently from us."

The rabbi exhibited a similar blend of concern and caution on the Palestinian issue, which boiled over with the outbreak of the Intifada during the same period. He endorsed the petition of ninety prominent local Jews—about a third of them university professors—which criticized Israel for its "iron fist" response to young stone-throwers in the West Bank and Gaza, and read it from the pulpit at a Friday evening service. He even accompanied the delegation of the six well-known Jewish academics who had organized the protest when they presented the petition in person to the Israeli consul-general. But Kirschner refrained from signing it himself, "because of the demoralizing effect of public denunciations of the Jewish state already so besieged and vulnerable." In the same vein, he became a charter member of the national editorial board of *Tikkun* magazine, the left-leaning periodical founded in Oakland by Michael Lerner which took a position highly critical of Israel. But he quietly resigned two years later, after having said that the journal "defined its political view more stridently than I prefer."

Kirschner, less partisan than Asher had been, frequently repeated the phrase "What unites us is more important than what drives us apart." More in the tradition of Martin Meyer, Louis Newman, and Alvin Fine, the young rabbi worked to narrow the theological and denominational rifts threatening Jewish unity. In the process, he also brought the temple, long regarded as holding itself aloof, closer to the rest of Bay Area Jewry.

KIRSCHNER SAW HIS MANDATE as one of increasing the membership rolls, and his bold initiatives in the Jewish and general community can be credited with raising the profile of the temple and bringing in many new congregants. But he and Irwin Wiener also targeted a number of fast-growing Jewish subgroups in the city: interfaith couples, Soviet émigrés, senior citizens, and young singles, among others. They designed and marketed programs to meet the special needs of these constituencies, beginning efforts of outreach that would last well beyond their own departure.

Above all, Kirschner and Wiener hoped to make the synagogue more attractive to families with young children. In 1986, they instituted the temple's first preschool, an ambitious project that would reap large rewards in the coming years. Rather than go through the long, bureaucratic process of obtaining a license, they quickly arranged for the San Francisco Jewish Community Center to open a branch of its premiere preschool at Emanu-El. The highly skilled Pam Schneider, an enthusiastic young specialist in early childhood education who had been a master-teacher at the JCC, came to the temple to inaugurate the new venture.

Opening with thirty-five toddlers, the nursery school's enrollment almost doubled in the next year and passed one hundred by the late '80s. The magnificent courtyard soon became its main outdoor space and, ever since, the first impression made upon visitors to the temple during weekdays has often been the joyful commotion of young children at play.

The majority of the parents have been congregants, who receive preference for the sought-after spaces as well as a small discount in fees. But among the unaffiliated, about a dozen families annually have decided to join the temple, accounting for a considerable part of the growth in membership in the past decade and a half.

RABBI KIRSCHNER WITH A CHILD
FROM THE EMANU-EL PRESCHOOL

Pam Schneider, who served for thirteen years, credits Kirschner for envisioning this "institution within an institution." His own children had attended the preschool at the JCC in the early '80s, and he saw the great impact it could make at Emanu-El. But he knew too that in addition to such new programs aimed at specific subgroups, the everyday workings of the synagogue—services, life-cycle events, pastoral counseling, and the religious school—would also be vital in drawing and retaining the unaffiliated.

With both goals in mind, he carefully assembled a team of clergy that, like him, was young and talented. For assistant rabbi he personally chose Yossi Liebowitz, his former classmate at Hebrew Union College and only eighteen months his junior. Liebowitz had been working for five years in Plattsburgh, New York, near the Canadian border, both as the spiritual leader of a tiny congregation and the chaplain in a prison that housed the Jewish serial murderer "Son of Sam." Liebowitz and his wife, now with two children, were eager to relocate to the Bay Area, the home of her family.

Although they both played the guitar well, the two rabbis could not have been more different in background and temperament. Having grown up in an Orthodox home in Brooklyn, Liebowitz exuded a kind of *Yiddishkeit* absent in Kirschner; the assistant rabbi sang Hasidic songs in the temple and often peppered his speech with Yiddish words and phrases. An exuberant, heavyset man with a hearty sense of humor (though he disliked being described as "jovial"), he remained for three years at Emanu-El and was promoted to associate rabbi before he left. He enlivened the religious school with many electives, taught the "Introduction to Judaism" course, planned programs for young adults, and even experimented with alternative "family-style" services, always bringing to his work a great deal of vitality. He was also at the forefront of the synagogue's new efforts to reach out to the unaffiliated; in 1987 he unveiled "Chag Emanu-El," a well-publicized, monthly educational program for non-members related to the Jewish holidays.

"His very [Hebrew] name showed that he differed from the usual Emanu-El profile," Kirschner recalls, "but I wanted to bring Yossi's sensibility [to the temple]; it wasn't an automatic fit, but I thought he would be a good counterweight to me."

In 1987, a new cantor was chosen, only the temple's fourth in the

RABBI KIRSCHNER AND RABBI YOSSI LIEBOWITZ

twentieth century. Roslyn Barak, like Liebowitz and Wiener, had grown up in a traditional family in New York and attended an Orthodox religious school. But her mother is Sephardi, and both Ladino and Yiddish were often spoken at home. Living near Tel Aviv for three years in her mid-twenties, where she married an Israeli and had a son, gave her fluency in Hebrew and further deepened her commitment to the Jewish people.

But it was singing that had been the passion of this lyric soprano from the time that she was a teenager. Trained at the Manhattan School of Music, she worked in the New York area as an opera singer and concert soloist, winning many awards before joining the Israeli National Opera Company in 1974.

Yet she was disappointed with the lack of professionalism there and eventually returned to New York. After a few years she found work in a synagogue—for the first time in her life—as a choir member at Shaaray Tefila, a Reform congregation on the Upper East Side. This experience was so rewarding that she decided to become a cantor. Now in her mid-thirties, she entered HUC's School of Sacred Music, despite the financial hardships involved in being a full-time student. In 1986, she graduated among an all-woman class of eight.

The members of Emanu-El's cantorial search committee, meanwhile, had been frustrated in their attempts to replace Joe Portnoy. A year had gone by since his retirement, and no one whom they auditioned around the country seemed to meet their high standards.

The following spring, Kirschner, accompanied by Walter Newman, Harold Stein, and James Schwabacher, the latter a professional singer and voice coach, flew to New York to audition several members of the cantorial school's class of 1987. Barak, then working as a part-time cantor in Forest Hills, asked to join the tryout and overwhelmed the San Franciscans. "Her voice was just like a bird," as Newman fondly recalls, a voice, in Schwabacher's glowing opinion, "that could do anything." She was brought out to the temple for an audition and interview, and easily won the job.

Barak fell in love with the Bay Area and thrived at her new post. From the outset she sought to maintain the majesty—and formality—of the Emanu-El worship service. "The music must have integrity that truly decorates the *mitzvah* of prayer," she has said. "People must leave the temple feeling uplifted."

But it also became evident that her repertoire, particularly on Friday evenings, would be much more diverse than that of Joseph Portnoy and Ludwig Altman. Reflecting her own richly textured Jewish background, she introduced a wide variety of music—the works of East European, Sephardi, Israeli, and contemporary American composers.

She enjoyed a great deal of latitude, for not only had Portnoy stepped down, but organist Ludwig Altman had also retired in 1986. His immediate successor was the able musician Michael Secour, but Barak felt a "terrific match" with the young David Higgs, one of the leading organists in the country, whom the temple engaged in 1989. Still, no one—and certainly not a recently arrived non-Jew—could have the influence of the legendary Altman, who had served for half a century. Barak, then (unlike Portnoy, who had been somewhat constrained not only by Altman but in his early years by Cantor Rinder, as well), was free to put her own stamp on the temple's musical program.

In the Emanu-El tradition of creating great music for the worship service, she used a grant from the Sisterhood to commission a work celebrating the temple's 140th anniversary in 1990. She invited the renowned

Canadian composer Ben Steinberg to compose the first Sabbath morning service for the female voice. With Barak's own soprano register in mind, he wrote *Avodat Hakodesh* (which also included parts for the choir, organ, and wind instruments), and came to the temple as scholar-in-residence for the gala weekend of its premiere.

At Kirschner's request, she also initiated an important educational program in the temple which is still flourishing today, adult B'nai Mitzvot. This had been introduced throughout the country in the past decade and the rabbi saw its potential for Emanu-El, where so many congregants regretted having missed this spiritual moment in childhood. Meeting every week for almost an entire year, the course begins with Hebrew and prepares adults to read their Torah and *haftarah* portions and lead parts of the service on the day of the ceremony. It has proven a profound experience for many of the roughly dozen people who participate annually.

The cantor admired Kirschner immensely, and recalls the late '80s as a time "crackling with excitement." A single mother, it meant a great deal to her too that her teenage son, whose Bar Mitzvah and confirmation were both performed by the senior rabbi, looked up to him as well.

Mark Schiftan, who like Barak joined the staff in mid-1987, also remembers the atmosphere as "electric with possibility." He had been chosen as the temple's third rabbi, a new position created by the board at Kirschner's request. With the proliferation of activities in the synagogue,

CANTOR ROSLYN BARAK TEACHES EMANU-EL'S FIRST
ANSHEI MITZVAH (ADULT B'NAI MITZVOT) CLASS, 1987

and its swelling ranks of members, there was little argument about the need for more staff.

A recent graduate of HUC, and only twenty-six, Schiftan had been born and raised in San Francisco and longed to come back home. He was also inspired by Kirschner's inclusive vision of Emanu-El. Schiftan led the first interfaith couples' support group in the temple, a workshop dealing with issues such as holiday celebrations, child-rearing, and acceptance in the Jewish community. He also offered an array of programs to the Soviet refugees who descended upon San Francisco in unprecedented numbers by the late '80s: an émigré friendship circle, a tutorial program to teach them English, and of course holiday celebrations. The annual Hanukah party and Passover seder for Russian newcomers each drew about five hundred people.

Schiftan, who was only beginning to develop his skills in the late '80s, was in awe of the senior rabbi, from whom he learned an enormous amount: "He always set the bar extremely high; he did it with every class he taught and every sermon he gave." Given his entry-level post, no one, least of all Schiftan, thought he would remain more than two or at most three years at Emanu-El. But he stayed for seven eventful years, being promoted to associate rabbi in 1990 and leading the temple for eighteen months as interim senior rabbi after Kirschner's sudden departure.

In 1989, Kirschner selected another recent HUC graduate for the position of assistant. Gayle Pomerantz, an intern at New York's large Central Synagogue, became the second female rabbi in the temple's history. She and her husband had been to San Francisco only once before—on their honeymoon.

She accomplished a great deal during her three years of service, an intense period which coincided with the Loma Prieta earthquake (causing her own apartment to be condemned), the birth of her first child, and of course the Kirschner resignation. She worked closely with the temple youth group; introduced the unaffiliated to the holiday cycle through a program called "First Steps," something similar to Liebowitz's "Chag Emanu-El"; and, like Schiftan, led workshops for interfaith couples. She also developed the first women's programs at Emanu-El, including not only courses but also a popular potluck feminist seder.

Like her colleagues, she was inspired by Kirschner's "compelling vision" and compared the atmosphere to "Camelot." But the demands of motherhood mandated her resignation in mid-1992 (six months after that of the senior rabbi), and she took a part-time post in the Jewish community of her native South Florida.

Kirschner believes his last appointment, in 1990, to have been his most important, that of the innovative Rabbi Peretz Wolf-Prusan for the newly created full-time position of educator. In point of fact, he was chosen after much deliberation by an active religious school committee, but he had the strong backing of the senior rabbi, who had known him well for more than a decade.

Wolf-Prusan had been the director of an outstanding program in the arts at Camp Swig in the mid-'70s, and later studied printmaking at the San Francisco Art Institute. An accomplished calligrapher, whose *ketubot* (Jewish marriage contracts) have been widely exhibited, he might well have made a career in the field of art education or graphic design had Kirschner not inspired him to study for the rabbinate.

They met at Beth Am in 1980, where Peretz taught in the religious school and encountered "a rabbi unlike any [he] had ever known." He remembers learning from Kirschner that rabbinical school did not really teach the texts, but rather *how to study* them. This notion appealed to Peretz, who at the time was studying not to *be*, but rather *how to become*, an artist. "The wall came down," he recalls of his sudden insight, and in 1982, shortly after his marriage to Becki Wolf, he decided to enter Hebrew Union College. Kirschner performed their wedding and signed the *ketubah* which still hangs in the Wolf-Prusans' bedroom.

Throughout rabbinical school Peretz kept in close touch with Kirschner, who had him in mind when he asked the board to allocate funds for a professional devoted entirely to the education of the temple's youth. Wolf-Prusan had gained valuable experience as the director of the Reform Jewish High School of Cincinnati in his last years at HUC, and now, planning a career as an educator, saw "the greatest challenge and the greatest promise" at Emanu-El.

Soon after his arrival, he enriched the Bar and Bat Mitzvah program, added a great deal of Hebrew to the school curriculum, and upgraded the early childhood activities. He experimented with family education and also offered the students opportunities to participate in the temple's

RABBI KIRSCHNER WITH HIS KEY STAFF MEMBERS IN 1990
FROM LEFT: RABBI KIRSCHNER, JUDI NEWMAN, IRWIN WIENER,
RABBI GAYLE POMERANTZ, RABBI PERETZ WOLF-PRUSAN,
CANTOR ROSLYN BARAK, RABBI MARK SCHIFTAN

community service initiatives. But he worked only a year and a half under Kirschner, and his greatest impact—not only on the religious school but also on the style of worship in the temple—would be made after his mentor's departure.

Toward the end of Kirschner's tenure the staff of clergy had grown considerably, from three to five. In effect, Cantor Portnoy had been replaced by two people, a full-time cantor and a full-time educator, and an additional rabbi had been engaged as well. Especially in contrast with the Asher era, the new team was remarkably young; in 1990, the average age of the five clergy was thirty-five. Led by "one of the most, if not *the* most gifted rabbi of his generation," as Schiftan put it, they thought there was nothing they couldn't accomplish.

IF THE PROFESSIONAL TEAM was completely different in 1990 than it had been less than a decade earlier, there were many new faces among the lay leadership as well. While a crop of baby boomers in their thirties and early forties became active in the temple's programs, and a number of them joined the board, the rabbi also worked hard to involve members of the temple's famous pioneer families, usually in their fifties and sixties, who had not been active in several decades. "I had a sense that the key families needed to lead," the rabbi recalls, "and that was missing when I came in." With much candor he admits that for positions of lay leadership, "I would always lean toward the big people, the rich people, the prominent people, because I felt that that was what was needed—we had all kinds of people on the board who were well-meaning…but that ain't gonna cut it, not at that level, not if you want to have a major impact on the community."

In this regard he feels that he was a more aggressive competitor of Brian Lurie than Asher had been, and energetically pursued major philanthropists who since the Six Day War had been "siphoned off" from the temple by the Federation. He was interested in more than money, however, pursuing people of "stature, and reach and clout." He says, "That's what would make it possible, if I had an idea, to get it going." He went after the sort of person who in Los Angeles would be called "a player."

But if Kirschner was instrumental in his choice of lay leaders, it is also true that he enjoyed genuine bonds of affection with them. He deeply appreciated the "charm and worldliness" of San Francisco's Jewish elite; he made many close and sincere friendships with eminent lay leaders, friendships that endure to this day.

Each of the three temple presidents in the Kirschner years came from families that go back to pioneer times. Walter Newman, of course, had become president shortly before Kirschner was chosen as senior rabbi. The two not only shared ambitious plans for the temple, but also enjoyed a personal relationship approaching that of father and son. Newman, who had lost his middle son, also named Robert, to a brain tumor, "loved" Kirschner; he could not have been more proud of the "young, brilliant, dynamic guy…who conveyed his thoughts in such beautiful style." As Harold Zellerbach and Ben Swig had greatly encouraged the young Rabbi Fine a generation earlier, so Newman "was there to help me," Kirschner recalls. And the gracious civic leader's "stature in the community…beyond the congregation" enabled him to bring other powerful people into the temple's orbit.

Newman's background in city planning and his shrewd business sense led to a financial boon for the temple—perhaps the greatest in its history. It involved the large tract of land in Colma, south of the city in suburban San Mateo County, which the congregation had bought in the 1880s. A portion of the grounds was used as the Home of Peace Cemetery, and the rest earmarked for use in the future. But by the latter part of the twentieth century, with the increasing preference for cremations over burials, it had become clear that dozens of acres would not be needed for many generations. The excess real estate, however, was zoned only for agricultural use, so it was leased to farmer tenants, most of whom grew flowers on the land. Collectively, they paid rent of roughly $3,000 a month through most of the early '80s.

In 1985, the City of Colma approached the temple, wanting to buy about seven acres of the property for the construction of a road. Newman, working closely with Irwin Wiener, offered to deed that land to them free of charge if they would change the zoning on eighteen other acres to commercial use. The town fathers agreed, and, as Newman recalls, "I knew that the value of our land had just gone from X to ten times X." As a result of the volunteer efforts of a number of congregants whom Newman enlisted, most notably the recently retired John Samter, who worked on the project for over a year, two-thirds of the commercially zoned land was leased to the giant Tom Price auto dealership for thirty-five years. The annual rent began at $370,000 and exceeded $500,000 by the early '90s—money that could augment the temple's operating income. "I thought, that's the best real estate deal I'll ever make in my life," Newman said recently with a warm smile.

Newman's successor as temple president was Mortimer Fleishhacker, whose probable forebear, Samuel Fleishhacker, signed the original charter of the temple in 1851. His grandfather, also named Mortimer Fleishhacker, was one of the city's leading bankers in the 1920s and a regent of the University of California. His father, Mortimer Fleishhacker Jr., was also a banker and had, over the objections of his family, married a "Polish" Jew, Janet Choynski, granddaughter of Isidore Choynski, the incorrigible newspaperman of the late nineteenth century. But they had an uncommonly successful marriage and by the mid-1950s devoted themselves almost exclusively to philanthropy: he was president of Mount Zion Hospital, as well as the American Conservatory Theatre; he also served as the first president of KQED, the Bay Area's premiere public television station, and as president of Emanu-El from 1952 to 1954. He later admitted, however, that he served "halfheartedly...[only] out of duty...[and] was not really prepared for it." But his son, a Princeton graduate and himself a civic leader—with a bit of his maternal great-grandfather's feistiness—would be a much more active president.

Like Newman, Mort Fleishhacker, who became temple president in 1988, aimed very high. As he said in one of his annual reports, "Emanu-El has always stood out as the leader, as the image, as the Reform Jewish presence,...as the major congregation in San Francisco." He felt "an obligation to continue our inherited responsibilities," and for him that meant a concerted effort to attract the unaffiliated, which he made a top priority of his presidency.

But "to create reasons for Jews to want to affiliate," he saw no alternative to a massive remodeling and refurbishing of the physical plant, rehabilitation which in any case was much needed after more than sixty years of use. With Kirschner and Wiener, he presided over an immense project to renovate the sanctuary and temple house, a four-year undertaking that ultimately cost more than eighteen million dollars. Fleishhacker was a maximalist; he "pushed" the board, in his words, "to create the finest, most beautiful facility in Northern California or the world....There are always those who say we could have done less. [But] my attitude was: this is our opportunity. We're on a roll. Don't stop now."

Even more persuasive, if less effusive, was the last president of the Kirschner years, Rhoda H. Goldman. She was unquestionably the most influential lay leader in the Bay Area's Jewish community; she was also regarded as one of the most prominent philanthropists in North America.

A fourth-generation San Franciscan, she was a relation of Levi Strauss and one of the owners of the company bearing his name—the largest apparel manufacturer in the world. As the daughter of the munificent Walter and Elise Haas, she was "bred" for benevolence and was active her entire life in a myriad of humanitarian causes. Widely admired for her gracious manner and good judgment, Goldman successfully led other major institutions, such as Mount Zion Hospital and the San Francisco Foundation, through difficult times of transition in the 1970s and '80s.

She and her husband, Richard (whose own parents and grandparents had been temple members), were profoundly affected by a visit in the late 1970s to Auschwitz, where they saw firsthand the remains of the Nazi death machine. A few years later, Mrs. Goldman was instrumental in creating San Francisco's Holocaust memorial, a haunting sculpture by George Segal near the Legion of Honor. But it was in the early '90s that the Goldmans impressed the entire philanthropic world with their ingenuity and ambition: they established a foundation that awards annual prizes for environmental protection—on all six inhabited continents.

Soon after he came to the temple as associate rabbi, Kirschner met Mrs. Goldman on a hospital visit, her name appearing on a list of patients Asher had asked him to see. The two of them "just hit it off," he recalls, talking not about her heart surgery but rather the prospects of a belated Bat Mitzvah. He learned only later, reporting on his visits to Joe Asher, of the prominence of the woman who was so easygoing and friendly.

Kirschner eventually prepared Rhoda for her Bat Mitzvah, taught her Hebrew, and formed a "precious friendship," not only with her but with her entire family. At the end of the '80s he was close by the side of the Goldmans during the greatest tragedy of their lives, comforting them after the death of one of their four grown children, Rick, who succumbed to a brain tumor.

RHODA HAAS GOLDMAN

Late in 1990, with the congregation facing the formidable task of completing the renovation, the rabbi asked her to become president. He knew of her health problems, and her many long-standing commitments, not least of all to the Federation and its burgeoning Endowment Fund, to which the Goldmans were the leading contributors. But at the Goldmans' home, with Richard present, he asked her on behalf of the congregation and himself personally, and the next day she accepted.

No one knew then, of course, that this would be one of the most trying presidencies in the history of the institution. In addition to the renovation, within a year she would see "her rabbi and her friend" at the center of a major scandal. Leading the temple "was a burden," as Richard recalls, "that she lived with all the time." As he recently remembered, "It took a lot out of her [because] when she got into something she wouldn't stop halfway. She put in whatever was required to get it done."

IT IS DIFFICULT TO IMAGINE how the temple's overwhelming demands upon Kirschner allowed him the time and energy to pursue his scholarship. But he continued his graduate work at UC Berkeley even after he became senior rabbi, and was awarded his doctorate in 1988. For his dissertation, he wrote a highly technical treatment of an ancient text on the tabernacle, *Baraita de-Melekhet ha-Mishkan*, an unusual codex, somewhat similar in structure to a tannaitic *midrash* on the Book of Exodus, but virtually unique in late antique rabbinic literature. He translated, annotated, and explained the significance of the rare document, and his critical edition was published as one of a series of scholarly monographs by Hebrew Union College Press.

He worked feverishly on his thesis in the mid-'80s, taking the one day a week he had "off" to spend twelve hours in Berkeley studying in the university library and conferring with his professors. Saving up his vacation time, he made short research trips abroad to Oxford, Cambridge, and Jerusalem. Beyond the dissertation, he published articles in such respected periodicals as the *Harvard Theological Review*, *Vigiliae Christianae*, the *Journal of Semitic Studies*, and the *Journal for the Study of Judaism*. In the tradition of Jacob Voorsanger and Martin Meyer, he also taught courses in Jewish studies at Berkeley, and in 1991 was announced as the inaugural winner of the Daniel Jeremy Silver Fellowship at Harvard.

Well aware of the gulf between the synagogue and the academy, Kirschner sought to bring Emanu-El closer in touch with the world of Jewish scholarship and thus link the two halves of his own remarkably productive professional life. He regularly printed the title page of his latest scholarly publication in the *Temple Chronicle* in order to acquaint the congregants with his academic pursuits, and he encouraged them to call his office for reprints. He expanded the congregation's Institute of Jewish Studies, adding a spring session of mini-courses to the high-quality offerings of the fall—adult education classes presented by some of the best teachers in the Bay Area. The course he himself taught each semester often drew more than a hundred students.

But Kirschner also envisioned something on an even higher plane: a well-endowed annual lecture that would bring to Emanu-El "only *the* stellar Jewish minds in the world." In addition, he wanted the presentations to be published and circulated among the members. Once again, he was able to enlist the support of a family of towering prominence. Sissy Geballe, the wife of a respected physicist and daughter of the revered philanthropist Daniel Koshland, spearheaded the effort to establish the lectureship in his memory. Only a few months earlier, her daughter, Alison, had agreed to chair the Back on Track tutorial program. The Geballes, closely intertwined with the Haas family (Rhoda Goldman was Sissy's first cousin), increased their involvement in the temple in the late '80s and also became warm friends of the rabbi.

Kirschner had the pleasure of inviting the two scholars who had most influenced him to deliver the first two Koshland Memorial Lectures. In 1988, to inaugurate the series, he chose Amos Funkenstein, with whom he had studied at Hebrew Union College. The brilliant medievalist and intellectual historian had just accepted a chair in Jewish studies at Stanford which the Koshland family had also endowed; a few years later, still in his fifties, he would win the coveted Israel Prize in history.

He was followed by Jacob Milgrom, professor of Bible at UC Berkeley and one of the world's leading authorities on the Book of Leviticus. Having been a pulpit rabbi for a decade and a half before entering academia, Milgrom was an important role model for Kirschner and his major professor at the university. The esteemed historians Saul Friedlander and Yosef Hayim Yerushalmi were the Koshland lecturers in 1990 and 1991, respectively, continuing the standards of academic excellence that distinguish the event to this day.

Kirschner also co-sponsored a variety of programs—often symposia devoted to ethical issues—with many of the finest institutions of higher learning in the Bay Area: UC Berkeley, the UCSF medical school, and Hastings College of the Law, among others. He established an especially close working relationship with the Jesuit-run University of San Francisco, whose Jewish studies program had been endowed by yet another Emanu-El family famous for its generosity in the academic world—the Swigs. Through USF, the rabbi arranged for the temple's post-confirmation class to receive college credit. In addition, he was regularly featured on the campus radio station, which every Sunday morning broadcast a prerecorded Emanu-El Sabbath service along with one of his sermons. In 1989, the two institutions co-sponsored a lecture by Nobel laureate Saul Bellow.

CONGREGANTS GREATLY APPRECIATED the opportunity to hear such luminaries, but it was Kirschner's own sermons that touched them most deeply. His exceptional abilities in the pulpit are recalled by Gary Shapiro, a well-known attorney in the city who joined the temple soon after Kirschner became senior rabbi and who expresses the thoughts of many members:

> Bob was not a good speaker—Bob was a *great* speaker, the best sermonizer I have ever heard in my life. Consistently [my wife] Dana and I would walk home after services and spend the afternoon talking about his sermon. There is no one else I ever heard that had that type of influence on us. They…achieved the purpose of the sermon—to give you something, to move a person.

Rhonda Abrams, speaking for the younger generation, was inspired by the unique way in which he articulated Jewish values: "Bob talked about what really mattered. I go to the synagogue to look into my soul and he challenged me to do just that."

Kirschner does not possess the sonorous voice of an Alvin Fine, and his sermons contained few of the cultured, continental flourishes of a Joe Asher. His style was different: thoughtful, reassuring, and, in the mind of a temple vice-president of that period, "almost soft and feminine." Above all, his words and thoughts were accessible to the audience. As accomplished academically as anyone who ever held the Emanu-El pulpit, he neither overestimated nor underestimated his listeners. He seemed to connect with them effortlessly.

But in truth Kirschner spent many hours each week "agonizing" over the sermon, for him a rabbinical task as important as any. He knew that Jewish preaching was in decline, that electronic media had largely eclipsed it, that many rabbis had done away with it. But for him the sermon, originating with the Hebrew prophets, represented a thoroughly Jewish mode of communication. In any case, the grand architecture of the temple and its tradition of distinguished preachers "required it."

His sermon would rarely be an analysis of current events ("Congregants can get that from *Newsweek*," he said), but rather flowed from the Torah. As he wrote in a recently published article entitled "Is There Still a Place for the Sermon?": "The challenge is to close the distance—chronological, conceptual, linguistic—between ancient wisdom and modern experience, without sacrificing one to the other."

At times, though, he misjudged the strength of the words he spoke from the pulpit, and he learned the "perils...of speaking from this height." His most painful lesson came during the High Holidays of 1987, only five days after the Pope's visit to San Francisco, when he delivered two powerful sermons on Catholic-Jewish relations, the second essentially recanting the first.

Like Jews throughout the world, Kirschner had been angered by John Paul II's reception of Kurt Waldheim in the summer of that year, making no reference to the Austrian president's well-documented Nazi past and actually praising him as a man of peace for his work as secretary-general of the United Nations. At first, though, the rabbi turned to his close friend Archbishop Quinn—to whom he had spoken a year earlier about inviting the Pope to Emanu-El—asking him to convey his concerns to Rome. But Kirschner's long-standing faith in ecumenicism was crushed by the archbishop's pastoral letter to local Jewish leaders, including several Holocaust survivors. It not only justified the papal audience with Waldheim, but also the Vatican's silence during the Holocaust and its four-decade-long refusal to recognize the State of Israel.

In early September, on the eve of the Pope's visit, the rabbi expressed his "deep, personal disappointment" to Quinn in a meeting that also included three survivors who related their personal stories to the Catholic leader. But the archbishop refused to alter his position, and Kirschner emerged as the most vehement voice of protest among all the rabbis in the Bay Area.

He spoke with fury at a raucous community-wide teach-in sponsored by *Tikkun* magazine, and then walked out of the hall in the middle of the event; he expressed his bitterness at the Church during an interfaith forum at the Graduate Theological Union in Berkeley, and bristled with anger and annoyance toward the others on the panel.

But it was his sermon on Rosh Hashanah Eve that would cause him the most regret; he counted it at the end of the '80s as "the most serious mistake" of his rabbinate up to that point. In a bellicose mood, he lashed out:

> Let the Church at last understand: the people of Israel lives—not in shadow, not in degradation but in our own place in the sun. We recognize your beliefs—but not as the fulfillment of ours. We grant you respect—but not at the price of ours. We welcome your friendship—but not if it means betraying the memory of six million Jews, who have already been betrayed enough.

Many congregants were wildly enthusiastic, and the sermon drew applause, unprecedented during worship services in the sanctuary. Kirschner received almost a hundred letters of support in the next few days.

Yet as soon as he finished speaking, he grew uneasy, and soon felt "devastated" when he realized how deeply he had wounded hundreds of intermarried couples who had heard him. He wept upon learning of a Catholic woman, visiting the temple with her Jewish husband for the first time, who became convinced that rabbis regularly attack Christianity, and vowed never to return to a synagogue again.

Feeling that he had "betrayed" his calling and himself, he chose Kol Nidre—precisely two years after the AIDS sermon, the moment of his greatest triumph—to offer a heartfelt apology to the congregation:

> What should have been spoken in love was spoken in anger. What should have been said in hope was said with bitterness. For this error, I...have come back to the very same place to ask the Holy One, blessed

be He, for His forgiveness, and you for yours....When anger runs too deep, it singes the borders of the heart. When it runs too deep for too long, it burns out the lining of the soul.

This time the response was largely negative. There were rumors that his retraction was due to pressure from leading board members, something that upset Kirschner even further. Holocaust survivors in particular were outraged and two yelled insults at him as he left the temple on Yom Kippur day. An astonishing two hundred letters of disapproval came to his office before the end of the year.

Kirschner's about-face, though, should not be seen as a complete fiasco. The entire Jewish community of the Bay Area had been polarized by the Pope's visit that summer, and his oscillation between the two poles of conflict and conciliation reflected the painful ambivalence many felt regarding the contemporary Church. Taken together, the sermons were highly educational; they illuminated much about the key issues dividing Catholic and Jew.

But there was something disturbing about this episode that went beyond the content of the rabbi's remarks. He had lost his temper at several public occasions during the week of the Pope's visit, and during the High Holidays had put himself—and his own seething struggle against the Pope—literally at center stage. Rarely had Rosh Hashanah and Yom Kippur been so eclipsed; never had the Emanu-El pulpit been so personalized.

It would not be fair to say that he was faltering in September 1987; many of Kirschner's major accomplishments still lay ahead. But the High Holiday reversal, "something seismic," in his words, showed that he was less surefooted and less at peace with himself than many had realized.

In the months that followed, he thought much about the contradictions inherent in sermonizing and wrote revealingly in the *Journal of Reform Judaism*, "There is something absurd about standing behind a pulpit and speaking without fear of contradiction, or hope of contradiction, as if our authority were immutable." He began to question other aspects of his work as well, such as the endless rounds of charitable functions he was expected to attend, and even the time he was required to stand in the receiving line after Sabbath services. It had been easier for the Ashers, he felt, because their two sons were already grown during most of the period when Joe was the senior rabbi. He and Reesa, and the young

Kirschner children, were paying a very high price for his interminably long hours.

He pondered as well another contradiction of his calling—its expectations of moral perfection. As he stated in 1988, "It is true we [rabbis] stand for Torah. But it is also true that no one can stand that tall."

ON TOP OF EVERYTHING ELSE in the crowded Kirschner years, the rapidly growing congregation embarked on a massive capital project.

It began at the end of 1988 with the extensive restoration of the sanctuary, called by the renowned architectural critic Allan Temko "the most majestic religious building in San Francisco." Since its opening in 1926, however, relatively little had been done to ensure that its beauty would last.

Repair of the enormous domed ceiling was considered most urgent; over time pieces of asbestos installed to enhance the acoustics had come loose. It all needed to be removed and replaced with a non-toxic material. But in addition to plastering and painting, the lay leaders hoped to take the opportunity to put in a new cork floor, new seat coverings, and an

INTERIOR OF THE MAIN SANCTUARY DURING THE RENOVATION

improved sound system. Repair of the stained-glass windows, weather-proofing, and seismic retrofitting were also incorporated into the project. A great deal of work would be have to be done on the sanctuary, but everyone agreed that the inspired conception of the original architect, Arthur Brown, should be maintained as much as possible.

The temple engaged the Southern California firm of Development Management Associates, first to conduct a feasibility study and later to coordinate the capital campaign. It was initially estimated that the renovation of the sanctuary would exceed two million dollars. But while the plans were being finalized, the board began to consider an even more ambitious undertaking: the remodeling of the temple house to accommodate the growing membership and its new needs. Including a proposed endowment fund for programs, "Campaign Emanu-El" announced a goal of 10.5 million dollars in September 1988, just before work was about to commence on the sanctuary.

It seemed a staggering sum, but one in line with the estimates of the consulting firm. Moreover, success seemed virtually guaranteed when the co-chairs of the campaign were named—Rhoda Goldman and Richard Swig. It was an ideal combination, with Goldman, the best representative one could have of the venerable German-Jewish families, and Swig, the grandson of an immigrant, epitomizing the postwar philanthropy of the East European Jews that had helped revitalize San Francisco Jewry. Kirschner and Wiener joined them and other lay leaders, such as Harold Stein, in a sustained effort to solicit the temple's membership.

They were able to make a persuasive case. The "Master Plan" of 1989 sought to reconfigure and refurbish the temple house to suit a congregation that itself had been transformed in just four years. With the increasing number of young families in mind, the plan called for a complete makeover of the school: the classrooms, library, and early childhood facilities would all be made more inviting. Guild Hall, on the ground floor, which had also deteriorated over the decades, would be remodeled, too. It was felt that with a major facelift the large social hall could serve as an attractive venue for wedding receptions, Bar and Bat Mitzvah celebrations, and congregational dinners—and in the process generate a considerable amount of income for the temple. During the day, its large, open area would accommodate the budding preschool.

The centerpiece of the project was the renovation of the Martin Meyer Auditorium. Designed in the 1920s as a theatre, the rather dreary room had been woefully underused for decades. Kirschner, meanwhile, had longed for an intermediate-sized hall both for cultural and educational programs and as a place of worship. On Friday evenings, for example, his popular services often brought overflow crowds to the long, narrow Rinder Chapel, which could seat only 135, even with folding chairs added in the aisles. The sanctuary, on the other hand, with a capacity of 1,700, was much too big a space; even a large turnout seemed small under the cavernous dome.

Irwin Wiener well understood this dilemma, but felt that rather than remodeling the Meyer Auditorium it would be more cost-effective simply to enlarge the Rinder Chapel. But he was overruled, both by the rabbi and the lay leaders, many of whom had an emotional attachment to the small, serene chapel and objected to altering it in any fundamental way. Moreover, they saw the value to the temple of a handsome, new, midsized and multipurpose room with an abundance of natural light. A second sanctuary, then, seating about three hundred on the main floor and over a hundred more in the balcony, was incorporated into the master plan.

There were no doubts at all, however, about the need for work on the main sanctuary. Just two weeks before construction was set to begin, part of the ceiling, damaged by leaks from recent rains, fell into the pews.

But the restored sanctuary, dedicated with a weekend of events in September 1989, did more than shore up a crumbling structure. Masterfully conceived by the local architectural firm of Robinson, Mills, and Williams, it was hailed as a "triumph" by the *San Francisco Chronicle*, and in some ways an improvement over the original. Congregants and the general public alike were awed by the color, light, texture, and sound they encountered. The vast interior, which Arthur Brown had rendered in a dull gray, was now brightened with a "warm beige" which went well with the new dark cork flooring and burgundy upholstery. The heavy leather and oak doors were remade with the same materials and the temple was further beautified with a band of polished brass along the walls.

The sound system was "the best in the world," according to a proud President Fleishhacker, who had visited the grand St. Thomas Church on New York's Fifth Avenue to hear it in operation. Known as "PewBack," it consisted of speakers mounted unobtrusively behind each seat, with the sound from the *bimah* electronically timed to reach every row at the optimal moment. Superb acoustically, this also obviated the need for large, hanging speakers that would have marred the interior design.

The lighting of the sanctuary was also much enhanced. A huge oculus, or circle of spotlights, was set into the very apex of the dome, adding not only illumination but a somewhat dramatic, even "dazzling" effect. The brilliant ring of lights was added rather late in the design process and proved to be the most controversial feature of the restoration. Allan Temko, who lauded the "otherwise flawless" makeover, felt the oculus to be its "one serious mistake." For him the genius of Brown's design in the 1920s was the upwardly curving dome—representing monotheism itself—and he believed that it should "continue unimpeded...calm, unified, unbroken."

But this was an arguable point, and it hardly detracted from what had been achieved by the architects and the dedicated building committee, headed by Helene Cohen and including John Samter, who oversaw the contractors, Plant Builders. The restoration soon won the Award for Excellence in Architectural Conservation from the Foundation for San Francisco's Architectural Heritage, and exactly one month after its opening came through the Loma Prieta earthquake virtually unscathed. Doubtless, its success emboldened the Emanu-El's leaders to "shoot for the stars" in the renovation of the temple house.

AS THE NEW DECADE DAWNED the lay leadership was "in euphoria," as Walter Newman remembers, "because everything was going so well." More had been accomplished in the past five years than anyone could have dreamed. A dynamic young rabbi—a consummate scholar, sermonizer, and social activist—leading a gifted team, had brought in hundreds of new members, including many baby-boomer couples. The cantor possessed the finest voice heard by the congregation since Edward Stark at the turn of the century. The new full-time educator, filled with energy and creativity, tackled the perennial problems of the school with a fervor not seen at Emanu-El since the days of Martin Meyer.

The size of the congregation swelled by about a half, rising from around a thousand to almost 1,500 families. But with the "Fair Share

NEWLY RENOVATED INTERIOR OF THE MAIN SANCTUARY

Plan" put in place by Irwin Wiener, a guideline for dues related to a family's income, this larger flock was also paying more per capita than it had in the first half of the '80s. The total annual amount taken in through dues roughly doubled during Kirschner's tenure, increasing from half a million to a million dollars a year. The Colma leasehold, of minor consequence until mid-decade, now produced more than $40,000 in net rents for the temple *every month*.

The most prominent Jewish families in Northern California had returned to the active role they had played in the congregation in past generations. They helped restore the exquisite sanctuary and were now turning their attention to the temple house.

Emanu-El seemed more of a leader in the Bay Area Jewish community and the national Reform movement than it had in the '70s and early '80s. The community service initiatives, the pulpit exchanges with the other denominations, the preschool, the Koshland Memorial Lecture, and the renovation all brought recognition and praise.

With Brian Lurie's departure from the Federation at the beginning of the decade for the top post at the United Jewish Appeal in New York, Kirschner was left as the most influential Jewish professional in Northern

California. But many spoke of even greater things for him in the near future: perhaps the presidency of HUC, or even the UAHC, both of which were due to become available in the next few years. The rabbi himself dreamed of one day holding the Koshland Chair in Jewish Studies at his alma mater, Stanford. It was a time when nothing seemed out of reach.

The fame of individual congregants in the late '80s added additional luster to the institution. When the Giants and the A's played the unlikely "Bay Bridge World Series" in 1989, it turned out that temple members owned both teams. Real estate magnate Bob Lurie had kept the Giants in San Francisco by buying the franchise in the 1970s, and Walter Haas Jr. (Rhoda Goldman's brother) later did the same for Oakland by purchasing the A's when it appeared that they might leave their East Bay home. A headline in the *Jewish Bulletin* on the eve of the first game was quoted in *Sports Illustrated*: "Emanu-El Wins Series Either Way."

Dianne Feinstein, meanwhile, won the Democratic nomination for governor in the spring of 1990. She would lose to Pete Wilson in the fall, but would be one of two Bay Area Jewish women elected to the United States Senate two years later. Other eminent congregants included Bill Honig, the state's superintendent of education; Richard Rosenberg, the CEO of Bank of America; Don and Doris Fisher, the founders and primary stockholders of the Gap; William Lowenberg, a real estate developer who served on the board of the Jewish Agency and as vice-president of the U.S. Holocaust Memorial Council; Claude Rosenberg, a highly regarded financier, author, and philanthropist; Milton Marks, a longtime state senator; Stephen Dobbs, the CEO of the Koret Foundation and Marin Community Foundation; and many, many others.

The temple was the site of moving memorial services for Cyril Magnin and Bill Graham. It also hosted one of the most inspiring events in Bay Area Jewish history: the address of Natan Sharansky in 1987, only a year after his release from the Soviet gulag. It would be hard to imagine an institution more central in the life of the city of San Francisco and its Jews.

BUT THERE WERE SERIOUS PROBLEMS emerging which the board members, perhaps too often blinded by Kirschner's brilliant achievements, failed to see.

First, the fiscal condition of the temple was far less rosy than it seemed on the surface. The commercially zoned property in Colma was a financial godsend for the synagogue, but it required huge development costs at the outset. A large outlay for landscaping had been anticipated, of course, but until the work began it was not known that the tenant farmers had long used the site as a dump. Over a period of many decades, they had buried vast quantities of nonbiodegradable trash and plastic sheeting in the soil. Its removal filled more than two thousand truckloads. The temple sued some of the major offenders and recovered part of its cleanup costs, but it still owed over a million dollars for the project, which it financed over a seven-year term. Servicing this debt cut deeply into the cash flow from the leasehold that it had hoped to realize in the late '80s and early '90s.

The cemetery's two-million-dollar endowment fund, meanwhile, which had financially buoyed the temple in the Asher years, had been largely invested in fixed-income securities and produced less and less revenue for the operating budget as interest rates declined sharply in the mid- and late '80s. More worrisome was the fact that the cemetery itself began losing money in this decade and regularly showed annual operating losses exceeding $100,000.

But most disturbing were the massive deficits of the temple's own operations, something "absolutely inexcusable," in the words of Stuart Aronoff, who became treasurer early in 1991, inheriting a "dire" situation. The synagogue had been hundreds of thousands of dollars in the red almost every year of the expansive Kirschner era, amounting to a cumulative deficit of well over a million dollars by the end of his tenure. And Aronoff was furious to learn that this shortfall had been covered with money borrowed from the cemetery endowment fund, an imprudent policy "by all measures of business judgment and fiduciary responsibility."

Kirschner's "programmatic requests were overwhelming relative to the resources," Aronoff recalls, but he holds the board much more responsible than the rabbi: "They just couldn't stand up and say no to him."

An even larger and more immediate fiscal crisis—if one that was more understandable—resulted from the capital project. Along with the operating deficit, this was the second half of what Aronoff ruefully termed the "double-headed snake." By mid-1990, it was clear that the renovation of the temple house had been far under-budgeted, and that the amount Campaign Emanu-El needed to generate was not the 10.5 million dollars that had been announced the previous year but almost twice that sum. Certainly the earthquake, which occurred shortly before work on the temple house was set to begin, drove up the costs considerably by convincing everyone of the need for extensive seismic bracing, a huge item that had not been foreseen.

But there were many other unexpected costs as well—which were discovered only while the construction was already underway. Just as the unanticipated extent of the asbestos problem in the sanctuary was largely responsible for raising the expenses of that phase of the renovation from about two to three million dollars, so the discovery of lead-based paint in Guild Hall drove up the price of the temple house rehabilitation. Similarly, installing more and larger elevators than had originally been planned, reconfiguring the exits and entrances in the light of very strict new city codes, and repairing the immense roof with its surprisingly complicated drainage system added millions to the initial estimate. Even parts of the magnificent Skinner organ had worn out at this time; meticulously replacing them with the same natural materials of wood and leather cost more than $300,000.

Unfortunately, most of this work could not be done on an incremental basis. "Each part depended on another," Mort Fleishhacker explained to a concerned membership in his last annual report, "and there was no intelligent way that we could do part of the construction now and hope to do more later." He made the telling point that since the walls on each of the five floors of the temple house needed to be opened for the seismic retrofit, there would actually be a great savings in completing the rest of the remodeling at the same time.

But if there was no turning back, how would the temple meet the colossal financial commitment it had made? At the board retreat in August 1990, it was noted that even if most of the proposed two-million-dollar endowment fund for community service programs were dropped, over eighteen million would still be required for the capital project. But only 9.3 million had been pledged, and campaign consultants told the board that barely three million more could reasonably be expected. Even if that money could be raised, hardly a foregone conclusion, this left a spine-chilling shortfall of close to six million dollars, not including the rapidly mounting carrying costs.

Despite Fleishhacker's eagerness "to complete the entire project now," there were powerful "naysayers," such as Stuart Aronoff, who actually recommended shutting down the construction "rather than spending money [the temple] didn't have." The board seriously considered this at several meetings in the second half of 1990 and early 1991, but in the end—after assurances had been received from leading donors—voted to proceed with the renovation. At the same time the temple refinanced its commercial property in Colma (which had been appraised at twelve million dollars), sought a bridge loan from private lenders, and planned a second phase to the fundraising campaign.

Many were calmed by Rhoda Goldman's assumption of the presidency in February 1991. She redoubled her efforts at soliciting other major donors, and later that year made a dignified plea for the capital campaign at the High Holiday services. She also held a meeting in her home to mollify a group of members who were worried that the scale of the capital project was compromising the temple's programs and who were angry that the congregation had not been fully informed of the spiraling costs.

Most important, she was instrumental in obtaining an unexpectedly large grant—three million dollars—from the Walter and Elise Haas Fund, as well as a 1.5 million dollar loan from that foundation, $500,000 of which was eventually forgiven. This massive infusion of cash "saved the temple" as Kirschner and countless others later put it. The Goldmans could have had the sanctuary named for them by the grateful board, but the family felt it was inappropriate and declined the honor.

The renovation of the temple house, also designed by Robinson, Mills, and Williams, was as much an architectural achievement as the restored sanctuary and arguably an even greater factor in the institution's vitality during the rest of the decade. The renamed Martin Meyer Sanctuary in particular proved invaluable as the venue of countless innovative programs and religious services.

But even with the Goldmans' extraordinary efforts, the synagogue still owed more than five million dollars for the renovation when the temple house was rededicated in March 1992. "We had gotten in over our heads," said a member of the executive board who confirmed Aronoff's grim assessment of the synagogue's financial health at the time. Combined with the huge operating deficit, which could no longer be ignored, it meant that the early '90s would be a period of retrenchment. It also showed the need for better fiscal management.

IN HINDSIGHT, it is also clear that staff management was far from ideal. Although his colleagues had the utmost admiration for Kirschner's many talents, nearly all of them chafed under his mode of leadership, described as "top-down," "autocratic," and even "abusive." He was a "perfectionist," several members of the staff recall, and had to have his hand in every detail, from the style of punctuation in the *Temple Chronicle* to the configuration of the seating for Sabbath services. Except for the youngest member of the senior staff, Gayle Pomerantz, for whom Kirschner was always an encouraging mentor, every other key employee of that period refers to him as having lacked warmth and collegiality. Most remember him as being quick to anger and stinting on praise. Obviously he was not the first senior rabbi to be seen as overbearing and imperious by his subordinates. But this was something more—"leadership by inducement of fear, and with very little joy," according to Rabbi Schiftan.

Yossi Liebowitz, himself an unsettled personality, resigned his position of associate rabbi in the fall of 1988, giving little advance notice. He left in order to lead his own congregation, a midsized synagogue in Palm Desert. But his departure was also due to increasing friction in his relationship with Kirschner, and the dwindling prospect that he could ever truly share in the spiritual leadership of the temple. The sudden resignation—perhaps related to a heated exchange between the two at Yom Kippur services only days earlier—required a major realignment of staff responsibilities. Schiftan now became the director of the religious school, and the synagogue had two rabbis rather than the three planned for the busy program year of 1988–89.

Even more serious was the departure—again with relatively short notice—of Irwin Wiener late in 1990, in the midst of the temple house renovation and capital campaign. He became the head of the Hebrew Free Loan Association, and has performed admirably in this vital communal post ever since. But he would have left the temple even if that opportunity had not arisen.

To be sure, the popular executive director was squarely in the line of fire of a few lay leaders who felt that both the operating and capital budgets had gotten out of control. But many more saw him as a voice of prudence and moderation in dealing with complex fiscal problems that were largely not of his making. They viewed him too as an essential element in the success of the temple's many new programs, and deeply regretted his loss at such a critical time.

But Wiener, like Liebowitz, with whom he was quite close, could not envision a satisfactory future for himself as Kirschner's partner. Wiener and the senior rabbi had been "inseparable" for their first four years together, and went to lunch, often with Liebowitz, almost every day. But by the end of the '80s, as the former executive director recalls, Kirschner grew distant, "arrogant," and inaccessible. Wiener felt excluded from the rabbi's plans for the future of the temple, and slighted by the much younger man on numerous occasions. Fortunately, the temple was able to find a replacement in Gary Cohn, a young banker with experience in cost control and crisis management, who with the newly elected treasurer, Stuart Aronoff, began a process of zero-based budgeting as soon as he assumed his post early in 1991.

Kirschner was "shocked" by Wiener's resignation, something he neither wanted nor anticipated. In retrospect, he acknowledges that most of the criticism of his leadership style is valid, and that supervision of the large and varied senior staff was not his strong suit:

> One of the ways in which I was not very good at being a rabbi was that I tended to be oblivious...to how the rest of [the staff] felt. I tended not to be aware; it's as if one is driving and has a blind spot....That explains some of my conduct in this period...in terms of Irwin's growing sense of disappointment or feelings of rejection, in terms of Yossi's personal problems....Each [member of the staff] required a different touch; I tried to apply the same to all.
>
> I didn't have any experience in that regard. I hadn't ever had a congregation of my own. I'd only been an assistant rabbi myself for two years, and an associate for four more....I didn't have lessons on how to do this.

He regrets that he failed to create the kind of atmosphere in which his colleagues felt that they could freely come to talk to him about their problems—or his.

KIRSCHNER'S INNER LIFE was in turmoil while he was senior rabbi of Emanu-El; he recently shed much light on his mental state during those years in an interview for this volume.

By his own admission, he had many adulterous affairs, several of them with congregants, which he consummated in the temple. In one sense, his actions may be seen as a mirror of his times. He belonged to a generation known for its self-indulgence, and had reached the top during a decade marked by excess, in a city that celebrated sexual freedom. It was a period too when his marriage was deeply troubled and when the pressures of his work were most intense.

Yet he feels all of these were actually minor factors in his downward slide. Not wanting "to make any excuses," he points rather to his own long-standing psychological pathology as having been far more important:

> When you are elevated—literally—on this pulpit, with the light on your face, kind of the way I remember thinking in my youth of Jesus, you get that look from people...of admiration and even more. It can be very seductive; it can be toxic for someone like me....
>
> I was called to that pulpit and succeeded in certain respects because I had certain talents...but I didn't have the most important attributes needed to serve in that capacity: that is self-knowledge, humility, experience....
>
> I climbed too far, too fast and seemed to develop a certain form of narcissism, arrogance, obliviousness to the feelings of others that was in retrospect quite hurtful to [them] and to me and my own family. I wasn't aware of it and [that] was part of the problem.

At times he was exhilarated by his self-destructive conduct, his oversized ego further inflated by a sense of invincibility. At other times he was tormented by the hypocrisy of his behavior, painfully aware of the massive contradiction between his public and private life, and full of dread of being found out—by his wife, by the temple family, and by the general public. Mostly, though, he was in a state of denial, refusing to admit to others or to himself that he was speeding down a highway to ruination.

Some of the women he approached were initially flattered and gave in to his overtures. A few may have initiated the sexual contact. But many more women—especially within the context of the congregational setting—felt confused, disgusted, and degraded by the advances. And no matter how it began, or where it led, it invariably resulted in a violation of trust and a burdensome secret. About all of that he was in denial as well.

He was privately cautioned twice about his sexual misconduct, first by his mentor, Professor Jacob Milgrom, who had learned of alleged advances Kirschner had made toward a UC Berkeley student and two women from the Graduate Theological Union. Malcolm Sparer, president of the Northern California Board of Rabbis, also confronted him with a complaint he had received. Milgrom and Sparer, both rabbis a generation older than Kirschner, urged him to seek counseling for his problem, something he admits he "desperately" needed. But he remembers that he denied his misdeeds to both men, and quickly put their warnings out of his mind.

A few of the region's pulpit rabbis also had at least passing knowledge of his indiscretions, as did a number of Jewish communal workers and academics. While these individuals were not among his closest friends, it is still troubling that, with the exception of Sparer and Milgrom, not one of them advised Kirschner to get therapy. No one at all brought his problem to the attention of the temple board.

The failure was not the result of any "conspiracy of silence," but rather the judgment, made very much on an individual basis, of each person who was privy to this knowledge. In this period before the sensational Clarence Thomas–Anita Hill hearings—to say nothing of President Clinton's misconduct—Kirschner simply didn't fit the "profile" of someone who would abuse his exalted office in this manner. Some could envision a discreet affair, perhaps, but a pattern of unwanted sexual advances, risking the destruction of a stellar career, seemed preposterous.*

But even for those who overcame their disbelief, taking action was something else again, a vexing and perilous process that they chose to avoid. Some feared that their motives for bringing the matter to light would be questioned within the Jewish community. Others worried about retaliatory measures, legal or otherwise, that Kirschner or his powerful

---

*Within the next few years several local Christian ministers and two other Bay Area rabbis, all facing charges of sexual misconduct, resigned their pulpits, their cases no less painful but much more believable in light of the well-publicized Kirschner matter.

lay supporters might take. The lack of a proper mechanism for raising such charges, whether within the congregation or the Reform movement's national organizations, compounded the problem still further.

All of these factors were even more salient for Kirschner's colleagues at the temple. Most of them knew absolutely nothing of his improprieties. Two of those who did hear of indiscretions, Irwin Wiener and Rabbi Mark Schiftan, actually approached the rabbi on separate occasions but found him unwilling to discuss the issue. In neither instance, they both recall, was he open for a meaningful conversation; in neither case does he remember those meetings today. As for taking the matter further, perhaps to the Central Conference of American Rabbis or the temple board, Wiener "agonized over the situation," but in the end concluded that "there was no way I could pit myself against him....I was not going to be the messenger; the messenger gets killed."

But Kirschner, "emotionally isolated," as Gayle Pomerantz remembers with compassion, was increasingly in need of help. Looking back on his sermons and writings as senior rabbi, it is clear that amidst the shower of accolades he struggled mightily with the fact of his flawed character. For as he has come to realize, his narcissism was actually fuelled by deep-seated feelings of inadequacy: "I was such a poor example," he now says, "and knew deep down that I was."

His installation sermon began with words from Jacob in Genesis— "How unworthy I am of all your kindnesses"—before he prayed, "May it be Thy will, O Lord, that I never debase Thy teaching nor misrepresent it to others, that I never utter a word to dishonor Thee or Thy people."

Two years later he wrote at length about the contemporary rabbi who fails to measure up to the ancient standards of the "holy man," to some degree still expected by the laity: "There is something pathetic about comforting others with words that do not even comfort us, or counseling others who probably should be counseling us." Providing a clue to his private demons, he added, "On the one hand we represent what is holy; on the other hand we are anything but."

His remarks at the Kol Nidre service of 1991 may also be seen as a veiled acknowledgment of his dilemma. Entitled "Defects," it focused mainly on physical imperfections—Moses' stutter, Jacob's limp, and the courageous story of a contemporary youth, mute, paralyzed, and spastic. But then the rabbi continued:

> We too have defects, limitations, and obstacles to overcome. If it is not a limp or a stutter, then it is an illness or a disease, a cataract or a tumor, a weak heart or an aching one. It is a bereavement or a burden or a silent sorrow. We are not as flawless as the ancient priests....Maybe we have been hurt by life in such a way that it is not the body but the soul that limps from day to day.

Kirschner, a classic example of the "wounded healer," concluded the last of his memorable Yom Kippur Eve sermons at the temple with the thought, "Our defects can teach us what our blessings cannot."

But when it came to his own failings, he had not learned the lesson that he was trying to teach others. He neither sought therapy nor changed his ways until it was too late.

THE TIME OF RECKONING ARRIVED at the end of 1991. It began on a cold, damp Friday evening, December 6, at Sabbath services held in the main sanctuary because the temple house was still closed for renovation.

A congregant entered late, walked conspicuously down the long, sloping aisle, and took a seat in the front row, directly opposite Kirschner, who was seated on the *bimah*. The man did not pick up a prayerbook, but rather glowered at the rabbi throughout the rest of the brief service. Afterwards, on the receiving line, he threatened him with obscenities within earshot of several worshippers and other clergy. The agitated member, a prominent attorney and a fierce litigator, evidently believed Kirschner had made unwelcome sexual advances toward his wife, a woman active in the temple during the past few years and often seen with the rabbi at classes, services, and meetings. Deeply shaken by the episode, Kirschner told his colleagues that the eruption resulted from her having been denied a seat she had sought on the board of directors.

In the middle of the following week, on December 11, every member of the board of directors received at his or her home by courier a packet from the prestigious law firm in which the irate husband was a partner. It contained sworn affidavits from four anonymous women—three of them Emanu-El congregants—detailing unwanted sexual advances on the part of the rabbi. The alleged overtures were of a nonviolent nature, but the plaintiffs reported severe distress upon being approached sexually while in counseling, including grief counseling, as well as in other congregational settings. An accompanying letter demanded his removal. It added that the accusers would identify themselves and meet with the board if necessary, and that there were others who were prepared to come forward as well.*

The reaction of most of the board members was one of utter shock. Gary Shapiro received a jolt that was similar to that of many who read the sworn declarations, including veteran attorneys like himself: "It was a nightmare. I was devastated, absolutely devastated. This was the most unexpected, off-the-wall experience I've ever had."

As for the merit of the allegations themselves, an academic on the board initially thought them "vague," and a businessman characterized them as "just weird, bizarre." But the many lawyers on the board tended to feel that the plaintiffs had made a credible case for a pattern of behavior on the part of the rabbi, and they understood at once the professionalism and thoroughness of this opening salvo. As Don Buder recalls, "I knew immediately that this had to be taken very seriously."

An emergency board meeting was held two days later at the downtown law offices of temple vice-president Paul Matzger, like Rhoda Goldman a person with the deepest feelings of admiration and gratitude for Kirschner. The atmosphere that Friday morning was one of gloom, with several members weeping openly for their rabbi and their temple. But there was also a sense of apprehension in the air as the ten men and seven women on the board came to understand the extent and complexity of the predicament they faced, and the nature of the decisions they would have to make.

A few members voiced their incredulity at the allegations and wondered aloud if a "cabal" were "out to get the rabbi." At the other extreme, a few immediately accepted the accusations at face value and focused almost exclusively on the plight of the women who had brought the

---

*Also included in each thick envelope was a recent book by the local psychiatrist Peter Rutter, *Sex in the Forbidden Zone*, an exploration of the widespread problem of "sexual boundary violation" by therapists, doctors, clergy, and teachers, and the serious, long-term harm it does to the women they betray.

charges. But most followed the judicious lead of Matzger, whose law firm would represent the temple in this matter, in trying to keep in mind all of the "concentric circles of interest."

In addition to the distress of the plaintiffs, and the suffering that could befall the rabbi and his family, there was also the institution to consider. Would it become hopelessly divided between those defending Kirschner and those supporting his accusers? Was the temple legally liable for any misconduct on the part of its spiritual leader? Would the other clergy be demoralized and unable to function? Beyond all of this loomed a public relations disaster. An enormous amount of effort had been expended in recent years to enhance the temple's reputation in both the Jewish and the general community. Would that now be for naught?

Thus it was reasoned that in the best interest of all concerned—above all, the rabbi's wife and four children—every effort should be made to avoid public disclosure of the matter. But there was another important decision taken at the same time: at Matzger's insistence, any synagogue considering engaging Kirschner in the future would have to be fully informed of his troubles at Emanu-El. The attorney was furious that the temple's lay leadership had been "the last to know" of the rabbi's alleged misconduct. If it turned out that Kirschner was culpable, Matzger would not be party to the all-too-common practice, in his view, of the Reform movement foisting off a wayward rabbi on some unsuspecting congregation.

He was also angry with the CCAR and the UAHC on another matter: despite his pleas to both organizations, they provided a paucity of guidance to the temple in dealing with the disaster. The CCAR seemed solely concerned with the needs of the rabbi; the executives of the UAHC "fell on their faces," as far as Matzger was concerned, with the temple left "operating in a no-man's-land." So the board struggled with a problem that was unprecedented, unexpected, and exceedingly perilous—largely by instinct and with little outside help.*

Further complicating matters, of course, were the legal ramifications which were present from the outset. Temple board member and former ADL director Rhonda Abrams, herself no stranger to conflict resolution,

*For his part, Rabbi Morris Hershman, the longtime regional director of the UAHC who retired in 1996, claims that his organization did make its good offices available during the crisis "in subtle ways...and behind the scenes."

deeply regrets that the complainants began their attack "with the nuclear bomb" of a law firm's packet of affidavits. Although no lawsuit had yet been filed, it still meant that the temple needed legal representation, that the rabbi had to retain an attorney, and that "from that moment on," as she puts it, "every conversation had three lawyers present, whether they were physically in the room or not." All communication among the parties would now be tightly constrained, and Abrams, who describes herself as "an ardent feminist," feels that even the women who brought the charges ultimately did themselves a disservice by choosing such an adversarial approach. Others, though, continue to feel that nothing short of the legal broadside would have received much notice. Knowledge of Kirschner's indiscretions gleaned by colleagues and professional organizations had not produced results, they argue; perhaps without the legal prod, even the temple board—comprised largely of the rabbi's supporters—might not have given the matter the attention it deserved.

Whether or not one can attribute it to the manner in which the charges were brought, the gravity of the situation was never in doubt. The board decided at its initial meeting that, in light of the allegations, the rabbi should be suspended immediately, pending a thorough outside investigation. Matzger was empowered to confront Kirschner with the accusations later that day and to report his response at a meeting scheduled for the following week.

But most board members felt that even if the allegations were basically true, the rabbi could be given an extended period of leave—perhaps a year or even more—to undergo a supervised course of therapy, and then return to the temple to resume his duties. The time would also be used to make amends to the women involved and to heal the congregation. This would certainly be a difficult route to take, fraught with serious legal risks, among other dangers. Yet Kirschner was held in such high regard that the board endeavored to find a way for him not to have to leave the temple permanently.

But he chose instead to resign. Immediately after Matzger outlined the nature of the charges to his close friend, urging him to engage his own attorney, Kirschner denied the allegations but told him that now that they had been made, he could no longer function as a rabbi. A few days later the board accepted the resignation, "regretfully, but without hesitation."

His severance package still needed to be worked out. Stuart Aronoff represented the temple in negotiations with Kirschner's lawyer, the prominent John Keker, who represented him *pro bono*. The rabbi received a settlement that some would later criticize as unduly large under the circumstances; in point of fact, however, much of it was based on pre-existing contractual arrangements, such as the one granting him a portion of the equity in his Fifth Avenue home, which he owned jointly with the synagogue. He and his family were allowed to remain in the house for six months, and he received about a year's salary and his accrued pension. Aronoff considers the terms of the separation to have been "fair and reasonable" and stresses the need he felt to avoid "lingering negotiations" in this area during the most acute weeks of the crisis. Moreover, he and most others on the board felt a great deal of compassion for the rabbi and his family. As Matzger later said, "What are you going to do? Put him on the welfare rolls? We are a Jewish institution."

Some board members, most of them older men, also had doubts about how egregious his conduct had really been. He had not been accused of using physical force or coercion; and assuming he had made unwelcome sexual advances, hadn't he been punished enough? Having lost his pulpit, his reputation, and likely his marriage, did he not deserve some help in rebuilding his life?

In a similar vein of "trying to move forward," the board made the key decision not to conduct an investigation. There were a couple of adamantly dissenting voices on this point, but the majority felt that the resignation had eliminated the need for an inquiry since the accusers' sole demand was the rabbi's removal. And no longer being an employee of the temple, it was unlikely that Kirschner would voluntarily participate in such an investigation, or that he could be compelled to do so. Thinking that a full-scale probe of the charges would be "disruptive and divisive," and very possibly inconclusive, the board dispensed with it. Years later, however, some would have second thoughts about this decision, realizing that the lack of any formal, official closure to the matter—coupled with Kirschner's repeated denials—added much to the confusion of the congregants and the anger of the plaintiffs.

With the severance package concluded and the investigation shelved, on December 30 President Goldman wrote a letter to all temple members informing them that Rabbi Kirschner had asked to resign "for personal reasons," effective January 1. Understanding that this phraseology would be acceptable to the complainants—who had no desire to see their own names made public, nor the synagogue embarrassed—she intentionally offered no further details, hoping to keep the issue of sexual misconduct out of the press and spare everyone a great deal of anguish.

MUCH EARLIER, OF COURSE, the other key staff members had had to be informed of the allegations and the imminent resignation. The day after the affidavits were received by the board, the rabbi summoned to his study his secretary, the elderly Muriel Cohn, and the new executive director, Gary Cohn (no relation). Mrs. Cohn, one of the longest-serving and most dedicated employees in the temple's history, revered Kirschner and was convulsed upon hearing the charges that she later said had come "out of the blue." Although she would continue to work at the temple as the devoted secretary to his successor almost until her death in 1998, she would continue to believe Kirschner's denials for several years and would never overcome the profound loss she felt with his departure. Gary Cohn, then on the job only nine months, was also shocked, thinking, "This can't be happening." But he quickly went into an analytic mode; his efforts would be directed toward limiting the damage to the temple.

The clergy—with Kirschner conspicuously absent—was called to a special meeting at the Goldmans' Pacific Heights home the next day, late in the afternoon of December 13, following the emergency board meeting at Paul Matzger's office and the encounter the attorney had had with Kirschner at mid-day.

They were all shattered by the news that Matzger delivered. Each of them had been brought to the temple by the senior rabbi; each of their lives was bound up with his, through ties both personal and professional. Roz Barak broke into uncontrollable sobs and was comforted by Rhoda Goldman, herself despondent over the terrible turn of events. For Rabbi Pomerantz, "it was like the floor being taken out from under us…really like a death." Rabbis Schiftan and Wolf-Prusan were similarly stunned and horrified; they knew that they would soon be on the front lines in trying explain this to the congregants—and their children.

After the meeting, Wolf-Prusan decided to go to Kirschner's home and speak to him about the charges. Barak, Pomerantz, and Schiftan composed themselves and returned to the temple. They had to summon the strength to lead the Sabbath services beginning at 5:30.

Crushed though they were about the resignation of their leader under these circumstances, the clergy at this early stage had serious doubts about the truth of the accusations. Even in light of the disturbing incident at the temple the previous Friday evening, it seemed to most of them inconceivable that the man they thought they knew so well could have been conducting himself as alleged. Even for Mark Schiftan, the only one among them who had heard rumors of untoward remarks Kirschner had made to congregants, it was a "giant leap" to the immediate resignation of the senior rabbi in the face of sworn declarations of sexual misconduct.

Yet in the days following the meeting at the Goldmans' home, each of the clergy became convinced of the basic credibility of the plaintiffs' stories. The cantor would later characterize this realization of Kirschner's "betrayal" as the greatest trauma of her life. "Betrayal" was also the word used by each of the three rabbis in describing their feelings toward the man who had set such exacting standards.

This is not to say that they accepted as fact every accusation hurled at Kirschner, and to this day Gayle Pomerantz in particular believes some of the charges to have been "trumped up" and questions the motives of some of the women who came forward. But conversations which she and her colleagues had with close, trusted friends in the congregation—who told of other cases of unwanted sexual advances—soon persuaded her and the other clergy of Kirschner's malfeasance. Even those who most wanted to believe the rabbi's denials had their faith in him shaken by his swift resignation.

This was also the case for some of the top lay leaders. As Mortimer Fleishhacker recalls,

> He said "I didn't do it, but I'm not going to go through a process where you investigate me." That didn't make a lot of sense. Everything that Bob did forced us to say, "I guess it's true." There's no explanation of why, if he didn't do it, he wouldn't be completely willing to say, "This is ridiculous....How dare anybody say that, and you go and prove it!"

But for some with whom Kirschner was especially close, such as Walter Newman, it would take much longer to accept the accusers' version of the facts. For Newman, even the merit of the charges was less important than the profound sense of grief that overtook him, not unlike that following the death of a loved one: "There are few things in my life that have really broken my heart, and that was one of them because I looked on Bob almost like a son....I had such a fatherly affection for him...and I thought I had his confidence. And then to have this happen!"

THE STORY OF KIRSCHNER'S DEPARTURE was ultimately too explosive to be kept out of the press; the agreement to protect everyone's privacy with the term "personal reasons" depended on the accord of too many high-strung personalities just at a time when their emotions were most inflamed. In little more than a week after the resignation, the basic outlines of the story came out in print.

And once the newspapers entered the equation, it was, for Kirschner, "worse than I ever could have thought—my life as I knew it ended." Emanu-El too was scorched under the spotlight of the media, and for years to come would be the subject of all sorts of accounts—in both the Jewish and the general press—about the sensational case. The institution would eventually recover, but the rabbi and his family, who suffered "permanent and irreparable damage" from the media barrage, would not.

Ironically, the coverage began harmlessly enough. On January 7, 1992, the religion reporter of the *San Francisco Chronicle*, Don Lattin, who had written extensively, and often glowingly, about Kirschner's activities over the years, contributed an article citing "personal reasons" as the cause of the resignation. But in a brief interview with Lattin, the rabbi elaborated on the cause of his leaving, emphasizing his upcoming fellowship at Harvard and his desire to enter academic life, "a welcome respite from the arduous labors of leading a large congregation."

It may well have been that this self-serving version of recent events triggered someone—possibly one of the complainants, or perhaps a board member in the minority camp of those wanting full disclosure—to approach the press with the entire story. For on the following day the city's other daily, the afternoon *Examiner*, published a front-page, "above the fold" article under the headline "S.F. Rabbi Quits Amid Sexual Charges." The story disclosed that four women had charged Kirschner with sexual misconduct and went on to summarize their accusations, along with his denial. It also revealed that the temple had decided not to pursue an investigation and had structured a generous severance package for the rabbi. Don Lattin, upset that Kirschner had misled him earlier in the week, weighed in with a second *Chronicle* article on January 9, this time focusing on the scandal and Kirshner's disavowal. The next day saw a similar story on the front page of the *Jewish Bulletin*.

With the revelations in the press, Rhoda Goldman was now in the awkward position of having to send a second letter to the congregation, explaining why the board chose "not to go into the details of the 'personal reasons'" on December 30. It acted, she noted, "out of respect for the privacy of family members of the congregation, Rabbi Kirschner and his family, and others." She then outlined the sequence of events since the allegations had been made and provided a detailed description of the board's actions.

At this moment, which had to be among the most difficult in her distinguished lifetime of community service, she remained remarkably calm and fair, giving voice not only to her feelings of loss, but also to her concern for those who had leveled the charges:

> In view of Rabbi Kirschner's significant contributions during his tenure—and the regard in which he is held by countless members of the congregation—the events of the past month have been traumatic to us all. At the same time, we are acutely aware of the distress felt by the individuals [and their families] who brought these matters to our attention.

The rash of newspaper articles induced other women to come forward, who became the subject of still more articles. Perhaps most damaging to Kirschner was the front-page piece in the next issue of the weekly *Jewish Bulletin*, that of January 17, which shifted attention to his conduct toward women in the academic world. Two students from the Graduate Theological Union claimed that he had made unwelcome verbal sexual advances toward them a short time after they had come to his temple office to consult with him. The article also unearthed an earlier incident at UC Berkeley, where Kirschner was a visiting lecturer in 1986: one of his students had made a similar accusation regarding a conversation the two of them had had on campus.

Four highly respected professors of Jewish studies, two from the GTU and two from Berkeley, were quoted in the story, stating that they had long known of these complaints. Anyone still suspecting that there had been some sort of "conspiracy" to topple the rabbi now had to take into account the fact that charges had been made years earlier by at least three women—from outside the congregation.

By this time Kirschner was unavailable to the press even for a denial. The excruciating pain of confessing his infidelities to his wife and children, and the never-ending agony of the media coverage, had brought him to a point approaching paralysis: "I didn't know what to do; I didn't know where to turn; I had many friends who wished to help but were confused by what was happening, what was being said, what was being rumored....I just wanted to crawl into the darkness and be forgotten." It is this desperation, he recently said, that clouded his judgment in the first half of 1992 and resulted in his failure to acknowledge his indiscretions publicly: "It turned out to be a disastrous response, but it was the best I could do at the time; I was shamed and humiliated; I was terrified of this kind of exposure."

Not until mid-1994 did he express "contrition" to the ethics committee of the CCAR for his "sexual misconduct," a statement that was not made public for another sixteen months, when it was quoted in an article syndicated by the Jewish Telegraphic Agency and carried in the *Bulletin*. The apology was part of a long process toward rehabilitation which has included years of therapy as well as counseling sessions with rabbinic mentors. Suspended by the CCAR in 1995, Kirschner may be reinstated in the future if he successfully completes the rehabilitation program.

But his initial denials, the long silence that followed, and even the belated, partial apology, bitterly disappointed many—including his former colleagues, a large number of his former congregants, and most notably the women who brought the original charges against him. Some of the accusers, joined by activists in the women's movement as well as a number of academics and young Reform rabbis, felt strongly that he had "no place in a classroom or a pulpit." In a concerted effort, they successfully blocked his attempts to secure a rabbinical post in Stockton and a part-time teaching job for the summer semester of 1993 at Hebrew Union College in Los Angeles. The latter had been arranged by Rabbi Lee Bycel, then dean of HUC, Kirschner's former classmate and for years his closest friend and confidant: "Without him," Kirschner said, "I'm not sure I would have made it through." But angry protests at the college forced Bycel reluctantly to withdraw the appointment.

Then an explicit article on the front page of the joint Sunday edition of the *Examiner* and *Chronicle*, more than a year and a half after his resignation, tarnished him even further. Carrying an interview with his estranged wife, who acknowledged that he had admitted to her that he had had "affairs," the exposé also included the first public comments of two of his accusers as well as those of a disgruntled young temple board member who lamented the "lack of concern for [Kirschner's] victims." With lurid details, it also described a long-term liaison he had had with yet another woman, a deeply troubled congregant suffering from anorexia, whose forlorn picture was prominently featured.

The worst period, though, was the half year immediately following his departure. Kirschner separated from his wife—they would later divorce—and planned to go to Harvard, accompanied by his teenage son, for the fellowship he had won the previous fall. All the arrangements, including the flight plans, had been made, but in light of the scandal the university rescinded its offer. "Humiliated" by this indignity, and "not even functioning," he moved into his mother's house in Los Angeles. Here he was surprised one day when the camera crew of the tabloid television show *Hard Copy* alighted from a van to film him in the front yard as he returned from the grocery store.

Only that summer did he achieve a modicum of solace and stability by returning to the Bay Area and enrolling in an intensive course in ancient Greek at the Graduate Theological Union. Later he moved back to Los Angeles, where he has remained ever since. He ultimately found work at HUC's Skirball Cultural Center, serving for two years as a researcher supported by a fellowship funded by several of the leading families of Emanu-El. As the Skirball rapidly grew in the mid-'90s, eventually completing a spectacular new fifteen-acre facility designed by the world-famous architect Moshe Safdie, Kirschner took on greater responsibilities.

The center's ambitious director, Uri Herscher, asked his former student to prepare and oversee the museum's core exhibit, which focuses on the American-Jewish experience, first as a consultant and a year later as a permanent member of the staff. In 1996, in addition to being director of the core exhibit, Kirschner became the program director of the center, now one of the largest and most vibrant Jewish cultural institutions in the country. Even here, though, he continued to be dogged by the scandal at Emanu-El half a decade earlier. When the new Skirball finally opened to the public, flyers were found in the restrooms attacking Kirschner as a sexual predator.

But the former rabbi has succeeded in his new post. He is justifiably proud of the role he has played—which includes a good deal of fund-raising—in developing the flourishing Skirball Cultural Center, calling it "an outcome I might have hoped for in continuing to contribute to Jewish life, to Jewish history, Jewish culture...[which] I didn't imagine would be possible after what happened....Now instead of sermons, it's museum exhibitions....I still feel I have something...to offer."

He also remarried in Los Angeles. His new bride is a computer specialist around his age, the child of Austrian-Jewish refugees who has one son from a former marriage.

Yet despite the promising fresh start in his professional and personal life, Kirschner remains a man filled with anguish and regret about the past. Now well into middle age, portly and without the neatly trimmed red beard he sported in San Francisco, he could almost be unrecognizable to those who knew him at the temple.

He himself hardly recognizes the man who was the rabbi of Emanu-El: "Who I am now is somebody who feels very different, has a different life....I'm not ashamed of who I was, but I don't feel very acquainted with him." And, perhaps as a further indication of his return to a pre-rabbinic sense of himself, he now dresses casually and drives a pickup truck again, without, of course, the reproach he heard in the 1980s—"This will not do for a rabbi of Emanu-El."

He seems chastened and subdued, "painfully divested" of the grandiose ambitions he had as a young man:

> I had this image of myself—it turns out perhaps a flawed one....I felt I was destined for something. I wanted to make a difference in the world.... A

big struggle for me now is to try to figure out how to live without this kind of self-image....I feel that kind of winnowing...and the humbling that came with it—really beyond humbling—needed to happen.

He is also profoundly saddened by the pain his actions caused others, above all his former wife and children, "whom [he] hurt deeply and whose hurt was multiplied beyond description by the media coverage." He keenly regrets the pain his conduct caused the congregation, and the "dilemmas" it left for the lay leaders, for his former colleagues, and for the rabbinate as a whole.

But while in general he also takes "responsibility...for having created in any of the conversations or meetings that [he] had with anybody, an atmosphere that would lead them to feel offended by anything [he] said or did," he strongly qualifies any apology to his accusers:

I will not accept responsibility for allegations that were falsely and maliciously brought, that were simply untrue. I paid the price for all of this; I continue to pay the price for all of this, but only some of it is true...and the part that is true, I have said publicly, is that I engaged in marital relations outside of my marriage; this was wrong in every way. Unfortunately, the nature of the media coverage and the subsequent attention this garnered from people with their own agendas left me portrayed in a way that is not either accurate or fair.

He is especially embittered by the "spin of harassment" that the newspaper and television reporters—who descended upon him in the "fevered social and cultural climate" following the Thomas-Hill hearings—gave to his case. He resents the term "victim" being applied to any of his accusers and stresses that "these were acts between consenting adults; that's the limit of it."

BUT CAN THERE BE AUTHENTIC CONSENT for a sexual relationship between a rabbi and a counselee, a student, a potential convert? Certainly not, argued the ethicist Rachel Adler in a seminal article in the *CCAR Journal* in the spring of 1993, with the recent Kirschner case unnamed but apparently very much on her mind. She contended that in the setting of a rabbi's study—where congregants are so often vulnerable and unguarded, where there is a maximum discrepancy in power between the clergy and the laity—genuine consent is impossible, and a sexual overture inherently exploitative. With the powerful title "A Stumbling Block Before the Blind," her essay framed the issue not as adultery but rather as abuse.

Adler's was the first of no fewer than six articles on the subject which appeared in the Reform movement's professional journal in the mid-'90s, in the wake of several troubling cases of sexual misconduct in the rabbinate which had surfaced earlier in the decade. The commentators shed much light on a matter that had rarely been discussed openly. As Rabbi Jeffrey Salkin began his piece, "There's an elephant in the living room and no one wants to speak about it."

But his emphasis differed from Adler's in holding that not every sexual relationship between a rabbi and congregant is necessarily unethical. He expressed the fear that too rigid a prohibition could leave the impression of women as fragile and dependent beings. Yet there is little doubt that he too would consider the crossing of sexual boundaries in pastoral counseling most grievous, even aside from any violation of marital vows that may also have taken place.

In 1993 Rabbi Julie Spitzer joined Adler in bewailing the "utterly inadequate" process of the CCAR in dealing with allegations of sexual impropriety. She wrote of the lack of a clear definition of sexual misconduct, the absence of definitive guidelines for congregations to follow in this matter, and, most urgently, of the need for a single address for complaints. While all three issues were finally addressed by the CCAR in a lengthy document published in 1998, it is clear that the Reform movement is still struggling to frame the proper response to a problem more damaging and widespread than the laity had realized.*

Part of this response must also address the repentance and reinstatement of offenders. In the *CCAR Journal*, Rabbi Howard Kosovske examined rabbinic texts for guidance in this area and, drawing on Maimonides, seemed to take a somewhat lenient view: "The later tradition always holds the door open to—and thus hopes for—a total rehabilitation of any rabbinic colleague who would cross the boundaries of sexual

---

*In the mid-1980s, Rabbi Mark Winer of New York, a trained sociologist and a member of the CCAR's executive committee, conducted a study of the sixty largest Reform congregations and found that in the prior two decades charges of sexual misconduct had caused almost as many rabbis to leave their pulpits as had deaths and retirements combined.

propriety that at all times are dictated by the profession. I believe we can do no less."

But he was countered by Arthur Gross Schaefer, a professor of law and ethics as well as a pulpit rabbi, whose reading of Maimonides and others led him to focus less on the open door to the rabbinic house than on the difficulty of passing through it. *Teshuvah* (repentance), he states, must include "recognition of the sinful act, sincere remorse, confession, restitution, and resolve." Specifically naming the abuse and making amends to those aggrieved, he contends, are essential elements in this "arduous process."

Having completed five years of therapy, there can be no question that Kirschner has come a long way on his journey of self-examination, drawing not only upon modern psychology but also classical Judaism. As he has said, "The rabbis teach that with sin you begin with one thread, and before long it becomes a rope. The rabbis also say that one sin leads to another, so the first time you sin you're distraught; by the second or third time it becomes part of who you are, part of what you do, and it becomes its own pathology." But in terms of Gross Schaefer's requirements for *teshuvah*—which are shared by the current clergy at Temple Emanu-El— the former senior rabbi still appears to have a way yet to go.

Robert Kirschner—with the title of "doctor" rather than "rabbi"— would return to the Emanu-El pulpit only once, in early 1996, to deliver a eulogy for Rhoda Goldman.

LOOKED AT THROUGH THE PRISM of its nightmarish ending, there is a natural tendency to agree with Kirschner himself that the way his rabbinate collapsed "has ruined everything." "Deep down," he says, "I don't have any illusions about having done anything [at Emanu-El] that matters."

But in this instance, he is being much too hard on himself. True, he left a large deficit, and worse, a hurt and saddened temple family. But he also left an array of creative community service programs, a gifted staff, a booming preschool, and a magnificently restored and remodeled physical plant—all in the service of a younger and much larger congregation. Most important of all, he gave Emanu-El a new sense of itself—innovative in its programs, inclusive in its outreach, and involved in its community— that long survived his own calamitous fall. Certainly 1992 and 1993 would be dark and difficult, with the atmosphere still permeated by scandal, and the financial picture remaining clouded. But by the mid-'90s stability would be restored, and the cycle of innovation and expansion that began in the Kirschner years, though interrupted for a while, would resume at full speed.

But if the overall resilience of the institution was reassuring, there were painful lessons to be learned as well. And these went beyond the personal failings of one individual—though that was obviously the major cause of the tragedy—to the culture of the temple in which this misfortune occurred.

Thoughtful lay leaders began to revise their understanding of the senior rabbi's role and of the pressures and isolation of the position that had broken not only Kirschner but, in very different ways, most of his predecessors. Self-understanding, maturity, and modesty, they came to realize, were prerequisites that perhaps had not been given their due. Charisma, intellect, and stature had possibly counted for too much. Many of the older congregants in particular now expressed their disappointment that while the rabbi had enjoyed a high profile in the larger community, he didn't even know their names when he met them in the synagogue. Leaders of the Sisterhood, as well as other long-standing temple auxiliaries, felt that he was less than enthusiastic when it came to meeting their needs; several also spoke of him at times lacking the "social graces" that seemed to come so naturally to Rabbis Asher and Fine.

The role of the board was reexamined as well. The lay leadership in the late '80s had understandably been filled with pride by the success of new programs and the flood of new members. But for an institution seeking to be a sacred place, a house of God, a larger view was required, one that would take into account the quality and genuineness of the human interactions under its roof.

Likewise, the channel of communications between Kirschner and his colleagues had been impaired. They were in awe of his abilities and achievements, and learned a great deal from him. But they also functioned in an unduly hierarchical—and at times intimidating—environment which isolated the senior rabbi and deprived him, and the congregation, of any warnings that might have been sounded.

Both the impact of Kirschner's achievements and the lessons of his failures would be keenly felt during the rest of the '90s. But the immediate task following his departure was to deal with the confusion, anger, loss, and distrust that came in its wake. These were wounds that would require more than time alone to heal.

chapter eleven

STEPHEN PEARCE

Temple of the Open Door

T he newly designed temple house was rededicated in March 1992,
with a weekend of events marking the completion of the massive capital project that had begun with the restoration of the sanctuary
four years earlier. With its refurbished school, its rehabilitated social
hall, and especially its renovated midsized sanctuary, the facility spoke of
a new emphasis for the congregation in the '90s: warm and intimate, participatory and pluralistic.

The post-Kirschner years would be among the most consequential in
the temple's history. Departing from the model of a single, magnetic
leader, the synagogue would put forth a vast array of programs under the
direction of a large team of innovative professionals. It would put its
financial house in order and strengthen itself institutionally in countless
other ways as well. Not least of all, it would participate in the popular
spiritual revival sweeping the Reform movement, American Judaism, and
the country in general.

But in the spring of 1992, only a few months after Kirschner's painful
resignation, it was difficult to focus on the promise which the future
held. A disquieting pall still hung over the congregation. Many of the lay
leaders were exhausted both by the capital campaign and the recent scandal, neither of which had been fully resolved. Much of the membership
was hurt and dismayed by the sudden departure of the charismatic figure
who had not only been the unquestioned leader of the synagogue, but

who in their minds had also come to embody Judaism itself. Before the temple could move ahead, it needed to look back at what had happened and take a series of measures to restore stability and credibility.

At the center of this healing process, "cleaning up the mess," as he termed it, was Mark Schiftan, who quickly assumed the role of interim senior rabbi. The thirty-year-old, a cheerful and easygoing person, was "a godsend," as Stuart Aronoff recalls, a dedicated rabbi who demonstrated much good judgment during an uncommonly difficult eighteen-month period. Junior rabbis had had to serve in the top position before with little notice—Richard Zionts' outstanding contribution during Irving Hausman's illness in the mid-1960s is perhaps the best example—but no Emanu-El rabbi had ever borne the burden Schiftan now carried. He not only had to replace Kirschner as the temple's spiritual leader, but he also had to contend with widespread doubt and despair in the wake of the senior rabbi's downfall.

Schiftan had been born and raised in San Francisco, but in an environment far from that of Emanu-El. His parents, German-speaking refugees who had arrived on the West Coast via an extended stay in Shanghai, joined B'nai Emunah in the outlying Sunset District. As a boy, he "got [his] passion for Judaism" from that Conservative synagogue's rabbi, Ted Alexander, himself a German refugee who had come through Shanghai and met Mark's mother on the ship to California. But Schiftan later gravitated toward the Reform movement as a result of his summers at Camp Swig, where he met his future wife. He was also greatly influenced by one of his professors at San Francisco State—Rabbi Alvin Fine.

Working under Kirschner for four and a half years, first as assistant rabbi and later as associate, Schiftan grew rapidly as a preacher and teacher. But only when he was called upon to head the temple in the midst of one of the greatest crises in its history did his skills as a leader also become evident. As Paul Matzger aptly put it, Schiftan passed "the critical, yet intangible dividing point...between inspired initiate and insightful, mature rabbi."

But the winter of 1992 had many "lonely, dark days" for the young rabbi, "a bone-chilling" time in which his ethical principles were often put to the test by his and others' political and practical considerations. The emotional support of his wife, Harriet, a social worker employed by

THE MANAGEMENT STAFF AT THE END OF THE '90S. FROM LEFT:
CANTOR ROSLYN BARAK, RABBI HELEN T. COHN, RABBI PERETZ
WOLF-PRUSAN, TERRI FORMAN, RABBI SYDNEY B. MINTZ, RABBI
STEPHEN S. PEARCE, PAM SCHNEIDER, GARY S. COHN

the Jewish Vocational Service, was much needed as he tried to shape the temple's response to the tragic events of the year just passed.

Schiftan differed from many of the lay leaders, and even some of his rabbinical colleagues, in that he felt less compassion for Kirschner and more of an imperative to address the needs of those who had brought the charges. He believed that the congregation "did not [properly] understand the difference between the victim and the perpetrator." Absolutely appalled by his predecessor's behavior, Schiftan did not speak to Kirschner for the next six years, and felt not the slightest obligation to help him as he struggled to find a new job. He couldn't even bring himself to move upstairs to the senior rabbi's office, which in his mind had been "tainted" by the immoral conduct that had taken place there. As he recently reflected,

> It does not matter that he was an *illui* [a genius] and how many things he accomplished. Yes, he was a great rabbi in that sense, but it still does not equal the violation of that office and the damage that he did....At the end of the day what really matters are not the innovations, and not the new programs; what really matters is the rabbi's strength of character....What [Kirschner] learned painfully, what his congregation learned regrettably, what his board learned ultimately is that no one is above the law and everyone is accountable to it.

RABBI MARK SCHIFTAN

Schiftan was in favor of an investigation of the charges even after the resignation, and he also thought that public disclosure of the issue benefited rather than hurt the congregation in the long run. But, mindful of the sensitivities of the temple's most powerful lay leaders, he himself rarely spoke publicly about the matter. Instead, he chose privately to prod them toward a deeper understanding of what had happened; he acted as a counterweight to those who thought they could easily and painlessly put this matter behind them.

Along with the other clergy, Schiftan's strategy for healing emphasized one-on-one meetings with congregants. "What each of us did in the privacy of our offices," he remembers, "was to acknowledge the pain... both of those who were victims and [others] who were hurt by the experience. We listened to them without judgment; where appropriate we added our own insights and our own feelings."

It was particularly difficult to comfort the youngsters of the congregation, many of whom had idolized Kirschner and were close friends with one or more of his four children. His eldest, Nily, was a senior in high school and especially popular among the temple's teenagers. Over the strong objections of several lay leaders, the students in the religious school chose to dedicate their annual yearbook, the *Scroll*, to Kirschner (as well as to Rabbi Gayle Pomerantz, who announced her resignation effective in June 1992). The second page of the booklet carried a loving inscription to the departed senior rabbi, and a large picture of him dancing with Nily at the Simchat Torah celebration the previous fall.

Emanu-El's educator, Rabbi Peretz Wolf-Prusan, took over Kirschner's confirmation class in the middle of the academic year, and recalls the sobbing of the tenth-graders, week after week. "Having just come into adolescence," he explains, "they were very disturbed that a rabbi had not behaved properly sexually." Wolf-Prusan had meetings with parents and teachers as well; he likens his work in those days to grief counseling, for "this was the loss of a rabbi, the loss of an icon, the loss of confidence."

The staff and the lay leadership agreed on the need for two open congregational meetings to enable the bewildered membership to gain more information and air their feelings. These were held on weekday evenings in mid-January, at the height of the media coverage of the episode. Rhoda Goldman and Paul Matzger calmly performed the difficult and at times unpleasant task of chairing the gatherings of about 150 people, though there was little that they could add to the newspaper reports that had run the week before.*

The meetings, while less rancorous than expected, reflected a deep division in the congregation: several of those who spoke from the floor expressed anger at the rabbi for his behavior, while many others sharply criticized the board for accepting his resignation and not finding a way for him to remain at his post. The strong difference of opinion correlated less with gender than with age; the older members of the congregation were generally more forgiving of Kirschner than the younger generation was. But the women present were much more vocal than the men—on both sides of the issue.

Rabbi Schiftan had to use all of his powers of persuasion to convince the weary and anxious board of the need for a series of three meetings of a different kind. This was the opportunity for congregants to discuss the events of the past month in small groups with a therapist, the respected psychologist Norman Sohn, who had served more than two decades as the director of adult services at the Jewish Family and Children's Services and who was now in private practice. For Dr. Sohn, an authority on the psychological problems of children of Holocaust survivors, the group meetings at the temple were among the most "emotionally intense" encounters of his entire career. The situation was one of "tremendous immediacy," he recalls, requiring "critical incident debriefing." He saw his greatest challenge as that of breaking through the thick wall of denial—on the part of older couples in particular—that Kirschner could have behaved in the way alleged. He had to raise the hypothetical case of a woman committing suicide after being sexually abused by a clergyman in order to make real for them the danger, in his professional opinion, that the rabbi's conduct could conceivably have posed.

Therapy was also made available, at the temple's expense, to the staff members and their spouses, most of whom felt the need for it. Cantor

*Although the two complainants from the Graduate Theological Union arrived at the temple for one of the meetings, Matzger thought it best to exclude them. He felt that the proceedings should focus on the needs of the congregants and that little could be gained at that point from hearing "a bill of particulars" directed against the rabbi. Their story, however, would be published in the *Jewish Bulletin* at the end of that week.

Barak became so preoccupied with the causes of Kirschner's fall that she soon went back to school part-time and took a master's degree in clinical psychology. The board of directors also set aside funds for the counseling of any congregant who needed professional help in processing the disturbing events.

The temple's insurance company paid for the long-term therapy of a number of the women who suffered emotional distress after their encounters with Kirschner. This issue—reimbursement for extended psychological counseling—was the major element in the several civil claims that the temple quietly settled over the next two years.

A member of the executive board was also dispatched to contact the plaintiffs personally and reassure them of the temple's willingness to make amends. But he and a number of clergy and lay leaders felt that still more could have been done on the synagogue's part to reach out to the women who had been harmed. As Rabbi Schiftan later stated, "The primary obligation [ought to have been] rectifying the damage to the victims, the secondary consideration [ought to have been] the health of the congregation as a whole, and [only] the third and final concern should have been the rabbi."

There is no question, however, that in the aftermath of the scandal the temple focused its energies on preventing a similar disaster from occurring in the future. In the spring of 1992, a committee including Rabbi Pomerantz, as well as one of the women who filed the original charges, drafted a comprehensive sexual harassment policy for the institution. It was approved by the board in June, posted in the temple, and mailed to all congregants the following month.

After much debate among those who drafted the declaration, the final version stopped short of prohibiting sexual contact between a member of the clergy and a congregant under any circumstances. But it stressed that no employee should be permitted "to use a position of trust or influence to coerce a congregant or prospective congregant to engage in a sexual relationship." Most importantly, it set up a grievance procedure by which the plaintiff would have a choice of directing a complaint either to the executive director, a member of the board, a member of the clergy, or the executive director of the Jewish Family and Children's Services. It would then be taken to the temple board's executive committee, which would

investigate the charges and report back to the entire board. "Grievants
will be informed of the status of the investigation," the policy stated, and
"should feel free to assert a complaint without fear of reprisal."

With the help of such measures, the temple gradually emerged from
the shadows of the scandal. The program year of 1992–93 was one of
transition, of course, as the congregation conducted a search for a permanent senior rabbi. But while about seventy-five members resigned due
to the Kirschner matter, the day-to-day workings of the temple continued
unabated. Gayle Pomerantz's departure in the summer of 1992 was
regretted, but she was replaced as assistant rabbi by the creative, articulate
Misha Zinkow, who had served for seven years as the director of Camp
Swig. Along with Wolf-Prusan, who performed a good deal of the rabbinical work in this period, and the unflagging efforts of the new executive
director, Gary Cohn, Schiftan was able to keep intact virtually all of the
temple's programs and life-cycle events.

This was essential in restoring a sense of trust in the clergy. As Schiftan remembers, "We didn't miss a beat; I didn't want one thing to drop,
[because] the normal routine itself was part of the healing." Paul Matzger,
who assumed the presidency early in 1993, agrees completely with this
assessment. Like the members of the clergy, he and his predecessor, Rhoda
Goldman, listened attentively to vexed congregants, faced the scrutiny of
the media, and took a number of actions aimed at easing the pain of all
concerned. But no less important was the unbroken continuity in the life
of the institution: "We healed," according to Matzger, "service by service,
Bar Mitzvah by Bar Mitzvah." By September 1993, when the new senior
rabbi was installed by the revered Alvin Fine—a reassuring symbol of
rabbinical strength and integrity at Emanu-El—the worst was over.

Only six weeks earlier, Matzger, evaluating his board's handling of the
matter for a reporter of the *San Francisco Examiner*, was quoted as saying,
"We did the best we could." His words, however, were taken out of context and made to sound like a lame excuse; the article also quoted the
letter of resignation of another executive board member, Secretary Elaine
Petrocelli, in which she alleged a "cover-up" of the issue. The wife of an
attorney who had recently published a book on sexual harassment in the
workplace, her distress with the temple's handling of the Kirschner matter

would not be allayed even by the conciliatory Rhoda Goldman, who tried in vain to keep her from stepping down.

It is true that the board could have been more forthcoming earlier; the lay leaders made a serious error in thinking they could control the situation. And while they quickly acceded to the demands of the women who came forward, the board also could have shown a deeper sensitivity to their plight. But it is also the case that many salutary measures were taken in the weeks and months following Kirschner's departure, such as congregational meetings, counseling sessions, and the drafting of a strong sexual harassment policy. The board deserves credit for each of these actions, which were rarely reported in the Jewish or general press.

Still, the crisis was not handled in an ideal manner, a point Matzger himself concedes. But given the emotional ties of many on the board to the rabbi and to the temple, it can hardly be surprising that helping Kirschner and protecting the institution were uppermost in their minds. Guarding the privacy of the Kirschner family and of the complainants was also a prime consideration. The wisdom and morality of the board's decisions are debatable but, in the end, understandable. Amidst a sudden, unthinkable calamity, aided neither by past experience nor by Reform movement policy and constrained by serious legal and financial consider-ations, the temple's lay leaders indeed did the best they could.

MATZGER, WHO BECAME TEMPLE PRESIDENT a year after Kirschner's resignation, expresses the mood of many lay leaders in 1993: "I saw a need for normalcy. After I became president, for months and months I wanted *calm* [his emphasis]." This longing for stability was clearly in the minds of the search committee when it chose the new senior rabbi. To be sure, some sought another "daring, young visionary" to replace their fallen idol; others hoped to engage a woman as spiritual leader, thus sending a message of assurance to the female congregants. But for the majority, trustworthiness was the key requisite trait. After much deliberation, the committee finally selected the eleventh senior rabbi in the temple's history.

Stephen Pearce, who was in his late forties, had served more than twenty years as the rabbi of two midsized congregations in the North-east. He impressed the Emanu-El leadership not with the youth and

dynamism that had characterized Kirschner, but rather with a steadiness
and maturity that were especially welcome after a time of trauma. With
his emphasis on pastoral work more than preaching, and his preference for
team leadership rather than solo performances, his selection seemed a
classic example of the "pendulum principle" of engaging a rabbi: the congregation was ready for a spiritual leader with a temperament completely
different from the one before.

Married for almost two decades, and the father of two children, there
was not the hint of a blemish on his personal life. But the appeal for
Emanu-El of the native New Yorker went far beyond the sense that he
was "safe" in a way Kirschner had not been. For Pearce was well known
in Reform circles as a healer, both of battered souls and of troubled congregations.

Until he moved to San Francisco—a city he had never even seen
before interviewing for the position at Emanu-El—with his family in the
summer of 1993, virtually his entire life had been spent in the New York
metropolitan area. He grew up in postwar Brooklyn, the grandchild of
East European immigrants. With the death of his father when Pearce
was three, his strong and devoted mother shouldered all the responsibilities
of raising two children. The family joined a large, neo-Reform congregation, but young Stephen, like so many of his generation, had a miserable
time in its religious school. He was active in the youth group, however,
becoming president both of the synagogue's chapter and of the entire
region. Here he met young rabbis "who took their Judaism seriously";
they left their mark on the youth, who chose to enter Hebrew Union
College after his graduation in 1967 from City College, at that time one
of the finest public institutions of higher learning in the country.

Although it was not yet required of HUC students in the early '70s,
Pearce elected to spend a year of his training in Israel, where he worked
on his rabbinical thesis, an exploration of Jewish messianism. After his
ordination, he obtained a one-year interim post at Temple Isaiah in Forest Hills, Queens, a middle-income congregation of about four hundred
families. Here, on short notice, he filled in for a much older rabbi who
had failed his flock both personally and professionally, and whose contract
had been terminated. By the end of the year, the twenty-six-year-old had
made such a favorable impression that the synagogue chose to engage

STEPHEN PEARCE POSES FOR A PHOTO IN *MICROCOSM*,
THE YEARBOOK OF THE CITY COLLEGE OF NEW YORK,
WHICH HE EDITED DURING HIS SENIOR YEAR

him as its permanent spiritual leader rather than conduct a search for a more seasoned rabbi. The board had to ask the Central Conference of American Rabbis to make an exception in allowing a man only one year out of rabbinical school to head a congregation of that size.

Pearce remained for five eventful years at Isaiah. Early on, he decided to study counseling psychology on the graduate level, a field in which he later made an important contribution with several articles and a book, *Flash of Insight,* on the uses of narrative and metaphor in therapy.* He had long been interested in the workings of the human mind, but his choice to pursue a doctorate in the subject arose from an incident at the synagogue, where people frequently "saw the rabbi as someone who knows everything." A man came to discuss an intimate sexual problem with Pearce, who was still unmarried and "a novice, inexperienced." He was at first aghast when he heard the graphic details, but then decided to enroll in a post-graduate program in counseling psychology at nearby

*Published in 1996, after four years of research, this volume contains a readable analysis of the complex theories of psychotherapist Milton Erickson, as well as a compendium of parables for clinical use. "Metaphor," as Pearce wrote, "deeply permeates those realms of an individual's psyche that harbor ideas that would otherwise be repugnant or unacceptable."

RABBI STEPHEN S. PEARCE

RABBI FINE WITH RABBI PEARCE AT HIS INSTALLATION

St. John's University. He went on to receive a Ph.D. in 1978 and taught at St. John's as well as at HUC, where he served as an adjunct faculty member for almost two decades.

While in Queens he also met his wife, Laurie, then a student in Assyriology at Yale. The Pearces eventually moved to Connecticut, where Stephen took a pulpit in Stamford, less than an hour's drive from New York City, and for the second time in his career healed a congregation that had felt betrayed by his predecessor. Laurie, after receiving her Ph.D., taught classical mythology and ancient history at the state university.

By the early '90s, the rabbi assumed that he would spend the rest of his career at Stamford's Temple Sinai, where he had served for a decade and a half, increasing its membership rolls by a third, to about four hundred families, and righting its finances. But the suburban synagogue had a major disadvantage: a high turnover of congregants, who were transferred to and from corporate positions with great frequency or who moved to Florida upon retirement. "A person who remained in the community for seven years was considered an old-timer," he remembers. He also missed the stimulating diversity of the urban congregation he had served in Queens, and longed for the kind of intellectual challenges posed by Emanu-El, with its long succession of erudite rabbis. So he took his "entire life, put it in cardboard boxes, put it in a truck, and all of a sudden was in a place [he] had never visited before."

Once again he faced the task of shepherding a congregation through a period of distrust and disillusionment. But this time he was in the position of following a rabbi who was not only a fallen spiritual leader, but also a brilliant one. Even while he sought to close the wounds of the scandal and make his own impress on the temple, Pearce would often be compared to a man who had few peers in the Reform rabbinate. Succeeding Robert Kirschner would be a tall order.

ALTHOUGH PUBLICLY HE GENERALLY REFRAINED from mentioning his predecessor by name, Pearce frequently referred to the recent disaster by stressing the need for rabbis to be moral exemplars. This was part of a conscious "rebuilding" effort in his first two years, because, he later reflected, "the image of the rabbi had been shattered; [Kirschner had been] not just like everyone else, but worse than everyone else—a victimizer. I just wanted to let people know that's an aberrant experience. Not every rabbi is that way; [the large majority] know and understand boundaries."

"You have a right to expect more from a rabbi," he said from the *bimah*, "than you do from your dry cleaner, grocer, or accountant." In a tribute to Mark Schiftan (who further aided the congregation by remaining at the temple during Pearce's first year, before accepting a post at San Jose's Emanu-El), the new senior rabbi stated,

> To influence others a rabbi must truly be a role model. He must be devoted not only to Jewish learning and Jewish values, he must be devoted to his family. Rabbis must be *morei derech*—teachers of the way through all of their being. People can learn best from those they believe in and admire.... I see [in Schiftan] the model that...is not always present in other rabbis.

But while Pearce has often focused on the "sacred trust" between rabbi and congregant, this is only one aspect of his emphasis on human relations in general. The essence of his rabbinate may be described as "matters of the heart," constituting for this rabbi-psychologist nothing less than "the purpose of Judaism." His deepest concerns revolve around the individual—questions of personal integrity, family dynamics, death and dying, acts of *tzedakah* (Hebrew for both charity and justice), and, above all, connectedness to faith and a caring community.

In his first Kol Nidre sermon, Pearce encouraged his congregants to write ethical wills for their children and grandchildren, explaining that this age-old (though little-known) Jewish practice was "designed to allow us to focus on the meaning of our lives." Ethical wills "force us to confront ourselves," he said, and he asked each member to take almost the entire Jewish year to think about their spiritual legacy. Eleven months later, just before the *Selichot* services on the Shabbat preceding Rosh Hashanah, he led a workshop guiding participants as they put down on paper the most important values in their lives.

The following Yom Kippur Eve, he again addressed "the lasting legacy we leave behind." Analyzing the concept behind the Yiddish word *kaddishil*—the term for the child who will ultimately recite the *kaddish*, the prayer for the dead, for its parents—Pearce thought aloud about the reason many congregants refrained from coming to the synagogue to mark the departure of their loved ones. Probing the mysteries of the human mind, his sermon offered the membership much to consider:

> Relationships struggle on in spite of the death of one of the players, in spite of the wish to forget, to be free, not to be haunted by words we find ourselves unconsciously speaking to our own children—words that do not allow our loved ones to rest in peace and do not allow us to rest in peace. That is why some do not come to recite *kaddish*, why they do not wish to be the *kaddishil*—the rememberer. Some of us wish to forget what cannot be forgotten; we wish peace from the struggles that were not resolved by death any more than they were in life....And so when I do not see some of you here to recite *kaddish*, ever, I wonder if unfinished business keeps you away and dooms you to struggle on and on, looking for some resolution that you never find.

In other respects as well, Pearce has been brutally frank in discussing from the pulpit life's most personal and profound issues. In one sermon, he strongly asserted the right to die, noting that in certain circumstances "assisted death may truly be an act of sanctifying and reaffirming life rather than denying or desecrating it." On Kol Nidre of 1997, he turned to the topic of divorce, a subject that discomfited some in the sanctuary that evening. The rabbi acknowledged that many members had been touched in one way or another by a failed marriage, but he nevertheless spoke of the "casual acceptance of divorce [as] cause for profound alarm." Characteristically stressing the importance of interpersonal relations, he went on: "It is painful to see some people treat marriage and other familial relationships like old cars, fit only for recycling. We are dealing with human beings, love and intimacy, shared experience, and we cannot be unconcerned with the consequences of disposable marriages and family estrangement for partners, children, and extended families."

Even in speaking out on political issues, Pearce has often focused on the human soul rather than cold statistics, on feelings and emotions more than academic arguments. In 1994, he wrote an op-ed piece for the *San Francisco Examiner* which expressed joy at the signing of the Oslo accords the year before. But looking back at decades of violent conflict in the region, he also revealed his deep personal disappointment with the Jewish state:

Jews have proved that once they acquired guns there would be no distinction from anyone else who has power. This is what the shedding of
Arab and Israeli blood has done to the Jewish ideal....Many Jews
rejoice in the return of the land to the Palestinians and the return of
Arab prisoners to their families. We Jews celebrate the return of our
captive souls.*

For Pearce the treatment of the Palestinians, who "in some instances
have been totally disregarded," is essentially an ethical question. "I expect
more of Israel," he said recently. "I want it to be great, a nation of priests."

He has devoted far more of his time and energy to a territorial dispute
much closer to home—the bitter struggle over sixty thousand acres of
old-growth redwoods in the Headwaters Forest near the north end of
California. Working with an interfaith coalition, he testified in Sacramento, prodded Senator Dianne Feinstein to do more on a national level,
and led a symposium on the crisis for almost a hundred religious leaders
and environmental activists at the temple. He held candlelight vigils,
generated a massive letter-writing campaign, published articles in the
press, and addressed numerous rallies on the issue. He jokes that at one
demonstration at which he spoke, he "followed a guy who was dressed as
a salmon."

But the rabbi could not have been more serious about stopping the
clear-cutting of the last fragment of the redwood ecosystem that once
covered the north coast, calling it "an issue that speaks so clearly to me
that I cannot rest." Ironically, the Maxxam Corporation, which owned
the land and planned to log the two-thousand-year-old trees, is headed by
a Jew, Charles Hurwitz. Pearce even called Hurwitz' rabbi in Houston to
bring pressure to bear on the corporate raider, but to no avail.**

*Although the piece was sharply attacked in a letter to the editor written by two lay lead-
ers (one of them a well-known congregant who was president of the regional Jewish
National Fund), there was nothing approaching the firestorm of controversy which had
greeted Rabbi Asher's similar stance on the Jewish state a decade and a half earlier. By the
1990s there was much more tolerance for criticism of Israel by local Jewish leaders, even in
the general press.
**An agreement was eventually reached, however, in early 1999. The state agreed to buy
thousands of acres, nearly matching a similar acquisition by the federal government, and
required Maxxam to take certain conservation measures on its remaining lands. Some envi-
ronmentalists denounced the deal, but for Pearce it constituted a "realistic compromise."

For Pearce, ecologically minded since his youthful involvement with the famed Brooklyn Botanic Garden, "saving the forest [was] more than a politically correct action. It [was] a moral obligation." He devoted his sermon on Rosh Hashanah, 1997, to the issue, which he explained was "emblematic" of a much larger problem—"the decline of the sacred"—throughout our society: "What is happening to the Headwaters…is not a new phenomenon….It is the result of a deep-seated feeling that all of the earth's riches are there for our personal and collective exploitation. It is an act of hubris to consider that the earth and its fullness exist simply for our whim." He concluded by asking the congregation to join him in a moving prayer for the redwoods, an interfaith plea to God to "protect these ancient trees from all who would harm them."

Whether it is caring for the earth or caring for souls, Pearce believes strongly in the power of ecumenism. In some respects he has gone even further than his predecessors in forging vital alliances with non-Jewish clergy and in enunciating the common values of the Judeo-Christian tradition. He has continued the rewarding annual pulpit exchanges with the Unitarian Church and the African American Third Baptist, of course, but has added several other denominations as well. In 1994 alone, he led

RABBI PEARCE LEADS A PRAYER FOR THE REDWOODS IN THE HEADWATERS
FOREST WITH INTERFAITH LEADERS AND ENVIRONMENTALISTS

joint services with Presbyterians, Catholics, and even an Arab Christian church. He expanded the Koshland Memorial Lecture to include a clergy institute so that the distinguished speaker can also address spiritual leaders from the entire community.

He also accepted the challenge of co-authoring a volume on American values with a sociologist and two eminent Christian pastors, Father John Schlegel, president of the Jesuit-run University of San Francisco, and William Swing, the Episcopal bishop of California, whose home pulpit is Grace Cathedral. Entitled *Building Wisdom's House*, the book grew out of discussions the four had had over the course of a year. It is in large part a rejoinder to the shrill fundamentalists who have claimed to speak for American religion in recent years; it examines such issues as gun control, welfare, the death penalty, and, of course, the environment in an attempt to restore faith in governmental institutions under attack. But above all it is a plainspoken plea for human decency. Beginning each chapter with an inspirational story, the authors tried "to show...a personal and human side to American religious institutions."

> Ours is a history of emotion, from transcendent joy so great that one's life is remade, to a single tear of sadness, so small that it is immediately lost in the cheek's fold. Sometimes the church doors look big and impenetrable. This book says that these institutions are yours. They are as strong as your courage and as weak as your despair. Love them. Care for them. We say the same for America's institutions. America is more than a piece of land. We are blessed with a people so diverse, almost anywhere you turn you can learn from your neighbors and grow wise together....
>
> We have written this book together, to get to know one another better. We could have written separately. We could have followed our single traditions and argued for charity, faith, awe, and community. Together, though, our voices are stronger....We live together, Christian and Jew, black and white, rich and poor, man and woman, north and south, urban and rural, gay and straight, newcomer and first family. There are those who say otherwise. They say it is not a community and that each man, woman and child must live and die alone. One day they will be proven wrong. One day those voices of hate will be reduced to no more than the rumblings of cranks and the whine of opportunists. Then America will live free, and the law of kindness will prevail in this land.

THERE HAS BEEN WIDESPREAD APPRECIATION for Pearce's ardent ecumenism and environmentalism. As the president of the Northern California Board of Rabbis, as well as of the regional chapter of the National Conference for Community and Justice (formerly the National Conference of Christians and Jews), he has been able to generate broad-based support for his efforts. His frequent columns on the weekly Torah portion in the *Jewish Bulletin* have further raised his profile in the community. But he does not claim to have electrified the congregation from the pulpit as Kirschner did on several occasions, most notably on the AIDS issue. He knows that following his heartfelt Headwaters sermon, for example, there were some members who went away still wondering, "Why the big fuss for the sake of a bunch of trees?"

But if he has not been the "mesmerizing" orator that his predecessor was, virtually everyone recognizes his exceptional ability as a pastor: his uncommon skill, on a one-to-one basis, in comforting congregants—from whatever walk of life—who are ill, grief-stricken, or troubled.

A number of baby boomers who joined the synagogue in the second half of the '80s, swept up in the excitement of Kirschner's sermons and community service initiatives, often sought something else a decade later: succor at the time of the death of a parent. Invariably, they have referred to Pearce's soothing, caring manner during their time of grief, as well as his penetrating insights into the mentality of the bereaved. As one member who recently lost his father reflected on the consolation the rabbi provided, "It was worth more to me and my family than twenty inspiring sermons."

While Pearce has made a deep impact on the lives of countless individuals through his pastoral work, he has also had a profound effect on the workings of the institution as a whole. Perhaps his most important contribution has been in changing the very culture of the congregation. He has put his knowledge of human nature to use in reversing the proverbial image of Emanu-El as a cold, forbidding place of wealth and privilege, transforming it into a welcoming, accessible community of diversity and innovation.

The changes in this regard have been legion. They include small things, such as personalized letters to congregants from the senior rabbi marking the *yahrzeit* (anniversary of death) of a loved one, or displaying pictures in the foyer and in the *Temple Chronicle* not only of the clergy, but of the entire support staff—even the hardworking maintenance men. And each year on Purim the institution not formerly known for its sense of humor now publishes and mails to every member-household an uproarious parody of its newsletter—the *Temple Comical*. But there are also major undertakings that have redirected the course of Emanu-El, such as an unprecedented array of alternative worship services, a voluntary dues initiative, a greatly enlarged *havurah* (friendship group) program, and a concerted attempt not only to attract but also to integrate and retain new congregants.

The thread that connects these and many other new ventures over the past half-decade has been that of a warm, human touch, with a friendlier, more embracing temple being the goal of Pearce and his growing staff. As the rabbi recently described his vision of Emanu-El, "This a place for matters of the heart, matters of the soul; I don't want people to say, 'If you have money you're important, if you don't you're not.'"

In his leadership style, Pearce's rabbinate has differed not only from that of Kirschner, but from that of nearly all of his predecessors. During most of the temple's history, the senior rabbi placed his personal stamp on almost every aspect of the synagogue's operation; he stood far above anyone else, alone at the apex of the staff structure, directing the theological, ideological, and liturgical course of the institution. Through his High Holiday sermons in particular, he could reach people as could no other staff member or layperson.

As one among Emanu-El's five clergy and a member of its nine-person management staff (as the "senior staff" of Kirschner's day is now known), Pearce has inaugurated a decentralized, team approach to replace the top-down model of the past. Of course, he reserves the power to make the final decision at the weekly meetings, but everyone present is given an equal hearing, and not infrequently he defers to the opinions of others.

He generally gives free rein to his colleagues, "capable people" in whom he has great trust. He resists micromanaging their work: "In a large corporation, an executive is responsible for all the division heads, but he doesn't say, 'Let me see your calendar, what are you doing today?' [He says], 'You have a job to do; get it done.'" He welcomes the fact that each member of the high-powered clergy has developed his or her own loyal following, and he is aware that some congregants may be better served in certain respects by one of his colleagues than by him: "I benefit when my staff looks great," he offers.

The overwhelming majority of the staff is deeply grateful for the wide berth they have been given, and for the tone of collegiality Pearce has set. One employee with a great deal of responsibility recently considered the new mode of management and the impact it has had:

> Some of the older members of the temple are used to a single leader—charismatic or not—who was *the voice* of the congregation; what you're seeing now is a different leadership style. Some people think it's not leadership, but in fact it's very empowering on the part of Steve Pearce to allow a group of very talented people to do what they know how to do best, and to reach constituencies that they have expertise in reaching.

This kind of leadership—which, beginning in the mid-'70s, took hold at a number of large Reform congregations—has been essential in achieving the goals Pearce has set.* No single person can attract all the diverse subgroups of San Francisco Jewry, he feels. To lure the unaffiliated, not only must the style be welcoming, but the substance of the synagogue's offerings must be rich and varied. So each member of the staff must be a leader in his or her own distinct way, and each must be given the latitude to "have a stake" in the outcome.

NO ONE HAS THRIVED MORE under this power-sharing arrangement than Gary Cohn, the most influential executive director in the history of the temple. Since assuming his post in the difficult year of 1991, the former banking executive has strengthened the institution immeasurably through a series of shrewd fiscal moves. Working closely with Stuart Aronoff, treasurer of the board of directors in the early '90s and elected president in 1996, Cohn succeeded in balancing the budget and reducing the debt while attracting new members and establishing new endowment funds.

---

*A good example is Chicago's Temple Sholom, where Rabbi Frederick Schwartz even dispensed with the designations "senior," "associate," or "assistant." Each of the temple's spiritual leaders is referred to simply as "rabbi" in the congregation's publications.

The stout, middle-aged Cohn, who often wears suspenders as he strides through the temple, has the manner of a man at home in the business world. Less obvious is his instinctive grasp of the popular cultural predilections of the baby boomer generation. His passion for *Star Trek*, the Rolling Stones, and college football has kept him in close touch with the sensibility of many of the young families who joined the synagogue in the '90s. He is also a product of the Reform movement, and in the past half decade has had a major impact on the temple's programs as well as its finances.

Born and raised in Los Angeles, where his family was a member of the Wilshire Boulevard Temple, he frequently attended its summer camp (where, coincidentally, he met the young Bob Kirschner), and later taught for ten years in its religious school. An active congregant at Emanu-El after he moved to the Bay Area in 1987 to take a position with Union Bank, he was recruited by several friends and professional colleagues in the temple for the job of executive director after Irwin Wiener suddenly announced his resignation at the end of 1990.

Cohn's immediate task was that of applying the brakes to an operating budget that had gotten "out of control," with six-figure deficits during almost every year since the mid-'80s. With the cooperation of the fiscally conscious Aronoff, major cost-cutting measures were taken during the next few years: secretarial positions were eliminated; the large advertising budget was cut in half; and, until the financial picture improved in 1997, the temple left unfilled the rabbinical post vacated by Gayle Pomerantz in 1992. It meant that—including the educator, Wolf-Prusan—there would be three rather than four rabbis on the staff in the mid-'90s. Cohn also encouraged the board to increase the dues substantially—resulting in a gain of $200,000 in just two years—and to raise the religious school tuition as well.

He then turned to the cemetery, which had been a drain on the temple's finances for the better part of a decade. Here the strategy was to combine the operation with Sherith Israel's adjacent Hills of Eternity, which led to vast savings; within a few years, the cemetery was generating a considerable profit for the synagogue. A major addition to the indoor mausoleum in 1999 has further increased sales.

As early as 1992, the annual temple operating budget was balanced;

not one year of the Pearce era has seen red ink. But Cohn and Aronoff needed both good luck and good business sense in tackling the five-million-dollar debt which hung over the congregation after the completion of the giant capital project. The Kirschner scandal and resignation had naturally hindered fundraising efforts in 1992 and early 1993, and temple leaders were concerned that the huge outlay required to service the notes could cripple operations for the rest of the decade.

But in mid-1993, a developer came forward proposing to buy about three acres of the congregation's commercially zoned property in Colma at a price of 2.4 million dollars. None of this land had ever been used as a cemetery; almost all of it had been purchased by the temple for about $250,000 in the mid-1980s in order to complete the much larger parcel, which the City of Colma had agreed to rezone for commercial use. There was, however, a thorny ethical dilemma that needed to be resolved before the deal could be consummated: the buyer was seeking a permit to build a card parlor on the site. This form of gambling, allowed by a number of California municipalities, including Colma, is perfectly legal, but, as Aronoff recently quipped, "I would have preferred a Jiffy Lube."

After eliciting rabbinical input—including that of Stephen Pearce, who at the time had been appointed but had not yet arrived in town—Aronoff and Cohn persuaded the board to approve the sale. President Paul Matzger recalls "the feeling that we had no choice.…We desperately needed to pay down debt." The treasurer and executive director considered the moral question, but after weighing their fiduciary responsibility concluded, in Aronoff's words, that "it would have been almost foolhardy not to go ahead with it; there are certain things to which you have to apply common sense." They point out, too, that this was an outright sale; they did not feel it appropriate to pursue the developer's initial proposal of leasing the land and paying the temple a percentage of the gross proceeds of the card house.

The windfall from the sale cut the massive debt almost in half, and the balance may soon be erased by yet another major gain generated by the Colma leasehold. In the early 1990s, BART began planning a line to the San Francisco Airport's international terminal, using the old Southern Pacific right-of-way which runs through the temple's property. This too was land acquired for a modest sum during the rezoning on the astute recommendation of the temple's attorneys. It is now being sold to BART, which has agreed to build the airport extension sixty feet below ground, for several million dollars.* With this transaction, the temple, almost miraculously, will enter the new century free of debt.

Upon assuming his post, Cohn saw that "no long-range financial or strategic planning had been done." In order to generate a larger income for the temple, he soon focused on avenues beyond simply increasing membership dues. He encouraged the board to create the full-time position of development director, which was filled in 1993 by the thoughtful, well-traveled Terri Forman, an Emanu-El congregant who had worked for eight years for the United Way. Under Cohn's guidance, Forman has defined her role as one of educating the temple family about the Jewish tradition of *tzedakah* and about specific needs of the synagogue that individuals can meet now through the annual giving program, inaugurated in 1994. As she wrote in the *Temple Chronicle,*

> It is a new idea to give annually to Congregation Emanu-El. We have been perceived as a place of great wealth. The pride with which we maintain our beautiful buildings certainly reinforces that perception. However, it has been through the generosity of a few families that we have been able to do this. Today's reality is that in order to serve our members in the best way possible...the Congregation needs funds beyond [what] dues and a few big givers can provide.

Since its inception, the amount produced by annual giving has risen almost every year, approaching $100,000 in 1998 with more than 250 households participating. The money is used to enhance the temple's extensive youth and education program, as the religious school is now known. "Annual giving is still not a big component in a 3.5-million-dollar budget," Cohn allows, but he and Forman consider it a success in "trying to get people to change the way they think about giving to a synagogue." To get the attention of the congregation in 1997, Forman sent every member a small packet of honey along with the annual appeal letter, both to mark the Jewish New Year and to recall the traditional treat given to small children beginning their study of Torah.

---

*Cohn, enlisting the support of many cemeteries in the area, led a successful three-year campaign to dissuade BART from its original proposal to construct the tracks above ground, a plan that would have badly marred the serenity of the hillside setting.

Enlarging the temple's endowment has also been one of Cohn's primary goals. A survey of the Emanu-El membership conducted by independent researchers in 1993 revealed that congregants were most likely to give to youth education and activities, a category which out-polled community service programs. At Rabbi Pearce's suggestion, a religious education endowment fund was created (with the help of most of the proceeds of the annual giving program's first drive) and a second fund, to endow other programs, was set up as well. A third fund, for the long-term maintenance of the physical plant, is being planned.

The executive director is naturally pleased that the Colma leasehold produces about half a million dollars each year for temple operations, but he would like to see a much more substantial endowment to supplement the real estate, "something like twenty-five to thirty million dollars." Currently, he says, Emanu-El's endowment "pales in comparison" with large Reform congregations in New York, Los Angeles, Cleveland, and Chicago.

Forman has also obtained local foundation grants for a myriad of temple programs, including Rabbi Pearce's campaign to save the redwoods. This, too, is a departure from years past, when both lay and professional leaders generally assumed that Emanu-El would be perceived by grantors, including the Federation's giant Jewish Community Endowment Fund, as too wealthy to require outside financial support. With a few exceptions, such as Rabbi Kirschner's community service programs and Rabbi Asher's unsuccessful attempt to create a retirement community, the synagogue rarely even applied for institutional funding.

But Cohn is determined to correct this long-held misconception, which remains "pervasive in the community." Despite the serious financial setbacks the temple endured in the early '90s, he says,

> the myth is still out there, that we have all the money we could possibly need....It really hurts me...when I do Super Sunday and make calls for the Federation and I find that Lion of Judah givers [of more than $5,000 annually to the UJA] are on adjusted dues with Emanu-El. They say, "Well, you don't need my money."...I guess the only way to eliminate the myth is to go raise the money; then it'll be true!

Changing people's perceptions of the temple was also the goal of Jackie Levi, another key full-time employee whom Cohn added even before Terri Forman joined the staff, and who served until 1999. Engaged with the job title of director of membership services and program coordinator, the personable young woman initially oversaw many of the community service initiatives but increasingly focused on recruiting, integrating, and retaining new members. In this way, Levi filled a gap in the temple's operation which Cohn had recognized earlier than most of his counterparts at other large urban synagogues across the country.

Levi, and now her successor, Pam Schneider (formerly the preschool director), have provided the "human touch" that Rabbi Pearce stresses as being essential for the temple's viability. They have amiably welcomed potential congregants and, with the aid of a new member's questionnaire, have matched their needs and interests with the many programs and services offered. Once a person has joined, he or she can look forward to an orientation meeting preceding a Shabbat dinner, and even periodic calls from one of the clergy, just "checking in" to see that all is well. The temple's large *havurah* program serves as yet another means of integration.

Even the payment of dues for the first year is now optional, an innovation launched by Cohn and Pearce in 1996 which received national attention. The rolls now stand at more than 1,700 households, the highest number in the temple's history—an increase of over 250 from the dark days of 1992. But while the size of the congregation has grown by about 17 percent, almost 1.5 million dollars in annual dues is now generated by the membership, a gain of nearly 50 percent from Kirschner's last year.

No part of the temple has grown more during the '90s than the "secular" arm under Cohn, who reports directly to the board of directors, rather than to the senior rabbi, on several important matters. While the clergy consists of five, as it did at the beginning of the decade, the addition of both development and membership directors raises from one to three the number of administrators on the management staff of nine. Cohn, along with Rabbi Peretz Wolf-Prusan, is also the co-supervisor of the *havurah* and preschool directors.

While in one sense Cohn's rise has been made possible by the change in leadership style ushered in by Rabbi Pearce, his ascent is also part of a national trend which has seen the emergence of powerful executive directors in similar synagogues such as the Wilshire Boulevard Temple and New York's Emanu-El. There has been a growing realization that such a

EXECUTIVE DIRECTOR GARY S. COHN (LEFT) CONSULTS
WITH HAROLD S. STEIN JR. (ELECTED TEMPLE PRESIDENT
IN 1999) BEFORE A MONTHLY BOARD MEETING

large and complex institution as a great urban synagogue needs an administrator more akin to a CEO than to a social worker.*

Cohn clearly fits that mold. He sees his task as "bringing the best of the business world" to temple administration and has drawn upon the latest principles of corporate management theory. Like many other successful non-profit organizations in the 1990s, the temple has been infused with an entrepreneurial spirit. As Cohn recently wrote in the *Jewish Bulletin*, "marketing" should not be "a dirty word."

NEVER HAS THE TEMPLE BEEN SO CONSUMER-CONSCIOUS as in the Pearce era; never has there been such a heavy emphasis on reaching the "customer" or the "client," words freely used by staff members and lay leaders. Kirschner, of course, wanted to create a new image for Emanu-El, and with Irwin Wiener's help was able to present the temple to the public as an exciting, growing institution. But the current leadership—influenced no doubt by the competitive, free-market ethos of the '90s—has been even more enterprising.

---

*Standards have been elevated in recent years through a strong professional organization, the National Association of Temple Administrators, on whose executive board Cohn serves. NATA even confers a degree, the Fellow in Temple Administration (FTA), which Cohn earned in 1995.

To be sure, some of their outreach efforts had been tried before, such as Friday evening services in Marin, intended to make worship more convenient for those living north of the Golden Gate Bridge—more than 10 percent of the temple's members. Similarly, a popular course on Talmud taught by Rabbi Wolf-Prusan is held weekly during the lunch hour in a downtown office building, making it easier for business and professional people to spend part of their day in study. Building upon the success of Rabbi Kirschner's outdoor celebrations, Cohn has coordinated street fairs for Sukkot along several blocks of Arguello Boulevard which have attracted thousands of visitors.

But some of the new ventures, especially in the areas of fundraising and membership recruitment, have been more controversial. No congregant who heard Stuart Aronoff's address on Rosh Hashanah in 1997 could fail to appreciate the aggressive new thrust. Instead of merely delivering the president's traditional perfunctory remarks, Aronoff spoke for about twelve minutes at each of the two services in the main sanctuary. He asked the worshippers, among them some of the leading philanthropists in the Bay Area, to "tour the city with [him] for a moment."

> We have a beautifully renovated opera house, thanks to many of you. We have an enhanced ballet and a top-notch symphony, again, thanks to many of you. We have a Jewish Federation that exceeded its fundraising goals, thanks to you. We have organizations like Hebrew Free Loan and Jewish Vocational Services that continue to serve the

VISITORS TO EMANU-EL'S ANNUAL SUKKOT STREET FAIR

RABBI PERETZ WOLF-PRUSAN (CENTER) LEADS
DOWNTOWN LUNCHTIME TALMUD

community, thanks to you. At this point, you could breathe a satisfied sigh and rest contented that many of you have helped make San Francisco a world-class city from all perspectives....Now let me ask you this: doesn't a world-class city deserve a world-class synagogue?

He then enumerated the plethora of giving opportunities available at the temple and concluded with the phrase he chose as the title of the talk: "Shrouds have no pockets." He explained that "this [maxim] is to encourage us to give away everything before we die." Some were offended by what they considered "a pitch for money" during the High Holidays, but Aronoff remained unmoved by the criticism: "I've got to keep in front of people that we [must] focus on fundraising in the future, or else we'll stagnate."

This unusual High Holiday appeal was only one of several audacious experiments designed to strengthen the temple's financial position, heighten its visibility in the community, and increase the ranks of its members. A year earlier, the board embarked on a plan to offer a gift certificate to any congregant who provided a list of eighteen prospective new members to the temple, and a reduction of dues to any household whose referral actually resulted in a new family joining. Several members, among them some of the leaders of the Sisterhood, objected to the "offering of rewards [as] contrary to the dignity of our prestigious House of Worship." But it was primarily because the idea "just didn't work" that

Cohn and Aronoff soon announced that the congregation had to pull back from the program of financial incentives.

In 1998, Cohn devised a plan for the expanded Sisterhood gift shop—recently relocated to the main floor of the temple house—to sell matzah for Passover, "literally a ton" of unleavened bread. He was convinced that prices for matzah in San Francisco were "artificially high," with a five-pound box selling for $15.99, and dealt directly with a local food wholesaler to obtain them for sale at the temple. The concept was well received at Emanu-El, where spirited members of the Sisterhood briskly sold five-pound packages for $10.40, both to congregants and non-members who appreciated the reasonable price. But Cohn drew the ire of part of the Orthodox community, which felt that Emanu-El was undercutting J. Sosnick and Company, the Bay Area's leading year-round distributor of kosher food. No other congregation would join the temple in this venture, and an angry Jeffrey Sosnick was able to use the vehicle of an interview on the front page of the *San Francisco Chronicle* to chide Emanu-El: "Why do they make such a big deal over a dollar or two for matzo? They are doing it to play to the people, to get them to affiliate with the congregation."

The "matzah wars" constituted a minor episode, though, in comparison to an entrepreneurial effort in 1996 that also drew criticism from some quarters in the Jewish community, but proved to be an unqualified success with major implications. Cohn and Pearce, seeking out "Jews on the margin" and "looking for a way to make it impossible for them to say no" to affiliation, hit upon the idea of voluntary dues for the first year of membership. With a large bequest from the Caro-Serensky family, they were able to advertise the incentive, integrate the new members, and assess the results.

Well over two hundred households signed up within the first year of the program, the large majority reporting that the offer of a year's free membership was "important" or "very important" in their decision. An outside study of the initiative, conducted by Brandeis University's Institute for Community and Religion, not only revealed a highly effective marketing tool, but also showed the entire temple—four years under Pearce's influence—to be a genuinely warm and friendly place.

Through a mail survey and two focus groups, new members spoke again and again of the receptivity of the senior rabbi and the rest of the staff. The majority of the diverse group of newcomers expressed an intention to stay at the end of the trial period, largely because of the efforts made to welcome them. As one man said of the senior rabbi, "He wanted me to be there and he was extending himself, and I think an awful lot of him....This has a lot to do with the feeling of being drawn [in]." Another observed that "the people who work here enjoy being here," and pointed to "the ease by which they interact with one another." A single woman in her late forties had clearly changed her image of the temple: "I always had a perception of...Emanu-El and I did not fit into that. I mean, it was always...the rich Jews of San Francisco. I felt like I'd have to go out and buy a whole new wardrobe to go to...Shabbat services. Of course, that's not true....It makes me happy."

The study, conducted by Dr. Joel Streicker under the direction of Professor Gary Tobin, showed too that the fears of a number of congregational rabbis who had publicly opposed the program were unfounded. They felt that the prospect of a year's free membership, rather than attracting the unaffiliated, would cause some of their own congregants merely to switch their allegiance to Emanu-El. One rabbi countered the temple's publicity campaign by taking out an ad in the *Jewish Bulletin* decrying the voluntary dues program and touting his own synagogue as the one without "a million-dollar dome." But Streicker found that only one in twenty new Emanu-El members had dropped their membership in another congregation to join the temple, and that nearly three-quarters of those who enrolled under the plan had never belonged to a synagogue.

It was for this reason—its great attraction for the unaffiliated, who deeply appreciated the lack of pressure to make an initial financial commitment—that the voluntary dues policy generated such widespread interest. Inquiries came into the temple from across the country, and the *Forward*, a nationally respected weekly newspaper, ran a glowing front-page article on the program entitled "Rx for Shul Absentees: End Dues."

The voluntary dues program also showed that there needn't be a contradiction between aggressive marketing and fundraising on the one hand, and creating a warm and inviting atmosphere on the other. The deep concern demonstrated by the staff for every person who walks through the door is a major factor in attracting and retaining congregants—a good "business practice" as well as an ethical imperative. In this connection, the example of the Walt Disney Company has been invoked by several Emanu-El professionals; they see in the phenomenal success of the theme parks—in which every employee, even the janitors, excel at serving the public—an important lesson for the temple.

At the same time, the emphasis on expanding the membership rolls and financial base is necessary for the temple to thrive, and perhaps even to survive; its ability to carry out its sacred mission depends in large measure on its fiscal health. As Rabbi Pearce recently said, "We're doing more than we ever have before; there has to be a way to pay for that."

Almost from the time of its inception, one could say that the temple has, to a greater or lesser degree, competed in "the marketplace of souls," vying with Jewish and non-Jewish institutions throughout the city. Today it appears to be gaining ground, but the struggle is more demanding than ever.

IN THE MID-'90S, key staff members and lay people worked hand in hand toward the goal of "opening up" the temple: improving the lines of communication, increasing the receptivity to members' needs, and re-defining its value system. Rhoda Goldman perceived the need to change the ambience of Emanu-El, making it more genial and homelike. As immediate past-president, she played a major role in this regard at a pivotal day-long board retreat in the fall of 1993. With the new senior rabbi in place, Goldman, "the visionary," grasped the opportunity, as Gary Cohn recalls, "to change the way we do business."

As president she had given her approval for the hiring of membership and development directors, and chaired a series of focus groups in order to glean congregants' ideas about the direction of the temple and the traits they felt most essential in the hiring of Kirschner's successor. Now she encouraged the development of a far-reaching strategic plan "to set the direction of the congregation for the next five to ten years."

She understood that with the addition of hundreds of young households during the Kirschner years, the membership was more amenable to change than it had been earlier. To be sure, she had been one of the "old guard" that a decade before had backed Rabbi Asher in his struggle to maintain the status quo. But now she recognized that the number of longtime members, families that had belonged for a generation or more, was rapidly dwindling as a proportion of the congregation as a whole. The dynamism of the late '80s and early '90s had also convinced her of the malleability of the institution; she was not afraid of charting a new course.

One of the most important tools in the process was a survey conducted by an outside consulting firm in late 1993 "to learn how members view the temple...and their own involvement." Given that the data were collected at the very outset of the Pearce era, the survey is a good indication of the mood of the congregation upon his arrival and the challenges he and his staff faced.

The large majority of respondents agreed strongly with the statement "I take pride in the work of this congregation and am committed to its future well-being." This received an average rating of 4.23 out of a possible 5, the highest of the questionnaire's fifteen propositions. But for the statement "Our congregation is responsive to the diverse needs of our current and prospective multi-generational membership," the agreement rating dropped to 3.78. An alarmingly low level of agreement—2.51—was registered in response to the statement "I have a voice in the decisions about the direction of the congregation." This was all the more disturbing because of the likely "halo effect" of the survey itself, given that it was soliciting the members' input. Prior to that, congregants may have felt that they played an even smaller role in the institution.

Unsettling, too, was that more than half of those completing the inquiry rated their participation as "low"; only 11 percent characterized it as "high." This was especially troubling for a synagogue trying to shed its image as a place for "minimalist Judaism," and it raised the serious question of whether the clergy and board had not overestimated the involvement of the rank and file in recent years. Barely a third of the respondents indicated that they came to the temple at least a dozen times a year for services or programs. Beyond the High Holidays and life-cycle events, such as a wedding or Bar Mitzvah, could it be that only a thin layer of the membership was truly active?

The results of the survey were not lost on the staff and lay leadership. Three ad hoc committees were formed to develop the strategic plan: one to redefine the congregation's mission, vision and goals; a second to address membership recruitment, integration, and retention; and a third to face the issue of leadership development.

Emanu-El had not updated its mission statement since the days of Jacob Voorsanger at the turn of the century. The 1993 declaration pronounced the temple "dedicated to advancing lifelong involvement in Judaism guided by Jewish values." Significantly, first on a list of eight means for achieving this goal was "upholding the core value of the individual's ability to choose the manner of his/her religious identification and expression." This ringing affirmation of diversity and personal autonomy would prove to be an important guideline in the temple's decision-making for the rest of the decade. The second means enumerated, "providing access and resources to all Jews who seek to nurture and renew their faith," similarly validated the temple's efforts—begun by Kirschner and Wiener and to be carried even further by Pearce and Cohn—to reach ever-widening constituencies. "Providing resources and support for interfaith families" was specifically articulated as part of the mission as well.

The committee on membership did not yet consider the voluntary dues policy that would be developed three years later. But with Jackie Levi's input, it recommended a host of measures that she quickly implemented: targeting specific subgroups through well-placed advertisements, asking members to invite their unaffiliated friends and family members to join, and creating a database of potential congregants. This would be comprised both of newcomers to the area and anyone coming to the temple for any social, religious, or cultural activity. The committee also endorsed Levi's emphasis on "the personal touch," which has helped make people feel welcome throughout the years of their membership.

The leadership development committee, working to improve the effectiveness of the board of directors and the many standing committees of the temple, recommended a program to better prepare congregants to serve on these levels. This ultimately led Cohn to conceive Leadership Emanu-El, a year-long training course inaugurated in 1996, in which potential board and committee members, most of them people in their forties, meet monthly at the temple to learn the workings of the synagogue and the larger Jewish community. Participants typically gather on a Friday afternoon, study with a variety of teachers, including the Emanu-El clergy and outside specialists, and then remain for evening services. In the past, says Executive Director Cohn, "we've had people on the board who didn't even know we operate a preschool, but now we're building a cadre of graduates, all of whom have a better connection to the temple."

Terri Forman, who had a great deal of input into the member survey and staffed the strategic planning process, sums up the change in the direction of the temple that they signaled. She stresses a new responsiveness on the part of the staff since 1993: "It means constantly staying in touch, being aware of shifts in demographics [and] of needs that arise, narrowing the gap between the clergy and the temple management and the congregation; it's bringing us all much closer together; it makes it all more accessible."

Part and parcel of this effort to "put a new face on the temple" is an extensive *havurah* program, inaugurated in 1996. Fifteen affinity groups, each of about eighteen people, now meet monthly in private homes, offering an intimate setting for study, holiday celebration, and fellowship.

Emanu-El had been slow to appreciate the value of the small fellowship circles in overcoming the sense of alienation that many felt in a large and often impersonal congregation. True, one *havurah* did come into existence toward the end of the Asher era. "Tikvah," a study-based group, has often invited clergy to lead discussions. Especially vibrant and cohesive has been Havurah Mishpacha, a cohort formed in the late '80s of families with young children. Created by the Bureau of Jewish Education, Mishpacha initially used Emanu-El as a meeting place, but later its members, many of them well-versed in Judaism, joined the temple, enriching it with their knowledge and enthusiasm.

By the mid-1990s, Tikvah and Mishpacha were among five functioning *havurot* at Emanu-El. In 1996, a substantial grant from the Zellerbach Family Fund supported a concerted effort that has resulted in the tripling of the number of groups. A new full-time staff member was engaged for this purpose, the effervescent Jody Seltzer of Berkeley, who used the success stories of the existing *havurot* to motivate congregants to form new ones. These "intentional communities," which now include almost three hundred people, usually revolve around shared interests and needs; there are groups aimed at singles and young couples, families with small children, empty nesters, retirees, and many other social categories. Consistent with the congregation's emphasis on individual autonomy, *havurah* members themselves set the agenda of their activities, ranging from Passover seders to community service, from camping trips to Bible study.

Nurtured by the *havurah* experience, participants have become part of an "extended family." This is especially important, Rabbi Pearce has written, "as our society has become more mobile and people live further away from their cities of birth, their families of origin and their longtime friends."

THE NATIONAL *HAVURAH* MOVEMENT was initiated by young people in the late 1960s as a communitarian alternative to organized Judaism. It is one of many examples in the Pearce years of the full-scale adoption of religious forms that had once been shunned at the temple. Belatedly but wholeheartedly, the door has been thrown wide open to the multifaceted popular revival that has invigorated American Jewry in the past generation.

Rabbi Asher had set his face against most of the non-synagogue-based expressions of Judaism that emerged during his tenure. Kirschner, revitalizing the congregation largely through the power of his own personality, also appropriated little from Jewish mysticism or feminist Judaism, and he barely changed the mode of worship at the temple. But the middle and late '90s have seen a borrowing, indeed an embrace, of some of the freshest innovations in Jewish practice, particularly in the area of liturgy. While the standard Emanu-El service, with its many Classical Reform features, remains largely intact, it has now become but one of a large variety of worship opportunities.

The most striking new option, offered in the Martin Meyer Sanctuary, is the Shabbat La'Am service inaugurated by the temple's popular educator, Rabbi Peretz Wolf-Prusan, in 1996. It is an informal, participatory experience, which includes a guitar, a liberal amount of Hebrew, and even an infusion of the "spirituality" often associated with the Jewish renewal movement. Still, as Wolf-Prusan rightly states, "it is not a wild, New Age service," and would hardly be unusual in a camp setting or an up-to-date suburban synagogue. But at Emanu-El it is in sharp contrast to the decorous, "high church" mode of worship—including a cantor, organist, and professional choir—that had been virtually the sole religious expression of the congregation since the late nineteenth century.

In one sense, Peretz (who, even in professional settings, is often referred to only by his first name) created part of the constituency himself.

Because he infused the school curriculum with more Hebrew and enriched family education, many congregants have felt their needs no longer met by the largely English-language Classical Reform service. Likewise, the graduates of Cantor Barak's adult Bar and Bat Mitzvah program have often wished to use their newly gained familiarity with Hebrew in a prayer experience.

In addition, the Shabbat La'Am service begins at 7:30 PM, rather than 5:30, allowing working families some time at home before going out to the temple in the evening. It is these families, including both baby boomers and people in their twenties and thirties, as well as many singles, who comprise most of the service's audience. But the primary draw, especially for those under fifty, is the nature of the service—intimate and interactive, spirited and spontaneous. Often described as "seekers," this younger generation of Jews has recast Reform ritual life across the country. They have left in place the underlying theological content, but have revolutionized the form of religious expression. The alternative service is part of "a second reformation," in the words of one expert on Jewish liturgy. According to another, "it puts prayers back into the hands and hearts and lips of the worshippers."

Despite this powerful national trend, it is hard to imagine the Shabbat La'Am service succeeding as it has without the talented Peretz. His easy, open style is well-suited to the Meyer Sanctuary, with its low *bimah* and short distance between the clergy and congregation, and its backdrop of brightly colored batiks. Rather than delivering a formal sermon from a pulpit, he walks into the aisles, speaks without notes, and engages the audience in dialogue. He uses his gifts as a storyteller, comedian, and, occasionally, even as a mime.

With colloquial language, he often touches upon the most familiar trappings of the fast-paced urban lifestyle of his young listeners—cellular phones, computers, high-rise elevators, traffic jams, and airports—to make a point about Jewish values and belief. In contrast to the service in the main sanctuary, where the black-robed clergy speak with an intonation that reinforces the notion of a sacred setting *apart* from the outside world, the everyday speech of the new "holistic" worship experience seems to fuse the sacred with the secular.

A consummate teacher, Peretz also takes advantage of the loose

LEFT: THE NEW MARTIN MEYER SANCTUARY
RIGHT: RABBI WOLF-PRUSAN LEADING A SERVICE

structure of the service to explain the rationale behind a particular Jewish prayer or practice. And he encourages people to move their bodies: clapping their hands, swaying back and forth, and joining in the Israeli dancing that usually follows. The music of the service is highly contemporary, drawing upon popular composers such as Debbie Friedman who have been strongly influenced by American folk songs written since the '60s. But even more than the melodies, it is the group singing that most differentiates this mode of worship; with the accompaniment of a song leader playing the guitar, literally everyone in the room has a voice in the service.

In its initial year, the Shabbat La'Am service was held once a month, its small turnout relegating it to the Rinder Chapel. But it steadily grew to 150 people, was transferred to the larger Meyer Sanctuary, and was preceded by a communal dinner in Guild Hall. A second, mid-month service was added as well. Even some of the temple's Bar and Bat Mitzvah ceremonies have been held during the Shabbat La'Am service on Friday evening, rather than in the main sanctuary on Saturday morning.

In 1997, Shabbat La'Am services were offered to members on Rosh Hashanah and Yom Kippur mornings. These were so well attended that the decision was taken to expand the new service in the following year, placing it opposite *each* of the eight daytime and evening services in the main sanctuary throughout the entire High Holiday period. They were all filled to capacity.

Far from feeling threatened by the acclaim Peretz has received, Rabbi Pearce welcomes the ability to offer a choice to his congregants. He even foresees a day when the alternative service will move to the main sanctuary for the High Holidays. Instead of repeating each Classical Reform service—at 9:00 and then 11:30 on Yom Kippur morning, for example—one of the two slots would go to Wolf-Prusan. The guitar would replace the organ and professional choir; a song leader would likely fill in for the cantor.

The elevation of the Shabbat La'Am service, which was unthinkable in the past, has implications beyond liturgy and ritual. Among other things, it means that a large fraction of the congregation will not hear the senior rabbi's High Holiday sermons, which since the days of Voorsanger have often been the high point of the congregational calendar. But Pearce is willing to pay that price, and possibly face a few empty pews in the service he leads, to meet the disparate spiritual needs of today's Jews.

He is proud of other worship opportunities as well. In addition to those led by two of the temple's *havurot*, there are monthly "Tot Shabbats" for families with preschoolers, "Birthday Shabbats" for children, and a "Service of Peace and Comfort" for those needing emotional support during a difficult time.

All in all, it has resulted in a remarkable multiplicity of prayer experiences under one roof. It is not unusual for a total of five hundred people to participate in the several services now offered on a Friday evening, twice as many as used to attend the one option available in the early '90s. "The tradition here was, if you don't like the service, go elsewhere," Pearce says. "There was the feeling the *shul* was unresponsive." To describe the temple's new approach, he cleverly coined a term that was picked up by the national Jewish press in a story highlighting the new phenomenon of multiple minyans at Emanu-El as well as a few other pioneering congregations across the country. Consistent with his emphasis on religious pluralism, consumer-consciousness, and team leadership, Rabbi Pearce calls the new paradigm "the synaplex."

PERHAPS NO MEMBER OF THE CLERGY has done more to put the temple in touch with the wave of spirituality engulfing Reform Judaism than Rabbi Helen Cohn. Through mysticism and meditation, healing services and outdoor retreats, interfaith work and conversions, she has tried to guide people in their quest for community and personal meaning. She uses the temple as her "living room" to bring individuals together and often to introduce the congregation to an array of grassroots groups that have sprung up in recent years in response to changing religious needs.

Like many whom she serves, her own life story is that of a journey of "return" to Judaism. When she was appointed assistant rabbi in 1994, immediately following her ordination from Hebrew Union College, she was past the age of fifty. Less than a decade earlier, her Jewish identity had been so attenuated that she didn't even know the dates of the High Holidays or the meaning of such basic concepts as Shabbat.

She had received an excellent secular education, at UC Berkeley, Brandeis University, and in Florence, Italy. But as she told the congregation in her first Yom Kippur sermon, "When I left for college, I left my Jewish involvement behind." She married a non-Jew, raised two children, and had a productive career in the burgeoning computer industry, but religion was not a part of her family life.

Yet, on a business trip far from home in 1984, more out of curiosity than anything else, she attended Rosh Hashanah services in a small synagogue, and her life was changed forever. Not unlike the German theologian Franz Rosenzweig early in the century, she had an epiphany that transformed her Jewish identity from one of assimilation to affirmation:

> I drove through the dark night on unfamiliar streets, in a rented car. An archetypical journey. When I arrived, the place was blazing with light. The greeters on the steps were expecting me; they welcomed me with open arms, me a stranger in their midst....I had no idea what was happening during the service, all the standing and sitting and singing in Hebrew. None of it was familiar. I watched my neighbors for cues. I was the outsider. Yet I could tell that something very deep in me was touched, because I couldn't stop crying....So I came back...and started studying.... I was an explorer who had landed on the shores of a lush country that stretched further than the eye could see...and that country was *my* country....The more I learned about Judaism, the deeper it settled in my soul.

Within a few years, she entered rabbinical school in Jerusalem. It was a choice not without great costs. She had long been divorced by this time, and though her ex-husband agreed to shoulder all the responsibility of child-rearing during her year abroad, her absence was an extremely painful blow to her teenagers.

Cohn, today a grandmother only a few years older than the baby boomers, brings her unusual life experience to bear upon her rabbinate. Pearce anticipated this when he selected her: "I realized that [she] would have to deal with many Jews on the fringe, Jews who were only marginally connected to Jewish life but who...had deep spiritual hungers."

To that end, she has taken traditional rituals once rejected by the Reform movement as useless relics and imbued them with new meaning. One such custom is *tashlich*, a communal gathering near a body of water late in the afternoon of Rosh Hashanah to symbolically cast away sins. Beginning in 1997, each year she has led a group of about a hundred congregants to San Francisco's Baker Beach, where they take part in this ancient rite in view of the Golden Gate Bridge. In the same vein, she has conducted services (along with Rabbi Wolf-Prusan) for the fast day of Tisha B'Av; led a colorful seder for the holiday of Tu B'Shevat, ushering

A LARGE GROUP OF CONGREGANTS GATHERS AT BAKER BEACH
TO OBSERVE THE ANCIENT RITUAL OF *TASHLICH*

in the spring; and marked the first day of the month of Elul with a meditative day-long retreat in tranquil Marin county, setting the tone for Rosh Hashanah four weeks later. Beyond all of this, she leads an annual Shabbat weekend at a serene retreat center in the East Bay hills, again linking the natural beauty of Northern California with Jewish tradition and spiritual expression.

Rabbi Cohn has also found mysticism and meditation effective in awakening an appreciation of Judaism. Taking advantage of the remarkable strength of the Jewish renewal movement in the Bay Area, she has brought to the synagogue some of its leading teachers, such as Avram Davis, the founder of Chochmat Ha'Lev ("wisdom of the heart"), an institute for spiritual growth which merges elements of Zen Buddhism and transpersonal psychology with medieval Kabbalism and neo-Hasidism.

Responsible for most of the adult education at the temple in the second half of the '90s, she has frequently programmed courses and lectures not only on the history and literature of Jewish mysticism but on its practice as well. "Jewish Mysticism You Can Use" was the title of one such talk given at the temple in the fall of 1997 by Rabbi David Cooper, whose recently published book, *God Is a Verb*, distinguished him as one of the country's major exponents of New Age Judaism. Leading up to this presentation, Cohn herself taught a four-session introduction to Jewish meditation, which, she says, "aids us in connecting with the Divine." The following year, she co-led a workshop on meditation with the abbess of the San Francisco Zen Center. In a Yom Kippur sermon, Cohn explained to some who could still remember the unyielding rationalism of Rabbi Asher that "the arena of logic and reason" is sometimes insufficient: "The spiritual side of life can't be proven; it can only be experienced."

Her creation of a monthly Shabbat "Service of Peace and Comfort" also owes much to the experimentation that has characterized Bay Area Jewish life in the '90s. With the aid of Rabbi Nancy Flam, founder of the pathbreaking Ruach Ami, a San Francisco healing center providing spiritual support and guidance to the ill, Cohn inaugurated a special worship experience including prayers of thanks as well as those of entreaty. About a dozen people usually attend the service, which includes guided meditation and communal singing led by guitarist Dr. Richard Nathan, a dedicated congregant.

Most of Cohn's work, however, is in the interfaith area. She performs about two dozen weddings a year, the large majority of them mixed marriages. Consistent with temple policy, she requires the couple to take an intensive "Introduction to Judaism" course and pledge to raise their children as Jews. Many of those married by Cohn, as well as others from within and outside the temple, study with her for conversion. In guiding potential converts, she again stresses the experiential rather than the intellectual side of Judaism: "It's more than about books. In the year or more that I have these people, I try to give them the experience of being Jewish. [I tell them to] get out into the community; attend services; do home practices."

Cohn is delighted with the enthusiasm shown by many "Jews by choice," still another factor contributing to the revitalization of Jewish life both locally and nationally in recent years. "Converts are going to save American [Jewry]," she predicts, "because they don't take Judaism for granted. They see the beauty of it; they bring a commitment to it." Like Pearce, she is in complete agreement with the call in 1993 of Rabbi

RABBI COHN PERFORMS AN
INTERFAITH WEDDING CEREMONY

Alexander Schindler, then president of the UAHC, for Reform Jews to proselytize the "religiously non-preferenced."

But many non-Jewish spouses choose not to convert, and the temple currently has more interfaith families than ever before; they comprise about a third of the congregation, according to the estimates of several clergy and staff members. Cohn sees this more as an opportunity than a crisis, and seeks to welcome non-Jews into the temple family with warmth and respect. Like her predecessors Schiftan and Pomerantz, she conducts a support group, co-sponsored by still another innovative local agency, the Interfaith Connection. But she envisions a much greater effort to reach this rapidly growing constituency: an interfaith institute under temple auspices that, among other initiatives, would bring intermarried couples to Israel for a study tour.

The confident Cohn, who was promoted to associate rabbi in 1997, reflects the way the entire congregation has accommodated itself to a new era in the American Jewish experience. Echoing many contemporary observers, Executive Director Gary Cohn (no relation) recently wrote of the shifting landscape,

> The survival of Israel, the Shoah, and the rescue of Jews from the former Soviet Union, the three tenets which have guided the Jewish community for so many decades, no longer speak as clearly to the new generation of Jews as they once did. As we enter the twenty-first century, new issues and concerns such as spirituality, worship, rituals, Jewish continuity and interfaith marriage have been placed on our community agenda, even though these new issues are difficult for some Jews to embrace.

In many respects Helen Cohn's rabbinate is a response to such thoroughgoing change. It mirrors not only the shift in emphasis from the cerebral to the emotional and from the collective to the individual, but also the rise of Jewish spirituality and piety sometimes at the expense of Jewish ethnicity and nationality—a dichotomy sometimes referred to as that of faith vs. fate. For much of the congregation—and for the growing number of converts and non-Jewish spouses in particular—external issues such as the Holocaust, oppressed Jewry, and the Mideast crisis, while still significant, have had less salience in recent years than internal questions of personal belief, family ties, or the desire to improve one's local community. One prominent Reform rabbi pointed out the emergence of this trend over a decade ago: "There is a growing involvement in the personal, pastoral rabbinate, in devotion to the life and pain of individuals, but a leveling off—if not a decrease—in concern with...*klal Yisrael* [the overall unity of the Jewish people]. The national rabbi is being replaced by the devoted congregational rabbi."

None of this means, though, that Emanu-El has relinquished its long-held role as a major public forum for the serious discussion of political issues; celebrities spoke in the sanctuary no less frequently in the 1990s than in prior decades. Race relations in particular has received a great deal of attention, and fundraising events for the Back on Track program have brought a remarkable array of the nation's preeminent African American intellectuals to the temple: Henry Louis Gates Jr., Cornel West, Maya Angelou, Marian Wright Edelman, and even the radical Angela Davis.

Whereas in the past such big-name speakers, a few top-flight classes and symposia, and, of course, the outstanding exhibitions in the Elizabeth Fine Museum constituted almost the entirety of the adult education offered by the temple, in recent years both the form and the content have been much more varied. Workshops and support groups, *havurot* and retreats now abound as never before. And the topics that are explored are "matters of the heart" as much as of the mind.

THE TEMPLE IN THE LATE '90S has not only embraced many alternative expressions of Jewish life, it has also shown a marked tolerance for alternative lifestyles. In 1997, Stephen Pearce appointed Emanu-El's first openly homosexual rabbi, Sydney Mintz.

Pearce and Wolf-Prusan, who assisted in the search, emphasize that Mintz was engaged solely because they considered her to be the most qualified person for the job, that of the fourth rabbi on the staff—not to make a statement about gay rights.* Yet the fact that Mintz' sexual orientation did not preclude her selection is significant. It is hard to imagine an openly gay rabbi being chosen much earlier in the temple's history.

Most congregants were fully in accord with the decision, but Pearce

---

*This position had been held by Gayle Pomerantz early in the decade, and with the aid of a grant from the Koret Foundation's Synagogue Initiative could now be filled again.

nonetheless had to field many angry phone calls, especially from older members. With President Aronoff's approval, he had not brought the matter before the board, in part because assistant rabbis have generally been selected exclusively by the senior rabbi. Pearce patiently explained to his critics that the Reform movement had gone on record several years earlier allowing the ordination of homosexuals.

More than anything else, he was vindicated by the outstanding work done by Mintz from the outset. Most of those who did have reservations about her as "a proper role model" changed their minds when they encountered her as a preacher, teacher, or social activist. A thirty-two-year-old with a wry, self-effacing sense of humor, she recounts, "People came up to me and said, 'That was a great sermon; I even forgot that you're a lesbian.'" She also speaks of a welcome of "warmth, generosity, and support" that far exceeded her expectations.

While still a teenager, Mintz knew that she wanted to be a rabbi. A fourth-generation Chicagoan, she was very active at North Shore Congregation Israel, a large Classical Reform synagogue not unlike Emanu-El. She was strongly influenced by the rabbis she met there, but, above all, by her grandmother, Harriet Gerber Lewis. A well-known philanthropist and activist for Jewish causes, Lewis served on the temple's board along with young Mintz, who held a seat as president of the youth group.

She avidly pursued Jewish studies both at the University of Wisconsin–Madison and during a year abroad at Oxford. But before entering HUC, she lived in San Francisco for three years, working as the teen director of the Jewish Community Center and program director of Camp Tawonga. Here she met Deborah Newbrun, the director of the camp, and the two soon entered into a long-term relationship.

In 1994, while Mintz was a rabbinical student, she and Newbrun exchanged Jewish wedding vows at a moving ceremony performed by Rabbi Wolf-Prusan, the first Emanu-El rabbi to sanctify a same-sex union. Peretz—with Rabbi Pearce fully in accord—gave his "wholehearted support" to the wedding, held in Mintz' father's home on the Peninsula, which included the *huppah* (bridal canopy), the *ketubah* (marriage contract), and the traditional breaking of a glass.* "If I had married a man,"

---

*The two had also been called up to the Torah on the previous Shabbat at Netivot Shalom, Newbrun's Conservative congregation in Berkeley, in a festive prenuptial rite known as an *aufruf*. But this ceremony, performed by Rabbi Stuart Kelman, seriously divided the congrega-

says Sydney, "it would have been the same ceremony, [except that] there would have been a bride and groom on the cake instead of two brides."

Half of Mintz' classmates and several of her professors from HUC were in attendance—in the front rows, many of them taking copious notes. Her beloved grandmother was also present. But those most deeply affected were the newlyweds' gay and lesbian friends who had rarely seen two homosexuals convey their love and support for each other in such an open and Jewish way. Many of them wept openly out of the pain in their own lives of having been shunted aside and ostracized even by their families. Two gay men, who had been together for twenty-five years, had never before danced with one another at a wedding.

Mintz and Newbrun soon had a child, Eli, who is Deborah's biological son and whom Sydney adopted. The family is often seen together at services and other temple functions. Eli is enrolled in the congregation's preschool. But while Mintz is completely honest about her sexual orientation, it has played virtually no role in her rabbinate. "I'm not an 'in your face' kind of person," she says, knowing that "timing is everything" when she mentions she is a lesbian.

But she has discussed from the pulpit another unusual aspect of her young life: following the divorce of her parents when she was eight, her father married an Episcopalian, with the result that Mintz' step-family, including her three half-sisters, are Protestant. She feels this has given her "a unique vantage point" in working with the many interfaith families at the temple; she has personally been "faced with the Hanukah-Christmas dilemma every day." Like her rabbinical colleagues at Emanu-El, Mintz marries Jew to non-Jew. But her experience has led her to add a requirement beyond the guidelines of the temple: she will not perform an intermarriage if the non-Jewish spouse is actively practicing another religion.

Mintz co-leads the Shabbat La'Am service with Wolf-Prusan, and her enthusiasm and humor are well-suited to the lively worship experience. She also works closely with the growing, revitalized youth group (still known as ETY, pronounced "Eddy"), the religious school, and the *havurot*. But she has been most visible in the areas of community service and social action, passionate interests for her since childhood.

tion. In his controversial twenty-five-page *teshuvah*, or rabbinical treatment of the issue, Kelman claimed that the same-sex *aufruf* was within the bounds of Jewish law—for which he received national attention and much approbation in Conservative circles outside the Bay Area.

Most of Rabbi Kirschner's outstanding initiatives in this realm continued after his departure; the Back on Track program in particular has flourished. Without his leadership, though, programs such as outreach to the deaf and to the Asian communities ceased. Hospitality House, AIDS relief organizations, and many other local benevolent agencies have continued to receive needed financial support from the temple's Community Service Fund, but by the mid-'90s these efforts were no longer in the spotlight as they had been earlier.

Rabbi Pearce arrived with his own approach to *tikkun olam* ("healing the world"), however, and it went well beyond his hard-fought campaigns to improve the environment. His inaugural High Holiday sermon at Emanu-El, in 1993, was a moving plea—the first of its kind in the temple's history—for congregants to take a shopping bag home with them after the service and bring it back on Yom Kippur filled with food for the poor. Linking this act of personal piety to the fast on the Day of Atonement, Pearce thus inaugurated a custom that annually generates tens of thousands of pounds of groceries for the San Francisco Food Bank, which distributes meals to hundreds of non-profit organizations serving the needy. The following Rosh Hashanah, he delivered another sermon on "doing God's work on earth." This soon led to the imaginative project known as Pe'ah, referring to the Talmudic injunction to set aside for the hungry the harvest of the corner of one's field. Dozens of volunteers, cultivating a plot of vacant land near the Home of Peace Cemetery in Colma, grow more than a ton and a half of organic vegetables every year, produce that is also donated to the busy Food Bank.

Pearce appointed Mintz to reinvigorate the community service arm of the congregation even further; she has sought to provide opportunities for members "not only to write checks" to worthy causes, but also "to get their hands dirty...to volunteer...to be a part of running an agency rather than just visiting once a year."

Building upon a program inaugurated the previous spring, she accomplished a great deal with an expanded "Mitzvah Day" early in her first year. On a Sunday in November, she attracted five hundred volunteers from the congregation, including the Sisterhood and the religious school, to tackle thirteen different projects throughout the city, such as cleaning up a beach, painting a homeless shelter, and feeding the poor. "It was one

RABBI MINTZ (SECOND FROM RIGHT) WITH
EMANU-EL COMMUNITY SERVICE VOLUNTEERS

day, but I looked at it as a kickoff," she says. She soon organized the Adult Mitzvah Corps, a "hands-on" volunteer effort, mirroring the Youth Mitzvah Corps which Wolf-Prusan had founded several years earlier.

In addition to fulfilling the basic Jewish obligation of "making the world a better place," the perceptive young rabbi has identified an institutional benefit arising from the renewed emphasis on social action. In a congregation larger and more diverse than ever before, and now variegated in terms of its worship experience, community service can cut across all lines and unite the membership as one.

Although she is a staunch feminist, Mintz has been careful not to place women's issues at the center of her rabbinate. But she has nevertheless played a key role in bringing the creative energies of feminist Judaism to the temple. On the seventh night of Passover in 1998, she co-led a Bay Area women's seder in Guild Hall, sponsored by five congregations, which drew over 150 participants. Along with Rabbi Jane Litman of Sha'ar Zahav and Rabbi Zari Weiss of Berkeley's progressive Kehilla Community Synagogue, she used the festival's overall theme of liberation to put women in touch with their own struggles throughout the world, not least of all their fight for equality within Judaism.

While the feminist seder was not the first in the temple's history (it was initiated by Rabbi Pomerantz and followed by several conducted by

Cantor Barak and the Anshei Mitzvah graduates in the mid-'90s), Mintz is breaking entirely new ground at Emanu-El in appropriating another holiday for an exclusively female service—that of Rosh Hodesh, the new moon. Popular with Jewish feminists across the country since the early 1970s, and requested by several congregants, the experimental liturgy draws upon the festival's traditional association with women and provides an opportunity to meet their unique spiritual needs.

Mintz' appointment also meant that women now constituted the majority of the clergy for the first time in the temple's history; they now hold six of the nine positions on the management staff. It would be an exaggeration to speak of the "feminization" of Emanu-El, given the vast influence of the men who hold the other three posts—Pearce, Gary Cohn, and Wolf-Prusan. Moreover, the six female leaders are a highly diverse group, anything but a monolithic bloc within the staff advocating feminism or any other issue.

Still, the predominance of women as decision-makers in the second half of the '90s, especially in the context of Rabbi Pearce's collegial, collaborative style of team leadership, may be a contributing factor in the evolution of the temple as a warm and nurturing environment. Connectedness, an ethics of care, and the wish to make synagogue life less hierarchical have each been identified by scholars (albeit drawing largely upon anecdotal evidence) as values that tend to be championed more by women than men; in any case, they are all explicit goals of the entire Emanu-El staff.

Mintz, bringing up a small child, raises a more tangible women's issue: a rabbi who is also a mother balancing the needs of the synagogue with those of her family. Aware of the fact that her predecessor resigned precisely because of the difficulties of reconciling these demands, she is determined to succeed both as a full-time congregational rabbi and as a parent. It may be that the increasing proportion of female rabbis, both across the country and at Emanu-El, will change the prevailing expectation that for a member of the clergy the congregation will always come before the family. Just as Pearce has consciously redefined the role of the senior rabbi, his female colleagues may succeed in altering long-held notions about the rabbinate as well.

IN MANY RESPECTS, Cantor Barak is the member of the clergy with the strongest link to the congregation's fabled past. Now well into her second decade of service, she has the longest tenure of anyone on the management staff. Far more important, though, is the role she consciously plays as the guardian of the temple's extraordinary musical heritage.

Barak serves in a position previously occupied by some of the greatest cantors in American history, and, like them, is not only an exceptional talent but also a passionate and skillful advocate for synagogue music with "a sound like no other." She is committed to opening the gates of the temple to experimental composers, but unwilling to jettison the overall style—dignified and decorous, powerful and profound—that has characterized the music at Emanu-El for well over a century. She has written that continuing this proud legacy depends upon "the employment of choirs, … first class organists, and…trained, invested cantors."

Like her distinguished predecessors, she has commissioned new music for the synagogue. The successful Shabbat service of Ben Steinberg, performed in 1990, was followed in the Pearce years by two important works by the Southern California-based Ami Aloni. For Alvin Fine's eightieth birthday, a joyful event celebrated in the main sanctuary in 1996, the composer set to music the rabbi's fervent "Birth Is a Beginning," with a fluid, melodic piece for organ and cello.

On the same afternoon, the audience of over a thousand of Fine's well-wishers was also treated to one of Aloni's seven "Haftarot of Consolation." Commissioned by Barak, the piece was made possible by a gift from an adoring Sisterhood in recognition of her seventh year with the temple. She asked Aloni—who had been raised in an Orthodox home in Israel—to compose music for all seven of these comforting passages from the Book of Isaiah which mourn the destruction of the First Temple.* Even as he interpreted the prophet's response to the catastrophe, Aloni, also a jazz pianist and a writer of film scores for Hollywood, provided some lighthearted moments. But his work, like that of Steinberg before him, was based on the deep meaning of the text and was built upon a centuries-old tradition of synagogue music. "I wanted to enhance the

---

*The Haftarot of Consolation are read in succession at each of the Shabbat services following Tisha B'av, the solemn day commemorating the loss of Solomon's temple.

experience of prayer," Aloni recently said of his pieces for the temple, "and I would never want to lose sight of the past."

Sacred music, though, is only one element of a program under Barak's direction that has been the envy of synagogues across North America. She has brought to the temple renowned choirs from Russia and Japan, arranged for countless recitals and chamber concerts, and invited popular singers ranging from Debbie Friedman and Julie Silver to the vocal group Safam. There has been a festival of klezmer (Yiddish folk music) virtually every year, as well as numerous opportunities to hear cabaret and Broadway show tunes, often performed by the versatile Barak herself.

As in the past, a number of the congregation's leading families have come forward not only to underwrite individual concerts, but to endow the remarkably rich musical program as a whole. Beginning in the early '90s, two brothers, Drs. Ben and A. Jess Shenson, distinguished themselves as the temple's leading patrons of great music. The highly respected physicians, both graduates of Lowell High School and Stanford Medical School, were inseparable. Until Ben's death in 1995, they lived together for many decades in a spectacular Nob Hill home where they displayed their outstanding collection of Asian art. Well known for their wide-

LEFT: CANTOR BARAK AND COMPOSER AMI ALONI IN THE TEMPLE COURTYARD
RIGHT: CANTOR BARAK AND ORGANIST DAVID HIGGS (LEFT) MEET WITH
DRS. BEN AND A. JESS SHENSON TO CELEBRATE THE ESTABLISHMENT
OF THEIR MUSIC ENDOWMENT FUND

ranging philanthropy, they made a sizeable contribution to the temple in 1992—a big boost during a hard year for the synagogue—both to repair the great organ in the main sanctuary and to purchase a new one for the renovated Martin Meyer Sanctuary. Their endowed fund, which they established in memory of their parents, was also used to sponsor musical events at Emanu-El for the rest of the decade, including annual concerts dedicated to the late Ben.

The Shensons also voiced their deep personal admiration for Barak, whose career flowered in the '90s. She was well received at the UAHC Biennial, held in San Francisco in 1993, both as the cantor for the convention's main Shabbat service and as a performer in a special concert at the temple featuring some of the most eminent cantors in the country. In the same year, she sang and taught at the American Jewish Choral Festival at the Concord Hotel in New York's Catskill Mountains, and was soon appointed a permanent member of the festival's faculty, appearing regularly at the prestigious week-long summer institute. She traveled to Germany in 1995 to participate in an interfaith festival of religious music held in a Benedictine monastery in Munich, and was prominently featured in the recording made of the performance. The following year her own CD, *The Jewish Soul*, was released. Presenting liturgical music, Yiddish songs, and Israeli tunes, it captures the marvelous strength and flexibility of her operatic voice.

But even while her stature has grown, she has been increasingly concerned about the near revolution that has shaken Reform synagogue music in recent years. She takes a dim view of the rise of informal services across the country, with their folk tunes and guitar accompaniment. She laments the worshippers' new "fondness for camp music, for banal melodies which make everybody feel 'good' but not at all uplifted," and concurs with a critic who has dubbed this style "Have a nice day, God."

At the beginning of the '90s, as the "accessible" began to replace the "awe-inspiring" at many Reform congregations, Barak wrote an incisive column in the *Temple Chronicle* about the "musical crisis":

> The focus is [now] on folk, or folk-rock, or vaguely off-Broadway, or Chassidic *niggunim* with their endless refrains of "bim, bam, ya ba bai biddi biddi bam." I am not saying that this can't be fun, or even spiritual at times, to chant syllables along with everyone, with hands held and

eyes closed—but do we really believe this can replace the glorious tradition of the Reform synagogue?...To accommodate our children's
feelings of comfort in the temple, we employ more trendy tunes and
use the guitar, for this is acceptable to them and more in keeping with
their own experience of worship services at Jewish camps. However, as
adults, it is hoped we have grown to realize that the worship of the
God of Israel should be elevated to a higher plane.

This is not to say that she is displeased with communal singing. Indeed,
she welcomes audience participation: "There's nothing more depressing
than a silent congregation, especially for me, because I grew up in an
Orthodox synagogue with the constant noise of davening; it's frustrating
not to hear people, especially during a tune where there's a congregational
refrain." She is gratified that there has been more singing in her Friday
evening service, in the Meyer Sanctuary, but is disappointed with the
dearth of people lifting their voices on Saturday mornings, under the great
dome, where "they feel overwhelmed." When there is no Bar or Bat
Mitzvah, the Saturday morning service is now usually held in the more
intimate Meyer Sanctuary. But it may be that the professional choir—in
the Emanu-El tradition, comprised of some of the best voices in the city—
unwittingly acts as a stumbling block to congregational participation.

Barak, responding to the desire of many a congregant to sing the inspiring choral music, formed a volunteer choir in 1992. Later called Kol
Emanu-El, the group performs at Friday evening services once a month
and at many other congregational events. The dedicated choir of about
twenty has also given numerous recitals throughout the Bay Area, including one at Grace Cathedral in 1995 at a celebration marking the
founding of the United Nations in San Francisco fifty years earlier.

The volunteer choir has also been a means for the cantor to guide
promising young singers hoping to make a career in Jewish music. In the
mid-'90s, Margaret Bruner came under Barak's wing not only as a member of Kol Emanu-El, but also as an adult Bat Mitzvah student. "As soon
as I met Roz, one door after another opened for me," she recalled, and
within a few years she entered HUC's School of Sacred Music in New
York. In the summers of 1997 and 1998, while still a student, she
returned to her native Bay Area to substitute for her mentor while Barak
was in Israel. These were opportunities for Bruner to perform the classic

Reform repertoire, she said, "music that [she had] studied at school, but that is sung in few places anymore."

Since 1992, Emanu-El's organist has been Charles Rus, a deeply spiritual man from an Episcopal background who spent a year preparing for the exacting job before succeeding his young friend, the renowned David Higgs. The mix of liturgical music presented by Barak and Rus, a blend of choral and solo compositions and classical and contemporary pieces, is much more heterogeneous than that of Joseph Portnoy and Ludwig Altman. While often selecting time-honored giants such as Lewandowski, Freed, Shalit, Helftman, and Binder, they also bring in some of the best composers working today, innovative artists such as Steinberg and Aloni, of course, and Meir Finkelstein and Michael Isaacson. Even the work of Debbie Friedman, the songwriter most identified with the loose new style of folk music for the synagogue, is heard on occasion.

Barak has also welcomed the removal of some of the Classical Reform trappings from the worship experience, something that "was bound to happen," she notes, because "the younger people were not comfortable with them." Even some of the older lay leaders have been discomfited by the playing of "My Country 'Tis of Thee," for example. While this has continued on Yom Kippur (when the cantor segues into a Sephardi rendition of "Oseh Shalom"), the patriotic hymn ceased being a part of the Sabbath service with Barak's arrival in 1987.

Five years later, Mark Schiftan, as interim senior rabbi, became the first spiritual leader at Emanu-El in more than a century to wear a *kippah* on the *bimah*, a custom continued by Helen Cohn, Peretz Wolf-Prusan, and Sidney Mintz. Further concessions were made toward a more normative Jewish service with the appointment of Rabbi Pearce, who is "much more accommodating" in this regard, Barak says, than Kirschner had been. The Saturday morning service now has *aliyot* during a Bar or Bat Mitzvah, if the family requests them; up to four individuals (or couples) may be called up to the *bimah* to read the Torah blessings. Reflecting a change in many Reform congregations during the past few years, prayers such as the *V'ahavta*, the *Aleinu*, and the *Avot* are now chanted in a traditional style. Often the reader's *kaddish* is chanted as well, a prayer that was not even recited before the late 1970s. Perhaps the most visible innovation, begun by Barak's Anshei Mitzvah classes, is that of marching up and down the aisles of the main sanctuary with the Torah scrolls, a rite that is also practiced when congregants request it for the Bar or Bat Mitzvah of a child. Moreover, Barak is training a handful of members to read or even chant the Torah, and she looks forward to the day when they will lead part of the service on a regular basis.

These are not insignificant changes, but the essence of the service, especially on Saturday morning, is largely the same as it was a generation ago. It is viewed by many primarily as a performance—brilliantly conceived and executed, and full of majesty and power—but nonetheless at odds, to some extent, with the younger generation's hunger for more participation.

Given the sea change in Reform liturgy across the country, and the premium placed on experimentation at Emanu-El, questions have naturally arisen about the place of the Classical Reform service among the temple's many priorities. Every one of Barak's colleagues on the management staff expresses pride in working alongside one of the leading Reform cantors in America, but several of them have wondered aloud about the future of the Saturday morning service in its present form. Without a Bar Mitzvah, the attendance can dip well below a hundred; staff members question whether that justifies the participation of a professional choir and an organist on those occasions. The board of directors has addressed this delicate issue as well, with some of the members contending at one meeting that "even though the music is more complex and interesting with the professional choir, it [does not offer] a participatory role for the congregation. [It] is quite steeped in [Reform] tradition but doesn't necessarily represent the broad congregational view of today."

The fact remains that except for its exquisite architecture, nothing distinguishes Emanu-El more than its august music—the soul of the synagogue, in a sense. And precisely because the Classical Reform service is unique in Northern California, it fills an important niche and will likely always have a constituency. Rabbi Pearce agrees; his notion of the "synaplex" makes it possible for the grandeur of the past to coexist with the changing tastes of the present. To use another metaphor, Cantor Barak's magnificently rendered work may perhaps be compared to a rare jewel. It has lost none of its luster, but it is no longer the only one in the crown.

JUST AS THE MODE OF WORSHIP at the temple has been put to the test by new trends and preferences, so has Jewish education been deeply affected by altered attitudes. Peretz Wolf-Prusan, who assumed the newly created post of rabbi-educator in 1990, knew that the lay leadership "was looking for a change" and that he had not been engaged "to keep the status quo." For despite the vitality of the Kirschner years, the academic standing of the religious school still lagged behind those of other local congregations. Many of the baby boomers who had grown up at Emanu-El—notwithstanding the admiration they felt for the temple clergy—felt deprived by the inadequate training they had received and wanted something better for their children and themselves.

Wolf-Prusan has worked on many levels to raise the level of Jewish content, not in an attempt "to go backward to Orthodoxy," as he recently put it, but rather "to go forward to competency." Appalled at the low level of Hebrew proficiency that he found among the students, he chose to integrate the language into the entire curriculum, introducing key words as early as kindergarten. He no longer permits parents to register their children solely in the Sunday school to avoid the Hebrew instruction that was given in the mid-week sessions. Not all were pleased with the change, but the rabbi remained firm: "Families called up and asked, 'Why are my kids doing Hebrew and not ethics?' I said, 'Because there's no such word as ethics in Hebrew. *Mitzvah, tzedakah, g'milut hasidim*—that's how Jews discuss social justice.'" Some parents even had objections to the core curriculum of the fourth grade being "The Land and People of Israel." To that complaint, Peretz dryly answered, "We study it because this is the twentieth century."

From the beginning, he focused on family education, "the heart and soul of our educational program," offering parallel tracks for parents and children followed by joint study sessions. On Sundays, family members worship together before their morning of study. On weekday evenings, an hour of learning is followed by a communal dinner. Families with children in the school are required to attend several of these programs during the year; if the parents cannot participate, Wolf-Prusan welcomes adult siblings, aunts, uncles, and grandparents.

Education at the temple has been enriched in other respects as well. The rabbi launched an extensive arts camp for the summer and winter

RABBI WOLF-PRUSAN EXPLAINS THE *HAVDALAH* CEREMONY

RABBI WOLF-PRUSAN DISCUSSES *TZEDAKAH* WITH A CLASS OF EIGHTH-GRADERS

vacation periods, established the Youth Mitzvah Corps to involve students in community service projects, and reinvigorated the high school by joining forces with two other congregations, Sherith Israel and the Conservative Beth Sholom.

Nothing has changed more than the Bar and Bat Mitzvah program, however. Before the 1990s it was rare for a youngster to attempt more than a few lines of Torah. The verses were memorized from tapes and many students also relied on transliterations. Parental involvement in the process was minimal. Peretz, working closely with Cantor Barak, has succeeded in endowing the rite of passage with far greater meaning, an important goal for Stephen Pearce as well. As the senior rabbi recently wrote in the *Jewish Spectator*, "Each ceremony is touching in its own special way. Each may hold a secret power that we may not know about for years to come, if ever."

There is now a two-year schedule of preparation, including nine months of study with one of the synagogue's four rabbis as well as the cantor. The child not only reads ten to fifteen verses of Torah, and a considerable amount of the *haftarah*, but also delivers a three- to five-page speech on his or her Torah portion. This is a key feature of the program, as Wolf-Prusan explains with his usual directness: "I can teach a clever dog to chant the blessings," he says, but the *D'var Torah*, as the presentation is called, "is really a test of a thirteen-year-old's ability, motivation, and willingness to struggle with the text. They don't have to agree with it, they don't have to like it, but they have to struggle with it."

The youngster is also required to complete eighteen *mitzvot*, good deeds that are often in the realm of community service. Along with their child, the parents study the Torah portion with the "guide rabbi" for a minimum of three sessions. They participate in the Friday evening service the night before the Bar or Bat Mitzvah, and they may speak at the Saturday morning ceremony as well. As recently as a decade and a half ago, roughly one out of every three Emanu-El households with a thirteen-year-old child chose not to celebrate the Bar or Bat Mitzvah. Today, no doubt due to the importance attached to it by Wolf-Prusan and his colleagues, the level of participation is nearly 100 percent.

The improved training is reflected in the confirmation ceremony for tenth-graders. On the morning of Shavuot in 1998, almost half of the twenty-six confirmands read the Torah or *haftarah* with the traditional cantillation. "These are our kids," Peretz beamed, noting that nearly all of them had benefited from the strong curriculum he had developed during the decade, as well as the high standards set by Cantor Barak. He is also justifiably proud that the school has roughly doubled in size since the mid-1980s, to an enrollment of about five hundred.

An additional 150 children attend the preschool. In 1995, Gary Cohn, working with temple board vice-president Ann Blumlein Lazarus, completed a three-year process of separating the school from the San Francisco Jewish Community Center. They retained the preschool's talented founder, Pam Schneider, who became the temple's director of early childhood education and a member of the management staff. She took over the "Building Blocks" program for infants up to eighteen months, which Peretz had created earlier, and also inaugurated "Stepping Up," for children of nineteen months to two-and-a-half years, both of which require the child to be accompanied by a parent. The preschool itself, enrolling children up to age five and a half, offers five other programs, all of them emphasizing learning as an interactive process.

Independence from the JCC gave the veteran educator Schneider—under the guidance of both Gary Cohn and Wolf-Prusan—a freer hand in developing the popular institution that now has a long waiting list for admissions. Its staff has grown to twenty-four, and its annual budget to more than $600,000, comprising about a sixth of the temple's entire operation. Perhaps most impressive is the active parents association, which raises funds for scholarships, special equipment, staff development, and parent education programs.

Financially self-sustaining, the preschool has been a boon for the temple. About three-quarters of the children enrolled come from Jewish homes, but roughly half of these families are intermarried and not infrequently have tenuous ties to Judaism. So it is important that, in addition to a solid early childhood curriculum, Jewish values, traditions, holiday celebrations, and songs form a major part of the learning experience of both the children and their parents. Schneider, who recently left her post to become the temple's membership services director, was highly conscious of this while head of the preschool: "We have a responsibility to bring them into the fold, so to speak, in a very safe, non-threatening way. Sometimes what happens in the preschool can make or break it for families in terms of their commitment to Judaism and the temple."

The immense success of the preschool led many at Emanu-El to consider the establishment of a Jewish day school. With 95 percent of the preschoolers going on to private elementary education, it was clear that a feeder for a day school already existed under the synagogue's roof. For a while in the mid-'90s it appeared that this would be the next great project of the temple that had taken on so much in the past decade.

Rabbi Kirschner had opposed the concept during his tenure (and still does today) because of his unwavering commitment to public education. Despite the endorsement of Reform day schools by the Union of American Hebrew Congregations in 1985, he has argued that Jews should fight to improve the nation's beleaguered public school systems, not abandon them.

But Rabbi Pearce took the opposite view, and forcefully advocated it from the pulpit on Rosh Hashanah Eve in 1994. He articulated the arguments that were most compelling in the minds of the day school's proponents—that it would both stem the exodus of young Jews from the city and infuse the temple with an energetic cadre of new members.

> One thing I can tell you is that Jewish families continue to flee the city to the suburbs because many believe that their children cannot be assured of a place for quality education....If we hope to stabilize the Jewish population of San Francisco, we have no choice but to proceed. The day school movement is spreading through most urban Reform congregations in this country. Most report a resurgence of temple membership and the development of a core of parents and families deeply committed to synagogue life.

Most congregants supported Pearce's position, but many were surprised that the new rabbi had issued such a bold challenge. It was well known that a number of Emanu-El's most influential lay leaders had been on record against the concept of Jewish day schools in general, to say nothing of opening one under the auspices of the temple. The Orthodox Hebrew Academy, founded in 1964 by the strident East European immigrant Rabbi Pinchas Lipner, had often been at odds with powerful temple members such as Mel Swig, Peter Haas, Frances Green, and Richard Goldman in their capacity as Federation presidents in the 1970s and early '80s. Although they reluctantly came around to the view that Lipner's school was deserving of an annual allocation, they expressed fears that the day school movement could lead to separatism and even, as Goldman then put it, "ghettoize" the Jewish community.

Yet by the 1990s, a day school seemed squarely in line with the temple's priorities. "Harnessing the energy" of hundreds of young families, in Gary Cohn's words, was an attractive proposition. During the seven-year period of a child's elementary education, he noted, the school and the synagogue would necessarily become an important part of the parents' lives as well. The result would be more knowledgeable and active Jews and more "invested" and loyal temple members.

The scale of the venture was daunting, requiring an initial outlay of several million dollars to create an institution which one day might have an operating budget almost as large as that of the temple itself. Moreover, the project faced a hurdle which most of the two dozen Reform day schools already in existence did not have to surmount: because of strict city regulations, the school could not be housed in the temple; a suitable off-site location near the synagogue would have to be found. But while "the challenges in starting up...[were] overwhelming," as one observer opined, the late '80s and early '90s had proven that ambition was not in short supply at Emanu-El.

Events moved rapidly during the year that followed Pearce's sermon. In May 1995, a feasibility study commissioned by the temple and prepared by Dr. Gary Tobin concluded that there was substantial demand for a Reform day school. A telephone survey of one hundred families with children in one of the Jewish Community Center's network of nursery schools during the prior four years revealed that 61 percent would have been "interested" or "very interested" in sending their child to a day school at Emanu-El had one existed.* Two-thirds of the sample expressed their unwillingness to spend more than twenty minutes driving their

*Bearing out Rabbi Pearce's contention in the fall of 1994, more than half of the respondents indicated that schools had been an "important" or "very important" factor in their choice of residence, and half of this group indicated that they planned on moving out of San Francisco within the next three years.

child to school. This seemed to mitigate the attractiveness for many families of the liberal, nondenominational Brandeis Hillel Day School, a large and well-regarded institution located on the periphery of the traffic-clogged city.

The study also analyzed five day schools at comparable Reform congregations across the country and in each case found a "major beneficial qualitative impact on synagogue life." Quoting responses such as "invigorating," "energizing," "rejuvenating," and "lending vitality," Tobin asserted that "the day school helps build community around the synagogue." He pointed out a range of advantages, including the congregational leaders that had come from the ranks of day school parents, the increased attendance and enthusiasm at services resulting from the involvement of these families, and not least of all the special attraction for interfaith households seeking to raise their children as Jews: mixed couples, he found, tended to rely on the day school to provide the "Jewish knowledge and competence" that they themselves often lacked.

Close on the heels of Tobin's positive report came an initial gift for the creation of the day school, $500,000. The donor (who for several years preferred to be anonymous) was a Holocaust survivor, Dr. Lazlo Tauber of Washington, D.C., a prominent surgeon and real estate developer. He made the gift in honor of his daughter, Ingrid Tauber, a refined, soft-spoken psychologist who had joined the temple in the mid-'80s, one of the many baby boomers drawn in by Rabbi Kirschner's commitment to social action. She studied with Cantor Barak to become an adult Bat Mitzvah, joined the board in 1994, and championed the day school as a means of strengthening Reform Judaism in the generations to come.

A task force comprised of eighteen leading congregants, some of them with children in the preschool, was formed by the board to move the project forward. A two-year timeline was developed, which scheduled the opening of a kindergarten for the fall of 1997. Through a series of meetings, the task force sought to raise another half million dollars in start-up expenses and to develop the philosophy of the future Emanu-El Academy. While every effort would be made to provide secular studies of the highest quality, by far the primary concern of the preschool parents Tobin had queried, Judaica would not be slighted. As in other Reform day schools, Jewish studies would be "integrated" throughout the entire curriculum. "Everything would have a Jewish focus," says Ingrid Tauber, recalling the planners' early enthusiasm.

But by the end of the crowded year of 1995, the impetus to create a day school had lost its momentum, disappointing many. No further meetings of the task force were called and the project would be less and less frequently discussed during the rest of the decade. One reason for the reversal was the question of finances. Rhoda Goldman, who also had highly principled ideological reservations about the plan, expressed her concern at a board meeting that, with the temple still many millions of dollars in debt from the renovation, a huge undertaking such as a day school could be fiscally imprudent. President Stuart Aronoff quickly agreed. He has since expressed a willingness to "reopen" the day school issue, which he acknowledges as being one "of extreme importance to the congregation," but only when the synagogue is free of debt and has much stronger financial commitments for the project from its lay leaders. For Gary Cohn, a day school is inevitable: "I know we should have one; the writing's on the wall." Yet because it would need its own freestanding physical plant, he estimates an initial cost of at least five million dollars, a goal toward which the Tauber gift—welcome though it is—represents but a promising start.

Although he has termed the defeat of one of his most important initiatives "an unqualified failure," Rabbi Pearce is philosophical, stating that "a rabbi doesn't have to get everything he or she wants." But he feels that in shelving the day school "the congregation made a gross error," one that it will come to regret in the future.

Of course, the very fact that it received serious consideration is telling of the transformation of the temple since the mid-1980s, when such an initiative would have been inconceivable. But its failure as yet to materialize also shows the limits of change taking place at Emanu-El. The model of team leadership, so successful in other respects, may have undercut the senior rabbi's ability to impose his will on the congregation in the way that Fine and Kirschner had often done. Then, too, the recent memory of the overextended finances of the early '90s acted as a brake on such a large, open-ended project. Finally, concerns about abandoning the public schools—and these ought not to be dismissed as disingenuous—seemed to outweigh the desire to open a promising new avenue of Jewish continuity.

Rabbi Pearce, who was dealt this blow less than two years after his arrival in San Francisco, saw how formidable would be his struggle "to turn the congregation around."

THE SETBACK OVER THE DAY SCHOOL has not been the only difficulty for Pearce and his team. Although the response to their efforts has been largely positive, a very small but vocal group has been critical of the changes and anxious about the shape of the temple in the future. They tend to be older people, and not infrequently members of the pioneer families. Some still have fond recollections of Kirschner, who had cultivated this set in particular. They miss his boyish charm, his intellectual gravitas, and above all his inspiring sermons. They also voice the sort of complaints that even the greatest pulpit rabbis sometimes hear from congregants—ranging from a seating mix-up separating a member from his friends and family during the High Holidays, to an error in scheduling precluding the rabbi from attending an important community event in its entirety.

More importantly, some of the longtime San Franciscans, dubbed the "ancient mariners" by the Southern Californian Stuart Aronoff, disagree with the direction the temple has taken in the Pearce years. They feel its aggressive marketing ventures are undignified, its outreach to new constituencies unwarranted, its emphasis on alternative services unnecessary. In sum, they feel that "the temple is doing too much," that it has evolved into an institution resembling a high-powered Jewish Community Center more than a synagogue. They are also left cold by the mysticism and meditation courses, by the increasing amount of Hebrew in the school curriculum, and by the removal of more and more of the Classical Reform trappings from the Saturday morning service. A couple of them still question the wisdom of hiring an openly lesbian assistant rabbi.

Rabbi Pearce is anything but unmindful of the temple's history and its distinctive place in the American Reform movement and the city of San Francisco. He has written no fewer than eighteen articles on the synagogue's heritage in the *Temple Chronicle*, and has made a point of honoring the luminaries of the past. He was instrumental in naming the choir and organ loft for Ludwig Altman, in arranging for Alvin Fine to receive the title of "rabbi laureate," and in holding a dinner at the temple

celebrating the award of an honorary doctorate in music to Cantor Portnoy. Pearce has also paid tribute to longtime members at special Shabbat
services. Moreover, he feels that with his "synaplex" model, the old guard
may continue to experience a familiar service even while the temple
introduces new options for the younger generation.

But he is nevertheless committed to change, even if it is "assaultive" to
some, in order to ensure the viability of the institution in the new century.
In a hard-hitting sermon on the eve of Rosh Hashanah in 1997, he defended his "controversial" programs as "the ultimate response to the
message of the Jewish past: change or die!"

But what is the likelihood that Pearce and his colleagues can continue
to recast the temple, changing it from Rabbi Asher's notion of an opera
house to that of a synaplex, moving it, so to speak, from "high church" to
"mega-church"?

For the history of the temple is not an unbroken trajectory toward
inclusiveness and innovation. Rather, one sees an oscillation between
periods of expansion and consolidation. Throughout the entire twentieth century, each of the eras of growth, democratization, and relatively
normative Judaism was followed by an equally long phase of contraction,
elitism, and reaffirmation of Classical Reform, an echo of the Voorsanger
period, which often distanced the congregation from the larger Jewish
community.

Interestingly enough, these cycles—each one a bit shy of twenty years
in length—ran their course even when there was a sudden departure of the
senior rabbi. Martin Meyer's impressive outreach efforts, begun in 1910,
were continued after his suicide with no less ardor by his protégé Louis
Newman, who served until 1930. But Irving Reichert's seventeen years
reversed this course, with a rabbinate rejecting Jewish nationalism, ethnicity, and culture. Then the popular Alvin Fine, appointed in 1948, renewed
the spirit of Meyer and Newman with his Zionist and neo-Reform orientation. Yet after Irving Hausman's brief tenure, Fine was followed by
Joseph Asher, who—somewhat like Voorsanger and Reichert—maintained
Classical Reform Judaism even at the risk of shrinking membership rolls
and the antipathy of key segments of the rest of the community. The
third era of dynamism in the century began with Robert Kirschner in
1985; not unlike Meyer's suicide, his precipitous fall could not stem the

vigor and progress of his six and a half years—bold experimentation and rapid expansion have continued under Rabbi Pearce and his team.

The Meyer-Newman, Fine, and Kirschner-Pearce periods, each a generation apart, are the rabbinates of innovators: native-born men, most of them very young and from the Pacific Coast, who through ambitious initiatives sought to enlarge the temple and make it more diverse, to build or renovate the physical plant, and to put the congregation in sync with the great changes taking place in American Jewish life. The Voorsanger, Reichert, and Hausman-Asher eras, also each a generation apart, are characterized by leadership of no less strength, dedication, and intellectual rigor. But these older and mostly foreign-born rabbis are more properly thought of as guardians—protectors of a distinctive Emanu-El style which crystallized in the late nineteenth century. Their vision of Reform Judaism emphasized elegance, erudition, and generally a universalistic theology revolving around prophetic ethics. The Congregation Emanu-El of the guardians tended to be relatively small and homogeneous, and at times combative in tone toward various elements of San Francisco Jewry.

Of course the outlook of the senior rabbi was hardly the only factor accounting for the congregation's alternating posture. It is the lay leaders who select the rabbi in the first place; at times they have terminated his contract as well. Their support, or lack of it, for rabbinical initiatives has often been decisive, and at times they have imposed their own vision on Emanu-El. Individuals such as Henry Seligman and Martin Heller in the nineteenth century, and Harold Zellerbach, Walter Newman, and Rhoda Goldman in the twentieth, were indispensable in shaping the institution. Indeed, Zellerbach and Newman, in 1948 and 1985, respectively, were instrumental in replacing one senior rabbi with another, thus helping to inaugurate a long period of innovation.

Moreover, the lay people and the clergy must be seen in a context both global and local. While Reichert's rabbinate was constrained by the Depression and World War II, for example, clearly the Fine years were enhanced by postwar prosperity and the baby boom. By the same token, Asher's era was negatively affected by the exodus to the suburbs, while Kirschner and Pearce have benefited from the revitalization of the city and a return to spirituality among young families in particular. The vicissitudes of the national Reform movement and the ebb and flow of competing Jewish institutions, most notably the Federation and Congregation Sherith Israel, also enter into the equation.

Complex as this picture is, we are nevertheless left with a marked periodicity in the temple's history, a fluctuation in the balance of power almost every two decades. It is a swing of the pendulum between those who would affirm the late-nineteenth-century vision of the Bavarian families who founded the congregation, and those who would fundamentally depart from it.

If this schema is still operable we should expect a retrenchment early in the new century and a spirited defense of the vestiges of Classical Reform Judaism that still remain. Yet that is actually one of the least likely of all scenarios. The turn in the direction of the temple since the mid-1980s is so pronounced, the changes in the Reform movement—and indeed in American religious life—so thoroughgoing, the financial needs of the institution so great, that Emanu-El cannot in the foreseeable future return to a limited and monochromatic mission. It must continue to cast as broad a net as possible in reaching new constituencies; it must continue to be open to new expressions of Jewish identity.

Comparable Reform synagogues around the country—Emanu-El of Dallas is perhaps the best example—have undergone a similar experience in the 1980s and '90s. Many of the large urban congregations, founded by German Jews in the nineteenth century and, for most of their history, bastions of Classical Reform, have built midsized sanctuaries, introduced alternative services, and encouraged the participation of an ever-widening number of subgroups. Responding to the spiritual needs of the younger generation of "seekers," in particular, they have experimented creatively with music, liturgy, and adult education.

In San Francisco, those in the old guard who resist this model are aging, and their children, mostly baby boomers, generally feel less passionate about maintaining the status quo. Moreover, the longtime members, respected and influential though they are, constitute a declining percentage of the congregation as a whole. Recent statistics reveal that no fewer than 42 percent of the membership joined the temple in the years following the departure of Rabbi Kirschner at the beginning of 1992. Only 28 percent of the congregants belonged before 1970.

But there are far greater reasons to say that there will be no going back to the way things were before 1985. Much of the transformation on Lake Street, especially in the second half of the 1990s, may be seen as the temple's response to powerful social forces, perhaps even stronger on the West Coast than elsewhere, which have profoundly affected organized religion along with virtually everything else in our society.

One of the most important of these "catalysts," in the words of historian Jack Wertheimer, is a "spirit of religious individualism which encourages every person to make a personal choice about religious involvement." Sociologists often refer to this as a shift from "ascribed" to "achieved" identity, ascription meaning values that are innate or inherited, achievement designating individual choice and action. Put another way, it is the difference between religious practice justified by the statement "That's who I am" or "That's the way I was brought up," on the one hand, and "I am getting something meaningful out of this," on the other. At its most extreme, it can be the difference between regarding the synagogue as a nagging obligation (as many old-timers admitted they once had) and seeing it as a source of spiritual refreshment. A leading authority on contemporary American religion almost seems to have Temple Emanu-El in mind when he writes,

> The shift from ascription to achievement in congregations means that a greater sense of individual ownership and responsibility is likely to follow. Taking part in something that has "always been done this way" can be a deadening experience compared with doing something because one chooses it....The quality of programs, as well as the level of fervor, is likely to increase when people take the view that they have chosen to do this so they had better do it well.

If "choice" is so vital, naturally a great array of options must be offered, which in turn draws people from more and more segments of the population. Feminists and gays, converts and non-Jews, émigrés and poor people, young parents and old pensioners are all amply represented under the dome. They study subjects ranging from meditation to Talmud; they worship to the sound of a mighty organ or a lively guitar; they participate in community service projects or a spiritual retreat in the woods.

Not surprisingly, the criticism has been raised that the temple "is trying to be all things to all people," that the "synaplex" of Rabbi Pearce and

his team is a "smorgasbord," lacking a unifying theme other than pluralism itself. Indeed ideological coherence is not the strong suit of today's
pragmatic and eclectic Emanu-El. And perhaps the greatest challenge for
the temple in the new century will be to avoid the fragmentation, if not
balkanization, that can threaten a large congregation comprised of so
many disparate constituencies and spiritual preferences. Before 1985,
boundaries of class, and to some extent age and ethnicity, often separated
Emanu-El from the rest of San Francisco Jewry; today, social differences
exist *within* the synagogue as never before. Maintaining a sense of communal cohesiveness will no doubt be a major test.

Yet the day-to-day vitality of the temple in recent years strongly sug-
gests that it has been on the right track in responding to the new direction
in Jewish life. A keen observer who heads an interdenominational project
known as "Synagogue 2000," Professor Lawrence Hoffman of Hebrew
Union College, has indicated several ways in which synagogues need to
"overcome...outmoded habits of thought" if they are to flourish in the
future; his ideas are very similar to those of the temple leadership. Stressing that we live in a "new world where religious identity is elective," he
sees the old concept of ethnic Jewish solidarity as "a thing of the past,"
giving way to spirituality, a passionate seeking for meaning and belonging. In this connection, he argues that "liturgy in the 1990s that sounds
like the 1960s should be suspect." He also urges far-reaching changes in
the way the synagogue is structured and "how it feels to be there. Beyond
the coldness [there lies] a place where people feel welcome, connected
and spiritually alive." Two groups in particular, he feels, will enrich the
synagogue of tomorrow: women and "Jews by choice."

Hoffman, who has influenced the thinking of both Rabbi Pearce and
Executive Director Gary Cohn and who has consulted with the entire
management staff, has himself been impressed by the long strides taken at
the temple to renew itself throughout the 1990s: "In an age that makes
even 'future shock' seem commonplace, synagogues will rise or fall with
their ability to thrive on innovation," he says, "and Emanu-El has demonstrated a phenomenal capacity to take the need for change seriously."

Rabbi Pearce, in discussing the complex dialectic between continuity
and change taking place at Emanu-El, typically employs a parable to

penetrate his listeners' psychological defenses: "When Rabbi Noah, Rabbi Mordecai's son, assumed the succession after his father's death, his disciples noticed that there were a number of ways in which he conducted himself differently from his father, and they asked him about this. 'I do just as my father did,' he replied. 'He did not imitate and I do not imitate.'"

In sum, Pearce and his team stand in a line of innovators going back to Martin Meyer. Their vision of a synagogue that is inclusive and accessible, diverse and dynamic, is a twenty-first-century version of the "Temple of the Open Door" first envisioned when the incomparable Lake Street temple was conceived eighty years ago.

But in another sense, today's Emanu-El may be placed on a continuum that goes back even further, to the founding of the congregation during the Gold Rush. For while the visions of Reform have greatly differed during a period of seven generations and eleven senior rabbis, the overall aim has been the same: to adapt an ancient faith to contemporary reality, to modify Judaism in order to preserve it. This has been the goal of the guardians no less than the innovators. Indeed, the Classical Reform Judaism that Jacob Voorsanger built upon the foundations laid by Elkan Cohn was nothing if not a daring experiment, an "alternative to assimilation" responding to the culture of the late nineteenth century. That it was later in need of reform itself should not detract from its initial inventiveness and flexibility. Even in the twentieth century, those rabbis who were conservators in the area of prayer and praxis were also among the most courageous voices for social justice in the temple's history.

The guardians and the innovators, then, have their similarities as well as their differences. In virtually every period of the synagogue's experience, one finds artistic creativity and scholarly excellence, pastoral dedication and community involvement. All of it has gone into the creation of a special setting for worship and life-cycle events, for educational, cultural, and spiritual enrichment. The temple has had its share of adversity and yet enjoys the passionate loyalty of countless members of all backgrounds, for whom it is a primary locus of meaning and purpose in their lives.

The singular spirit of the synagogue has perhaps best been captured by its oldest living president, Louis Heilbron, now well into his nineties, who recently reflected upon the temple's sesquicentennial:

I think of the majestic dome, one of the centers of the city; the great windows of "Fire" and "Water" filtering the sunlight and lighting the pews; the precious, jeweled Ark of the Covenant; the quiet Rinder Chapel; the main sanctuary as the crowning successor of a twin-towered former house of worship. I think of the eloquent rabbis of Reform who have preached here about great issues: of Judaism and of our times, and of responsible personal conduct and social action; of the cantors and choir who have sung the music of the ages, and of Bloch and Lavry; of impressive confirmations, bright weddings, and compassionate memorials. I think of more than seven generations of congregants beginning with the creation of the state of California and the city of San Francisco and growing and interacting with both for close to 150 years. I recall many of those leaders and their lasting contributions to the Jewish and general community, to philanthropy, and to interfaith understanding and cooperation. And I think of the children playing in the courtyard who will carry on the traditions of the temple through most of the twenty-first century.

At one hundred and fifty, Congregation Emanu-El has attained something rare in the American West: a seamless continuity overlaying its many cycles of change, a sense of permanence even as it reinvents itself.

Abbreviations

Am. Israel.	*American Israelite* (Cincinnati)
AJHQ	*American Jewish Historical Quarterly* (Waltham, Mass.)
Fine Papers	Papers of Alvin I. Fine, Western Jewish History Center, Judah L. Magnes Museum (Berkeley, Calif.)
JBNC	*Jewish Bulletin of Northern California* (San Francisco), formerly *NCJB*
NCJB	*Northern California Jewish Bulletin* (San Francisco), formerly *SFJB*
Newman Papers	Papers of Louis I. Newman, Western Jewish History Center, Judah L. Magnes Museum (Berkeley, Calif.)
Reichert Papers	Papers of Irving F. Reichert, Western Jewish History Center, Judah L. Magnes Museum (Berkeley, Calif.)
Reichert Sermons	Irving Reichert, *Judaism and the American Jew: The Sermons and Addresses of Irving Frederick Reichert* (San Francisco, 1953).
Rinder Papers	Papers of Reuben Rinder, Western Jewish History Center, Judah L. Magnes Museum (Berkeley, Calif.)
SFJB	*San Francisco Jewish Bulletin* (San Francisco)
Temp. Chron.	*Temple Chronicle of Temple Emanu-El* (San Francisco)
Temple Minutes	Minutes of Congregation Emanu-El, Temple Emanu-El Archives (San Francisco)
WJHC	Western Jewish History Center, Judah L. Magnes Museum (Berkeley, Calif.)
WSJH	*Western States Jewish History* (Santa Monica, Calif.), formerly WSJHQ
WSJHQ	*Western States Jewish Historical Quarterly* (Santa Monica, Calif.)

Notes

CHAPTER 1 / INSTANT METROPOLIS

1   fifteenth-largest city...sixth-busiest port: Peter R. Decker, *Fortunes and Failures: White-Collar Mobility in Nineteenth-Century San Francisco* (Cambridge, Mass., 1978), pp. 32–33.

1   "the ubiquitous Hebrews": Hubert Howe Bancroft, *The Works of Hubert Howe Bancroft*, vol. 23 (San Francisco, 1888), p. 222.

2   "spending half a year in a floating tenement": Kevin Starr, *Americans and the California Dream, 1850–1915* (New York, 1973), p. 52.

2   "numbered in the thousands...": Robert E. Levinson, *The Jews in the California Gold Rush* (New York, 1978), p. 4.

2   On the Polish origins of the Jews of Posen: Hasia R. Diner, *A Time for Gathering: The Second Migration, 1820–1880* (Baltimore, 1992), pp. 28–31; Norton B. Stern and William M. Kramer, "The Major Role of Polish Jews in the Pioneer West," *WSJHQ* 8 (July 1976): 326–44.

3   immigration as a "substitute for emancipation": Avraham Barkai, *Branching Out: German-Jewish Immigration to the United States, 1820–1914* (New York, 1994), p. 25.

3   poorer Jews in southern German states who "could neither work nor marry": Diner, *Time for Gathering*, p. 43.

4   first generation twice as likely as non-Jews to remain in the area permanently: Peter R. Decker, "Jewish Merchants in San Francisco: Social Mobility on the Urban Frontier," in Moses Rischin, ed., *The Jews of the West: The Metropolitan Years* (Berkeley, 1979), p. 21.

4   early Jewish businessmen rarely drank to excess and usually kept within the bounds of the law: Decker, *Fortunes and Failures*, pp. 115–16.

5   Of fifty-four cases of homicide, not one punished: Ibid., p. 121.

5   norms of behavior...were severely tested: Malcolm J. Rohrbough, *Days of Gold: The California Gold Rush and the American Nation* (Berkeley, 1997), p. 69–70.

5   On the role of pioneer women: Ibid., pp. 172–84.

5   writers on the Gold Rush, and the Jewish experience in particular: Harriet Rochlin and Fred Rochlin, *Pioneer Jews: A New Life in the Far West* (Boston, 1984), p. 98; Irena Narell, *Our City: The Jews of San Francisco* (San Diego, 1981), p. 124.

5   men outnumbered women 6.5 to 1: Decker, *Fortunes and Failures*, p. 211.

5*   demographic imbalance would right itself only gradually: Ibid.

5   "Through the mud and stink and immorality": Rohrbough, *Days of Gold*, p. 160.

6   first Jewish services on the West Coast: Norton B. Stern and William M. Kramer, "A Search for the First Synagogue in the Golden West," *WSJHQ* 7 (October 1974): 3–20.

6* another version of the first service places the site on Montgomery Street: Jacob Voorsanger, *The Chronicles of Emanu-El* (San Francisco, 1900), p. 16.

6* contemporary research authenticates the tent-room on Jackson: Stern and Kramer, "Search for the First Synagogue."

6–7 August Helbing quotation: Voorsanger, *Chronicles*, pp. 17–18; quoted in Leslie

Brenner and Ava F. Kahn, *Birth of a Community: Jews and the Gold Rush* (Berkeley, 1995), p. 50.

7   "cheering presence of…daughters of Judah": Voorsanger, *Chronicles*, p. 16.

7   Yom Kippur sermon delivered by Lewis Franklin: Lewis A. Franklin, "The First Jewish Sermon in the West: Yom Kippur, 1850, San Francisco." Reprinted in *WSJHQ* 10 (October 1977) and *WSJH* 25 (January 1993): 169–79.

7   presence in city of two kosher boardinghouses: Brenner and Kahn, *Birth of a Community*, p. 21.

8   serious rift between Eastern and Western Europeans on matters of liturgy: Stern and Kramer, "Search for the First Synagogue."

8   one of the factions…probably the Bavarians…walked out: I am grateful to the late Norton B. Stern for clarifying this point for me.

8   meeting called for April 6: Ibid; Stern and Kramer, "Search for the First Synagogue."

8   disagreements between Bavarians and Poseners were common: Leon A. Jick, *The Americanization of the Synagogue, 1820–1870* (Hanover, N.H., 1976), pp. 102–3.

9   one leading researcher uses the word "arrogance": Barkai, *Branching Out*, p. 98.

9   French Catholics worshipped apart from Irish…American-born Presbyterians divided: Roger W. Lotchin, *San Francisco, 1846–1856: From Hamlet to City* (Urbana, 1997), p. 129.

9*   controversy over oldest congregation…Voorsanger adamantly claimed distinction: Voorsanger, *Chronicles*, p. 19.

9*   two researchers convincingly demonstrated Voorsanger's conclusion was based on a misdated document: Stern and Kramer, "Search for the First Synagogue."

9   drafted a charter on April 8, and filed it with the county clerk three days later: Voorsanger, *Chronicles*, pp. 11–12.

9**   signers of the charter: Ibid., pp. 24–25.

9–10   recent study of the founders: Alan Silverstein, *Alternatives to Assimilation: The Response of Reform Judaism to American Culture, 1840–1930* (Hanover, N.H., 1994), pp. 13–14. Silverstein found a sample of twenty-five "founders" in the census records and city directories of 1860. At that time, nine years after the birth of the congregation, their average age was 31.2. Although several of the older founders, particularly the American-born Sephardim, may no longer have been in San Francisco by 1860, Silverstein's data is most useful.

10   Emanu-El began with sixty members, Sherith Israel with forty-two: Stern and Kramer, "Search for the First Synagogue," p. 12.

10   Emanu-El's "Constitution" of 1851: Voorsanger, *Chronicles*, pp. 26–28.

10–11   On Abraham Labatt: Norton B. Stern and William M. Kramer, "The Historical Recovery of the Pioneer Sephardic Jews of California," *WSJHQ* 8 (October 1975): 7–10.

11   Less than a month after the founding…came the "Great Fire" of May 1851: John B. McGloin, *San Francisco: The Story of a City* (San Rafael, Calif., 1978), p. 7.

11   destroying one-fourth of the entire "cloth and board" city: Lotchin, *San Francisco*, p. 176.

11   "Thefts, robberies, murders, and fires follow each other in such rapid succession…": H. Eastman, quoted in Robert M. Senkewicz, *Vigilantes in Gold Rush San Francisco* (Stanford, 1985), p. 73.

11   leading citizens…formed the first Vigilance Committee: Decker, *Fortunes and Failures*, pp. 120–25.

11   No fewer than seven hundred men—among them thirty Jews: Rudolf Glanz, *The Jews of California: From the Discovery of Gold Until 1880* (New York, 1960), p. 41.

12   the congregation's entire income was barely $1,500: Voorsanger, *Chronicles*, p. 31.

12   A *Sefer Torah* was donated in 1851: Edgar M. Kahn, "The Saga of the First Fifty Years of Congregation Emanu-El," *WSJHQ* 3 (April 1971): 131.

12   reacting to an outside threat in advocating a synagogue: Voorsanger, *Chronicles*, p. 33.

12   committee announced that a site had been bought: Ibid., p. 34.

12–13   On Henry Seligman: Stephen Birmingham, *Our Crowd: The Great Jewish Families of New York* (New York, 1967), pp. 29–36.

13   the congregation committed itself to raise $20,000 to build a house of worship: Voorsanger, *Chronicles*, p. 38.

15*   almost "instant spatial ordering" of the city: Decker, *Fortunes and Failures*, p. 196.

15   Seligman convinced his fellow members to pledge an additional $3,500 a year: Ibid., p. 39.

16   On Isaac Mayer Wise: Michael A. Meyer, *Response to Modernity: A History of the Reform Movement in Judaism* (New York, 1988), pp. 242–43; James C. Heller, *Isaac Mayer Wise: His Life and Thought* (New York, 1965).

16   On Rabbi James Gutheim: Voorsanger, *Chronicles*, pp. 40–42.

17   Dr. David Steinberg declined to come: Ibid., pp. 42–43.

17   Julius Eckman was soon asked to perform the ceremonies of laying the cornerstone both for Emanu-El and for Sherith Israel: Voorsanger, *Chronicles*, p. 46.

17   His credentials could not have been better…he had also spent three years in London: Joshua Stampfer, *Pioneer Rabbi of the West: The Life and Times of Julius Eckman* (Portland, Ore., 1988), pp. 1–23.

17   neither Gutheim nor Isaac Leeser could put forward any other name: Voorsanger, *Chronicles*, p. 45.

17   the salary was reduced…the Labatt family knew him: Ava F. Kahn, *The Gold Rush Decades: The Jewish Community Documents Itself* (forthcoming).

19   "The new focus of their lives was San Francisco…": Lotchin, *San Francisco*, p. 134.

19   By the 1850s there were no fewer than twenty-two Protestant churches: Ibid., pp. 322–23.

19   leading Jews…had to be aware of the dedicated, broad-minded preachers among the Protestants: Starr, *Americans and the California Dream*, pp. 69–109.

21   "There are no innovations…a gallery for the ladies": Daniel Levy, in a collection of his letters published as "Letters about the Jews of California: 1855–1858," *WSJHQ* 3 (January 1971): 95.

21   Isaac Mayer Wise favored not only universal suffrage but also the inclusion of women as synagogue board members: Charlotte Baum, Paula Hyman, and Sonia Michel, *The Jewish Woman in America* (New York, 1974), p. 35.

21   Eckman viewed their "so-called Emancipation" as "ridiculous foolery": Stampfer, *Pioneer Rabbi*, p. 173.

21   Eckman on observance and on changing the name to "temple": Ibid., pp. 153–62.

21   "the cultivated ear of our generation wants the aid of the refined arts…"; "Fifty years hence our successors will wonder more at the question than the reply": Quoted in I. Harold Scharfman, *The First Rabbi: Origins of Conflict Between Orthodox and Reform* (Malibu, Calif., 1988), p. 383.

21   Eckman was sharply criticized by the Orthodox Henry A. Henry: Ibid.

22   Eckman once told a friend that Judaism "is on the eve of great changes": Ibid., p. 468.

22   Eckman seemed always at odds with his new surroundings: Voorsanger, *Chronicles*, p. 143.

22   "I do not think he ever felt at home...": O. P. Fitzgerald, quoted in Stampfer, *Pioneer Rabbi*, p. 191.

22   Eckman appalled that congregants would throw wedding receptions in downtown taverns or leave the synagogue upon hearing that a steamer had arrived; "madness in raving after riches": Julius Eckman to Samuel Nunes Carvalho, 15 March 1855, quoted in A. Kahn, *Gold Rush Decades*.

22*   Eckman never made the trip to Asia: Stampfer, *Pioneer Rabbi*, pp. 126–29.

23   Eckman published a haughty letter in the *Daily Herald*: *Daily Herald* (San Francisco), 20 December 1854, p. 2.

23   Eckman called the proposed *schochet* an "ignoramus" and a "worthless character": Scharfman, *First Rabbi*, pp. 587–88.

23   Henry Seligman declared, "We are Reformers...": Ibid., p. 588.

23   Henry Labatt said that the only point of contention was whether Eckman should be asked to resign or just be summarily dismissed: Ibid., p. 323.

23   Eckman's role model was Joshua Baer Herzfeld: Stampfer, *Pioneer Rabbi*, pp. 3–4.

24   "It was a ramshackle, weird old building...": Mary Goldsmith Prag, quoted in ibid., pp. 71–72.

24–25   On the *Weekly Gleaner*: Ibid., pp. 77–93; Robert E. Levinson, "Julius Eckman and the *Weekly Gleaner*: The Jewish Press in Pioneer America," in Bertram Korn, ed., *A Bicentennial Festschrift for Jacob Rader Marcus* (New York, 1976), pp. 323–40.

25   On Eckman in Portland: Stampfer, *Pioneer Rabbi*, pp. 177–80, 184–90.

25   Eckman complained that he was dismissed from Emanu-El for being a "Polock": Quoted in Diner, *Time for Gathering*, p. 97.

25   "All these [synagogues on the West Coast]...hence in POPULARITY": Quoted in Levinson, "Julius Eckman and the *Weekly Gleaner*," p. 334.

25   On the day of the dedication Emanu-El numbered 147 families: Voorsanger, *Chronicles*, p. 47.

26   A number of resignations resulted from the rabbi's ill-considered outburst: Ibid., p. 48.

26   The indebtedness of the synagogue mounted...reaching $6,000: Ibid., p. 50.

26   the sexton was ordered to "take four dollars when he can get it...": Eckman to Carvalho, 15 March 1855, quoted in A. Kahn, *Gold Rush Decades*.

27   Herman Bien could not have been more different from Rabbi Eckman: Reva Clar and William S. Kramer, "Julius Eckman and Herman Bien: The Battling Rabbis of San Francisco," *WSJH* 15 (January/April/July 1983): 107–30, 232–53, 341–59. I am indebted to the authors for their insights on the contrast between the two men.

27   Wise called a halt to the fray, scolding both: *Am. Israel.*, 10 October 1856, p. 108; quoted in Clar and Kramer, "Julius Eckman and Herman Bien," p. 116.

28*   Bien's death likely by suicide: Ibid., p. 358.

28   On Daniel Levy: Voorsanger, *Chronicles*, pp. 55–56.

28**   With refreshing modesty...returned to France: Ibid., p. 56.

29   lay committee charged with "recommending a new mode of worship": Ibid., p. 54.

29   "ritual still teems"; "all the synagogues accept a single superior authority"; "a certain number of Jews find that they have the same principles..."; "the future belongs to Reform": Daniel Levy, in "Letters," pp. 103–4.

29   Levy knew that systematic and lasting changes awaited the arrival of a respected rabbi who "could find here a fertile field for the seeds he would sow": Ibid., p. 107.

29–30	Three prominent members wrote Wise…that "Orthodoxy seems to have but little sway": E. Kahn, "Saga," p. 139.
30	Wise himself considered the Emanu-El pulpit: Voorsanger, *Chronicles*, p. 56.
30	On Dr. Elias Greenebaum: Ibid., pp. 58–59.
30	By 1860 there were roughly ten thousand Jews in the western states, half of them in the Bay City: I. J. Benjamin, *Three Years in America*, 1859–1862, vol. I (Philadelphia, 1956), p. 232.
30	On the Jewish population of New York, Baltimore, and Philadelphia: Barkai, *Branching Out*, p. 136.
30	On the Eureka Benevolent Society: Benjamin, *Three Years in America*, pp. 210–27.
31	On the Masons: Norton B. Stern, "The Masonic Career of Benjamin D. Hyam: California's Third Grand Master," *WSJHQ* 7 (April 1975): 251–52, 260.
31	Jews comprised 12 percent of the San Francisco membership…a particularly high degree of integration: Tony Fels, "Religious Assimilation in a Fraternal Organization," *AJHQ* 74 (June 1985): 375.
31	Emanu-El congregants flocked to the Masons, about half the men of the synagogue joining: Ibid., p. 401.
31	one scholar has emphasized theological congruence: Ibid., pp. 395–96.
31*	about a third of all Jewish Masons belonged to a congregation…the majority chose Emanu-El: Ibid., p. 392.
32	Masons adamantly opposed "ignorant superstition"; "emotional fanaticism": Quoted in ibid., p. 388.
32	On Dr. Jacob Regensburger: Benjamin, *Three Years in America*, p. 241.
32	On the Concordia-Argonaut: *Concordia-Argonaut Centennial* (San Francisco, 1963); Bernice Scharlach, *House of Harmony: Concordia-Argonaut's First 130 Years* (Berkeley, 1983).
32	Jews were active in civic affairs: Benjamin, *Three Years in America*, p. 233.
32	"Whenever an undertaking of public interest or benefit is to be carried out, the Jews…are always ready to contribute": Quoted in ibid.
32	vigilantes…termed a revolution by contemporary historians: Decker, *Fortunes and Failures*, p. 139; Lotchin, *San Francisco*, pp. 245–75.
33	Jews such as the well-known journalist Seixas Solomons served as officers: Narell, *Our City*, p. 44.
33	They also formed a new political party which dominated San Francisco politics for the next two decades: William Issel and Robert W. Cherny, *San Francisco, 1865–1932: Politics, Power and Urban Development* (Berkeley, 1986), pp. 207–8.
33	In this "Revolution of 1856," Jesse Seligman played a major role: Decker, *Fortunes and Failures*, pp. 138, 300.
33	changing of the political guard…clearly in the class interest of Jewish merchants: Issel and Cherny, *San Francisco*, p. 208.
33*	On historiography of the vigilantes: Lotchin, *San Francisco*, pp. xvi–xxi.
33	On Isaac Cardozo and Elkan Heydenfeldt: Stern and Kramer, "Pioneer Sephardic Jews," pp. 14–15.
33	On Solomon Heydenfeldt: Ibid., p. 15; Stanley Mosk, "A Majority of the California Supreme Court," *WSJHQ* 8 (April 1976): 227–31; Albert M. Friedenberg, "Solomon Heydenfeldt: A Jewish Jurist of Alabama and California," *Publications of the American Jewish Historical Society* (New York, 1902), pp. 130–40.
33	On Henry Lyons: Mosk, "Majority," pp. 224–27.
34	On Washington Bartlett: Stern and Kramer, "Pioneer Sephardic Jews," p. 15.

34	Heydenfeldt disallowed the testimony of Chinese witnesses: Friedenberg, "Solomon Heydenfeldt," p. 135n.
34	"There was no aristocracy in California in 1849…": Earl Raab, "There's No City Like San Francisco," *Commentary* 10 (October 1956): 371.
35	One historian puts forth the relatively benign image of the aquarium: D. Michael Quinn, "Religion in the American West," in William Cronan, George Miller, and Jay Gitlin, eds., *Under an Open Sky: Rethinking America's Western Past* (New York, 1992), p. 164.
36	William Stow viciously slandered the Jews: "Anti-Jewish Sentiment in California: 1855," *American Jewish Archives*, April 1960, pp. 15–33.
36	Labatt's incisive letter to the Speaker: Reprinted in ibid., pp. 22–23.
36	Jews used their political power, a bloc of 1,500 votes: Benjamin, *Three Years in America*, p. 232.
37	The court held that he should be exempt from having to close on Sunday: Friedenberg, "Solomon Heydenfeldt," pp. 136–37.
37	"Jews were assumed not to possess character unless they proved otherwise…": Decker, *Fortunes and Failures*, p. 100.
37	In 1859, Emanu-El congregants raised nearly $3,700: Voorsanger, *Chronicles*, p. 96.
37	On the Edgardo Mortara case: Bertram Korn, *The American Reaction to the Mortara Case: 1858–1859* (Cincinnati, 1957).
38	More than three thousand people gathered to hear fiery speeches and resolutions: "Proceedings in Relation to the Mortara Abduction" (pamphlet reprinting news clippings and speeches, San Francisco, 1859).
38	Solomon Heydenfeldt condemned the "act of tyranny" and reminded his audience of "the power of public opinion…": Ibid., p. 5.
38	"their endeavors to suppress religious intolerance…": Ibid., p. 13.
38–39	Full text of Eckman's speech: Ibid., pp. 8–9.
39*	The evening was not without another indignity for Eckman: Stampfer, *Pioneer Rabbi*, p. 138.
39	Isaac Mayer Wise took the opportunity to castigate all priests: Korn, *American Reaction*, p. 24.
39	The event revealed the good will of a number of prominent Christians, including several clergymen: Ibid., pp. 13–16, 18–19.
39	the local press lauded the mass meeting; a *San Francisco Times* editorial chastised Secretary of State Cass: Ibid., pp. 28–29.
40	"Almost all of them are doing well…a large part of the wealth…is in their hands": Benjamin, *Three Years in America*, pp. 232–33.
40	Decker contends that economic opportunity was actually no greater: Decker, *Fortunes and Failures*, p. 253.
40	Jews "were more successful than others…": Decker, "Jewish Merchants," p. 22.
40–41	"Anyone leaving California in those days…": Levy, in "Letters," p. 110.
41	"Nowhere else…are [the Jews] regarded with as much esteem…": Benjamin, *Three Years in America*, p. 233.

CHAPTER 2 / ELKAN COHN: TEMPLE ON A HILL

43	On Elkan Cohn: Voorsanger, *Chronicles*, pp. 151–68; Meyer, *Response to Modernity*, pp. 84–85.

43   On Cohn's sermons: Philo Jacoby, *American Hebrew* (San Francisco), 27 December 1912, p. 2.

44   On Thomas Starr King: Starr, *Americans and the California Dream*, pp. 97–105.

44   Cohn spoke at King's church: Charles W. Wendte, *Thomas Starr King: Patriot and Preacher* (Boston, 1921), p. 96.

46   Cohn seemed like a man well past eighty: Voorsanger, *Chronicles*, p. 163.

46   On Cohn's reorganization of the religious school: Ibid., pp. 135, 162.

46   In 1861, Cohn inaugurated the confirmation program: E. Kahn, "Saga," pp. 140–41.

46   On the alterations Cohn made in the sphere of ritual: Voorsanger, *Chronicles*, p. 97; Benjamin, *Three Years in America*, pp. 204–10.

46   He chose a Sabbath sermon to justify the change, invoking a well-known verse from Deuteronomy: Scharfman, *First Rabbi*, p. 395.

46   the rabbi went on to complain that Judaism had far too long "excluded women from...many privileges to which they are justly entitled...": Quoted in ibid.

47   Benjamin listed Emanu-El as one of eight Reform congregations: Benjamin, *Three Years in America*, p. 82.

47   Cohn received a stinging rebuke from the Orthodox Isaac Leeser: Scharfman, *First Rabbi*, p. 419.

47   annual report of October 1860: Ibid., pp. 205–9.

47   Only one year later, the board of trustees approved the purchase of a choice site: Voorsanger, *Chronicles*, p. 99.

47   Seligman...stressed the happy fact..."I say we here on the Pacific Coast have been more fortunate...": Quoted in ibid., p. 101.

47   Solomon Heydenfeldt urged the diplomatic recognition of the Confederacy and gave up the practice of law: Friedenberg, "Solomon Heydenfeldt," p. 138.

47–48   Rabbi Eckman sympathized with the Confederacy: Robert J. Chandler, "Some Political and Cultural Pressures on the Jewish Image in Civil War San Francisco," *WSJH* 20 (January 1988): 151.

48   bitter strife erupted over the election of the sexton: Voorsanger, *Chronicles*, p. 105.

48   During the High Holidays cantorial parts of the service were rendered by a celebrated Catholic concert singer: *Occident* (Philadelphia), December 1863, p. 429.

48   Hoshanah Rabbah not observed at Emanu-El: Ibid., p. 431.

48   Cohn ridiculed by Jewish press as far away as Mainz in the Rhineland: Voorsanger, *Chronicles*, p. 61n.

48   The *Occident* of Philadelphia deplored "the inroads and injuries...": *Occident*, December 1863, p. 430.

48   Eckman's *Gleaner* criticized Cohn for sermons such as the one in which he deprecated the wearing of *tefillin*: Levinson, "Julius Eckman and the *Weekly Gleaner*," p. 333.

48–49   On the Merzbacher prayerbook: Hyman Grinstein, *The Rise of the Jewish Community of New York: 1654–1860* (Philadelphia, 1945), p. 357.

49   On the November 1864 annual meeting: Voorsanger, *Chronicles*, p. 109.

49   notice in the local newspapers "to all...who are in favor to organize a new Congregation": First Minute Book of Congregation Ohabai Shalome, 6 November 1864–13 October 1870, p. 1. WJHC.

49   Solomon Wangenheim wrote, "no satisfactory settlement could be had...": Ibid., p. 4.

49   Ohabai Shalome not strictly Orthodox: Ibid., pp. 4–5.

50   Joseph Mayer's inaugural address...paraphrased by the secretary: Ibid., p. 11.

50*   On Ohabai Shalome: Meyer, *Response to Modernity*, pp. 50–53.

50   In June 1864, the congregation approved the expenditure of $134,000: Voorsanger, *Chronicles*, p. 106.

50   Emanu-El counted 302 member-families in November 1864: Ibid., p. 108.

50   member rolls in October 1865 stood at only 267: Ibid., p. 111.

50   Cohn and his lay leaders raised the needed capital in a variety of ways: Ibid., p. 120.

51   strong earthquake of October 1865: Ibid.

51–53   On William Patton: Allan Temko, "Temple Emanu-El of San Francisco: A Glory of the West," *Commentary* 26 (August 1958), pp. 114–15.

53   as Temko has written, "the arches, the pillars,…a truly medieval church": Ibid., p. 116.

53   Patton wove many Jewish symbols into the Gothic plan: Ibid.

53   domes a prominent landmark: Ibid., p. 117.

53   domes probably meant to symbolize the headpieces of the Torah: Ibid.

54   On the ceremony consecrating the temple: Voorsanger, *Chronicles*, pp. 115–16.

54   Weisler's "faultless" baritone: Ibid., p. 115.

55   reporter for the *Alta California* wrote, "The stranger became aware of how grand and beautiful…": Quoted in ibid., pp. 115–16.

55   United States census shows the value of synagogue property rising more than 450 percent: Jick, *Americanization of the Synagogue*, p. 179.

55   New York's Emanu-El spent $600,000: Ibid.

55   Wise's Plum Street Temple built at a cost exceeding a quarter of a million dollars: Ibid.

55   The grand scale of the Sutter Street temple indicated that a Jewish commercial elite had crystallized…They had come very far indeed: Ibid. I am indebted to Leon Jick, who, in writing of New York's Temple Emanu-El, afforded me this insight.

55–56   wartime demand for finished goods…contributed to the emergence of a diversified manufacturing sector: Issel and Cherny, *San Francisco*, pp. 24–25.

56   On Levi Strauss and David Stern: Decker, *Fortunes and Failures*, p. 187.

56   San Francisco now "rebuilt with Nevada silver": Oscar Lewis, *San Francisco: Mission to Metropolis* (San Diego, 1980), p. 112.

56–57   In 1864 alone, no fewer than a thousand new buildings were constructed: Ibid., p. 113.

57   ten members of Emanu-El were reputed to have had an aggregate wealth of forty-five million dollars: Glanz, *Jews of California*, p. 43.

57   On Jewish pioneer fortunes: Meyer, *Response to Modernity*; Leon Harris, *Merchant Princes* (New York, 1979), pp. 237–59.

57   Isaac Magnin aided immensely by his wife, Mary Ann: Rochlin and Rochlin, *Pioneer Jews*, pp. 177–79.

58   Aaron "Honest" Fleishhacker…"grubstaked" the future "Silver Kings": Narell, *Our City*, p. 62.

58   On Michael de Young: Ira Rosewaike, "The Parentage and Early Years of M. H. de Young: Legend and Fact," *WSJHQ* 7 (April 1975): 210–17.

59   On the High Holidays they filled the Sutter Street temple to capacity: Homer S. Henley, "Yom Kippur in the Temple Emanu-El," *WSJHQ* 4 (October 1971): 11–19.

59   "Many of our Christian friends were present": Isaac F. Bloch, Annual Report, 27

October 1867. Temple Emanu-El Archives. This handwritten speech by Vice-President Bloch, delivered in President Martin Heller's absence, is one of the few extant annual reports from the nineteenth century.

59   Socially, the Jewish elite were a group unto themselves: Gertrude Atherton, *My San Francisco* (New York, 1946), p. 152; Frances Bransten Rothmann, *The Haas Sisters of Franklin Street: A Look Back With Love* (Berkeley, 1979).

59   all but one percent were merchants or professionals: Silverstein, *Alternatives to Assimilation*, pp. 80–81.

59*   On Wise's visit to San Francisco; Wise reported that *every* member paid $100 a year: William M. Kramer, ed., *The Western Journal of Isaac Mayer Wise, 1877* (Berkeley, 1974), p. 58.

59*   minute books of Sherith Israel: Minute Books of Congregation Sherith Israel, 1877, WJHC.

59   the synagogue was segregated ethnically: Ibid., pp. 75–76.

60   aloofness of the Bavarians toward the "Polacks" continued unabated: Benjamin, *Three Years in America*, p. 211; Rudolf Glanz, "The 'Bayer' and 'Pollack' in America," in *Studies in Judaica Americana* (New York, 1970), p. 119.

60   B'nai B'rith lodge lists: *Proceedings of District Grand Lodge No. 4 of the Independent Order of B'nai B'rith* (San Francisco, 1865), pp. 106–9.

60   Benish and Yetta Levy born in West Prussia: Charlene Akers, introduction to *920 O'Farrell Street: A Jewish Girlhood in San Francisco*, by Harriet Lane Levy (Berkeley, 1996), p. ix.

60   "That the Baiern were superior to us, we knew. We took our position…": Harriet Lane Levy, *920 O'Farrell Street* (Berkeley, 1996), p. 151.

60   Harriet Lane Levy felt "uncomfortable"…"Pleasure was rarely simple…'No Baier marries a Pole…'": Ibid., p. 153.

61*   Kohut writes of "unhealthy rivalry"; "to even a larger extent" than in Richmond, Virginia: Rebekah Kohut, *My Portion* (New York, 1927), p. 47.

61   Jews "are welcome members…and form an inner group of their own": Atherton, *My San Francisco*, p. 152.

61   Harriet Lane Levy could also sense this "pleasant disassociation…": Quoted in Akers, introduction to *920 O'Farrell Street*, p. viii.

61   exclusive haunts admitted very few Jewish members: J. B. Levison, *Memories for My Family* (San Francisco, 1933), p. 235; Isidore Choynski, *Am. Israel.*, 24 March 1882, p. 309.

61   Bay Area's first *Elite Directory: The Elite Directory for San Francisco and Oakland* (San Francisco, 1879); Decker, "Jewish Merchants," p. 22.

61   *Blue Book: The San Francisco Blue Book 1888* (San Francisco, 1888).

61   By World War I the city's Jewish aristocracy was so inbred that it resembled the royalty of Europe: See Narell, *Our City*, passim.

62   Louis Sloss invited to join Stanford board of trustees: Ibid., pp. 230–31.

62–63   wealthiest Jews and non-Jews fawned over Ada Isaacs Menken: Ibid., pp. 81–82; Rochlin and Rochlin, *Pioneer Jews*, pp. 173–74.

63   Jessica Peixotto forced to delay her studies due to her father's objections: William Kramer, "Jessica Peixotto: UC Professor and Pioneer Women's Activist," 28 *WSJH* (April 1996): 265.

63   Yetta Levy lived in "a world where variation was perversity…": H. Levy, *920 O'Farrell Street*, p. 50.

63   Harriet Lane Levy's adult life: Akers, introduction to *920 O'Farrell Street*, p. x.

63   Alice Toklas raised by her widowed grandfather: Rochlin and Rochlin, *Pioneer Jews*, pp. 190–91.

64   Deborah Hirsh, "a nobody on O'Farrell Street...now Mrs. Orton of London": H. Levy, *920 O'Farrell Street*, p. 30.

64   pattern of "second-generation Jewish women in the West...": Rochlin and Rochlin, *Pioneer Jews*, p. 104.

64   Hannah Marks Solomons brought out West to marry a man she had never seen: Narell, *Our City*, p. 394.

64   "cattle matching project...": Quoted in Rochlin and Rochlin, *Pioneer Jews*, p. 99.

64   Seixas Solomons became an alcoholic: Narell, *Our City*, p. 394; Rochlin and Rochlin, *Pioneer Jews*, p. 100.

64   the Solomons offspring went far: Narell, *Our City*, p. 394; Rochlin and Rochlin, *Pioneer Jews*, pp. 100, 104–5.

64   "She appears always well-dressed...": Rebecca Gradwohl, "The Jewish Woman in San Francisco" (1896), in Jacob Rader Marcus, *The American Jewish Woman, 1654–1980*, vol. I (New York, 1981), p. 365.

65   Jewish women accounted for six local physicians: Rochlin and Rochlin, *Pioneer Jews*, p. 104.

65   "the Jewess developed not alone physically...": Gradwohl, "Jewish Woman," p. 365.

65   Choynski's "San Francisco Letter" studded with incidents of humbug: See, e.g., *Am. Israel.*, 5 October 1877, p. 6; 29 October 1880, p. 138; 21 January 1881, p. 237.

65   Choynski ridiculed Cohn's ostentatious confirmation ceremony..."with its floral display that would do credit...": *Am. Israel.*, 4 June 1880, p. 6.

65   "the handsomest and wealthiest misses...shine for an hour as professors": *Am. Israel.*, 9 May 1879, p. 20.

65   One well-to-do Jewish woman asked Rosenthal for a discount: *Am. Israel.*, 21 March 1879, p. 6.

66   On Joshua Norton: Allen Stanley Lane, *Emperor Norton: The Mad Monarch of America* (Caldwell, Idaho, 1939).

66   Choynski told tales of blackmail, adultery, suicide, and even homicide: See, e.g., *Am. Israel.*, 15 September 1882, p. 90; 5 May 1882, p. 355; 17 February 1882, p. 270; 8 September 1882, p. 82; 1 January 1881, p. 210.

66   He also attacked women, the Orthodox, the poor, Chinese, American Indians, Christians, and all rabbis as a class: See, e.g., *Am. Israel.*, 24 February 1882, p. 227; 23 June 1882, p. 413; 30 June 1882, p. 417; 21 April 1882, p. 341; 5 May 1882, p. 357; 16 June 1882, p. 402; 17 November 1882, p. 167.

66–67   On Michael Reese's death: William M. Kramer, "The Stingiest Man in San Francisco," *WSJHQ* 5 (July 1973), pp. 265–66.

67   "These fellows...on a pair of aces": *Am. Israel.*, 21 April 1882, p. 341.

67   On the Eureka Benevolent Society: *The Annual Report of the Eureka Benevolent Society* (San Francisco, 1890).

67   On the Pacific Hebrew Orphan Asylum: Meyer, *Response to Modernity*, pp. 23–27.

67   On the Hebrew Home for the Aged Disabled: Ibid., p. 42.

67–68   On Mount Zion Hospital: Barbara Rogers, "To Be or Not to Be a Jewish Hospital?" *WSJHQ* 10 (April 1978), pp. 195–201.

68   formation of a San Francisco chapter of the Alliance Israélite Universelle: *American Hebrew*, 7 April 1864, p. 4.

68   Choynski published a list of donations to show that orphan asylum supported more by poor Jews: *Am. Israel.*, 17 November 1882, p. 167; 24 February 1883, p. 276.

69   Calls for centralization voiced in the Jewish press: S. Bachrach, *The Progress* (San Francisco), 5 April 1878, p. 2.

69   Jews comprised the most charitable group in the city: Mary Watson, *San Francisco Society* (San Francisco, 1887), p. 27.

69   Cohn played the unofficial role of "Grand Rabbi": Philo Jacoby, "Rev. Dr. Elkan Cohn," *American Hebrew*, 27 December 1912.

69   In 1883, Cohn traveled to Los Angeles, were he addressed the B'nai B'rith Congregation: Max Vorspan and Lloyd P. Gartner, *History of the Jews of Los Angeles* (Philadelphia, 1970), p. 86.

69   Cohn enjoyed several deep friendships with non-Jewish clergymen: Mary Goldsmith Prag, 9 April 1929, Temple Emanu-El (San Francisco) Papers, WJHC.

69   Cohn took a stand on public aid to parochial schools: Ibid.

70   Cohn's eulogy for Lincoln: William M. Kramer, "They Have Killed Our Man But Not Our Cause," *WSJHQ* 2 (July 1970), pp. 194–95.

70   Cohn found initiating reforms easier after defection of more religiously observant families: Voorsanger, *Chronicles*, p. 120.

70   Rabbi Aaron Messing called Cohn a "false prophet…a 'messiah' who has converted the whole town…": *Am. Israel.*, 6 May 1870, quoted in Norton B. Stern, "An Orthodox Rabbi and a Reforming Congregation," *WSJHQ* 15 (April 1983), p. 276.

70*   Messing underestimated reformist tendencies at Sherith Israel: Stern, "Orthodox Rabbi," p. 276.

71   Choynski on replacement of the shofar with a cornet: *Am. Israel.*, 3 November 1876, p. 6.

71*   trombone often used in place of the shofar: Jeffrey S. Zucker, "Cantor Edward Stark at Congregation Emanu-El, Part I," *WSJH* 17 (April 1985), p. 237.

71   visitor who insisted on wearing his hat removed from the temple by Maier Steppacher: *Am. Israel.*, 9 December 1881, p. 186.

71   Emanu-El joined a handful of congregations in moving Friday evening services to Sunday: *Emanu-El*, 29 November 1895, p. 5.

71   Cohn also departed from tradition at weddings and funerals: *Am. Israel.*, 8 April 1881, p. 318; 1 September 1882, p. 67.

71–72 On Wise's 1877 visit to San Francisco: Kramer, *Western Journal of Isaac Mayer Wise*, passim.

72   Jews feared for the safety of the Chinese: Ibid., p. 34

72   Social unrest hardly restrained Wise's enthusiasm for "the city of miracles": Ibid., p. 25.

72   Wise bewailed the fact that "two hundred dollars per annum pays a millionaire's bills…": Ibid., p. 61.

72   Wise deeply gratified by the "gorgeous" temple: *The Progress*, 27 July 1887, p. 2.

72   Wise's plea for unity "on this American soil…our Mount Moriah": Ibid.

72   Important benefits reaped by the synagogue…another Protestant-style model: Silverstein, *Alternatives to Assimilation*, pp. 35–70.

73   Emanu-El's Sabbath school the largest in the city, with an enrollment of more than four hundred: Voorsanger, *Chronicles*, p. 136.

73   "Our children grow up in ignorance…": Benjamin Franklin Peixotto, quoted in Barkai, *Branching Out*, p. 168.

73   Peixotto ardently supported Wise: Kramer, *Western Journal of Isaac Mayer Wise*, p. 67.

73   By the end of the 1870s only 16 percent of Jewish families belonged to one of the seven synagogues in town: Fels, "Religious Assimilation," p. 392.

73–74	Sherith Israel had close to the same number of congregants as Emanu-El; Ohabai Shalome was about half the size: Kramer, *Western Journal of Isaac Mayer Wise*, p. 58.
74	Jews reaching intellectual maturity in the last third of the nineteenth century "felt alienated": Silverstein, *Alternatives to Assimilation*, p. 82.
74	Jewish interest in Christian Science: H. Levy, *920 O'Farrell Street*, pp. 55–57.
74	Jewish interest in Ethical Culture: Silverstein, *Alternatives to Assimilation*, p. 82.
74	Jewish interest in fortune-telling: H. Levy, *920 O'Farrell Street*, p. 33.
74	"liberal-minded people...peruse at length": Passage from *Am. Israel.*, 25 November 1887, quoted in the *San Francisco Examiner* and in *WSJHQ* 4 (July 1972), p. 198.
74	Henry U. Brandenstein a self-proclaimed "agnostic" who refused to join the temple: David G. Dalin and John F. Rothmann, "Henry U. Brandenstein of San Francisco," *WSJH* 18 (October 1985), p. 14.
74	On Henry U. Brandenstein (biographical): Ibid., pp. 3–21.
74	Jews favored strong remedies ranging from school reform and urban planning to anti-vice crusades: Issel and Cherny, *San Francisco*, pp. 102–11.
75	in the 1870s international recognition came for San Francisco's cuisine: Lewis, *San Francisco*, p. 146.
75	On the opening of Golden Gate Park: Ibid., pp. 161–65.
75–76	On the establishment of a new cemetery: Voorsanger, *Chronicles*, pp. 139–40.
76	On Martin Heller: Ibid., p. 140.
76	On Max Wolff: Ibid., pp. 121–22.
76	On Abraham Illch: Ibid., pp. 168–69.

CHAPTER 3 / JACOB VOORSANGER: AXIOMS OF REFORM

79	Voorsanger never received rabbinical ordination; his degrees were honorary: Kenneth C. Zwerin and Norton B. Stern, "Jacob Voorsanger: From Cantor to Rabbi," *WSJHQ* 15 (April 1983), pp. 195–200.
79*	Voorsanger portrayed as not only a graduate of the Jewish Theological Seminary, but one of its finest students: Meyer, *Response to Modernity*, pp. 157–58.
79*	biographical details repeated by more than one historian since: Fred Rosenbaum, *Architects of Reform* (Berkeley, 1980), p. 45; Marc Lee Raphael, "Rabbi Jacob Voorsanger of San Francisco on Jews and Judaism: The Implications of the Pittsburgh Platform," *AJHQ* 63 (December 1973), p. 185.
79–80	Voorsanger worked initially as a cantor: Ibid., pp. 196–97.
80*	Zwerin and Stern found no reference to Voorsanger in seminary records: Zwerin and Stern, "Jacob Voorsanger," p. 195.
80–82	Pittsburgh Platform excerpt: *Encyclopaedia Judaica*, s.v. "Pittsburgh Platform."
82	Voorsanger's notion of "progressive, rational Judaism": Raphael, "Rabbi Jacob Voorsanger," p. 188.
82	Voorsanger taught the theory of two Isaiahs, the non-existence of Ezra, a Second Commonwealth date for Daniel, and the Gospels as *midrash*; suggested a "power politics" interpretation of the canonization of the Hebrew Bible: Ibid., p. 187.
83	"We find greater comfort in the struggle toward high ideals...": *Emanu-El*, 18 November 1898, p. 5.
83	Voorsanger quotation pondering Reform's decline: *Emanu-El*, 27 December 1895, pp. 6–7.

83   "Does a cigar stand between Reform and radicalism?": *Emanu-El*, 31 January 1896, p. 7.

84   Voorsanger argued that Krauskopf had gone "too far": *Emanu-El*, 17 January 1896, pp. 6–7.

84   Rabbi Hirsch...removed the scrolls from his Chicago sanctuary: Gunther Plaut, "Reform as an Adjective: What Are the Limits?" in Aron Hirt-Manheimer, ed., *The Jewish Condition: Essays on Contemporary Judaism Honoring Rabbi Alexander Schindler* (New York, 1995), p. 352.

84   "Our objections to Sunday services are of no religious character": *Emanu-El*, 20 November 1896, p. 5.

84   Voorsanger considered the Sabbath question "the greatest issue of our modern religious life": Jacob Voorsanger, "The Sabbath Question," in *Sermons and Addresses* (New York, 1913), p. 258.

84   "to throw a three-thousand-year-old tradition overboard...": Ibid., p. 272.

84   "Israel...must be a distinct spiritual entity": Ibid., p. 277.

84   "solidarity and identity...false ambition of becoming founders of the latest": Ibid., p. 278.

85   Stark hailed in the local press: Zucker, "Cantor Edward Stark," p. 248.

85   On Stark's early years: Jeffrey S. Zucker, "Edward Josef Stark at Emanu-El, 1893–1913," *Journal of Synagogue Music* (June 1983), pp. 14–16.

86   Stark's job description at Emanu-El: Zucker, "Cantor Edward Stark," p. 234.

86   visitors to the temple sometimes mistook him for an assistant rabbi: Ibid., p. 236

86   Stark paid singers well but rehearsed them mercilessly: Zucker, "Edward Josef Stark," p. 18.

86   Stark known to be "quick in temper": Zucker, "Cantor Edward Stark," p. 232.

86   Stark had the pulpit outfitted with an electric buzzer: Ibid., p. 235.

86   Stark invariably received raves in the press: Ibid., p. 237.

86   one contemporary described him as "a squat, thickset dwarf": S. Homer Henley, quoted in ibid., p. 235.

87   Stark's repertoire thrilled audiences with its "magnetic power": Ibid., p. 239.

87   on Yom Kippur afternoon he "sang as he sang but once in the whole year": Ibid., p. 236.

87   Stark exhibited an uncommon depth of feeling, "heavy with passionate sorrow": Ibid.

87   "An organ in the hands of a master...": Stark, quoted in Zucker, "Edward Josef Stark," p. 20.

88   "he wanted to return the *nusach* to its rightful place...": Ibid., pp. 22–23.

88   Stark's "Shofar Service" performed throughout America: Zucker, "Cantor Edward Stark," p. 240.

88*   On the cantor's magnum opus: Zucker, "Edward Josef Stark," p. 14.

88   "short-breathed sectionalism": Albert Weissler, *The Modern Renaissance of Jewish Music* (New York, 1954), p. 141.

88   one authority hears in the cantor's harmonic language the barbershop quartet: Zucker, "Edward Josef Stark," p. 23

88   Stark was "head and shoulders above his contemporaries...": Weissler, *Modern Renaissance of Jewish Music*, p. 141.

88   Voorsanger condemned bicycle races along with prizefights: *Emanu-El*, 17 February 1899, p. 6.

88	Voorsanger prayed to be free "from the terror of the automobile": *Emanu-El*, 22 November 1907, p. 2.
88	Voorsanger fearful of the women's suffrage movement as well as labor unions: *Emanu-El*, 9 October 1896; Raphael, "Rabbi Jacob Voorsanger," p. 187.
89	"The Chinese belongs to a non-assimilative race...": *Emanu-El*, 28 August 1896, p. 6.
89	Jewish press uniformly opposed to the Chinese: Rudolf Glanz, "Jews and Chinese in America," in *Studies in Judaica Americana*, p. 322.
89	"We are confronted by an invasion...Russian Orthodoxy represents retrogressive forces...": *Emanu-El*, 17 June 1904, p. 5.
90	Voorsanger called East European Jews "blackguards," "hypocrites," "schnorrers": *Emanu-El*, 27 December 1895, p. 6; 7 August 1896, p. 7; 17 February 1899, p. 5.
90	On the Russian-Jewish Alliance: Meyer, *Response to Modernity*, p. 124.
90	Voorsanger sought to provide Jewish education to "children of the proletariat": Michael Zarchin, *Glimpses of Jewish Life in San Francisco* (Berkeley, 1952), p. 168.
90	religious schools operated by the Jewish Educational Society earned Voorsanger's praise and encouragement: *Emanu-El*, 12 August 1904, p. 5.
90	Emanu-El Sisterhood founded in 1894: *Emanu-El*, 27 March 1896, p. 8; 15 January 1904, p. 10.
91	On Voorsanger's son, William: Barbara S. Rogers and Stephen M. Dobbs, *The First Century: Mount Zion Hospital and Medical Center, 1887–1987* (San Francisco, 1987), pp. 42–43.
91	Sadie American launched the NCJW with an inspirational address: Martin Meyer, *Western Jewry: An Account of the Achievements of the Jews and Judaism in California* (San Francisco, 1916), p. 32.
91	Voorsanger sometimes viewed the NCJW as a competitor of the Sisterhood: *Emanu-El*, 14 February 1896, p. 6.
92	nearly every Emanu-El household employed at least one live-in servant: Silverstein, *Alternatives to Assimilation*, p. 89.
92	many women sought "an outlet for the growing restlessness...": Caroline Sahlein, quoted in Meyer, *Western Jewry*, p. 32.
92	women quietly began "a radical redefinition of behavioral norms...": Beth Wenger, "Jewish Women and Voluntarism: Beyond the Myth of Enablers," *AJHQ* (Autumn 1989), p. 17.
92	as the hospital's historians recount, "the auxiliary members...": Rogers and Dobbs, *Mount Zion Hospital*, p. 16.
92	the Ladies' Auxiliary threatened to disband...the directors capitulated: Ibid.
92	"the ladies have been of inestimable assistance...": J. B. Levison, quoted in ibid., p. 17.
92–93	Voorsanger felt that union of relief organizations was necessary; one check would "free every contributor from promiscuous begging...": *Emanu-El*, 13 November 1903, p. 6.
93	Voorsanger threw up his hands at this plot "to dump the riff-raff of Europe...": *Emanu-El*, 26 August 1904, p. 5.
93	Voorsanger urged that East European Jews be "distributed over the full length and width of this country": Voorsanger, quoted in Raphael, "Rabbi Jacob Voorsanger," p. 197.
93	Voorsanger encouraged such projects as Rabbi Krauskopf's National Farm School and carried reports in the *Emanu-El* on Jewish agricultural colonies: See, e.g., *Emanu-El*, 29 November 1895, p. 5; 10 June 1904, p. 6.

93   Voorsanger favored the scheme putting forward Baja California for Jewish immigration: Norton B. Stern, *Baja California: Jewish Refuge and Homeland* (Los Angeles, 1973), pp. 11–17.

93   Voorsanger warned, "Our people are in no humor...": *Emanu-El*, 7 May 1897, p. 5.

93–94   "this mad-cap affair"; "The bringing of shiftless creatures..." : *Emanu-El*, 21 May 1897, p. 7.

94   "Those who remain will have to shift for themselves...": *Emanu-El*, 15 October 1897, pp. 6–7.

94   Voorsanger chastised some refugees of the Kishinev pogrom: *Emanu-El*, 24 June 1904, p. 5.

94   "We must defeat this nefarious scheme...": *Emanu-El*, 12 November 1897, p. 5.

94   "the processes of adaptation are already underway...": *Emanu-El*, 27 March 1908, p. 1.

94   Voorsanger agitated by a new "grave danger to the American-Jewish community...": Ibid.

94   Accusing Emma Goldman of "moral insanity" and apostasy...Jews should cooperate with the most rigid interpretation: Ibid.

94   Voorsanger believed the return to the ancient homeland to be "one of the wildest of all wild dreams": *Emanu-El*, 11 June 1897, p. 5.

94   Voorsanger's open letter to Simon Wolf: *Emanu-El*, 31 December 1898, p. 7.

94   "Turk-ridden land": *Emanu-El*, 15 January 1904, p. 8.

94–95   On Voorsanger's 1907 trip to Palestine: *Emanu-El*, 24 May 1907, p. 2.

95   "We refuse to believe that the divine intention...edge of civilization"; "the degrading confession...a beaten dog": *Emanu-El*, 2 December 1898, p. 5.

95   Voorsanger believed that the Russian people would overthrow authoritarian rule and put in its place a democratic government: *Emanu-El*, 8 January 1904, p. 6.

95–96   Voorsanger passage describing California as Zion: *Emanu-El*, 10 July 1896, p. 6.

96   "when suddenly the abyss yawned...": *Emanu-El*, 6 September 1907, p. 6.

96   The earthquake destroyed more than half the city's buildings: Judd Kahn, *Imperial San Francisco: Politics and Planning in an American City, 1897–1906* (Lincoln, Nebr., 1979), pp. 130, 132.

96   The earthquake claimed about three thousand lives: Gladys C. Hansen and Emmet Condon, *The Denial of Disaster* (San Francisco, 1989), p. 153. Although U.S. military officials counted around five hundred dead, Hansen and Condon convincingly demonstrate that a far higher number of fatalities may be attributed to the earthquake and fire.

96   Levison's description of the earthquake and fire: Levison, *Memories for My Family*, p. 122.

97   Voorsanger fought to spare San Francisco from famine, "the worst anarchist in existence": Jacob Voorsanger, "Relief Work in San Francisco after the 1906 Earthquake and Fire: An Overview," in William M. Kramer, ed., *California: Earthquakes and Jews* (Los Angeles, 1995), p. 194.

97   Voorsanger "commandeered store after store"; "I was the biggest thief...": Ibid., p. 196.

97   "How widespread was the shock...": Paul Sinsheimer, "Paul Sinsheimer's Letter on the San Francisco Earthquake-Fire of 1906," in Kramer, *Earthquakes and Jews*, pp. 165–66.

98   Levison writes of "the grinding noise on the sidewalks...": Levison, *Memories for My Family*, p. 127.

98	ten thousand Jews homeless: Voorsanger, *Emanu-El*, 18 March 1908, p. 1.
98	total fire loss approached a billion dollars: Hansen and Condon, *Denial of Disaster*, p. 127.
98	Jewish institutions were ravaged: *Emanu-El*, 28 December 1906, p. 4.
99	Voorsanger wept only as he realized the extent of the damage: *Emanu-El*, 18 May 1906, p. 3.
100	"houseless, helpless, totally ruined, destitute": *Emanu-El*, 4 May 1906, p. 1.
100	when the Jewish community of Portland sent $5,000, Voorsanger returned the money: *Emanu-El*, 16 November 1906, p. 3.
100	periodicals such as the *American Israelite* and *American Hebrew* were sympathetic: Ibid.
100	by April 18, 1907, no money had been received: *Emanu-El*, 19 April 1907, p. 2.
101	Voorsanger argued that Magnes and Frankel did not "take the time" to interview refugees: *Emanu-El*, 13 March 1908, p. 1.
101	donations held up "in the high and mighty East": *Emanu-El*, 24 August 1906, p. 2.
102	Voorsanger deemed the appeal "indiscreet, injudicious, ill-advised"; dubbed Oakland "a village"; ridiculed Friedlander..."the only Jewish theologian on the West Coast": *Emanu-El*, 8 June 1906, p. 2.
102	Voorsanger encouraged plans for improved lighting on Fillmore and an electric streetcar line across Van Ness: *Emanu-El*, 10 August 1906, p. 1; 13 July 1906, p. 1.
102	Voorsanger outraged by press reports describing San Francisco as "a total wreck"..."a despairing mob": *Emanu-El*, 17 August 1906, pp. 1–2.
102	the congregation would remain on Sutter Street "until the future looks brighter and more secure": *Emanu-El*, 26 October 1906, p. 8.
102*	On Gustave Albert Lansburgh: Meyer, *Response to Modernity*, p. 201.
103	"Russian domes have no place on a synagogue": *Emanu-El*, 6 September 1907, p. 11.
103	On the temple's restoration: *Emanu-El*, 6 September 1907.
103	Voorsanger took a voluntary cut in salary: Martin Wiener, "Jewish Life in San Francisco: 1905–1910" (typescript, 1962), p. 6.
104	Kevin Starr on the earthquake and fire: Starr, *Americans and the California Dream*, p. 294.
104	Voorsanger's sermon at the rededication: *Emanu-El*, 6 September 1907, pp. 6–7.
105	On the Ruef case: Walton Bean, *Boss Ruef's San Francisco: The Story of the Union Labor Party, Big Business, and the Graft Prosecution* (Berkeley, 1952).
105	The *Emanu-El* ran a rare banner headline...front-page editorial: *Emanu-El*, 31 January 1908, pp. 1–2.
106	Voorsanger demanded "a square deal for the indicted": *Emanu-El*, 7 June 1907, p. 1.
106	Pleasure at their acquittal was expressed by Rabbi Bernard Kaplan: *Emanu-El*, 14 August 1908, p. 5.
106	Voorsanger and Kaplan attacked the "perverse" press, which they felt had "poisoned the public mind": *Emanu-El*, 13 September 1907, p. 3.
106	Voorsanger reported from Paris..."exposure of all the political filth...considered one of the most infamous communities extant": *Emanu-El*, 11 January 1907, p. 2.
106	Voorsanger urged his readers to ride the trains despite scab labor: *Emanu-El*, 10 May 1907, p. 1; 17 May 1907, p. 1.
106	Kaplan attacked...P. H. McCarthy: *Emanu-El*, 27 December 1907, p. 3.
106	The *Emanu-El* supported a little-known Republican businessman: *Emanu-El*, 24 September 1909, p. 5.
107	The *Emanu-El* carried letters urging Ruef's parole: *Emanu-El*, 3 July 1914, p. 5.

107	an editorial demanded his early release: *Emanu-El*, 7 August 1914, pp. 2, 62–63.
107	"Israel is not responsible for Ruef's sins"; "Wise is a brilliant and eloquent young man but not of a well-balanced frame of mind": *Emanu-El*, 15 October 1909, p. 1.
107	Heney replied that "some of the best men" on the panel were Jewish: Bean, *Boss Ruef's San Francisco*, p. 203.
107	"He is an ex-convict and he is a Jew…"; the *Emanu-El* expressed deep sympathy for Haas: *Emanu-El*, 1 October 1909, p. 5.
107	Voorsanger's reproach elicited a letter of apology: *Emanu-El*, 4 April 1907, p. 2.
107	Ruef characterized as "a small, weak, nervous Jew": *Emanu-El*, 19 July 1907, p. 2.
107*	On Heney, Haas, Biggy: Bean, *Boss Ruef's San Francisco*, pp. 282–86.
108	Ruef himself contributed to the suffering of the Chinese: Ibid., p. 126.
108	an even greater controversy erupted regarding the Japanese: Ibid., p. 182.
109	On the impact of Rachel's death: Henrietta Voorsanger, interview by author, 1978.
109	Voorsanger anticipated that California would one day be "the star of the American Empire": *Emanu-El*, 10 July 1896, p. 7.
109	Russian Jews numbered less than one percent of temple membership: Silverstein, *Alternatives to Assimilation*, p. 76.
109	the average age of temple members had risen to fifty-three; only one in seven was under forty: Ibid., p. 79. This data refers to the men of the congregation; women were still not permitted to join in their own right.
110	"swindlers who trade on the credulity of society": *Emanu-El*, 6 October 1899, p. 5.
110	Cantor Stark's health ruined by overwork; he resigned in 1913 after suffering a stroke: Jeffrey S. Zucker, "Cantor Edward Stark at Congregation Emanu-El, Part II," *WSJHQ* 17 (July 1985), p. 321.
110	Stark's elaborate cantorial work seems to have been a low priority for Martin Meyer; Stark's role in the service cut down and his salary reduced: Ibid., pp. 319–20.

CHAPTER 4 / MARTIN MEYER: TEMPLE AND COMMUNITY

114	On Elkan Voorsanger: Henrietta Voorsanger, interview by author, 1978.
114	On Mount Zion Hospital's new facility: Meyer, *Response to Modernity*, pp. 27–30.
114	On the Federation of Jewish Charities: *Emanu-El*, 18 April 1913, pp. 10–11, 32–35.
115–16	On Martin Meyer: Meyer, *Response to Modernity*, pp. 313–14; *Emanu-El*, 27 August 1909, p. 2; Daniel J. Moskowitz, "Martin Meyer: His Life and Its Lessons, Part I," *WSJH* 26 (April 1994), pp. 194–216.
115*	Wangenheim offered the job to Rosenau and Rabbi Abram Simon: *Emanu-El*, 26 February 1909, pp. 212–13.
116	Meyer attacked the typical "evils" of his day: *Emanu-El*, 28 April 1911, p. 2.
116	Frances Bransten Rothmann's intimate memoir; "they knew little about Jewish rites…": Rothmann, *Haas Sisters*, p. 71.
116–17	Meyer expressed his dismay that many temple members celebrated Christmas…and were attracted to Christian Science: *Emanu-El*, 18 December 1914, p. 2; 23 June 1911, p. 2.
117	Meyer sought to restore a number of Jewish ceremonies: Temple Minutes, January 1917.
117	Meyer urged the temple choir to recruit a higher proportion of Jews: *Emanu-El*, 4 August 1911, p. 2.

117   Meyer refused to sanctify intermarriage: *Emanu-El*, 3 March 1911, p. 2.
117–18   On Wise's Free Synagogue: Melvin I. Urofsky, *A Voice That Spoke for Justice: The Life and Times of Stephen S. Wise* (Albany, 1982), pp. 59–72.
118   Meyer "greatly liked and admired" by Wise: Ibid., p. 89.
118   Wise refused the post of head rabbi after learning that the pulpit was not "free"; he credited Louis Marshall as "author and founder": Ibid., p. 57.
119   "the accident of history that brought so-called German Jews to this land...to perpetuate the traditions of his people": *Emanu-El*, 5 February 1915, p. 2.
119   Meyer viewed internal dissension as American Jewry's "greatest folly and weakness": *Emanu-El*, 18 November 1910, p. 2.
119   "If we are not the children...": Ibid.
119   Esther Hellman Settlement House erected at the end of 1918: *Emanu-El*, 25 October 1918, p. 4.
120   A rally for the war sufferers in 1915 packed the sanctuary: *Emanu-El*, 19 March 1915, p. 8.
120   a committee raised more than a quarter of a million dollars: *Emanu-El*, 4 February 1916, p. 2.
120   protests against the pogroms led by Justice Sloss: *Emanu-El*, 6 June 1919, p. 4.
120–21   On Reuben Rinder: Rose Rinder, "Music, Prayer and Religious Leadership" (WJHC, oral history, typescript, 1971).
120   Rinder briefly attended the Hebrew Theological Seminary: I am indebted to the late Rabbi Kenneth Zwerin for informing me that Rinder never graduated from the seminary.
121–22   On "the Club": Vivian Solomon, interview by Ruth Rafael, tape recording, WJHC.
122   "they certainly could not imagine us mixing with their children": Ibid.
122   Meyer's year in Palestine made him doubt the Zionists' "rosy accounts": *Emanu-El*, 5 August 1910, p. 2.
122   By 1915 he had been won over to the Zionist cause: *Emanu-El*, 7 January 1916, p. 4; 17 March 1916, p. 2.
122   Meyer chaired a mass meeting at Dreamland Rink on behalf of the Jews of Palestine: *Emanu-El*, 26 November 1915, p. 13.
122*   Meyer had to be assured by Brandeis that non-Jews would have the right to become citizens: Brandeis to Louis Edward Kirstein, 10 September 1915, *Letters of Louis D. Brandeis III, 1913–1915*, ed. Melvin Urofsky and David Levy (Albany, N.Y., 1973), p. 587.
123   Sokolow spoke at the temple...but Weizmann was spurned: Michael Zarchin, *Glimpses of Jewish Life in San Francisco*, 2nd ed. (Berkeley, 1964), p. 223.
123   Kahn's petition to President Wilson signed by Hellman and Sloss: Moshe Menuhin, *The Decadence of Judaism in Our Time* (Beirut, 1965), pp. 76–79.
123   "For me the United States is my Zion...": Julius Kahn, quoted in the *Emanu-El*, 14 February 1919, p. 10.
123   "the twentieth century will be notable in Jewish history...": *Emanu-El*, 11 April 1919, p. 2.
123   "Rowie" Rinder initiated San Francisco's first Hadassah chapter: Rinder, "Music, Prayer and Religious Leadership," pp. 161–63.
124   "Had we the proper spirit we would not wait...": *Emanu-El*, 26 August 1910, p. 2.
124   On the founding of the Emanu-El Correspondence School: Temple Minutes, October 1913.

125   Meyer expressed concern about an imminent exodus to "the suburbs"; "The rapacity of the landlords of San Francisco has made the rents so high...": *Emanu-El*, 25 November 1910, p. 2.

125   On Meyer's efforts to help the struggling Jewish communities of the suburbs: Temple Minutes, October 1913.

125   On the founding of the Menorah Club: *Emanu-El*, 18 September 1916, pp. 10–12.

125   On the Jewish Committee for Personal Service: Frieda Mogerman, "Pioneers in Social Service: The Jewish Committee for Personal Service in State Institutions in the 1920s," *WSJHQ* 6 (January 1974), pp. 83–89.

126   "the ignorant men who occupy the pulpits": *Emanu-El*, 1 April 1910, p. 12.

126   Meyer castigated American Jewry for its "indifference" to the support of scholarship; "We get as much from Europe...as we get here in a dozen years"; "a Jewish public which will encourage it...": *Emanu-El*, 18 September 1914, p. 3.

127   Women now permitted to join in their own right: Temple Minutes, January 1921.

127   Sophie Lilienthal and Caroline Sahlein the first female members of the board of directors: *Emanu-El*, 29 April 1921, p. 4.

127   "Woman the world over has come out of her classical and medieval seclusion...": *Emanu-El*, 2 June 1922, p. 1.

127   Meyer insisted on a new schoolhouse: Temple Minutes, June 1910.

127   The new building housed the "Free Synagogue": Temple Minutes, October 1911.

128   By 1917 the annex itself had become overcrowded: Temple Minutes, January 1917.

128   children of the unaffiliated accepted at Emanu-El's school without charge: Ibid.

128   The Sutter and Van Ness building alone boasted 545 registrants: Temple Minutes, January 1922.

129   On Arthur "Pie" Myer: Marshall Kuhn, interview by author, 1978.

129   Meyer developed a personal bond with a cadre of young men: Rinder, "Music, Prayer and Religious Leadership," pp. 82–83; Louis Freehof, interview by author, 1978; Eugene Block, interview by author, 1978.

130   On William Stern: Mrs. William (Rae) Stern, interview by author, 1978.

130–31   Newman-Meyer correspondence: Newman Papers.

131   Meyer saw the schoolhouse become inadequate, with over fifty children crowding into a single classroom: Temple Minutes, January 1915.

131   "the Temple of the Open Door"; "Community service is the word of the day...": Temple Minutes, January 1920.

132   Meyer would soon call for a $50 fee...angered without that without exception non-members were required to pay $200: Temple Minutes, January 1921.

132   The decade following World War I ushered in an unprecedented period of synagogue building...the number of structures doubling: David Kaufman, *Shul with a Pool: The "Synagogue-Center" in American Jewish History* (Hanover, N.H., 1999), p. 244.

132   "will endeavor to have us work, play, love and worship as Jews": Quoted in Mel Scult, *Judaism Faces the Twentieth Century: A Biography of Mordecai M. Kaplan* (Detroit, 1993), p. 155.

132   recent research has revealed that the idea of the "open temple" was first broached decades earlier: Kaufman, *Shul with a Pool*, pp. 10–50.

133   "a new spirit is widening the walls...": Quoted in ibid., p. 42.

133   "amusement and spiritual entertainment...": Gotthard Deutsch, quoted in ibid., p. 44.

133   the idea of a synagogue-center rapidly gained ground and was heartily endorsed by the Central Conference of American Rabbis: Ibid., p. 48.

133   The previous spring Meyer had been given a raise to $14,400 a year: Temple Minutes, March 1919.

133   By the end of August the committee had a list of many possible locations: "Memo of services rendered by Messrs. Sam Baer et al. to the Congregation Emanu-El in the matter of the selection of a building site for a new temple," memorandum, n.d., Temple Emanu-El Archives.

133   the site committee had difficulty making a final decision: Ibid.

134   Bloch on the new sanctuary: Temple Minutes, March 1923.

134   Rabbi Meyer found dead: *Emanu-El*, 29 June 1923, p. 1.

134   the coroner found potassium cyanide in his stomach: Eugene Block, interview by author, 1978.

134   Much more likely, in the opinion of those who knew him, was that he was driven to suicide: Eugene Block, interview by author, 1978; Louis Freehof, interview by author, 1978.

135   "harrowing labors with the wounded and dying burned their impress...": Quoted in Daniel J. Moscowitz, "Martin A. Meyer: His Life and Its Lessons, Part I," *WSJH* 26 (April 1994), p. 213.

135   Meyer's health had been poor and he was hospitalized due to "stress and exhaustion": Daniel J. Moscowitz, "Martin A. Meyer: His Life and Its Lessons, Part II," *WSJH* 26 (July 1994), p. 350.

135   He was also suffering from a serious hearing loss: Eugene Block, interview by author, 1978; Narell, *Our City*, p. 408.

135   Other congregants believed that he had had an inoperable brain tumor: Louis Heilbron, interview by author, 25 October 1997.

135   rumor that Meyer was culpable of sexual misconduct: Louis Freehof, interview by author, 1978. Freehof was convinced that Meyer was guilty of serious wrongdoing in this regard, a claim he also made in separate discussions with John Rothmann and Rabbi Alvin Fine, among others. Although Freehof did not arrive at Emanu-El until 1946, as its first executive secretary, he named as his sources deeply respected lay leaders of his era who had been in the rabbi's confirmation class in the early 1920s. Unfortunately, by 1978 each of his informants had either passed away or were too ill to discuss the matter. In 1997, Louis Heilbron—who in 1923 was a sixteen-year-old, active in the temple—affirmed that a rumor of sexual misconduct did circulate after Meyer's death, the truth of which he can neither verify nor deny. But disagreeing with the late Freehof, he believes that the proximate cause of the suicide was an inoperable brain tumor.

135   Meyer's obituary for Krauskopf: *Emanu-El*, 22 June 1923, p. 2.

CHAPTER 5 / LOUIS NEWMAN: THE RENASCENT TWENTIES

137   "tall, erect, and spare," he spoke with a dramatic delivery: Louis Heilbron, interview by Anita Hecht, 21 May 1998.

137   a collection of his sermons was published, "typical illustrations of what is preached...": Louis I. Newman, foreword to *Anglo-Saxon and Jew: Jewish Questions of the Day* (New York, 1923).

137   Newman's doctoral dissertation in Semitics was published as a monumental seven-hundred-page volume: Louis I. Newman, *Jewish Influence on Christian Reform*

Movements (New York, 1925).

138   Newman's dissertation attacked by George Foote Moore: George Foote Moore, *American Historical Review* (October 1926), p. 100.

138   Newman's dissertation attacked by Paul Radin: Paul Radin, "Books," *N.Y. Herald Tribune*, 4 July 1926, p. 6.

138   His "valuable mine of material" was praised as "compilation and research unusual in this day of outlines": Sidney S. Tedesche, "A Useful Work," *Saturday Review of Literature*, 4 December 1926, p. 374.

138   "Men move in groups; hence I will accept my own group...": Newman, "On Being a Jew," in *Anglo-Saxon and Jew*, p. 25.

140   "The Temple House movement with its basketball games, dramatics, dancing classes...": Louis I. Newman, *Biting on Granite: Selected Sermons and Addresses* (New York, 1946), p. 37.

140   "The Temple House is a 'piece of Palestine'...": Ibid., p. 38.

140   Newman was opposed by Harold Zellerbach: Harold Zellerbach, interview by author, 1978.

141   the Martin A. Meyer Auditorium in particular bore Newman's stamp: Rinder, "Music, Prayer and Religious Leadership," p. 88.

141   the price tag for the entire complex was more than fifteen times the average cost: Kaufman, *Shul with a Pool*, p. 244.

142   The status-conscious finance committee established sixteen different categories of seats: Temple Minutes, November 1924.

142   A special meeting was held on December 9, 1924, to collect pledges: *Temp. Chron.*, 19 December 1924.

142*   Temple Sholom of Chicago took out a mortgage of $700,000: Elliot Lefkowitz, *Temple Sholom: 125 Years of Living Judaism* (Chicago, 1993), p. 41.

142   A published list of the donors of December 9: *Temp. Chron.*, 19 December 1924.

143   "Here shall stand one of the rarest buildings...": *Temp. Chron.*, 27 February 1925.

143   The elaborate exercises included speeches...: *Temp. Chron.*, 16 April 1926.

144   "Of all the architectural forms yet imagined...": Arthur Brown Jr., "Building a Temple," *Pacific Coast Architect* 30 (September 1926), p. 31.

144   "a great, golden bubble, lofty, soaring in the sky": Harris Allen, "Sermons Cast in Stone," *Pacific Coast Architect* 30 (September 1926), p. 10.

145   described by Rabbi Newman as "autumn red": Louis I. Newman, "The New Temple Emanu-El of San Francisco," *Pacific Coast Architect* 30 (September 1926), p. 55.

145   The symbol of the dome also has its place in the variegated world of synagogue architecture: Rachel Wischnitzer, *Synagogue Architecture in the United States: History and Interpretation* (Philadelphia, 1955), pp. 84–89, 104–17.

145   Mumford on the dome: Louis Mumford, "Towards a Modern Synagogue Architecture," *Menorah Journal* 11 (June 1925), pp. 225–40.

147   "everything in architecture is either a cube or an egg": Ibid., p. 233.

148   "There is a rugged and potent barbaric splendor in the edifice...": Newman, "The New Temple Emanu-El," p. 57.

148   "a great quiet auditorium...": Allen, "Sermons Cast in Stone," p. 10.

148–49   On the ark: *Temp. Chron.*, 17 December 1926; 11 February 1927.

149   On the organ: Newman, "The New Temple Emanu-El," p. 57; Rinder, "Music, Prayer and Religious Leadership," p. 54.

149   "a glorious building...": Quoted in the *San Francisco Chronicle*, 6 June 1927, p. 10.

149   Newman remarked in 1930 that five thousand people were in some way affiliated: Temple Minutes, January 1929.
150   the board of directors voted to cease all advertising in the *Emanu-El: Temp. Chron.*, 30 April 1926.
150   On the Temple Players: Mortimer Fleishhacker and Janet Choynski Fleishhacker, "Family, Business and the San Francisco Community" (WJHC, oral history, typescript, 1975), pp. 105–6, 315–16, 328, 330.
150   On S. An-Ski's *Dybbuk:* Rinder, "Music, Prayer and Religious Leadership," p. 89.
150   Critics were unanimous in their praise: *Temp. Chron.*, 9 November 1928.
151–52 On the Pathfinders and Troop 17: Marshall Kuhn, interview by author, 1978.
152   the school had difficulty competing with "the California out of doors": *Temp. Chron.*, 9 November 1928.
153   "Nothing in this world is perfect...": Temple Minutes, January 1927.
153   Marshall Kuhn remembered his own Sunday school experience as "just horrible": Marshall H. Kuhn, "Catalyst and Teacher: San Francisco Jewish and Communal Leader, 1934–1978" (WJHC, oral history, typescript, 1978), p. 187.
153   model Passover seder erupted into a raucous food fight: Ibid., p. 32.
153   "social life"; "I'm not sure it was religious fervor that brought them to religious school...": Louis Heilbron, interview by Anita Hecht, 21 May 1998.
153   Newman lashed out at what he termed "the new paganism": *Temp. Chron.*, 6 February 1925.
153–54 His favorite foe was Freud: *Temp. Chron.*, 10 April 1925; 22 May 1925; 11 April 1930.
154   Newman's talks before young people stressed fidelity: *Temp. Chron.*, 10 April 1925; 22 May 1925; 11 April 1930.
154   "Judge Lindsey dismisses the need for continence too lightly": *Temp. Chron.*, 4 February 1927,
154   Newman blamed "the young girl for the troublesomeness...preferable to the life of the home and the family": *Temp. Chron.*, 21 January 1927.
154   "nature worship": *Temp. Chron.*, 1 October 1926.
154   "Jewry, like other religious groups...is being overborne...": *Temp. Chron.*, 16 August 1929.
154   Newman upheld the principle of separation of church and state in a widely circulated pamphlet: Louis I. Newman, *The Sectarian Invasion of Our Public Schools* (San Francisco, 1925).
154–55 "This may be the age of hysteria...": Ibid., p. 14.
155   "You shall not crucify mankind upon a cross of ignorance": *Temp. Chron.*, 29 May 1925.
155   Newman joined the nationwide protest against *King of Kings: Temp. Chron.*, 23 December 1927.
155   Two years later he condemned the American tour of the Freiburg Passion Play: *Temp. Chron.*, 17 May 1929.
155   "True liberalism does not encourage the breakdown...": Newman, *Anglo-Saxon and Jew*, pp. 14–15.
155   Louis Bloch's daughter married a non-Jew without the rabbi's blessing: Eugene Block, interview by author, 1978.
155   "Newman would have been better off...": Harold Zellerbach, interview by author, 1978.
156   "The most flagrant blunder of Reform Judaism...": *Temp. Chron.*, 27 May 1927.

156   Newman was the first Reform rabbi to endorse Jabotinsky's militant Revisionism: Louis Freehof, interview by author, 1978.

156   "colossal blunders": *Temp. Chron.*, 13 September 1929.

156   "The catch phrases of the last ten years...": Melvin Urofsky, *American Zionism from Herzl to the Holocaust* (Garden City, N.Y., 1975), p. 364.

157   "the center of centers": Temple Minutes, January 1930.

157   "the amazing city": *Temp. Chron.*, 20 April 1928.

158   Newman asked the price of shipping the piano to New York: Rose Rinder, interview by author, 1978.

158   Dinkelspiel tried desperately to convince Newman to stay: Rinder, "Music, Prayer and Religious Leadership," p. 91.

CHAPTER 6 / REUBEN RINDER: MUSIC AND HUMANITY

160   "the peculiar sensitivity which marks the musician...": Reuben R. Rinder, "Albert Schweitzer: Musician and Humanitarian," 1949, Rinder Papers.

160   From 1928 to 1940 Rinder presented a concert at the mansion of Marcus Koshland's widow: Rinder, "Music, Prayer and Religious Leadership," pp. 40–42.

160   The temple organist...would play the ample organ which Mrs. Koshland had installed: Louis Freehof, interview by author, 1978.

160   annual musical events held at the temple beginning in 1922: Ibid., p. 76.

162   "the most thrilling episode, an extraordinary example...": Marjory M. Fischer, quoted in Rinder, "Music, Prayer and Religious Leadership," p. 78n.

162   "American Israel contents itself with a meagre musical output"; "a Jewish Palestrina": Reuben R. Rinder, "The Society for the Advancement of Synagogue Music: Its Aim and Scope," Rinder Papers.

162   His own liturgical output: Rinder, "Music, Prayer and Religious Leadership," pp. 122–25.

163   The cantor decided "on the spur of the moment"; "Anyone coming from San Francisco...": Ibid., p. 47.

163   Rinder informed Bloch that a director was being sought: Ruth Rafael, "Ernest Bloch at the San Francisco Conservatory of Music," *WSJHQ* 9 (April 1977), p. 195.

164   "I have felt around me, in Frisco, an atmosphere...": quoted in ibid., p. 201.

165   Bloch's *Helvetia* was completed in 1929 and named co-winner: Robert Strassburg, *Ernest Bloch: Voice in the Wilderness* (Los Angeles, 1977), pp. 64–65.

165   Bloch needed another decade to "absorb America": Ernest Bloch, introduction to *America: An Epic Rhapsody in Three Parts* (Vanguard recording, New York, 1975).

165   This composition was chosen as winner of yet another contest: Strassburg, *Ernest Bloch*, p. 63.

165   a number of critics ridiculed the piece, and there were even those who wondered if a foreign-born Jew ought to be writing: Rafael, "Ernest Bloch," p. 202.

165   "the greatest symphonic work...": Alexander Fried, quoted in ibid.

165   "the Indians...dance with Hasidic feet": David Ewen, quoted in ibid.

165   "It is the Hebrew spirit that interests me...": *Encyclopaedia Judaica*, s.v. "Bloch, Ernest."

166   "It is not my purpose, not my desire to attempt a 'reconstruction'...": Quoted in Rafael, "Ernest Bloch," p. 213.

166   Rinder succeeded in soliciting a gift of $3,000....Ten thousand dollars were soon added: Ibid., p. 207.

166–67   Bloch's letters to Rinder: 26 November 1930 and 5 March 1931, Rinder Papers.

167   A portion of the morning service which the cantor had set to music appeared *in toto*: Rinder, "Music, Prayer and Religious Leadership," p. 51.

167   "The service is built up from the vast, primordial roots...": Alfred Frankenstein, "Bloch's 'Sacred Service' Heard First Time in S.F.," *San Francisco Chronicle*, 29 March 1938, p. 14.

168   "It seems *yesterday* to me that *you* approached me with the idea...": Bloch to Rinder, 18 May 1938, Letters of Ernest Bloch, Music Library, University of California, Berkeley.

168   Leonard Bernstein was one who refused: Ludwig Altman, interview by author, 1979.

168   On Darius Milhaud: Darius Milhaud, *Notes Without Music* (New York, 1953).

169   The Milhauds attended the Rinder seder each year: Rinder, "Music, Prayer and Religious Leadership," p. 72.

169   Mrs. E. S. Heller hastily offered to fund the project: Ibid., p. 71.

169–70   "I want performers of my work, not interpreters"; "big number": Ludwig Altman, interview by author, 1979.

170   Milhaud fails even to mention the *Sacred Service* in his autobiography: Milhaud, *Notes Without Music*.

170   Frankenstein was overwhelmed by the work's "simplicity, dignity, magnificently fluent melody," and "classical clarity": *San Francisco Chronicle*, 20 May 1949, p. 8.

170   Fried stressed the "subtle beauty" of the "deep-felt and original" composition: *San Francisco Examiner*, 20 May 1949, p. 77.

170   "like a never-ending carpet": Ludwig Altman, interview by author, 1979.

171   Rinder met Marc Lavry...commissioned him to write a service: Ibid.; Rinder, "Music, Prayer and Religious Leadership," p. 73.

171   "I have indeed labored nights and days...": Lavry to Rinder, 25 October 1954, Rinder Papers.

171   "angel-music...": Press release, Temple Emanu-El, n.d., Rinder Papers.

171   others were disappointed with the work: Ludwig Altman, interview by author, 1979.

172   "outstanding merit": Rinder to Rabbi Herman E. Schaalman, 26 January 1955, Rinder Papers.

172   "The work occupies a unique place...": Kaelter to Rinder, 11 March 1955, Rinder Papers.

172   Rinder persuaded Congregation Beth El of Detroit to present Lavry's service: Rinder to Rabbi Richard C. Hertz, 31 March 1958, Rinder Papers.

172   "You really opened before me...": Lavry to Rinder, 8 October 1957, Rinder Papers.

172   On Paul Ben Haim: Rinder, "Music, Prayer and Religious Leadership," pp. 74–75.

172   Ben Haim's "themes and tunes are unmistakably Israeli...": Leonard Bernstein, 23 April 1959, Rinder Papers.

172   "A mood of fresh, melodious innocence...": Alfred Frankenstein, *San Francisco Chronicle*, 19 May 1963, p. 14.

173   Altman held that the composition may be ranked alongside Bernstein's famous *Chichester Psalms*: Ludwig Altman, interview by author, 1979.

173   "One child after another sprang up...": Rinder, "Music, Prayer and Religious Leadership," p. 66.

173   On Rinder's discovery of Yehudi Menuhin: Ibid., pp. 56–64.

174   Rinder arranged for Persinger to take Menuhin on: Ibid., p. 57.

174   "who [set] high my sites from the beginning…took extraordinary pains with me":
        Yehudi Menuhin, *Unfinished Journey* (New York, 1976), pp. 29, 33.

174   "He adopted us…": Ibid., p. 59.

175   On Rinder's discovery of Isaac Stern: Rinder, "Music, Prayer and Religious
        Leadership," p. 67.

175   Rinder found Stern a patron in the form of Jennie Baruh Zellerbach: Ibid., p. 68.

175   Rinder arranged for his friend to treat Isaac's ailing father: Dr. Henry Harris to
        Rinder, 19 December 1929, Rinder Papers.

175   Only after Rinder "begged her" did Lutie Goldstein agree to support Stern: Rose
        Rinder, interview by author, 1978.

176   Ruth Slenczynski was so tiny that her father had to devise an extension of the foot
        pedal: Rinder, "Music, Prayer and Religious Leadership," p. 65.

176   On Miriam Solovieff: Ibid., p. 64.

176   On Leon Fleisher: Ibid., p. 69.

176   On Bronislaw Huberman: Ibid., p. 79.

176   A reception at the home of Hattie Sloss yielded $5,000: Ibid.

176   on Huberman's plate were a hard-boiled egg and a check: Rose Rinder, interview
        by author, 1978.

177   "So, you see, your future does not depend on this": Rinder, "Music, Prayer and
        Religious Leadership," p. 55.

177   Rinder raised funds for Amiram Rigai: Ibid.

177   Rinder aided Itzhak Perlman: Ludwig Altman, interview by author, 1979.

177–78 On Ludwig Altman's early life: Ludwig Altman, interview by author, 1979;
        Ludwig Altman, "A Well-Tempered Musician's Unfinished Journey Through
        Life" (WJHC, oral history, typescript, 1990).

178   Altman's "main job" was that of organist at Temple Emanu-El: Altman,
        "Unfinished Journey," p. 154.

178   On Altman's wife, Emmy: Emmy Altman, interview by Anita Hecht, 11 May 1998.

178   Altman met Thomas Mann and played in orchestras conducted by such luminar-
        ies as Bernstein, Ozawa, Fiedler, and Walter: Robert Kirschner, "Ludwig Altman:
        In Memorium," *Temp. Chron.*, January 1991.

179   Altman uncomfortable with any praise save that he was "the best organist in the
        Richmond District": Ludwig Altman, interview by author, 1979.

179   Altman "diplomatically" let the cantor select the pieces for each service: Altman,
        "Unfinished Journey," p. 67.

179   "If the cantor had worried…": Ibid., p. 154.

179   it would be difficult not to "outshine" the rabbi: Ibid., p. 67.

180   Rinder's only book appeared at the end of his career: Reuben R. Rinder, *Music and
        Prayer for Home, School and Synagogue* (New York, 1959).

180   Naming Rinder "Cantor for Life" was largely Rose Rinder's doing: Rinder,
        "Music, Prayer and Religious Leadership," p. 113.

181   "It is said in the Zohar…": Louis Newman, eulogy for Rinder, Rinder Papers.

181   Newman declared Reform Judaism "sterile of inspiration, poetry, and art": *Temp.
        Chron.*, 27 May 1927.

CHAPTER 7 / IRVING REICHERT: YEARS OF RANCOR

184   "fundamental fact that Judaism is a religion, *and a religion only*": "Getting Back to
        Fundamentals," 4 April 1952, *Reichert Sermons*, p. 9.

184   "either a phrase or a fetish, no more than that...": Ibid.
184   "a retreat from the highway of Jewish destiny...": Ibid., p. 15.
184   "the decline of an historical mission": "Judaism in Eclipse," 13 April 1951, *Reichert Sermons*, p. 155.
184   "Why this revival of archaic Orthodox ceremonies and customs...": Ibid., p. 168.
184   Reichert's Judaism came very close to the teachings of the Unitarian Church: Irving Reichert Jr., interview by author, 1978.
184   "a quest, a vision, and a goal": "The Fool Hath Said It in his Heart," May 1936, *Reichert Sermons*, p. 80.
184   "from Moses to Lincoln"; "co-worker": "Getting Back to Fundamentals," p. 11.
186   Reichert included Jesus among the Hebrew prophets: Louis Freehof, interview by author, 1978.
186   "the masses could be aroused...": "The Duty of Hating," 1 May 1937, *Reichert Sermons*, p. 68.
186   "How much liberty...": Ibid., p. 73.
186   "time- and energy-consuming activities...a digression": "The Spoken Word as Part of the Worship," 15 January 1937, *Reichert Sermons*, p. 19.
186   "Preaching that claims to be interested...": Ibid., p. 24.
186   Reichert's passion for liberal causes: Irving Reichert Jr., interview by author, 1978.
187   Reichert appointed to the state advisory board of the National Recovery Administration: Zarchin, *Glimpses of Jewish Life* (1952 edition), p. 133.
187   Reichert sent a telegram to the press holding Rolph responsible "for any further outrages": *San Francisco Chronicle*, 12 October 1933, p. 1.
187   The rabbi threatened the growers with a cutoff of federal farm relief: *San Francisco Chronicle*, 10 October 1933, p. 1; Irving Reichert Jr., interview by author, 1978.
187   "the best lesson California has ever given...": *San Francisco Chronicle*, 27 November 1933, p. 1.
187   "humiliation and shame"; "laudation": *San Francisco Chronicle*, 30 November 1933, p. 1.
188   "unpardonable attacks and outrages...": *Temp. Chron.*, 19 December 1941.
188   On the American Committee on Fair Play: Zarchin, *Glimpses of Jewish Life* (1952 edition), p. 134.
188   "Ask any Jew what he thinks of tyranny...": *Temp. Chron.*, 2 March 1934.
188   "hopeless lot"; "of 600,000 of our fellow Jews": "The New Year and the Nazi Terror," 20 September 1933, *Reichert Sermons*, p. 118.
188   "the most moving and impressive sermon...": Louis Heilbron, interview by Anita Hecht, 21 May 1998.
188–89   "German Jewry, like Israel of old...": "The New Year and the Nazi Terror," p. 119.
189   "incomprehensible" complacency; "appalling niggardliness"; "There is no longer any justification..."; "subsidize his own degradation": Ibid., p. 120.
189   Reichert held that further persecution would result from domestic prosperity: Ibid., p. 121.
189–90   "ambassador to the gentiles"; Reichert's speaking engagements and participation in civic associations: Temple Minutes, January 1933 and January 1934.
190   Reichert able to prevail upon the San Francisco Board of Education to remove all religious references from Christmas celebrations: *Temp. Chron.*, 6 January 1933.
190   Reichert and other leading Jews formed the Survey Committee; "invaluable..."; "one man of the cloth to another": Eugene Block, interview by author, 1978.

190   Reichert personally sponsored many immigrants: Irving Reichert Jr., interview by author, 1978.

191   By 1937, fourteen German-Jewish children were enrolled in the religious school; Emanu-El's programs for immigrants were replicated: Temple Minutes, January 1938.

191–92   Reichert clashed publicly with Hugh Johnson: *Temp. Chron.*, 1 November 1940.

192   "You blind men, fumbling with your broom-straws...": "How Much Do We Want Liberty?" 13 April 1940, *Reichert Sermons*, p. 218.

192   Reichert declared that American Jews "were prepared to give everything": *Newsweek*, 22 December 1941, p. 62.

192   servicemen invited to High Holiday prayers: Temple Minutes, January 1942.

193   "They were not killed on the battlefield...": "Futile Weapons," 1 May 1943, *Reichert Sermons*, p. 98.

193   "compassion and courage..."; "Not the captives but the conquerors...": Ibid., p. 97.

193   "the real problems will come after the last shot has been fired": *Temp. Chron.*, 30 January 1942.

193   Reichert opposed Britain's White Paper of 1939: *Temp. Chron.*, 28 January 1944.

194   On Reichert's speech before the local chapter of the Zionist Organization of America: Eugene Block, interview by author, 1978.

194   nationalism "alien to the historic traditions of Israel"; "Jewish states may rise and fall...": "One Reform Rabbi Replies to Ludwig Lewisohn," 11 January 1936, *Reichert Sermons*, p. 133.

194   "Israel took upon itself the yoke of the Law...": Ibid., p. 131.

194   "One wonders what the Gentile world makes of all this...": Ibid., p. 132.

194–95   "No swashbuckling, sabber-rattling Nazi...": Ibid., p. 132.

195   "extortion, character assassination...": "Judaism in Eclipse," p. 169.

195   CCAR resolved to "take no official stand...": Samuel Halperin, *The Political World of American Zionism* (Detroit, 1961), p. 78.

195   The rabbinical conclave in Atlantic City countered with a manifesto of its own: Ibid., pp. 83–86; *Temp. Chron.*, 9 October 1942.

195   The gathering also led to the formation of the American Council for Judaism: Halperin, *Political World of American Zionism*, p. 87.

196   On Edward Nathan Calisch: Myron Berman, "Rabbi Edward Nathan Calisch and the Debate over Zionism in Richmond, Virginia," *AJHQ* 63 (March 1973), pp. 295–305.

196   Reichert drew his leadership almost exclusively from the board of directors: San Francisco Records of the American Council for Judaism, 1943, WJHC.

197   "No more serious issue will face us as Jews...": "Where Do You Stand?" 8 October 1943, *Reichert Sermons*, pp. 135–36.

197   "at every point"; "it is on the basis of such a vote...": Ibid., p. 138.

197   "make a decision...and take a place on one side or the other": Ibid., p. 142.

197   servicemen dismayed by Reichert sermon; heated exchanges ensued: Rose Rinder, interview by author, 1978.

198   Rose Rinder compared the rabbi to Hitler: Ibid.

198   San Francisco section boasted enrollment of over a thousand: San Francisco Records of the American Council for Judaism, 1943, WJHC.

198   membership peaked at somewhere approaching 1,400: Fred Rosenbaum, "Zionism and Anti-Zionism in San Francisco," in Moses Rischin and John

Livingston, eds., *Jews of the American West* (Detroit, 1991), p. 123. I wish to thank Wayne State University Press for permission to include here part of the text of my previously published article.

198   "while Israelite, it had known no other nationality...": Quoted in ibid., p. 124.

198   The leading families in particular rallied to the cause: Ibid., p. 122.

198   "sense of well-being": Kevin Starr, *The Dream Endures: California Enters the 1940s* (New York, 1997), p. 125.

199   a third of the mayor's appointments: David G. Dalin, "Jewish and Non-Partisan Republicanism in San Francisco, 1911–1963" in Rischin, ed., *Jews of the West*, pp. 123–24.

199   "could not be matched in any other American city": Earl Rabb, quoted in ibid., p. 124.

199   "Does anyone who has not completely surrendered...": "The Policy and Program of Reform Judaism," 3 March 1946, *Reichert Sermons*, p. 34.

200   Zionists held rallies...Saul White reprimanded the ACJ by name: Rosenbaum, "Zionism and Anti-Zionism," p. 124.

200   "There are still a few thousands of European Jews on the march...": Anita Freed to Reichert, 11 June 1945, John F. Rothmann Archives, San Francisco.

200   "I do not believe that a Jewish state in Palestine...": Reichert to Anita Freed, 3 July 1945, John F. Rothmann Archives, San Francisco. I am indebted to John Rothmann for making these letters available to me.

201   Reichert sought out Bartley Crum; Sloss reported an attempt to change the opinion of Hoover: San Francisco Records of the American Council for Judaism, 1943, WJHC.

201   Reichert conducted less than half the temple's funerals: Harold Zellerbach, Report to the Board of Directors (manuscript, December 1947). Temple Emanu-El Archives.

201   "reluctant to face him frankly": Temple Minutes, January 1933.

201   woman threatened resign...on the death of her poodle: Irving Reichert Jr., interview by author, 1978.

201   Reichert's bad memory for names and faces damaged him: Ibid.

201   Most glaring was the deterioration of the institution itself: Zellerbach, Report to the Board of Directors.

202   Most important was the addition of a new sacred space: Stephen Pearce, "Historical Highlights: The Reuben R. Rinder Chapel," *Temp. Chron.*, April 1994, p. 14.

203   Zellerbach's first task was "hearing complaints": Harold Zellerbach, interview by author, 1978.

204   "in the minds of many non-members is a citadel of snobbishness": Gene K. Walker, Report to the Board of Directors (manuscript, 15 May 1947). Temple Emanu-El Archives.

204   "attitude"; "warmth and friendliness"; "a ship with many propellers..."; "honorary office"; "grave responsibility"; "The publication of a price list...": Ibid.

204   a net gain of 104 members during the year 1947: Temple Minutes, January 1948.

204   In 1947, Zellerbach held a day-long hearing: Harold Zellerbach, interview by author, 1978; Marshall Kuhn, interview by author, 1978; Louis Freehof, interview by author, 1978.

205   "A rabbi is not a janitor or a street-sweeper...": Monroe Deutsch, speech before the board of directors, Reichert Papers.

206   Morris Lazaron forced to step down: *Encyclopaedia Judaica, s.v.* "Lazaron, Morris Samuel."

206   "If it's good enough for my country...": Lloyd Dinkelspiel, quoted by Marshall Kuhn, interview by author, 1978.

206   doubts about the ACJ which letters from Berger could not allay: San Francisco Records of the American Council for Judaism, 1943, WJHC.

206   Zionist leanings of Rhoda and Richard Goldman: Richard Goldman, interview by Anita Hecht, 27 May 1998.

206   ACJ had virtually no members under thirty: Rosenbaum, "Zionism and Anti-Zionism," p. 127.

206   "Certainly all of our members belong to the Reform": Sloss to Berger, quoted in ibid.

207   "reactivate"; "difficulty in maintaining the interest..."; "the group needs constant attention..."; "appears to be coming apart...": Reichert, quoted in ibid., p. 128.

207   Ehrman discontinued his annual gift to the UJA: Marshall Kuhn, interview by author, 1978.

207   Berger voiced criticism of George Levison: Rosenbaum, "Zionism and Anti-Zionism," p. 129.

207   "Let us be sure...": Sloss to Berger, quoted in ibid., p. 131.

207   "First of all, they're both philanthropic...": Lilienthal, quoted in ibid.

208   "Ashamed" of themselves, as Dan Koshland admitted: Koshland, quoted in ibid., p. 132.

208–9   "indoctrinated"; "developing a split-personality neurosis": Reichert, "Policy and Program of Reform Judaism," p. 37.

209   "Zionizing"; "Zionism uses the state as a sort of haven...": Lasky, quoted in Rosenbaum, "Zionism and Anti-Zionism," p. 125.

209   letter to Goodman: Berger to Reichert, San Francisco Records of the American Council for Judaism, 1943, WJHC.

209   "bears an ominous resemblance": San Francisco Records of the American Council for Judaism, 1943, WJHC.

209   Reichert planned an advertising campaign: San Francisco Records of the American Council for Judaism, 1943, WJHC.

211   Zionists in Seattle and Portland had tried to cancel Reichert's speaking tour: San Francisco Records of the American Council for Judaism, 1943, WJHC.

211   "The Jewish nationalists have a lot of money....": Reichert, "Getting Back to Fundamentals," p. 14.

211   "incredible and outrageous": Reichert to Clarence Coleman Jr., 19 July 1956, Reichert Papers.

211   "The bulk of funds raised by the UJA...": Moses Lasky, *Between Truth and Repose* (1956), front flyleaf.

212   the ACJ rendered "a pariah...": Reichert to the *San Francisco Jewish Bulletin*, Reichert Papers; published in *SFJB*, 15 June 1956, p. 8.

212   "turn back the clock..."; "history has made its decision...": Ibid.

212   Reichert never ceased from pointing out Zionism's "dangerous" implications: Irving Reichert Jr., interview by author, 1978.

212   Lasky too resigned from the ACJ; "the [ACJ's] strident public affairs campaign...": Stephen Pearce, "Historical Highlights: The American Council for Judaism and Its Relationship to Congregation Emanu-El," *Temp. Chron.*, June/July 1994, p. 11.

212   Charles Tanenbaum remained on the rolls: Ibid.

212   Reichert's personal life also caused him unbearable pain: Irving Reichert Jr., interview by author, 1978.

213   Reichert wounded most deeply by his career-long fight against Zionism….he took
        his own life: Ibid.

        CHAPTER 8 / ALVIN FINE: POSTWAR REVIVAL AND NEO-REFORM

215   membership increased by more than half while Fine served as its rabbi: Temple
        Minutes, January 1964.
215–16 On Alvin Fine (biographical): Alvin Fine, interviews by author, 1978 and 25 July
        1998.
216   "They want you, Alvin": Fine, interview by author, 25 July 1998.
216   Zellerbach's promise of a big gift to HUC: Harold Zellerbach, interview by
        author, 1978.
216   Fine's Zionist inclinations "raised some eyebrows": Fine, interview by Anita
        Hecht, 1 June 1998.
216   "We'd like you to become our rabbi.": Fine, interview by author, 25 July 1998.
216   Heller played "Mr. Inside" to Fine's "Mr. Outside": Meyer Heller, interview by
        author, 1978.
217   "Neo-Reform": Marshall Sklare and Joseph Greenblum, *Jewish Identity on the
        Suburban Frontier: A Study of Group Survival in the Open Society* (New York, 1967),
        p. 110.
217   "transplanted *shtetl*": Fine, interview by author, 1978.
217   "wouldn't let a day go by": Fine, interview by author, 25 July 1998.
218–19 Fine was the first rabbi in eighty years to wear the *tallit*…reinstituted actual blow-
        ing of the shofar…attempted to introduce at least a modicum of Hebrew…mem-
        ber of the Labor Zionist Organization of America: Fine, interview by author,
        1978.
219–20 "American democracy, in its best and highest definition, does not reduce…": "The
        State of Israel and the American Jew," 14 October 1949, Fine Papers.
220   the major forum for the often heated discussions of these ideas became the reli-
        gious school committee: Meyer Heller, interview by author, 1978.
220   Fine letter on the Berger incident: letter dated 4 January 1952, Fine Papers.
220   Eisendrath waging a struggle: Avi M. Schulman, *Like a Raging Fire: A Biography of
        Maurice N. Eisendrath* (New York, 1993), pp. 36–37.
220   Eisendrath invigorated the movement, which tripled its membership: Ibid., p. 38.
221   "I know such delegates will reflect your inspiration…": Eisendrath to Fine, 12
        March 1957, Fine Papers.
221   Fine was able to withhold the invitation: Fine, interview by author, 25 July 1998.
222   "At the end of each year we would empty it…": Meyer Heller, interview by author,
        1978.
222   complaints greatly exaggerated the extent to which Fine had altered the service:
        Fine, interview by author, 1978.
222   "racehorse"; "Coach": Fine Papers; Fine, interview by author, 1978.
222   "I want the lights on seven nights a week": Ibid.
222   the extended "Levi Strauss family" accounted for one-quarter of all funds: Louis
        Weintraub, interview by author, 1979.
223   early study missions to the Middle East were far more exciting than temple com-
        mittee meetings: Fine, interview by author, 1978.
223   "The Federation…faces a choice…": Fine to Treguboff, 31 July 1962, Fine
        Papers.

224   On Walter Haas: Walter A. Haas Sr., "Civic, Philanthropic and Business Leadership" (WJHC, oral history, typescript, 1975).

224   On Benjamin Swig: Walter Blum, *Benjamin H. Swig: The Measure of a Man* (San Francisco, 1968).

224   Up to that point his life had been spent in Boston...anti-Semitism of his neighbors: John F. Stack Jr., *International Conflict in an American City: Boston's Irish, Italians and Jews, 1935–1944* (Westport, Conn., 1979).

224   "master's degree": Blum, *Benjamin H. Swig*, p. 3.

225   Swig's gifts of luxury automobiles to Ben-Zvi and Ben-Gurion: Ibid., p. 53.

225   Swig "practically a father" to Fine: Fine, interview by author, 1978.

225   On Camp Swig: Ibid.; Blum, *Benjamin H. Swig*, pp. 54–55.

226   On Jesse Colman: Dalin, "Jewish and Non-Partisan Republicanism," p. 115.

226   Swig worked for Adlai Stevenson; rallied the California contingent at the Democratic National Convention: Blum, *Benjamin H. Swig*, pp. 45–49.

226   Swig the first to console Brown after his loss: Ibid., p. 77.

226   Swig invited the Warrens and the Fines on a cruise: Fine, interview by author, 1978.

226   Fine's eulogy for Warren: Address by Rabbi Alvin I. Fine at the Funeral Service of Chief Justice Earl Warren in the Washington Cathedral, 12 July 1974, Fine Papers.

226   "If the shoe fits...": Fine, interview by author, 1978.

226   Swig played a major role in San Francisco mayoral elections: David G. Dalin, "Public Affairs and the Jewish Community: The Changing Political World of San Francisco Jews" (Ph.D. diss., University of Michigan, 1977), pp. 162–63.

227   Until 1974, other San Francisco politicians were the beneficiaries of large donations: Ibid., pp. 164–66.

227   social justice "as much of a *mitzvah*...": Fine, interview by author, 1978.

227–28 "It is for us to seek the *right* way...": "The Essence of the Matter," 27 February 1955, Fine Papers.

228   Fine affected profoundly by Rabbi Jacob Weinstein: Fine, interview by author, 1978.

228   Weinstein forced to resign: Zarchin, *Glimpses of Jewish Life* (1952 edition), p. 94; Janet Weinstein, interview by author, 1979.

228   "idealistic": Fine, interview by author, 1978.

228   Fine publicly voiced his doubts about the rearmament of Germany and Japan: "Religion and World Crisis," Fine Papers.

228   Dr. Hewlett Johnson known as "the Red Dean of Canterbury": Fine, interview by author, 1978; Louis Freehof, interview by author, 1978.

229   Fine speech at the convention of the ILWU: "Democracy in Danger," 4 May 1949, Fine Papers.

229   Fine lobbied against the "Tenney Bills" and was a sponsor of the statewide Federation for the Repeal of the Levering Act: Fine, interview by author, 1978; personal correspondence, Fine Papers.

229   Fine attacked the loyalty oath required by the University of California; presented a debate on the subject: Marshall Kuhn, interview by author, 1978.

229   an FBI agent came to the temple: Fine, interview by author, 1978.

230   Fine refused to take an active role in defending Morton Sobell: Patrick Murphy Malin to Fine, 23 May 1960, Fine Papers.

230   George Christopher referred to the protesters as "dupes of known communists": Ernest Besig to Mayor George Christopher, 11 February 1961, Fine Papers.

230   "If the film is a fraud...in this matter": Ibid.

230   in 1962, Fine again assailed Christopher: Fine to Christopher, 26 January 1962, Fine Papers.

231   "I believe that the extremist ideology of the reactionary right...": 13 September 1960, Fine Papers.

231   "concern with the dangers and pitfalls...obscene literature": Fine to Supervisor Jack Morrison, 25 January 1962, Fine Papers.

231–32   Fine and Pike disagreed on the Court's decision: "Fine Disputes Pike on the First Amendment," *Pacific Jewish Press*, 10 August 1962, p. 1, 10; *SFJB*, 17 August 1962.

232–33   Fine able to convey his views during Second Vatican Council through letters to Hurley: Fine, interview by author, 1978.

233   in 1953 only five landlord-tenant disputes could be mediated: the Reverend James O'Shea to Joseph A. Brown, 6 November 1953, Fine Papers.

233   Fine constantly bombarding every member of the board of supervisors with letters: Ibid.

233   "Being a religious man, it is my conviction...": Statement of Rabbi Alvin I. Fine to the County, State, and National Affairs Committee of the Board of Supervisors, 30 January 1957, Fine Papers.

233   Fine attacked degrading blackface minstrel shows: Ibid.

233   Fine publicly opposed the overly harsh sentence meted out to a black physician: July 1964, Fine Papers.

234   Fine extolled Martin Luther King Jr. as "a modern Moses": Fine, interview by author, 1978.

234   "I took him into the temple...": Fine, interview by Anita Hecht, 1 June 1998.

234   On Howard Thurman: Howard Thurman, *With Head and Heart* (New York, 1979).

235   On Sammy Davis Jr.: Sammy Davis Jr., Jane Boyar, and Burt Boyar, *Yes I Can: The Story of Sammy Davis Jr.* (New York, 1966), pp. 237–38, 280–86; Fine, interview by author, 1978.

236   Joseph Weinberg arrested and jailed for protesting; ninth-grade class presented the assistant rabbi with a plaque: Joseph Weinberg, interview by author, 1979.

236   "Bigotry, however polite...": Reynold Colvin, "Meditation" (1963), Fine Papers.

237   "Our fellow citizens—our brothers of the Negro community...": "A Sermon on Religion and Race—1963," *Temp. Chron.*, October 1963.

237   the rolls swelled to a high of 1,540 households by 1964: Temple Minutes, January 1964.

237   Zellerbach predicted two thousand families: Annual Report, 16 January 1951, Temple Emanu-El Archives.

237*   Massarik's report on Jewish population: Fred Massarik, *Report on the Jewish Population of San Francisco, Marin County and the Peninsula* (San Francisco, 1959), p. 5.

238   "democratization": Fine, interview by author, 1978.

238   the board adopted the "Fair Share Plan": G. Marvin Schoenberg, interview by author, 1978.

238   The Home of Peace Cemetery showed a surplus: Ibid.

239   Funds were raised in special anniversary drives every five years: Ibid.; Temple Minutes; *Temp. Chron.*

240   "Membership was up and inflation was down": G. Marvin Schoenberg, interview by author, 1978.

240   Heller organized the spirited Emanu-El Temple Youth; its newsletter reflects a wide range of activities: Jeffrey Keyak, interview by author, August 1998.

240–41 Religious school enrollment figures: Temple Minutes, January 1961.

241 Yet the religious school had severe problems: Meyer Heller, interview by author, 1978; John Rothmann, interviews by author, 1978 and 4 November 1997.

242–43 "We know that the amount of information that we can impart...": Meyer Heller, Temple Minutes, January 1960.

244 "make sure that everything you ever say...": Fine, interview by author, 25 July 1998.

244 Fine's letter of resignation: Fine to Jacobs, 21 January 1963, Temple Minutes.

244 Fine did not want to "diminish" the role of spiritual leader; "Anybody who wanted anything...": Fine, interview by author, 1978.

244 "discouraged...with the meager interest...": Fine to Jacobs, October 1961, Fine Papers.

244 Friday evening prayers and Saturday mornings each drew an average of about 225 worshippers: Temple Minutes, 1948–1964.

244–45 Heller handed in his resignation just weeks after Fine: Heller to Jacobs, 5 March 1963, Temple Minutes.

245 Fine was offered many attractive posts: Fine, interview by author, 1978.

246 acting mayor Dianne Feinstein asked him to address a mass meeting: Fine, interview by author, 25 July 1998.

246 Fine's eightieth birthday celebration: transcripts of tributes by Lou Heilbron, Paul Matzger, and Rabbi Meyer Heller made available by Alvin Fine.

247–48 "Birth Is a Beginning": made available by Alvin Fine. (This version, which Rabbi Fine preferred, differs slightly from that published in *Gates of Repentance*.)

248 "I wanted to move...into the next century...": Fine, interview by Anita Hecht, 1 June 1998.

248 "The universal principles are like windows...": "State of Israel" (1949), Fine Papers.

248 "We learn from the past, but we do not live in it...": Fine, interview by Anita Hecht, 1 June 1998.

CHAPTER 9 / JOSEPH ASHER: VERITIES FOR A VOLATILE WORLD

251 On Irving Hausman: Irving Hausman, interview by author, 1979; Alvin Fine, interview by author, 25 July 1998.

252 met with students in his home; rested on a cot: John Rothmann, interview by author, 1978.

254* On Rabbi Jonah Ansbacher: Joseph Asher, "An Incomprehensible Puzzlement," in Moses Rischin and Raphael Asher, eds., *The Jewish Legacy and the German Conscience* (Berkeley, 1991), pp. 25–37.

254–56 On Joseph Asher (biographical): Joseph Asher, interview by author, 1979.

255 On Asher's experience on the HMT *Dunera*: Peggy Isaak (Gluck), "'Internee' Talks About 'Dunera Incident,'" *SFJB*, 19 October 1979, pp. 19–20; Benzion Patkin, *The Dunera Internees* (Erskineville, Australia, 1979).

255* Asher called in a reporter to unburden himself of his story: Peggy Isaak (Gluck), interview by author, 1979.

256 On Cone Mills: William H. Chafe, *Civilities and Civil Rights: Greensboro, North Carolina and the Black Struggle for Freedom* (New York, 1980), pp. 51–54.

257 "the time [had] come for those who hate Germany...": Asher, "Isn't It Time We Forgave the Germans?" *Look*, 20 April 1965, p. 84.

257 "spiritual victory in reducing bitterness...": Ibid., p. 92.

257 Asher felt no "animosity...only compassion": Ibid., p. 86.

257   *Look* printed replies from two former concentration camp inmates: *Look,* 1 June
       1965, pp. 18, 22.
258   In his sermons Asher frequently dealt with questions often ignored by the Jewish
       community: Asher, sermon, 3 October 1976; *Temp. Chron.,* June 1980; Joseph
       Asher, *Moral Choices: A Religious Perspective* (San Francisco, 1984).
258   He was annoyed by the question "Is it good for the Jews?": Joseph Asher, inter-
       view by author, 1979.
258   "I would regret the Council to fall into the trap of single-issue orientation…":
       Joseph Asher, *Temp. Chron.,* Summer 1980.
258   Asher rarely missed a meeting of the U.S. Holocaust Memorial Council…estab-
       lished a close friendship with Elie Wiesel: Fae Asher, interview by author, 5
       November 1997.
259   Asher referred to Jimi Hendrix and Janis Joplin and wrote at length on the sub-
       ject of hallucinatory drugs: *Temp. Chron.,* October 1970, November 1970.
259   "veneer of flower petals…love and peace generation"; "Viewing the event, there
       came to mind the picture of the proverbial lemmings…": *Temp. Chron.,* January
       1970.
259   "assaulting our senses and intellects": Asher, sermon, 17 September 1972.
260   Asher felt that graphic movies contributed to the atmosphere which led to terror-
       ist acts: Asher, sermon, 8 September 1972.
260   "penetrates,…saturates, strangles our lives at every turn": Asher, sermon, 24
       September 1976.
260   "'Telling it like it is' leaves little to our imagination.…"; "All we shall have accom-
       plished…": *Temp. Chron.,* December 1970.
260   rhetorical "excesses" of feminism: Joseph Asher, interview by author, 1979.
260   Nor did he feel an affinity with San Francisco's homosexual community, whose
       leaders he viewed as contentious and provocative: Joseph Asher, interview by
       author, 1979; Fae Asher, interview by author, 5 November 1997; Michal Bourne,
       interview by author, 7 September 1998.
261   "the newest challenge to the Bill of Rights": *Temp. Chron.,* December 1975.
261   "exercise in showmanship"; "if a giant menorah really intensifies Jewish values…":
       Temp. Chron., November 1975.
261   The Jewish Community Relations Council formed a committee to try to reach a
       compromise: John Rothmann, interview by author, 1978.
261   "pied-pipering": Raphael Asher, "In My Father's House," in Rischin and Asher,
       eds., *Jewish Legacy and the German Conscience,* p. 42.
261   On Zalman Schachter-Shalomi: Joseph Asher, interview by author, 1979.
262   "spiritual bankruptcy"; "Jewish militants, Jewish radicals, Jewish communes…":
       Asher, sermon, 9 September 1972.
262   For Asher, interest in Jewish mysticism and meditation "represented a primitive
       sentimentality…": *Temp. Chron.,* September 1977.
262   "an idealized shtetl culture…": Joseph Portnoy, "The Quest for Jewish
       Spirituality: My Personal Search," *Temp. Chron.,* May 1986, p. 6.
263   Asher and Portnoy introduced traditional practices such as the *hakafot:* Joseph
       Asher, interview by author, 1979.
263   Asher "very ambivalent" about many liturgical changes: Joseph Portnoy, interview
       by author, 2 April 1998.
263–64 "there is something to be said for the majesty of that old English style…"; "the
       [revised] text retains a poetic character": *Temp. Chron.,* December 1978.

264   Asher refrained from making a recommendation on replacing the old prayerbook: Joseph Portnoy, interview by author, 2 April 1998.

264*   Portnoy saw no reason to jettison the hymn: Joseph Portnoy, interview by author, 1979.

264   "'high church'...we offer some of the world's greatest liturgical music...": Ibid.

265   Portnoy "wouldn't have *dared* to introduce" a different style of music: Joseph Portnoy, interview by author, 18 November 1997.

265   Asher lambasted the inconsistent "pick and choose" mentality: Joseph Asher, "Mindless Traditionalism," *Temp. Chron.*, February 1982.

265   Asher questioned the motives of those advocating "the restoration of customs and rituals...": *Temp. Chron.*, February 1983.

265   "I know there are only a few congregations like this left...": Joseph Asher, interview by author, 1979.

266   Asher and Lurie launched the first annual confirmation class trip to Israel: Brian Lurie, interview by author, 1979; Joseph Asher, interview by author, 1979.

266   Asher annually contributed about a tenth of his salary to the UJA campaign: Fae Asher, interview by author, 5 November 1997.

266–67 "zealots...who impose their prejudices upon the people"; "kosher level": *Temp. Chron.*, March 1973.

267   Asher also expressed his concern about the conflicts between young and old, Arab and Jew, Ashkenazi and Sephardi, soldier and civilian: Asher, sermon, 13 September 1977.

267   "tantamount to treason": Asher, sermon, 25 September 1976.

267   "we have the right—nay, the duty...": *Temp. Chron.*, October 1973.

267   A lengthy pamphlet circulated by the ZOA drew parallels between Breira and the ACJ: Rael Jean Isaac, "Breira: American Counsel for Judaism?" (New York, 1977).

267   A conspicuous article in the *Jewish Bulletin* on Asher's Breira connection: *SFJB*, 11 March 1977, p. 22.

267   Asher resigned from the ZOA board of directors; Federation executives unhappy; Asher the recipient of death threats: Joseph Asher, interview by author, 1979.

268   Asher expressed dismay with "the dramatic rise of resentment against Israel"; "odious and malicious" comparisons: *Temp. Chron.*, November 1982.

268   "It is one thing to be sharply critical...": *Temp. Chron.*, Summer 1982.

268   Jews of the diaspora have an "obligation to speak out"; acting "as a goad"; "only now [are] the very voices ignored for so long...": *Temp. Chron.*, Summer 1985.

268   "a secular, or civil religion replacing the sacerdotal"; "precisely because the synagogue applies a test beyond the financial one...": *Temp. Chron.*, January 1984.

269   Asher argued that the Federation too closely resembled a giant corporation: Joseph Asher, interview by author, 1979.

269   Jewish federations across the country had "drained away substantial resources": Reynold Colvin, interview by author, 1979.

269   Rabbi Asher wrote ruefully that he could not organize missions to meet Talmudic sages: *Temp. Chron.*, January 1984.

270   Lurie asked whether caring for the aged or finding someone a job is not a religious act; "instrumentality for creating community": Brian Lurie, interview by author, 1979.

271   Asher freely admitted that he was on the defensive: Joseph Asher, interview by author, 1979.

271   "Rabbi Asher was by aptitude and temperament a true intellectual...": Robert

Kirschner, "A Singular Elegance," in Rischin and Asher, eds., *Jewish Legacy and the German Conscience*, p. 49.

272   "that dances across the sanctuary…": Stephen Pearce, "Historical Highlights: The Main Sanctuary's Stained-Glass Windows," *Temp. Chron.*, October 1994, p. 14.

272   "seems to say…[that] only by entering the temple…": Robert Flynn Johnson, Paul Mills, and Lorna Price, *Mark Adams* (San Francisco, 1985), quoted in ibid.

273   Sylvia Stone influenced by Hattie Sloss: Sylvia L. Stone, "Lifelong Volunteer in San Francisco" (WHJC, oral history, typescript, 1983), p. 42.

274   Shifrin's work declared "monumental" by a local reviewer: David Noble, *Patriotic Ledger* (news clipping, n.d.), made available by Joseph Portnoy.

275   Portnoy worked closely with Natra: Sergiu Natra to Joseph Portnoy, letters dated 28 November 1975 and 20 April 1976, made available by Joseph Portnoy.

275   "It spreads warmth and lyric appeal…": Alexander Fried, "Natra's Gates of Prayer Premiere," *San Francisco Examiner*, 17 May 1976, p. 19.

276   a significant number were really inactive members who had neither paid dues nor attended temple events in years; it was later estimated that the actual size had dipped to around a thousand: Mortimer Fleishhacker, interview by author, 11 November 1997; Irwin Wiener, interview by author, 29 October 1997.

276   Muriel Cohn freely admitted that many religious school instructors wandered from the curriculum: Muriel Cohn, interview by author, 9 December 1997.

276   "When I first got on the *bimah*, I looked out at the audience and saw nothing but gray hair": Walter Newman, interview by author, 19 November 1997.

276   A demographic study revealed that the city had lost 26.5 percent of its Jewish population since 1959: Fred Massarik, *The Jewish Population of San Francisco, Marin County and the Peninsula, 1970–1973: Basic Findings* (San Francisco, 1974), p. 2.

276**   Jewish children under fifteen numbered only about four thousand: Ibid., p. 6.

277   two temple presidents even mentioned merger with Sherith Israel as a distinct possibility: Raymond Marks, *Temp. Chron.*, January 1975; Myer Kahn, interview by author, 1979.

277   Another Federation-sponsored study offers a snapshot of the situation: Gary Tobin and Sharon Sassler, *Bay Area Jewish Community Study* (Waltham, Mass., 1988).

277   the sheer size of the Bay Area Jewish community was impressive; the city had more than replaced the steep losses of the 1960s and '70s: Ibid., pp. 22–23.

277–78   On changes in the size and composition of Jewish households: Ibid., pp. 24–29.

278   Jewish men outnumbered Jewish women by a ratio of 3 to 2: Ibid., pp. 67–68.

278–79   On the city's low rate of synagogue affiliation: Ibid., pp. 47–53.

279   San Francisco's Jews had a relatively high rate of mobility: Ibid., p. 42.

279   Almost seven thousand Jewish children lived in the city in the mid '80s: Ibid., pp. 66–68.

279*   The city's economy had been transformed since the '60s: Chester Hartman, *The Transformation of San Francisco* (Totowa, N.J., 1984), pp. 1–5.

280   almost half of the city's unaffiliated Jews were considering a synagogue in the future: Tobin and Sassler, *Bay Area Jewish Community Study*, p. 64.

280   Reform Jews far outnumbered any other designation; number of Orthodox dropped to one in twenty: Ibid., pp. 27–35.

280   On the soaring rate of intermarriage: Ibid., p. 139.

280   half the unaffiliated intermarried families said they were considering synagogue membership: Ibid., p. 147.

281   There were very few younger congregants at Emanu-El by the mid-'80s: John Rothmann, interview by author, 4 November 1997.

281   "it has become increasingly difficult to ask...": G. Marvin Schoenberg, interview by author, 1978.

282   major conflict with the UAHC over dues: Myer Kahn, interview by author, 1979; G. Marvin Schoenberg, interview by author, 1978; *Temp. Chron.*, 1975.

282   "the most important accomplishment": Myer Kahn, interview by author, 1979.

282   The compensation of the clergy and other staff were kept relatively low: Joseph Portnoy, interview by author, 18 November 1997; Temple Minutes, 1968–1984.

282   "We were constantly discussing funding...": Joseph Portnoy, interview by author, 18 November 1997.

283   "as an empty house"; criticism "that our congregation is of the senior-citizen variety"; changes "to provide activity for every age and interest group": Nadine Rushakoff, Annual Report, 20 January 1981, Temple Emanu-El Archives.

283   the early service was conducted in precisely thirty-three minutes: John Rothmann, interview by author, 4 November 1997.

283–84 "a wonderful way to wind down..."; "You always knew who you would see there...": Andrew Colvin, interview by author, 6 February 1998.

284   Bourne's job description didn't "play to [her] strengths": Michal Bourne, interview by author, 7 September 1998.

284   "trainee": Nadine Rushakoff, Annual Report, 20 January 1981, Temple Emanu-El Archives.

285   Kirschner's rabbinic thesis won the praise of Rabbi Alexander Schindler: Robert Kirschner, interview by author, 3 February 1998.

286–87 On Walter Newman (biographical information): Walter Newman, interview by author, 19 November 1997.

286–87 "deadly...where things weren't happening"; "Through Cyril Magnin I learned..."; "felt strongly that youth had to be attracted to the temple..."; "great, great rabbi"; "As happens in so many different organizations...": Ibid.

287   Asher received a raft of honors: Fae Asher, interview by author, 5 November 1997.

287–88 Asher was tiring from his many battles and faced a rough, uncertain road ahead: Joseph Portnoy, interview by author, 18 November 1997.

288   Asher's health beginning to flag; a yet-undiagnosed case of prostate cancer: Fae Asher, interview by author, 5 November 1997.

289   "Not that I am obsessed with my age...": Joseph Asher, annual meeting address, 17 January 1984, Temple Emanu-El Archives.

289   Portnoy too felt that he "had had enough"; he and Asher "had tried to make certain changes...": Joseph Portnoy, interview by author, 18 November 1997.

290   "I can envisage our temple...": Joseph Asher, annual meeting address, March 1983, Temple Emanu-El Archives.

290   Asher's model for the retirement community was the Sequoias: Fae Asher, interview by author, 5 November 1997.

290   extensive feasibility and marketing studies were conducted; hundreds of Bay Area Jews expressed interest: Crown Research Corporation, "Proposed Retirement Center: Questionnaire Survey, Analysis and Interpretation" (Gresham, Ore., 1984).

290   Asher advanced the proposal from the pulpit and in print: See, e.g., *Temp. Chron.*, October 1984.

290–91 "very, very close to culminating a deal": Stuart Aronoff, interview by author, 19 November 1997.

291   "Everyone there loved him": Charlotte Fonrobert, interview by author, August 1998.

291   "incomprehensible puzzlement": Joseph Asher, "An Incomprehensible Puzzlement," p. 25.

292   the festschrift: Moses Rischin and Raphael Asher, eds., *The Jewish Legacy and the German Conscience* (Berkeley, 1991), pp. 25–37.

292   Asher's own piece discussed his scholarly father; "fierce attachment to the world around them...": "In My Father's House," ibid., p. 38.

293   "a *Seelsorger* who took special care of every bride and groom...": Raphael Asher, "Rabbi Joseph Asher: In Memorium" (Eulogy, Temple Emanu-El, 1 June 1990).

293   "My father considered this sanctuary to be holy ground...": Raphael Asher, "Dedication of the Joseph Asher Courtyard (March 21, 1992)," *Temp. Chron.*, May 1992, p. 8.

294–95   "when the synagogue tailors its style..."; "the spiritual and durable anchor...": *Temp. Chron.*, January 1984.

CHAPTER 10 / ROBERT KIRSCHNER: FALLEN STAR

298–300   On Robert Kirschner's origins and early years: Robert Kirschner, interview by author, 3 February 1998.

300–1   "bastion of privilege"; "It seemed like a church..."; "had the necessity of being elected..."; "much more privileged backgrounds..."; "spiritualized figures who somehow had an aura of goodness..." "You see him from the back..."; "these *figures*..."; "There was something narcissistic...": Ibid.

301   Kirschner's rabbinic thesis was published: Robert Kirschner, *Rabbinic Responsa in the Holocaust Era* (New York, 1985).

301–2   "worried about religious school teachers..."; "It wasn't a good fit..."; "on a bit of a lark"; "a full-time mom": Kirschner, interview by author, 3 February 1998.

302   Emanu-El's congregation "still look[ed] to the rabbi as a kind of holy man"; "I was prepared for the grandeur...": Robert Kirschner, "R. Meir's Neck," *Journal of Reform Judaism* 35 (Fall 1988), p. 35.

302   Kirschner thrived under Joe Asher, "everything a senior colleague could be": Kirschner, interview by author, 3 February 1998.

302   "so distressed"; "This will not do for a rabbi of Emanu-El": Ibid.

303   "I found that I liked...the opportunities I had...": Ibid.

303   Kirschner's wife was "thrilled," but "had a lot of trepidation...": Ibid.

303   "I had the feeling that people were just waiting for something to ignite...": Ibid.

304   Kirschner's installation was a grand event: "1,000 Attend Rabbi's Installation at Emanu-El in S.F.," *NCJB*, 13 September 1985, p. 4

304   "profound honor to receive this sacred responsibility...": Robert Kirschner, sermon at installation, 8 September 1985.

305   On Irwin Wiener (biographical): Irwin Wiener, interview by author, 29 October 1997.

305   Kirschner "*thought* [his sermon] was quite enlightened at the time": Kirschner, interview by author, 3 February 1998.

306   Kirschner decried the *Jewish Gaily Forward* as making a mockery of the great New York newspaper: Michael Rankin, interview by author, March 1998.

306   "very much in the closet": Ibid.

306　　"The words of the Torah and the sages...have not changed...": Robert Kirschner, sermon, August 1984. (Excerpts of this sermon, to which Dr. Rankin was invited, were also reprinted by Congregation Sha'ar Zahav.)

306　　Kirschner later told Rankin he would visit AIDS patients: Kirschner, interview by author, 3 February 1998.

307　　"It had to be ashamed to speak its name"; "Where's your yarmulke?"; "knew exactly what to talk about": Ibid.

307　　Passages from the AIDS sermon: Robert Kirschner, "AIDS," *Temp. Chron.*, November 1985, pp. 6–7.

309　　a month after Kirschner spoke the UAHC passed a strongly worded resolution, later endorsed by the Northern California Board of Rabbis: Peggy Isaak Gluck, "Board of Rabbis Makes AIDS Jewish Priority," *NCJB*, 31 January 1986, p. 66.

310　　"We felt for the first time that we weren't alone in this": Michael Rankin, interview by author, March 1998.

310　　"passion and compassion"; "I can still picture him and what he said...": Andrew Colvin, interview by author, 6 February 1998.

310　　"God has no other hands than ours...": Kirschner, "AIDS."

311　　"there are still wounds that take generations to heal..."; "We need you, brother": Kirschner, interview by author, 3 February 1998.

311　　"[He was] suspended there...": Quoted in Winston Pickett, "Bay Area Jews See 'Racism at its Rawest' at GA Rights March," *NCJB*, 30 January 1987, p. 62.

311　　"It occurred to me...": Quoted in Don Lattin, "How Jews and Blacks Got Together," *San Francisco Examiner*, 12 January 1988.

311–12　"something concrete and lasting"; "the huge divide between the Western Addition and Presidio Heights": Kirschner, interview by author, 3 February 1998.

313　　"every kid should have a mentor": Alison Geballe, interview by author, March 1998.

313　　Back on Track "has been a wonderful way of cementing better race relations": Walter Newman, interview by author, 19 November 1997.

313　　"People across generational boundaries were willing to participate...": Don Buder, interview by author, 16 March 1998.

313　　"lighthouse effect"; "on the moral and spiritual horizon of our community": Robert Kirschner, annual meeting address, 20 January 1987; published in *Temp. Chron.*, March 1987, p. 3.

313　　"I didn't even see him...": Kirschner, interview by author, 3 February 1998.

313　　"a continuing commitment to help the needy...": Robert Kirschner, "Cosmetic Compassion," 26 November 1987; published in *Temp. Chron.*, January 1988, p. 2.

314　　the shelter conducted an extensive program in the creative arts: Kirschner, interview by author, 3 February 1998.

314　　Lou Kamen stressed the complexity of social problems such as homelessness: Lou Kamen, "Dealing with Homelessness: A Response to Stephen Dobbs," *Temp. Chron.*, October 1988, p. 4.

314　　the Federation felt that the temple was beginning to compete: Kirschner, interview by author, 3 February 1998.

314　　"not only the conduit of money..."; "restoring, not inventing": Ibid.

314　　"The synagogue should not be confined to where people are married...": Quoted in "Emanu-El Members Share With Homeless," *Inside View*, October 1988, p. 10.

315　　"Concerned about Jewish insularity": Quoted in Peggy Isaak Gluck, "Emanu-El

Reaches Out to Its Asian Neighbors," *NCJB*, 25 April 1986, p. 1.

316   By 1990, Asians comprised almost a third of the city's population: Sam Roberts, *Who We Are: A Portrait of America Based on the Latest U.S. Census* (New York, 1993), p. 76.

316   "little lasting effect": Kirschner, interview by author, 3 February 1998.

316   "holding out our hands...": Gluck, "Emanu-El Reaches Out," p. 1.

316   Kirschner brought a deaf rabbinic intern to lead Sabbath services: Don Plansky, "Deaf Rabbinical Student Tells of Frustration, Successes," *NCJB*, 17 March 1989.

316   On the Bar Mitzvah of a deaf boy: Peggy Isaak Gluck, "Deaf 13-Year-Old Overcomes Challenge to Become Bar Mitzvah," *NCJB*, 9 November 1990.

316   Kirschner took a strong stand in the local press on statewide political issues: Robert Kirschner, "Open Forum: Proposition 63—Against: Veiled Attack," *San Francisco Examiner*, 1 November 1986.

316   Kirschner's plea for contributions netted $40,000: Jane Gross, "Californians Fill Churches Seeking Solace and Life," *New York Times*, 23 October 1989, p. 1.

317   Buder and Kirschner set up a charitable foundation: Don Buder, interview by author, 16 March 1998.

317   Judi Newman reported that the list of volunteers had grown steadily: Judi Leff Newman, "Volunteer Shabbat," address during service, 2 May 1992; published in *Temp. Chron.*, Summer 1992.

317–18 Rhonda Abrams "joined the temple because of Bob"; "He touched a chord...": Rhonda Abrams, interview by author, 24 April 1998.

318   "was able to connect...": Andrew Colvin, interview by author, 6 February 1998.

318   "responsible social force"..."congregation of conscience": Stephen Dobbs, interview by author, 7 November 1997.

318   Kirschner's initial experience with the Classical Reform service was "very negative": Kirschner, interview by author, 3 February 1998.

318   Kirschner didn't think worship services "mattered very much...": Ibid.

319   His incisive essay, "Halakhah and Homosexuality": Robert Kirschner, "Halakhah and Homosexuality: A Reappraisal," *Judaism* 37 (Fall 1988), pp. 450–58.

320–21 "the disgraceful squabbling..."; "For the sake of Torah...": Robert Kirschner, "A Single Garment of Destiny," *Temp. Chron.*, November 1986.

321   The San Francisco experiment was hailed as "unprecedented": Rabbi Irving Greenberg, quoted in Winston Pickett, "CLAL Founder Sees Slowdown in Threat of Jewish Split," *NCJB*, 3 April 1987.

321   "any effort to divide our people..."; "resolve to defend Jewish pluralism": Robert Kirschner to congregation, letter dated 6 December 1988.

321–22 Feinstein voiced "pain and outrage...": Winston Pickett, "Who Is a Jew? Forum With Four Jewish Leaders Draws 800," *NCJB*, 23 Dec 1988, p. 3.

322   "the ultra-religious are not villains...": Robert Kirschner, quoted in ibid.

322   "because of the demoralizing effect of public denunciations of the Jewish state...": Robert Kirschner, quoted in Winston Pickett, "90 Prominent Jews in Bay Area Criticize Israel—With Regrets," *NCJB*, 5 February 1988 p. 41.

322   *Tikkun* "defined its political view more stridently than I prefer": Robert Kirschner, quoted in Marshall Krantz, "Tikkun Magazine Draws Praise, Ire After First Year," *NCJB*, 26 June 1987, p. 28.

322   "What unites us is more important...": Kirschner, interview by author, 3 February 1998.

323 the nursery school opened with thirty-five toddlers: Pam Schneider, interview by author, 19 March 1998.

324 On Yossi Liebowitz (biographical): Yossi Liebowitz, interview by author, 25 November 1997.

324 "His very [Hebrew] name showed that he differed...": Kirschner, interview by author, 3 February 1998.

325 On Roslyn Barak (biographical): Roslyn Barak, interview by author, 20 November 1997.

326 "Her voice was just like a bird...": Walter Newman, interview by author, 19 November 1997.

326 "that could do anything": James Schwabacher, quoted by Stephen Pearce, interview by author, 21 September 1998.

326 "The music must have integrity..."; "terrific match": Roslyn Barak, interview by author, 20 November 1997.

327 "crackling with excitement": Ibid.

327 "electric with possibility": Mark Schiftan, interview by author, 4 November 1997.

328 On Mark Schiftan (biographical): Ibid.

328 "He always set the bar extremely high...": Ibid.

328 On Gayle Pomerantz (biographical): Gayle Pomerantz, interview by author, 26 November 1997.

328–29 "compelling vision"; "Camelot": Ibid.

329 On Peretz Wolf-Prusan (biographical): Peretz Wolf-Prusan, interview by author, 18 November 1997.

329 "a rabbi unlike any [he] had ever known"; "The wall came down"; "the greatest challenge...": Ibid.

330 "one of the most, if not *the* most gifted rabbi of his generation": Mark Schiftan, interview by author, 4 November 1997.

331 "I had a sense that the key families needed to lead..."; "I would always lean toward the big people..."; "siphoned off"; "stature, and reach and clout..."; "a player"; "charm and worldliness": Kirschner, interview by author, 3 February 1998.

331 Newman "loved" the "young, brilliant, dynamic guy...": Walter Newman, interview by author, 19 November 1997.

331 Newman "was there to help me"; "stature in the community...": Kirschner, interview by author, 3 February 1998.

332 "I knew that the value of our land had just gone from X to ten times X"; "I thought, that's the best real estate deal...": Walter Newman, interview by author, 19 November 1997.

332–33 On Mortimer Fleishhacker (1866–1953) and Mortimer Fleishhacker Jr. (1907–1976), temple president Mortimer Fleishhacker's grandfather and father: Narell, *Our City*, pp. 311–23.

333 Fleishhacker admitted that he served "halfheartedly": Fleishhacker and Fleishhacker, "Family, Business and the San Francisco Community," p. 33; Narell, *Our City*, p. 311–12.

333 "Emanu-El has always stood out as the leader...": Mortimer Fleishhacker, Annual Report, 25 February 1991; published in *Temp. Chron.*, April 1991, p. 2.

333 Fleishhacker felt "an obligation..."; "to create reasons for Jews to want to affiliate..."; "pushed"; "to create the finest, most beautiful facility in Northern California...": Mortimer Fleishhacker, interview by author, 11 November 1997.

333   Rhoda Goldman was "bred" for benevolence: Rhoda Goldman, remarks upon receiving Lehrhaus Judaica's Genesis Award for Community Service, 7 November 1993.

334   Richard and Rhoda Goldman were profoundly affected by a visit to Auschwitz: Richard Goldman, interview by Anita Hecht, 27 May 1998.

334   Rhoda Goldman and Robert Kirschner "just hit it off"; they formed a "precious friendship": Kirschner, interview by author, 3 February 1998.

335   at the Goldmans' home, Kirschner asked Mrs. Goldman to become president: Kirschner, interview by author, 3 February 1998; Richard Goldman, interview by Anita Hecht, 27 May 1998.

335   "her rabbi and her friend": Kirschner, interview by author, 3 February 1998.

335   For Rhoda Goldman, leading the temple "was a burden"; "it took a lot out of her...": Richard Goldman, interview by Anita Hecht, 27 May 1998.

335   Kirschner's dissertation: Robert Kirschner, *Baraita de-Melekhet ha-Mishkan: A Critical Edition With Introduction and Translation* (Cincinnati, 1992).

335   Kirschner worked feverishly on his thesis in the mid-'80s: Kirschner, interview by author, 3 February 1998.

335   Beyond the dissertation, Kirschner published articles in respected periodicals: "Apocalyptic and Rabbinic Responses to the Destruction of 70," *Harvard Theological Review* 78 (1985), pp. 27–46; "Imitatio Rabbini," *Journal for the Study of Judaism* 17 (June 1986), pp. 70–79; "Three Recensions of a Baraitha: An Analysis and Theory of Development," *Journal of Semitic Studies* 33 (Spring 1988), pp. 37–57; "Two Responses to Epochal Change: Augustine and the Rabbis on PS. 137 (136)," *Vigiliae Christianae* 44 (1990), pp. 242–62.

336   Kirschner envisioned an annual lecture that would bring "only *the* stellar Jewish minds in the world": Kirschner, interview by author, 3 February 1998.

336   Milgrom an important role model for Kirschner: Ibid.

337   "Bob was not a good speaker—Bob was a *great* speaker...": Gary Shapiro, interview by author, 11 November 1997.

337   "Bob talked about what really mattered....": Rhonda Abrams, interview by author, 24 April 1998.

338   Kirschner spent many hours "agonizing" over each sermon; the nature of the temple "required it": Kirschner, interview by author, 3 February 1998.

338   "Congregants can get that from *Newsweek*": Ibid.

338   "The challenge is to close the distance...": Robert Kirschner, "Is There Still a Place for the Sermon?" *Conservative Judaism* 48 (Spring 1996), pp. 20–21.

338   "perils...of speaking from this height": Ibid., p. 16.

338   the rabbi turned to Archbishop Quinn: David Biale and Fred Rosenbaum, "The Pope Comes to San Francisco: An Anatomy of Jewish Communal Response to a Political Crisis," in Seymour Martin Lipset, ed., *American Pluralism and the Jewish Community* (New Brunswick, N.J., 1990), p. 257.

338–39 Kirschner conveyed his "deep, personal disappointment": Kirschner, quoted in ibid.

339   Kirschner spoke with fury, then walked out; he expressed bitterness; bristled with anger: Ibid., p. 258.

339   Kirschner considered his Rosh Hashanah Eve sermon "the most serious mistake" of his rabbinate up to that point: Kirschner, quoted in ibid.

339   "Let the Church at last understand: the people of Israel lives...": Kirschner, quoted in ibid.

339	Kirschner soon felt "devastated"; felt that he had "betrayed" his calling and himself: Kirschner, quoted in ibid.
339–40	"What should have been spoken in love was spoken in anger....": Kirschner, quoted in ibid., p. 259.
340	There were rumors that his retraction was due to pressure; Holocaust survivors in particular were outraged: Ibid.
340	"something seismic": Kirschner, quoted in ibid., p. 256.
340	"There is something absurd about standing behind a pulpit and speaking without fear...": Kirschner, "R. Meir's Neck," p. 36.
340	Kirschner felt that it had been easier for the Ashers: Kirschner, interview by author, 3 February 1998.
341	"It is true that we [rabbis] stand for the Torah...": Kirschner, "R. Meir's Neck," p. 36.
341	"the most majestic religious building in San Francisco": Allan Temko, "The Restoration of a True San Francisco Landmark," *San Francisco Chronicle*, 1 January 1990, p. A8.
341	Repair of the ceiling was considered most urgent: Irwin Wiener, interview by author, 29 October 1997.
342	"Campaign Emanu-El" announced a goal of 10.5 million dollars: Temple Minutes, 29 September 1988.
343	Kirschner had longed for an intermediate-sized hall: Kirschner, interview by author, 3 February 1998.
343	Wiener felt that it would be more cost-effective simply to enlarge the Rinder Chapel: Irwin Wiener, interview by author, 29 October 1997.
343	two weeks before construction was set to begin, part of the ceiling fell into the pews: Ibid.
343	the restored sanctuary was hailed as a "triumph"; "warm beige": Temko, "Restoration."
343	The sound system was "the best in the world": Mortimer Fleishhacker, interview by author, 11 November 1997.
344	"dazzling"; "otherwise flawless..."; "continue unimpeded...": Temko, "Restoration."
344	the success of the restoration emboldened Emanu-El's leaders to "shoot for the stars": Kirschner, interview by author, 3 February 1998.
344	As the new decade dawned the lay leadership was "in euphoria": Walter Newman, interview by author, 19 November 1997.
345	The total annual amount taken in through dues roughly doubled during Kirschner's tenure: Temple Minutes, 1985–1992.
346	Kirschner dreamed of one day holding the Koshland Chair in Jewish Studies at Stanford: Kirschner, interview by author, 3 February 1998.
346	A headline in the *Jewish Bulletin* was quoted in *Sports Illustrated*: "Emanu-El Wins Series Either Way," *NCJB*, 13 October 1989, p. 1; Steve Wulf, "On a Roll," *Sports Illustrated*, 23 October 1989, p. 34.
347	tenant farmers had long used the site as a dump: Walter Newman, Annual Report, 20 January 1987; published in *Temp. Chron.*, March 1987, pp. 7–8.
347	The cemetery's endowment fund had been invested in fixed-income securities; the cemetery itself began losing money: Gary Cohn, interview by author, 20 November 1997; Temple Minutes, passim.
347	massive deficits in the temple's own operations were "absolutely inexcusable"; "dire"; "by all measures...": Stuart Aronoff, interview by author, 19 November 1997.

347 Kirschner's "programmatic requests were overwhelming..."; "They just couldn't stand up and say no to him"; "double-headed snake": Ibid.

348 the earthquake drove up costs; there many other unexpected costs as well: Mortimer Fleishhacker, Annual Report, 25 February 1991; published in *Temp. Chron.*, April 1991, pp. 3–4.

348 Even parts of the magnificent Skinner organ had worn out: Ibid.

348 "Each part depended on another"..."and there was no intelligent way...": Ibid., p. 4.

348–49 Even if that money could be raised, this left a spine-chilling shortfall of close to six million dollars: Temple Minutes, August 1990.

349 Despite Fleishhacker's eagerness "to complete the entire project now," there were powerful "naysayers": Mortimer Fleishhacker, interview by author, 11 November 1997.

349 Stuart Aronoff recommended shutting down the construction "rather than spending money [the temple] didn't have": Stuart Aronoff, interview by author, 19 November 1997; Temple Minutes, 24 January 1991.

349 Rhoda Goldman held a meeting in her home to mollify a group of members: Dr. Allan M. Unger to Rhoda Goldman, 27 May 1991. Letter made available by Dr. Allan Unger.

349 This infusion of cash "saved the temple": Kirschner, interview by author, 3 February 1998; Gary Cohn, interview by author, 20 November 1997.

350 Kirschner's leadership style described as "autocratic": Mark Schiftan, interview by author, 4 November 1997.

350 Kirschner's leadership style could even be "abusive"; he was a "perfectionist": Irwin Wiener, interview by author, 29 October 1997.

350 Kirschner was always an encouraging mentor for Gayle Pomerantz: Gayle Pomerantz, interview by author, 26 November 1997.

350 Kirschner demonstrated "leadership by inducement of fear...": Mark Schiftan, interview by author, 4 November 1997.

350 Liebowitz's departure due to the dwindling prospect that he could ever truly share in spiritual leadership of the temple: Yossi Liebowitz, interview by author, 25 November 1997.

351 Wiener and the senior rabbi had been "inseparable"; Kirschner grew distant, "arrogant"; Wiener felt excluded and slighted: Irwin Wiener, interview by author, 29 October 1997.

351 Kirschner was "shocked" by Wiener's resignation; "One of the ways in which I was not very good at being a rabbi...": Kirschner, interview by author, 3 February 1998.

352 By his own admission, Kirschner had many adulterous affairs: Ibid.

352 Not wanting "to make any excuses": Ibid.

352 "When you are elevated—literally—on this pulpit...": Ibid.

352 Mostly, Kirschner was in a state of denial: Ibid.

353 Kirschner was cautioned twice about his sexual misconduct, first by Jacob Milgrom: Ibid.; Tamar Kaufman, "Students Reveal New Allegations Against Kirschner," *NCJB*, 17 January 1992, p. 32.

353 Malcolm Sparer also confronted him: Kirschner, interview by author, 3 February 1998; Malcolm Sparer, interview by author, April 1998.

354 Wiener approached the rabbi but found him unwilling to discuss the issue; he "agonized..."; "there was no way I could pit myself against him...": Irwin Wiener, interview by author, 29 October 1997.

354   Schiftan approached the rabbi: Mark Schiftan, interview by author, 4 November 1997.

354   In neither case does Kirschner remember those meetings today: Kirschner, interview by author, 3 February 1998.

354   Kirschner was "emotionally isolated": Gayle Pomerantz, interview by author, 26 November 1997.

354   "I was such a poor example...": Kirschner, interview by author, 3 February 1998.

354   "How unworthy I am of all your kindnesses...": Kirschner, sermon at installation, 8 September 1985.

354   "There is something pathetic...": Kirschner, "R. Meir's Neck," p. 36.

354   "On the one hand we represent what is holy...": Ibid., p. 40.

355   "We too have defects, limitations..."; "our defects can teach us what our blessings cannot": Kirschner, "Defects," *Temp. Chron.*, November 1991, p. 3.

355   The man glowered at the rabbi throughout the service and threatened him with obscenities: Mark Schiftan, interview by author, 4 November 1997.

355   Kirschner told his colleagues that the eruption resulted from her having been denied a seat on the board of directors: Ibid.

355–56 The packet contained sworn affidavits from four anonymous women detailing unwanted sexual advances of a nonviolent nature; the plaintiffs reported severe distress: Paul Matzger, interview by author, 29 October 1997.

356*   Also included in each envelope was a recent book on "sexual boundary violation": Peter Rutter, *Sex in the Forbidden Zone: When Men in Power—Therapists, Doctors, Clergy, Teachers and Others—Betray Women's Trust* (New York, 1989).

356   "It was a nightmare. I was devastated...": Gary Shapiro, interview by author, 11 November 1997.

356   "I knew immediately that this had to be taken very seriously": Don Buder, interview by author, 16 March 1998.

356   A few members wondered if a "cabal" were "out to get the rabbi": Mortimer Fleishhacker, interview by author, 11 November 1997.

357   "concentric circles of interest": Paul Matzger, interview by author, 29 October 1997.

357   at Matzger's insistence, any synagogue considering engaging Kirschner in the future would have to be fully informed; the attorney was furious that the temple's lay leadership had been "the last to know": Ibid.

357   Matzger was also angry with the CCAR and the UAHC; the executives of the UAHC "fell on their faces..."; "operating in a no-man's-land": Ibid.

357*   Rabbi Morris Hershman claims that his organization helped "in subtle ways...and behind the scenes": Morris Hershman, interview by author, 6 November 1997.

358   Rhonda Abrams regrets that the complainants began their attack "with the nuclear bomb" of the law firm's packet; "every conversation had three lawyers present"; "an ardent feminist": Rhonda Abrams, interview by author, 24 April 1998.

358   The board decided that the rabbi should be suspended immediately, but most felt that he could be given an extended period of leave to undergo therapy and then return: Paul Matzger, interview by author, 29 October 1997.

358   But Kirschner chose instead to resign; denied the allegations; could no longer function: Ibid.

358   the board accepted the resignation "regretfully, but without hesitation": Rhoda Goldman to congregation, letter dated January 1992.

359   "fair and reasonable"; "lingering negotiations": Stuart Aronoff, interview by author, 19 November 1997.

359   "What are you going to do? Put him on the welfare rolls? We are a Jewish institution": Quoted in Natalie Weinstein, "How a Synagogue Heals Itself," *JBNC*, 25 October 1996, p. 48.

359   "trying to move forward"; a full-scale probe would be "disruptive and divisive": Stuart Aronoff, interview by author, 19 November 1997.

359–60 President Goldman wrote that Rabbi Kirschner had asked to resign "for personal reasons": Rhoda Goldman to congregation, letter dated 30 December 1991.

360   Muriel Cohn was convulsed upon hearing charges that had come "out of the blue": Muriel Cohn, interview by author, 9 December 1997.

360   "This can't be happening": Gary Cohn, interview by author, 20 November 1997.

360   Roz Barak broke into uncontrollable sobs: Roslyn Barak, interview by author, 20 November 1997.

360   "it was like the floor being taken out from under us...really like a death": Gayle Pomerantz, interview by author, 26 November 1997.

361   the clergy had serious doubts; it was a "giant leap" to immediate resignation: Mark Schiftan, interview by author, 4 November 1997.

361   The cantor would later characterize the realization of Kirschner's "betrayal" as the greatest trauma of her life: Roslyn Barak, interview by author, 20 November 1997.

361   Gayle Pomerantz believes some of the charges to have been "trumped up": Gayle Pomerantz, interview by author, 26 November 1997.

361   But conversations she and her colleagues had with close, trusted friends soon persuaded them of Kirschner's malfeasance: Ibid.; Mark Schiftan, interview by author, 4 November 1997; Roslyn Barak, interview by author, 20 November 1997; Peretz Wolf-Prusan, interview by author, 18 November 1997.

361   "He said, 'I didn't do it...'": Mortimer Fleishhacker, interview by author, 11 November 1997.

362   "There are few things in my life that have really broken my heart...": Walter Newman, interview by author, 19 November 1997.

362   "worse than I ever could have thought—my life as I knew it ended"; "permanent and irreparable damage": Kirschner, interview by author, 3 February 1998.

362   Don Lattin contributed an article citing "personal reasons" as the cause of the resignation: Don Lattin, "Temple Emanu-El's Rabbi Resigns," *San Francisco Chronicle*, 7 January 1992, p. A12.

362   "a welcome respite...": Kirschner, quoted in ibid.

363   The story disclosed that four women had charged Kirschner with sexual misconduct: Candy J. Cooper, "S.F. Rabbi Quits Amid Sexual Charges," *San Francisco Examiner*, 8 January 1992, p. A2.

363   Don Lattin weighed in with a second *Chronicle* article: Don Lattin, "S.F. Rabbi Denies Sexual Allegations," *San Francisco Chronicle*, 9 January 1992, p. A16.

363   The next day saw a similar story on the front page of the *Jewish Bulletin*: Tamar Kaufman, "Emanu-El's Rabbi Quits, Denies Sex Allegations," *NCJB*, 10 January 1992, pp. 1, 41.

363   Rhoda Goldman was now in the awkward position of having to send a second letter; "In view of Rabbi Kirschner's significant contributions...": Rhoda Goldman to congregation, letter dated January 1992.

363   Perhaps most damaging to Kirschner was the piece in the *Jewish Bulletin* which

shifted attention to his conduct toward women in the academic world: Tamar Kaufman, "Students Reveal New Allegations," *NCJB*, pp. 1, 32.

364   "I didn't know what to do..."; "It turned out to be a disastrous response...": Kirschner, interview by author, 3 February 1998.

364   Not until mid-1994 did he express "contrition" for his "sexual misconduct"; suspended by the CCAR in 1995: Debra Nussbaum Cohen and Natalie Weinstein, "Rabbi Robert Kirschner Apologizes," *JBNC*, 18 October 1996, p. 27.

364   Some of the accusers felt that Kirschner had "no place in a classroom or a pulpit": Plaintiff quoted in Elizabeth Fernandez, "Temple's Bitter Taste of Scandal," *San Francisco Examiner*, 11 July 1993, p. A8.

365   "Without him I'm not sure I would have made it through": Kirschner, interview by author, 3 February 1998.

365   Kirschner had admitted to his wife that he had had "affairs"; "lack of concern for [Kirschner's] victims"; a long-term liaison with a deeply troubled congregant suffering from anorexia: Fernandez, "Temple's Bitter Taste of Scandal."

365   "Humiliated...not even functioning"; the camera crew from *Hard Copy* alighted from a van: Kirschner, interview by author, 3 February 1998.

365   As the Skirball grew, Kirschner took on greater responsibilities: Ibid.; Herbert Muschamp, "Architecture of Light and Rembrance," *New York Times*, 15 December 1996, Arts and Leisure section, p. 1.

366   When the new Skirball opened to the public, flyers were found in the restrooms attacking Kirschner as a sexual predator: Kirschner, interview by author, 3 February 1998.

366   "an outcome I might have hoped for...": Ibid.

366   "Who I am now is somebody who feels very different...": Ibid.

366 67 "painfully divested"; "I had this image of myself...": Ibid.

367   "whom [he] hurt deeply and whose hurt was multiplied..."; regrets the pain his conduct caused and the "dilemmas" it left: Ibid.

367   takes "responsibility..."; "I will not accept responsibility for allegations that were falsely and maliciously brought...": Ibid.

367   Kirschner is especially embittered by the "spin of harassment"...in the "fevered social and cultural climate"; resents the term "victim" being applied: Ibid.

367   Rachel Adler's seminal article in the *CCAR Journal*; "maximum discrepancy": Rachel Adler, "A Stumbling Block Before the Blind: Sexual Exploitation in Pastoral Counseling, " *CCAR Journal* 40 (Spring 1993), pp. 16–17.

368   "There's an elephant in the living room..."; Salkin would consider the crossing of sexual boundaries in pastoral counseling most grievous: Jeffrey Salkin, "Response (to Rachel Adler)," *CCAR Journal* 40 (Spring 1993), p. 47.

368   "utterly inadequate": Adler, "Stumbling Block," p. 37.

368   Rabbi Julie Spitzer's response; need for a single address for complaints: Julie Spitzer, "Response (to Rachel Adler)," *CCAR Journal* 40 (Spring 1993), p. 53.

368*   sexual misconduct had caused almost as many rabbis to leave their pulpits as had deaths and retirements: Debra Nussbaum Cohen, "Rabbinic Sexual Misconduct—Breaching a Sacred Trust," *JBNC*, 18 October 1996, p. 26.

368–69 "The later tradition always holds the door open...": Howard Kosovske, "Sexual Exploitation: A Jewish Response," *CCAR Journal* 41 (Summer 1994), p. 16.

369   *Teshuvah* must include "recognition of the sinful act, sincere remorse...": Arthur Gross Schaefer, "Teshuvah and Rabbinic Sexual Misconduct," *CCAR Journal* 42 (Summer/Fall 1995), p. 77.

369   naming the abuse and making amends are essential elements in this "arduous process": Ibid., p. 75
369   "The rabbis teach that with sin you begin with one thread...": Kirschner, interview by author, 3 February 1998.
369   the way Kirschner's rabbinate collapsed "has ruined everything...": Ibid.

11 STEPHEN PEARCE: TEMPLE OF THE OPEN DOOR

374   "cleaning up the mess": Mark Schiftan, interview by author, 4 November 1997.
374   Mark Schiftan "a godsend": Stuart Aronoff, interview by author, 19 November 1997.
374   On Mark Schiftan (biographical); "got [his] passion for Judaism": Mark Schiftan, interview by author, 4 November 1997.
374   Schiftan passed "the critical, yet intangible dividing point...": Paul Matzger, "Message From the President," *Temp. Chron.*, June/July 1994, p. 3.
374   "lonely, dark days"; "a bone-chilling" time; emotional support of his wife much needed: Mark Schiftan, interview by author, 4 November 1997.
376   Schiftan believed that the congregation "did not [properly] understand..."; Schiftan did not speak to Kirschner; felt not the slightest obligation to help him: Ibid.
376   "tainted": Peretz Wolf-Prusan, interview by author, 18 November 1997.
376   "It does not matter that he was an *illui*...": Mark Schiftan, interview by author, 4 November 1997.
377   "What each of us did in the privacy of our offices was to acknowledge the pain...": Ibid.
377   "Having just come into adolescence..."; "this was the loss of a rabbi...": Peretz Wolf-Prusan, interview by author, 18 November 1997.
378*   Matzger felt that little could be gained from hearing "a bill of particulars": Paul Matzger, interview by author, 29 October 1997.
378*   The story of the two GTU complainants would be published in the *Jewish Bulletin*: Kaufman, "Students Reveal New Allegations."
378   Schiftan had to use all of his powers of persuasion: Temple Minutes, 23 January 1992; Mark Schiftan, interview by author, 4 November 1997.
378   "emotionally intense"; "tremendous immediacy"; "critical incident debriefing": Norman Sohn, interview by author, 8 June 1998.
378   He had to raise the hypothetical case of a woman committing suicide: Ibid.
379   reimbursement for extended counseling was the major element in the several civil claims that the temple quietly settled: Temple Minutes, 25 September 1992 and 22 April 1993.
379   "The primary obligation [ought to have been] rectifying the damage...": Mark Schiftan, interview by author, 4 November 1997.
379   a committee drafted a comprehensive sexual harassment policy: Temple Minutes, 15 May 1992 and 25 June 1992.
379   the final version stopped short of prohibiting sexual contact: Gayle Pomerantz, interview by author, 26 November 1997.
380   "We didn't miss a beat; I didn't want one thing to drop...": Mark Schiftan, interview by author, 4 November 1997.
380   "We healed service by service...": Paul Matzger, interview by author, 29 October 1997.

380   "We did the best we could": Quoted in Fernandez, "Temple's Bitter Taste of Scandal," p. A8.

380   Elaine Petrocelli alleged a "cover-up": Ibid.

380   The wife of an attorney who had recently published a book on sexual harassment in the workplace: William Petrocelli and Barbara Kate Repa, *Sexual Harassment on the Job* (Berkeley, 1992).

381   the crisis was not handled in an ideal manner: Paul Matzger, interview by author, 29 October 1997.

381   "I saw a need for normalcy....": Ibid.

382   On Stephen Pearce (biographical): Stephen Pearce, interview by author, 20 November 1997.

382   "who took their Judaism seriously": Ibid.

383   Pearce made an important contribution to counseling psychology with a book on the use of narrative and metaphor: Stephen Pearce, *Flash of Insight: Metaphor and Narrative in Therapy* (Needham Heights, Mass., 1996).

383*   "Metaphor deeply permeates...": Ibid., p. xiii.

385   conscious "rebuilding"; "the image of the rabbi had been shattered...": Pearce, interview by author, 9 December 1997.

386   "You have a right to expect more from a rabbi...": Stephen Pearce, "Rabbi's Message," 27 August 1994; published in *Temp. Chron.*, October 1994, p. 2.

386   "To influence others a rabbi must truly be a role model...": Stephen Pearce, "Tribute to Rabbi Mark Schiftan," 8 October 1993; published in *Temp. Chron.*, December 1993, p. 3.

386   "sacred trust"; "matters of the heart": Pearce, interview by author, 20 November 1997.

386   "the purpose of Judaism": Stephen Pearce, "New Beginnings," *Temp. Chron.*, September 1993, p. 2.

386   practice of ethical wills was "designed to allow us to focus on the meaning of our lives": Stephen Pearce, Kol Nidre sermon, 24 September 1993.

386–87   The following Yom Kippur Eve, Pearce again addressed "the lasting legacy we leave behind"; "Relationships struggle on in spite of the death of one of the players...": Stephen Pearce, "To Be a Kaddish," sermon, 14 September 1994; published in *Temp. Chron.*, September 1995, p. 3.

387   "assisted death may truly be an act of sanctifying...": Stephen Pearce, "Questions of Life and Death," sermon, 19 February 1994; published in *Temp. Chron.*, April 1994, p. 3.

387   the rabbi spoke of the "casual acceptance of divorce [as] cause for profound alarm"; "It is painful...": Stephen Pearce, "The Sacred at Home," sermon, 10 October 1997.

388   "Jews have proved that once they acquired guns...": Stephen Pearce, "The Triumph of Justice Over Violence," *San Francisco Examiner*, 18 May 1994, p. A15.

388*   the piece was sharply attacked in a letter to the editor: Julie Brandt and John Rothmann, "Israel Seeks Peace," *San Francisco Examiner*, 3 June 1994, p. A18.

388   the Palestinians "in some instances have been totally disregarded"; "I expect more of Israel...": Pearce, interview by author, 20 November 1997.

388   at one demonstration, Pearce "followed a guy who was dressed as a salmon": Ibid.

388   "an issue that speaks so clearly to me that I cannot rest": Stephen Pearce, "The Decline of the Sacred," sermon, 2 October 1997.

389   "saving the forest [was] more than a politically correct action...": Stephen Pearce

and Ted Nordhaus, "Saving Headwaters Is a Moral Issue," *San Francisco Chronicle*, 9 September 1997, p. A21.

389   "emblematic"; "the decline of the sacred"; "What is happening to the Headwaters…"; "protect these ancient trees…": Pearce, "The Decline of the Sacred."

390   "to show…a personal and human side…"; "Ours is a history of emotion…": Bonnie Menes Kahn, Stephen S. Pearce, John P. Schlegel, and William E. Swing, *Building Wisdom's House: A Book of Values for Our Time* (Reading, Mass., 1997), p. 206.

391   Pearce does not claim to have electrified the congregation; "Why the big fuss for the sake of a bunch of trees?": Pearce, interview by author, 20 November 1997.

391   "It was worth more to me and my family…": Stephen Dobbs, interview by author, 7 November 1997.

392   "This is a place for matters of the heart, matters of the soul…": Pearce, interview by author, 7 December 1997.

392–93   "In a large corporation, an executive is responsible…"; "I benefit when my staff looks great": Ibid.

393   "Some of the older members of the temple are used to a single leader…": Terri Forman, interview by author, 20 March 1998.

393*   Rabbi Frederick Schwartz dispensed with the designations "senior," "associate," or "assistant": Lefkowitz, *Temple Sholom*, p. 89; Ed Alpert, interview by author, 20 November 1998.

393   Pearce believes that each member of the staff must be given the latitude to "feel that they have a stake": Pearce, interview by author, 7 December 1997.

394   On Gary Cohn (biographical): Gary Cohn, interview by author, 20 November 1997.

394   Cohn's immediate task was apply brakes to an operating budget that had gotten "out of control": Ibid.

395   "I would have preferred a Jiffy Lube": Stuart Aronoff, interview by author, 19 November 1997.

395   President Paul Matzger recalls "the feeling that we had no choice": Paul Matzger, interview by author, 29 October 1997.

395   "it would have been almost foolhardy not to go ahead with it…": Stuart Aronoff, interview by author, 19 November 1997.

396*   Cohn led a campaign to dissuade BART: Gary Cohn, interview by author, 10 December 1997.

396   Cohn saw that "no long-range financial or strategic planning had been done": Ibid.

396   "It is a new idea to give annually…": Terri Forman, "Repairing the World a Deed at a Time," *Temp. Chron.*, October 1995, p. 2.

396   "Annual giving is still not a big component…": Gary Cohn, interview by author, 10 December 1997.

397   A survey of the Emanu-El membership revealed…: Performance Audits, Inc., "A Survey of Temple Emanu-El Members," January 1994, p. 14.

397   "something like twenty-five to thirty million dollars"; Emanu-El's endowment "pales in comparison": Gary Cohn, interview by author, 10 December 1997.

397   Forman has also obtained local foundation grants: Terri Forman, interview by author, 20 March 1998.

397   Cohn is determined to correct this long-held misconception, which remains "pervasive in the community"; "the myth is still out there, that we have all the money we could possibly need...": Gary Cohn, interview by author, 10 December 1997.

398   almost 1.5 million dollars in annual dues is now generated: Temple Minutes, 1998.

399   Cohn sees his task as "bringing the best of the business world" to temple administration: Gary Cohn, interview by author, 10 December 1997.

399   "marketing" should not be "a dirty word": Gary Cohn, "What Are Our Priorities?" *JBNC*, 19 September 1997, p. 13.

400–1   "tour the city with me for a moment. We have a beautifully renovated opera house..."; "this [maxim] is to encourage us to give away everything before we die": Stuart Aronoff, "Shrouds Have No Pockets," Rosh Hashanah address, 1 October 1997.

401   "I've got to keep in front of people...": Stuart Aronoff, interview by author, 19 November 1997.

401   Several members objected to the "offering of rewards [as] contrary to the dignity of our prestigious House of Worship": Temple Minutes, 25 April 1996.

401   the idea "just didn't work": Gary Cohn, interview by author, 30 October 1998.

402   Cohn devised a plan to sell matzah for Passover, "literally a ton" of unleavened bread: Don Lattin, "Kosher Grocer, Temple in Spat Over Matzo," *San Francisco Chronicle*, 26 March 1998, p. A18.

402   Cohn was convinced that prices for matzah were "artificially high": Gary Cohn, quoted in ibid.

402   "Why do they make such a big deal over a dollar or two for matzo?...": Jeffrey Sosnick, quoted in ibid.

402   Cohn and Pearce sought out "Jews on the margin," "looking for a way to make it impossible for them to say no": Pearce, interview by author, 10 December 1997.

402   Well over two hundred households signed up within the first year: Gary Cohn, interview by author, 30 October 1998.

402   the large majority reported that the offer of a year's free membership was "important" or "very important": Joel Streicker, *An Assessment of a Synagogue Voluntary Dues Policy: The Temple Emanu-El Experience* (San Francisco, 1997), p. 11.

403   "He wanted me to be there...": Quoted in ibid., p. 15.

403   "the people who work here enjoy being here..."; "I always had a perception of...Emanu-El and I did not fit...": Quoted in ibid., p. 16.

403   Streicker found that only one in twenty new members had dropped their membership in another congregation: Ibid., p. 10.

403   the *Forward* ran a glowing front-page article on the program: E. J. Kessler, "Rx for Shul Absentees: End Dues," *Forward*, 29 August 1997, pp. 1, 4.

404   "We're doing more than we ever have...": Pearce, interview by author, 20 November 1997.

404   "the marketplace of souls": Silverstein, *Alternatives*, p. 204.

404   Rhoda Goldman, "the visionary," grasped the opportunity "to change the way we do business": Gary Cohn, interview by author, 10 December 1997.

404   Rhoda Goldman encouraged the development of a strategic plan "to set the direction of the congregation...": Paul Matzger and Stephen Pearce to congregation, letter dated December 1994.

405   One of the most important tools was a survey conducted "to learn how members view the temple...": Performance Audits, Inc., "Survey," p. 1.

405   "I take pride in the work of this congregation…"; "Our congregation is respon-
       sive…"; "I have a voice…": Ibid., p. 5.
405   more than half rated their participation as "low"; only 11 percent characterized it
       as "high": Ibid., p. 2.
406   The 1993 declaration pronounced the temple "dedicated to advancing lifelong
       involvement…"; "upholding the core value of the individual's ability…"; "provid-
       ing access and resources to all Jews…"; "providing resources and support for
       interfaith families": "The Congregation Emanu-El Mission Statement," in "Our
       Vision for the Future," December 1994, p. 5.
406   The committee on membership recommended a host of measures: Ibid., p. 9.
406–7 "we've had people on the board who didn't even know we operate a preschool…":
       Gary Cohn, interview by author, 10 December 1997.
407   "It means constantly staying in touch…": Terri Forman, interview by author, 20
       March 1998.
407   Jody Seltzer used the success stories of existing *havurot* to motivate congregants;
       "intentional communities": Jody Seltzer, interview by author, 23 July 1998.
408   the *havurah* experience has become more important "as our society has become
       more mobile…": Stephen Pearce, "Havurah," *Temp. Chron.*, February 1997,
       insert.
408   The Shabbat La'Am service "is not a wild, New Age service": Peretz Wolf-Prusan,
       interview by author, 18 November 1997.
409   Often described as "seekers": Lawrence A. Hoffman, "From Ethnic to Spiritual,
       A Tale of Four Generations," *The Synagogue 2000 Library* (New York, 1996), p. 24.
409   The alternative service is part of "a second reformation": Lawrence Hoffman,
       quoted in Diane Winston, "Searching for Spirituality: Reform Judaism
       Responds," *Moment*, June 1992, p. 29.
409   "it puts prayers back into the hands…": David Klepper, quoted in David
       Mermelstein, "Pop Culture," *Reform Judaism* 17 (Spring 1988), p. 43.
411   Pearce welcomes the ability to offer a choice: Pearce, interview by author, 10
       December 1997.
411   He even foresees a day when the alternative service will move to the main sanctu-
       ary for the High Holidays: Pearce, interview by author, 19 March 1998.
411   "The tradition here was, if you don't like the service…": Stephen Pearce, quoted
       in E. J. Kessler, "Rabbis Bucking for Friday Nights at the 'Synaplex,'" *Forward*, 5
       June 1998, p. 2.
411   "the synaplex": Stephen Pearce, "Synaplex and the Compound Influence of
       Change," annual meeting address, 10 February 1997; published in *Temp. Chron.*,
       April 1997, p. 9.
412   Helen Cohn uses the temple as her "living room": Helen Cohn, interview by
       author, 9 December 1997.
412–13 On Helen Cohn (biographical): Ibid.
413   "When I left for college, I left my Jewish involvement behind": "I drove through
       the dark night on unfamiliar streets…": Helen Cohn, sermon, 15 September
       1994.
413   "I realized that [she] would have to deal with many Jews on the fringe…": Stephen
       Pearce, "Installation of Rabbi Helen T. Cohn," 27 August 1994; published in
       Temp. Chron., November 1994, p. 3.
414   Cohn taught an introduction to Jewish meditation, "which aids us in connecting with
       the Divine": "Lifelong Learning Fall Series," *Temp. Chron.*, October 1997, p. 5.

414   Cohn explained that "the arena of logic and reason" is sometimes insufficient: Helen Cohn, sermon, 23 September 1996.

415   Cohn performs about two dozen weddings a year, the large majority of them mixed marriages; "It's more than about books..."; "Converts are going to save American [Jewry]...": Helen Cohn, interview by author, 9 December 1997.

416   "The survival of Israel, the Shoah, and the rescue of Jews from the former Soviet Union...": Gary Cohn, "What Are Our Priorities?" p. 13.

417   "There is a growing involvement in the personal, pastoral rabbinate...": David Polish, "Assessing the Reform Rabbinate Today," *Journal of Reform Judaism* 33 (Fall 1986), p. 2.

417–18   Mintz was considered to be the most qualified person; Pearce had to field many angry phone calls; most who had reservations changed their minds: Pearce, interview by author, 10 December 1997.

418   "People came up to me and said, 'That was a great sermon; I even forgot that you're a lesbian'"; "warmth, generosity, and support": Sydney Mintz, interview by author, 16 April 1998.

418–19   On Sydney Mintz (biographical): Ibid.

418   Peretz gave his "wholehearted support"; "If I had married a man...": Ibid.

419   "timing is everything"; "a unique vantage point": Ibid.

419   Mintz has personally been "faced with the Hanukah-Christmas dilemma every day": Sydney Mintz, "Parashat Miketz," sermon, 27 December 1997.

420   Pearce's inaugural High Holiday sermon: Stephen Pearce, "Is This the Fast I Have Chosen?" Rosh Hashanah sermon, 15 September 1993.

420   The following Rosh Hashanah, he delivered another sermon on "doing God's work on earth": Stephen Pearce, "FORGET ABOUT GOD! Forget about God!" Rosh Hashanah sermon, 5 September 1994.

420   Pearce appointed Mintz to reinvigorate community service: Temple Minutes, 27 February 1997.

420   she has sought opportunities for members "not only to write checks...": Sydney Mintz, interview by author, 16 April 1998.

420–21   "It was one day, but I looked at it as a kickoff"; "making the world a better place": Ibid.

421   Mintz has been careful not to place women's issues at the center: Ibid.

422   connectedness: Catherine Keller, quoted in Ellen M. Umansky, "Feminism and American Reform Judaism," in Robert M. Seltzer and Norman Cohen, eds., *The Americanization of the Jews* (New York, 1995), pp. 272–73.

422   ethics of care: Carol Gilligan, quoted in ibid.

422   the wish to make synagogue life less hierarchical: Sandy Eisenberg Sasso, quoted in Janet Marder, "How Women Are Changing the Rabbinate," *Reform Judaism* 20 (Summer 1991), p. 8.

422   Mintz is determined to succeed both as a full-time congregational rabbi and as a parent: Sydney Mintz, interview by author, 16 April 1998.

423   Barak advocates synagogue music with "a sound like no other": Roslyn Barak, interview by author, 20 November 1997.

423   Barak has written that continuing this legacy depends upon "the employment of choirs...": Roslyn Barak, "The Music of the Synagogue," 17 November 1990; published in *Temp. Chron.*, January 1991, p. 3.

423–24   On Ami Aloni (biographical); "I wanted to enhance the experience of prayer...": Ami Aloni, interview by author, 2 July 1998.

424–25   On Drs. Ben and A. Jess Shenson (biographical): Stephen Pearce, "Historical Highlights: Remembering Dr. Ben Shenson," *Temp. Chron.*, January 1996, pp. 10–11.

425   Barak laments the worshippers' new "fondness for camp music…"; "Have a nice day, God": Barak, "Music of the Synagogue," p. 3.

425   "accessible"; "awe-inspiring": Mermelstein, "Pop Culture," p. 43.

425–26   "musical crisis"; "The focus is [now] on folk, or folk-rock…": Barak, "Music of the Synagogue," p. 3.

426   "There's nothing more depressing than a silent congregation…"; "they feel over-whelmed": Roslyn Barak, interview by author, 20 November 1997.

426–27   "As soon as I met Roz…"; "music that [she had] studied at school, but that is sung in few places anymore": Margaret Bruner, interview by author, 6 July 1998.

427   removal of some of the Classical Reform trappings was "bound to happen…younger people were not comfortable with them": Roslyn Barak, inter-view by author, 20 November 1997.

427   Even some of the older lay leaders have been discomfited by the playing of "My Country 'Tis of Thee": Temple Minutes, 24 April 1997; Paul Matzger, interview by author, 29 October 1997.

427   Pearce "much more accommodating" of changes toward a more normative Jewish service: Roslyn Barak, interview by author, 20 November 1997.

427   Reflecting a change in many Reform congregations, prayers are now chanted in a traditional style: Daniel Freelander, Robin Hirsch, and Sanford Seltzer, *Emerging Worship and Music Trends in UAHC Congregations* (New York, 1994), p. 13.

428   "even though the music is more complex…": Temple Minutes, 24 April 1997.

428   Rabbi Pearce agrees: Pearce, interview by author, 9 December 1997.

429   Peretz Wolf-Prusan knew that the lay leadership "was looking for a change": Peretz Wolf-Prusan, interview by author, 18 November 1997.

429   Wolf-Prusan has worked on many levels to raise the level of Jewish content, not in an attempt "to go backward to Orthodoxy…": Peretz Wolf-Prusan, Rosh Hashanah address, 21 September 1998.

429   "Families called up and asked, 'Why are my kids doing Hebrew and not ethics?'…"; "We study it because this is the twentieth century": Peretz Wolf-Prusan, interview by author, 18 November 1997.

429   From the beginning, Peretz focused on family education, "the heart and soul of our educational program": "Youth Havurah Curriculum Guide, 1998–1999," p. 5.

431   "Each ceremony is touching…": Stephen Pearce, "Bar/Bat Mitzvah From the Other Side of the Pulpit," *Jewish Spectator* 62 (Summer 1997), p. 44.

431   "I can teach a clever dog to chant the blessings…": Peretz Wolf-Prusan, interview by author, 18 November 1997.

432   "These are our kids": Peretz Wolf-Prusan, interview by author, 23 July 1998.

432   An additional 150 children attend the preschool; its staff has grown; most impres-sive is the active parents association: Pam Schneider, interview by author, 19 March 1998.

432–33   "We have a responsibility to bring them into the fold…": Ibid.

433   Kirschner had opposed the concept (and still does today): Kirschner, interview by author, 3 February 1998.

433   "One thing I can tell you is that Jewish families continue to flee the city…": Stephen Pearce, "The Future of the Jewish Future," sermon, 4 September 1994.

434   they expressed fears that the day school could lead to separatism and even "ghet-toize" the Jewish community: Richard Goldman, quoted in Natalie Weinstein, "Candid S.F. Leaders Recall Controversies," *NCJB*, 21 November 1997, p. 48.

434   "Harnessing the energy"; "invested": Gary Cohn, interview by author, 10 December 1997.

434   a feasibility study concluded that there was substantial demand for a Reform day school: Gary A. Tobin and Joel Streicker, *Reform Day School Feasibility Study* (Waltham, Mass., 1995), p. 2.

434   A telephone survey revealed that 61 percent would have been "interested" or "very interested": Ibid., p. 15.

434*   more than half indicated that schools had been an "important" or "very important" factor: Ibid., p. 16.

434   Two-thirds expressed unwillingness to spend more than twenty minutes driving their child to school: Ibid., p. 9.

435   The study found "major beneficial qualitative impact..."; responses such as "invigorating," "energizing," "rejuvenating," "lending vitality": Ibid., pp. 18–19.

435   Dr. Tobin asserted that "the day school helps build community..."; mixed couples tended to rely on the day school to provide "Jewish knowledge and competence": Ibid., p. 20.

435   Close on the heels of Tobin's report came an initial gift: Ingrid Tauber, interview by author, 24 November 1997.

435   A task force was formed: "The Temple Emanu-El Day School Task Force," *Temp. Chron.*, September 1995, p. 5.

435–36   Jewish studies would be "integrated" throughout the entire curriculum; "Everything would have a Jewish focus": Ingrid Tauber, interview by author, 24 November 1997.

436   Rhoda Goldman expressed concern; Aronoff quickly agreed; Aronoff has since expressed willingness to "reopen" the issue, which he acknowledges as being "of extreme importance": Stuart Aronoff, interview by author, 19 November 1997.

436   "I know we should have one..."; the Tauber gift represents but a promising start: Gary Cohn, interview by author, 10 December 1997.

436   Pearce termed the defeat "an unqualified failure"; "a rabbi doesn't have to get everything he or she wants"; "the congregation made a gross error": Pearce, interview by author, 9 December 1997.

437   Pearce saw how formidable would be his struggle "to turn the congregation around": Ibid.

437   "ancient mariners": Stuart Aronoff, interview by author, 19 November 1997.

437   they feel that "the temple is doing too much": Stephen Pearce, "Re-envisioning Emanu-El in the Coming Millennium and Beyond," annual meeting address, 3 February 1998; published in *Temp. Chron.*, April 1998, p. 7.

437–38   Pearce is anything but unmindful of the temple's history; but he is committed to change, even if it is "assaultive" to some: Pearce, interview by author, 9 December 1997.

438   "controversial"; "...change or die!": Stephen Pearce, "The Transformation of the Sacred," Rosh Hashanah sermon, 1 October 1997.

440   Comparable Reform synagogues around the country have undergone a similar experience; Emanu-El of Dallas perhaps the best example: Daniel Freelander, interview by author, July 1998; Diane Winston, "Searching for Spirituality."

440   Recent statistics reveal that no fewer than 42 percent of the membership joined following Kirschner's departure; only 28 percent belonged before 1970: Demographic data made available by Terri Forman, March 1998.

441   One of the most important of these "catalysts" is a "spirit of religious individualism...": Jack Wertheimer, *A People Divided: Judaism in Contemporary America* (New York, 1993), p. 191.

441   Sociologists often refer to this as a shift from "ascribed" to "achieved": Ibid.

441   "The shift from ascription to achievement in congregations means...": Robert Wuthnow, *Producing the Sacred: An Essay on Public Religion* (Urbana, 1994), p. 66.

442   Lawrence Hoffman has indicated several ways in which synagogues need to "overcome...outmoded habits of thought": Lawrence A. Hoffman, "Imagine: A Synagogue for the 21st Century," *Reform Judaism* 25 (Fall 1996), p. 22.

442   we live in a "new world where religious identity is elective"; ethnic Jewish solidarity "a thing of the past": Lawrence Hoffman, interview by author, 1 September 1998.

442   "liturgy in the 1990s that sounds like the 1960s should be suspect": Hoffman, "Imagine," p. 21.

442   Hoffman also urges changes in the way the synagogue is structured and "how it feels to be there....": Ibid., p. 25.

442   "In an age that makes even 'future shock' seem commonplace, synagogues will rise or fall...": Lawrence Hoffman, interview by author, 1 September 1998.

443   "When Rabbi Noah, Rabbi Mordecai's son, assumed the succession after his father's death...": Stephen Pearce, "The Transformation of the Sacred," sermon, 1 October 1997.

443   "alternative to assimilation": Silverstein, *Alternatives to Assimilation.*

444   "I think of the majestic dome...": Louis Heilbron, interview by Anita Hecht, 21 May 1998.

Sources of Illustrations

217	Courtesy of Michelle Ackerman
219	Courtesy of Francis Taylor
232	Photo by Ken McLaughlin, 1965 / Courtesy of Michelle Ackerman
234	Courtesy of Michelle Ackerman
239	(left and right) Photo by Milton Mann Studios / Courtesy of the Fine Museum
241	Photo by Roy Flamm / Courtesy of the Fine Museum
242	Photo by Gunther (Max Reichmann Associates), San Francisco,
245	Courtesy of Michelle Ackerman
253	Photo by Mimi Jacobs / Courtesy of Fae Asher
255	Courtesy of Fae Asher
259	Courtesy of Fae Asher
275	Photo by Gary Haas / Courtesy of the Fine Museum
285	(left) Photo by Gary Haas / Courtesy of the Fine Museum (right) Courtesy of the Fine Museum
288	Courtesy of Fae Asher
292	Courtesy of Fae Asher
299	Courtesy of the Fine Museum
304	Courtesy of Robert Kirschner
309	Photo by Gary Haas / Courtesy of the Fine Museum
312	Courtesy of the Fine Museum
315	Photo by Lance Woodruff, Worldwide Documentations, San Francisco / Courtesy of the Fine Museum
320	Courtesy of Robert Kirschner
323	Courtesy of the Fine Museum
325	Photo by Gary Haas / Courtesy of the Fine Museum
327	Courtesy of the Fine Museum
330	Photo by Mike Richman, 1991
334	Courtesy of the Fine Museum
341	Photo by Bob Swanson, 1989 / Courtesy of the Fine Museum
345	Photo by Bob Swanson, 1989 / Courtesy of the Fine Museum
375	Photo by Sharon Beals, 1999 / Courtesy of the Fine Museum
376	Courtesy of Rabbi Mark Schiftan
383	Courtesy of Rabbi Stephen S. Pearce
384	(top) Photo by Kendra Luck. Copyright © 1999 San Francisco Chronicle (bottom) Courtesy of Rabbi Stephen S. Pearce
389	Photo by Sharon Beals, 1997 / Courtesy of the Fine Museum
399	Courtesy of the Fine Museum
400	Courtesy of the Fine Museum
401	Courtesy of Rabbi Peretz Wolf-Prusan
410	(left) Courtesy of the Fine Museum (right) Photo by Susanne Floyd / Courtesy of Heather Harrell
413	Courtesy of Rabbi Helen T. Cohn
415	Courtesy of Rabbi Helen T. Cohn
421	Courtesy of the Fine Museum
424	(left) Courtesy of Cantor Roslyn Barak (right) Courtesy of the Fine Museum
430	(top) Courtesy of Rabbi Peretz Wolf-Prusan (bottom) Photo by Tom Wachs / Courtesy of Rabbi Peretz Wolf-Prusan

Photo researcher: Dana Zimmerman

Selected Secondary Sources

Adler, Rachel. "A Stumbling Block Before the Blind: Sexual Exploitation in Pastoral Counseling." *CCAR Journal* 40 (Spring 1993).

Ahlstrom, Sydney E. *A Religious History of the American People*. 2 vols. Garden City, N.Y.: Doubleday, 1975.

Barkai, Avraham. *Branching Out: German-Jewish Immigration to the United States, 1820–1914*. New York: Holmes and Meier, 1994.

Bean, Walton. *Boss Ruef's San Francisco: The Story of the Union Labor Party, Big Business and the Graft Prosecution*. Berkeley and Los Angeles: University of California Press, 1974.

Benjamin, I. J. *Three Years in America, 1859–1862*. 2 vols. Philadelphia: Jewish Publication Society, 1956.

Biale, David, and Fred Rosenbaum. "The Pope Comes to San Francisco." In Seymour Martin Lipset, ed., *American Pluralism and the Jewish Community*. New Brunswick, N.J.: Transaction Publishers, 1990.

Birmingham, Stephen. *Our Crowd: The Great Jewish Families of New York*. New York: Harper and Row, 1967.

Clar, Reva, and William S. Kramer. "Julius Eckman and Herman Bien: The Battling Rabbis of San Francisco." Parts 1–3. *WSJH* 15 (January, April, and July 1983).

Decker, Peter R. *Fortunes and Failures: White Collar Mobility in Nineteenth-Century San Francisco*. Cambridge, Mass. and London: Harvard University Press, 1978.

Diner, Hasia R. *A Time for Gathering: The Second Migration, 1820–1880*. Baltimore and London: Johns Hopkins University Press, 1992.

Feingold, Henry L. *Zion in America: The Jewish Experience from Colonial Times to the Present*. New York: Hippocrene Books, 1974.

Fels, Tony. "Religious Assimilation in a Fraternal Organization." *AJHQ* 74 (June 1985).

Flamm, Jerry. *Good Life in Hard Times: San Francisco's '20s and '30s*. San Francisco: Chronicle Books, 1988.

Fortune, Marie. *Is Nothing Sacred? The Story of a Pastor, the Women He Sexually Abused, and the Congregation He Nearly Destroyed.* San Francisco: Harper and Row, 1989.

Franklin, Lewis A. "Out of Our Archives: The First Jewish Sermon in the American West: Yom Kippur, 1850, San Francisco." *WSJH* 25 (January 1993).

Glanz, Rudolf. *The Jews of California: From the Discovery of Gold Until 1880.* New York: Waldon Books, 1960.

———. *Studies in Judaica Americana.* New York: Ktav, 1970.

Hoffman, Lawrence A. "Imagine: A Synagogue for the 21st Century." *Reform Judaism* 25 (Fall 1996).

Isaak, Peggy A. "'Internee' Talks About 'Dunera Incident,'" *SFJB*, 19 October 1979.

Issel, William, and Robert W. Cherny. *San Francisco, 1865–1932: Politics, Power and Urban Development.* Berkeley and Los Angeles: University of California Press, 1986.

Jick, Leon A. *The Americanization of the Synagogue, 1820–1870.* Hanover, N.H.: Brandeis University Press and the University Press of New England, 1976.

Kaufman, David. *Shul with a Pool: The Synagogue-Center in American Jewish History.* Hanover, N.H.: Brandeis University Press and the University Press of New England, 1999.

Kirschner, Robert. "R. Meir's Neck." *Journal of Reform Judaism* 35 (Fall 1988).

Kolsky, Thomas A. *Jews Against Zionism: The American Council for Judaism, 1942–1948.* Philadelphia: Temple University Press, 1990.

Kramer, William M., ed. *The Western Journal of Isaac Mayer Wise, 1877.* Berkeley: Western Jewish History Center, Judah L. Magnes Memorial Museum, 1974.

Levinson, Robert E. *The Jews in the California Gold Rush.* New York: Ktav, 1978.

———. "Julius Eckman and the *Weekly Gleaner:* The Jewish Press in the Pioneer American West," in Bertram Korn, ed., *A Bicentennial Festschrift for Jacob Rader Marcus.* New York: Ktav, 1976.

Levy, Daniel. "Letters about the Jews of California: 1855–1858." *WSJHQ* 3 (January 1971).

Levy, Harriet Lane. *920 O'Farrell Street: A Jewish Girlhood in San Francisco.* Berkeley: Heyday Books, 1996.

Lewis, Oscar. *San Francisco: Mission to Metropolis.* San Diego: Howell North Books, 1980.

Limerick, Patricia, Clyde A. Milner II, and Charles Rankin. *Trails Toward a New Western History.* Lawrence: University of Kansas Press, 1991.

Lotchin, Roger W. *San Francisco, 1846–1856: From Hamlet to City.* Urbana and Chicago: University of Illinois Press, 1997.

Massarik, Fred. *The Jewish Population of San Francisco, Marin County and the Peninsula, 1970–1973: Basic Findings.* San Francisco: Jewish Welfare Federation of San Francisco, Marin County and the Peninsula, 1974.

Meyer, Michael A. *Response to Modernity: A History of the Reform Movement in Judaism.* New York: Oxford University Press, 1988.

Milner II, Clyde A., Carol A. O'Connor, and Martha A. Sandweiss, eds., *The Oxford History of the American West.* New York: Oxford University Press, 1994.

Moore, Deborah Dash. *To the Golden Cities: Pursuing the American Jewish Dream.* Cambridge: Harvard University Press, 1996.

Moscowitz, Daniel J. "Martin A. Meyer: His Life and Its Lessons." Parts 1–2. *WSJH* 26 (April and July 1994).

Narell, Irena. *Our City: The Jews of San Francisco.* San Diego: Howell North Books, 1981.

Quinn, D. Michael. "Religion in the American West." In William Cronan, George Miller, and Jay Gitlin, eds., *Under an Open Sky: Rethinking America's Western Past.* New York and London: W. W. Norton and Company, 1992.

Raab, Earl. "There's No City Like San Francisco." *Commentary* 10 (October 1956).

Rafael, Ruth. "Ernest Bloch at the San Francisco Conservatory of Music." *WSJHQ* 9 (April 1977).

Raphael, Marc Lee. "Rabbi Jacob Voorsanger of San Francisco on Jews and Judaism: The Implications of the Pittsburgh Platform." *AJHQ* 63 (December 1973).

Reichert, Irving F. *Judaism and the American Jew: The Sermons and Addresses of Irving Frederick Reichert.* San Francisco: Grabhorn Press, 1953.

Rischin, Moses, ed. *The Jews of the West: The Metropolitan Years.* Waltham, Mass.: American Jewish Historical Society; Berkeley: Western Jewish History Center, Judah L. Magnes Memorial Museum, 1979.

Rischin, Moses, and Raphael Asher, eds. *The Jewish Legacy and the German Conscience: Essays in Memory of Rabbi Joseph Asher.* Berkeley: Judah L. Magnes Museum, 1991.

Rochlin, Harriet, and Fred Rochlin. *Pioneer Jews: A New Life in the Far West.* Boston: Houghton Mifflin Company, 1984.

Rogers, Barbara S., and Stephen M. Dobbs. *The First Century: Mount Zion Hospital and Medical Center, 1887–1987.* San Francisco: Mount Zion Hospital and Medical Center, 1987.

Rohrbough, Malcolm J. *Days of Gold: The California Gold Rush and the American Nation.* Berkeley and Los Angeles: University of California Press, 1997.

Rosenbaum, Fred. *Architects of Reform: Congregational and Community Leadership, Emanu-El of San Francisco, 1849–1980.* Berkeley: Western Jewish History Center, Judah L. Magnes Memorial Museum, 1980.

———. *Free to Choose: The Making of a Jewish Community in the American West.* Berkeley: Western Jewish History Center, Judah L. Magnes Memorial Museum, 1976.

———. "San Francisco–Oakland Native Son," in William M. Brinner and Moses Rischin, eds., *Like All the Nations? The Life and Legacy of Judah L. Magnes.* Albany: SUNY Press, 1987.

———. "Zionism and Anti-Zionism in San Francisco." In Moses Rischin and John Livingston, eds., *Jews of the American West.* Detroit: Wayne State University Press, 1991.

Rothmann, Frances Bransten. *The Haas Sisters of Franklin Street: A Look Back With Love.* Berkeley: Judah L. Magnes Museum, 1979.

Scharlach, Bernice. *House of Harmony: Concordia Argonaut's First 130 Years.* Berkeley: Judah L. Magnes Museum, 1983.

Silverstein, Alan. *Alternatives to Assimilation: The Response of Reform Judaism to American Culture.* Hanover, N.H.: Brandeis University Press and the University Press of New England, 1994.

Sklare, Marshall, and Joseph Greenblum. *Jewish Identity on the Suburban Frontier: A Study of Group Survival in the Open Society.* New York: Basic Books, 1967.

Stampfer, Joshua. *Pioneer Rabbi of the West: The Life and Times of Julius Eckman.* Portland, Ore.: IJS, 1988.

Starr, Kevin. *Americans and the California Dream, 1850–1915.* New York: Oxford University Press, 1973.

———. *The Dream Endures: California Enters the 1940s.* New York: Oxford University Press, 1997.

———. *Endangered Dreams: The Great Depression in California.* New York: Oxford University Press, 1996.

Stern, Norton B., and William M. Kramer. "The Historical Recovery of the Pioneer Sephardic Jews of California." *WSJHQ* 8 (October 1975).

———. "A Search for the First Synagogue in the Golden West." *WSJHQ* 7 (October 1974).

Streicker, Joel. *An Assessment of a Synagogue Voluntary Dues Policy: The Temple Emanu-El Experience.* San Francisco: Institute for Community and Religion, 1997.

Temko, Allan. "Temple Emanu-El of San Francisco: A Glory of the West." *Commentary* 26 (August 1958).

Tobin, Gary A., and Gabriel Berger. *Synagogue Affiliation: Implications for the 1990s.* Waltham, Mass.: Cohen Center for Modern Jewish Studies, 1993.

Tobin, Gary A., and Sharon Sassler. *Bay Area Jewish Community Study.* Waltham, Mass.: Cohen Center for Modern Jewish Studies, 1988.

Tobin, Gary A., and Joel Streicker. *Reform Day School Feasibility Study.* San Francisco: Institute for Community and Religion, 1995.

Urofsky, Melvin I. *A Voice that Spoke for Justice: The Life and Times of Stephen S. Wise.* Albany: SUNY Press, 1982.

Voorsanger, Jacob. *The Chronicles of Emanu-El: Being an Account of the Rise and Progress of the Congregation Emanu-El Which was Founded in July, 1850 and Will Celebrate its Fiftieth Anniversary December 23, 1900.* San Francisco: Geo. Spaulding and Co., 1900.

———. "Relief Work in San Francisco after the 1906 Earthquake and Fire: An Overview." In William M. Kramer, ed., *California: Earthquakes and Jews.* Los Angeles: Western States Jewish History, 1995.

Vorspan, Max, and Lloyd Gartner. *History of the Jews of Los Angeles.* Philadelphia: Jewish Publication Society, 1970.

Wertheimer, Jack, ed. *The American Synagogue: A Sanctuary Transformed.* New York: Cambridge University Press, 1987.

———. *A People Divided: Judaism in Contemporary America.* New York: Basic Books, 1993.

Zucker, Jeffrey S. "Cantor Edward Stark at Congregation Emanu-El." Parts 1–2. *WSJH* 17 (April and July 1985).

Zwerin, Kenneth C., and Norton B. Stern. "Jacob Voorsanger: From Cantor to Rabbi." *WSJHQ* 15 (April 1983).

Index

Boldface type indicates a photograph. *Italic type* indicates a title; where possible, an identifier ("newspaper" or "book," etc.) has been added for clarity. Musical titles are followed by the composer's name.

United Jewish Appeal of Greater New
York, 270, 345
United Palestine Appeal, 156
United States Holocaust Memorial
Council, 258, 287
United States Holocaust Museum
(Washington, D.C.), 258
United War Work Drive, 112
United Workman (fraternal group), 31
University of California, Berkeley, 62, 151,
337
chorus, 162, 170
Cowell Hospital, 143n
faculty and officers, 196, 229, 243,
321, 332
Haas Business School, 224
Haas Pavilion, 224
Hillel Foundation, 125, 130, 243
and Kirschner scandal, 353, 363–64
Library Annex, 143n
loyalty oath controversy, 229
Martin Meyer's commencement
address, 133
Menorah Club, 125
Near Eastern Studies Department, 285
and San Francisco Conservatory of
Music, 164
Semitics Department, 82, 125
Strawberry Canyon Recreation Area,
224
Zellerbach Hall, 223–24
University of California, San Francisco
Medical School, 337
University of California Extension, 128
University of San Francisco, 337
University of Santa Clara, 224

Vallejo, California, 125
Vidaver, Henry, 74
Vietnam War, 257
Vigilantes, 11, 32–33, 34
Voice of Israel (newspaper), 27
Voorsanger, A. W., 123, 150n
Voorsanger, Elkan, 109, 114, 115–16
Voorsanger, Eva, 109
Voorsanger, Jacob (1852–1908)
death, 108
early years and education, 79–80

family, 91, 109, 114
health, 108–109
photograph, **81**
See also Voorsanger rabbinate
Voorsanger, Rachel, 109
Voorsanger, William, 91
Voorsanger Memorial Library, 239
Voorsanger rabbinate (1889–1908), 9n,
79–110, 198, 222, 294, 438, 439, 443
as assistant rabbi, 77, 80, 152
building projects, 102–104, 153
earthquake and fire (1906), 96–102
economy, 102, 106
innovations and reforms, 83–84
Jewish community, 90–92, 108
religious education and schools, 90
social and community work, 90–93,
97, 100–102
women's groups and programs, 90–92
on Zionism, 94–95, 109, 110

Waldheim, Kurt, 338
Walker, Gene K., 203
Walker Report, 204
Walt Disney Company, 404
Walter, Edgar, 62, 147
Walter, Isaac, 62
Walter and Elise Haas Fund, 349
Wand, Samuel, 50, 57
Wangenheim, Henry, 100, 102, 133
Wangenheim, Solomon, 49, 50
War Memorial Opera House, 143, 162,
176
Warburg, Gerald, 166
Warenskold, Dorothy, 160
Warren, Earl, 226, 239
Wascerwitz, Philip, 127
Washington Hebrew Congregation,
227–28, 236n
Waskow, Arthur, 267
Watson, Mary, quoted, 69
Watters, Abraham, 6n, 9n
Weekly Gleaner (newspaper). *See Gleaner*
Weil, Abraham, 61
Weill, Raphael, 57
Weinberg, Joseph, 235–36, 240
Weiner, Martin, 281
Weinstein, Jacob, 228

Weisler, Alexander, 54–55
Weiss, Zari, 421
Weizmann, Chaim, 123, 156
Weizsaecker, Richard, 287
Welhof, Max, 12
Wells Fargo Bank, 58
Wertheimer, Jack, quoted, 441
West, Cornel, 417
Western Jewish History Center, 50n
Western Jewry (book), 79n, 115
Wheeler, Benjamin Ide, 109
White, Saul, 200, 228
White House department store (San
  Francisco), 57
White House (Washington, D.C.), 287
White Paper (on Palestine, 1939), 193
Wiener, Grace, 122
Wiener, Irwin, 305, 316, 322–23, **330**, 332,
  333, 342, 343, 345, 350–51, 354, 394, 399
Wiesel, Elie, 258, **259,** 292, 300
Wilbur, Ray Lyman, 143
Williams, Cecil, 304, 309, 311
Wilshire Boulevard Temple (Los Angeles),
  69, 202, 298, 300, 318, 394, 398
Wilson, Pete, 346
Winer, Mark, 368n
Wise, Isaac Mayer, 16, 18, 21, 27, 29, 36,
  39, 44, 49, 55, 59n, 71–72, 76, 137, 184
Wise, Stephen, 107, 110, 117–18, 121,
  131, 132, 157, 187n, 189
  and Free Synagogue, 137, 138
Wolf, Becki, 329
Wolf, Simon, 94
Wolf-Prusan, Peretz, 360–61, 380, 394,
  408–10, 411, 413, 417, 418–19, 427
  early years and education, 329
  photographs, **330, 375, 401, 410, 430**
  religious education and schools, 377,
    398, 400, 429, 431–32
  See also Shabbat La'Am service
Wolfe, Edward, 108
Wolff, Max, 76, **77**
Wolsey, Louis, 196
Women
  Gold Rush era, 5, 64
  in Jewish community, 62–65
  and Panama-Pacific International

  Exposition, 111–12
  in synagogue life, 21, 46, 75, 127
  twenties era, 126–27, 154
  women's groups, 30–31, 90–92, 273–74
  and Zionism, 123–24
  See also specific women's groups
Woolf, I. E., 9n
Works Project Administration Federal
  Music Project, 167
The World of Sholom Aleichem (play), 274
World Union for Progressive Judaism, 254
World War I, 112, 114, 120, 122, 134–35
World War II, 188, 191–93, 254–56, 315
Wyman, Rudolph, 9n
Wyner, Yehudi, 251

Yerushalmi, Yosef Hayim, 336–37
Yom Kippur War (1973), 267, 271
Young Men's Hebrew Association, 120

Zangwill, Israel, 80
Zellerbach, Anthony, 58
Zellerbach, Harold, 175, 196n, **203**, 274,
  286, 439
  and Asher rabbinate, 274, 286–87
  and Fine rabbinate, 215, 216, 221,
    222, 226, 237
  and Newman rabbinate, 140, 155
  and Reichert rabbinate, 196n,
    203–204, 205
Zellerbach, J. D., 175, 196n
Zellerbach, Jennie Baruh, 175, 274. *See
  also* Zellerbach (Jennie Baruh) Fund
Zellerbach Family Fund, 407
Zellerbach (Jennie Baruh) Fund, 274, 275
Zemach, Nahum, 150
Zinkow, Misha, 380
Zionism and anti-Zionism, 94–95, 122–24,
  155–57, 194–212, 213, 218–20, 221–22,
  266–68, 322. *See also* American Council
  for Judaism; "Dual loyalties" argument
Zionist Organization of America, 156–57,
  194, 197, 200, 211, 267
Zionts, Richard, 252, 374
Zucker, Jeffrey, 87–88
Zunz, Leopold, 17, 44
Zwerin, Kenneth, 79n, 80n